ANARCHY AND LEGAL ORDER

This book elaborates and defends the idea of law without the state. Animated by a vision of peaceful, voluntary cooperation as a social ideal and building on a careful account of nonaggression, it features a clear explanation of why the state is illegitimate, dangerous, and unnecessary. It proposes an understanding of how law enforcement in a stateless society could be legitimate and what the optimal substance of law without the state might be, suggests ways in which a stateless legal order could foster the growth of a culture of freedom, and situates the project it elaborates in relation to leftist, anticapitalist, and socialist traditions.

GARY CHARTIER is Professor of Law and Business Ethics and Associate Dean of the Ton and Vi Zapara School of Business at La Sierra University in Riverside, California. He is the author of *Economic Justice and Natural Law* (2009), *The Conscience of an Anarchist* (2011), and *The Analogy of Love* (2007), as well as the coeditor (with Charles W. Johnson) of *Markets Not Capitalism: Individualist Anarchism against Bosses, Inequality, Corporate Power, and Structural Poverty* (2011).

Anarchy and Legal Order

LAW AND POLITICS FOR A STATELESS SOCIETY

GARY CHARTIER
La Sierra University

CAMBRIDGE
UNIVERSITY PRESS

32 Avenue of the Americas, New York NY 10013-2473, USA

Cambridge University Press is part of the University of Cambridge.

It furthers the University's mission by disseminating knowledge in the pursuit of education, learning and research at the highest international levels of excellence.

www.cambridge.org
Information on this title: www.cambridge.org/9781107661615

First published 2013
First paperback edition 2014

A catalogue record for this publication is available from the British Library

Library of Congress Cataloguing in Publication data
Chartier, Gary.
Anarchy and legal order: law and politics for a stateless society / Gary Chartier.
p. cm.
Includes index.
ISBN 978-1-107-03228-6 (hardback)
1. Law—Philosophy. 2. Rule of law. 3. State, The. 4. Anarchism. I. Title.
K250.C43 2013
340'.1–dc23 2012024350

ISBN 978-1-107-03228-6 Hardback
ISBN 978-1-107-66161-5 Paperback

For

Kevin Carson, Stephen R. L. Clark, Sheldon Richman,
Jeffrey Cassidy, Annette Bryson, and Wonil Kim

Justice being taken away, then, what are kingdoms but great robberies? For what are robberies themselves, but little kingdoms? The band itself is made up of men; it is ruled by the authority of a prince, it is knit together by the pact of the confederacy; the booty is divided by the law agreed on. If, by the admittance of abandoned men, this evil increases to such a degree that it holds places, fixes abodes, takes possession of cities, and subdues peoples, it assumes the more plainly the name of a kingdom, because the reality is now manifestly conferred on it, not by the removal of covetousness, but by the addition of impunity. Indeed, that was an apt and true reply which was given to Alexander the Great by a pirate who had been seized. For when that king had asked the man what he meant by keeping hostile possession of the sea, he answered with bold pride, "What thou meanest by seizing the whole earth; but because I do it with a petty ship, I am called a robber, whilst thou who dost it with a great fleet art styled emperor."

– AUGUSTINE OF HIPPO (354–430)

When Adam delved and Eve span, Who was then the gentleman? From the beginning all men by nature were created alike, and our bondage or servitude came in by the unjust oppression of naughty men. For if God would have had any bondmen from the beginning, he would have appointed who should be bond, and who free. And therefore I exhort you to consider that now the time is come, appointed to us by God, in which ye may (if ye will) cast off the yoke of bondage, and recover liberty.

– JOHN BALL (1338–81)

Those who make laws, appropriate wealth in order to secure power. All the legislative classes, and all the classes whose possessions depend not on nature, but on the law, perceiving that law alone guarantees and secures their possessions, and perceiving that government as the instrument for enforcing obedience to the law, and thus for preserving their power and possessions, is indispensable, unite one and all, heart and soul to uphold it, and, as the means of upholding it, to place at its disposal a large part of the annual produce of labour.

– THOMAS HODGSKIN (1787–1869)

[A] very large portion of the people of this country do not believe that the government is doing "equal and exact justice to all men." And some persons are earnestly promulgating the idea that the government is not attempting to do, and has no intention of doing, anything like "equal and exact justice to all men"; that, on the contrary, it is knowingly, deliberately, and wilfully doing an incalculable amount of injustice; that it has always been doing this in the past, and that it has no intention of doing anything else in the future; that it is a mere tool in the hands of a few ambitious, rapacious, and unprincipled men; that its purpose, in doing all this injustice, is to keep—so far as they can without driving the people to rebellion—all wealth, and all political power, in as few hands as possible; and that this injustice is the direct cause of all the widespread poverty, ignorance, and servitude among the great body of the people.

– LYSANDER SPOONER (1808–87)

When Warren and Proudhon, in prosecuting their search for justice to labor, came face to face with the obstacle of class monopolies, they saw that these monopolies rested upon Authority, and concluded that the thing to be done was, not to strengthen this Authority and thus make monopoly universal, but to utterly uproot Authority and give full sway to the opposite principle, Liberty....

– BENJAMIN R. TUCKER (1854–1939)

The State's criminality is nothing new and nothing to be wondered at. It began when the first predatory group of men clustered together and formed the State, and it will continue as long as the State exists in the world, because the State is fundamentally an anti-social institution, fundamentally criminal. The idea that the State originated to serve any kind of social purpose is completely unhistorical. It originated in conquest and confiscation—that is to say, in crime. It originated for the purpose of maintaining the division of society into an owning-and-exploiting class and a propertyless dependent class—that is, for a criminal purpose.

– ALBERT JAY NOCK (1870–1945)

What we call a government is after all nothing but a group of individuals, who, by a variety of sanctions, have acquired the power to govern their fellows. The sanctions range from the fraud of divine right to that of sheer conquest; from the imbecility of hereditary privilege to the irrationality of counting voters. In most cases the extent to which these sanctions produce capable legislators, judges, and administrators will not bear critical examination. Nominally, government exists and functions for the public. Actually it exists and functions for the benefit of those who have in one of these absurd ways acquired power to govern. It is accepted mainly because of the sheer inertia of great masses of people. Ostensibly, of course, it is accepted because it confers a sufficiency of visible benefits upon society to make the officials who operate it tolerated in spite of the selfish and idiotic exercise of the powers conferred upon them.

– RALPH BORSODI (1886–1977)

My political opinions lean more and more to Anarchy (philosophically understood, meaning abolition of control not whiskered men with bombs)—or to 'unconstitutional' Monarchy. I would arrest anybody who uses the word state (in any sense other than the inanimate realm of England and its inhabitants, a thing that has neither power, rights nor mind); and after a chance of recantation, execute them if they remained obstinate!

– J. R. R. TOLKIEN (1892–1972)

You've asked me, "What might you be?" Now I answer you: "I am a Wobbly." I mean this spiritually and politically. In saying this I refer less to political orientation than to political ethos, and I take Wobbly to mean one thing: the opposite of bureaucrat.... A Wobbly is not only a man who takes orders from himself. He's also a man who's often in the situation where there are no regulations to fall back upon that he hasn't made up himself. He doesn't like bosses—capitalistic or communistic—they are all the same to him. He wants to be, and he wants everyone else to be, his own boss at all times under all conditions and for any purposes they may want to follow up. This kind of spiritual condition, and only this, is Wobbly freedom.

– C. WRIGHT MILLS (1916–62)

Contents

Preface

The "anarchistic socialism" of Benjamin Tucker and the "Ricardian socialism" of Thomas Hodgskin lie behind this book, which is in significant part an attempt to defend contemporary descendants of their ideas. As I seek to articulate an anarchist position that is identifiably leftist, anticapitalist, and socialist, while also hospitable to robust possessory claims and to mutually beneficial exchange as a valuable variety of peaceful, voluntary cooperation, I am deeply grateful for the intellectual inheritance I have received from Tucker and Hodgskin and those who learned from and dialogued with them—Voltairine de Cleyre, Lysander Spooner, Dyer Lum, Herbert Spencer, and William B. Greene, among others.[1]

I've dedicated *Anarchy and Legal Order* to six people from whom I have learned and continue to learn about politics and philosophy.

- Kevin Carson's brilliant synthesis of ideas from diverse radical traditions and his ability to draw effortlessly on a wealth of material from economics, history, political philosophy, and organizational theory have grounded an approach to anarchism that I realized could accommodate both my visceral antiauthoritarianism and my opposition to exclusion, subordination, and deprivation. He continues to stimulate and challenge me, and to exemplify an enviable commitment to scholarly productivity. This book would be unimaginable without the inspiration his work has provided.
- As a source of insight during my dissertation research, as the external examiner of my dissertation, and as a continuing interlocutor in subsequent years, Stephen R. L. Clark has served as an exceptional model of clear thinking and elegant writing, of the effective integration of moral passion and reflective faith

[1] I direct those who are convinced that Spencer does not belong in this group to a number of essays by Roderick T. Long, all available via his website, Praxeology.net, http://www.praxeology.net. *Cf.* Thomas Hodgskin, Book Review, THE ECONOMIST, Feb. 8, 1851, at 149 (reviewing HERBERT SPENCER, SOCIAL STATICS [1851]).

with careful analysis. He was among the first anarchist thinkers to help me see that the authority of the state was indefensible. Stephen's nimble mind ranges over a remarkable range of topics, and I remain delighted by the ongoing opportunity to learn from him about all of them, even when we disagree.

- Sheldon Richman has been a constantly available conversation partner, challenging me, posing difficult questions, directing me to unfamiliar sources, and serving as a vital link to the history of American radicalism. His dry wit, good sense, wisdom, and breadth of knowledge have made our constant exchanges both pleasurable and instructive.
- A treasured friend for more than thirty years, Jeffrey Cassidy has helped to expand my horizons even as he has offered consistent warmth, loyalty, understanding, and innumerable opportunities to banter about pop culture; to reflect on vital human relationships; to explore issues in theology, philosophy, politics, science, and society; and to engage in a welcome and continuing process of mutual radicalization.
- Annette Bryson has engaged and listened and dreamed with me as I have confronted an enormous number of personal and intellectual challenges. It has been a delight to know her since college, to officiate at her wedding, and to reflect with her on our shared past and our many overlapping connections. She has invited me into the world of her own philosophical scholarship, very different from my own. And while she may not embrace all of the positions I take here, we have happily shared a wide range of political convictions and, more than that, an underlying sensibility marked by concern for inclusion and opposition to aggression, subordination, and deprivation. Wise and compassionate and movingly trusting, she enriches my life in diverse ways.
- Wonil Kim, warmly decent and generous friend and dedicated campaigner for peace and for the well-being and dignity of immigrants and workers, has offered for many years the perspective of a humane, antiauthoritarian Marxist on my politics, of an informed scholar of the Bible on my theological ruminations, and of a sensitive pastor on my personal struggles. It is an honor and a pleasure to work with him as a colleague, to team-teach with him a course on social change that links our diverse perspectives, and to share my angst and my joy with him.

I am fortunate to be able to call Kevin, Stephen, Sheldon, Jeffrey, Annette, and Wonil my friends and to continue to be able to draw on their insights and their personal support.

My comrades at the Center for a Stateless Society—including Sheldon, Kevin, Charles W. Johnson, Roderick T. Long, Brad Spangler, Chris Lempa, Joseph Stromberg, James Tuttle, Roman Pearah, Anna O. Morgenstern, Tom Knapp, Darian Worden, David S. D'Amato, Tennyson McCalla, Mike Gogulski, Ross

Kenyon, Mariana Evica, Stephanie Murphy, Wendy McElroy, Stephan Kinsella, William Gillis, Julia Riber Pitt, and Jeremy Weiland—deserve my ongoing thanks for, among other things, their enthusiastic encouragement of this and other projects. They have been engaging conversation partners as well as valued friends. Their ideas are reflected throughout this book. I'm also very thankful for the stimuli for my work provided by John Finnis, Germain Grisez, Carole Pateman, Michael Taylor, Anthony de Jasay, Stephen Munzer, Fritz Guy, John Hick, Brian Hebblethwaite, Charles Teel, Jr., David Schmidtz, David D. Friedman, Murray Rothbard, Karl Hess, and Randy Barnett. Gene Callahan deserves credit for prompting the reflections that led to what is now Chapter 5. While I am unsympathetic to David Hume's metaethical posture, I have drawn appreciatively on his general account of justice in possession at multiple points. Thanks are due, too, to Matt Zwolinski, Pete Boettke, Steve Horwitz, John Tomasi, Fernando Tesón, Andrew Jason Cohen, Jason Brennan, Danny Shapiro, Jacob Levy, James Stacey Taylor, Brian Doherty, Riley O'Neill, Gene Berkman, and Kevin Vallier for listening, reacting, supporting, and challenging; to Sky Conway and Joyce Brand for fostering good conversation; and to Sandy Thatcher and Roy Carlisle for being the seasoned publishing professionals they are.

My parents did not live to see this book published, and no doubt each would have responded to it with mixed feelings. But they deserve repeated thanks for bequeathing me a passion for freedom, a skepticism about authority, and a disgust at elite mischief—all of which are, I hope, deeply embedded in this book.

Anarchy and Legal Order builds on, even as in some ways it departs from, the account of ethics in economic life I developed in *Economic Justice and Natural Law*. It differs especially in allowing the anarchist ideas that played minor roles in the earlier book to occupy center stage and in focusing specifically on the moral limits on the use of force—and so on the development of a natural-law version of the moral requirement of nonaggression.[2] Credit for the refinement of my position goes first of all to Kevin Carson, who addressed a number of pointed questions to me about the links between *Economic Justice* and my more explicitly anarchist work, but I am also grateful to the other participants in an author-and-critics session devoted to the book that took place at the 2011 San Diego meeting of the American Philosophical Association's Pacific Division—Roderick Long, who organized the session, as well as Douglas Den Uyl, Douglas Rasmussen, David Gordon, and Jennifer Baker. Carson also provided detailed, helpful comments on a draft version of *Anarchy and Legal*

[2] Other differences include (*i*) greater development of the desiderata underlying just possessory claims and the implications of these desiderata, (*ii*) a clearer distinction between the justifications for the use of force with and without consent, (*iii*) a change in focus from direct legal mandates to the indirect impact of institutional change as the central means of fostering workplace democracy and nondiscrimination, and (*iv*) an explicit acknowledgment of the importance of mechanisms for encouraging social change quite apart from the legal system.

Order. Sandy Thatcher offered a wide range of helpful suggestions on parts of the manuscript, as did Jonathan Crowe, John Clark, Richard Broughton, Stephen R. L. Clark, Roderick T. Long, Mark Pennington, Douglas B. Rasmussen, Michael Stokes, Joseph Stromberg, David Gordon, and several anonymous readers. I am grateful as well to Neera Badhwar for giving me the chance to think about well-being in dialogue with a chapter of her forthcoming book on virtue and happiness, and to Hillel Steiner, David Schmidtz, Matt Zwolinski, Fernando R. Tesón, Mark Pennington, and Jonathan Crowe for being willing to endorse the book.

Thanks are also due, of course, to the usual suspects: Elenor Webb and (in addition to Jeffrey, Annette, Sheldon, and Wonil) Aena Prakash, Alexander Lian, Andrew Howe, Angela Keaton, Anne-Marie Pearson, Bart Willruth, Carole Pateman, Chelsea Krafve, Craig R. Kinzer, David B. Hoppe, David R. Larson, Deborah K. Dunn, Donna Carlson, Ellen Hubbell, Eva Pascal, Fritz Guy, Heather Ferguson, Jan M. Holden, Jesse Leamon, Joel Sandefur, John Elder, John Thomas, Julio C. Muñoz, Kenneth A. Dickey, Lawrence T. Geraty, Less Antman, Ligia Radoias, Maria Zlateva, Michael Orlando, Nabil Abu-Assal, Patricia Cabrera, Roger E. Rustad, Jr., Ronel Harvey, Ruth E. E. Burke, Sarvi Sheybany, Sel J. Hwahng, and W. Kent Rogers. I especially appreciate the moral and logistical support Elenor provided as I completed this book. As usual, Dean Thomas ensured that La Sierra University's Zapara School of Business was a congenial place in which to complete work on a project of this kind.

I am very thankful to Cambridge University Press editors John Berger and Finòla O'Sullivan for their support for this book, and to production editor Paul Smolenski, senior editorial assistant David Jou, copy editor Brooke Smith, Bhavani Ganesh (of Newgen Knowledge Works Pvt Ltd. Chennai), and other participants in the production process for facilitating the rapid production of the book, ensuring its æsthetic appeal, and helping to make my writing accurate and clear.[3]

All of the author royalties I receive for this book will be donated to AntiWar.com. This exceptional source of news and inspirer of activism, cross-ideological but staffed by a disproportionate number of anarchists, performs a vital service by promoting peaceful, voluntary cooperation in a conflict-ridden world, and I urge all those who find my arguments in *Anarchy and Legal Order* appealing to support it.

[3] In addition, I am grateful for permission to make use in this book of material published elsewhere: *Enforcing the Law and Being a State*, 31 L. & PHIL 99 (2012) (Springer); *Government Is No Friend of the Poor*, THE FREEMAN: IDEAS ON LIBERTY, Jan.– Feb. 2012, at 15; *Response to Charles Clark*. 9 CONVERSATIONS IN REL. & THEOL. 188 (2011); SOCIALIST ENDS, MARKET MEANS: FIVE ESSAYS (Tulsa Alliance of the Libertarian Left, 2009); ADVOCATES OF FREED MARKETS SHOULD EMBRACE "ANTI-CAPITALISM" (Tulsa Alliance of the Libertarian Left, 2011); *Intellectual Property and Natural Law*, 36 AUST. J. LEG. PHIL. 58 (2011); *Pirate Constitutions and Workplace Democracy*, 18 JAHRBUCH FÜR RECHT UND ETHIK 449 (2010); *Natural Law and Non-Aggression*, 51 ACTA JURIDICA HUNGARICA 79 (2010); and *Natural Law and Animal Rights*, 23 CAN. J.L. & JURIS 33 (2010).

Introduction

Embodying Freedom

People cooperate peacefully and voluntarily when they interact without aggression.[1] A just society, a society rooted in peaceful, voluntary cooperation, is both possible and desirable.[2] Because the state precludes and preempts this kind of cooperation, aggressing or threatening to engage in aggression against those who disobey it, a peaceful, voluntary society must be a stateless society—an anarchist society.[3] The

[1] By "aggression," I mean, roughly, nondefensive, non-remedial harm to people's bodies and nondefensive, nonremedial interference with their just possessory interests; *see* Chapter 2, *infra*. "Peace" as nonaggression is a necessary condition for peace in other, more elaborate senses, and it can reasonably be expected to promote peace in these senses.

[2] Events and states of affairs are not proper subjects for moral evaluation, which is concerned with *choice*. Moral choices are made by particular people, even if in concert and cooperation with others. Thus, while it is possible to talk about a "just legal system" or even a "just society," this kind of language is shorthand. A just *institution* is one that characteristically functions in accordance with reasonable choices by particular people. Similarly, to call a legal *rule* just is simply to say that someone can enforce the rule consistently without doing anything unjust.

[3] I take a state to be, in roughly Weberian terms, an entity that claims, and exercises something reasonably like, a monopoly over the determination, adjudication, and enforcement of legal rights in a given geographic area. Thanks to Charles Johnson for emphasizing the importance of referring to legal rights here and to Heather Ferguson for stressing the need to clarify the meaning of "state" as I use it in this book. In the interests of convenience, I refer at various points to states as doing things; in reality, of course, states as such don't do things—rather, particular people, engaged in certain kinds of cooperative activities and proceeding with the benefit of certain kinds of legitimation, do things in their roles as state actors, and it should be clear throughout I have the actions of such people in mind when I talk about state action.

By "anarchy," I do not, of course, mean *chaotic violence* but rather *social order rooted in peaceful, voluntary cooperation, and so without the state*. *Cf.* Patricia Crone, *Ninth-Century Muslim Anarchists*, 167 PAST & PRESENT 3, 3 (2000) (referring to "anarchists in the simple sense of believers in an-archy, 'no government'."). While my primary focus here is on opposition to social order created and maintained by aggressive force, support for anarchy is naturally and intimately associated with opposition to social hierarchies maintained by nonaggressive means (*see* Charles W. Johnson, *Liberty, Equality, Solidarity: Toward a Dialectical Anarchism*, *in* ANARCHISM/MINARCHISM: IS A GOVERNMENT PART OF A FREE COUNTRY? 155, 179–83 [Roderick T. Long and Tibor Machan eds., 2008]); as I argue in Chapter 6, ending institutionalized aggression and various complementary varieties of nonaggressive

general character of the kind of legal and political order compatible with anarchy can be specified and justified in light of a plausible conception of what it means for people to live fulfilled, flourishing lives.

Contemporary natural law theory offers such a conception. It incorporates both a rich and variegated understanding of human well-being and a set of principles that can guide our attempts to foster our own welfare and that of others—the Principle of Fairness, the Principle of Respect, and the Principle of Recognition (Chapter 1). People's obligations to each other with respect to physical things are both sources of conflict and (while too frequently invoked to legitimize unjust privilege) useful guarantors of autonomy and sources of flourishing; just possessory claims serve to demarcate those interests people can reasonably defend using force from those they can't—and, properly understood, they help to explain why the state is illegitimate. Rooted both in basic moral principles and in a set of desiderata derived from these principles and from truisms about human existence, these obligations, embodied in what I call the *baseline possessory rules*, can play a crucial instrumental role in fostering people's welfare. However, while there are good reasons to respect people's possessory interests in physical things, people often claim that they are entitled to treat other kinds of things as possessions. Though people often claim that other people or other sentients are among their legitimate possessions, arguments that our fellow sentients, human or nonhuman, are raw material we can use at our discretion are unconvincing. And the notion that someone can justifiably control how other people embody abstract ideas in their own legitimate possessions finds little support in a credible account of people's just possessory claims. The strong prima facie presumption in favor of respecting people's claims to their justly acquired physical possessions—those acquired in accordance with the baseline rules[4]—combined with everyone's right not to be the object of purposeful, instrumental, or otherwise unreasonable physical attack, can be usefully summarized in the form of a maxim of *nonaggression* (Chapter 2).[5]

protest can reasonably be expected to lead to significant reductions in the frequency and influence of such hierarchies.

[4] On just acquisition, *see* Chapter 2.IV, *infra*. To anticipate: just acquisition is acquisition in accordance with the baseline rules. Someone justly acquires a physical object if she takes effective possession of it when it is not justly claimed by anyone else, or when she receives it through voluntary transfer from another just possessor.

[5] The natural-law approach to moral theory I take here combines something resembling an Aristotelian account of personal flourishing, a Kantian account of duties with respect to basic aspects of others' well-being, and a Humean account of obligations with respect to others' possessory claims. The understanding of the prohibition on violence against basic aspects of flourishing which the natural-law approach grounds is thus straightforwardly deontological, similar to that enshrined in the Formula of the End-in-Itself. By contrast, the account of possessory rules I defend has (as applied to institutional actors) obvious affinities with a sort of practice-consequentialism; while I do not believe that global or aggregating consequentialism is defensible, persons reasoning in accordance with the Principle of

To reject aggression is to embrace a model of social interaction rooted in peaceful, voluntary cooperation. This kind of cooperation can occur without the state; it can be fostered effectively by a variety of nonaggressive social institutions, including, in particular, institutions upholding consensual legal rules, resolving disputes, and providing protection against aggression, which I'll refer to as *legal regimes*.[6] Unlike these institutions, the state is premised on the denial of human moral equality and is inimical to peaceful, voluntary cooperation (and the flourishing such cooperation facilitates) because of the state's nonconsensual character and its inefficiency, destructiveness, rapacity, and penchant for aggression—especially in the service of elite groups (Chapter 3).

The state is unjustified, illegitimate, and dangerous. But life without the state need not be thought of as organized purely on the basis of ad hoc cooperation or persistent social norms. There would be good reason for people in a stateless society to maintain just legal regimes. Such regimes (which might serve geographically localized or virtual and widely distributed networks of people) would of necessity be rooted in actual rather than implied or hypothetical consent; and even when they employed force against outlaws, they would be morally distinguishable from states in important ways (Chapter 4).

Though different actual legal regimes in a stateless society would doubtless adopt different rules, the maxim of nonaggression and the prohibitions on violating people's bodies and on interference with their possessory claims that underlie it provide a clear and intelligible framework for the legal rules it would be reasonable for just institutions in a stateless society to implement. A central role in maintaining justice and preventing aggression should be played by simple tort-law rules precluding attacks on bodies and possessions and requiring compensation for injuries when such attacks occur. Such rules would leave no room for attempts to foster virtue using the force of law or to employ the law to prevent or end nonaggressive injuries—often important, but appropriately addressed by non-forcible means. Just legal rules enforced in a stateless society would not feature the separate category of *crime*, which is essentially statist. A stateless society could deal effectively not only with direct interpersonal injuries but also with environmentally mediated injuries to

Fairness would surely take expected consequences into account when determining what it was and was not reasonable for them to do, and the general tendency of the baseline rules to foster certain kinds of consequences would (I believe) tend to make it reasonable for people to endorse them and to render it unreasonable for people to decline to so. Given the importance of simplicity and reliability, among other values, legal regimes would have every reason to treat the baseline rules as if they were deontological requirements, and ordinary moral actors would have good reason to treat them as generally exceptionless.

6 I'll refer throughout to those who voluntarily agree to accept the authority of a legal regime as *participants* in the regime. For a model of how legal regimes in a stateless society might be structured, *see* Peter T. Leeson, *Government, Clubs, and Constitutions*, 80 J. Econ. Behav. & Org. 301 (2011).

bodies and to possessions and with harms to human persons with limited capacities as well as to sentient nonhuman animals (Chapter 5).[7]

The maxim of nonaggression rules out purposeful, instrumental, or unfair injuries to bodies and interference with just possessory interests even in pursuit of desirable objectives,[8] requiring compensation for both intentional and unintentional injuries. But legal rules and institutions precluding aggression could make possible a range of effective responses to the problems of dispossession, deprivation, subordination, and exclusion. Just institutions in a stateless society could engage in and foster multiple forms of wealth redistribution, for instance, employing both legal mechanisms and various nonaggressive means not dependent on the force of law. And a combination of structural change and nonaggressive direct action could help to humanize workplaces, to liberate people from stultifying social pressure, and to create opportunities for the embodiment of diverse forms of human flourishing in ways that would help to nourish a culture of freedom (Chapter 6).[9]

[7] I think it may plausibly be maintained that some nonhuman animals, even on our own planet, qualify as genuinely *personal* creatures (the obvious candidates would be cetaceans, primates, and elephants). But I seek to argue at more than one point that sentient creatures that are not fully personal may still deserve moral standing and legal protection. *See* GARY VARNER, PERSONHOOD, ETHICS, AND ANIMAL COGNITION: SITUATING ANIMALS IN HARE'S TWO LEVEL UTILITARIANISM (2012).

[8] I interfere unreasonably with your just possessory interests when I damage your justly acquired possessions or limit your control over those possessions, except when doing so is (in light of the various interpersonal and systemic considerations noted in Chapter 2) consistent with the Principle of Fairness (since the Principle determines in what sense possessory interests are just).

[9] *Freedom* is, of course, a complex and open-textured concept, even when the vexed (though profoundly important) question of free will in the metaphysical sense is bracketed. In general, freedom in the sense(s) in which I am concerned with it here is the ability to do what one wants. (Metaphysical freedom builds on a similar sense of subjection to another, with the difference that the other is God or Nature.)

More specifically, (*i*) I take someone to enjoy what I will call *freedom from aggression* when she is not prevented from doing what she wants to do by someone else's actual or threatened aggression. (At least under ordinary circumstance, the bandit who points a gun at you and demands, "Your money or your life!" is violating your freedom in this sense.) (This sort of freedom is often called *political freedom*, but I avoid labeling it that way here because the realm of the political as I refer to it in this book has to do with more than just the use of force—it's also concerned with voluntary collective action, and efforts designed to shape and influence the behavior of institutions.)

(*ii*) Someone enjoys *social freedom* when she is not only free from aggression but also not (*a*) presented with an attempt to motivate her that focuses primarily on an appeal to the would-be motivator's position or status rather than to the inherent value of the action in which she is being urged to engage or (*b*) faced with a dilemma of the following sort: if she does what she wants, someone else will do something nonaggressive but inconsistent with the principles of practical reasonableness as I elaborate them in Chapter 1. (The boss who threatens to fire you if you fail to adhere to an arbitrary, humiliating work rule by which she would be unwilling to live herself is violating your social freedom.)

Freedom from aggression and social freedom both involve the absence of constraints imposed on one's choices by other people's choices—of subjection to other people's *wills*. We might also consider broader senses of freedom that involve the absence of limits on one's ability to do what one likes posed by (*iii*) *resources* (I am not currently free to buy an island), (*iv*) *culture* (someone in a traditional society

The project of building a society free from the privileges secured by the state may initially seem difficult to classify. It embraces freedom and challenges the hierarchical management of the economy, while also rejecting capitalism. It exhibits obvious affinities with classical liberal and libertarian thought, but unequivocally repudiates the affirmation of corporate power and statist privilege too many classical liberals and libertarians seem inclined to offer. It shares modern liberalism's challenge to non-statist forms of subordination and exclusion while declining the modern liberal's Mephistophelean invitation to use the state to provide remedies for them. It is a leftist, anticapitalist project appropriately seen as an expression of the strand of the socialist tradition developed by a range of nineteenth-century American radicals (Chapter 7).

There is nothing inherently contradictory about the idea of using law to structure a stateless society. Rooted in the requirements of practical reasonableness, just legal rules enforced by a network of overlapping, consensual legal regimes could foster peaceful, voluntary cooperation by restraining aggression, rectifying injury, and coordinating people's actions where necessary, even while allowing considerable room for variety in lifestyles and patterns of interaction. They could deal effectively with the problems of exclusion, deprivation, subordination, and dispossession, and in this way lay the groundwork for the emergence of a culture of freedom (Conclusion).

In one sense, the shape of freedom—of peaceful, voluntary cooperation—will be given by the basic rules and norms that structure interaction in a stateless society. But the shape of freedom *as lived* is not, cannot be, determined by a mandate issued by statist bureaucrats or revolutionary ideologues. The contours of life in a stateless society will be the product of innumerable free choices by people engaged in peaceful, voluntary cooperation. Such a society need not and will not be a society of isolated atoms: people do not need the state to equip them to form thriving networks of mutual support and interdependence. Absent the state's threat of aggressive force,

might confront inhibitions that prevent her from marrying outside her social class, ethnic group, or religious community), (*v*) *emotions* (a victim of childhood violence may in a practical sense lack the freedom to trust, even though she very much wants to do so), or (*vi*) the laws of *nature* (I am not free to fly without mechanical assistance or to vary my height at will). (*vii*) Finally, one might say that someone enjoys *moral freedom* in a case in which there is no conflict between her preferences and the requirements of practical reasonableness.

A society rooted in peaceful, voluntary cooperation is one in which people consistently and predictably enjoy freedom from aggression. Its institutions could reasonably be expected (*see* Chapter 6, *infra*) to facilitate the achievement of social freedom as well as, in varying degrees, resource freedom, freedom from cultural constraints, and emotional freedom. I leave it to transhumanists to consider the degree to which it might foster freedom from the laws of nature. Moral freedom is not, per se, a matter for decision or influence, given that moral requirements are not products of our wills and that our preferences are not legitimately subject to authoritarian meddling.

On the varieties of freedom, *see, e.g.*, Mortimer J. Adler, The Idea of Freedom (2 vols., 1958–61); David Schmidtz & Jason Brennan, A Brief History of Liberty (2010).

people will be free to be, not atomic, but (as Sheldon Richman suggests we say) *molecular*,[10] linked with each other in innumerable arrays of fruitful relationships. Together, on an ongoing basis, they will form and *re*form their own lives and *in*form the choices of others through their voluntary interactions. Together, they will determine the shape of freedom.

[10] For this phrase, *see* Sheldon Richman, *Molecular Individualism*, THE FREEMAN: IDEAS ON LIBERTY, March 1, 1998, http://www.thefreemanonline.org/columns/perspective/perspective-molecular-individualism/. Since Richman refers specifically to molecular *individualism*, it is worth emphasizing that individualism comes in multiple varieties: political, methodological, moral, and metaphysical, among others. *Political individualism* is the thesis that force should not be used to prevent, end, or sanction nonaggressive conduct. *Methodological individualism* is the thesis that ultimate explanations of human events refer to the characteristics and actions of particular persons. *Moral individualism* is the thesis that only particular creatures have moral worth. *Metaphysical individualism* is the thesis that persons (and other creatures) are importantly distinguishable from each other and from their relationships with each other. It is important to emphasize that in *none* of these senses is individualism incompatible with the recognition that (*i*) we have robust moral responsibilities, *positive* as well as negative, to others; (*ii*) relationships help to determine who we are; (*iii*) relationships both constitute and contribute to our flourishing; and (*iv*) institutions significantly affect our self-understandings, our perceptions, our choices, and the possibilities we confront. *Cf.* MURRAY N. ROTHBARD, MAN, ECONOMY, AND STATE WITH POWER AND MARKET 3 n.6 (2d scholar's ed., 2009) (acknowledging "that [agents] are influenced in their desires and actions by the acts of other individuals" and refusing to make the assumption that they "are 'atoms' isolated from one another").

1

Laying Foundations

I. A REASONABLE CONCEPTION OF THE GOOD LIFE WILL INVOLVE AN UNDERSTANDING OF BOTH WELFARE AND RIGHT ACTION

A credible account of human flourishing and reasonable human action can ground the law and politics of a society rooted in peaceful, voluntary cooperation. The elaboration and justification of such an account is not the purpose of this book; what I offer here is a brief overview rather than the extensive argument that would be required in a study focused on the explication of the normative approach I adopt.[1] In brief: a satisfactory understanding of the good life will, I maintain, feature a

[1] The general approach to moral reasoning I defend here is outlined and applied in GARY CHARTIER, ECONOMIC JUSTICE AND NATURAL LAW (2009), though I have refined and in some ways altered here the position elaborated in that book. In both books, I draw freely on, and with equal freedom depart from, the stimulating and helpful work of the "new classical natural law" theorists and other contemporary exponents of natural law ethics; *see, e.g.*, JOHN FINNIS, NATURAL LAW AND NATURAL RIGHTS (1980) [*hereinafter* FINNIS, LAW]; JOHN FINNIS, FUNDAMENTALS OF ETHICS (1983) [*hereinafter* FINNIS, ETHICS]; John Finnis, *Commensuration and Practical Reason*, *in* INCOMMENSURABILITY, INCOMPARABILITY, AND PRACTICAL REASON 215, 225–28 (Ruth Chang ed., 1997) [*hereinafter* Finnis, *Commensuration*]; 1 GERMAIN GRISEZ, THE WAY OF THE LORD JESUS: CHRISTIAN MORAL PRINCIPLES (1983) [*hereinafter* GRISEZ, PRINCIPLES]; GERMAIN GRISEZ & RUSSELL SHAW, BEYOND THE NEW MORALITY: THE RESPONSIBILITIES OF FREEDOM (3rd ed., 1988); JOHN M. FINNIS, JOSEPH M. BOYLE, JR. & GERMAIN G. GRISEZ, NUCLEAR DETERRENCE, MORALITY, AND REALISM (1987) [*hereinafter* FINNIS ET AL., DETERRENCE]; 2 GERMAIN G. GRISEZ, THE WAY OF THE LORD JESUS: LIVING A CHRISTIAN LIFE (1994); JOHN FINNIS, AQUINAS: MORAL, POLITICAL, AND LEGAL THEORY (1998) [*hereinafter* FINNIS, AQUINAS]; GERMAIN GRISEZ & JOSEPH M. BOYLE, JR., LIFE AND DEATH WITH LIBERTY AND JUSTICE: A CONTRIBUTION TO THE EUTHANASIA DEBATE (1979); ROBERT P. GEORGE, IN DEFENSE OF NATURAL LAW (2001); Germain Grisez, Joseph M. Boyle & John Finnis, *Practical Principles, Moral Truth, and Ultimate Ends*, 32 AM. J. JURIS 99 (1987); John M. Finnis, Germain G. Grisez & Joseph M. Boyle, *"Direct" and "Indirect": A Reply to Critics of Our Action Theory*, 65 THOMIST 1 (2001); MARK C. MURPHY, NATURAL LAW AND PRACTICAL RATIONALITY (2001) [*hereinafter* MURPHY, RATIONALITY]; MARK C. MURPHY, NATURAL LAW IN JURISPRUDENCE AND POLITICS (2006); TIMOTHY CHAPPELL, UNDERSTANDING HUMAN GOODS: A THEORY OF ETHICS (1995). While my work, like the work of these theorists, clearly lies within the broader natural law tradition, it should be clear that it differs from that of other natural law theorists in a variety of ways.

substantive and *pluriform* conception of well-being (Part II) and a set of constraints governing the flourishing of moral agents and moral patients (Part III).[2] A credible conception of welfare—featuring a diverse array of basic aspects of well-being—and of what reason requires with respect to our own flourishing and our attempts to help others flourish (including acknowledging the reality of the varied dimensions of welfare, acting fairly, and declining to cause harm purposefully or instrumentally) can ground a rich and attractive conception of the good life (Part IV).[3]

II. WELFARE IS MULTIDIMENSIONAL

A. Well-Being Is Diverse and Lacks a Substantive Essence

Talk about welfare, well-being, flourishing, or fulfillment (I use the terms synonymously) is generic and abstract.[4] Saying that something is an aspect of welfare is just a way of saying that one has a reason to experience it or engage in it or embody it, or to help another do so.[5] In other words, there's no substantive *essence* of what it is for something to be an aspect of welfare other than this.

People often talk as if there were such an essence. Two common approaches to specifying it are unsatisfactory: (*i*) the notion that something is an instance or aspect of welfare if it counts as the satisfaction of a *preference* (Section B), and (*ii*) the idea that something is an instance or aspect of welfare if it produces some hedonic psychic state (Section C). Rather, welfare is a multidimensional reality without a substantive essence that can be identified using a range of complementary approaches (Section D). Its aspects are incommensurable and non-fungible (Section E). And well-being *matters* in any particular case precisely because it is the well-being of a

[2] For present purposes, I count as a moral *agent* if I am capable of making morally responsible choices; I count as a moral *patient* if I am owed moral consideration.

[3] *See* CHARTIER, *supra* note 1, at 6–23 for a further discussion of the approach to moral theory represented here and further references to sources of insight on which I draw here. Though there are not dramatic differences, there are some, and of course the present account, rather than its predecessor, represents the current state of my thinking about the contours of an appealing moral stance.

[4] *Cf.* THOMAS M. SCANLON, WHAT WE OWE TO EACH OTHER 95–100 (1998).

[5] We *participate* or *engage in* friendships; we *experience* æsthetic form and sensory pleasure; we *are* alive; we *acquire and embody* practical reasonableness and knowledge. While we can reasonably talk about friendship, æsthetic experience, sensory pleasure knowledge, life, and practical reasonableness, among others, as aspects or dimensions of welfare or well-being, some are activities; some are relationships; some are experiences; some are qualities of our existence. It's awkward to talk about all of them, viewed as a class. In this book, I've decided to avoid talking about *participating* in the various aspects of well-being (except when, as in the case of friendship, participation-language has an obvious and non-confusing meaning), because, while it need not be read as doing so, it too easily suggests that aspects of well-being are preexisting impersonal realities. I use a variety of alternatives (talk about *flourishing* will be especially common) in hopes of emphasizing that particular relationships, experiences, activities, and states of being are worthwhile goals.

particular moral patient (Section F). In brief, welfare or well-being or flourishing or fulfillment is what it is, independent (at least in general) of our reactions to it,[6] and it is inescapably diverse (Section G).

B. Welfare Is Not Preference-Satisfaction

The notion of welfare (like the similar notions of well-being, flourishing, and fulfillment) is essentially *normative*.[7] By contrast, talk about preferences is straightforwardly *descriptive*. To report a preference is simply to note a particular attitude or disposition on someone's part. For any preference, it will always be reasonable to ask whether it ought to be satisfied; the question of what action it is reasonable for me to take in light of the preference always remains open. To the factual report, "I prefer X," it will always make sense to respond, "But is it *reasonable* for you to prefer X?" The only basis on which it would make sense to equate welfare with preference would be a synthetic judgment to the effect that I *ought* (at least presumptively) to prefer what I prefer (not in the sense that I ought to ratify some particular preference, but that I should prefer things simply because I do in fact prefer them). And there are too many instances of things which people do prefer but which we ordinarily suppose that they have good reason *not* to prefer for this to be an attractive option.

In any event, the equation of preference with welfare misses the point that, when I do prefer something, I ordinarily prefer it under some description other than the description "preferred by me." My preference typically presupposes the judgment that what I am preferring is actually *worth* preferring—good for me or for another. It might seem that this isn't always the case: sometimes I select one option from among a menu of possibilities simply because I experience some sort of psychic inclination to do so. And there is a sense in which acting on my preference in this case needs no further justification than that I prefer what I prefer. But notice that, even here, not just anything is on the menu of possibilities. The fact that something is treated as reasonably included on the menu suggests that it's already been vetted as reasonable, as worth preferring; it's easy to imagine a case in which I express a preference for myself or another that might seem (or be) unintelligible or undesirable, and so in need of justification. Justifying something *simply* by saying that I prefer it only makes sense in the limit-case in which I'm choosing it from among a set of possibilities any

6 Peace of mind, æsthetic experience, and sensory pleasure might all be thought to be exceptions here.

7 This is not true, of course, in the specialized discourse of welfare economics, which is concerned precisely with determining how best to satisfy preferences. My goal here is not to correct economists in their use of language; my focus is on welfare in what I take to be the ordinary-language sense. Thanks to Sandy Thatcher for emphasizing the need to make this point.

of which might merit being selected. Preferring ordinarily presupposes preferability, so preference-satisfaction can't reasonably substitute for preferability.

C. Welfare Is Not a Pleasant Emotional Reaction

1. *It Is a Mistake to Identify Well-Being with a Positive Emotional State*

Well-being isn't the same thing as some sort of positive emotional reaction. For a mental state to qualify as an emotion, it must be associated with a cognition (Subsection 2). Thus, it makes no sense, at least ordinarily, to perform an action *for the purpose of* experiencing a particular emotion (Subsection 3). There is certainly no reason to think of well-being itself as a subjective, emotional state (Subsection 4). Well-being is neither dependent on nor constituted by one's emotional states (Subsection 5).[8]

2. *Emotions Necessarily Involve Cognitions*

It's important to recognize that pleasant psychic states come in (at least) two varieties: sensations and emotions. A *sensation* carries no particular cognitive content; it is what it is, and we characteristically seek (or avoid) sensations just because of their phenomenal qualities—just, that is, because of how they *feel* in a narrow sense. An emotion, by contrast, is a sensation allied with a *cognition*—that is, with a *thought* about value or meaning or appropriate response. When I experience an emotion, I'm experiencing a sensation that serves as a signal either pointing to or prompted by a judgment about what might be an appropriate response to a given situation. Judgments about appropriateness—inherently normative judgments—are inextricable from emotions.

There's a complex relationship between the sensation and the cognition that make up an emotion. The sensation characteristically serves as a *signal* that encapsulates or points to the cognition.[9] In some cases, a logically prior *judgment* about a situation triggers a conscious sensation. In others, the sensation is triggered unconsciously, without any intervening thought, but then goes on to prompt the relevant sort of thought. In either kind of case, the emotion embodies useful information about the significance of our circumstances. Emotions provide us with compressed insight into those circumstances, insight that may sometimes reflect our awareness of factors we haven't allowed into consciousness. In addition, they tell us about ourselves,

[8] For an extended discussion of the relevant issues, *see* FINNIS, ETHICS, *supra* note 1, at 26–55.

[9] *Cf.* ANTONIO DAMASIO, DESCARTES' ERROR: EMOTION, REASON, AND THE HUMAN BRAIN (1994) (discussing the notion of emotions as "somatic markers" efficiently encapsulating relevant information).

about what—quite apart from our beliefs about how we *ought* to react—we *actually* prize and fear.

But although emotions do embody information related not only to ourselves but also to our circumstances, it's important to see that any information about our circumstances conveyed in an emotion hasn't necessarily been weighed and scrutinized critically. It is often helpful to take seriously the signals about our surroundings embedded in an emotion, but careful, critical reflection is still often in order to determine whether the assessment the emotion conveys is accurate.

3. *Experiencing an Emotion Is Not Ordinarily the Goal of a Reasonable Action*

Although an emotion is a source of information (however accurate) about oneself and one's surroundings, the fact that doing something will enable one to experience a particular emotion is not ordinarily a credible reason to do it. One ordinarily has perfectly good reasons to do things which one knows will, in fact, evoke positive emotions: one knows, say, that one will experience emotional satisfaction in the course of going home for the holidays. But one's reason for going isn't the emotional satisfaction, but rather the activities, relationships, and experiences that one expects to give rise to the satisfaction.

It's important to seek good information about oneself and one's surroundings, and such information may be accessible by means of an emotion. However, an emotion involves a cognition, characteristically the judgment (not necessarily fully conscious) that a given object or event merits a particular sort of physical or mental reaction. Such a judgment is either appropriate or inappropriate, and its fittingness cannot ordinarily be the direct object of an action.

If I understand what an emotion is, I cannot reasonably seek to experience a different emotion in response to a particular situation without also making a different associated judgment about the situation. And I cannot make a different judgment unless my understanding either of the relevant facts or of their significance alters. I might wish that I experienced a different emotion in a given case—I might, say, want the feelings associated with fear to go away—but I can't change the *emotion* without changing the allied cognition (whether the feeling is a product or a cause of the cognition).

Sometimes an environmental trigger—rather than deliberation, perception, or intuition, any of which might be the source of a reasonable belief—generates a belief one takes to be unreasonable, and in this case, one can surely attempt to manipulate the trigger to end the belief.[10] Most of the time, however, beliefs are

[10] I can, of course, sometimes reason in precisely this way. Suppose I'm walking through a forest at night and hear a sound that triggers intense fear. Perhaps I'm paralyzed by the fear; or perhaps I begin

not, nor can they be, under our volitional control. A belief-forming mechanism that gave us the beliefs we chose rather than the beliefs that actually followed from our encounters with the world outside the process of conscious reflection would be thoroughly unreliable, because the beliefs would be unrelated to their putative objects. What one wants from one's beliefs is precisely that they be *accurate*, that they in some sense count as correct *responses* to a world that exists independently of one's beliefs and preferences. A belief presents itself as *about* something, but it does no good if it's shaped primarily by one's will rather than by the object it's supposed to be about.[11] So it will make sense to seek volitionally to undermine a belief associated with an emotion (and so to alter the emotion itself) only when one takes the belief-forming mechanism responsible for the belief to be generally unreliable or when one has good reason in a particular case to judge that the mechanism has produced a dubious belief.

Under ordinary circumstances, a reasonable action is an action that seeks to realize or protect—in one's own life or another's—some aspect of well-being. Such an action may well yield a particular emotional response—say, satisfaction at the achievement of something valuable. Indeed, it *should* characteristically yield such a response if one's emotions are in good working order. But it will be the aspect of well-being that makes the response appropriate, and *that* will thus be the reasonably chosen object of one's action.

Again, of course, we do sometimes seek to change emotions directly. I might, say, visit a new and interesting place in order to boost my spirits. But when my feelings are the direct object of my action, this would seem to be either because (*i*) I am seeking unreasonably to alter an evaluation of my circumstances which I can see no way to undermine cognitively, in which case I run the risk of disconnecting myself from reality; (*ii*) my feelings do not match my beliefs about the way things are or about how it might be desirable to respond to the way things are, and I am trying to bring the two into alignment; (*iii*) I am uncertain how best to evaluate a situation I confront, but am trying, at minimum, to avoid being paralyzed by negative feelings (which can feed back into and warp accurate judgment) and am therefore trying to alter my feelings *without* impeding my capacity for judgment; or (*iv*) I am seeking an experience of imaginative immersion (as in the world of a film or book), in which case it is *that* world, rather than the world of my everyday experience, to

running in particular direction. The fear, we may suppose, leads to a cognition of some sort: say, the judgment that my flight or paralysis, as the case may be, is warranted by the situation. I may quite reasonably challenge this judgment directly, because I regard it as inaccurate, or else put myself in a situation in which environmental stimuli no longer trigger the fear that leads to the judgment I regard as inappropriate.

[11] Obviously, in a case in which an emotion involves a cognition that is *triggered by* a sensation, one may indirectly affect the cognition by seeking to alter the sensation, as when one knows that a certain event will yield irrational fear.

which I seek to make my judgment and my feelings, aligned in an emotion, responsive. Case (*i*) is an instance of unreasonable action, and the frequency with which choices of this kind occur does nothing to count against their unreasonableness. By contrast, cases (*ii*), (*iii*), and (*iv*) do not involve any denial that accurate cognition is the appropriate basis for reasonable action and that it makes no sense to want the feeling-cognition pair that is a given emotion when one regards the cognition that would be an integral element of the emotion as false. Thus, none of these cases provides a counterexample to the claim that it is at least ordinarily unreasonable to desire to experience an *emotion*, which necessarily incorporates a judgment, as the goal of an action.

4. *Welfare Is Not an Emotion*

The (dubious) claim that welfare, well-being, is, just as such, a pleasant psychic state can't sensibly be the claim that welfare *is* a particular emotion. That's because the emotion—whichever emotion is purportedly the right one—embodies judgments about appropriateness that will likely unavoidably amount to or involve judgments about welfare. So the claim that welfare amounts to an emotion would be question-begging: to make sense of the cognition involved in the emotion would require making sense of welfare, so it wouldn't work to appeal to the emotion itself as a way of making sense of welfare.

Clearly this is true of the special case in which the pleasant psychic state is *happiness*, which can be understood as the pleasure associated precisely with preference-satisfaction. Understood as an emotion, happiness obviously involves a cognition—roughly, the belief that the object of one's happiness is an appropriate object of happiness. One can always ask about this belief whether it is accurate.

One can also always ask of one's satisfaction with any given state of affairs "Should I be happy about this?" "Does it make sense to be happy about it?" "Is it worth being happy about?" If one's preferences are actually worth satisfying, then it makes sense to be pleased that they have been satisfied. But, in this case, what matters—and so what seems actually to constitute one's well-being—is whatever it is that makes it worthwhile that the preference has been satisfied—and not *either* the satisfaction of the preference qua preference *or* the sensation associated with the satisfaction of the preference. On the other hand, if one's preferences are not worth satisfying, there will be no more reason to seek to be pleased at their having been satisfied than there will be to seek that they be satisfied in the first place. What's important to see in either case is that the question of the reasonableness of one's reaction to the satisfaction of one's preferences is always on the table, and that its reasonableness depends on the reasonableness of satisfying the preferences.

An obvious example of the frequent conflation of well-being with a psychic state is the assumption that *being in love* is inherently valuable apart from the worth of the relationship to the existence and value of which this emotional state is a pointer. Being in love is a particular mental state that involves both feelings of excitement, euphoria, and delight in the beloved and the desire to be united—usually both psychically and sexually—with the beloved; it necessarily involves judgments about the beloved as, for instance, worth desiring, worth pursuing, worth finding attractive, worth uniting with, worth admiring, and so forth. It can be triggered in a variety of ways; it seems to be realized in the brain and the rest of the nervous system through the release of chemicals including oxytocin and phenylethylamine.[12] The chemically induced high associated with being in love is phenomenally pleasurable, but relatively transient, with the result that many people find the prospect of pursuing the high, by repeatedly beginning new relationships, quite irresistible. But although romantic passion is reasonably regarded as evidence that something important is occurring or could occur (for the experience of being in love need not come at the beginning of a relationship), it's *the something*—the actual or prospective relationship, the prospect or the reality of creating a "we" with someone—that's important, worthwhile, valuable, not the psychic state that *highlights* its value.[13] There is no reason not to relish the pleasure associated with being in love, as long as it's not treated as an end in itself—*or* as the only possible evidence of a relationship's worth, because a chemical high can dissipate even as a relationship remains very real and valuable. But the temptation, unfortunately, is often to treat the high as valuable in its own right, and thus both to regard a relationship that no longer provokes it as being somehow itself deficient and to seek a new relationship with the potential to birth a new high at the cost of an existing one. Remembering the relationship between emotions and well-being may help to reduce the likelihood that the value of existing relationships will be discounted or ignored in this way.

5. *Well-Being Is Not Identical with or Dependent on One's Emotional Reaction to One's Condition*

Listening to one's emotions is important and informative. But although sensory pleasure—an *aspect* of a positive emotion—is an aspect of well-being, well-being isn't the same as a particular emotional state. An emotion is an emotion precisely because it involves—in any of several ways—a cognition, a judgment, which frequently presents itself as an accurate evaluation. The aptness of the evaluation is

[12] *See* HELEN FISHER, WHY WE LOVE: THE NATURE AND CHEMISTRY OF ROMANTIC LOVE (2004).

[13] *See* ROBERT C. SOLOMON, ABOUT LOVE: REINVENTING ROMANCE FOR OUR TIME (1988). Despite the title's gesture at contemporaneity, Solomon's basic understanding of emotion is Aristotelian.

dependent on factors external to the evaluation itself, so it makes no sense to seek an emotion as such as the goal of one's action.

D. Welfare Is Pluriform

1. *Multiple, Complementary Approaches Help Us Identify Basic Aspects of Well-Being*

Among the reasonable approaches to identifying good reasons for choice may be locating the things we characteristically take to be basic justifications for our actions (Subsection 2) or the aspects of our lives that are affected by what we confidently judge to be real harms (Subsection 3). We might reasonably judge some claims about putative aspects of well-being to be correct if rejecting them would involve us in self-contradiction (Subsection 4). That some beliefs about well-being seem relatively consistent across cultures may provide limited evidence for the truth of those beliefs (Subsection 5). And the process of seeking and achieving reflective equilibrium might enable us to justify claims to identify particular aspects of well-being (Subsection 6). These approaches might all reasonably figure in efforts to provide credible support for the tentative identification of multiple aspects of well-being (Subsection 7).

2. *We Take Something to Be a Dimension of Well-Being if We Treat It as a Basic Reason for Action*

Identifying something as an aspect of welfare, or as an instance of such an aspect, is ultimately a matter of identifying good reasons for making choices. So one way to think about what might or might not be a good reason for action is to think about what might or might not be a good reason to choose. And perhaps we can begin to get at this more clearly by thinking about how we actually *do* make choices.[14]

Very often, it makes sense, when someone else proposes that I do something, or when I experience an inner impulse to make a particular choice, to ask, "Why should I?" or "What would make that a sensible choice?" And usually, in turn, we can offer underlying reasons for our choices. Why should I get in the car? *To drive to the park*. Why should I want to drive to the park? *Because I'm supposed to meet Chris there*. Why should I want to meet Chris in the park? *Because the park will provide us with a comfortable environment in which to talk*. Why should I want to talk with Chris? *Because, by talking, we'll grow closer, achieve greater mutual understanding, amuse each other, or perhaps discover ways of helping each other*. Why should I want

[14] *See, e.g.*, GRISEZ, PRINCIPLES, *supra* note 1, at 122; CHAPPELL, *supra* note 1, at 35–36.

to do those things with Chris? *Because those things are important constituents of friendship; Chris is my friend, and I want to nourish our friendship.*

But suppose I ask, "Why should I want to nourish a friendship—not this friendship in particular, but any friendship?" What answer can I give, apart from the relatively uninformative report on the way things seem to me: *friendship matters*. Of course there are various ways in which friendship matters instrumentally: friends help each other in various ways. But we do not seem in general to want friendship just because of the aid friends can offer, so that friendship turns out to be important just because it conduces to our other purposes. Connecting with others, knowing others, incorporating them into our lives and our identities, seems often to be something we actually choose for its own sake.

And the same seems to be true of lots of other things as well. Take sensory pleasure.[15] Perhaps I consume a bar of chocolate as a source of energy, or as part of a social ritual. But more often I do so simply because of its flavor. There is nothing odd about choosing to eat a bar of chocolate because the taste of chocolate is pleasurable, and this fact, offered in justification of my action, seems to require no further rationale. It's worth emphasizing, again, that an experience of sensory pleasure is on its own a bare *sensation*, not an *emotion*; while it might be accompanied by a judgment, it need not be, and it can serve on its own as an independent reason for action despite the fact that experiencing an emotion ordinarily cannot function in this way.

Or consider knowledge. If I want to learn about the behavior of a particular molecule, or determine how mind and body are related, or understand Chinese tort law, I may be pursuing some independent goal: perhaps I am trying to justify a promotion or a new job, or impress a date. But I can just as sensibly pursue my goal for its own sake. Someone else can reasonably ask why finding out about something in particular is appealing to me—a question that requires explanation, but not justification—but simply wanting to know, wanting to understand, seems to provide as much *justification* as is needed.

What about æsthetic experience? To seek to see the beauty of a painting, to relish the artistry of a gymnast, to catch the interplay of themes in a fugue, to appreciate the artistry involved in combining flavors and textures in a meal, or to trace the elegance of a mathematical proof—in each case, one's action seems perfectly intelligible, perfectly reasonable, without needing any additional rationale. And the same seems true of other dimensions of our lives and experiences, any of which might seem—like friendship, knowledge, and æsthetic experience—to be sufficient to end a chain of justification for a choice. Play, the capacity for practical reasoning, religion (in the broad sense of being in harmony with reality, whether the cosmos is the whole of reality or not), imaginative immersion in a fictive narrative and the

[15] *See* CHAPPELL, *supra* note 1; THOMAS NAGEL, THE VIEW FROM NOWHERE 156–62 (1986).

lives of its characters (perhaps this is an aspect of æsthetic experience), life, bodily well-being, and peace of mind all seem to provide sensible reasons for doing things that don't need to be justified or rendered intelligible by reference to any deeper reasons.[16]

Thinking through our own (or other agents') reasons for action, and seeing where chains of justification and explanation stop, is perhaps the most natural way of identifying what we take to be genuinely worthwhile aspects of welfare, *basic*—in the sense of irreducible—aspects of well-being. Perhaps we're mistaken about this, of course: we're not infallible. But we can at least make our own understanding more luminous; we can clarify what makes sense to us. Notice that at no point in this process do we attempt to derive a judgment about what we *ought* to pursue, about what really is an aspect of well-being, from a *descriptive* claim about what we do, in fact, pursue. Rather, we're simply trying to find the most basic normative judgments we do, in fact, make regarding our own well-being and other people's and ask what follows from these judgments.

To be sure, there will be variations among persons and groups in this regard, and some of these variations will quite possibly be explicable with reference to personality or cultural difference of one sort or another. But in trying to determine whether a putative aspect of welfare really is intrinsically valuable, a particular moral agent will still need to ask herself whether it seems to her on due reflection to be a genuinely final end or not. And, if she judges that it is, she will thereby be committed to maintaining that it is, in fact, an authentic aspect of well-being—for her and for anyone relevantly similar to her.[17]

3. *Our Judgments about Harms Point Us to Insights about the Nature of Well-Being*

There are other, complementary approaches to reaching the same kind of understanding. For instance: we can begin by focusing on what's going on when we believe another has been harmed, when we believe we're being threatened, and so forth. What's the locus of the actual potential loss? What does the harm amount to? Again, we can work our way down to the most basic level of understanding, asking at each stage if further illumination would be offered by a recharacterization of what has been or might be harmed. The destruction of an archive of irreplaceable documents, for instance, might be seen as (among other things) impeding an opportunity

[16] Perhaps bodily well-being should be thought of as an independently valuable aspect of flourishing. Alternatively, it might make sense to regard bodily well-being as valuable to the extent needed to make life and the other kinds of flourishing possible.

[17] Thanks to Sandy Thatcher for highlighting the need to clarify this point.

for *knowledge* or *æsthetic experience* on the part of those who might consult it. Lying about one person to another might damage a *friendship*. Torture seems to be an attack on *peace of mind*, and sometimes, of course, on *life*. And so on. By analyzing our judgments about situations in which harms occur or are threatened, we can again identify what we in fact take to be fundamentally worthwhile aspects of our lives.[18]

4. *It May Be Self-Contradictory to Deny That Some Putative Aspects of Welfare Provide Reasons for Action*

In some cases, we can do more than this: we can show that it is actually self-contradictory to attempt to deny the value of one or another aspect of welfare. Most fundamentally, of course, it makes no sense to say, "Nothing is valuable for its own sake," for, if an infinite regress is to be avoided, the process of valuing one thing with reference to another thing must finally come to rest. Nothing can be valuable instrumentally unless something is valuable intrinsically. And something must be valuable intrinsically or there will be no reason to act at all (and so, of course, no reason to choose to assert that nothing is valuable).

It won't do to respond that something can be valuable instrumentally as long as something else, something to which it is instrumental, is *valued* for its own sake. For if the focus is on the act of valuation rather than its justification, the question, "But is this valuable?" will continue to be appropriate. The answer to the question must be either "Yes" or "No." And if it is "No," then it seems that anything instrumental to whatever it is that has been judged not to be inherently valuable can't be seen as intrinsically valuable itself. Unless something else farther along the chain of justification does prove to be genuinely worth valuing, action still seems pointless.

In addition, a person actively nurturing a friendship, seeking bodily well-being, engaging in play, is estopped from claiming that the putative aspect of welfare that is the object of her action isn't, at any rate, worthwhile for *her* to value; if it weren't, why would she choose it as the object of her action? However one might be inclined to view other people's actions, one can't view one's own, from the inside, as simply *happening* to one. Rather, one has to choose. And if one has to choose, it will at minimum be difficult not to select the object of one's action under some description such that it is *worth* pursuing under that description. Further, if one judges that something is a worthwhile aspect of one's own life, it will be difficult to resist the conclusion that it is also potentially a worthwhile aspect of another's.

Denying some aspects of well-being may be self-contradictory for deeper reasons. Someone who denies that knowledge is inherently valuable appears to be making

[18] *See* Grisez, Principles, *supra* note 1, at 123; Murphy, Rationality, *supra* note 1, at 40.

a truth-claim, a claim about knowledge, that might seem to presuppose the worthwhileness of things.[19] Someone who embraces skepticism about the objectivity of the ends of action but who *argues* for this conclusion might seem to be presupposing the inherent worth of truth, and so to be caught in a contradiction.[20]

And rejecting the possibility that there might be objective reasons for action—and so of reasons to seek to flourish or to help another to flourish—is at least very close to rejecting the possibility that there might be objective reasons for *judgment* as well. Certainly, the reasons characteristically offered for rejecting this possibility—as that actions and dispositions must be accounted for in causal terms and that normativity can play no part in explaining them—seem fairly clearly to count against reasons for judgment as much as against reasons for action. And this means that claims about (at least) logical, mathematical, and epistemic norms are undermined by these arguments. But when an argument appears to undermine the possibility of argumentation itself, something—even if we cannot agree on what—seems pretty clearly to have gone seriously wrong. And this obviously gives us reason to question the underlying argument, and so to doubt the effectiveness of its in-principle challenge to normative claims about reasons for action.[21]

5. *Cross-Cultural Consensus May Help Us to Identify Basic Aspects of Well-Being*

The fact that another *finds* something valuable does not mean, of course, that it *is* valuable—either for her or for you. Nonetheless, the existence of a widespread, cross-cultural consensus on basic aspects of well-being is perhaps evidence of a certain kind that humans either have correctly identified multiple, diverse aspects of well-being or are systematically deceived. Whether one concludes that such a consensus *does* serve to support particular claims about well-being will depend, of course, at least in part, on how one evaluates the possibility that there are normative

[19] *See* FINNIS, LAW, *supra* note 1, at 73–75.

[20] *See* FINNIS, AQUINAS, *supra* note 1, at 58–61. *Cf.* FINNIS, ETHICS, *supra* note 1 at 4–5, 51–53.

[21] The analogy between reasons for judgment or belief on the one hand and reasons for action on the other has been explored effectively by a variety of philosophers, notably Hilary Putnam. It is developed extensively in TERENCE CUNEO, THE NORMATIVE WEB: AN ARGUMENT FOR MORAL REALISM (2007) and Nathan Nobis, Truth in Ethics and Epistemology: A Defense of Normative Realism (2004) (unpublished PhD dissertation, University of Rochester). The approach defended by Cuneo and Nobis rightly forms part of an ensemble of defenses available for moral realism, and I believe these defenses are worth taking quite seriously. An alternative understanding of metaethics—say, an expressivist one—might be seen successfully to ground the kinds of normative claims I make here, although I am inclined to think that expressivist approaches undermine the force of moral requirements rather more substantially than their proponents often suppose. I take no position here on questions of moral *epistemology*: whether a sentimentalist epistemology, for instance, turned out to be correct need have no implications for the realism–irrealism debate.

truths and that one might actually succeed in knowing some of them.[22] In any case, it does not seem unreasonable to pay some attention to cross-cultural evidence for the endorsement of particular ends of action.

6. *We May Be Able to Justify Claims about Well-Being by Seeing How Well They Fit into Coherent Webs of Belief*

Finally, we might reasonably pursue a piecemeal strategy of assessing—and so of validating or invalidating—particular claims about putative aspects of well-being in much the way we assess most claims in our lives. The piecemeal approach has famously been described as a matter of seeking "reflective equilibrium."[23] Unavoidably, we begin (our conscious lives, and each of the successive moments in those lives) with particular beliefs. When we encounter challenges to those beliefs, we resolve them—by rejecting or modifying the beliefs we hold, by reinterpreting or rejecting the challenging evidence or argument, or by finding a way in which both new and old beliefs can coexist consistently.[24] There is no rigid formula for doing this; rather, one seeks to achieve an elegant fit among all of one's beliefs. One is not responsible, surely, for constantly searching for potential defeaters for one's beliefs, but one *is* surely responsible for taking appropriate account of potential defeaters when they come to one's attention.[25]

This general approach is surely available with respect to one's beliefs about basic aspects of well-being. Self-reflection will reveal that we do, in fact, seem often to have particular beliefs about what is and isn't a basic dimension of welfare. We can retain those beliefs that seem correct to us absent particular challenges to them (challenges which may focus, of course, either on specific putative aspects of welfare or on the notion that there are objective aspects of welfare at all). In the face of such challenges, we may need to alter or abandon our beliefs about what makes for well-being; alternatively, we may find that they emerge from the process of scrutiny more obviously correct than before.[26]

[22] *See* FINNIS, LAW, *supra* note 1, at 81–90 (1980). *Cf.* DONALD BROWN, HUMAN UNIVERSALS (1991); MORRIS GINSBERG, ON THE DIVERSITY OF MORALS (1962).

[23] *See* JOHN RAWLS, A THEORY OF JUSTICE 18–19, 42–45 (2d ed. 1999); *cf.* W. V. O. QUINE & J. S. ULLIAN, THE WEB OF BELIEF (2d ed., 1978).

[24] *See, e.g.*, ALASDAIR MACINTYRE, WHOSE JUSTICE? WHICH RATIONALITY? (1988); Nicholas Wolterstorff, *Can Belief in God Be Rational if It Has No Foundations?*, *in* FAITH AND RATIONALITY: REASON AND BELIEF IN GOD 135 (Alvin Plantinga & Nicholas Wolterstorff eds., 1983).

[25] Taking appropriate account obviously does not mean seeking to resolve every problem immediately: one may surely place on the back burner a major challenge to some trivially important belief.

[26] *Cf.* CHARLES LARMORE, THE MORALS OF MODERNITY 55–64 (1996); Gary Chartier, Comment, *Righting Narrative: Robert Chang, Poststructuralism, and the Limits of Critique*, 7 UCLA ASIAN PAC. AM. L.J. 105 (2001).

7. *Varied Approaches to Identifying Aspects of Well-Being May Prove Mutually Supportive*

Analyzing what we take to be good reasons for action and loci of what we take to be real harms, recognizing that denying the value of some arguable instances of well-being would be self-contradictory, drawing inferences from cross-cultural beliefs about well-being, and seeking to determine how well particular convictions about well-being fit into coherent webs of belief can all help us to provide secure foundations for our identifications of various aspects of welfare, flourishing, or fulfillment. In many cases, it seems likely that we will find that different approaches reinforce parallel identifications of particular dimensions of well-being. Bodily well- being seems to be a source of basic reasons for action; bodily well-being seems to be what events which we would likely recognize as authentic injuries in fact injure; there is widespread cross-cultural support for the view that bodily well-being is valuable; and the notion that bodily well-being is a fundamental aspect of well-being fits well with our other beliefs about our lives and our convictions about what is worthwhile.[27] I believe the same kind of case might arguably be made for the other aspects of welfare I have considered, including friendship, knowledge, æsthetic experience, play, practical reasonableness, religion, imaginative immersion, life, sensory pleasure, and peace of mind.[28] Rational reflection can provide at least some plausible grounding for claims about well-being.

E. The Various Dimensions of Welfare Are Incommensurable and Non-Fungible

There is no underlying *thing* that well-being *is*. "Well-being" or "welfare" or "flourishing" or "fulfillment" should simply be seen as a summary label for all the different aspects of a life that goes well. There is no quantity, no substance, that underlies all dimensions of well-being qua dimensions of well-being. And the absence of such a substratum, a definable common element, means that the various aspects of well-being are *incommensurable*—that there is no way of measuring them in relation to each other.[29] It makes no sense to say that æsthetic experience is worth more

[27] *Cf.* Bryan Turner, Vulnerability and Human Rights (2006).

[28] Thus, it is unreasonable to treat *pleasure*, or some particular sort of pleasure, as the only valuable thing, or the substratum underlying other putative aspects of welfare; rather, sensory pleasure—as over against emotional pleasure, which is not independently valuable, but is, instead, a pointer to the putative value of an action, quality, relationship, characteristic, or experience—is simply one among many dimensions of well-being. *Cf.* Finnis, Law, *supra* note 1, at 95–97.

[29] *See, e.g.*, Finnis, Law, *supra* note 1 at 92–95; Finnis, Ethics, *supra* note 1, at 86–90; Grisez & Shaw, *supra* note 1, at 132.

than play, or practical reasonableness more than life. There is thus no way of weighing some particular instance of one against some particular instance of another, as if there were an objective fact of the matter about whether a solitary trip to a museum, say, was more worthwhile than a day spent with friends. And there is no way, either, of weighing some particular instance of the same kind of flourishing against another: my friendship with Sheldon and my friendship with Jeffrey and my friendship with Annette are all different from each other, even though each is a friendship. The point is *not* that there is no reliable procedure for determining what the fact of the matter might be, as if the problem were in essence epistemic. Rather, the point is that there *is* no fact of the matter, any more than there is a fact of the matter about whether orange is faster than up.[30] Thus, attempting to aggregate the putative values of various instances of diverse kinds of welfare "is senseless in the way that it is senseless to try to sum together the size of this page, the number six, and the mass of this book."[31]

Similarly, particular instances of the various aspects of well-being are *non-fungible*: there is no objective basis for trading one off against another. It is silly to suppose that it is either true or false that listening to Bach's third Brandenburg Concerto involves more æsthetic value than contemplating the *Mona Lisa*, that knowing about theoretical physics is better than knowing about history, or that one friendship is more *intrinsically* worthwhile than another.

Obviously, we make choices among different kinds of well-being and different instances of different kinds of well-being, in light of our preferences and circumstances and characters and dispositions.[32] And as long as we're choosing reasonably among real goods, that seems entirely appropriate. We can't do everything, we shouldn't try to do so, and we're free to choose how we will shape our lives. It's just important to remember that, when I make a choice among particular kinds of welfare, I'm not selecting, because I can't be selecting, the best option for any human, or the best option for anyone in my situation, or the best option for me: I'm selecting one of a number of possibilities, none of which can be ranked ahead of any of the others because they're all fundamentally different, because each is fundamentally unique, and any of which I can freely embrace. And of course it's not as if the only way to generate moral requirements regarding choices among aspects of well-being is to show that they can be objectively ranked: there are constraints on our choices imposed by specific requirements of practical reasonableness. Seeking to participate in a friendship and enjoying the dietary benefits and sensory pleasures associated

[30] Thanks to Fritz Guy for this example.

[31] FINNIS, LAW, *supra* note 1, at 113; *cf. id.* at 115.

[32] *See, e.g.*, FINNIS, ETHICS, *supra* note 1, at 90–94; *cf.* DAVID L. NORTON, PERSONAL DESTINIES (1976).

with consuming a good meal are both ways of flourishing, but it may be inconsistent with the requirement of practical reasonableness I label the Principle of Fairness to opt for the meal over helping a friend.[33]

F. To Recognize Something as an Aspect of Welfare Is to See a Reason to Pursue It for the Benefit of the Moral Patient of Whose Welfare It Is an Aspect, Not a Reason to Try to Realize "Impersonal Value"

The claim that there are multiple basic aspects of well-being or flourishing or fulfillment can certainly risk sliding into "Platonism"—the sense that the various aspects of welfare are important independently of the people whose goods they are, that their logically prior existence exerts some sort of claim on us, that they demand their own realization in the world and in our lives. I do not wish to defend this sort of view. On my view, what matters most about the sort of account of welfare I have offered here is simply this.

(i) There are truths about my welfare, or yours, that are strongly independent of our preferences.[34]

(ii) The aspects of a moral patient's welfare are diverse—there are different ways in which her life is or isn't going well at any given time, and different ways in which it could go well over time.

(iii) While one is quite free to seek flourishing and fulfillment in an infinite variety of ways, there are meaningful continuities among the things that make for welfare in humans (and others).

(iv) Whatever one's welfare amounts to, there are some things *no one's* welfare amounts to, including preference-satisfaction and the cluster of emotional states we call happiness (since only if the preferences being satisfied are preferences for real instances of flourishing is satisfying them going to be a real instance of flourishing, and since only if the states of affairs regarding which one is happy are real instances of welfare is it going to be reasonable to be happy about them).

I strenuously deny that there is only one kind of good life for persons or groups of persons. There are many, many different kinds of good lives, and the attempt to claim that one is objectively better for persons in general or, often enough, for

[33] *But cf.* Roderick T. Long, comment under Sheldon Richman, *Do Ends Justify Means?*, THE FREEMAN: IDEAS ON LIBERTY, Feb. 24, 2012, http://www.thefreemanonline.org/columns/tgif/do-ends-justify-means/#comment-89490.

[34] With whatever allowances, if any, are needed for peace of mind, æsthetic experience, and sensory pleasure.

any particular person, is simply false. There is no single, unique *summum bonum* that is the same for every person; flourishing is not a summum bonum or an agent-neutral good at all, but rather a placeholder for all the diverse ways in which people can flourish. There are many different ways in which creatures, human and otherwise, can flourish, many different ways in which their lives can go well and be worthwhile. However, there are limits on reasonable choices and reasonable lives: some putative aspects of well-being are not genuine constituents of flourishing—they are in one way or another unreal, and so not worth pursuing—and there are universally applicable requirements of reasonable action that apply to all moral agents.[35]

G. Welfare Is Reaction-Independent and Varied

For most purposes, it is not particularly important to identify an exhaustive list of the various aspects of welfare. What matters is rather that (*i*) there is some fact of the matter about what makes for well-being, (*ii*) one's well-being is not reducible either to the fact that one's preferences have been realized or that one experiences some particular emotion or other sensation, (*iii*) well-being is not a unitary quantity, but rather one that is multiform and variegated, and (*iv*) an action is reasonable if and only if its goal is one's own flourishing or another's.

Well-being is a function of how one's life actually goes, and not, per se, of how one *reacts* to one's choices, relationships, and experiences. Whether one's preferences are or aren't satisfied, whether one experiences positive or negative emotional reactions to particular aspects of one's life, may provide some *evidence* about, but doesn't generally *determine*, whether one is flourishing or helping another to flourish. (To be sure, however, a *failure* to experience a positive emotional response to one's own flourishing may often be rightly regarded as a deficiency: to fail to recognize an instance of flourishing as an instance of flourishing is to be deficient with regard to knowledge, while to fail to experience a positive sensation when one is flourishing may be a deficiency with regard to bodily well-being.) Reasonable choices are choices intended to foster one's own well-being, or another's; positive emotional responses may be concomitants of such choices, but they are ordinarily not reasonable *objects* of such choices. The objects of such choices are instances of the various dimensions of welfare. The diverse aspects of welfare are incommensurable, and particular instances of each are both incommensurable and non-fungible. They matter precisely because they are aspects of the welfare of particular moral patients, and not because they are, somehow, impersonally valuable.

[35] *See* Part III, *infra*. Thanks to an anonymous reader for prompting me to clarify my position in the way I seek to do in this paragraph.

III. REASONABLY SEEKING TO FLOURISH OR TO HELP ANOTHER TO FLOURISH REQUIRES RECOGNITION, FAIRNESS, AND RESPECT

A. Living Well Means Acting Reasonably

Reasonable action begins in free and reasonable *choice*.[36] Particular agents, and only particular agents, make choices and are morally responsible for conforming those choices to the requirements of practical reasonableness. Neither the issuance of commands by authority figures nor the fact that other participants in a common enterprise take a particular view of what ought to be done absolves anyone of responsibility for acting reasonably or confers on her any moral privileges she wouldn't otherwise have.[37]

Recognizing something as an instance of an authentic dimension of welfare, well-being, fulfillment, or flourishing means taking it as a reason (not necessarily decisive) to choose to realize it in one's own life or another's. But not all actions in pursuit of instances of basic aspects of well-being are reasonable. It's important to seek genuine aspects of well-being, rather than illusory ones (Section B). We pursue genuine aspects of well-being reasonably only when we do so fairly (Section C). And we act in accordance with reason only when we avoid attacking any aspect of well-being purposefully or instrumentally (Section D). The principles of practical reasonableness generate different sorts of prohibitions—some absolute, some relative and qualified (Section E). Taken together, they outline the contours of a reasonable life, while leaving considerable freedom for personal creativity and experimentation (Section F).

B. The Principle of Recognition Calls for the Acknowledgment of All and Only Real Aspects of Well-Being as Worthy Objects of Action

What I'll call the Principle of Recognition can be summed up this way: *do not act except in order to foster what one recognizes as a genuine aspect of well-being in one's own life or another's*.[38]

[36] On free choice, *see, e.g.*, JOSEPH BOYLE, JR., GERMAIN GRISEZ & OLAF TOLLEFSEN, FREE CHOICE: A SELF-REFERENTIAL ARGUMENT (1976); CARL GINET, ON ACTION (1989); DAVID RAY GRIFFIN, UNSNARLING THE WORLD-KNOT: CONSCIOUSNESS, FREEDOM, AND THE MIND–BODY PROBLEM (1998); ROBERT KANE, THE SIGNIFICANCE OF FREE WILL (1998); JOHN THORP, FREE WILL: A DEFENSE AGAINST NEUROPHYSIOLOGICAL DETERMINISM (1980); AUSTIN FARRER, THE FREEDOM OF THE WILL (1957). *Cf.* BENJAMIN LIBET, MIND TIME: THE TEMPORAL FACTOR IN CONSCIOUSNESS 123–56 (2004).

[37] There may, of course, be an exception with respect to anyone whose preferences are such that she consents to the exercise, with respect to her, of a privilege the agent wouldn't otherwise have had. The point is that the relevant sort of privilege needs to be rooted in consent, at minimum, if it is to be legitimate. (It may not be legitimate in any case: even if I genuinely consent, and so relinquish any claim to *legal* recompense, it is still *morally* wrong of you to chop off my fingers for your pleasure.)

[38] *Cf.* FINNIS, ETHICS, *supra* note 1, at 40–42.

It is clearly reasonable to seek to flourish or to foster flourishing—one's own or another's. Seeking to flourish or to foster flourishing provides an intelligible reason for action; there's nothing puzzling about the claim that one acts in a given way in order to participate in a friendship or to help another have an æsthetic experience. By contrast, it is hard to see why one would pursue something one does not regard as contributing to the well-being of any sentient.[39] What would be one's reason for doing so? It is easy to see how a chain of justifications for an action might terminate in an appeal to a basic aspect of flourishing. But when the rationale for an action involves no reference to any sentient's flourishing, it seems as if it would make sense to keep asking for further justification.

Sometimes people do things seemingly for inanimate objects. In some cases, this may be because they want to benefit humans or other animals. People attempt to foster life and bodily well-being by seeking to control pollution. They work to protect particular sites or regions in order to enable themselves or others to experience natural beauty. Perhaps they seek to preserve objects or spaces that have particular significance for them—that they've incorporated into their identities. (And this would include a case in which someone welcomed the fact that a particular natural object might be in existence well after the end of her own life.) In all these cases, they're doing things that they intend to contribute to well-being in one way or another; and so, even if it might initially appear otherwise, what they're doing can be perfectly intelligible and reasonable.

Often, I suspect, people attempts to benefit some non-sentient reality for its own sake simply because they reflexively treat it, or some aspect of it, as sentient, and it's hard not to see this as an instance of false belief. But it's also imaginable that someone might not have any finite creature's well-being in mind and still be acting rationally and intelligibly when seeking to enhance some aspect of the nonhuman world. At least, it's possible to conceive of the actor intending to contribute in some way to the enjoyment of beauty in the world which God might be thought to experience. And on the view that there is God, this is hardly unreasonable. On the other hand, someone who supposes that there is no God and that she is not fostering the well-being of any actual or potential sentient *does* seem to me to be acting irrationally if she seeks to enhance or protect some bit of the non-sentient world for its own

[39] Note, by the way, that, doing something for the well-being of a nonhuman sentient is not an instance of irrationality, for there are ways in which the sentient's life can go well or not *for the sentient itself*. The sentient's life can go well in various ways (even if fewer than yours or mine can), and, as a sentient, it can in some sense be aware that things are going well or not. So there's nothing irrational or unintelligible about fostering the animal's well-being. On nonhuman sentience, *see, e.g.*, Gary Varner, Personhood, Ethics, and Animal Cognition: Situating Animals in Hare's Two Level Utilitarianism (2012). On the more general question of taking moral account of nonhuman animals, *see, e.g.*, Stephen R.L. Clark, The Moral Status of Animals (1977).

sake. (Even if she understands the world in pantheistic fashion as somehow divine in its totality, but without any conscious center, it's not clear that the notion of conferring a benefit on it is genuinely intelligible.[40])

Apart from efforts to benefit the non-sentient world, it seems as if an attempt to act for some purpose other than honoring or promoting the well-being of sentients might either reflect (*i*) a mistake about what counts as well-being or (*ii*) an unconcern for well-being, rooted in the notion that preference-satisfaction is on its own a sensible reason for action. The most likely sort of mistake of the first sort, I suspect, will involve the misidentification of emotional satisfaction as a goal that's inherently worthwhile on its own. What I've already said should make clear why I regard the second option as an error.

To be sure, while particular goals can be distinguished for analytical purposes, we often pursue them in tandem—as when beauty provides an occasion for the pursuit of friendship, for instance. However, although there are vastly many reasonable but diverse ways of flourishing, people sometimes act for reasons which can reasonably be judged not to be, and not to conduce to, instances of flourishing at all (though there are certainly good reasons not to interfere with people's nonaggressive attempts to pursue these putative goods).

Instances of basic dimensions of well-being provide good independent reasons for action. Other aspects of reality do not. The Principle of Recognition embodies the requirement that we acknowledge the difference.

C. The Principle of Fairness Calls for the Avoidance of Arbitrary Distinctions among Those Affected by Our Actions

1. *The Principle of Fairness Protects the Basic Moral Equality of Sentients Capable of Flourishing*

Sometimes, we act to flourish or to foster our own flourishing (directly or indirectly). Sometimes, we act to foster the flourishing of others. Sometimes, we act for the benefit of ourselves *and* others. In principle, all such actions can be reasonable, as long as they don't involve arbitrary choices among those affected by our actions (including ourselves).

The Principle of Fairness reflects the reality and importance of shared characteristics (Subsection 2). This Principle requires that an agent *avoid discriminating arbitrarily among those affected by her actions*; it entails that she treat them equivalently except when doing so is a way of fostering authentic well-being (Subsection 3) *and* when she would be willing to see herself or her loved ones subjected to the

[40] *But cf.* Paul Taylor, Respect for Nature (1986). Thanks to Sandy Thatcher for this reference.

same sort of discrimination in which she proposes to engage were roles reversed (Subsection 4). The Principle of Fairness does *not* require that we opt for consequentialist maximizing (Subsection 5) or that we abandon particular projects, loyalties, relationships, and attachments (Subsection 6). But it nonetheless provides important safeguards against unreasonable partiality (Subsection 7).

2. *The Principle of Fairness Is Grounded in the Recognition of Shared Characteristics*

There seems to be no *essential* difference between oneself and another sentient, presuming both are capable of flourishing. It seems clear that "intelligence and reasonableness can find no basis in the mere fact that A is A and not B (that I am I and am not you) for evaluating his (our) well-being differentially."[41] And so, when one's actions might affect oneself and others differently, or when they might affect several others in different ways, it's important to avoid unreasonable, arbitrary choices. The Principle of Fairness precludes such choices.

3. *The Principle of Fairness Precludes Distinctions Not Made in Pursuit of Genuine Aspects of Well-Being*

If it is to be reasonable, a choice ought to be for the purpose of seeking to experience or do or be something inherently worthwhile, or of helping another to experience or do or be something inherently worthwhile, rather than simply the expression of a preference unrelated to one's own flourishing or another's. This follows, of course, from the fact that the point of an intelligible, justifiable choice should always be one's own welfare or another's. Deliberately choosing to allocate the costs and benefits of a risky policy on the basis simply of ethnicity, for instance, seems like a fairly obvious example of a choice animated by a preference unrelated to real well-being.[42]

Of course, one may reasonably select capable players for a football team in order to foster the good of play; one may reasonably select good art over trash in order to foster the good of æsthetic experience; friendship requires distinctions between friends and non-friends; and so forth. By contrast, distinctions related to membership in arbitrary—say, national or ethnic—groups would be difficult to defend, since discriminating in favor of these groups, or in favor of particular people on the basis of their memberships in these groups, does not obviously serve any intelligible aspect of welfare.[43]

[41] Finnis, Law, *supra* note 1, at 107 (italics supplied); *cf.* Finnis, Aquinas, *supra* note 1, at 140.

[42] *See* Finnis, Law, *supra* note 1, at 107–08, 304–05; Finnis, *Commensuration*, *supra* note 1, at 227.

[43] The notion of friendship is stretched to the breaking point if one can be said to be able to participate in friendship with fifty million fellow citizens. A soldier may be friends, at least in some attenuated sense,

4. *The Principle of Fairness Precludes Distinctions an Actor Would Be Unwilling to Accept If Roles Were Reversed*

A reasonable choice with disparate effects is a choice which one would be willing to accept were one to exchange positions with one of the others affected by it.[44] To make a choice one would *not* be willing to accept were roles reversed would be precisely to imply that one is in a different position from, is more privileged or morally worthy than, those impacted by one's choice (or that one or a group of those affected should be seen as privileged in ways that another affected, or another group of those affected, should somehow not be).[45] "From one's way of conducting oneself here and now it should be possible to derive a universal norm applicable to every case involving no rational consideration other than those involved in this case."[46] Thus, it would be unreasonable for me, say, to dump carcinogens into a stream from which people draw drinking water if I would be unwilling to accept the dumping of similar chemicals by someone else into a stream from which *I* drew drinking water.

It is certainly correct that I sometimes might be unwilling to accept being treated in a given way without its being the case that my treating another in a seemingly similar way should be seen as morally troubling. But this intuitively plausible conclusion need not count against the Principle of Fairness as I have formulated it.

Consider someone who desires very strongly not to perform a certain kind of work.[47] She could perfectly reasonably *offer* the same kind of work to someone else. In this case, however, the offeror presumably knows that others do not all share her preferences, and that the offeree need not have the same aversion to performing the work that she herself does. Thus, the offeror and the offeree are *not similarly situated*. Further, while the work itself is, in the example, detestable to her, there is no reason

with the other members of her unit, but she can hardly be said to be able to be friends with an entire army. And so forth. An alternative would be to treat *community* as an independently valuable aspect of well-being, with a given community identified, perhaps, by common purposes and other interconnections. Despite common talk about ethnic, cultural, gender, and other communities, I'm not sure any of these qualifies as a community in any interesting sense, given that none has a common purpose, a shared conception of the good, and so on. An army might qualify as a community, depending on how a community was understood; but given the dubious purposes shared by most armies and the myriad unjust injuries caused in the course of pursuing or facilitating the pursuit of those objectives, discriminating in favor of an army would seem to be inconsistent with the Principle of Fairness and perhaps, on occasion, the Principle of Respect. Thanks to Sandy Thatcher for conversation leading to my clarification of this point.

[44] Thus, even if it *were* the case that discriminating in the interests of, say, a state were somehow to foster flourishing, such discrimination would likely be unreasonable, given that most reflective moral agents would be unwilling to be disadvantaged on the basis of such discrimination.

[45] *See* Finnis, *Commensuration*, *supra* note 1, at 227–28; Finnis et al., Deterrence, *supra* note 1, at 284–85; Finnis, Ethics, *supra* note 1, at 91–92.

[46] Grisez & Shaw, *supra* note 1, at 120.

[47] I owe this example to David Gordon.

to think that under ordinary circumstances *being given the opportunity* to do the work would be. She could thus quite consistently offer a similar opportunity to someone else and wait to see how that person responds without being in any way unfair.

5. *Accepting the Principle of Fairness Does Not Mean Embracing Impartial Consequentialism*

The Principle of Fairness might be thought to require that we reason like consequentialists—that we maximize well-being in the world, or something similar. But it doesn't. We're not required to choose "the best overall option" because, typically, at least, there isn't any such thing. There is ordinarily no way of showing that reason *demands* that one choose a given kind or instance of flourishing over another. There's no necessary, rationally required ranking of options in light of the putative quantity of welfare each is likely to realize.

This is not because value is subjective, though this claim is sometimes advanced by some economists. The confusion here is a probably unavoidable consequence of cross-disciplinary equivocation about the use of the world *value*. For a typical economist, the value of a product is whatever it is about an actor's psyche in virtue of which she is disposed to pay whatever it is she is, in fact, disposed to pay for the product in a peaceful, voluntary transaction.[48] Economic value, in this sense, is obviously subjective: what plays an explanatory or interpretive role in economic analysis is simply an aspect or set of aspects of each relevant economic actor's motivational set, of her subjectivity.

People speaking as moralists may also use the word *value*, and sometimes they use it in this explanatory or interpretive way. More frequently, however, they use it in an objective sense. In this sense, value is the same as *inherent, intrinsic* worth. Real aspects of welfare can be spoken of as "basic values," and calling something valuable can be a way of identifying it as an authentic dimension of well-being.

Basic aspects of well-being are, as I've already argued, incommensurable and non-fungible. And that means that all varieties of consequentialism, which assumes

[48] This would often be framed in counterfactual terms, so that the focus would be on whatever it is that explains what she would be *willing* to pay under particular circumstances. There are two related problems with this formulation from the perspective of natural law theory: (*i*) The use of "explains" might be thought to amount to an appeal to a sufficient condition for the actor's behavior. But natural law theory is committed to belief in a robust view of free will, with the result that no factor apart from the agent's free choice itself, at least under ordinary circumstances, will be sufficient to explain the choice. (*ii*) If the agent's choice is genuinely free, then no claim what the agent would do or would have done under various envisioned non-actual circumstances will necessarily be true. Natural law theory can reasonably talk about the aspects of a person's motivational set that might dispose her to choose in a certain way, as long as it is clear that the relationship is, roughly, probabilistic, and that disposition is a far cry from necessitation.

that the states of affairs which might be produced by various choices can be ranked and requires that one make a choice such that no other choice has a higher rank, is fundamentally a nonstarter. Because different states of affairs typically involve different aspects of well-being, and different instances of both the same and different aspects of well-being, there's no way of measuring them, and so of comparing them quantitatively (whether cardinally or ordinally) in the way consequentialism seems to require.[49]

There is no rationally inescapable way to combine all of the goods realized in a given state of affairs. There *cannot* be, because the assignment of weights to different instances of different goods must be a matter of calculation in light of one's prior commitments (to oneself and others) rather than of rational necessity constraining such commitments (apart, of course, from the rational necessity imposed by the requirements of practical reasonableness themselves). So there will be, can be, no objectively required ranking of states of affairs in the way standard consequentialism demands.[50]

So avoiding arbitrariness, choosing in accordance with the Principle of Fairness, does not, cannot, mean promoting the overall good in all one's actions, for the simple reason that there isn't any such thing. There is no meaning to the notion of "the sum of all the goods realized in a given state of affairs." Thus, there can be no way of reasoning in genuinely consequentialist fashion.[51]

[49] There are, of course, various other problems with consequentialism, notably the fact that it requires predictions about the future which almost certainly cannot be made with any confidence, and that it will often require actions inconsistent with what I am calling here the Principle of Respect.

[50] Classical utilitarianism offers the possibility of objective ranking by focusing on the amount of pleasure embodied in each possibility to be ranked; but as early as Mill it was becoming apparent that this sort of Benthamite project was inattentive to crucial aspects of the human experiences of valuation and moral judgment. A more common recent approach has been to appeal to a putatively "impartial" or "objective" point of view from which it might be possible to rank states of affairs objectively. A frequent response has been to suggest that a moral agent need not adopt, or need not always adopt, this point of view. But my claim in the text is intended to offer a more radical critique of consequentialism: the kind of objective ranking envisioned is simply not *possible*, and it is not magically rendered conceivable through the adoption of one point of view or another. There is no point of view from which states of affairs can be seen to be objectively ranked.

[51] *See, e.g.*, Paul Hurley, Beyond Consequentialism (2009); Alasdair MacIntyre, After Virtue: A Study in Moral Theory 61–63, 67–68, 185 (2d ed., 1984); Finnis, Law, *supra* note 1, at 111–19; Finnis, Ethics, *supra* note 1, at 80–108; Finnis et al., Deterrence, *supra* note 1, at 177–296; Grisez & Shaw, *supra* note 1, at 111–14, 131–33; Germain Grisez, *Against Consequentialism*, 23 Am. J. Juris 21 (1978). *Cf.* David S. Oderberg, Moral Theory: A Non-Consequentialist Approach 65–76, 97–101, 132–33 (2000); Nel Noddings, Caring: A Feminine Approach to Ethics and Moral Education 86–87, 151–54 (1984); Alan Donagan, The Theory of Morality 172–209 (1977); Bernard Williams, Morality: An Introduction to Ethics (2d ed., 1993); Bernard Williams, *A Critique of Utilitarianism*, *in* Utilitarianism: For and Against 77–150 (J.J.C. Smart & Bernard Williams eds., 1973); Stephen R.L. Clark, *Natural Integrity and Biotechnology*, *in* Human Lives 58 (Jacqueline A. Laing & David S. Oderberg eds., 1997). The new classical natural law

6. *Fairness Is Quite Compatible with Pursuing Particular Projects*

The Principle of Fairness does not rule out the pursuit of particular projects adopted in light of personal preference, whether for oneself or others. I acknowledge the reality and value of the various aspects of well-being precisely by choosing to realize them in one way or another, in my own life or another's.[52] Obviously, others matter, in the same way and for the same reasons, that I matter. But I can reasonably seek to foster flourishing in various ways, and I will obviously be able to seek to flourish and to influence my own flourishing in ways in which I cannot affect the flourishing of anyone else.[53] Similarly, fostering the flourishing of particular others is very much an expression of the worth of friendship and of other aspects of welfare.[54] Furthering the good of particular others reflects (in no particular order) the importance (*i*) of friendship and loyalty as aspects of one's own flourishing, (*ii*) of friends themselves as constitutive of one's own identity, (*iii*) of aspects of well-being shared with friends, and (*iv*) of the independent reality and value of the particular others one benefits.[55]

7. *Reasonableness Requires Fairness*

A particular moral agent's particular characteristics and circumstances can and should shape her own establishment of her priorities and her determination of what it makes sense for her to do or not do. But these characteristics and circumstances can reasonably play this role only *within* the constraints established by the Principle of Fairness (and the other principles of practical reasonableness). Universality is not the sine qua non of any moral action: being moral does not mean aspiring to be a legislator. However, to the extent that there *are* common characteristics that unite moral agents and moral patients, it would be unreasonable to ignore them.

People seem to be capable of acting to benefit themselves, to benefit others, or to realize shared goods that simultaneously benefit themselves *and* others. Shared natures enable people to understand others' well-being by analogy with their own (though it is obviously crucial to recognize that others' preferences and circumstances may differ from one's own), and so to see what it might mean to pursue it. And training, cultural environment, developmentally relevant experiences, and

theorists' critique of consequentialism is similar to, albeit not identical with, economists' critiques of the attempt to make interpersonal utility comparisons in welfare economics; *see, e.g.*, Murray N. Rothbard, *Toward a Reconstruction of Utility and Welfare Economics*, *in* ON FREEDOM AND FREE ENTERPRISE: ESSAYS IN HONOR OF LUDWIG VON MISES 226 (Mary Sennholz ed., 1956); Walter Block, Art Carden & Stephen W. Carson, Ex Ante *and* Ex Post: *What Does Rod Stewart Really Know Now?*, 111 BUS. & SOC'Y REV. 427 (2006).

[52] *See* FINNIS, LAW, *supra* note 1, at 107.

[53] *See id.* at 304.

[54] *See id.* at 108.

[55] *Cf.* Finnis, *Commensuration*, *supra* note 1, at 227.

biological inheritance all dispose people to appreciate the independent significance of others' well-being,[56] and so to adhere to the Principle of Fairness.

To acknowledge the basic moral equality of the sentients capable of flourishing is to see that arbitrary distinctions among them cannot be justified. While this does not require that one seek to perform the impossible task of maximizing the quantity of good in the universe or abandon one's particular projects and commitments, it does require that one avoid discriminating arbitrarily—that one make distinctions only when doing so is a way of flourishing or helping oneself or others to flourish and only when one would not be willing to accept a given distinction if roles were reversed.[57]

D. The Principle of Respect Calls for the Avoidance of Purposeful and Instrumental Harm

1. *Recognizing the Value and Incommensurability of Basic Aspects of Well-Being Rules out Making Harm to Any the Goal of One's Action or a Means to One's Goal*

Because aspects of well-being are valuable, it makes no sense to attack them purposefully (Subsection 2), and because they are incommensurable it makes no sense to attack them instrumentally (Subsection 3). These dual requirements do not rule

[56] *Cf.* Yochai Benkler, The Penguin and the Leviathan: How Cooperation Triumphs over Self-Interest (2011); Robert Axelrod, The Evolution of Cooperation (rev. ed., 2006); Stephen Jay Gould, *Kropotkin Was No Crackpot*, 106 Natural Hist. 12 (1997); Matt Ridley, The Origins of Virtue: Human Instincts and the Evolution of Cooperation (1996); Alfie Kohn, The Brighter Side of Human Nature: Altruism and Empathy in Everyday Life (1992); Kristen Renwick Monroe, The Heart of Altruism: Perceptions of a Common Humanity (1996); Frans B. M. de Waal, Good Natured: The Origins of Right and Wrong in Humans and Other Animals (1997); Elliott Sober & David Sloan Wilson, Unto Others: The Evolution and Psychology of Unselfish Behavior (1997); Robert Wright, The Moral Animal: Why We Are the Way We Are (1995); Samuel Bowles, A Cooperative Species: Human Reciprocity and Its Evolution (2011).

[57] The Principle of Fairness certainly leaves room for a reasonable agent to prioritize friends by investing time, energy, and resources in nourishing her friendships. It seems likely to leave less room for her to give priority to others based simply on national or ethnic commonalities. The Principle requires that I avoid discriminating except in pursuit of a genuine good. Acting for the sake of a relationship with a person or a group of people is a matter of acting for the good of friendship—but simply acting for their sake when such a relationship isn't in the air is not. Thus, the Principle seems likely to rule out prioritizing others simply on the basis of their membership in large-scale and medium-scale groups. By contrast, membership in small-scale groups clearly could matter here. Further, even if particular nationalistic and quasi-nationalistic choices could be seen as narrowly appropriate in some cases vis-à-vis the Principle of Fairness, I think it would be hard to implement those choices non-destructively given the constraints imposed by not only the Principle of Respect but also the baseline possessory rules that I suggest can be derived from the Principle of Fairness; *see* Chapter 2, *infra*. Thanks to Sandy Thatcher for calling to my attention the need to make this point.

out the use of force to defend oneself or others (Subsection 4). They do, however, provide crucial protections for multiple, valuable aspects of our lives (Subsection 5). Together, they yield what I'll call the Principle of Respect: *do not purposefully or instrumentally harm any instance of a basic aspect of well-being, and do not cause harm to anything out of hostility.*[58]

2. *Purposefully Harming an Instance of an Authentic Aspect of Well-Being Is Unreasonable*

Something like the Principle of Respect is sometimes expressed in this form: *don't do evil, even to bring about good.* The principle is often treated as presupposing a set of rules (say, in a religious context, the Ten Commandments); in this case, the principle can be understood as stipulating that the rules should be treated as exceptionless, so that they may not be violated even in pursuit of particularly good consequences. But understood in this way, the principle appears unavoidably arbitrary. Why should I accept the relevant moral rules in the first place? And what reason, exactly, does the principle give me to treat them as exceptionless?

Thus the strength of the Principle of Respect. This principle doesn't begin with a set of specific moral rules treated as givens or with a prior understanding of evil. Rather, it is derived in large part simply from the idea that there are objective aspects of human welfare which it is unreasonable to harm.

Think about how one might reason if one sought to attack another's well-being (or one's own). One reason for which one might do so would be to cause harm for its own sake. Acting for this sort of reason seems unjustifiable.

To make attacking an instance of any aspect of well-being one's *purpose*, to attack it for the sake of attacking it, might make sense if it lacked value, if it weren't inherently worthwhile. Attacking it can be seen as presupposing a denial of its inherent worth. Once that intrinsic value is granted, the attack seems unreasonable (as does choosing to maintain an attitude of hostility toward any instance of any aspect of well-being). Any purposeful attack on an instance of welfare, and so any action rooted in hostility toward the welfare of the one being affected by one's action, won't make sense because it will involve treating a genuine aspect of welfare as if it weren't a genuine aspect of welfare at all. In addition, an attack on a basic aspect of well-being for the purpose of harming it is, by definition, undertaken for no intelligible reason: one seems to be seeking no ultimate benefit, but only a harm, and doing so appears to be inconsistent with the Principle of Recognition.

[58] *See* MURPHY, RATIONALITY, *supra* note 1, at 204–07; FINNIS, ETHICS, *supra* note 1, at 109–27; GRISEZ & SHAW, *supra* note 1, at 129–39; FINNIS ET AL., DETERRENCE, *supra* note 1, at 286–87; FINNIS, LAW, *supra* note 1, at 118–25.

3. *Instrumentally Harming an Instance of an Authentic Aspect of Well-Being Is Unreasonable because Aspects of Well- Being Can't Be Objectively Rank-Ordered*

One might also attack a basic aspect of well-being not because one doesn't think it's valuable, but instead *in order* to flourish or to foster another's flourishing. This, too, seems hard to defend,

An instrumental attack on an instance of flourishing will still be—one must still think of it as being—an attack on the relevant aspect of well-being. Since it is unreasonable to attack a basic aspect of anyone's welfare—to the extent that an attack seems to involve treating it mistakenly as valueless or worse—it seems as if there will be good reason not to attack, *whatever one's reason*.

Perhaps this argument might be thought to count against a direct attack but not an instrumental one. In the case of an instrumental attack, one might correctly understand what one was doing as an attack on some aspect of another's good but not as involving a denial of its value. In this case one will presumably see one's attack as justified in virtue of the good one seeks to realize or pursue. It can't be because the aspect of welfare one is attacking is valueless. However, the good one is attempting to realize doesn't, couldn't, *outweigh* the good one is attacking: it's not commensurable with it. So any instrumental attack on an instance of an acknowledged aspect of well-being in the service of another such instance would seem to be unreasonable: it would need to be grounded on the assumption that a basic aspect of well-being could be objectively less valuable than another genuine aspect of well-being—despite the fact that this can't be the case.[59] Instances of well-being are incommensurable and non-fungible, so none can outweigh any other.[60]

[59] Of course I may reasonably choose one real good rather than another simply because I like the good I choose and don't like the one I don't. We do this sort of thing all the time, and I didn't mean to imply that we don't, or that we don't act sensibly when we do. But I can't *cause harm* to one aspect of someone's well-being as a means to furthering some other aspect of someone else's well-being (or my own) on the assumption that the aspect of well-being I'm choosing to harm is somehow objectively less important than, say, the one in the interests of which I'm causing the harm.

Thus, it is not unreasonable to pursue something one likes in preference to something one doesn't: for instance, I may reasonably pursue a research program in biophysics that is so demanding that I will have little time to devote to personal friendships, with the unintended but foreseen consequence that my friendships suffer, perhaps irremediably. But this can be reasonable in a way that, say, forcibly subjecting a friend to a burst of harmful radiation in pursuit of that program would not be. My point is *not* that choosing one good over another can only be rational if one is worth more than the other—this would leave us paralyzed. Rather, I believe various aspects of welfare are incommensurable, and that one can choose one over another without making any false judgment about their relative merits—as if they were, in fact commensurable. But one *does* need to treat one as more valuable than another in order to justify purposefully or instrumentally attacking it.

[60] Obviously, this does not mean that one cannot in some cases reasonably *choose* to promote one rather than another without attacking the instance of well-being not chosen, but one does not do so on the basis of any objective weighting. Thus, the possibility of preference does not provide a backdoor

This doesn't apply, of course, when the harm one causes is merely incidental. But it *does* apply when one harms one good *in service to* another: in this case, it would seem that one must judge the good one harms as less important than the good one is seeking to foster, provided one acknowledges that directly harming the good isn't reasonable. And doing this can never be reasonable because of the incommensurability and non-fungibility of the various aspects of well-being and the various instances of those aspects.

A critic could argue that one might choose to harm one aspect of flourishing in order to foster another, not because one judged the latter superior to the former, but only because one *preferred* the latter to the former. On this view, one wouldn't fall foul of the criticism that one was unreasonably treating one as inherently more valuable than the other. But it is not clear that this response would be satisfactory. While one may certainly choose some aspects of flourishing (one's own or others') in preference to others, one must still judge what one chooses to be valuable, and to be worth choosing because of its value, if one is to choose reasonably (in accordance with the Principle of Recognition). The preference amounts, as it were, to a proposal that one opt for something, but one can reasonably accept that proposal only if that for which one opts really *is* valuable. So it doesn't seem one could escape considering the actual worth of the object of one's choice. In addition, whatever the role of one's preference in motivating one's action, to proceed in the envisioned way would still involve choosing to attack a genuine aspect of flourishing. One's preference wouldn't be sufficient to justify the attack, since it wouldn't provide a justification for action at all—only the value of what one preferred would. But the value of what one preferred would be, ex hypothesi, incommensurable with the value of what one attacked and therefore incapable of providing the needed justification.[61]

Harming something—say, a physical object—that isn't itself an instance of a basic aspect of well-being, but doing so on the basis of *hostility* to another's well-being (as when the object is attacked because it is a means to another's well-being, which one intends to affect adversely), is also inconsistent with the Principle of Respect. Even though one isn't attacking a basic aspect of welfare, one is choosing *on the basis of* hostility to a basic aspect of welfare. And doing so amounts, again, to the denial that something valuable—the well-being of the person toward whom one is being

rationale for direct attacks on basic aspects of well-being. (Thanks to Sandy Thatcher for a useful exchange on this point.) Suppose, for instance, that one seeks to end spectacles of public torture in the arena that strike some people as æsthetically appealing. Eliminating these spectacles has an adverse affect, ex hypothesi, on the æsthetic experiences of those who appreciate them. But this is a foreseen but unintended side effect of eliminating the spectacles, not a means to their elimination. One chooses in this case to promote the well-being of the spectacles' victims rather than that of the victimizers (a preference mandated, surely, by the Principle of Fairness).

61 Thanks to David Gordon for discussion of these points.

hostile, the indirect target of one's hostile action—really *is* valuable. Something that is inherently worthwhile isn't a reasonable object of hostility, even if the hostility isn't expressed in a direct attack on whatever it is that's worthwhile, but rather in an assault on something else. The Principle of Respect doesn't rule out causing incidental harms to things that aren't aspects of welfare, but it *does* rule out causing purposeful harms to such things *in order to* hamper another's well-being.

4. *Accepting the Principle of Respect Is Consistent with Using Force Defensively*

The Principle of Respect does not itself rule out causing harm as a foreseen but unintended by-product or side effect of doing something else.[62]

Often enough, we do things with consequences that we do not intend, that we do not choose purposefully. A dentist may knowingly disturb a patient's peace of mind by drilling into one of his teeth, but she may *intend* only to improve his health by doing so. The Principle of Respect does not rule out causing this kind of harm. It governs *how* we choose, how particular reasons *figure* in our deliberation and our selection of options. It precludes making injury the *object* of our action because doing so amounts to a denial of the value of inherently worthwhile aspects of well-being and their incommensurable, non-fungible character. Knowingly but unintentionally bringing about some harm to some instance of well-being need not involve *either* treating the instance of well-being as if it weren't an instance of well-being *or* treating it as less intrinsically valuable than some other instance of well-being.

Thus, while the use of force as a means of intimidation or retribution or retaliation is ruled out by the Principle of Respect, the use of force to defend oneself or another is not. Using force against an assailant for the purpose of stopping her attack may, in fact, result in her injury or death. But the structure of one's action need not involve injuring or killing purposefully: one need not use force *in order to* injure or kill her. And it need not involve injuring or killing *instrumentally*: one can act in a way one knows will injure or kill without selecting the attacker's injury or death as a *means* to the goal of stopping her.[63] Instead, one's goal may be, say, to stop the other's unjust action, using a method one expects to result in harm, but without willing the harm itself. One's action might be "directed at resisting and reducing unjust force, ... [while] unavoidably ... [resulting] in the injury or death of another"[64]—it might be designed "to stop the attack, accepting as a side-effect the attacker's death"[65]

[62] *See* FINNIS, ETHICS, *supra* note 1, at 132; GRISEZ & SHAW, *supra* note 1, at 140–46; FINNIS ET AL., DETERRENCE, *supra* note 1, at 312–13; FINNIS, LAW, *supra* note 1, at 123–25.

[63] *Cf.* FINNIS, ETHICS, *supra* note 1, at 132.

[64] GRISEZ & SHAW, *supra* note 1, at 151.

[65] FINNIS ET AL., DETERRENCE, *supra* note 1, at 312.

instead of involving the proposal "to kill ... as a means to an end."[66] So, for instance, the point of the Stauffenberg plot was "that Hitler be incapacitated from participating in the ongoing Nazi tyranny whose murderous violence he directed." It involved the use of a bomb just as someone on a battlefield might employ "a rifle or grenade to stop the assault of enemy soldiers, or a howitzer to disrupt enemy formations assembling far behind the lines."[67]

None of this implies, of course, that there's never a problem with foreseeably causing harm as long as one doesn't intend to do so. For, even if one doesn't, one may still be imposing harm, or the risk of harm, unreasonably. The Principle of Fairness may rule out a choice to impose harm even if the Principle of Respect does not. But the absolute prohibition on purposeful or instrumental harm embodied in the Principle of Respect leaves open the possibility of using force defensively.

5. *The Principle of Respect Safeguards the Basic Aspects of Well-Being*

Any purposeful or instrumental attack on any instance of a basic aspect of well-being is unreasonable, as is any indirect harm to an aspect of well-being that is rooted in hostility. For a purposeful or instrumental attack on an aspect of well-being (or an act rooted in hostility to an instance of well-being) to be justified, it would have to be the case that a putative aspect of welfare wasn't *really* valuable, in which case it wouldn't really be an aspect of welfare at all, or that a genuine aspect of welfare could reasonably be treated as objectively less important than another—which it could be only if aspects of well-being, or instances of such aspects, could be rank-ordered, as they cannot be. The Principle of Respect does not rule out causing harm as the anticipated but unintended consequence of an otherwise reasonable action, but it does provide very secure protection against purposeful or instrumental harm and injury rooted in hostility.[68]

[66] Grisez & Shaw, *supra* note 1, at 151.

[67] Finnis, Aquinas, *supra* note 1, at 291.

[68] The Principle of Respect fairly clearly tracks common moral intuitions at some points. But it might seem not to do so at others. For instance, it might be asked whether one could choose in a manner consistent with this requirement of practical reasonableness while clipping fingernails, trimming hair, or cutting through someone's skin for the purpose of facilitating access to a tumor one hopes to remove: do these not seem to be attacks on bodily well-being in the interests of logically subsequent good consequences? Perhaps the easiest way to deal with these sorts of problems would be to treat bodily integrity and well-being, not as basic aspects of well-being, but as valuable to the extent necessary to safeguard life and other varieties of flourishing. Alternatively, these actions might be judged not to be instances of *attacking* or *harming* bodily well-being, though I would wonder whether a clear line could be drawn. Perhaps in some cases the harm to bodily well-being might be seen as a side effect of choices make in pursuit of other sorts of fulfillment rather than as means

E. The Principles of Practical Reasonableness Yield Some Absolute Prohibitions and Some Relative Ones

The Principle of Recognition, the Principle of Fairness, and the Principle of Respect are themselves absolute and exceptionless. That is, there is never a time when it is reasonable to ignore or disregard any of them. But there's one fairly obvious difference between the Principle of Recognition and the Principle of Respect on the one hand and the Principle of Fairness on the other. The Principle of Recognition and the Principle of Respect rule out certain generically specifiable action-types absolutely. For example: any instance of targeting noncombatants in wartime is fairly clearly an instance of purposefully causing harm to one or more basic aspects of well-being. So it's possible to be quite clear in general terms about various sorts of conduct that will always be inconsistent with the Principle of Respect: any time I choose to injure any basic aspect of well-being purposefully or instrumentally, and any time I act out of hostility, I violate this principle and so act unreasonably. By contrast, the Principle of Fairness leaves open a much broader range of possibilities. It creates, for instance, a general presumption in favor of honoring promises; but, in the absence of quite specific information about a given situation, it can provide only limited guidance about whether a particular promise might reasonably be broken or not. The Principle of Fairness does not yield exceptionless, specific rules of conduct in the way the Principle of Respect does, though it is itself exceptionless, and though it may provide reason for *institutions* to adopt rules which it makes sense for them to enforce exceptionlessly.

F. We Act Reasonably When We Accept the Reality and Diversity of the Basic Aspects of Well-Being and the Essential Moral Equality of Those Capable of Flourishing

Acting reasonably means acting in full view of reality. The Principle of Recognition mandates attentiveness to the genuine worth of the objects of one's actions, and thus avoidance of the pursuit of illusory goals. The Principle of Fairness entails that a moral agent accept the moral equality of those capable of flourishing, and thus that she

to these ends, though, again, I am doubtful that this would always be true in the sorts of instances I've envisioned here.

The principle poses fewer problems in other cases than might initially be thought. Going on a diet to lose weight may unsettle my peace of mind, causing physical or emotional distress. But the distress is a by-product of a choice undertaken in the interests of life (and the various kinds of flourishing which bodily well-being facilitates), not a means to flourishing. What if the point of the diet is to prepare myself for an anticipated period of privation? If the only harm involved is likely to be to my peace of mind, I need not choose to cause *this* harm as a means to my purpose; rather, it could (and likely would) be a foreseen but unintended consequence of my decision to diet. By contrast, if depriving myself really amounted (as it need not amount) to attacking my bodily well-being, then I think it would be unreasonable. Thanks to an anonymous reader for suggesting the importance of addressing these issues.

avoid discrimination which is not rooted in the pursuit of actual goods and which she would not be willing to accept were roles reversed. The Principle of Respect requires that a moral agent acknowledge the incommensurability of the aspects of welfare and the non-fungibility of the particular instances of those aspects, and thus avoidance of purposeful or instrumental attacks on basic aspects of welfare. (Of course, simply because the various dimensions of welfare can be distinguished for this and other analytic purposes, it does not, of course, follow that in reality they occur or can be realized in isolation from other aspects.) Moral rules derived from the Principle of Recognition and the Principle of Respect are exceptionless; the Principle of Fairness itself is, like the others, exceptionless, but rules for personal conduct (a rule enforced by institutions over a wide range of cases may, of course, be another matter) derived from it will of necessity be more flexible and responsive to particular circumstances. As negative principles, the requirements of reasonableness leave actors with considerable latitude—with a great deal of freedom to choose the ways in which they will seek to flourish and those in which they will seek to help others flourish. But they do rule out choices that attack basic aspects of well-being, ignore the importance of flourishing, and preclude peaceful, cooperative interaction. Thus, they provide a framework that allows for the reasonable resolution of conflicts among actors' various attempts to flourish and to foster the flourishing of others.[69]

The principles of practical reasonableness do not, in general, *direct* agents' choices; rather, they constrain those choices, leaving agents free to pursue real aspects of welfare in light of their preferences and identities. It is the aspects of well-being that provide agents with reasons for action, but the reasonableness and the subjective appeal of a potential choice to realize a particular aspect of well-being in a particular way will depend on the temperament, circumstances, talents, endowments, interests, and commitments of the agent. Reasonable agents will accept the moral limits on their choices that flow from the principles of practical reasonableness; they must assess options in light of their preferences *within* these constraints. This kind of assessment is not, of course, in the ordinary sense an objective process, since the various dimensions of flourishing are incommensurable and non-fungible; but it amounts to the establishment of reasonable priorities by agents in light of their own unique characteristics and circumstances.[70]

IV. A FLOURISHING LIFE IS A REASONABLE LIFE

The point of morality is to acknowledge, in tandem with an awareness of the reality and variety of the modes of flourishing and fulfillment, (*i*) the irreducible diversity

[69] Thanks to an anonymous reader for making clear the need to make the points I seek to express in this sentence and the following paragraph.

[70] *Cf.* FINNIS, LAW, *supra* note 1, at 111–12; FINNIS, *Commensuration*, *supra* note 1, at 227–28.

of those affected by our actions (and so, in accordance with the Principle of Respect, to refuse to turn any into an object to be manipulated, an aspect of an aggregate, or a fungible unit exchangeable with others) and, at the same time, (*ii*) their common possession of those characteristics that render them (equally) morally considerable (and so, in accordance with the Principle of Fairness, to avoid arbitrary distinctions). The point of morality is, in short, a life lived well.

Such a life is a life lived in accordance with reason. This does not mean that reasonableness is itself the only sensible goal of action or that it is pointless or destructive to attend to our emotions. It *does* mean that we need to think carefully, reflectively, and critically about how and why we act. The right is neither logically prior nor logically subsequent to the good. Rather, rightness—practical reasonableness—is an ineliminable aspect of goodness, of flourishing.

When we reason well, we recognize that some aspects of our lives and those of others are inherently valuable for us, that it is reasonable to seek them for their own sake; by contrast, we can see that other aspects matter precisely because, and just to the extent that, they *enable* us to flourish. We can sensibly disagree about just what which aspects of well-being are intrinsically and instrumentally valuable, but there is good reason to think that it is *not* the case that things go well for us just because our preferences are satisfied or that we experience pleasant emotions. Instead, we flourish when we have inherently worthwhile experiences, join in inherently worthwhile relationships, engage in inherently worthwhile activities, acquire and maintain inherently worthwhile qualities, and so forth. There may be good, even if not unquestionable, reason to treat friendship, knowledge, æsthetic experience, play, practical reasonableness, religion, imaginative immersion, life, bodily well-being, and peace of mind, and perhaps other kinds of well-being, too, as among these aspects of well-being that are inherently worthwhile for us. What is clear, in any case, is that there is no substratum that underlies these varied dimensions of welfare: each is different from the others. Thus, the various aspects of welfare can't be weighed against each other using the same metric, and particular instances of each can't be objectively traded off against each other or against instances of others.

We *do* make choices among ways in which we seek to flourish, among ways in which we seek to help others flourish. But we do not, cannot, do so on the basis of objective rank-ordering or quantitative weighing, which are simply impossible.[71]

[71] Thus, talk about *personal utility* in the context of economic analysis is not best read as pointing to any sort of discriminable psychological state capable of doing explanatory work. It is relatively harmless, if confusing, to refer to an option chosen by a given agent as the one, of those available to her, with "the greatest utility." But this can mean neither that she felt more strongly about it than alternatives (for she might have chosen one she judged to be preferable even though, as an empirical matter, she desired it less; she might also simply have desired the two options with qualitatively different desires incapable of quantitative comparison) nor even that it best met her preferred objectives (since, absent

Reason leaves us free to choose in light of our preferences, as long as we opt for real aspects of flourishing rather than illusory ones, avoid discriminating arbitrarily among those affected by our actions, and decline to attack any aspect of well-being—either directly or as a means to some other goal—and to act out of hostility.

Thus, morality as I conceive of it has both personal and interpersonal dimensions, which are inextricably linked: it is concerned with personal flourishing and with what we can reasonably be said to owe others.[72] As I will maintain in more detail subsequently, institutional actors choose reasonably when their decisions are constrained by the requirements of interpersonal morality in ways that reflect the scope and impact of their decisions. It is not the case, then, that there is any sort of specially institutional morality or that institutions have special moral prerogatives. Institutional actors' role-specific duties flow from the same moral principles that constrain all interpersonal moral choices, even as they also reflect the distinctive situations in which such actors find themselves.

a set of commitments ordering those objectives, they would be, because incommensurable, incapable of being ranked objectively and since she might well be fully aware of their incommensurable attractions). Similarly, it will ordinarily be meaningless to talk about the utility of options not chosen, not only because this ranking, if it existed, would likely be inaccessible to others but because it might well not exist at all—one may simply not have fully formed preferences about the relevant options on the basis of which a ranking of the options could be constructed. And since talk about utility is finally just a convenient way of pointing to people's choices, it will make no sense to claim that someone *would have* chosen a particular option when she didn't, in fact, do so, given that, in general, counterfactual propositions concerning free choices are either false or lacking in truth-values. In some cases, commitments or felt preferences *will* indeed yield subjective rankings of alternatives, but personal choice can be entirely intelligible without any reference to such rankings, as long as it involves a recognition of the chosen option as an instance of or a means to flourishing, and claims about rankings of this kind will often be indefensible.

[72] Personal flourishing and what we owe others are linked in at least two ways: acting reasonably, and so acting reasonably in relation to others, is an expression of practical reasonableness, which is an aspect of personal flourishing; and it is precisely the flourishing of persons that the principles of practical reasonableness serve to safeguard. I do not say a great deal here about the constraints reason imposes on purely self-regarding action. While action that harms unreasonably warrants guilt, I don't think this is appropriate in the case of action that harms or deprives oneself—in this case, regret seems more appropriate. But there *are* multiple constraints on reasonable behavior with respect to oneself. For instance: (*i*) the Principle of Respect obviously precludes causing oneself purposeful harm; (*ii*) one owes it to oneself, as well as the others affected, to make commitments and to nourish constitutive attachments (even thought of course one can reasonably absolutize neither); (*iii*) one ought to pursue one's goals in appropriately efficient ways. For a discussion of the latter two constraints in the context of contemporary natural law theory, *see, e.g.*, CHARTIER, *supra* note 1. For a more general discussion of reason's constraints on one's treatment of oneself, framed with respect to "reflective rationality," *see* DAVID SCHMIDTZ, RATIONAL CHOICE AND MORAL AGENCY (1995). In general, I would be inclined to see Schmidtz's analysis as complementing and supplementing mine, though I would tend to approach questions about personal flourishing in a somewhat different way. The dual focus of Schmidtz's theory on personal well-being and social institutions is also in some ways parallel to the joint concern with personal and institutional morality I adopt here, though I think there's something to be said for emphasizing a bit more sharply a distinction between institutional moral requirements and interpersonal but noninstitutional ones.

These moral principles serve to referee conflicts among different people's attempts to flourish. And, in tandem with what we know about ourselves and our environment, we can use the basic principles of reasonable action to generate rules limiting the reasonable imposition of injuries on others and their justly acquired possessions, rules that can be summed up in what I call the *nonaggression maxim*, which provides a framework for reasonable interpersonal choices in both institutional and noninstitutional settings. I turn to the justification of this generalization and an introduction to its implications in Chapter 2.

2

Rejecting Aggression

I. ACTING REASONABLY MEANS AVOIDING AGGRESSION AGAINST OTHERS AND THEIR JUSTLY ACQUIRED POSSESSIONS

An understanding of well-being and the requirements of practical reasonableness, in tandem with a set of truisms about human beings, yields a maxim barring aggression—the basic guideline for a society rooted in peaceful, voluntary cooperation: *avoid aggression against people's bodies and just possessory interests.*

Roughly speaking, I engage in aggression when I injure another's body or interfere with her just possessory interests (except when defending myself against or securing a remedy for her unjust attack); the Nonaggression Maxim (NAM) summarizes the prohibition on aggression (Part II). The NAM highlights some of the requirements implicit in the Principle of Respect, which rules out all purposeful and instrumental attacks on others' welfare, and the Principle of Fairness, which precludes harming people's bodily well-being (and other aspects of their welfare) unreasonably (Part III). The Principle of Fairness also grounds robust protections of others' just possessory claims—claims rooted in initial acquisition through effective possession or in voluntary transfer (Part IV). Just possessory claims do not extend to other sentients (human or nonhuman) or to abstract patterns (Part V). They are not exceptionless (Part VI), but the constraints on harm to others' bodies and their possessions encapsulated in the NAM are both robust and consistent (Part VII).

II. AGGRESSION INVOLVES UNREASONABLY INJURING OTHERS' BODIES OR INTERFERING WITH THEIR JUST POSSESSORY INTERESTS

As I will use the term here, an act is an act of *aggression* if, roughly, it is a voluntary act (or a voluntary inaction in violation of voluntarily assumed duty) that (*i*) causes injury to another's body or interferes with her just possessory interests or her control over her body; (*ii*) occurs without her consent (harming someone in certain ways can be *wrong* even with her consent, but she can reasonably be regarded as being estopped from demanding forcible compensation if she has consented); and (*iii*) is not undertaken to prevent, end, or remedy an actual or threatened unjust injury to another's body or just possessory interests. Aggression need not be morally culpable, but, whether it is or not, it will trigger the duty to compensate for action (or inaction in breach of voluntarily assumed duty) to bodies and possessions.

Aggression need not be morally culpable because it may be negligent or inadvertent (in this case, the negligence itself may be morally culpable, of course). It may also not be morally culpable because the Principle of Fairness—which grounds the basic constraints on just possessory claims and their legal enforcement, constraints I call the *baseline possessory rules*—may not preclude infringements on possessory interests in some cases, though the reasonableness of such infringements will not void the corresponding requirement to compensate.

There will, of course, be choices of various kinds (involving both action and inaction) that are not instances of aggression but that are nonetheless varieties of moral wrongdoing—perhaps very serious moral wrongdoing. As instances of wrongdoing, they will be blameworthy, and it will be entirely reasonable for people to use nonaggressive social pressure of various kinds to prevent, end, or remedy them. However, in virtue of the considerations that ground the prohibition on aggression, it will *not* ordinarily be appropriate to prevent, end, or remedy nonaggressive injuries *by using force* against the bodies or the justly acquired possessions of others. What distinguishes aggressive from nonaggressive wrongdoing is *not* that the former is always more serious than the latter, but rather that ordinarily only the former can reasonably be met using force against people's bodies or forcibly interfering with their just possessory claims.

The *nonaggression maxim* (NAM) is the injunction that moral agents should avoid harming the bodies and interfering with the just possessory interests of others. Generally ruling out the use of force against others and their justly acquired possession, this maxim summarizes key implications of the principles of practical reasonableness.

III. THE REQUIREMENTS OF PRACTICAL REASONABLENESS PRECLUDE MANY CHOICES CAUSING INJURIES TO BASIC ASPECTS OF WELFARE

A. The Requirements of Practical Reasonableness Safeguard the Basic Aspects of Well-Being

Taken together, the Principle of Respect and the Principle of Fairness rule out purposeful (including instrumental), reckless, and negligent injuries to basic aspects of others' well-being and require compensation for essentially all injuries. The Principle of Respect requires that an agent always avoid causing injury to any basic aspect of welfare deliberately—for its own sake, as a means to an end, or out of hostility (Section B). The Principle of Fairness requires that an agent always avoid causing injury to any basic aspect of another's well-being in a case in which she would not be willing to permit herself or her loved ones to be injured were roles reversed, and that she accept responsibility for remedying injuries she causes even when they are justified (Section C). The requirements of practical reasonableness provide sturdy protection for the basic aspects of well-being (Section D).

B. The Principle of Respect Imposes an Absolute Prohibition on Purposeful or Instrumental Harm to Basic Aspects of Welfare

The Principle of Respect rules out in principle any purposeful or instrumental attack on any basic aspect of another's well-being, including her life, bodily well-being, and peace of mind. This kind of conduct is wrong under any circumstances.

The Principle of Respect imposes an absolute prohibition on injuring people's bodies, and other basic aspects of their welfare, purposefully, instrumentally, or out of hostility. Thus, this principle grounds a significant prong of the nonaggression maxim.

It does not follow, of course, that all such attacks ought to be legally remediable. Legal remedies (as I argue subsequently) ought to involve compensation for economic losses constituted by harms to bodies and injuries to or interference with justly acquired possessions, together with reasonable costs of recovery. Not all violations of the Principle of Respect will amount to attacks on bodies, and few will likely amount to attacks on people's possessions. Thus, only some violations of the Principle of Respect will be remediable using force—though other social institutions can and should address violations not remediable in this way. To the extent that the NAM is understood to refer to legally remediable injuries, therefore, it rules out only injuries to life and bodily well-being. But while the NAM is narrowly focused, concerned only with injuries for which compensation ought to be available at law, the Principle of Respect which helps to undergird it clearly does preclude a broader range of injuries.

C. The Principle of Fairness Precludes Unreasonable, Albeit Unintentional, Harms to Basic Aspects of Well-Being, and Requires Compensation even for Nonculpable Injuries

The Principle of Fairness imposes further limits on causing injury.

Many injuries are not purposeful or instrumental or rooted in hostility. For instance, using force to defend oneself or another against an unjust attack will often be reasonable. Doing so need not involve causing purposeful or instrumental harm. Rather, any harm one causes may be incidental—anticipated but unintended. Even if an injury resulting from a defensive action *is* unintentional, however, one must still also inquire whether inflicting it is consistent with the Principle of Fairness.

Causing injuries of various kinds will likely be ruled out by the Principle of Fairness. Consider some examples.

(*i*) A violent thug is hiding in a crowd while randomly shooting at passersby when she can do so; impatiently, I spray the entire crowd with a machine gun. My *purpose* is not to cause the injuries that result, but, rather, to stop the thug; and the occurrence of the injuries is not a means to my purpose. It's a reasonably predictable side effect of my attempt to stop the thug. But I have chosen to try to stop the thug in a way that harms lots of people. Doing this would be reasonable, per the Principle of Fairness, only if I would be willing for someone else to spray the crowd with machine-gun fire to stop the thug even if I or a loved one were part of the crowd, rather than behind the gun. In most cases, I surely would not be, so my attack on the crowd would be inconsistent with the Principle of Fairness.[1]

(*ii*) I use force to stop another from idly grazing me lightly with her fingertips. If she succeeds in touching me she will, in current legal terms, have committed a battery. And I'm not seeking to harm her. But I would not be willing to accept this kind of treatment of my loved ones (or of myself). So I can hardly have good reason to treat another in this way.

(*iii*) The members of a cooperative operate a factory. Because doing so reduces their expenses, they dispose of chemicals used in the manufacturing process in a nearby community's stream. Residents of the community develop serious illnesses as a result. The members of the cooperative don't *intend* to cause the illnesses. And causing the illnesses isn't a way of achieving some other goal. Rather, causing injuries to the victims is a by-product, an unintended consequence, of disposing of the chemicals in the stream. It should be obvious that, if the members of the cooperative know or strongly suspect that the chemicals are toxic, they almost certainly act unreasonably by dumping the chemicals in the stream. No member of the cooperative would likely be willing that others dump similar chemicals in a stream providing the water *she* used to cook and bathe and clean. And, if she wouldn't, it would be unreasonable of her to support or participate in the dumping of the chemicals in a stream providing water others used for these purposes. However, even if the members of the cooperative don't know the risk to which they're subjecting the people who use the stream, perhaps they *should* know: perhaps it's unreasonable of them not to conduct the investigation required to determine that the chemicals

1 *Cf.* John M. Finnis, Joseph M. Boyle, Jr. & Germain G. Grisez, Nuclear Deterrence, Morality, and Realism 313 (1987).

pose a serious risk to others. This will be true, obviously, if they would be unwilling for others to dump the chemicals under similar circumstances without conducting certain kinds of tests or engaging in certain kinds of inquiry; it will be unfair of them, in these circumstances, not to conduct these sorts of tests or to engage in the relevant sort of inquiry. And, having done so, if they learn that the chemicals pose serious risks, it will, again, be unreasonable to impose these risks on others when they would not be willing that others impose comparable risks on them or their loved ones.

Of course, it may be the case that the members of the cooperative conclude in good faith, after reasonable investigation, that the chemicals don't pose a serious risk of harm when in fact they do. In this case, they will not be morally culpable for dumping the chemicals. But causing injuries by dumping the chemicals into the stream will *still* count as aggression. People will still, ex hypothesi, be harmed. And, because they are responsible, the Principle of Fairness suggests that the members of the cooperative should still be liable for remedying the harms: their acts caused the harms, and, given this, it is more reasonable that the risk of liability fall on them than on those they have harmed. (I leave to one side the interesting question of whether this should still be the case, and, if so, why, if those injured opted to live near the factory fully aware of the dumping and the risks.) Aggression is not limited to deliberate choice.[2]

Injuries that are unfair, but not caused purposefully or instrumentally, are (like purposeful and instrumental injuries) not limited to harms to life and bodily well-being. Perhaps you expose some sort of venality on my part in order to keep me from acquiring a position in which you believe I would engage in corrupt conduct; as a result of the exposure, I lose some friends. Or perhaps you and a partner close the coffeehouse you've been operating, a coffeehouse that displays paintings by local artists; along with other patrons, I'm denied opportunities to have æsthetic experiences I could have had if the coffeehouse had stayed open. In these cases, of course, causing the injuries will be reasonable if the actor is willing that similar injuries be caused to her or her loved ones under similar circumstances (or, to put the point differently, if she is willing that everyone operate under a rule allowing the foreseen but unintended causing of similar injuries under similar circumstances). As in the case of harms inconsistent with the Principle of Respect, however, *compensation* in these cases should be available for injuries to life and bodily well-being (and, as I'll argue subsequently, justly acquired possessions), leaving other institutions and mechanisms to provide remedies for injuries to other aspects of well-being.

[2] *Cf.* Chapter 5.II.C.2.iii, *infra*.

D. The Principle of Respect and the Principle of Fairness Preclude Aggression against Basic Aspects of Well-Being

The basic aspects of sentients' well-being are protected from attack by the requirements of practical reasonableness. Causing injury purposefully or instrumentally—especially, though not exclusively, to life and bodily well-being—is inconsistent with the Principle of Respect. Causing injury arbitrarily, or refusing to accept legal liability for any injury to life or bodily well-being one has demonstrably caused under any circumstances, is inconsistent with the Principle of Fairness. These principles serve as vital safeguards against aggression.

IV. THE PRINCIPLE OF FAIRNESS PROVIDES GOOD REASON TO AVOID INTERFERING WITH OTHERS' JUSTLY ACQUIRED POSSESSIONS

A. The Justice of Possessory Claims Is a Function of Their Consistency with the Principle of Fairness

The Principle of Fairness imposes substantial limits on the treatment of people's possessions. Given the way in which they flow from the requirements of practical reasonableness, just possessory claims should be seen as in one sense contingent, derivative, and instrumental—but also as narrowly limited by the Principle of Fairness (Section B). There is good reason to respect simple possession (Section C), but multiple considerations help substantially to extend and constrain just possessory claims (Section D)—providing support for a stable, robust set of rules governing such claims (Section E). Thus, a relatively narrow range of *baseline rules* governing the initial acquisition, control, and transfer of physical objects, and so determining when such objects have been justly acquired, can be seen to be consistent with the requirements of practical reasonableness (Section F).

B. Rules Regarding Possession Can Be Seen as Conventions That Are Contingent, Instrumental, and Derivative, but Tightly Constrained by the Principle of Fairness

Rules regarding possession are not themselves basic moral norms. From a moral standpoint, they are at least to some degree *contingent*, because they can take somewhat different forms. They are *instrumental*, designed to foster, and justified to the extent that they foster, general participation in the basic aspects of well-being. And they are *derivative*, flowing from the Principle of Fairness (in tandem with a variety of facts about our natures and circumstances).[3] They come into being through the actions of moral agents in community (in community because the notion of a possessory claim necessarily involves just claims against other agents).[4]

The meaning and justification of possessory claims must be understood with reference to the well-being of everyone. In particular:

- Physical objects (the only reasonable foci of just possessory claims, because a scheme of such claims serves to resolve problems of scarcity, and only physical objects are scarce in the relevant sense) must be appropriated in order to be justly claimed; before appropriation, they are unclaimed and available to anyone.[5]
- Rules governing the acquisition, control, and disposition of possessions can promote widespread well-being in a variety of ways.
- The specific rules regarding the acquisition, control, and disposition of possessions which it is reasonable for institutional actors to identify, articulate, and uphold ought to be framed in light of the Principle of Fairness, so that the interests of all those affected by a given rule are taken reasonably into account.

While possessory claims are contingent, instrumental, and derivative, what counts as a reasonable possessory rule will be substantially constrained by the Principle of Fairness in tandem with a set of truisms regarding human nature and existence, which yield multiple desiderata for a scheme of just possessory rules. Thus, while they might first appear to be a matter of unconstrained decision, it turns out, on closer inspection, that their content—given a set of facts about humanness—is quite narrowly limited by the Principle of Fairness.

This principle will not constrain just possessory claims simply by governing two-person relationships. Rather, its primary role will be to limit what general *rules* governing possession will count as reasonable. Most decisions about the origins, natures, and implications of possessory claims are not made in the context of freestanding interpersonal interactions. Rather, they will characteristically reflect judgments about whether one ought to respect particular *general rules* regarding possession. That's *both* because the Principle of Fairness applies generically to all similarly

[3] *Cf.* Harold Demsetz, *Toward a Theory of Property Rights*, 57 AM. ECON. REV. 347, 347 (1967) (emphasizing the social context and significance of possessory claims).

[4] Thanks for insights on this point from Douglas Rasmussen and Douglas Den Uyl.

[5] "A physical object" here means anything physical, whether mobile and immobile, and so includes land and space. And, to anticipate, (*i*) possession can be continuous, but need not be, provided the absence of continuous possession is not reasonably interpreted as abandonment, and (*ii*) a just possessor can be someone who personally controls a physical object *or* someone who is the partner or principal of someone else who does so.

situated people, and thus lends itself naturally to the generation and assessment of rules of practice applicable to generically equivalent situations rather than just particular choices—given the commonalities that link situations—*and also* because there are good reasons for rules about possession to be general, stable, reliable, and predictable. While one thus has responsibilities to others with respect to objects one comes or might come to possess, one fulfills those responsibilities first by adhering to and supporting a just system of possessory rules.

C. Actual Possession Itself Deserves Protection under the Principle of Fairness

A physical object has to be *possessed* if it's going to be *justly possessed*. Whatever counts as just possession, it can only reasonably apply in the case where something actually *is* possessed. When someone is in actual possession of something, she characteristically is unwilling that others deprive her of it. Someone who would not be willing to be deprived of a particular possession in a given set of circumstances cannot reasonably deprive another of a relevantly similar possession in comparable circumstances. There is thus a strong presumption against interference with the things people actually possess.

This presumption must be defeasible, of course. At least, there is reason to think so if at least some deprivations of people's possessions are inconsistent with the Principle of Fairness and ought to be remedied, for, in this case, someone depriving an otherwise just possessor of something will become a possessor herself, and it will be important to be able to distinguish between the two cases.[6]

The injunction to respect people's claims to the things they currently possess is insufficient to determine how conflicts over possessions are to be resolved. If the presumption in favor of existing possession is to have any weight, then, when a rule embodying that presumption is violated unreasonably, it will at least often be appropriate to return the unreasonably taken possession to the person from whom it was taken in violation of the rule. Returning the possession, however, will mean taking the possession away from the person who has taken it. And no doubt *she* may be unwilling to be dispossessed as well. If the only relevant rule were, *Avoid taking people's possessions*, there would be no way to provide a remedy for unjust taking.

The need to decide how to sort out problems posed by cases of this sort requires a reasonable scheme of rules regarding agents' relationships with each other vis-à-vis physical objects. To be useful, such a scheme would need to make clear when possession itself was reasonable in the first place, so that it could be ascertained when

[6] It is not crucial that we identify at this stage just what circumstances would or would not make depriving someone of something incompatible with this principle.

someone currently in possession of something was its just possessor, someone whose possessory claim ought to be protected, and when her possessory interest deserved no particular respect because she was an unjust possessor. Thus, rules specifying what will count as just acquisition, determining just what further entitlements ought to be associated with just possession, and governing the disposition of justly held possessions are all important.

D. Truisms about the Human Situation Ground Multiple Desiderata That Provide Further Reasons for Narrowing the Range of Possible Just Possessory Rules

While the presumption in favor of current possessors is strong, it requires augmentation in light of the Principle of Fairness and a range of facts about human behavior and the human condition. Taken together, these "truisms" or "'rule[s]' of human experience"[7] help to generate a set of rules that provide reasonable limits on choices regarding possessions.

It might be possible to formulate any of several schemes of possessory rules building only on the Principle of Fairness and the fact that people are not willing that others deprive them of their possessions. However, without canceling or ignoring the basic, if defeasible, presumption in favor of retaining what one possesses, it is possible to identify a set of more extensive and nuanced norms regarding possession. These norms ground reasonable and substantial limits on the contents of just possessory rules. Several desiderata derived from a range of useful truisms about the human situation, in tandem with the Principle of Fairness,[8] can serve (*i*) to explain

[7] The notion of *truisms* about human existence as providing the basis for legal rules lies at the root of H.L.A. Hart's minimalist account of natural law; *see* H.L.A. HART, THE CONCEPT OF LAW 191–200 (2d ed., 1994). Hart's list of truisms—human vulnerability, approximate equality, limited altruism, limited resources, limited understanding and strength of will—is somewhat more modest than the one I offer in this chapter, and is obviously less moralized; but, like Hart, I seek to build on relatively obvious data of human experience. It seems reasonable to view each of the truisms to which I attend as, to draw on an analysis offered by John Finnis that in some ways parallels the one I offer here, "a 'rule' of human experience"; *see* JOHN FINNIS, NATURAL LAW AND NATURAL RIGHTS 170 (1980) (referring, in particular, to the notion that particularized control leads to more extensive and effective stewardship).

[8] On this general approach to justice in possession, *see, e.g.*, ARISTOTLE, POLITICS II.5 (Benjamin Jowett trans., 1905); FINNIS, *supra* note 7, at 169–67; GARY CHARTIER, ECONOMIC JUSTICE AND NATURAL LAW 32–33 (2009) [hereinafter CHARTIER, JUSTICE]; Gary Chartier, *Natural Law and Non-Aggression*, 51 ACTA JURIDICA HUNGARICA 79 (2010). The new classical natural-law theorists emphasize the significance of incentivization, stewardship, and autonomy as reasons for the recognition of possessory claims. The additional considerations I adduce here further constrain the range of reasonable options regarding just possessory claims, I believe. *Cf.* 2 ARMEN ALCHIAN, THE COLLECTED WORKS OF ARMEN ALCHIAN 3–144 (Daniel K. Benjamin ed., 2006) (discussing the economic logic of possessory claims); L.W. SUMNER, THE MORAL FOUNDATIONS OF RIGHTS (1987) (seeking to show how robust, reliable rights might be provided with a perhaps unexpected consequentialist grounding).

why supporting and adhering to *some system* of rules protecting and regularizing possession might be a requirement of practical reasonableness, (*ii*) to determine whether *a given system* of possessory rules will count as reasonable, and so (*iii*) to establish, at least in some cases, whether *a given claim* to possess some physical object in particular should be regarded as reasonable.[9] The relevant desiderata include at least those I identify by talking about concern with:

- accessibility;
- autonomy;
- connection;
- coordination;
- desert;
- experimentation;
- generosity;
- identity;
- incentivization;
- norm maintenance;
- peacemaking;
- reciprocity;
- reliability;
- simplicity;
- specialization;
- stability;
- stewardship; *and*
- trustworthiness.

The desiderata sometimes overlap in justification and substance as well as in implications, but it seems useful nonetheless to distinguish them analytically.

A system of rules that increases the number, variety, and quality of desired goods and services—for simplicity's sake, we can refer to their *accessibility*—to most people is, all other things being equal, to be preferred to one that does not. Most people will want, and will have reason to want, it to be easier rather than harder to obtain the goods and services they desire.[10] While some people might prefer that others

[9] In effect, I seek to show that supporting *some* set of rules is reasonable—and so to fulfill goal (*i*)—by arguing directly for the constraints limiting the range of available options—and thus meeting goal (*ii*). My general view regarding particular claims is that arguing for *their* justice—fulfilling goal (*iii*)—should ordinarily be a matter of appealing to the considerations adduced in fulfillment of goal (*ii*), though it will of course be reasonable to argue that the proper way to understand a given rule in a given case is in light of the considerations underlying the rule as they are made relevant in that case.

[10] *Cf.* Stephen R. Munzer, A Theory of Property 191–226 (1991). Of course, there are many sorts of uses, and deliberate noninterference can be a kind of use.

not have access to specific goods or services, everyone will favor the existence and operations of rules that increase the chances that the goods and services *she* wants, in particular, will be accessible to her (and this will be especially true of such widely valued goods as food, clothing, shelter, transportation, and communication, and of such widely valued services as health care, education, and culture). It will be therefore be unreasonable for her to object, at least on the whole, to rules that increase others' access to the goods and services *they* want.

One way of talking about, and in some sense measuring, an increase in the accessibility of desired goods and services is as an increase in societal wealth (where societal wealth is simply the wealth realized in whatever population is affected by the rules). Despite the fact that flourishing is hardly limited to the realization of monetizable value, and even though monetary wealth itself is only of instrumental value, an increase in monetary wealth, in particular, can obviously provide the means for people to flourish in genuine, objectively valuable ways, since such wealth gives them the latitude to pursue their own preferred conceptions of flourishing.[11] Further, when it is invested in worthwhile projects, these projects will necessarily have positive consequences that extend beyond the welfare of the immediate participants and beneficiaries and that will often help to boost the well-being of the worst-off in a given society. In addition, the more wealth available in a given group, the more is available for people to use to exhibit generosity, and the more likely it is that generous actions will take place. This means that an increase in societal wealth will increase the resources available for sharing with economically vulnerable people, in particular, and increase the likelihood that such sharing will take place. Because everyone has reason to seek flourishing, there will be good reason for most people to value the availability of increased *means* to flourishing, for themselves and for others, and so of increased societal wealth.

[11] The concern with societal wealth generally parallels the focus on *wealth-maximization* as a basis for the relevant sorts of legal protections, a notion ably defended by Richard Posner; *see, e.g.*, RICHARD A. POSNER, THE ECONOMICS OF JUSTICE 13–115 (1981). But where appeals to wealth-maximization often seem framed in such a way that maximizing wealth is seen as the primary or exclusive purpose of law, I simply suggest that economic productivity benefits many people and should thus be taken into account when possessory rules are being framed, not that it is or should be the sole objective of such rules. I resist the consequentialist and monist reduction of flourishing to monetarily measurable wealth; it seems clear that there are multiple kinds of things that matter, or ought to matter, to us, and wealth is an imperfect proxy for these things because it offers access to them. Obviously, there is no entity that holds societal wealth—"society" names a set of people and relationships and activities, and it is the people who hold the wealth; but, given just rules of acquisition and transfer, the presence of a given level of wealth held by all the members of a group can provide information of limited but real value in determining the prosperity of the group's members.

Concern with societal wealth is obviously closely related to concern with incentivization, but incentivization has to do with the impact of a just scheme of possessory rules on the behavior of particular actors; one key reason for regarding this kind of impact as significant is its impact on societal wealth, but presumably there might be other reasons as well.

People tend to prefer that they be able to realize their goals without being prevented from doing so by others—that others not interfere with their doing what they want to do. As long as we don't introduce contestable understandings of what the term might mean, laden with assumptions about the origins and contents of the preferences people can be expected to attempt to realize, we can sum this up by saying that they seek *autonomy*. Anyone who values the opportunity to realize her own preferences has reason to value her own autonomy, and so, in accordance with the Principle of Fairness, to respect the autonomy of others. And people have reason to value institutions that foster autonomy because they recognize that some people seek to control others for selfish ends and that other people seek control for putatively benevolent ones: autonomy-enhancing institutions limit the damage these would-be controllers can do.[12] In addition, practical reasonableness cannot be cultivated or exercised without autonomy. Autonomy is at times instrumental and at times best seen as—to some indeterminate degree—constitutive of various other aspects of well-being, especially practical reasonableness. In any case, it is essential to reasonable living.[13] Autonomy is not only something people happen to desire but also something that allows people to create lives that are truly their own and to make use effectively of their unique knowledge and insights, and which is also an essential prerequisite for moral agency.[14] Most people thus have reason to favor the existence and operation of possessory rules that safeguard and enhance everyone's autonomy.

People have good reason to favor possessory rules that foster what I'll call, for summary purposes, *connection*. Possessory rules can, in principle, help to bridge gaps among disparate groups of people. They can provide opportunities for people who are strangers, even enemies, to become allies, and in some cases friends. They can do this in at least several interconnected ways. (*i*) Rules that facilitate (direct and indirect) exchanges among people who would otherwise be strangers or enemies create mutual interdependence, something that makes hostility and distance more costly. (*ii*) Such rules provide occasions for people to interact, even if, at first, unwillingly, and thus for greater understanding and personal relationships between them to develop. (*iii*) Rules of this kind also enable people to see each other occupying

[12] *See* MARK PENNINGTON, ROBUST POLITICAL ECONOMY: CLASSICAL LIBERALISM AND THE FUTURE OF PUBLIC POLICY 5 (2011). Pennington's concern here is with the absence of altruistic behavior, rather than with abuses of power, but his observations suggested to me the need to emphasize this point.

[13] *Cf.* GERMAIN GRISEZ & JOSEPH M. BOYLE, JR., LIFE AND DEATH WITH LIBERTY AND JUSTICE: A CONTRIBUTION TO THE EUTHANASIA DEBATE 454–55 (1979).

[14] *See* FINNIS, *supra* note 7, at 168–69, 172, 192; 2 GERMAIN G. GRISEZ, THE WAY OF THE LORD JESUS: LIVING A CHRISTIAN LIFE 794–95 (1994). If someone would be unwilling to accept someone else's infringing on her autonomy in particular circumstances, it would be inconsistent with the Principle of Fairness for her to violate another's autonomy in comparable circumstances: for such a person (who is, I would have thought, quite typical), disregarding the autonomy of others would be unreasonable quite apart from its role in making moral agency possible.

roles other than those determined by family, ethnicity, gender, religion, and other sources of identity that sometimes generate conflict—and thus to transcend unduly narrow classifications of others. (*iv*) Possessory rules that require cooperation as a means of achieving mutual benefit can encourage people to embrace norms favoring cooperative rather than conflictual interaction more generally, as cooperation comes to be seen to the ordinary mode of personal interaction. (*v*) Possessory rules fostering greater prosperity will reduce occasions for suspicion and conflict and create more room than would otherwise be available for the formation of friendship and community. Anyone who wants to be understood by others, to avoid enmity with them, and to foster friendship, fellow-feeling, and community will have some reason, in accordance with the Principle of Fairness, to favor possessory rules that encourage connection in the sense I have described it here.[15]

In any large-scale economy, it is crucial to ensure the ongoing *coordination* of the decisions of various producers, distributors, and consumers. Production and distribution are for the sake of consumption—which is to say, use by all of us (not everyone is a producer, but almost everyone is a consumer). And it is thus crucial that decisions about what is produced, how much of it is produced, and how it is distributed track the preferences people express through their consumption choices. To the extent that particular possessory rules can enable this kind of coordination to take place, they facilitate sensible decisions about production and distribution and make it more likely that consumers' preferences will be satisfied. Because each person qua consumer wants her preferences to be satisfied, she has good reason, in accordance with the Principle of Fairness, to favor arrangements that facilitate the coordination of producers', distributors', and consumers' decisions. But this is not simply another way of providing further specificity to the point that she has good reason to favor accessibility, which is fostered by coordination. She also has at least three additional reasons to favor rules that facilitate coordination: (*i*) Coordination facilitates social cooperation, interdependence, and what I have labeled *connection*—all of which are inherently valuable. (*ii*) Rules that facilitate coordination benefit not only consumers but also producers and distributors, who can make reasonable choices about the use of time and physical resources more readily when they can adjust their actions in light of consumers' preferences. (*iii*) In addition, such rules encourage social order more broadly, since social strife of all kinds is less likely (*a*) when

[15] *Cf.* Neera Kapur Badhwar, *Friendship and Commercial Societies*, 7 POLITICS, PHIL. & ECON. 301 (2008); MURRAY N. ROTHBARD, MAN, ECONOMY, AND STATE WITH POWER AND MARKET 100–101 (2d scholar's ed., 2009). Obviously, as regards (*iii*), some people will have countervailing desires for, say, homogeneous environments not disrupted by outsiders. It *may* not be unfair for them to disfavor possessory rules that foster communication of the sort I have considered *under the description* that they foster this kind of communication, provided they do so in pursuit of authentic fulfillment. On the other hand, they may nonetheless have good reason to favor such rules under other descriptions.

people have access to the goods and services they desire, (*b*) when producers and distributors have regular work, (*c*) when producers and distributors can use the best information available to them to predict the need for their work, and (*d*) when producers and distributors know their work is valued—as they will more readily when possessory rules that allow and encourage them to make decisions about production and distribution in light of consumers' revealed preferences are in place.[16]

The Principle of Fairness incorporates the recognition "that one good turn deserves another."[17] People value receiving, and want and expect to receive, benefits from others in accordance with the benefits they have conferred on others (at least when the beneficiaries have received the benefits in the course of a willing exchange—involuntarily conferred benefits are more problematic).[18] And, while they ought to be unwilling to accept retributive punishment as a putative expression of desert—just because one *good* turn deserves another, it doesn't follow that one *bad* turn deserves another—they will characteristically be willing to accept losses that flow from desert. They will thus have good reason to affirm, and little reason to

[16] *See, e.g.*, RANDY E. BARNETT, THE STRUCTURE OF LIBERTY: JUSTICE AND THE RULE OF LAW (1998); David D. Friedman, *A Positive Account of Property Rights*, 11 SOC. PHIL. & POL'Y 1 (1994).

[17] *See, e.g.*, JOHN FINNIS, AQUINAS: MORAL, POLITICAL, AND LEGAL THEORY 197 (1998); MUNZER, *supra* note 10, at 254–91.

[18] Peaceful, voluntary cooperation through exchange is presumptively beneficial to both parties: after all, if no one forces someone to make an exchange, it's likely that she regards it as beneficial—and there's good reason to assume that we are better positioned than are others to determine what's good for us.

But while, for purposes of *interpretation*, *explanation*, or *prediction*, it is reasonable to treat each choice, including each choice to participate in an exchange, as undertaken in pursuit of a goal the agent regards as important, there might be cases in which a peaceful, voluntary exchange is not mutually beneficial from a *normative* perspective. This might be because (*i*) a party to the exchange is mistaken about the relevant facts, (*ii*) a party mistakenly believes that what she receives in the course of the exchange is inherently worthwhile (an instance of an aspect of flourishing, or a reasonably sought means to such an instance) when it is not, or (*iii*) a party *chooses* unreasonably to receive something under the description that it is not objectively worthwhile (but perhaps objectively harmful).

Except in these cases, each party receives in the course of a peaceful, voluntary exchange something worthwhile she didn't have before. She chooses this because she does not have it and desires it—but *not* necessarily because she desires it *more strongly* or takes it to be somehow *more preferable* than any alternatives: she *may*, but she need not. And it almost certainly will not be *objectively* more preferable, given the incommensurability of the various aspects of flourishing.

This incommensurability means that no quantitative comparison will be possible when people exchange different goods with each other, so that one party cannot be said to have benefited more in objective terms than the other. However, when one party to an exchange would not be willing to accept an arrangement in which the terms were the same but the roles of the parties were reversed, she acts unreasonably in making the exchange on the current terms. If she makes the exchange anyway, it will qualify as unfair.

Obviously, the possibility of error or unreasonableness does not justify forcible interference with any instance of cooperation through exchange that is peaceful and voluntary (and so, among other things, non-fraudulent).

reject, possessory rules that make it possible for *desert* to be acknowledged and to be reflected in people's interactions.

People have good reason to value *experimentation*.[19] The ability to create or discover new products and processes and to test and evaluate them creates opportunities that benefit everyone. Anyone who believes she can benefit from experimentation will favor institutions that give her, and others, the chance to experiment and innovate.

Possessory rules can and should foster the expression of *generosity*. People who are the beneficiaries of generosity have reason to value it, not only because of the immediate benefits it confers but because of its capacity to convey attitudes and cement relationships. And those who act generously have reason to value it for the same reason. It would be unreasonable for anyone who valued generosity not to favor, all other things being equal, the existence and operation of possessory rules that made it possible.[20]

Someone will often have reason to favor possessory rules that foster the protection of her relationship with a possession that is a constituent of her *identity*.[21] Many possessions are surely not identity-constitutive, but it seems entirely possible that some might be—a farm or a painting that has been home to successive generations of family members, for instance. There is probably good reason for this fact not to give rise to independent, enforceable possessory claims at law. The possibility of confusion and conflict created by allowing someone to invoke an identity-based interest as an independent justification for a possessory claim makes treating such interests admissible at the level of a particular case ill-advised. There is good reason for someone considering what kinds of legal rules to support to prefer rules that themselves make no explicit reference to identity-linked interests. However, the possibility that there might *be* identity-constitutive attachments to particular possessions ought to influence the kinds of possessory rules it would be reasonable to support. Anyone who might value a particular possession as identity-constitutive will have reason to support possessory rules that will in fact provide some protection for her identity-constitutive possessory relationships and (in virtue of the Principle of Fairness) those of others, though probably not for ones that single out an object's identity-constitutive character as an independent reason for determining who should possess it.

People often respond well to *incentivization*. If they are enabled to retain possessions they receive in exchange for others or as gifts, they are likely to work more

[19] *Cf.* PENNINGTON, *supra* note 12, at 5.

[20] *See, e.g.*, ARISTOTLE, *supra* note 8, at II.5; FINNIS, *supra* note 7, at 175.

[21] *See, e.g.*, MARGARET RADIN, REINTERPRETING PROPERTY 35–71 (1993); CHARTIER, JUSTICE, *supra* note 8. The notion of selfhood involved here is articulated in RAZIEL ABELSON, PERSONS: A STUDY IN PHILOSOPHICAL PSYCHOLOGY 91 (1977).

diligently and so to produce goods and services others seek, in greater quantities and at lower costs than they otherwise would.[22] Incentivization can be seen as a *means* to the achievement of *accessibility* and the facilitation of *coordination*, and sometimes as an expression of regard for *desert*. But it is worth emphasizing separately because of its relationship to multiple goals. Anyone who has reason to want to be able to influence others' behavior using incentives, or to see others' behavior influenced in this way, or who recognizes that her own behavior can thus be influenced in ways she values, will have reason to favor possessory rules that foster incentivization.

Effective social order, especially nonviolent social order, depends on effective *norm maintenance*. People need to have a variety of mechanisms at their disposal to encourage cooperative behavior on the part of others. And they thus have good reason to value the kind of social order fostered by norm-maintenance strategies, and thus good reason to favor possessory rules that permit people to implement these strategies. Of course, it's important to note here, as with regard to the other desiderata, that the value of norm maintenance should inform the design of possessory rules to the extent that norm-maintenance strategies encourage people to uphold social norms consistent with the principles of practical reasonableness. To the extent that the same possessory rules will permit the use of norm-maintenance strategies to achieve a variety of ends, this constraint needn't matter much. But to the extent that some rules will tend to make it easier to uphold norms inconsistent with the requirements of practical reasonableness, while others will not, this will be a reason to favor the latter. In particular, upholding social norms that respect the particularity, essential equality, and diversity of persons is consistent with the Principle of Fairness in ways that upholding norms that foster conformity, hierarchy, submissiveness, and

[22] *See, e.g.*, FINNIS, *supra* note 7, at 170–71; GRISEZ, *supra* note 14, at 794; FINNIS, *supra* note 17, at 190. As Finnis observes: "a theory of justice is to establish what is due to a person in the circumstances in which he is, not in the circumstances of some other, 'ideal' world. And those many members of the community who reasonably depend for their livelihood upon the productive efforts and good husbandry of other members can rightly complain of injustice if a regime … is adopted, on the basis that it *would* enhance their well-being of the non-dependent members of the community had characters different from those that in fact they have, but which *actually* yields them (and everyone else) a lower standard of living than they would enjoy under a different regime … operated by the non-dependent members as they *actually* are"; LAW, *supra* note 7, at 170–71 (footnote omitted). To be sure, not everyone requires this sort of incentivization; some people will regard as intrinsically valuable tasks or objects others will view only as instrumentally or strategically valuable, and some people will act persistently for the purpose of fostering the well-being of others without the expectation of personal benefit. But rules that incentivize are important because they serve to promote desirable behavior on the part even of those who never act out of benevolent motives and of those who do act on the basis of altruistic motives but who do not, and are not morally required, to do so all the time; *cf.* PENNINGTON, *supra* note 12, at 5–6.

uniformity is not. To the extent that they differ, possessory rules that make it easier to uphold norms of the former sort are surely to be preferred.

Conflicts over possessions are persistent sources of violence and social unrest. Rules that allocate responsibility for and control over particular physical objects to specific, identifiable persons or groups can serve to reduce conflict (especially conflict over scarce resources). Good fences make good neighbors. By reducing ambiguity and signaling the existence of a consensus regarding what counts as predatory behavior, and what will therefore be met with consistent resistance, possessory rules can contribute effectively to *peacemaking*.[23] Anyone who would prefer to avoid conflict and to see others avoid conflict will thus have reason to favor clear and stable possessory rules.

A crucial feature of a social order rooted in peaceful, voluntary cooperation is *reciprocity*. Reciprocating each other's good behavior is not only a matter of fairness; it is also a crucial mechanism for signaling to others that their behavior should be repeated. It is intrinsically valuable morally as an expression of practical reasonableness (which requires fairness) and, at the same time, instrumentally valuable as a means of sending useful information and prompting good behavior on the part of others that will benefit oneself, those encouraged to reciprocate (since they will benefit from others' positive responses to them, and from an overall social climate favoring reciprocation), and others who benefit from the reciprocating behavior of those encouraged to reciprocate.[24] People thus have good reason to favor possessory rules that facilitate and encourage reciprocity.

People can plan most effectively, achieve their goals most consistently, and be most productive in an environment in which background rules for social interaction, including possessory rules, are characterized by *reliability*—when, once in place, the rules can be expected consistently to be upheld without interference or situational adjustment.[25] Similarly, planning and coordination will be easiest when possessory claims safeguarded by the rules are themselves reliable, when people's possessory claims are not subject to interference. Since effective action characteristically requires planning, and since most people value the capacity to engage in effective action, most people will have reason to favor reliable possessory rules and reliable possessory claims.

[23] *See, e.g.*, John Hasnas, *Toward a Theory of Empirical Natural Rights*, 22 Soc. Phil. & Pol'y 111 (2005); Butler Shaffer, Boundaries of Order (2009); Friedman, *supra* note 16.

[24] *See, e.g.*, David Schmidtz, The Limits of Government: An Essay on the Public Goods Argument 138–56 (1991); Robert Nozick, Invariances: The Structure of the Objective World 240–84 (2001).

[25] *See, e.g.*, Charles M. Fried, Modern Liberty and the Limits of Government 156–60 (2006); Munzer, *supra* note 10, at 191–226. On the negative consequences of undermining the perceived reliability of possessory rules and claims, *see, e.g.*, Robert Higgs, *Regime Uncertainty: Why the Great Depression Lasted So Long and Why Prosperity Resumed after the War*, 1 Indep. Rev. 561 (1997).

Rules marked by *simplicity*—rules that are easy to identify, formulate, articulate, learn, and apply—make efficient use of people's cognitive capacities and their time as well as of resources devoted to preventing and remedying rule-violations.[26] They also reduce the transaction costs associated with defining and following possessory rules and remedying violations of those rules. And they reduce the likelihood that anyone will come into conflict with others or be subject to legal liability—which is particularly important given that legal liability might trigger the use of force, and there is good reason to ensure that cases in which someone's body or possessions might be subjected to force are few in number and clearly identifiable, as they would be likely to be when rules were simple. Anyone who values these goals—as most or all people should—will thus have reason to favor simple rules.

Everyone benefits from possessory rules that make possible *specialization* in economic activity.[27] Most people are better at some things than they are at others, and not especially good at many things. This means that everyone benefits when people concentrate on what they do best, leaving others, in turn, to do what *they* do best. This is true not only because the economy is thus rendered more productive but also because people can focus on using their skills in ways valued by others, so that (*i*) they need not devote time and energy to things at which they are not as adept; and (*ii*) they can be repeatedly assured, to the extent that their choices about productive activity are shaped by others' valuations (obviously, some people's will not be, since they will prefer less valued activities about which they are passionate—and of course there need be no objective reason for them not to do this), that they are contributing something worthwhile to others and that they are appreciated by others as a result. People flourish in a society marked by interdependence—a crucial aspect of peaceful, voluntary cooperation; they thrive when each is allowed and encouraged to specialize, with the result that everyone has reason to favor possessory rules that permit and encourage specialization. (This obviously does not mean that some people might not prefer to be generalists or that avocational opportunities to engage in a variety of pursuits wouldn't be available in a flourishing society. Quite the reverse. Specialization is valuable, but it is hardly the only thing that matters.)

A possessory rule may, but need not, exhibit a particular kind of *stability*—the sort that it possesses when it is or could readily become a self-enforcing convention. This kind of rule is likely to be less costly and intrusive to enforce than one that lacks this quality.[28] Further, since a convention would not *be* a convention if it

[26] *See, e.g.*, Richard A. Epstein, Simple Rules for a Complex World (2005); Demsetz, *supra* note 3, at 354–55.

[27] *Cf.* Alchian, *supra* note 8, at 38–43, 62–66, 96–98.

[28] *See, e.g.*, Anthony de Jasay, Against Politics: On Government, Anarchy, and Order 193–202 (1997); Anthony de Jasay, Political Philosophy, Clearly: Essays on Freedom and Fairness, Property and Equalities 320–33 (2010).

constantly provoked overt conflict—such conflict would seem to be incompatible with the existence of a stable equilibrium—a rule that tracks a stable convention might be expected to be more reductive of conflict than any alternative that was not, or could not readily become, a stable convention. And a possessory rule that tracks a self-enforcing convention may also enjoy greater perceived legitimacy, if only because people may be accustomed to the operation of the convention, and this fact may contribute to conflict prevention as well as to the persistence of the rule, which may, in turn, make it easier to uphold the rule reliably. There will thus be good reason for people to support possessory rules that track stable conventions, since there is good reason to want to reduce enforcement costs and the need for external enforcement of rules as well as to favor conflict reduction and the reliability of possessory rules.

Physical objects will be cared for most effectively when some particular person or group of people is responsible for caring for them—when possessory rules foster *stewardship*.[29] This is so both because objects will be better cared for when people control them sufficiently to be able to realize desired goals using these objects and because a significant level of control enables someone to be an effective steward. By contrast, rules that make lines of benefit and control less clear may tempt people to misuse, squander, and harm physical objects, often to the detriment of others.[30] Rules that foster stewardship are important whether particular objects are valued instrumentally or intrinsically, and whether they are valued for benefit to the possessors or to others, alive or unborn. Anyone who wants physical objects cared for thoughtfully and diligently will thus have reason to favor possessory rules that make stewardship possible and encourage it.

People need to be able to depend on others, even complete strangers, in at least minimal ways. If one assumes that one won't be manipulated or taken advantage of, one can feel much more free to pursue a range of mutually beneficial interactions with strangers, and that one is able to do so confers obvious benefits on everyone affected. [31] Thus, people have good reason to want others to be honest and to keep their promises, and so good reason to want to do so themselves. Similarly, they will have good reason to want others who interact with them to view them as partners in arrangements each can regard as equitable—to be able to trust others not to take advantage of them. And they will therefore have good reason to favor possessory rules that prompt those who engage in economic interactions to exhibit *trustworthiness*.[32]

[29] See, *e.g.*, FINNIS, *supra* note 7, at 70.

[30] *Cf.* Demsetz, *supra* note 3, at 355–58.

[31] *Cf.* DAVID C. ROSE, MORAL FOUNDATIONS OF ECONOMIC BEHAVIOR (2011).

[32] On exchange relationships as promoting equitable interaction, *see* Joseph Henrich et al., *"Economic Man" in Cross-Cultural Perspective: Ethnography and Experiments from 15 Small-Scale Societies*, BEH.

In general, the truisms suggest, a just system of possessory rules will be one that:

- promotes the accessibility of goods and services;
- facilitates people's autonomy;
- fosters interactions that help to convert strangers and enemies into allies and friends and facilitates fellow-feeling and community;
- coordinates people's interactions by making possible the aggregation of information about their interests and needs and the determination of appropriate production levels and distribution patterns for goods and services;
- makes it possible for people to receive, and likely that they will receive, compensation for the goods and services they provide to others and that, more broadly, one good turn will follow another;
- facilitates experimentation with new products and processes and ideas;
- makes it possible for people to be generous and likely that they will be;
- provides some security for people's interests in possessions that might be identity-constitutive;
- facilitates people's contribution to the performance of a community's economy by providing them with things they want when they contribute in ways that others value;
- equips people to uphold social norms nonviolently;
- minimizes conflict—notably by clearly allocating responsibility for particular things to particular people;
- ensures that possessions are put to productive use;
- fosters relationships marked by mutuality and reciprocity;
- enables people to depend on their expectations that otherwise just possessory rules will continue in force, that decisions made about particular claims in light of such rules will be respected, and that otherwise just possessory claims will be respected;
- features rules that are simple—that are easy to formulate, articulate, learn, and apply;
- encourages specialization;
- embodies norms rooted in self-enforcing conventions;
- facilitates stewardship—taking good care of physical objects, cultivating and developing them responsibly, and preventing them from falling into disrepair; *and*
- encourages people to be trustworthy.

& Brain Sci. 795, 808, 813 (2005). Thanks to Paul Zak, Jason Brennan, and David Schmidtz for this reference. *Cf.* Paul J. Zak & Stephen Knack, *Trust and Growth*, 111 Econ. J. 295 (2001) (highlighting the complex connections between trust and economic performance).

E. The Principle of Fairness and the Desiderata Provide Credible Support for the Baseline Possessory Rules

1. *The Principle of Fairness Constrains the Range of Reasonable Possessory Rules*

The Principle of Fairness can justify a system of robust possessory rules in virtue of which first possessors retain what they come effectively to possess, transfer it to others voluntarily, and control it while their claims under the rules persist.

Taken together with the Principle of Fairness, the basic presumption in favor of respecting current possessors' claims, and the various desiderata significantly limit the kinds of possessory rules that it might make sense for anyone to endorse. Indeed, they provide substantial overlapping and mutually reinforcing support for a simple set of rules with respect to physical objects, which I will call the *baseline possessory rules*: (*i*) the first person or group to establish effective possession of an object of which no one else is the just possessor *becomes* its just possessor (Subsection 2);[33]

[33] It is worth emphasizing both that (*i*) the first possessor may be a group (whose members act cooperatively to establish effective possession) rather than a particular person, and (*ii*) a particular person may combine her holdings with those of others or opt to share a possession with someone else in a way that renders it the justly acquired possession of both. The baseline possessory rules do not embody any in-principle bias in favor of personal as opposed to common possession, and certainly leave room for the emergence of common possessions. What matters is simply that just possessors, whether personal or collective, be (*i*) identifiable, (*ii*) able discretionarily to exclude others from the use of their possessions, (*iii*) responsible for internalizing the costs associated with harms done *using* their possessions, (*iv*) responsible for internalizing the costs associated with nonaggressive harms done *to* their possessions, and (*v*) able to reap the benefits derived from the uses of these possessions in which they engage or which they authorize. For a classic discussion of how groups might successfully manage shared possessions, especially natural resources, *see* ELINOR OSTROM, GOVERNING THE COMMONS: THE EVOLUTION OF INSTITUTIONS FOR COLLECTIVE ACTION (1990). I think there is clearly an argument for vesting control over a given possession in the smallest efficient unit possible. Obviously, there will be different ways of assessing the merits of different possessory arrangements, since incommensurable aspects of flourishing and uncertain futures will be at issue. But it seems clear that smaller possessory units will encourage greater flexibility, efficiency, and autonomy, which each decision maker involved will have reason to value, with the result that the Principle of Fairness will provide good reason for subsidiarity to be respected through the creation of possessory units as small as possible. For instance: it might make sense for all those living around a lake to exercise some control over some or all aspects of the lake, depending on the degree to which particular segments might or might not be efficiently controlled by smaller groups. But control over one aspect need not entail control over all, and it would often seem to make little or no sense for all lakes in a given region to be treated as the possession of, say, a group made up of all those living around all of them. For a careful analysis of collective possessory claims from a standpoint compatible with the one I take here, *see* KEVIN A. CARSON, COMMUNAL PROPERTY: A LIBERTARIAN ANALYSIS (Center for a Stateless Society, Paper 13, 2011).

It is also worth emphasizing that, while claims against unjust dispossessors ought not to be arbitrarily time-limited, there will be effective constraints on the instability of just possessory claims as long as there is a presumption in favor of the current possessor, so that someone who wants to maintain that the current possessor's claim is unjust will have the burden of demonstrating that it is.

(*ii*) the just possessor of a physical object may dispose of it freely by gift or as part of an exchange on any terms she wishes (Subsection 3);[34] and (*iii*) a just possessor is entitled to exclusive control over what happens to each physical object she has justly acquired (though she may not use it to cause harm to the bodies or justly acquired possessions of others) (Subsection 4). There is a strong presumption in favor of the baseline rules (Subsection 5).[35]

2. *The First Baseline Rule Provides for Initial Acquisition through Effective Possession*

The first rule, the rule of *initial acquisition through effective possession*, of "first come, first served" or "finders' keepers," serves to solidify and clarify the defeasible presumption, supported by the Principle of Fairness, in favor of respecting people's claims on the possessions they actually have. It is clearly supported by multiple desiderata.

This rule, recognizing effective possession as the basis for a just possessory claim to an object of which no one is the just possessor, would foster *accessibility* because it would allow people to come to possess objects easily and straightforwardly, in relatively unambiguous fashion. It would expedite the process of making good use of possessions. Establishing effective possession of a physical object may be time-consuming and demanding. But establishing that one's claim to the object is justified and will thus be legally recognized should not and need not be. The more efficient the process of claiming an object, the more rapidly it can be used by the possessor, transferred to others, or transformed and then exchanged, and so the more rapidly it can increase the overall stock of goods and services available to everyone. Further, the clearer the path to establishing a just possessory claim, the fewer resources people will expend on disputes regarding claims and the more will

[34] For a similar list, *see, e.g.*, ANTHONY DE JASAY, CHOICE, CONTRACT, CONSENT: A RESTATEMENT OF LIBERALISM 65–79 (1991). Jasay's account tracks Hume's. *See* DAVID HUME, A TREATISE OF HUMAN NATURE 3.2.2–5 (2d ed., 1749). Hume proposes three rules, but his proposed rules feature separate requirements that possessions be transferrable by consent *and* that agreements be kept. While the keeping of agreements is obviously of considerable moral importance, and the duty to keep promises clearly flows from the Principle of Fairness, the *legally enforceable* duty to keep agreements is simply the duty to honor transfers of possession, so there is no need for a separate rule governing agreements. *See* Chapter 5.II.C.2.iv, *infra*.

[35] Anthony de Jasay plausibly defends something like what I'm calling the first and third baseline rules; *see* JASAY, *supra* note 34, at 69–79 (Jasay characterizes what I'm calling the first rule as embodying the principle "first come, first served" and "finders' keepers"). Randy Barnett, David Schmidtz, and Carole Rose also defend version of the first rule. *See* BARNETT, *supra* note 14, at 68–71, 100–102, 112, 153–54; DAVID SCHMIDTZ, ELEMENTS OF JUSTICE 153–57 (2006); Carole Rose, *Possession as the Origin of Property*, 52 U. CHI. L.R. 73 (1985). On the second and third rules, *see, e.g.*, ALCHIAN, *supra* note 8, at 105–07; curiously, Alchian seems to devote little attention to rules of acquisition.

be put to useful purposes. In addition, allocation of a possessory claim to a given object to someone who has exerted the effort needed to establish effective possession of the object seems likely to lead to more effective use of the object than alternatives that pay less, or no, attention to this kind of effort. Those who have exerted this sort of effort are likely both to care more about the objects they come to possess, and so to use them carefully and responsibly, and to be willing to exert the further effort needed to put the objects to use in cooperation with others.

Barriers to taking possession of unclaimed possessions would likely lead to marginal reductions in accessibility. They might have this effect because they could discourage people from seeking to claim such possessions and because they might reduce the probability that people with the skills to make use of particular potential possessions and significant interest in making use of them were actually the ones who claimed the possessions. Rules involving third parties constitutively in the establishment of just possessory claims would make it more likely that possessions would go to those uninterested in or incapable of using them to foster accessibility.[36] Rules that allow people to claim possessions only after surmounting ritual or other hurdles, perhaps with third-party involvement, seem likely to reduce at least to some extent the degree to which unclaimed possessions are claimed and used to make desired goods and services more accessible.

The proposed first rule would foster *autonomy* by allowing people to establish possession of objects, and so to create spheres of existence and activity under their own control. It would also foster autonomy by providing a mechanism by which they could do so without obtaining anyone's permission and without employing complex ritual or other procedures that themselves reduce autonomy and create opportunities for autonomy-reducing abuses by those overseeing and administering them. By conferring power on other persons or institutions, alternative rules would *reduce* autonomy. The proposed first rule could also, arguably, increase autonomy indirectly given the operation of the proposed second rule, allowing for unhindered exchanges: a wider range of objects would be available for exchange if a claim to any unclaimed object could be established through effective possession than might otherwise be available, and the fact that the range was greater could expand the scope of personal choice, and so of autonomy.

[36] The requirement that one fulfill simple *evidentiary* requirements to establish that one is, indeed, in effective possession of something, or that one meet simple *registration* requirements to ensure that a given agency is aware of and will defend one's claim would not amount to a grant of meaningful discretionary authority to a third party in the sense in which I am objecting to such grants here; *cf.* BARNETT, *supra* note 14, at 100–02. My focus here is on what *constitutes* a just claim, and simple, non-discretionary constraints on verifying and seeking defense for claims would not change the fact that effective possession of an unclaimed object constituted a just claim to that object.

The rule would foster *connection* by serving as an unencumbered prerequisite to the establishment of the kinds of exchange relationships that can bridge social, cultural, and economic gaps. Similarly, it would foster *coordination* to the extent that it laid the groundwork for the kinds of exchanges that, operating within the framework of a price system, can foster sensible production, distribution, and consumption decisions. Rules that complicated the process of acquiring unclaimed objects would at least marginally reduce their availability for use in the course of exchange and would thus undermine connection and coordination.

The proposed first baseline rule would serve as a kind of acknowledgment of *desert*, insofar as it recognized the effort (of one sort or another) invested in establishing effective possession. (This obviously might include personal physical effort, the effort spent coordinating others, and the effort spent acquiring other possessions exchanged with others in return for their assistance in establishing effective possession.) Alternative rules could impede the acknowledgment of desert in this sense, to the extent that they attenuated the link between effort and reward: either effort would not be rewarded, or it would be rewarded only in conjunction with something else. And this would be true even of a rule that sought to reward desert in some other arena not directly related to the acquisition of the unclaimed object in question, by conferring a particular possession: this sort of rule would acknowledge one sort of desert only by nullifying another.

The rule would offer some indirect support for *experimentation*, insofar as it would ensure that those who wanted to experiment could obtained unclaimed objects useful for experimentation if they were willing to take effective possession of those objects. It would also foster experimentation to the extent that allowing people to take the initiative to secure unowned objects would make it more likely than would alternate rules that people who wanted those objects could acquire them without interference, provided they were willing to work for them. The proposed rule would minimize random interference with would-be experimenters' acquisition of unclaimed objects relevant to their experimental activities. Further, insofar as experimentation not only fosters but is fostered by autonomy (since freedom of decision creates more space for experimentation), the operation of a simple rule governing claims on unclaimed objects, a rule that would foster autonomy, would also foster experimentation.

The proposed baseline rule would be a simple way of making *generosity* possible—one could acquire a physical object in order to give it away. Alternate rules could also, obviously, make generosity possible. However, ones that entirely cut the link between effective possession and the acquisition of previously unclaimed physical objects might make generosity marginally less meaningful: giving as a gift something one was assigned by a third party might be less appreciated by the recipient than giving as a gift something acquired through the efforts of the giver (or, if the giver was not the first possessor, whoever lay at the beginning of the chain of possession). I do not claim that this consideration weighs heavily in favor of the first rule, of course, only that it might be thought to provide it with limited support.

The proposed baseline rule would also protect some *identity* interests—those established through the self-investment required to take effective possession. Since the proposed rule applies only to unclaimed objects, it would obviously not be relevant to objects with long histories of possession (unless they were judged to be abandoned), and it is in such objects that people can reasonably be expected to have most identity interests. But to the extent that people *did* have identity interests in previously unclaimed objects they have come effectively to possess, a rule rooting just claims in effective possession would protect their interests. And it would certainly do so more than alternative rules that placed barriers in the way of effective possessors seeking acknowledgment of their claims to their possessions, and certainly more than alternatives that ignored effective possession and authorized third parties to assign claims to previously unclaimed possessions.

Allowing people to establish claims through effective possession would serve as a means of *incentivization*, encouraging them to invest time, energy, and resources in establishing just possessory claims (which benefit not only them but those with whom these claims might be exchanged and those who might benefit from these exchanges) and so to lay the groundwork for the use of physical objects in exchange relationships with the potential to benefit large numbers of people.[37] Obviously, systems that featured different rules regarding first possession could also go on to incentivize people to produce for the benefit of others, though something like the first baseline rule would incentivize them particularly to transform unclaimed objects into justly claimed possessions.

The proposed baseline rule would facilitate *norm maintenance* to the extent that it made the acquisition of unclaimed objects easy, and thus gave people ready access to possessions they could use to maintain social norms. (Its very simplicity might, of course, mean that its implementation would limit the capacity of some groups and structures to maintain norms *if* those norms weren't embraced by the persons and associations taking possession of particular objects. But the fact that a set of arrangements made it harder to compel these persons and associations to support norms they didn't want to support seems like an advantage, not a disadvantage, in light of the Principle of Fairness.) It would also would be an effective means of *peacemaking*, since it would establish a clear and simple mechanism for identifying who was and who wasn't the just initial possessor of a given object and for tracing later claims back to just initial ones, and also because it would put others on notice regarding

[37] *See id.* at 153–54.

a just possessor's claim.[38] More complex rules would offer more opportunities for conflict.

The proposed first rule would serve as a useful precondition for *reciprocity* to the extent that it offered a straightforward mechanism for people to acquire the possessions of which they then disposed when engaged in reciprocal exchanges. Obviously, other rules of initial acquisition could play this role as well; the main advantage of this one would be that the rule would make it easy for people to establish just claims to unclaimed possessions, so that they could then focus on cooperating with others through peaceful, voluntary (direct and indirect) exchange.

The proposed rule could be expected to help to ensure the *reliability* of the system of possessory rules and of people's various specific possessory claims: the rule is simple to apply and understand and tracks a stable convention, factors which would reduce the likelihood of its being altered. Alternative rules that allowed discretionary involvement by third parties would increase uncertainty and so decrease reliability. (Alternatives that created hurdles people needed to surmount in order to qualify as just possessors of unclaimed objects might be objectionable on other grounds, but would raise reliability problems only to the extent that they allowed third parties to exercise arbitrary discretion.)

The rule's *simplicity* should be obvious. Given that objects are open for possession at all, establishing effective possession will be a less complex means of acquiring a just claim than any conceivable alternative that involves *both* establishing effective possession *and* some discretionary act by someone else (as also than one that gives no one else discretion, but requires some unduly complex signaling mechanism to make others aware of the just possessor's claim). It will not necessarily be less simple than some alternatives that involve no action by the putative possessor but simply an action by some third party. (Say: a priestess points her finger at a plot on a map and announces, "This one's yours!") But any rule vesting discretionary authority over the assignment of claims to possessions in one or more third parties will be obviously objectionable for multiple reasons.[39]

[38] *See id.* at 70; Rose, *supra* note 35, at 78–82.

[39] This kind of rule would appear to justify evicting someone who was an effective possessor, and so to fall foul of the presumption in favor of respecting actual possession. (This would be true, of course, only if actual possession were deemed irrelevant to establishing a just claim. If a rule instead provided that actual possession *would* establish a claim, but that the action of a third party of the sort I've envisioned could *also* establish a just claim, the rule would be problematic at least because it wasn't simpler than the obvious alternatives and because it would increase the likelihood of conflict. A variety of other objections noted below to third-party allocation would also apply.) Given the basic defensibility of this presumption, it seems as if actual possession should be overturned only when someone else has a better claim rooted, at least originally, in actual possession.

Giving third parties discretionary authority over the assignment of possessory claims would undermine autonomy by giving people the authority to determine others' holdings. In so doing, they would count against accessibility, since people's incentives for use of their possessions would be reduced. It

The rule would indirectly encourage *specialization* since it would offer an easy, straightforward way for someone to take possession of an unclaimed object that might enable her to make effective use of her distinctive skills in light of her distinctive interests. The easier it is to claim an unclaimed object, the easier it is, in turn, at least in general, for objects to be claimed by those whose specialties allow them to make effective use of these objects. By contrast, the more barriers impede the establishment of a claim on an unclaimed object, the less likely it is, in general, that the ultimately validated claim on the object will reflect the claimant's penchant for specialization in some activity for which the object will be useful, and the more likely it is that the claim will reflect ritual, familial, political, or other factors orthogonal to the object's use to someone specializing in making effective use of objects of its kind. Alternative rules regarding acquisition might well make specialization possible as well. However, the more barriers any rule places in the way of an unclaimed

would undermine connection, since people might be less likely to engage in exchange relationships, given the reduced incentives for effective possessors to make use of their possessions, the reduced incentives for beneficiaries of third parties' assignment of possessory claims to work to develop their resources, and the possibility that the third parties might use their assignment authority to reduce connection. It would undermine coordination, since the authority granted to third parties under these envisioned alternatives would reduce predictability and the capacity to coordinate. It would seem to ignore the importance of desert by disregarding the effort involved in establishing actual possession. It would undermine generosity, since gifts could be unsettled by third-party action and people might be less likely to take initial action to acquire possessions that could be used as gifts. It could affect the protection of identity interests, since people would run the risk of being denied access to identity-constitutive possessions. (It may be more likely that one will have an identity-constitutive interest in a physical object one has claimed oneself through effective possession than in one which one has been allocated by a third party.) It would adversely affect incentivization: third-party allocation of unclaimed possessions would reduce incentives for people to establish effective possession over unclaimed physical objects; people simply assigned claims to such objects might not do anything with them. Further, people who expected that they might receive claims allocated by third parties might not be incentivized to perform, to the benefit of others, in other contexts since they would know that they might be awarded possessions by third parties as an alternative to receiving them in virtue of their own effort or work. A rule permitting the allocation of possessions by third parties would undermine the peacemaking function of the possessory rules: effective possessors would likely come into conflict with the third parties and with those to whom they claimed to assign possessory rights. A rule vesting allocative authority over possessory claims in third parties would reduce productivity, since people would have less incentive actually to establish effective possession through actual use of potentially possessed objects. It would create an unequal distribution of power, and thus militate against reciprocity while encouraging self-dealing. It would reduce the reliability of the set of claims resulting from the system of possessory rules, since third-party involvement in the determination of the justice of possessory claims could create uncertainty. It would waste societal wealth on legal disputes over possessory claims and on efforts to manipulate those with the ability to assign possessory claims. It would certainly count against stability, since a rule allowing for third-party involvement would not be a stable convention. It could militate against stewardship, since people assigned possessory claims by third parties might care less for the objects assigned to them, and since effective possessors might care less in anticipation of being deprived of their claims by the third parties. And it could be expected to exert other problematic effects simply by making it harder for people to gain access to physical objects and thus to put them to use in cooperation with others.

object's being possessed by someone able to make use of it, the more likely it is that the object will not be used in the course of productive specialization. In particular, rules that vest authority over unclaimed objects in persons empowered to decide who merits possession of such objects run the risk of limiting access to these objects in various ways that do not reflect awareness of the potential to specialize. Such rules reduce people's ability to draw on their own knowledge regarding their potential for specialization and risk ensuring that authorities' judgments regarding potential specialty uses will predominate over users'.

The proposed rule's *stability* should also be apparent. A rule assigning claims to first possessors tracks a stable convention, not least because someone who takes effective possession of an object will be in a better position to defend her control over it than someone who has not taken effective possession of it. More complex rules are unlikely to prove as stable.

The rule could also be expected to contribute to *stewardship*—for instance, because, all other things being equal, someone might be expected to take better care of something she actually wanted, and going to the trouble to establish effective possession of something is good evidence of valuing it. It is not entirely clear how other methods of acquisition would affect possessors' propensities to engage in stewardship. Receiving a claim to a given possession as the fruit of some complex ritual process could obviously foster someone's attachment to the possession and prompt her to treat it well, for instance, though it is not obvious whether this would lead to the exhibition of significantly more care for the possession than would the proposed baseline rule. Simple assignment by a third party would likely lead, on average, to *less* engagement in stewardship, and hurdles not designed specifically to boost the possessor's sense of the possession's importance of sanctity seem unlikely to promote stewardship.

The rule could be expected to contribute in at least a limited way to the development of *trustworthiness*. It would provide a clear, reliable mechanism for the acquisition of unclaimed possessions, and clarity of expectations should make it easier for people to know what to expect from each other and to hold each other accountable than would alternatives offering less clarity. In addition, knowing that other people shared the baseline rule and would act to enforce it when others—whether carelessly or deliberately—ignored it would enable actors to trust those with whom they interacted in a less calculating way, aware that their decisions to interact need not be conditioned solely on their own ability to assess trustworthiness or to enforce rules when others behaved in untrustworthy ways; and a trusting attitude might be expected to breed trustworthy responses. People might be expected, therefore, to behave in a more trusting and trustworthy fashion in such a setting: some might be trustworthy simply to avoid social sanctions, but it's reasonable to expect that others would tend to internalize norms calling for trustworthiness even if they might initially have experienced those norms as externally imposed. And, of course, once internalized, such norms might be expected to be generalized, so that they applied in settings in which adherence to the first baseline rule wasn't directly at issue.

The proposed first baseline rule is clearly superior to possible alternatives with respect to autonomy and desert. And it is superior to realistically conceivable alternatives with respect to simplicity and accessibility. It is probably at least somewhat superior to available alternatives with respect to peacemaking (particularly since, as compared with alternatives which assume that all potentially claimable assets are the possession of everyone in a given community, it encourages members of the community to welcome outsiders—whose arrival would, by contrast, under the alternative rule being considered, reduce everyone else's claim on existing assets).[40] It is superior to most alternatives with respect to stability, and at least as good as others. It could well be marginally superior to other possible rules with respect to connection, coordination, experimentation, incentivization (at least as regards the transformation of objects from unclaimed to claimed), and specialization. It will be at least as satisfactory as other realistically likely rules with respect to generosity, identity, norm maintenance, reciprocity, reliability, stewardship, and trustworthiness. It would tend to facilitate norm maintenance by particular persons while perhaps in some cases undermining norm-maintenance efforts by groups and authority structures—a less-than-troubling feature to the extent that the norms in question were inconsistent with the Principle of Fairness. In short: the various desiderata would seem to support a strong presumption in favor of the first proposed baseline rule. Whether in highly irregular situations the requirements of practical reasonableness might render some alternative appropriate, in reasonably stable, peaceful societies, it is difficult to conceive of an alternative as reasonable.

Realistically conceivable objections will surely not focus on the desirability of third-party allocation schemes (though these present the most obvious counterexamples), much less on arbitrary assertions of control over objects by would-be possessors as means of asserting claims to them. Instead, they seem likely to rest on claims that putatively relevant groups should be able to control access to unclaimed objects. But these sorts of objections will tend to have to do with the *use* to which these objects are put; they will be framed on the assumption that, once acquired, the objects will be used in particular ways. If it is reasonable for legal rules to limit use, then it may be reasonable for them to limit use by limiting acquisition. But if it is not reasonable for legal rules to limit use, then it will not be reasonable for them to limit use by limiting acquisition. And whether it is reasonable for possessory rules to limit the use of possessions has to do with the second and third rules, rather than the first. The proposed second rule empowers just possessors to transfer their possessions

[40] *See* SCHMIDTZ, *supra* note 35, at 155.

freely, while the third gives just possessors exclusive control over their possessions. Presuming the second and third rules are defensible, it will be difficult to challenge the first rule on the basis that an alternate rule of acquisition is needed to limit the use of possessions. Further, if it were assumed that just possessors ought to control their possessions, but that the *number* of just possessors of certain kinds of things ought to be limited, this will be objectionable on multiple grounds. It seems to vest inordinate power in whoever is responsible for limiting access and in whoever is able to obtain access to the limited number of objects of the relevant class to which people are permitted to make possessory claims. It would also fall foul of many of the desiderata: accessibility, connection, coordination, and incentivization, in particular, are all fostered by widespread opportunities for just possession. It seems clear that the strong presumption in favor of the proposed first baseline rule could survive obvious challenges unscathed.

The proposed first rule leaves open the question of *how* effective possession is to be established and so of precisely how unclaimed objects might justly be acquired. Various sorts of procedures would likely be consistent with the spirit of the rule. Possession sufficient to allow someone to begin transforming an object in some way, or to make it easier to control the object than it would have been prior to one's possessory action, would seem likely to qualify. Thus, while transforming an object through one's labor would not establish a special metaphysical relationship with the object, transforming the object could certainly amount to possessing it effectively.

3. *The Second Baseline Rule Provides for Just Possessors' Unconstrained Transfer of Their Possessions to Others at Their Discretion*

The second rule, the rule of *voluntary transfer*, entitles a just possessor to transfer anything she possesses to another, for any reason, when she does so voluntarily. That is, she is always free to transfer, but can never be forced or fraudulently manipulated into doing so. The desiderata provide strong support for this rule.

A system of possessory rules that seeks to foster *accessibility*, *connection*, and *coordination* will be one that makes peaceful, voluntary exchange possible. This kind of exchange contributes to the production and distribution of goods and services people value, and to the creation of relationships rooted in, but extending beyond, exchange. Unburdened exchange can help possessions flow to those who want them most and can do the most with them. Rules that limit voluntary transfer are, obviously, rules that limit exchange, and thus rules that fail to be responsive to multiple desiderata. The more exchanges are burdened, the more burdens will be confronted by those seeking to obtain physical objects in order to use them productively, and the more difficult it will typically be for those most inclined to put them to productive use to acquire them.

The proposed second rule would obviously foster *autonomy*. Indeed, it is clear that no alternative transfer rule could enable a similar degree of autonomy. It would also make *generosity* more possible than would any alternative: not only would it make it easier for people to give without hindrance, but it would also boost opportunities for giving and dispositions to give by increasing the stock of available resources. It would effect *incentivization*, since transferrable objects can be used to incentivize those who wish to acquire them, while limits on transferability would reduce the capacity of transfers to incentivize. It would clearly exhibit greater *simplicity* than almost any obvious alternatives as well. Clearly, any rule that allowed in general for unencumbered transfer but required occasional interventions by some third party would be more complicated. The only obvious alternative that would be as simple would be one in which all transfers were handled in toto by a small number of third parties, but this sort of alternative poses so many other obvious problems that it is not a realistic candidate for adoption.

The proposed second rule would not ensure that possessions were transferred to people on the basis of generalized merit. But it would certainly make it *possible* for them to be transferred on the basis of regard for generalized merit, and more likely that they would be transferred on the basis of specific *desert*—as a reward for work performed in accordance with an agreement, say. Those in a position to transfer their possessions in an unconstrained manner can be expected frequently to take equity concerns into account, and this will mean honoring their agreements with others, and honoring work performed in fulfillment of such agreements, as well as honoring work conferring broader benefits on groups to which the transferors belong and particular members of those groups. Alternatives involving third-party intervention to foster desert presuppose an unlikely degree of knowledge on the part of those expected to intervene, and leave room for meddling that would be problematic on multiple fronts, undermining autonomy, connection, coordination, incentivization, and accessibility.

The proposed rule would encourage *experimentation* insofar as it made it likely that objects could find their way to those likely to experiment with them. In addition, since incentivization fosters experimentation, and the rule would encourage incentivization, it would also promote experimentation in this way. Further, the worth of experimentation presupposes that it is uncertain how a given object can be put to best use (if, in a particular case, there is, as there is unlikely to be, a best use at all), to efficient use, or to otherwise appropriate use. So deciding in advance with whom an object should be located, as a restraint on transferability would amount to deciding, would constitute an effective denial of the importance of experimentation.

The proposed rule would facilitate *norm maintenance* effectively. It would enable people to dispose of their possessions in ways that could serve to uphold various sorts of social expectations. Transferring or withholding possessions to others based on the conformity of their behavior to relevant norms could serve as a very effective motivator. By contrast, limiting transferability could impede people's capacities to influence others to conform to relevant social norms, because they could not respond as flexibly to situational specifics. (Of course, retention of possessions might itself *be* a social norm, and limits on transferability might serve various other goals some people might have. But the rule wouldn't prevent people from adhering to a social norm encouraging retention of possessions. It would, of course, keep some people from *controlling* others' transfers except by persuading them not to make these transfers, but this seems to reflect the kind of concern for equal treatment embodied in the Principle of Fairness.)

If *specialization* and *stewardship* happen because people are invested in, and can control, what happens to their possessions, the proposed rule, safeguarding the ability easily to transfer possessions, seems tailor-made to foster both. (*i*) When a current claimant doesn't want a possession at all and transfers it to someone who does, the recipient is likely to be someone who wants to care appropriately for the object and to employ it in a way reflective of expertise and interests. (*ii*) People may serve as stewards of objects, and will quite likely use and transform those objects in view of the objects' potential value in the context of exchange with others, which they couldn't realize were they not free to transfer their possessions to others. Thus, people will be able to specialize in activities at which they are particularly adept and on serving those they are particularly well situated to benefit. (*iii*) In addition, unhindered transferability ensures that others can exchange usefully with people with particular specialties in ways that enable them to concentrate on those specialties rather than needing to focus their efforts on economic tasks in which it would be more reasonable for others to specialize.

The rule might or might not foster the protection of *identity* interests. On the one hand, limits on transfer might keep some possessions in, for instance, some families for extended periods in ways that might protect identity interests people not yet in direct control of the possessions might have developed in them. On the other hand, of course, ease of transfer might make it simpler for those with identity interests to acquire possessions in which they had already gained such interests.

A convention permitting unencumbered transfer of possessions could clearly and readily emerge and prove stable. Thus, the proposed second rule would track a stable convention, and the fact that it exhibited the relevant sort of *stability* would provide a further reason to endorse it.

The absence of limits on transfers will make some kinds of conflicts, in some particular cases, more likely, while constraints on transfers will encourage other kinds of conflict between particular people in particular cases. To this extent, adopting the second rule might not seem to be an obvious means of *peacemaking*. However, someone who wants to transfer one of her possessions to someone else seems likely to react negatively in general to a third party's attempt to interfere with the transfer, so that a rule allowing for third-party limitations on transfers will itself tend to generate conflict in a way that a rule precluding such limitations would not. In addition, the proposed second rule would foster peacemaking because it would provide a simple standard for identifying just claims to previously claimed and justly possessed objects: *transfer from previous just possessors*. The availability of such a simple standard would tend to reduce conflict, while a more complex standard would create more opportunities for conflict. (To be sure, some people will want rules that allow them to restrain others' transfers. But (*i*) many of them will want their own transfers to occur without restraint, and it will obviously be inconsistent of such people to want to restrain others'; and (*ii*) given the broad range of reasons for which people might want to transfer possessions, it seems likely that those wishing to restrain others' transfers would be significantly smaller than those who want to be able to transfer their own possessions at will.)

The proposed second rule would undoubtedly foster *reciprocity*. Unhindered exchange is an effective mechanism of reciprocating others' behavior. The more unencumbered exchanges are, the more readily people will be able to equilibrate their behavior in relation to each other's actions, and so to reflect their responsiveness to, and their desire to influence, each other's choices.

The fewer the constraints on voluntary action, and so on voluntary cooperation in exchange, the greater *reliability* a system of possessory rules and people's particular possessory claims will exhibit: people will be able to count on the persistent enforcement of rules that enable them to exchange at will, and they will be count on noninterference with their possessions. (A *system* featuring many complex exceptions to a general rule allowing voluntary transfers could be enforced consistently, of course; but in such a case the central rule would not itself be reliable and couldn't serve as a basis for effective planning, which would be much more difficult given the possibility of multiple exceptions. And of course particular possessory claims wouldn't be reliable. To the extent that the exceptions could be made on the basis of authority figures', or others', discretion, the reliability of rules and claims would be further undermined.) A rule allowing for unencumbered transfer, as opposed to one permitting various sorts of interferences with transfers, would obviously make the transactional environment less reliable, generating more uncertainty and thus inhibiting planning.

The proposed rule would encourage people to engage in ongoing patterns of exchange. And engaging in ongoing networks of exchange seems to have the potential to encourage people to develop habits of honesty, promise-keeping, and regard for equity, with likely spillover effects outside the narrowly economic sphere. (For instance: free transferability would give people a wide range of opportunities to exhibit trustworthy behavior, and so to encourage a culture of trust inside and outside the realm of economic exchange.) It would thus be worth endorsing as a means of promoting *trustworthiness*. By contrast, concern for equity, at any rate, seems less likely to be fostered in the absence of opportunities to participate in continuing exchange relationships, while other social forms seem no more likely, and quite possibly less likely, to foster honesty and promise-keeping among strangers.

The proposed second rule is obviously superior to reasonable alternatives from the standpoint of accessibility, autonomy, connection, coordination, generosity, incentivization, reciprocity, reliability, and simplicity. It seems likely to be preferable to alternatives from the standpoint of desert, experimentation, stability, peace-making, specialization, stewardship, and trustworthiness. And it is, at any rate, no worse than alternatives from the standpoint of norm maintenance, and identity; clearly, other arrangements might serve these values well, though it is not obvious that any would be superior to the proposed second rule. The sorts of adjustments to the second proposed rule needed to ensure that it was significantly more responsive to specific concerns related to (generalized) desert and identity, or that it met some goals related to the maintenance of particular norms the proposed rule might be thought to undermine, would involve considerable third-party meddling of a sort that would undermine the effectiveness of the rule with respect to the other desiderata. In addition, such adjustments would reduce the scope for people to engage in the kinds of behaviors in virtue of which ascriptions of desert would be appropriate in the first place. That is because in an economic context these behaviors often occur in the context of transactions or cooperative ventures, and the range of possible transactions and cooperative ventures would be limited were transactions more encumbered than they would be were the second rule adopted.

Since the various aspects of well-being involved and affected are not commensurable, there is no way to establish that no alternative rule could, in principle, be superior to the proposed second rule. But it can plausibly be maintained, with reference to all of the desiderata, that there is a very strong presumption in favor of the proposed second rule. It is difficult to imagine realistic arguments invoking the Principle of Fairness in support of alternate rules thought to be more likely to promote generalized desert and identity, given the importance most people will place on the other desiderata and the degree to which the alternate rules would undermine those desiderata.

Realistically, in any case, objections to the second rule are likely to be framed, not in terms of concern about identity or generalized desert, but rather with reference to injuries to or losses suffered by transferors or transferees. The availability of remedies for fraud and for injuries caused to the unwitting by dangerous products should suffice to render these possibilities less worrisome, and should thus leave the strong presumption in favor of the second rule intact.

4. *The Third Baseline Rule Provides for Just Possessors' Exclusive Control over Their Possessions*

The third baseline rule, the rule of *exclusive control of possessions* acquired in accordance with the first rule (or through voluntary transfers consistent with the second rule and ultimately rooted in acquisitions consistent with the first), entitles a just possessor to exclude others from access to her justly acquired possessions.[41]

The rule would foster *accessibility* because people confident that they could control their possessions and employ the results of their possessions' use as they saw fit, whether for others' benefit or their own, would typically be more inclined to invest time and effort and other possessions in acquiring these possessions than they would if they did not have exclusive control over them. And this in turn would encourage them to engage in mutually beneficial cooperative ventures and exchanges with others, in ways that will foster accessibility. In addition, the ability to control a possession means that one can transform it as needed in a way that may enhance its value either to the possessor, to others, or to both. While it might initially be thought that more access to goods and services might be fostered if possessory rules gave people ready access to others' possessions, it seems clear that, were this the case, people would be less inclined to engage in the kinds of relationships and activities likely to yield a greater stock of goods for everyone, since, given their reduced control over their possessions, they would be less able to realize their objectives.

The rule would clearly and unequivocally foster *autonomy*, since it would create a zone of control within which one could act without interference. No alternate rule would ensure anyone comparable autonomy: any other rule would give someone else at least partial control over each agent's justly acquired possessions. It might

[41] That one may justly control a possession means, among other things, that one may justly exclude others from access to it. And, because no one likes to be excluded, the Principle of Fairness might be thought to militate against allowing this sort of control. However, (*i*) those who do not wish to be excluded will characteristically wish to be able to exclude, so it will be difficult for them to object to a rule permitting exclusion (perhaps some will not want to be able to exclude either, seeing themselves as sufficiently weak-willed that they need to be restrained from excluding, and there will thus in their case be no inconsistency between their immediate preferences with regard to their own opportunities and those of others, though the Principle of Fairness may still ultimately entail, in view of other considerations, that they are being unfair for opposing opportunities for exclusion); (*ii*) while the right to exclude might be thought to pave the way for the creation of a vast array of landless paupers, the requirement a just possessory claim must be rooted in effective possession rules out legislated engrossment of land, in particular, and thus means that it can be expected to be available to those who might wish to homestead it in accordance with the first baseline rule; and (*iii*) similarly, the emergence of large numbers of landless persons reflects not only state-driven engrossment but also state-underwritten violence, *see* LUDWIG VON MISES, SOCIALISM: AN ECONOMIC AND SOCIOLOGICAL ANALYSIS 335 (1981), which the baseline rules prohibit and for which they imply the suitability of remedies; (*iv*) the ability of anyone to establish exclusive claims to resources is potentially beneficial to everyone (given all the truisms underlying the baseline rules) and thus worth affirming by everyone; *see* DAVID SCHMIDTZ, PERSON, POLIS, PLANET: ESSAYS IN APPLIED PHILOSOPHY 193–210 (2008).

be objected that the rule could also *undermine* autonomy, since access to others' possessions might sometimes increase some people's autonomy. However, there are several reasons not to prefer alternate rules allowing interference with people's exclusive control over their justly acquired possessions.

(*i*) While such alternative rules might foster autonomy in some cases, they would create multiple opportunities for infringement on autonomy in others. The more extensive the range of permissible exceptions, the more unreasonable it would be to permit them, since people would be less and less willing to accept as generally applicable rules creating multiple opportunities for their autonomy to be infringed. Despite the likelihood that autonomy in some sense might be fostered in particular cases by revised rules of various sorts, there would be good reason to favor a more general rule in virtue of its typically autonomy-enhancing character.

(*ii*) Such alternate rules would foster generalized uncertainty that would reduce people's ability to plan, because there would be more opportunities for interference with people's just possessory claims.

(*iii*) Evicting someone from one's home obviously restrains her autonomy in one sense. But the kind of interference with a person's autonomy involved in evicting her from one's own space is quite different from the interference involved in interfering with her body or what are undisputedly her possessions.

(*iv*) Creating exceptions would leave more room for discretion, and so for abuse, on the part of judicial and law enforcement agencies. The undesirability of such abuse is a reason not to favor exceptions that might be thought to enhance autonomy in particular cases.

(*v*) Although allowing exceptions might enhance (some kinds of) autonomy in particular cases, it is unlikely that it would be obviously and easily determined in the abstract in which cases this might be so. Thus, a rule that dealt with these cases would run the risk of being much too inclusive, and so of allowing autonomy-infringing interference with people's justly acquired possessions in many cases in which it might not be necessary even in light of the rationale advanced for the alternate rule.

(*vi*) Further, alternative rules would be harder for people to understand and apply because they would be more complex.

The rule would encourage *connection*, because it would provide substantial encouragement for people to engage in exchange relationships that would bridge cultural, ethnic, religious, and other sorts of gaps. It would also make *coordination* possible because it would help to ensure that people engaged in exchanges with each other and so participated in the wider coordinative framework that allowed them to meet each other's needs. It would foster people's being treated in accordance with the demands of *desert* to the extent that desert justified acquisition of some possession—since initial acquisition would seem pointless without the subsequent opportunity to control what one possesses. It would encourage *experimentation*, since the more control one has over an object, the more one is able to experiment with it (and if the claim is made that the present possessor of an object is ill-suited to experiment with it, it must be responded that, on the whole, to assume this is to assume that experimentation is unnecessary and that top-down decision making can substitute for it). And it would help to give a point to *generosity*, since the less the recipient of one's generosity could control what one gave, the less reason one would have to give to her in the first place. It would also foster generosity because it would contribute to an overall increase in wealth, and thus both to the availability of resources with which people could be generous and, probably, to an increase in generous impulses.

The rule could also be expected to safeguard *identity* interests in possessions already held. To the extent that one had such an interest, it would presumably matter to one especially intensely that one actually be able to control one's identity-constitutive possession. (Obviously, the rule would not protect identity interests in possessions held by others, and would militate against the recognition of identity-based claims to control the use of such possessions.)

It seems clear that the incentive to acquire something—whatever one's objective in relation to it—would be reduced in proportion to the degree that one was unable to control it. The third baseline rule would thus facilitate *incentivization*.

The proposed third rule could play a vital role in *norm maintenance*. The ability to exclude norm-violators from others' just possessions, especially land, would be a very effective means both of offering protection from the undesirable consequences of their norm-violating conduct and of encouraging them to alter their behavior. Of course, at the same time, it would prevent others from *requiring* that a just possessor maintain a given norm with respect to her own possessions; it would make it easier for particular persons and specific possessor groups to uphold the norms they in fact wanted to uphold, and the Principle of Fairness, with its concern for basic moral equality, would seem to provide good reason to secure this opportunity for them. While very different possessory rules could allow for effective norm maintenance as well, they would be less likely to do so for particular persons and groups. The proposed third rule would be, on average, an unequivocal boon to norm maintenance *given* a scheme of possessory rules responsive to the concerns underlying the other desiderata. And it could be expected to safeguard the values embodied in those desiderata more than alternatives. Norms that stress conformity and seek to repress difference will be harder to maintain in a legal regime that adheres to all three baseline rules. By contrast, the more social norms are respectful of the equality, diversity, and particularity of persons, the easier it will be to maintain these norms using the opportunities provided by the proposed third baseline rule, and the more the rule would tend to be attractive. The proposed rule would safeguard the maintenance of norms voluntarily *by* particular persons and groups and the maintenance of norms respectful of the particularity *of* specific persons and groups.

While being able justly to exclude someone from access to a possession could obviously be a source of conflict, denying someone exclusive control over her possessions is an invitation to meddling by others and an occasion for resentment, and so a potential trigger for conflict. It seems as if there will be good reason to favor a rule that provides for exclusive control in the interests of *peacemaking*.

The envisioned third baseline rule could make a difference as regards *reciprocity* to the extent that it encouraged exchange, which provides a crucial occasion for people to reciprocate. It is conceivable that people might sometimes also reciprocate, and encourage reciprocation, through nonexchange behavior having to do with their direct use of their own possessions—behavior made possible by the kind of control over their possessions facilitated by the proposed third rule.

The proposed rule would also exhibit *reliability*. People could count on the background orderliness of a transactional environment organized in accordance with the rule, and they would know that they could count on the availability of their own possessions and could also be sure they could control those possessions. They could probably also predict the behavior in which other people, as the exclusive controllers of *their* possessions, would be likely to engage more effectively than they could predict behavior in the absence of exclusive control. (It is possible to imagine fantastical scenarios, no doubt, in which pure predictability is maximized in the absence of control, but it seems obvious that there would be good reasons not to want these scenarios realized.)

It is obvious that the third baseline rule is the realistically conceivable rule exhibiting the greatest *simplicity*. The alternatives would seem to be *either* that a just possessor lacks any control over her possessions (in which case there is no real reason to call them her possessions) *or* that she controls them to a significant degree but others exert control over them as well. The former option is simpler, but nontenable (and probably incoherent), while the latter option (a family of options obviously) seems clearly more complex.

The rule seems likely to foster *specialization*. With the capacity to exercise exclusive control over a possession, someone will be freer to make effective use of it in light of her expertise and interests, while alternative rules would seem to reduce her ability to do so.

The rule also seems clearly to exhibit *stability*, since it could effectively emerge as a stable, self-enforcing convention. Alternatives would generate conflict that would yield ongoing instability. And the rule would also foster *stewardship*, since just possessors would be (*i*) *encouraged to care* for possessions when they could reap the benefits of doing so, which they would be better able to do with exclusive control of those possessions and (*ii*) *able to care* for possessions when they could control how the possessions were treated.

The proposed third rule could be expected to foster *trustworthiness* for several reasons: (*i*) Even if people were not *entitled* to control their possessions (as they would not be in the absence of the third proposed baseline rule or one closely resembling it), they could be expected to resent others for interfering with them. A rule that precluded this kind of interference would be likely to reduce resentment, and so to boost trust. (*ii*) Exclusive control would make it more likely that people would engage in exchange relationships, since the incentive to do so would be greater, and participation in networks of such relationships can be expected to foster trustworthiness. (*iii*) Support for the third rule or something close to it might mean that it was more likely than it would be otherwise that dishonesty and promise-breaking would be sanctioned, and the availability of sanctions can contribute directly (by generating fear of penalties) and indirectly (by leading to the internalization of relevant norms) to the development of a culture of trustworthiness. (*iv*) Exclusive control extends the range of promises people can make with regard to their possessions, thus giving them more opportunities to show themselves trustworthy and so to contribute to the creation of a climate of trust.

The third baseline rule seems much more likely than any alternatives to exhibit simplicity and reliability, and to foster accessibility, autonomy, connection, incentivization, specialization, and stewardship. It seems at least somewhat more likely than any realistic alternatives to foster coordination, regard for desert, experimentation, generosity, peacemaking, and reciprocity; to protect identity interests in possessions already held;[42] and to exhibit the right sort of stability. It would be at least as good as alternatives at fostering trustworthiness. The proposed third rule would be much better than alternatives at equipping particular people to maintain social norms effectively, though it might constrain the capacity of involuntary groups and authority structures to do so; structuring possessory rules to the advantage of such groups and structures would seem to fly in the fact of other desiderata, while limiting the use of a very powerful norm-maintenance strategy by specific people. There would seem to be very good reason to favor the third baseline rule.

Reasons to challenge the third baseline rule would not, realistically, concern its responsiveness to the various desiderata but rather the various particular cases in

[42] Obviously, the proposed third rule could cut in both directions where identity interests were concerned. One might have an identity-constitutive attachment to something justly possessed by someone else, and a rule that permitted one some control over it might thus allow for some protection of one's identity interest in it. However, there are multiple reasons not to favor such a rule, and a rule that provided for exclusive control over just possessions would indeed protect many, even if by no means all, identity-constitutive interests in possessions.

which people might be expected to favor violations of a strong presumption in favor of exclusive control. These will come in at least three varieties. In some cases, while the envisioned circumstances might evoke initial sympathy, it will be obvious that, even with regard only to the immediate facts, violating just possessors' exclusive control over their possessions would be unreasonable. In others, were particular instances considered on their own, violating just possessors' control might be judged to be reasonable; however, from a systemic perspective, it might reasonably be concluded that interference with possessors' control was unwarranted—that is, in a case of this kind, the potential interferer should judge that, taking systemic considerations into account, she should not interfere, even though she might have good reason to do so when ignoring these considerations. Finally, there may be cases in which, even allowing for systemic considerations to be relevant, a potential interferer judges that interference is reasonable. But this would not be a reason for adjusting the rule as such, but rather for understanding that the rule requires compensation to, and permits reasonable resistance by, just possessors even in cases of morally defensible interference.

The third baseline rule would obviously make it possible for some people to exclude others on arbitrary, unfair bases. On the other hand, so would a scheme that allowed for much more control by ethnic groups, traditional authority structures, and so forth, rather than by particular possessors. The difference is that, with the proposed baseline rules in place, those engaging in irrational discrimination would be subjected to constant pressures to opt for openness rather than inclusion. By contrast, when, as in the Jim Crow South or apartheid-era South Africa, particular groups are able to control how other people use their possessions, the dominant groups can, by cartelizing, block the pressures that would otherwise lead to greater openness and inclusion. The proposed baseline rules would make it difficult for people to impose their prejudices on others.

5. *The Various Desiderata Provide Strong Support for the Baseline Rules*

There is a strong presumption in favor of the baseline rules: the rule of initial acquisition through effective possession; the rule of voluntary transfer of possessions; and the rule of exclusive control of possessions.

- This cluster of rules would contribute to the accessibility of goods and services by giving people opportunities and motives to transform and exchange possessions, enabling them to direct these possessions to the uses for which they are most desired and most worthwhile and the users by whom they are most valued, and prompting them to shape possessions into the forms in which they are most valued. The rules could thus lead (through incentivization) to the optimization of production levels, and (through the preclusion of monopolistic privileges) the reduction of costs to end users.

- The set of baseline rules would foster autonomy by establishing a zone of control within which a person was able to choose without being constrained by others.
- It could encourage the development of unexpected forms of relationship and community linked by exchanges that undermined the effects of prejudice and distrust.
- It would make possible the exchange of goods at people's discretion, and therefore allow for the coordination of production and distribution effected by prices.
- It would give people the resources needed for them to make agreements and exchange goods and services, thus rewarding their labor.
- It would offer people the relatively unconstrained capacity to experiment and discover new possibilities, as well as the motive to do so.
- It would enable people to express generosity through gift-giving and increases the likelihood that they will do so.
- It would offer some protection to identity-constitutive possessory interests.
- It would create the opportunity for people to be incentivized by having the opportunity to acquire physical objects. It would thus encourage them to make resources more productive by taking initial steps toward rendering those resources apt for development.
- It would enable people to uphold valuable social norms by disposing or retaining control of their possessions.
- It would create conflict-reducing, peace-enhancing boundaries.
- It would encourage reciprocity by facilitating exchange and other kinds of behavior with signaling potential.
- It would generate a reliable background structure that enabled people to plan not just their economically productive activity, but also their lives more generally, in effective ways.
- It may plausibly be seen as exhibiting much greater simplicity than options that assigned putatively just claims to groups of people or parcel out different aspects of putatively just claims with respect to particular possessions to different people or that required more elaborate actions than those required to establish actual possession in order to secure claims.
- It would encourage and allow people to make the investments of time and resources needed to specialize in particular kinds of economic activities.
- It could exhibit the stability typical of rules tracking stable conventions: rules protecting acquisition through effective possession, control over possessions, and free exchange by possessors would tend to be self-enforcing.

- It would assign responsibility for particular physical objects in ways that rendered it more likely that they would be safeguarded for the benefit of anyone with the potential to benefit from them.
- It could encourage people to develop and exhibit honesty and a willingness to keep promises and to exhibit concern for equitable mutual benefit—at minimum in the context of peaceful, voluntary cooperation through (direct and indirect) exchange.

There is thus good reason to endorse each of the baseline rules. But the value of embracing the rules is most clearly apparent when it is understood that they function as interlocking, mutually supportive elements of a *system* that fosters peaceful, voluntary cooperation through (direct and indirect) exchange. Attempting to identify specific instances of the various aspects of flourishing to be furthered or not by the adoption of these or other rules would obviously be a fool's game: predicting outcomes would be impossible, and many of the relevant outcomes would be, in any case, indeterminate. But if the focus is instead on the proposed baseline rules as providing the structure for an endless variety of harmonious interactions, their appeal should be obvious.

The vindication of the baseline rules will necessarily include a key dialectical element. Positive arguments clearly help to establish their validity. But vindicating them also seems to involve demonstrating their superiority to alternatives, and it is not realistically possible to imagine all possible alternatives, or all possible kinds of alternatives, before they come on the scene. Still, I have considered alternatives throughout in ways that suggest that baseline rules are vindicable in the face of other realistically conceivable options.

Understood as precepts to be announced and enforced by the institutions of a legal system, the rules are exceptionless. That they are reflects the significance of desiderata including autonomy, simplicity, and reliability.[43] While reliability is fostered *by* each of the baseline rules, so that under the rules just possessors would be able to count on being able to retain, control, and dispose of their possessions, at least to some degree, just legal institutions will also foster reliability *with respect to* each of the rules and the possessory claims made in accordance with them. The rules (like any similar possessory rules) can be expected to function effectively to the extent that they, and the claims that flow from them, are undisturbed, to the extent, that is, that people are able to use them to plan and coordinate their actions.[44] This means that, from the standpoint of just legal institutions, they should be treated

[43] On the importance of exceptionlessness, *cf.* HENRY HAZLITT, THE FOUNDATIONS OF MORALITY 58, 72–73, 181–85, 258–61, 264 (1964); *cf.* SUMNER, *supra* note 8.

[44] As guides for personal conduct, they leave room for exceptions, as I argue below; *see infra*, Chapter 2.VI.

as uniformly applicable. None of the rules incorporates built-in exceptions—and simplicity dictates that none should. So enforcing these rules means treating them as limiting and liberating action in just the way they appear to do. (To be sure, the circumstances of legal institutions enforcing rules in repeated cases involving many different people and influencing the behavior of many others, directly and indirectly, are obviously different from those of particular persons, who may sometimes reasonably appeal to the Principle of Fairness underlying the rules to justify making exceptions to them, even while acknowledging the requirement of compensation owed in virtue of violations of others' justly protected interests.)

The rules' generality, and their focus on limiting actions without regard to specific outcomes, mean that they would obviously constrain ad hoc attempts to pursue particular outcomes. And this might be seen as an objection to the rules. However, (*i*) the rules themselves are shaped with a view to their likely positive contributions to a range of desirable outcomes, outcomes that might be rendered less likely were the rules ignored in the course of pursuing particular goals. They foster good consequences precisely by their focus on actions rather than on good consequences. And (*ii*) the goals it might be tempting to ignore the rules in order to foster can often be achieved using action within the constraints created by the rules.

This set of rules does not on its own resolve questions about emergencies, questions about de minimis infringements, questions about remedies, questions about the ways in which land ought to be treated differently from moveable possessions, and so forth. Thus, for instance, it does not seem to provide a definitive basis for deciding on a reasonable abandonment period: it certainly leaves open, say, the length of time that would need to pass, and the other events, if any, that would need to occur, before a possession once held by one person might be treated as abandoned and ripe for effective possession by someone else, and just what the would-be possessor of an abandoned possession would need to do to establish a claim.[45] It is

[45] A possessory rule will not count as just, will not be consistent with the Principle of Fairness, if (for instance) it denies homesteaders access to land that is unused, and so abandoned. This is simply because there is (I think) good reason, morally, for those with land and all others involved in interpreting and applying possessory rules to embrace and implement rules that give the homesteaders this access; the first baseline rule does not treat initial effective possession as valid without renewal, nor should it, for reasons related to autonomy, compensation, productivity, and other desiderata. Just what a legal regime's abandonment rules ought to be is unavoidably in part a matter of convention; *that* there ought to be such rules is, I think, more plausibly regarded as a matter of justice. My own view, for which I will not argue here, is that legal rules which treat just possessors and their agents as indistinguishable for purposes of determining whether abandonment has occurred are simpler to understand and apply than rules that require otherwise just possessors themselves to be persistently present on land for it not to be abandoned and are, at least for this reason, to be preferred to the alternatives. I do believe, however, that the period of disuse (by just possessors and their agents) required to constitute abandonment ought to be very short—perhaps one or two years. This kind of time line is desirable because it discourages unproductive use, ensures that social influence is less likely to be concentrated, and creates opportunities for more widespread economic betterment. But I obviously can't claim that a specific time line is required by practical reason.

compatible, more broadly, with a variety of subsidiary possessory rules.[46] Despite the degree to which the rules leave various secondary issues open for reasonable decision, however, they do provide a clear, stable, readily navigable framework for peaceful, voluntary cooperation.

F. The Principle of Fairness Supports Baseline Possessory Rules

The justice of possessory claims is rooted in the capacity of respecting people's possessions to foster reasonable action in furtherance of flourishing. Just possessory norms can be derived from the Principle of Fairness in tandem with basic truisms about human beings and their environment. A broad range of overlapping, mutually reinforcing considerations provide support for the affirmation of the baseline possessory rules, which permit people to acquire physical objects through meaningful first possession or through voluntary exchange, to transfer possessions voluntarily, and to control justly acquired possessions.

The baseline rules determine what counts as justice in acquisition. Someone acquires a physical object justly if she acquires it in accordance with these rules—*either*, roughly, (*i*) by taking effective possession of something (*a*) which has not previously been claimed by anyone else; (*b*) which has been claimed by someone else, but not in a manner consistent with the baseline rules; or (*c*) which has previously been claimed in a manner consistent with the baseline rules by someone who has now abandoned it; *or* (*ii*) by receiving a possession through voluntary transfer from a just possessor (that is to say, someone who has, in turn, acquired the possession in one of the ways specified here). The baseline rules flow from the

In general, I think rules treating just possessors and their agents as equivalent are fairly clearly preferable to ones that require a just possessor to occupy and use land to which she has a just possessory claim in order to avoid abandoning it. It is clear, however, that rules requiring occupancy and use do have one advantage over alternatives: they render impossible the occurrence of nightmare scenarios in which states or the equivalent are reestablished in a stateless society through some variety of landlordism. Prescriptive easement requirements, and other requirements flowing from the Principle of Fairness, might mitigate these risks to some degree, as would the availability of significant numbers of living options, which could be expected to increase the pressure on proprietors to avoid unwelcome impositions on tenants. And the concentration of land in a small number of hands in the real world seems to be rooted in unjust violence. *Cf.* note 41, *supra*.

[46] To be clear, I do not regard this as a criticism: some variability in possessory rules seems perfectly reasonable to me. (*i*) Some empirical facts and some implications of particular ideas are unclear and need still to be discovered or understood more fully, and experimentation among different possessory rules, within the constraints of justice, will facilitate greater understanding. (*ii*) Different people's personalities will obviously vary, and some people will simply be more comfortable with some rules than other people will be—and there seems no reason for them not to be able to proceed accordingly. At the same time, while people should be free to consent to any set of possessory rules they like, the voluntariness of their consent will be vitiated if it is not understood that, prior to their consent, any possessory claims they might have which would be consistent with the baseline rules will be respected; *see* Chapter 4, *infra*.

Principle of Fairness. Thus, the obligation to respect a possessory claim in accordance with these rules is an obligation to all those to whom one has duties that flow from this principle. Sometimes, a simple two-person application of the principle will be enough to establish that I am obligated to respect someone's claim to something. Sometimes, however, it would be unreasonable for me to decline to respect the claim because doing so, while not necessarily unfair to the possessor, would be unfair to others – say, those (including myself) affected by the existence and operation of a system of simple, reliable possessory rules (or, of course, those associated with a consensual legal regime that supports the baseline rules, with which I've agreed to affiliate, and by the rules which are upheld by the regime and by which I've agreed to be bound). The *duty* I owe under the rules is a duty *to* a just possessor; but the *justification* for this duty reflects fair respect for the interests not only of the possessor but also, potentially, of many or all others.

It does not follow, of course, that every use someone might make of the opportunities that are hers in accordance with legal standards embodying the baseline rules will be prudent or moral. Though connection, for instance, is a desideratum underlying the baseline rules, someone may use her control over her possessions to exclude others on unreasonable grounds. Though accessibility, too, is such a desideratum, someone may unfairly deny others access to material assistance out of stinginess or malice. The baseline rules are justified in virtue of their systemic effects—in full recognition that undesirable consequences will sometimes follow from their consistent enforcement, but that multiple desiderata militate strongly in favor of treating them as exceptionless and against authorizing people to use force to tinker with them on a case-by-case basis.

It may be too simple to talk about the baseline rules, which flow from a combination of moral requirements and truisms about the human situation, as "natural." But while justice in possession is in some sense a matter of convention, it is a matter of convention very tightly constrained by that combination of truisms and moral requirements—constrained tightly enough that it should be easy to distinguish between just and unjust claims.

One important feature of a just system of possessory rules is, as I have suggested, its reliability. And this means that proposals for various kinds of legal norms not consistent with the baseline rules can be understood most charitably not as suggestions for ad hoc exceptions but rather as proposals to *amend* or *alter* the baseline rules—as proposals that these generally applicable rules should not take quite the form I have outlined here. While I cannot demonstrate a priori that alternate forms of the rules could not be better than the ones I have outlined, I do believe I can show that a number of possibilities are *not* preferable. I consider one of these in Part V—a proposal to treat possessory claims on abstract patterns as acceptable—along with another idea worth rejecting: that the physical objects on which just possessory claims can be made might include the bodies of humans and other sentients.

V. JUST POSSESSORY CLAIMS DO NOT EXTEND TO OTHER SENTIENTS OR TO ABSTRACT PATTERNS

A. The Baseline Possessory Rules Do Not License Possessory Claims on Things Other than Non-Sentient Physical Objects

The Principle of Fairness and the associated desiderata on the basis of which it is possible to generate the baseline possessory rules warrant protecting people's possessions—when those possessions are non-sentient physical objects. They provide no justification for rules protecting putative possessory claims to anything else. In particular, they do not justify slavery—which involves possessory claims to other people's bodies (Section B). For similar reasons, possessory claims to nonhuman sentients are ruled out (Section C). So, too, are possessory claims to ideas or abstract patterns rather than on physical objects in which these ideas or patterns are embodied or expressed (Section D). More broadly, possessory claims on *others'* justly acquired possessions—say, ones designed to safeguard anticipated economic returns—are unjustifiable (Section E). In short, rules that make sense when applied to non-sentient physical objects cannot reasonably be extended beyond them (Section F).

B. There Can Be No Just Possessory Claims to Other Persons' Bodies or Labor

1. *Slavery Is Unjustified*

Treating another as the object of a just possessory claim—as a slave—is indefensible. To enslave another is to treat her as rightly subject to your absolute dominion: you may justly do anything to her body you like, you may use force and the threat of force to ensure that she behaves as you want her to, and she is obligated to obey you. A strong presumption against enslavement is established by the Principle of Fairness (Subsection 2). This presumption cannot be defeated by the claim that a particular instance of enslavement is appropriate as punishment, that it serves to enforce someone's obligations (even when assumed by means of actual consent), or that it is a means of self-defense (Subsection 3). A claim to someone's body can't be made under the first baseline rule (Subsection 4). No one else's body or labor can reasonably be claimed as one's just possession (Subsection 5).

2. *The Principle of Fairness Establishes a Strong Presumption against Slavery*

The Principle of Fairness will obviously militate against enslavement, since none of us wishes to be enslaved. If I would not be willing to be enslaved in particular circumstances, then it will be wrong for me to enslave another in comparable circumstances.

3. *Enslavement Cannot Be Justified as a Means of Punishment, as a Way of Enforcing a Putative Obligation, or as a Means of Self-Defense*

It will also be wrong to cause physical harm to another *in order to* cause her to behave as a slave, to submit to one's orders: to cause harm instrumentally in this way, as a deterrent or a means of disincentivization, will be to violate the Principle of Respect.

While it will be wrong to cause or threaten harm for its own sake or instrumentally—for the purpose of encouraging a slave to behave in a particular way—the Principle of Respect might be read as permitting three other kinds of force: force used as, or as incidental to, punishment; force undertaken in the course of enforcing obligations; and force used in self-defense. Thus, it could, on this view, be just to use force to compel compliance on the part of one enslaved as a matter of punishment; it could also, this view might suggest, be just to use force to enforce specific obligations assumed by a voluntarily self-enslaved person; and it could be just to defend oneself against the use of force by one resisting enslavement-as-punishment and enslavement-as-promissory-obligation.

Retributive punishment cannot be used to justify enslavement, for the simple reason that retributive punishment is itself morally objectionable.[47] Though it is true, therefore, that some instances of enslavement might also count as instances of retributive punishment, this does nothing to show that enslavement is just, given that retribution isn't, either.

It is difficult to see how one could be enslaved against one's will, and so come to have any sort of obligation which could be enforced by someone else's coercively requiring one to submit to her will. For in what would this obligation be rooted if not the Principle of Fairness? No one is naturally obligated to obey anyone else, so it seems as if a duty to obey would need to be rooted in one's actual commitment. And what would ground such a duty in the absence of a specific promise that severely constrained one's options? I cannot maintain in the abstract that there is no circumstance under which one might not be obligated, per the Principle of Fairness, to work for someone on an open-ended basis, but I cannot see what sorts of circumstances might be thought to give rise to the relevant sort of obligation. So, at least in the vast majority of cases, I am confident that only actual consent could, even in principle, establish the relevant sort of obligation.

[47] *See* Chapter 5.II.C.4, *infra*.

Further, even if, as seems most unlikely, I had—in virtue of a justly concluded agreement—a genuine moral obligation to serve someone permanently and comprehensively, she would *still* not be entitled to use force to compel my compliance with it, any more than it would be justifiable to use force against someone's body to compel performance of any other agreement to work. The fact that an obligation exists is insufficient to show that someone's body or possessions may be threatened or harmed as a means of enforcing the obligation.

As I will maintain in greater detail later,[48] the only just remedy for the violation of a justly concluded agreement is the return of possessions misappropriated under the agreement. An agreement to perform services, even if they are defined in open-ended fashion, is not a transfer of any possession. There is thus no possession to be returned if such an agreement is violated.[49] Other remedies will be available in such a case—forfeiture of a bond, loss of a risk-management policy, shunning, public shaming, and so forth. But forcibly compelling another to perform services will not be among them.

Perhaps a self-assumed obligation to be a slave might be thought to rest, not in an agreement to work for another indefinitely, but, rather, in the voluntary conversion of one's entire, animated body into another's possession. The would-be slave-owner's acceptance of this sort of conversion would likely be morally objectionable because it is inconsistent with the Principle of Fairness, and this means, in turn, that it would be morally objectionable, in light of the Principle of Respect, to use force to try to prevent violation of the relevant agreement. While there is clearly good reason for the law to provide remedies for violations of enforceable agreements that are immoral but otherwise valid, and though the repossession of an inanimate physical object by the transferor might justifiably be remedied with a requirement of specific performance, it might well be most reasonable in *this* kind of case to require forfeiture of any economic benefits rather than specific performance—to treat the transaction as functionally equivalent to an indefinite service agreement. (One obvious argument for this position is that transferring one's animate body to another's control is ultimately impossible because one's own capacity for agency cannot, under ordinary circumstances, be alienated, and would therefore persist even if one purported to transfer legal control over one's body to another. Another is that the cost to the transferor of enforcing such an agreement would be so great as to be precluded across the board by the Principle of Fairness.)

The use of force to defend oneself against a slave using force in the course of an attempt to escape might well be just *if* her enslavement were itself antecedently justified; but absent some prior justification—unavailable even in case of

[48] *See* Chapter 5.II.C.2.iv, *infra*.

[49] *See* BARNETT, *supra* note 14, at 78–82.

actual consent—the use of force to keep another enslaved or to keep her from using force to prevent one from stopping her escape could not be justified either, since any justification for the use of force in these sorts of cases would depend on its being just to enslave her in the first place. One cannot justify using force to keep another enslaved by maintaining that one needs to employ it to defend oneself if the need to do so arises only because one is perpetuating her unjust enslavement. And, of course, because specific performance should not be required in the case of a self-enslavement agreement, understood as an agreement to work indefinitely for another, any more than in the case of any other sort of work agreement, it would not be just to use force to prevent someone from violating the agreement, and it *would* therefore be just for the person one is seeking to enslave to use force to prevent one from forcibly compelling her to continue working (though one *could* use force to defend oneself if she sought to retaliate against one for making the agreement in the first place).

4. *A Just Possessory Claim on Another's Body Cannot Be Justified in Virtue of the First Baseline Rule*

The Principle of Fairness, together with the truisms that inform sensible judgments about just possessory rules, cannot reasonably be read as leading to the conclusion that my body could count as another's just possession. Among the baseline possessory rules is the provision that the first possessor of an unclaimed object may justly claim and retain possession of it; but it would be bizarre to treat another's body as an unclaimed object, whatever one's preferred ontology of embodied sentients. Either one's body *is* identical with oneself, or one's body is claimed by a mind, soul, self, or ego that is numerically distinct from it; in either case, it is not unclaimed.

5. *Others' Bodies and Labor Cannot Justly Be Subjected to Possessory Claims*

Enslaving another is generally going to be inconsistent with the Principle of Fairness. And even when it is not, the actions in which someone must engage to make and keep another a slave will generally be inconsistent with the Principle of Respect, since they will almost always involve actual or threatened instrumental harm to another's person; attempts to defeat this objection by maintaining that enslavement is justified as a method of retributive punishment, as a means of ensuring performance of some obligation (even in case of actual consent), or as a means of self-defense are unsuccessful. No one's body may be acquired, as if unclaimed, or transferred as a possession in accordance with the baseline possessory rules. Other persons are not appropriate objects of just possessory claims.[50]

C. Nonhuman Sentients May Not Be the Objects of Just Possessory Claims

1. *Nonhuman Sentients Cannot Be Enslaved*

A nonhuman sentient may not justly be made anyone's slave. That is because a nonhuman sentient has a life of its own, with a point of view and the capacity to flourish. Thus, it is not reasonable to cause or threaten harm to nonhuman animals for the purpose of using components of their bodies to make food or clothing or subjecting them to invasive experiments. Doing these things involves purposefully harming aspects of their well-being, and is thus inconsistent with the Principle of Respect. Arguments designed to deny moral standing to nonhuman sentients are unsuccessful. These include the claim that animals do not flourish; for, in fact, nonhuman sentients can be understood to do just that (Subsection 2). An indirect argument (often called the "argument from marginal cases") designed to leverage support for belief in animals' moral standing from belief about the status of some humans can withstand attack (Subsection 3). And it makes little sense to argue that affirming that animals have moral standing and legally protectable interests leaves one with no basis for maintaining that humans do (Subsection 4). The same kinds of arguments that can be advanced against enslaving humans count strongly against enslaving nonhuman sentients (Subsection 5). In short, because the interests of nonhuman sentients are reasonably safeguarded by the Principle of Respect and the Principle of Fairness, they cannot be others' just possessions (Subsection 6).

2. *Nonhuman Sentients Can Flourish*

John Finnis's rejection of the claim that animals have moral standing is brisk:

> Those who propose that animals have rights have a deficient appreciation of the basic forms of human good. At the root of their contention is the conception that good consists essentially in sentience … ; for it is only sentience that is common to human beings and the animals which are said to have rights. … Even if we consider

[50] My focus here is on sentience and personhood rather than (as will be apparent from Section C) species membership. Whether a fetus qualifies as a protectable sentient will be, on my view, a matter of degree; *see, e.g.*, Alan Gewirth, Reason and Morality 142–44 (1978); Harold Morowitz & James Trefil, The Facts of Life: Science and the Abortion Controversy (1994). Thanks to an anonymous reader for noting the significance of this point.

> the bodily human goods, and those simply as experienced, we see that the quality of this experience is very different from a merely animal consciousness, since it is experienced as expressive of decision, choice, reflectiveness, commitment, as fruition of purpose, or of self-discipline or self-abandonment, and as the action of a responsible personality. The basic human goods are not abstract forms, such as "life" or "conscious life": they are good as aspects of the flourishing of a person.[51]

I can, I hope, without prejudice to Finnis, reconstruct this argument as follows:

I.1. Humans have rights.
I.2. If animals have rights, this must be in virtue of whatever it is in virtue of which humans have rights.[52]
I.3. But humans and animals share nothing but sentience.
I.4. So, if animals were to have rights, this could only be in virtue of sentience.
I.5. But bare sentience cannot be a basis for right-claims.
I.6. So animals do not have rights.

This argument is unpersuasive.

Premise (I.2) needs to be understood carefully if it is to be plausible. Perhaps, for instance, we can say that some fairly general procedure might be used to identify rights of whatever sort; if this is so (and I am not sure that it is—perhaps what is involved is simply nonderivative judgment), then we might want to say that the relevant human and nonhuman characteristics shared the formal property of *being such that they can be picked out by this procedure*. Because humans and animals both had characteristics with this property, they would share something in virtue of which both had rights, but this property might not be particularly interesting.

In addition: to have a right in the relevant sense is for some aspect of one's (actual or potential) well-being to merit robust protection. So the claim that an animal has a right entails the view that the animal has at least this in common with a human person: the property (again formal) of being such *that some determinate content can be given to the notion of the well-being of each*.

[51] Finnis, *supra* note 7, at 194–95. To be clear: Finnis's primary goal here is not to articulate a position regarding the moral status of animals but rather to argue against the treatment of human beings with limited capacities as if they were no different from nonhuman animals. His argument is thus less well developed than it would be were animal rights his focus. I believe, nonetheless, that I have fairly represented the points he wants to make in the cited passage against any sort of moral equivalence between human and nonhuman animals. I focus on Finnis, and later Grisez, in order to respond to arguments articulated within the frame of the general approach to natural-law theory I employ throughout, on the view that my position might be thought to be particularly vulnerable to such arguments. It will be apparent why I do not examine, for instance, consequentialist arguments.

[52] Finnis does not articulate this assumption, but his argument seems to me to depend on it. Otherwise, the claim that sentience is the only thing humans and animals with rights have in common would seem to be irrelevant.

As far as I can see, however, nothing follows from all these considerations about whether the *content* of an animal's well-being must be anything like the *content* of a human's well-being. While humans and animals might both be moral patients, animals' well-being might comprise very different aspects or dimensions than humans'. Because rights (it may plausibly be maintained) safeguard various aspects of well-being, the specific rights animals might be thought to have could well in many cases be different from those humans have. All that it would be necessary for humans and animals to share would be the bare minimum required to make a being a moral patient.

As regards (I.3), a credible case can be made for the view that animals can flourish: they can live; they can join in friendship (both with each other and with humans)[53]; they can experience inner peace;[54] and they can play.[55] It may also, if more contentiously, be maintained that they can flourish in other ways—they can perhaps acquire knowledge and have æsthetic experiences.[56] If so, humans and animals have in common their capacity to flourish in common ways. So there seems to be good reason to reject (I.3). But, if (I.3) is implausible, then the argument provides us with no reason to affirm (I.4).

Finnis could seek to block this kind of move in more than one way. He could deny that animals were capable of flourishing at all or that they were capable of flourishing in a manner that warranted the ascription to them of rights.

The denial that animals can flourish in meaningful ways cannot, I think, amount simply to the claim that there is nothing that counts as the flourishing of an animal. The same intelligent reflection that identifies aspects of human well-being can and does discern aspects of canine flourishing, elephantine fulfillment. Many elements of human flourishing may not be among these aspects (the reverse may be true as well). But even if canine flourishing has fewer dimensions than human flourishing, it is no less real.

[53] *Cf.* Stephen R.L. Clark, The Political Animal: Biology, Ethics, and Politics 155–66 (1999) [hereinafter Clark, Animal]; Stephen R L. Clark, The Moral Status of Animals 24–25 (1977); Elizabeth Hess, Nim Chimpsky: The Chimp Who Would Be Human (2008); Jennifer Holland Workman, Unlikely Friendships: Forty-Seven Remarkable Stories from the Animal Kingdom (2011); Stephanie LaLand, Random Acts of Kindness by Animals (2008); Stephen R.L. Clark, *Can Animals Be Our Friends?*, Phil. Now, May–June 2008, at 13.

[54] *Cf.* Stephen R.L. Clark, The Nature of the Beast: Are Animals Moral? 59 (1982).

[55] *Cf. id.* at 16, 30.

[56] The new classical natural-law theorists' canonical lists of basic aspects of well-being do not include some aspects of existence which seem to me to qualify as basic and which are aspects of nonhuman animals' flourishing. I want to avoid the appearance of introducing them into my discussion of the moral and legal entitlements of nonhuman animals to salvage an argument incapable of being defended on other grounds. I do not need to introduce these elements to ensure that my argument is viable.

It is no argument against this conclusion to maintain that animals' well-being is recognized as such by humans rather than by the animals themselves, for there is no necessary connection between the capacity to flourish in a given way and the capacity intelligently to *recognize* one's flourishing as an instance of flourishing. And there are multiple reasonable ways of identifying varied aspects of animals' well-being.[57] Perhaps an aspect of well-being might simply be directly recognized. It might be possible to begin with a generally agreed-upon instance of lack or deficiency in an animal's existence and to reason from the lack or deficiency to the good of which it is a privation. It might also be possible to reach conclusions about animals' well-being by bringing various judgments about humans and animals into reflective equilibrium. Since the proposition that animals have rights is a proposition about the reasons human (and other) persons have to respect them and about the remedies that ought to be available when they are unjustly injured (and not, say, of their own ability to use the legal system to claim these rights), provided these persons can discern and acknowledge the good of an animal, they can act on their awareness of that good, and so respect the animal's rights. And provided that humans can act as proxies for nonhuman sentients, the legal system can vindicate these rights.[58]

If we grant, as it seems clear we should, that there is something that is *good for* a given animal, then we can say that the relevant good is or isn't realized in the animal's life. It seems on the face of it that animals' flourishing *is* analogous to humans' flourishing. Obviously, it does not involve the rational reflection—and probably (though not certainly) not the deliberate choice—that human flourishing involves (and which is required, at least on Finnis's view, to be morally significant). Finnis maintains that "the quality of … [human] experience is very different from a merely animal consciousness, since it is experienced as expressive of decision, choice, reflectiveness, commitment, as fruition of purpose, or of self-discipline or self-abandonment, and as the action of a responsible personality."[59] He grants that "there is a sense in which goods like life and mating are 'shared' with other animals," but argues that "only rational beings, capable (at least radically) of participating in these goods by understanding, deliberation, and free choice, can in the focal sense *have* goods and so, by sharing them live *in societate* and friendship with each other."[60]

[57] For parallels in the human case, *see* 1 GERMAIN GRISEZ, THE WAY OF THE LORD JESUS: CHRISTIAN MORAL PRINCIPLES 122–23 (1983); FINNIS, *supra* note 7, at 51–99; FINNIS, *supra* note 15, at 58–61; JOHN FINNIS, FUNDAMENTALS OF ETHICS 51–52 (1983) [hereinafter FINNIS, ETHICS]; 51–52. *Cf.* ALFONSO GÓMEZ-LOBO, MORALITY AND THE HUMAN GOODS: AN INTRODUCTION TO NATURAL LAW ETHICS 9–10 (2002); TIMOTHY CHAPPELL, UNDERSTANDING HUMAN GOODS: A THEORY OF ETHICS 35–36 (1995); MARK C. MURPHY, NATURAL LAW AND PRACTICAL RATIONALITY 40 (2001).

[58] *See* Chapter 5.III.C, *infra*.

[59] FINNIS, *supra* note 7, at 195.

[60] FINNIS, *supra* note 15, at 82 n.110; *cf.* GERMAIN GRISEZ & RUSSELL SHAW, BEYOND THE NEW MORALITY: THE RESPONSIBILITIES OF FREEDOM 24 (3rd ed., 1988). On the meaning of "radical"

Many of the differences between humans and other animals seem to be differences more in degree than in kind. But suppose there *were* differences in kind, so that animals were *entirely* incapable of reflection, moral deliberation, or free choice: it still seems as if animals could be understood to flourish in identifiable ways—to live, to join in friendship, to have æsthetic experiences, to play. If their flourishing is not reflective, then perhaps animals are not full moral *agents*, subject to full moral assessment. But I see no reason to say that they are not moral *patients*, capable of being helped or harmed by the actions of others—capable of flourishing in ways that moral agents can recognize as worthwhile and so respect.

The implausibility of (I.3), and so of (I.4) is, on its own, sufficient reason to reject Finnis's argument. But we can also ask whether (I.5) is persuasive. Certainly, any creature capable even of bare sentience could experience peace of mind, an aspect of well-being that can be attacked through the infliction of pain.

In any event, it is difficult to imagine an existence capable only of sensory pleasure and pain but not of any particular sort of flourishing. But it would only be to such an existence that (I.5) was relevant: any creature possessed of more than bare sentience might, at any rate, flourish in one way or another quite apart from those specifiable with reference only to the contents of consciousness.[61] So the focus on sentience seems to be a bit of a red herring.

Thus, we need not conclude that, provided we can kill animals without causing them to *suffer*, we have not violated their rights. For the rights of animals will include (*i*) in accordance with the Principle of Fairness, the right to be given respectful consideration when their interests are being affected, and (*ii*) in accordance with the Principle of Respect, the right not to be subjected to purposeful or instrumental harm (where any attack on an intelligible aspect of an animal's good will qualify as a harm). Purposefully causing psychic distress in a human person or a nonhuman animal violates the Principle of Respect (since it is certainly an attack on inner peace), but so does a purposeful attack on an animal's life, or friendships, or play, or any other aspect of the animal's existence that can intelligently be identified as an objective aspect of the animal's good.

We need not agree that sentience is *constitutive* of the good to suppose that animals have moral standing. But sentience does seem to me to be more significant as regards moral standing than Finnis here supposes. Certainly, there would be no

here, see FINNIS, *supra* note 15, at 179: "the essence and powers of the soul are given to each individual complete (as wholly undeveloped, radical capacities) at the outset of his or her existence as such. This is the root of the dignity we all have as human beings" (footnotes omitted).

[61] Of course, if sensory pleasure is rightly regarded as a basic aspect of welfare, then, because the bare sentience considered here could flourish by experiencing this aspect of well-being, an entity possessed of bare sentience could reasonably be understood to be a right-holder. But I do not think I need to show that sensory pleasure is inherently valuable to establish the claim I am trying to defend here.

reason sentience could *not* ground the equality of moral patients. As a rough approximation, we might say that, in order to have moral standing, a putative moral patient must *either* (*i*) be sentient *or* (*ii*) have been sentient and be capable of being sentient again. Meeting this requirement seems to be a necessary prerequisite for flourishing in any way apart from bare existence,[62] and existence in its absence seems likely to be deficient. Just how we think about the moral meaning of sentience has significant implications, of course, for other controversies, ones I do not wish here to join. So I simply offer what I have said about sentience as a sketch of a claim, rather than as the elaboration of an argument.

I believe we can reject (I.3) with a high level of confidence and (I.4) and (I.5) with a reasonable level of confidence. The move to (I.6) would appear to be blocked. So Finnis's argument, designed to undermine the morally relevant analogy between humans and animals, appears to fail.

3. *The Argument from Marginal Cases Withstands Challenge*

The analogy between human persons and nonhuman animals forms the focus of what is often referred to as the "argument from marginal cases." Finnis rejects this argument. He writes:

> [I]f the proponents of animal rights point to very young babies, or very old and decayed or mentally defective persons (or to someone asleep?), and ask how their state differs empirically from that of a flourishing, friendly, and clever dog, and demand to know why the former are accorded the respect due to right-holders while the latter is not, we must reply that respect for human good reasonably extends as far as human being, and is not to be extinguished by the circumstance that the incidents or "accidents" of affairs have deprived a particular human being of the opportunity of a full flourishing.[63]

The argument Finnis is rejecting could be reconstructed in something like the following manner (for simplicity's sake, I'll call "very young babies, or very old and decayed or mentally defective persons," *vulnerable persons*):

II.1. The actual condition of a vulnerable person does not differ empirically in great degree from the actual condition of a flourishing, friendly, and clever dog.

[62] The sentience criterion helps to explain why babies are moral patients and plants are not. The relationship between sentience and flourishing life helps to make the appeal to sentience here nonarbitrary. On animal sentience and its relevance for ethics, *see* GARY VARNER, PERSONHOOD, ETHICS, AND ANIMAL COGNITION: SITUATING ANIMALS IN HARE'S TWO LEVEL UTILITARIANISM (2012) (defending a range of conclusions frequently, but not uniformly, consonant with those I defend here, while providing detailed information regarding aspects of animal consciousness relevant to the moral assessment of our treatment of animals).

[63] FINNIS, *supra* note 7, at 195.

II.2. A right-claim is a function of the actual state of the putative right-holder.
II.3. So the same sorts of right-claims can be made on behalf of a vulnerable person and a flourishing, friendly, and clever dog.
II.4. But Finnis believes that vulnerable persons have rights.
II.5. So Finnis should accept that a flourishing, friendly, and clever dog has rights.

Finnis seeks to undermine this argument by, it appears, objecting to (II.2). He seems to want to reject (II.2) in favor of an alternate claim, one which blocks the argument from marginal cases and which goes something like this:

II.2a. A right-claim is a function of the *nature* of the putative right-holder.

Biologically speaking, humanity as a species is not a natural kind—a kind with a "nature." One is a member of a species not because one exhibits an essential nature but because one is a member of an interbreeding population.[64] But the claim here that a putative right-holder has rights in virtue of her nature is *not* the claim that she has the rights in virtue of her membership in a particular *species*. It seems rather to be the claim that she has them because, roughly, the capacity for reason and free choice are essential to who she is. Thus, human beings have rights "because every individual member of the species has the dignity of being [by nature] a *person*."[65] And "[i]f there are extra-terrestrial rational beings, they are persons, with the dignity and rights of persons...."[66] Human *nature* grounds human rights because, while "[t]he manifold activations of ... [a human individual's] bodily and rational powers are variously dependent upon the physical maturity and health of the individual," nonetheless, "the essence and powers of the soul are given to each individual complete (as wholly undeveloped, radical capacities) at the outset of his or her existence as such."[67] Not surprisingly, then, Finnis seems to intend something like (II.2a) when he says that "respect for human good reasonably extends as far as human being"[68] and that "every individual member of the [human] species has the dignity of being a person"—which "is a truth already grasped in one's understanding of basic reasons for actions: goods good for me and anyone like me—anyone who shares my nature, any human being."[69]

It is not obvious that there is something about one's possession of a nature that, were it fully actualized, would make for a particular sort of flourishing, which entitles one to the protections one would enjoy *if* one could flourish in the relevant

[64] *See* CLARK, ANIMAL, *supra* note 53, at 40–58.
[65] FINNIS, *supra* note 15, at 176 (footnote omitted) (my italics).
[66] *Id.* at 176 n.206.
[67] *Id.* at 179.
[68] FINNIS, *supra* note 7, at 195.
[69] FINNIS, *supra* note 15, at 176.

way—*even though* one can't.[70] But it is not necessary to determine whether rights are grounded in natures or in empirically ascertainable biological characteristics. In general, the same arguments that suggest that animals' empirical characteristics are such that they have rights would show that animal natures are such that animals have rights. All this follows if it is sufficient to show that animals flourish by nature, or that by nature they possess sentience, which is enough to render them part of a community with humans.

On the other hand, it is clear that, if the nature of a human person is what entitles her to rights, and that what is essential to human nature is rationality in a strong sense,[71] then premise (II.1) is simply irrelevant; (II.3) does not follow, and neither, therefore, does the ad hominem argument expressed in (II.4) and (II.5). If Finnis reasons in this way, identifying human nature rather than empirically ascertainable human characteristics as the ground of human rights claims, it seems as if he can avoid the implications of the argument from marginal cases. But it is not clear that we should reason just as Finnis seems to do.

He seems to be making something like the following set of moves:

III.1. Each human person actually has the capacity for rationality from the moment of conception.
III.2. All members of the human species are equal and all have rights in virtue of the fact that each possesses this capacity, whether or not it is currently actualized.
III.3. Nonhuman animals all seem to lack this capacity.
III.4. This capacity is absent from the *natures* of nonhuman animals.
III.5. Nonhuman animals are not equal with persons and so do not have rights.

The notion of human rights as grounded in human nature, and of human nature as characterizing all biologically human beings, provides a plausible justificatory account of a commitment to universal human rights, a commitment worth affirming. But the argument I have attributed to Finnis is not convincing. It clearly demonstrates—if its premises are true, which I am not sure they are—that nonhumans lack a quality in virtue of which humans are equal with each other and have rights. It does not, however, show *either* that there could not be some other morally relevant quality in virtue of which humans and nonhuman animals could be judged to be equal *or* that the absence of some such source of inter-species equality would be sufficient to show that animals could not have rights.

[70] *But cf.* CHAPPELL, *supra* note 57, at 127–42 (especially 141 n.37).

[71] FINNIS, *supra* note 15, at 82 n.110 ("only rational beings, capable [at least radically] of participating in these goods by understanding, deliberation, and free choice, can in the focal sense *have* goods and so, by sharing them live *in societate* and friendship with each other").

It seems to make sense to begin by wondering whether the presence of the capacity for rationality is *necessary* for human animals to be equal with each other and for them to have rights.[72] Clearly, humans could be equal with each other in virtue of some other capacity as well. We might, for instance, for the reasons I have suggested earlier, offer this substitute for (III.1):

III.1a. Each human person actually has the capacity for sentience from the moment of conception.

I am skeptical about this claim (at least if "human person" means the same thing as "biological individual"); I think we ought to be concerned with empirical characteristics rather than with natures. But, in any case, focusing on sentience rather than rationality would render (III.3) incorrect. Many nonhuman animals seem to be sentient, and "sentience," rather than "rationality," would now be intended by "this capacity." Thus, the inference to (III.5) would be blocked.

Obviously, if each human being possesses some aspect of human nature *radically* (to use Finnis's term), then, whatever the feature is, all members of the human species will be equal in virtue of possessing it. But the proposition "Humans are equal in dignity and rights" *could* be warranted even if the proposition "Humans are equal in dignity and rights because they are rational" were not. Finnis may be right that moral theories according to which persons deserve moral consideration because of their empirical characteristics have no basis for affirming the equality of human rights (though I believe such theories could have such a basis). Even if he is, however, it does not follow that the only possible nonempirical basis for doing so must be the equality of human nature *in its capacity for rational action*.

Finnis could—as he doubtless would not—grant that the possession of some other feature of human nature that is shared with animal nature, some feature such as sentience, might also prove sufficient to warrant belief in human *equality*. But, if he did, he could do so without agreeing that this feature alone would be sufficient to warrant the affirmation of human *rights*.

Human rights are, roughly, interests protected by the principles of practical reasonableness. One has a right to be given fair and respectful consideration when one's actions will or might be affected by a contemplated action, to not be an object of hostility, to not be harmed instrumentally or purposefully. For these I have a right of the sort protected by the Principle of Respect if there is something that counts as a basic aspect of my well-being; if something does, then it can be the object of purposeful or instrumental harm, which is precluded by the Principle of Respect.

[72] I do not intend anything I have said here to be treated as making a meaningful contribution to the debate over the question whether human nature is possessed by each human being from the moment of conception.

I have already argued that nonhuman animals flourish in various identifiable ways. And, provided this conclusion is itself plausible, I think it would be easy, if one were committed to believing in creaturely natures in an interesting sense, to defend the claim that animals flourish as they do *in virtue of their natures*. If an entity has rights in virtue of its capacity, in accordance with its nature, to flourish, then there is a plausible argument that animals have rights—both to respectful consideration and to freedom from purposeful or instrumental harm.

But Finnis seems to maintain that *dignity* is a necessary condition for the possession of rights and that it is the fact that the human soul radically possesses certain capacities that is the root of human dignity. Dignity, he maintains has two dimensions: superiority and intrinsic worth. Human beings' capacities make them *superior* to all other earthly creatures because they have the same basic capacities as those creatures and, in addition, the ability to understand, choose, and act rationally. And they are inherently *valuable* in virtue of, at least, the intrinsic worth of the ways in which they flourish and of the value a moral agent can discern in each "friend's (and thus in every human person's) very being."[73]

Humans can, however, be equal with each other whether or not they are superior to other creatures; they can be equal with each other even if they are also equal with or even inferior to others. So dignity in Finnis's first sense is not required to safeguard human equality, which does not depend on humans' putative superiority to other creatures. And the kind of inherent worth he identifies as an element of dignity can also be a characteristic of sentient nonhuman animals if they can, as I have argued, be reasonably understood to flourish. Human and nonhuman sentients might both reasonably be judged to possess the capacity to flourish, and this might be thought to be sufficient to ground the dignity of both.

There is good reason, therefore, to question (III.2). It is also possible to raise critical questions about (III.3) and (III.4).

As regards (III.3), it seems reasonable to view animal intelligence as lying along a continuum. Perhaps we could even grant, *arguendo*, that the capacity for rational action was inherent in human nature and provided the basis for human rights while leaving open the question of the rational capacities of other species. We might ask, for instance, just what level of rationality is essential to human nature (a crucial question for Finnis, since he suggests that the radically possessed capacity for rationality is a necessary condition for the possession of human rights). If some very low level of rationality were humanly essential, then this same level might well be characteristic of various nonhuman animals. And, even if a level of rationality greater than that possessed by most or all other animals were typical in fact of essential human nature, it could still be the case that some lower level—rather than mere

[73] FINNIS, *supra* note 15, at 179–80 (footnotes omitted).

sentience, if one were disposed to reject this criterion, but also rather lower than the human minimum—was required for moral standing, and that this level was reached by other animals. In this case, the claim would be that moral standing was a function, not of personhood, but of *minimal rationality*.

It is increasingly clear that many nonhuman animals are intelligent creatures. Some higher mammals clearly possess the capacity for *self*-awareness (elephants, for instance, have now been shown to be able to recognize themselves in mirrors[74]). And, even if one limits *rationality* to *linguistic rationality*, it is apparent that at least some hominids have limited capacities to use language. However, as I have already argued, it is not clear why some level of intelligence lower than (or simply different from) that characteristic of humans should not be sufficient to equip a creature to flourish. Lively flourishing seems to be going on around us and around our world constantly. I think we can see enough to give us good reason to be confident that many animals merit moral standing on this basis.

I have not ignored the meaning of *nature* here, but I have focused primarily on empirical characteristics as clues to its radical possession. Arguing directly on the basis of nature might offer even more possibilities for defending animal rights than focusing on empirical characteristics. If one is to argue as Finnis has, it must be the case not only that animals lack certain characteristics *empirically*, but that they do so by *nature*. And we might reasonably wonder whether, given the conception of nature for which Finnis argues, we can determine the contours of a creature's nature by examining its empirical characteristics. Perhaps, it would be open to an objector to argue, for all we know animal *nature* is rational in the relevant sense, even if empirical animals are not. Perhaps some systematic distortion of creaturely existence has prevented their realization of animals' full natural potentials.[75] Since it seems as if, on Finnis's view, we would do a great wrong by causing serious harm to a naturally rational creature, perhaps we would do well to avoid harming nonhuman animals on the view that their natures *might* be rational, whether or not we judged these creatures to be rational as empirical individuals.[76]

Finnis's rejection of the argument from marginal cases is unconvincing because it depends on an unpersuasive distinction between human nature and animal nature. The belief that human nature is essentially and radically rational in a strong sense may be sufficient, but is certainly not necessary, to ground belief in human equality or human rights. All that ought to be necessary is the capacity for flourishing; and

[74] *See* Joshua M. Plotnik, Frans B. M. de Waal & Diana Reiss, *Self-Recognition in an Asian Elephant*, 103 PROC. NAT. ACAD. SCI. 17053 (2006).

[75] For instance, farm animals obviously have not generally been bred for cleverness and independence of thought. Thanks to Stephen R.L. Clark for this point.

[76] *Cf.* CLARK, ANIMAL, *supra* note 53, at 40–58.

it is perfectly possible to see nonhuman animals flourishing (in ways, if you like, appropriate to their natures).

And, even if this were not enough, if rationally were essential, we can reasonably ask about degrees of rationality. If rationality is a characteristic in varying degrees of the natures of different creatures, there may be good reason to regard some nonhumans as sufficiently rational to warrant regarding them as equal (with each other and with humans) and possessed of basic rights appropriate to their natures, or to regard animal nature itself as fully rational in the necessary sense even if particular nonhuman animals were not. (And, of course, if the notion that being a right-bearer had to be a function of the possession of the right sort of *nature* were itself rejected in favor of a focus on a putative right-bearer's empirical characteristics, Finnis would need either to accept the argument from marginal cases or adopt an alternate conception of human rights.)

4. *Affirming That Nonhuman Animals Are Morally Considerable Does Not Undermine the Claim That Humans Are Morally Considerable*

Germain Grisez offers an argument against animal rights that is similar to the first one advanced by Finnis, albeit with a slightly different emphasis. According to Grisez, advocates "of animal rights cannot account for moral obligation." We may reconstruct his argument as follows:

IV.1. Animals cannot flourish.[77]

IV.2. As a result, any appeal to animal rights must involve an account of rights that does not refer to flourishing.

IV.3. However, every such account, by not focusing on what is shared by right-holders, provides no basis for understanding why putative right-holders should respect others' rights.

IV.4. Absent such a basis, right-claims are implausible.

IV.5. But defenses of animal rights presuppose the absence of such a basis.

IV.6. So any defense of belief in animal rights undermines all right-claims, and so undermines itself.[78]

There is, as I have already suggested, reason to reject (IV.1). Animals do seem to flourish, to realize, even if unreflectively, what are clearly basic aspects of welfare *for*

[77] *See* GRISEZ, *supra* note 11, at 785 (the requirements of practical reasonableness "direct action only toward intelligible human goods, and lower animals simply cannot be fulfilled by sharing in those goods").

[78] *Id.* at 784–85. Grisez does not make the explicit allegation of self-contradiction I make here; instead, he appeals to the belief he assumes he shares with his readers that there are moral norms, and suggests that the affirmation of animal rights undermines this belief.

them, basic aspects of animal well-being or flourishing. Humans can recognize these goods as good for the animals.

At minimum, animal goods have in common with human goods the quality of being constituents of animal flourishing as human goods are constituents of human flourishing. In addition, of course, there seem to be specific aspects of well-being that humans clearly share with nonhuman animals, personal and otherwise, including life, bodily well-being, friendship, play, and, perhaps æsthetic experience. Humans can flourish without reflection or deliberation, and it is not a satisfactory rejoinder to this obvious point to maintain that human nature is such that humans can also flourish deliberately and reflectively, or that flourishing without deliberation and reflection is deficient. For the fact remains that putatively deficient flourishing *is* still flourishing. Even, therefore, if (implausibly) all instances of flourishing by animals are judged to be deficient, they are not thereby shown to be nonexistent and nonconsiderable.

It is important, with respect to (IV.3) to understand just what is meant by the claim that a credible account of rights must focus on what is shared by right-holders. Grisez does not mean that right-holders acknowledge and respect each others' rights just because doing so will further their shared interests. The point would seem to be, rather, that the shared nature of a given way of flourishing enables each of those who flourish in the relevant way to *understand* how it is good for each of the others. Recognizing the intrinsic value of a good enables one to seek that good not only in one's own life but in the life of another.[79] According to Finnis:

> [T]he only *reasons* we have for choice and action are the basic reasons, the goods and ends to which the first practical principles direct us. These goods are *human* goods; the principles contain no proper names, no restrictions such as "for me". So it is not merely a fact about the human animal, but also and more importantly a testimony to people's practical understanding, that they can be interested in the well being of a stranger . . . ; for it is the same good(s) that the stranger can share in or lose and that I can: specifically human good(s).[80]

I can understand and recognize and further an aspect of another's well-being whether the other recognizes the relevant aspect of well-being or not. To acknowledge the well-being of an animal, I need to be able to discern that well-being, to have some understanding of it. But this is so even if the animal has no understanding of it. And I can grasp what it means for the animal to flourish even if the specific *manner* in which the animal flourishes would not be a form in which it would be

[79] *See id.* at 785; *cf.* Alan Dershowitz, Rights from Wrongs: A Secular Theory of the Origins of Rights 198–99 (2004) (acknowledging the moral arbitrariness of treating human and nonhuman animals differently).

[80] Finnis, *supra* note 15, at 111.

appropriate for *me* to do so—if, say, the animal's digestive system allows it to flourish by consuming something that would be poisonous to me. (Furthering an animal's fulfillment can also contribute to my development of cooperative and empathetic habits. It can help to dispose me to regard the animal's well-being as worthy of moral consideration, especially by building community between myself and the animal, just as is the case in our relationships with other humans.)[81]

The demand, expressed in (IV.4), that right-holders and those who respect their rights must share *something*, is, as I suggested in connection with Finnis's denial that animals flourish meaningfully, a thin one. To the extent that it does state a serious demand of practical reasonableness, it is met in the case of animals: nonhuman animals flourish in ways humans can acknowledge—and in ways in which humans themselves flourish. *Contra* what would have to be assumed by someone who affirmed (IV.5), the defender of animal rights ordinarily *does* believe—on my view, correctly—that humans and animals have something in common and that this something is morally relevant. However, the conviction that nonhuman and human animals share enough that animals deserve moral standing would be defensible even if what human and nonhuman animals shared could only be described as valuable in formal terms—as, in the case of humans and nonhumans alike, constituents of flourishing.

The acknowledgment of animal rights does not undermine the credibility of human rights. It is consistent with the notion that people are equal—even if they are also equal in moral worth to at least some animals. And there is a perfectly straightforward way of understanding animals' responsiveness to basic aspects of their own well-being which can certainly allow for dimensions of animals' welfare to be included among the intelligible aspects of well-being to which the moral agent responds, and so to provide a secure basis for animal rights.

5. *Given that Nonhuman Sentients Are Morally Considerable, They Cannot Reasonably Be Treated as Objects of Just Possessory Claims*

Nonhuman sentients cannot reasonably be the objects of just possessory claims. To treat them as such would be to enslave them. And to enslave them would be to subject, or threaten to subject, basic aspects of their well-being to instrumental harms, something that is ruled out by the Principle of Respect. As with humans, they cannot justly be kept in slavery in order to punish them, since retributive punishment is itself unjust. Whatever one thinks about nonhuman animals' capacities for moral action, there is no reason to think they have assumed obligations that could reasonably be enforced by enslaving them. And enslaving them is surely not a reasonable

[81] *See id.* at 111–12 (noting how friendship and cooperation counter egoism).

means of self-defense (though one might envision cases in which restraining them could be). As in the case of humans, the baseline possessory rules would not, in any case, permit treating them as the objects of just possessory claims, most fundamentally because a nonhuman sentient is its own first possessor. (This would not, I think, preclude the recognition that, as in the case of disabled humans, functional humans can at least to some degree restrain an animal in the animal's own interest—to a degree that would likely vary with the animal's capacity for understanding and responsible self-direction. Nor would it preclude the establishment of interdependent companion relationships with nonhuman animals.)[82]

6. *Nonhuman Sentients Are Protected by the Principle of Respect and the Principle of Fairness, and Thus Cannot Be Enslaved*

The conceptual price of denying that animals have moral rights (at least on natural-law grounds) seems to be commitment to the view that rights are grounded in radical natures that may entirely lack empirical manifestation and that essential to those natures must be the capacity not only to flourish in clearly discernible ways but also to do so rationally and reflectively. For those unwilling to pay this price, the similarities between humans and nonhumans will make treating them differently (at least in some fundamental ways) unreasonable. And the specific arguments offered by Finnis and Grisez to justify different treatment are unpersuasive. While most or all animals may not do so reflectively and deliberately, they do seem to flourish in ways which can be clearly intelligible to persons deciding how to treat them. The argument from marginal cases rightly highlights the meaningful continuity between some human and nonhuman animals and so, despite Finnis's criticisms, grounds a plausible case for the unreasonableness of denying moral standing to all animals. And arguments for animal rights need not undermine the credibility of human rights. Thus, I believe we can say with confidence that some animals—likely those capable of sentience and even more likely those capable of flourishing in appropriate ways—*have rights*. The specific content of those rights is another matter, but they will include, at minimum, the right not to be subjected to purposeful

[82] Gary Francione has argued that treating nonhuman sentients as objects of just possessory claims lies at the root of many other abuses; *see* GARY L. FRANCIONE, INTRODUCTION TO ANIMAL RIGHTS: YOUR CHILD OR THE DOG? 50–80 (2000). Jonathan Crowe suggests (in a prepublication review) that, just because "it is wrong to threaten basic aspects of animal welfare," it does not follow "that it is wrong to keep and use animals, provided their rights are respected." I suppose the question is what it means to "keep and use animals." To the extent that it is possible to "keep" an animal without attacking or threatening to attack its well-being and without treating it unfairly, this seems right, since in this case the relationship could reasonably be seen as a companionable one, at least if to "use" an animal here is understood as a matter of engaging in mutually beneficial and respectful cooperation. But it also seems apparent that much keeping and using will fall disastrously far from this moral minimum.

or instrumental harm and the right to be given respectful consideration when their interests are affected by human choices: in short, they are reasonably regarded as protected by the Principle of Respect and the Principle of Fairness.[83] As a result, it would be difficult to justify treating them as legitimate objects of just possessory claims—and so enslaving them.

D. Just Possessory Rules Would Be Unlikely to Permit a Possessory Claim on an Idea or Pattern as Such, or Some Sort of Equivalent Legal Protection

1. *A Reasonable Account of Possession Is Inhospitable to Possessory Claims on Abstractions*

A reasonable understanding of just possessory claims does not require legal protection for "pattern possession" (PP) claims—possessory claims on abstract (i.e., disembodied) patterns that offer putative possessors control over *others'* justly acquired physical possessions embodying these patterns—and, in fact, militates against such protection or anything similar.

Legal protection for PP claims would be inconsistent with the baseline rules, and could be defensible only if an exception or amendment to the rules were justified (Subsection 2). Defenses of the legal protection of PP claims might seek to ground a *PP exception* in the purported tendency of legally protected PP claims to encourage innovation or protect the interests of innovators (Subsection 3). The notion that the legal protection of such claims is justified because of their value in incentivizing innovators is implausible (Subsection 4), as is the argument that it is necessary to ensure that innovators receive "fair returns" (Subsection 5). Likely negative consequences of upholding a PP exception to the baseline rules provide further justification for doubting the reasonableness of such an exception (Subsection 6). Given the reasonable constraints on possible possessory claims, it is difficult to make a persuasive case for a PP exception to the baseline rules (Subsection 7). And legally enforceable claims designed to have PP-like effects and features but rooted in agreement are unlikely to offer the kinds of protections PP proponents characteristically

[83] Thus, subsequent references to those entitled to just treatment in light of the Principle of Respect and the Principle of Fairness should ordinarily be understood to refer to nonhuman sentients, unless the context suggests otherwise, even if I use language that might seem to refer more narrowly to persons (which some nonhuman sentients might be). Acknowledging the moral limits on the treatment of nonhuman sentients which I defend here would seem to have fairly practical consequences as regards the behavior of the meat industry and of institutions procuring goods from this industry; on the responsibilities of particular moral agents, *see* Gary Chartier, *Consumers, Boycotts, and Non-Human Animals*, 12 BUFFALO ENV. L.J. 123 (2005); Gary Chartier, *On the Threshold Argument against Consumer Meat Purchases*, 37 J. SOC. PHIL. 235 (2006).

desire (Subsection 8). A legal system rooted in the baseline rules thus seems unlikely to make room for PP, or anything much like it (Subsection 9).

2. *A PP Exception Seems Deeply Problematic in Light of the Baseline Rules*

The baseline possessory rules govern the just use of physical objects, safeguarding people's freedom to do as they choose with their justly acquired possessions. Attempts to protect PP claims would thus be straightforwardly inconsistent with the baseline rules: protection for PP claims would involve limiting people's control over their possessions and their freedom to dispose of their possessions, since such protection involves prohibiting people from embodying particular patterns in their own possessions and from giving away or exchanging some possessions embodying particular patterns. Legal protection for PP claims would involve limiting people's choices *with respect to what are acknowledged to be their own justly acquired possessions.*

Someone who favors legal protection for PP claims can justify this kind of protection only if the baseline rules include it. This means that the initial formulation of the rules as I've defended them would need to be understood as inadequate and that the proposed baseline rules would need to be altered or amended. A PP exception, allowing legal protection for PP claims, would provide that people were fully entitled to do whatever they like with their justly acquired possessions—*except* to configure them in certain patterns and to dispose of the objects thus configured. Legal protection for PP claims would be defensible only to the extent that this kind of exception could be justified.

3. *A PP Exception Might Be Defended on the Basis of an Argument from Incentives or an Argument from "Fair Returns"*

Legal protection for PP claims might be defended on multiple grounds, any of which might serve as a rationale for a PP exception. Consequentialist grounds have arguably been the most common.[84] Obligations to respect others' putative PP claims

[84] *See, e.g.*, Jerome Reichman, *Charting the Collapse of the Patent–Copyright Dichotomy: Premises for a Restructured International Intellectual Property System*, CARDOZO ARTS & ENT. L.J. 13 (1995) 475, 475 ("Governments adopt intellectual property laws in the belief that a privileged, monopolistic domain operating on the margins of the free-market economy promotes long-term cultural and technological progress better than a regime of unbridled competition."); Alan Devlin, *The Misunderstood Function of Disclosure in Patent Law*, 23 HARV. J.L. & TECH. 401, 407 (2010) ("In certain instances—those where the patented technology is so useful that no substitutes exist—the award of a patent creates a complete economic monopoly."); LUDWIG VON MISES, HUMAN ACTION 766 (4th ed., 1996) ("If the government objects to monopoly prices for new inventions, it should stop granting patents."); Richard A. Epstein, *A Perversion of Free Trade*, TCS DAILY, July 24, 2003, http://www.ideasinactiontv.com/tcs_daily/2003/07/a-perversion-of-free-trade.html ("Patented goods are subject to a lawful monopoly created by the state in order to induce their creation."). (Thanks to Stephan Kinsella for these

have also been defended as flowing from innovators' purported rights to reap returns on their investments of time and energy. Germain Grisez gestures at both kinds of defenses when he writes:

> For a long time, copyright laws have provided authors and/or publishers of books, sheet music, records, films, and so on with protection of their interest in receiving a fair return for their work and other investment that make such items available to those who can benefit from their use. At least in their general lines, copyright laws surely are reasonable, and fair-minded people recognize that they should be respected.[85]

The most obvious reading of Grisez's claim is that he thinks the provision of "a fair return" serves the function of incentivizing innovators so that they will produce for others' benefit; call this the *incentives argument*. But he can also be read as making the separate argument that PP is justified because it ensures that a creator can be reasonably compensated for her creation; call this the *fair return* argument. Both of these arguments could be used to defend a PP exception; I am disinclined to embrace either.

4. *The Incentives Argument Does Not Show That the PP Exception Is Necessary or Desirable*

i. The incentives argument is unpersuasive

The incentives argument attempts to demonstrate that a PP exception to the baseline rules is essential if innovation is to occur at an optimal level (Subsubsection ii). This rationale is unsuccessful. Innovators often respond to nonfinancial motives (Subsubsection iii). There is no objectively determinate optimal production level for various creations, and thus no basis for claiming that innovation levels absent a PP exception would be objectively suboptimal (Subsubsection iv). And, in any event, economic and historical evidence suggests that a PP exception is not needed to incentivize vigorous innovative activity, and that protection for PP claims sometimes undermines such activity (Subsubsection vi). The incentives argument provides little warrant for a PP exception (Subsubsection vii).

The incentives argument treats it as obvious that, once we really understand the consequences of implementing or not implementing patent and copyright protections, it will be clear that implementing these protections is required. But understanding various consequences is insufficient to show that a choice that leads to one set of consequences rather than another is necessarily obligatory.

references.) Since I reserve the term *monopoly* for those cases where alternatives are forcibly excluded by or on behalf of the monopolist, I believe Reichman is correct that what I am calling PP is *necessarily* monopolistic.

[85] 3 Germain G. Grisez, The Way of the Lord Jesus: Difficult Moral Questions 591 (1997).

As a general matter, someone can appropriately judge that supporting legal protection for PP claims is morally required only if she concludes that it would be unreasonable for her not to accept the failure to support this kind of protection were she among those affected by that failure. Clearly, there is no single right answer to the question whether she would so conclude, since different people will have different attitudes. But what is clear is that she can reasonably regard a PP exception as required only if she is unwilling that PP claims not be enforced. And to suggest that she should be unwilling that they not be enforced because of the incentival consequences of failing to enforce them is problematic both because of the good available evidence regarding people's behavior in the absence of legal protection for PP claims and because (as I'll emphasize subsequently) the incentival consequences of this kind of protection are not the only factors worth taking into account.

ii. The incentives argument seeks to show that innovation in artistic and technological creation will occur at suitable levels only if innovators anticipate receiving monopoly privileges

The incentives argument can be understood as proceeding, roughly, like this (with the understanding that sensible proponents of PP would be unlikely to argue in this fashion in a number of contexts and would often not wish to frame the relevant premises exceptionlessly):

V.1. It is not viable to produce a good or service unless people pay for it.
V.2. People will not pay for a good or service unless access to it can be limited to those willing to pay for it.
V.3. If it is not viable to produce a good or service, it will be produced, if at all, at a suboptimal level.
V.4. Access to artistic and technological creations cannot be limited to those willing to pay for them unless pattern possession claims receive legal protection.
V.5. It is crucial that artistic and technological creations be produced at optimal levels.
V.6. It is therefore crucial that pattern possession claims receive legal protection.

iii. Production may not depend on financial appeal

Both (V.1) and (V.2) are broadly empirical claims; neither seems likely to be true except, if at all, when seriously qualified. It is clearly possible to render the production of a good or service viable even if people don't pay for the good or service itself—as, for instance, by bundling it with something else for which they will pay. And people's motives for paying for things are diverse enough that the notion that people might pay for things even were they able to obtain these things for free—but might act out of gratitude or duty, for instance—cannot, at any rate, be ruled out in advance.

iv. The idea of an optimal overall state of affairs is generally vacuous, so a PP exception couldn't be shown to render the level of innovation optimal

There is little reason to accept (V.3): the notion of an optimal overall state of affairs is vacuous. This is because, as a general rule, there is no way of giving sense to the claim that more value is embodied in one global state of affairs than another, and thus no way of comparing possible states of affairs in the sort of way in which they would need to be compared to judge one possibility as optimal and another as suboptimal.[86]

Because the relevant aspects of flourishing are incommensurable, there is no fact of the matter about what is or isn't the "best possible overall state of affairs." Different states of affairs embody different instances of different aspects of welfare. In this sense, then, there may be many different, incommensurably valuable states of affairs. There is no one optimal state of affairs—but this is not because value in the sense in which I am concerned with it here is subjective. It is because there is almost never a meaningful way of rationally aggregating the various objective values realized in a given situation, and there is never a way of doing so when the situation is a large-scale one. Incommensurability rules out the appeal to optimality. If the consequences of adopting a particular rule give us reason to prefer that rule to others, it cannot be because the quantum of value brought about by the adoption of the rule is greater than that brought about by any alternative.

This does not mean, of course, that anything goes—so that, for instance, it would be just as reasonable to choose a system of possessory rules grounding legal protection for PP claims as to choose a system lacking this kind of protection. For choice among the various aspects of well-being is constrained choice. It is reasonable to the extent that it is consistent with the requirements of practical reasonableness, which constitute significant limits on what will count as a reasonable choice in pursuit of one's own or another's flourishing—especially, of course, when the Principle of Fairness is acknowledged as grounding the baseline rules.

v. Even when cashed without reference to optimality, concerns about incentives do not show that a PP exception is required by, or even obviously consistent with, the principles of practical reasonableness

a. A PP exception rests, at minimum, on shaky ground

An incentive-focused argument for a PP exception could seek to show that offering legal protection for PP claims was necessary or permissible (Subsubsubsection b). Alternatives seem perfectly reasonable, so it's difficult to see how PP protection

[86] *See, e.g.*, Chapter 1.II.E, *supra*; CHARTIER, JUSTICE, *supra* note 8, at 10–13.

could be *required* (Subsubsubsection c). And, given that it doesn't seem necessary as a driver of innovation, and may, in fact, be counterproductive, a PP exception may not even be permissible (Subsubsubsection d). Legal protection for PP claims is unlikely to form part of a just scheme of possessory rules (Subsubsubsection e).

b. A nonconsequentialist defense of PP protection might seek to show either that it was required or that it was permissible

The incentives argument as framed takes an essentially consequentialist form. And, since globally consequentialist reasoning is indefensible, the argument cannot succeed in its present form. However, while there is no coherent sense of optimality that would enable (V.5) in its current form to make sense, it might be recast in either of two ways:

V.5a. A PP exception to the baseline rules is *required by* the principles of practical reasonableness.

V.5b. A PP exception to the baseline rules is *consistent with* the requirements of practical reasonableness.

The strong version, (V.5a) is indefensible. The weak version, (V.5b), cannot be ruled out in principle, but support for it is weak at best.

c. The incentives argument for a PP exception cannot show that such an exception is required

Once a globally consequentialist case for a PP exception has been ruled out, it is difficult to see how PP protection could be judged to be *required* on incentival grounds, for the point of the incentives argument is to show that PP protection is necessary precisely because of the benefits it yields. However, because there is no way to show that these benefits are in principle superior to other potential benefits that might be yielded by alternate policies, a simple concentration on benefits cannot show that PP protection is superior to alternatives. Since the incentives argument is concerned with benefits, the incentives argument cannot be used to demonstrate the PP protection is superior to alternatives. By its own terms, therefore, it cannot show that PP protection is required: to show that this kind of protection *was* required, it would be necessary to introduce other considerations unrelated to incentives.

d. The incentives argument for a PP exception cannot show that such an exception is clearly desirable

To justify a PP exception to the baseline rules, it would be necessary to show that reasonable people would predictably be willing to endorse such an exception. It seems unlikely that they would be willing to do so on incentival grounds.

The argument from incentives for the conclusion that it would be reasonable to embrace a PP exception might be rooted in the judgment that consumers would have access to more artistic and technological creations, or to ones of noticeably higher quality, if a PP exception were in place than they would if it weren't. However, it seems clear that artistic and technological productivity do not depend unequivocally on legal protection for PP claims. It is not obvious, therefore, that it would be reasonable to endorse a PP exception.

"I doubt," Friedrich Hayek wrote in 1988, "whether there exists a single great work of literature which we would not possess had the author been unable to obtain an exclusive copyright for it ...."[87] "Similarly," Hayek went on,

> recurrent re-examinations of the problem have not demonstrated that the obtainability of patents of invention actually enhances the flow of new technical knowledge rather than leading to wasteful concentration of research on problems whose solution in the near future can be foreseen and where, in consequence of the law, anyone who hits upon a solution a moment before the next gains the right to its exclusive use for a prolonged period.[88]

There are, in fact, both theoretical support and historical and contemporary evidence for the view that artistic creations could be expected to be produced in large quantities in the absence of PP protection.[89] English authors found that it made sense to sell books to American publishers in the nineteenth century, for instance, despite the fact that, because they were in England, they enjoyed no protection under U.S. copyright laws.[90] Enthusiastic, active news reporting continues despite the minimal protection copyright affords to most news stories.[91] The pornography industry has flourished despite the fact that pornographers are unlikely to take advantage of copyright protections even when they are nominally entitled to them.[92]

[87] F.A. Hayek, The Fatal Conceit 36 (W.W. Bartley III ed., 1988). Before condemning patent protection in no uncertain terms, Hayek observes about copyright: "it seems to me that the case for copyright must rest almost entirely on the circumstance that such exceedingly useful works as encyclopædias, dictionaries, textbooks, and other works of reference could not be produced if, once they existed, they could freely be reproduced." *Id.* at 36–37. Questions about the usefulness of textbooks aside, it is worth wondering whether Jimmy Wales, who reports having been influenced by Hayek, was aware of the claim that encyclopedias could not be produced in the absence of copyright when he founded Wikipedia.

[88] *Id.* at 37.

[89] See Michele Boldrin & David K. Levine, Against Intellectual Monopoly 15–41 (2008).

[90] *See id.* at 22–3. This offers no proof that these authors would have published their books in England without copyright protection, of course, nor is it meant to. Thanks to Sandy Thatcher for emphasizing the need to make this point.

[91] *See id.* at 26–30. And it is increasingly evident that it is quite capable of continuing in the absence of traditional media; *cf.* Kevin A. Carson, "Intellectual Property": A Libertarian Critique 19 (2009), http://c4ss.org/wp-content/uploads/2009/05/intellectual-property-a-libertarian-critique.pdf.

[92] *See* Boldrin & Levine, *supra* note 89, at 36–39.

And efforts to sell effectively promoted versions of government reports—not subject to copyright—have proved viable despite the reports' availability from multiple, alternative sources and for free in downloadable form on the Internet.[93] Computer software was not patentable in the United States until 1981 but software production flourished before patent protection was available. Some software makers have not infrequently renounced conventional copyright protections in order to boost consumer acceptability, and thus sales.[94]

Patents have not played the role in technological development that their proponents have alleged, either.[95] The principal spur to industry innovation seems to be the desire to outperform others, rather than to achieve patent protection.[96] The high costs of developing pharmaceuticals that are said to make the availability of patents for such products necessary reflect the costs of government drug approval processes, the distorting effects of government subsidies, and efforts designed to "achieve patent lockdown on all the possible major variations" of patented products.[97]

Significant new technological developments took place through the nineteenth century, or even, in some cases, the twentieth, in multiple European countries in which patents weren't available.[98] In fact, documented productivity actually preceded the availability of patent protection.[99] The availability of patents has served as an incentive for potential innovators not so much to birth new technology as to focus on consolidating gains from their existing creations by eliminating the pressure created by the existence of alternatives and, indeed, to focus on the suppression of alternatives to the *detriment* of genuine innovation.[100] By contrast, when an invention is left unpatented, innovators working to improve the design of a particular product type can both contribute to and learn from the developments effected by the others.

Thus, for instance, the plant and animal breeding industries proved enormously productive in the years before plant and animal varieties could be patented.[101] While securities became patentable in the United States as of 1998, financial instruments were created in multiple varieties well before patent protection was available, arguably because first movers could reap significant rewards despite high up-front costs

[93] *See id.* at 24–26.

[94] *See id.* at 15–22. Obviously, this is not true of all software firms, and those represented by the Software Information Industry Association have made aggressive use of existing copyright legislation. Thanks to Sandy Thatcher for this point.

[95] *See id.* at 42–67, 212–42.

[96] *See* CARSON, *supra* note 91, at 27–28 (citing and quoting a variety of sources underscoring this point).

[97] *Id.* at 28.

[98] *See* BOLDRIN & LEVINE, *supra* note 89, at 45.

[99] *See id.* at 46.

[100] *See, e.g.*, *id.* at 49–51.

[101] *See id.* at 52–57.

and risks of imitation.[102] Despite the availability of some putative legal protections, designs in fields from clothing to architecture are not genuinely patentable, and successful ones are constantly mimicked, but the lack of effective legal protection for possessory claims on abstract patterns has hardly inhibited the occurrence of dramatic innovation in multiple design spaces.[103] Sports leagues have every reason to want to promote productive innovations, and they could, in principle, require member teams to treat new moves introduced by particular clubs as usable by only those clubs, but they have shown no inclination to do so.[104] The behavior of actors across multiple industries does not suggest that the potential availability of patent protection is the principal incentive for them to create new products.[105]

Copyright term extension did not substantially increase the production of copyrightable material.[106] Instead, it arguably *reduced* the incentive for media companies to create new content.[107] Over the long term, copyright can tend to keep works out of circulation, and thus to reduce the availability of diverse media content.[108] And contemporary content creators have devised a variety of ways to pay their bills without relying on copyright protection.[109]

There is little or no evidence that PP actually serves to boost the pace and quantity of technological and artistic creation.[110] But the problem with patents, in particular, extends beyond their lack of effectiveness: there is, at any rate, a strong argument to be made for the view that patents have sometimes actually *retarded* technological innovation, since it may be more efficient for patent-holders to focus their energies on suppressing innovative alternatives, thus simultaneously preventing others from making new developments and, if they are the creators of the items to which they hold the patents, avoiding the creative work needed to improve their creations.[111] Like all monopolists, PP beneficiaries, each with the putative right to

[102] *See id.* at 57–59.
[103] *See id.* at 59–60.
[104] *See id.* at 61.
[105] *See id.* at 62.
[106] *See id.* at 99–100. Term extension was not motivated by the desire to increase productivity, but the fact that it did not helps to cast doubt on the claim that copyright protection incentivizes creation.
[107] *See id.* at 101.
[108] *See id.* at 104–05.
[109] *See, e.g.*, CARSON, *supra* note 91, at 28–29; [Mike Masnick,] *The Future of Music Business Models (and Those Who Are Already There)*, TECHDIRT, Jan. 25, 2010, http://www.techdirt.com/articles/20091119/1634117011.shtml; Stephan Kinsella, *Examples of Ways Content Creators Can Profit without Intellectual Property*, STEPHANKINSELLA.COM, July 28, 2010, http://www.stephankinsella.com/2010/07/examples-of-ways-content-creators-can-profit-without-intellectual-property/. *But cf.* Bobbie Johnson, *Unbound's Struggle to Crowdfund Books*, BLOOMBERG BUSINESSWEEK, July 26, 2011, http://www.businessweek.com/technology/unbounds-struggle-to-crowdfund-books-07262011.html (detailing reasons for the contingent lack of success of an alternative book-funding model).
[110] *See* BOLDRIN & LEVINE, *supra* note 89, at 184–211.
[111] *See id.* at 68–96.

prevent others from offering certain kinds of products, can act in ways that foster their own acquisition of resources at the expense of the public—driving up prices and enjoying the absence of any pressure to deliver their products and services at lower costs.[112] The ability to reap monopoly profits from PP may incentivize them *both* to avoid innovating themselves—since it may be less costly to focus on protecting PP than on developing new products and services—*and* to try to limit innovation by others.[113] Holders of monopolistic PP "rights" may actually generate products of lower quality and greater cost—ones featuring built-in copy protections, for instance, which inconvenience users and add to prices, since they require innovative effort to create and install—in order to reduce the pressures posed by alternatives.[114]

Substantial resources are invested in acquiring and protecting patents, including patents designed primarily to serve as leverage to be used to secure licenses from other patent-holders.[115] Patents on particular items are frequently used to block the availability of alternatives to those items, a practice that can hardly be seen as contributing to the emergence of innovative products and services.[116] By raising start-up costs and conferring monopoly privileges permitting those who hold them to control previously public-domain items, seed patents keep poorer farmers from selling their products internationally and substantially limit their ability to use existing resources.[117] The profitability of patents enables "patenting ... to ... [serve as] a substitute for research and development."[118]

Contra PP defenders, we would not be dependent on the pure goodwill of innovators if we wanted to enjoy technological and artistic innovations in a PP-free world: in reality, there would be multiple incentives for creative work in such a world, just as there are multiple incentives in our world for people not protected by monopolies to innovate and serve consumers.[119] (Monopolies are not known to encourage consumer-friendly behavior.)

Incentivization is, of course, a key justification for the baseline rules. But the impact on consumers of not supporting the monopolistic privileges conferred by legal protection for PP claims makes it hard to see why it would be especially appealing to support a PP *exception* to those rules on incentival grounds. Given that consumers could benefit from innovative activities in the absence of such an exception, it is unclear why it would be reasonable for someone to support

[112] *See id.* at 68–69.
[113] *See id.* at 69.
[114] *See id.* at 71.
[115] *See id.* at 73–77.
[116] *See id.* at 77–78.
[117] *See id.* at 80.
[118] *Id.* at 83.
[119] *See id.* at 123–48.

such an exception. To be sure, someone *could* reason that, because she desired some *particular* innovation which she concluded would be available only were a PP exception in place, she ought to support such an exception. But she would need to support such an exception despite the costs to consumers associated with doing so and the other problematic consequences of accepting the exception—most fundamentally, the interference with people's justly acquired possessions it would license. In principle, she might find some reason to support a PP exception and some reason to be willing to accept its imposition. I cannot show that it would never be unreasonable for her to support such an exception on incentival grounds. However, the value of preserving the baseline possessory rules, the nonnecessity of a PP exception, and the considerations rendering such an exception undesirable should give her good, whether or not absolutely decisive, reason to avoid supporting the exception.

e. Defenses of PP protection as needed to foster innovation don't seem very appealing

A defender of PP not appealing straightforwardly to consequentialist maximizing might seem to show that PP was nonetheless *necessary* on incentival grounds or that it was at least legitimate, even if not required. But there is no realistic way to show that PP protection is necessary absent indefensible consequentialist arguments. And the fact that incentivization is possible in the absence of PP protection, and that PP protection seems potentially dangerous, makes it difficult to see why interfering with people's justly acquired possessions in the name of PP protection could even be defensible.

vi. The incentives argument provides little support for a PP exception

The incentives argument is designed to show that the level of innovation would be inadequate without a PP exception to the baseline possessory rules. But the argument is unsuccessful. It depends on dubious assumptions about people's motives for creation and about the possibility of objectively measuring overall adequacy. Even apart from these assumptions, however, it fails to convince. Empirical evidence and theoretical considerations both suggest that there would be incentives for content creators to produce artistic and technological innovations in the absence of PP protection. No doubt some patterns would not be embodied in physical objects without the particular incentives provided by PP protection. But it is not clear how many would not be, nor is it clear that we ought to be overly concerned. Certainly, there is little reason to think a PP exception would be desirable as a means of fostering innovation, and none to think it would be necessary. There would thus be little reason for someone to support a PP exception to the baseline rules. The incentives argument appears unsuccessful.

5. A PP Exception Would Not Be Justified by Its Putative Contribution to Securing "Fair Returns" for Innovators

i. The "fair return" argument for a PP exception seems unpersuasive

A defender of a PP exception to the baseline possessory rules might argue for the importance of providing innovators with "fair return[s] for their work and other investment," perhaps as an independent justification for the PP exception, but this attempted justification for a PP exception is unsuccessful. As a general rule, a fair return will be the return resulting from transactions conducted in accordance with the baseline possessory rules (Subsubsection ii). Provided background rules are fair, it is not clear that there is a consistent, nonarbitrary way of identifying a fair return apart from purchasers' demonstrated preferences (Subsubsection iii). While a transaction may be unfair despite the fairness of the background rules, a judgment about fairness that cannot reasonably be reflected in the rules themselves should be treated as an exception which these rules cannot be expected to incorporate (Subsubsection iv). There is good reason not to incorporate a PP exception into the baseline possessory rules, and the putative desirability of ensuring fair returns to innovators does not alter the relevant calculus (Subsubsection v).

ii. Judgments about the fairness of transactions depend on prior judgments about background rules governing the transactions

As a moral actor, I need to judge the fairness of my choices as I make them. There's a sense in which fairness is unavoidably determined on a case-by-case basis. Thus, someone's behavior in a given transaction is unfair if she would be unwilling to accept the behavior were her role and that of her transactional partner reversed. (This isn't the same thing, of course, as saying that unfair transactions should, just as such, be invalidated.)

However, there are good, general reasons for someone to opt, precisely as a matter of fairness (in light of the Principle of Fairness and the desiderata that flow from it), to endorse the baseline rules and so to regard the outcomes of transactions conducted in accordance with these rules as acceptable. It would ordinarily make no sense for someone to judge that the baseline rules were fair and worth supporting while simultaneously maintaining that the outcome of a given exchange consistent with those rules was not fair—while being unwilling that a transaction with this outcome occur. That's because my judgments about the fairness of the baseline rules themselves should enter into my judgments about what I might be willing to accept or not accept in a given case. I can hardly be unwilling to accept an outcome to the extent that it involves the rules functioning as they are supposed to function, given that the rules themselves are fair—are ones I am willing to accept as applied both to me and to others.[120]

[120] *See, e.g.*, CHARTIER, JUSTICE, *supra* note 8, at 57–58.

General rules are, among other things, simple, reliable, and autonomy-enhancing, and institutions enforcing such rules are worth supporting precisely because the rules have these characteristics. But the fact of generality does mean that, in principle, it is possible that, even after taking into account the merits of a given rule and agreeing that it is just the sort of general rule that ought to be in place, I might still judge that, in a particular instance, an action consistent with the rule would be unfair. The consistency of a transaction with the baseline rules doesn't *ensure* the fairness of the transaction.

Nonetheless, even if it could be shown that a given transaction involving the physical embodiment of a given pattern was unfair to the pattern's creator, it obviously wouldn't follow that a just set of legal rules should incorporate a PP exception. For there might be—as I think, in fact, there are—good reasons for endorsing and upholding the baseline rules, and therefore good reasons not to endorse exceptions or amendments to them.

iii. It is unclear what it means to talk about a "fair return" apart from what purchasers actually want

These general points about the relationship between general legal rules and particular cases aside, however, the question persists whether there is any particular means of specifying what counts as "a fair return for … work [on] and other investment" in a given creative project. Obviously, no innovator is entitled to any compensation at all *just* for creating something, for it may be that no one in a position to compensate her can use her creation or chooses to compensate her in exchange for access to the creation. Compensation for something is a reflection of its valuation by the person doing the compensating.

But suppose someone does want to use her creation, and *could* compensate her for doing so. It still does not follow that the user owes her anything. What, exactly, is supposed to count as a fair return? How much someone is willing to pay for something is a function of its importance to her. If it's trivially important, there is no obvious reason the user should be compelled to pay a great deal for it simply because its production was costly for the seller. Whether the user owes the seller anything will depend on just what the seller is entitled to do with respect to her creation.

If she were, as I deny, entitled to control any physical embodiment of the pattern she has created, then someone who used that pattern without her permission would doubtless owe her something. But the nature of her entitlements has to be sorted out before the question of fair return can be resolved; there seems to be no finally reasonable way of specifying what will count as a fair return apart from the fairness of the relevant background legal rules.[121] And there are, as I have suggested, good

[121] The behavior of others in the relevant industry is insufficient to establish fairness in a given transaction, which will unavoidably have features—including the preferences of the participants—that distinguish it from others. (This seems to me to be one good reason not to favor any sort of compulsory

reasons for a set of just legal rules to include the baseline possessory rules and not to feature the PP exception.

Put another way: even in a case in which someone acts unfairly by not paying a creator at a particular level for the use of a given pattern, there may be (as I think there are) good systemic reasons (themselves rooted in the Principle of Fairness) for the creator to be unable to force her to do so; even though the failure to pay the creator at a given level might be unfair, it might also be (as I believe it would be) unfair of the creator, or others acting on her behalf, to use force to secure payment at the relevant level.

iv. Judgments about ad hoc exceptions cannot readily be incorporated into the baseline rules

It is certainly possible that unfair conduct might be consistent with the baseline rules. But to claim that conduct that failed to treat creators as having possessory claims to the patterns embodied in their creations was *consistently* unfair would be tantamount to arguing that a set of just legal rules should incorporate the PP exception. Such an exception would fly in the face of multiple desiderata underlying the baseline rules.

The problem with the fair return argument is fundamentally the same as the problem with all arguments against legal protection for putatively unfair pricing. There will ordinarily be no objective measure of what counts as an unfair price.[122] Some buyers will, indeed, act unfairly in offering particular prices because they would be unwilling to accept standards permitting offers comparable to their own were the rules reversed. But it will be difficult to establish that they do so. There will be no way to build into the baseline rules situation-specific features designed to deal with these cases without undermining reliability, simplicity, autonomy, and other desirable features of a just system of possessory rules, and so without being unfair to all those affected. And, given that the rules themselves should be treated as exceptionless by a just legal system, there will be no way of offering situation-specific *legal* relief, since this would involve treating the rules as valid but as capable of being discretionarily ignored.

v. The "fair return" argument provides little reason to support a PP exception

As a general rule, transactions conducted in accordance with background rules shaped in accordance with the requirement of fairness embodied in the Principle of

licensing scheme.) Respect for the baseline rules will ordinarily be sufficient to show that a transaction is fair, but even when it can reasonably be judged that one of the transactors violated the Principle of Fairness—treating the other in a way she would not be willing to be treated—while respecting the baseline rules, the systemic effects of making ad hoc exceptions to the baseline rules should be avoided. Remedies in cases of this kind may be not only desirable but even obligatory, but they should be sought outside the legal system and without the use of force. Thanks to Sandy Thatcher for emphasizing the need to address this issue.

[122] *See supra* note 18.

Fairness will themselves be fair: if they weren't, it would be odd to say that the rules themselves were fair. And in order to serve the interests that underlie a just set of possessory rules, the rules themselves should be treated as exceptionless by a just legal system. Ordinarily, a return resulting from transactions conducted in accordance with fair rules will be a fair return. And even when it isn't, there is good reason not to allow for legal remedies for occasional instances of unfairness, given the importance, precisely from the perspective of fairness, of establishing and maintaining the baseline rules.

6. *Negative Consequences of Embracing a PP Exception Provide Further Reason Not to Endorse It*

i. A PP exception could be expected to yield a variety of problematic outcomes

Quite apart from the (dubious) merits of the proffered positive justifications for a PP exception to the baseline rules, there are several likely negative consequences of upholding such an exception, consequences that provide further reason to oppose it. These include increased consumer costs (Subsubsection ii), the discretionary power associated with the underdetermined character of PP claims (Subsubsection iii), the similarly troubling power that would be needed to enforce such claims (Subsubsection iv), and the control over information that could result from legitimizing such claims (Subsubsection v). The negative concomitants of a PP exception count strongly against embracing such an exception (Subsubsection vi).

ii. A PP exception would ground consumer-unfriendly monopoly privileges

A PP exception would, in effect, confer a monopolistic privilege. And, in the nature of the case, monopolies harm consumers. Consumers obviously pay more for products offered by monopolies than they would for products offered absent monopolistic privileges. So it stands to reason that consumers of artistic and technological creations would pay less for such works absent the monopolistic privileges conferred by legal protection for PP claims. Given that almost everyone is a direct or indirect consumer of such creations, almost everyone would have some reason to oppose a PP exception. And this reason ought to be decisive (presuming the issue of incentives can be dealt with satisfactorily), since to say otherwise would be to maintain, in effect, that the interests of creators trumped those of consumers, despite the fact that almost everyone is a consumer, and production is for the sake of consumption.

iii. PP claims could only be defined by entities with considerable discretionary power, with obvious potential for abuse

In addition, the essentially arbitrary character of PP claims would vest enormous discretion in the institutions responsible for upholding them. While there is, of course, a degree of arbitrariness in all possessory claims, the baseline rules tightly constrain ordinary possessory claims in physical objects. The various features a given pattern possession claim—how much resemblance would be required for a violation, how much time could elapse before a claim expired, and so forth—could be expected to be definable in much more varied ways (with persons and entities making such claims arguing, no doubt, for the most extensive possible interpretations). The result would be that institutions able to uphold PP claims could exercise a great deal of power over people's possessions. To the extent that the unconstrained use of power is troubling, legal protection for PP claims should be quite disturbing.

iv. PP claims could only be upheld by entities authorized to be highly, and troublingly, intrusive

The discretionary power that would be needed to uphold PP claims is troubling not only because of the relatively indeterminate character of PP claims themselves but also because of the kind of investigation and intrusion that would be required to uphold the claims flowing from a PP exception. An entity charged with upholding a PP claim would need to be empowered to examine the possessions of many people, subjecting them to careful scrutiny. Concerns with privacy and with what would under other circumstances count as trespass should prompt significant concern at the prospect of a PP exception.

v. Upholding PP claims would often mean restricting access to important information

A PP exception would also make it easier for people and institutions to control access to information, independent of its physical embodiment. Given the importance of information access in ensuring the exposure of aggression, fostering nonviolent social influence, and facilitating consumer choice, there is good reason to favor possessory rules that encourage the wide dissemination of information rather than creating opportunities for the dispersal of information to be impeded.

vi. Potential negative consequences provide independent reasons to oppose a PP exception

While positive arguments don't seem to provide strong support for a PP exception, even if they did, it would also be necessary to take into account a variety of negative results that might be expected to follow from the adoption of such an exception. These include increases in consumer costs, the likely behavior of entities charged with enforcing PP claims (entities which could be expected to define such claims broadly and to prove highly intrusive when enforcing them), and greater limits on access to information. All of these factors provide good reason not to support a PP exception.

7. *There Is Little Reason to Support a PP Exception to the Baseline Rules*

The Principle of Fairness and the truisms about human agents that, taken together with this principle, underlie the baseline rules do not require a PP exception, and they provide good reason for someone whose reasoning is guided by the Principle of Fairness to avoid supporting a PP exception to the baseline rules. Such an exception would not be a necessary or desirable means of prompting innovation. And it would not be an appropriate means of securing a putatively fair return for creators on their investments in their creations. It would also seem to ignore the negative consequences of establishing institutions needed to enforce legal PP protections. And it would seem to disregard the costs to consumers of admittedly monopolistic protections, with the consequent reduction in accessibility of desirable goods and services.

Some of the desiderata that ground the baseline possessory rules clearly count against a PP exception.

- The proposed exception would reduce the accessibility of at least some goods and services, even if it increased the accessibility of others.
- The proposed exception would involve more extensive restrictions on people's autonomous use of their possessions than would the baseline rules.
- Because it would impose limits on people's use of their own possessions, such an exception would make it harder for possessory rules to serve as peacemaking boundary markers, while impeding peacemaking by sparking conflict.
- Justly acquired physical objects may be less likely to be put to productive use if their possessors are prevented from configuring them in accordance with certain patterns.
- Similarly, a PP exception to the baseline possessory rules would reduce the reliability of the rules and of particular possessory claims, since people could be prevented from controlling their own justly acquired possessions.
- Rules incorporating a PP exception would be less simple than those without it.
- Such rules might in some cases reduce experimentation by limiting access to information.
- They might constrain people's ability to be generous with their own justly acquired possessions.
- They might also marginally affect opportunities for connection, specialization, and the development of trustworthiness.

Some of the other desiderata would not weigh directly against an exception, but provide no particular support for it.

- Rules incorporating an exception would not improve the coordination of producers' and consumers' plans and objectives.

- Such rules seem no more likely to track self-enforcing conventions than the unaltered baseline rules—and would arguably be less stable because they were less simple and produced tension with rules protecting control over physical objects.
- Such rules don't seem overly likely to increase stewardship of physical objects—and of course abstract patterns capable of being embodied in physical objects are not scarce resources capable of benefiting from stewardship.

Only a limited number of the desiderata might be thought to count in favor of an exception: *incentivization*, *desert*, and, perhaps, *reciprocity*. What I've already said about the incentives and fair return arguments should make clear why I don't think these considerations count strongly in favor of legal protection for PP claims.

Judging the fairness of a given rule means taking all of the relevant facts into consideration and asking oneself whether one would be willing to accept the imposition of the rule—or its nonimposition—were one affected by it in one way or another. Taking all of the relevant considerations into account, it would be quite reasonable for someone to be willing to endorse the baseline rules, which don't feature a PP exception and, indeed, for someone to be *unwilling* to accept the addition of such an exception to the baseline rules. Similarly, there would seem to be good reason for someone *not* to endorse such an exception in light of the impact of the various desiderata.

The desiderata weigh strongly in favor of the unamended baseline rules, which protecting PP claims would violate. The incentives and fair-return arguments provide at best weak support for amending the rules. And various independent considerations count against acknowledging PP claims. Thus, if just possessory norms emerge from the Principle of Fairness in tandem with the various truisms about the human situation and the desiderata that flow from them, there seems to be limited reason to conceive of the baseline rules as incorporating PP protection.

8. *The Likely Efficacy of Agreement-Based Sources of Legal Protection for PP Claims Is Limited*

i. Agreements are unlikely to provide effective substitutes for legal protections for PP claims

People could not, in general, achieve the effects of a PP exception to the baseline rules by making agreements with each other. They could seek to accomplish by agreement results that could not, in the absence of agreement, be *required* in a manner consistent with the baseline rules.[123] However, agreements could not secure the

[123] To be sure, people currently engage in agreement-based transactions that build on existing positive-law PP "rights." But the model envisioned in the text is not one that presupposes such rights, but rather an agreement-based alternative to them.

monopolistic protection a PP exception would afford. Imposing a limit on the sale of an item would not allow a seller to treat the copying buyer as a thief (Subsubsection ii). And while agreements could certainly feature liquidated damages clauses triggered by copying, such clauses would be difficult, at best, to enforce and would not be efficacious against all copiers (Subsubsection iii), especially when embodied in shrink-wrap or click-wrap agreements (Subsubsection iv). It is unlikely that attempts to use agreements to achieve the same effects as legal protections for PP claims would be successful (Subsubsection v).

ii. It is difficult to imagine that attempting to sell something minus the right to copy could provide a creator with the equivalent of PP protection

One agreement-based approach to copyright protection involves the supposition that the set of just claims associated with a given physical object includes the freedom to copy the object, and so that transfer of title to the object could involve the transfer of all the items in the bundle except this one. On this view, if someone wishes to secure copyright protection for a given work, she need simply sell it *minus* the permission to copy it.[124]

But this view seems clearly mistaken. To be able to copy a given creation is to be able to embody an abstract pattern in new material. To prohibit copying is to prohibit the use of this abstract pattern in a particular way. However, I could exclude the freedom to use this abstract pattern in the relevant way in the course of selling a physical object that embodied the pattern only if I already had the right to control the use of the pattern, and whether I do is precisely the point at issue. The notion that I can exclude the freedom to copy an object from the rights I convey when I transfer my just possessory claim to the object to another appears to be question-begging. On a plausible understanding of contract, the relevant set of provisions could be enforced only be requiring the return of the purchased item and the payment of whatever costs might have resulted from my not having had access to it (as well, perhaps, as the payment of reasonable costs of recovery),[125] so that copying could still perfectly well take place.

iii. An agreement featuring liquidated damages for copying would be unlikely to achieve the equivalent of PP protection

Perhaps a more straightforward agreement-based approach could be used to provide something like copyright protection.[126] Suppose the agreement I use to transfer a given physical object to you embodied a set of provisions something like these:

[124] *Cf.* Murray N. Rothbard, The Ethics of Liberty 123 (1982).
[125] *See* Chapter 5.II.C.2.iv, *infra*.
[126] *See* N. Stephan Kinsella, Against Intellectual Property 45–46 (2008).

1. If Buyer copies Creation, Buyer will pay Seller damages in the amount of $X for each instance of copying, as well as all reasonable costs associated with recovering these damages.
2. If anyone to whom Buyer transfers title to Creation through gift or sale, or anyone who acquires Creation in virtue of Buyer's negligence or abandonment, copies Creation, Buyer will pay Seller damages in the amount of $X for each instance of copying, as well as all reasonable costs associated with recovering these damages.

Here, there is no reference to question-begging duplication rights; instead, the buyer simply agrees to pay liquidated damages in a given amount should she copy the creation, and to impose a similar requirement on others.

However, while an agreement like this could offer some privileges currently conferred by copyright and patent law, making enforceable claims in accordance with it would be difficult. One problem: given that the proper remedy for the violation of an agreement is the return of possessions acquired under the agreement,[127] it might appear that only the return of a duplicated item and the payment of the reasonable costs associated with its loss and recovery could be ordered by a court, so that damages of the requisite sort would not be available absent a bond. In fact, though, a subsidiary agreement could transfer the damages amount conditionally, with the transfer condition being violation of the primary agreement.

But even were liquidated damages or a similar sort of remedy available, a creator would not ordinarily have any direct agreement with end users. The *copier's* legal relationship would almost certainly be with someone other than the creator—a retailer, say, or a friend. Thus, the creator would need to identify the ultimate buyer whose purchase provided an agreement-based link with the copier. Doing so could obviously be costly and time-consuming. The possibility of suit by a creator would obviously encourage initial buyers to impose indemnification requirements on successive purchasers, all the way to the end user. Tracking purchases and enforcing indemnification requirements would also be costly and otherwise difficult.

On the envisioned agreement-based model, those seeking to obtain payments when people copied creations covered by the applicable set of agreement-based rules (presuming the contemplated liquidated damages were available at all) would be forced to internalize the relevant administrative and enforcement costs. And it is reasonable to think that these costs would discourage creators and participants in the relevant supply chain from supporting the envisioned agreement-based scheme. Retailers, in particular, might be expected to be resistant. To avoid covering indemnification costs, they would need to require purchasers of inexpensive consumer items to agree to detailed agreements; the purchasers' likely objections could have

[127] *See* Chapter 5.II.C.2.iv, *infra*.

severe effects on sales. So retailers might be expected to resist the indemnification requirements, with consequences all along the supply chain.

And of course a good deal of copying need not involve direct access to any physical item transferred along a supply chain. An item need not be sold, given away, or abandoned in order to be copied. A patentable device might need only to be observed in operation. Reviews or a friend's description might provide all the information needed to replicate a film or a musical performance. An overheard conversation about a book might prompt a knockoff. A broadcast television program can be received, and so copied, without implicating any sort of agreement. These possibilities all limit the efficacy of attempted agreement-based alternatives to PP.

iv. Attempts to create the equivalent of PP protection by agreement could not realistically employ shrink-wrap or click-wrap agreements

Efforts to achieve the same results as those made possible by a PP exception to the baseline possessory rules by means of agreements would also be hampered if the mechanism chosen were not a personally negotiated agreement, or even a pre-written agreement, the buyer's review of which could be verified in person by a seller representative, but rather a "shrink-wrap" or "click-wrap" agreement.[128] A shrink-wrap agreement is a putative agreement, consent to which is supposed to be inferable from a customer's willingness to break the shrink-wrap covering of a disk. A click-wrap agreement is a similar agreement: consent in this case is supposed to be inferable from the customer's clicking a button that says, or is adjacent to text that says something like, "I have read and consented to the agreement governing access to the software I am about to download."

The general legal principle that the past behavior of people engaged in a dispute over an agreement will affect a court's interpretation of their responsibilities and just claims is perfectly consistent with the Principle of Fairness. And that principle has the potential to make click-wrap and shrink-wrap agreements unenforceable in many cases. To the extent, at any rate, that sellers know that wrappings will be broken and buttons pushed by consumers who do not read agreements' terms and nonetheless accept the sellers' purchases without challenging them, enforcement of any but the most obvious terms will presumably not be possible.[129] Thus, the kinds of provisions I've envisioned would likely not be enforceable if embodied in shrink-wrap or click-wrap agreements.

[128] Thanks to Kevin Carson and Stephan Kinsella for emphasizing the need to make this point.

[129] Thanks to Kevin Carson for this point. An anonymous reader suggests a supportive example of reasonable limits on agreement-based obligation: suppose I walk into a restaurant and order a simple meal without inquiring about the price; if the price turns out to be somewhat higher than I'd expected, I'm presumably on the hook; but if the price turns out to be, say, $1,000, then few courts could be expected to require me to pay.

v. Agreements probably wouldn't be able to serve as backdoor routes to the equivalent of PP protection

A cumbersome agreement-based alternative to patent and copyright would be unlikely to be available given a plausible theory of damages for violations of enforceable agreements, and given the nonviability of attempts to sell items minus copying privileges. Even if it *were* available, however, the costs of the alternative would often make employing it prohibitive. And even when it was available, identifying responsible parties would be much more difficult than under a scheme in accordance with which copiers were directly liable to creators. In addition, an agreement-based alternative would not provide any sort of protection against copying by people outside the chain of agreements linking a copied work with its creator. Agreements seem unlikely to enable people to accomplish what legal protection for PP claims might be thought to achieve.

9. *There Is Limited Justification for Legal Protection for PP Claims or the Equivalent*

Providing legal protection for PP claims would be reasonable only if the baseline rules as I've initially elaborated them were altered significantly.

PP proponents sometimes see themselves as defending a worker's entitlement to the product of her labor. But what labor produces is never a pattern as such, but rather a physical embodiment of a pattern. And there does not seem to be a reasonable way to control transactions in patterns as such—a way of doing so that does not depend on a disruptive, risky alteration of the baseline rules.

Making a PP exception to the baseline rules seems neither necessary nor particularly useful as a way of ensuring an optimal level of innovation—not only because there is no objective measure of optimality but also because incentives for innovation would certainly obtain in a world free of PP. The incentives argument for a PP exception is thus unsuccessful. But so, too, is the fair return argument—built on a notion of fairness in exchange that cannot, as a general rule, be specified apart from the preferences of actual people engaged in actual transactions. The desiderata underlying the baseline rules provide, in tandem with the Principle of Fairness, good reason to embrace those rules in their simple, reliable, autonomy-enhancing form, without any sort of PP exception. And making such an exception doesn't seem likely to achieve some desired level of innovation optimality or to secure putatively fair returns to creators. It *does*, however, seem likely to pose a variety of undesirable risks.

In principle, it is possible that someone might be able to achieve something resembling PP protection by agreement. It is clear, however, that the relevant sorts of agreements would not generate reasonably enforceable claims in many of the cases in which proponents of PP protection might want them, and that enforcing them would, in any event, be relatively costly.

There is little reason for a version of the baseline possessory rules incorporating protection for PP claims. Similarly, there is little space for agreement-based alternatives designed to achieve the same goals. A credible account of possessory claims is at best uncongenial to PP.

E. The Baseline Rules Do Not Provide Protection for Claims on Others' Justly Acquired Possessions

Not only PP claims but also all other possessory claims that do not concern physical objects are suspect and likely undeserving of legal protection in accordance with the baseline rules,[130] for any such claim will effectively amount to a claim on *another's* justly acquired possessions and so to an exception to the baseline rule permitting a just possessor to control her own possessions (provided she does not harm the justly acquired possessions of others) and to dispose of them at her discretion.

Consider two common examples. (*i*) A asserts that she should be entitled to control how her neighbor, *B*, maintains his lawn or paints his home because she believes that some choices on *B*'s part will reduce how much someone else will likely pay for her home. (*ii*) A cooperative, *C*, which provides a particular good to consumers, maintains that another cooperative, *D*, which provides the same good, should be fined for providing that good below cost to consumers (perhaps as a loss leader), on the grounds that doing so constitutes unfair interference with *C*'s revenue.

In each case, the claim being advanced is implausible. It depends *either* on (*i*) the view that a seller has a just possessory claim on a particular payment by a purchaser and so has a derivative claim on another's possessions if they are or might be used to interfere with that claim, *or* on (*ii*) the view that a seller has an underived just possessory claim on another's possessions. Either A has just claims with respect to particular purchasers with which *B*'s maintenance of his home and yard interferes, so that A has a just derivative claim with respect to *B*'s possessions, or A has a basic, underived just claim on those possessions. Either C has just claims with respect to consumers' payments for the goods it offers, so that C has a just derivative right with respect to *D*'s possessions, or C has a basic, underived just claim on those possessions. Neither sort of claim is defensible.

Both sorts of claims are obviously inconsistent with the baseline rules. Permitting them would fall foul of the rule permitting control over and free disposition of one's justly acquired possessions. A rule embodying an exception that made possible these sorts of claims would yield higher costs for consumers (and so reduce product accessibility), reduce autonomy, limit incentivization (the less discretion people have with respect to the use of their possessions, whether by way of investment or by way

[130] *Cf.* ALCHIAN, *supra* note 8, at 55, 96.

of consumption, the less they'll likely care about working to acquire them), increase the likelihood of conflict (and so precisely *not* serve the peacemaking function of possessory rules), reduce reliability (since predictability is constrained when multiple people can make decisions about a given possession), reduce simplicity, exhibit less self-enforcing stability, and reduce the motivation for stewardship. It would not reflect the demands of desert; foster connection, coordination, experimentation, generosity, reciprocity, specialization, or trustworthiness (by undermining exchange relationships, it might be expected to impede the realization of the values furthered by a number of these desiderata); give people the freedom to maintain the social norms of their choosing; or protect most identity interests.

The baseline rules require the internalization of negative externalities only when these externalities cause or constitute aggressive harms to bodies or aggressive interference with just possessory interests.[131] Thus, claims to returns on particular transactions or to the preconditions needed to achieve such returns are inconsistent with the baseline rules, and there is no good reason to understand the baseline rules as incorporating exceptions permitting such claims.

F. The Baseline Rules Limit Just Possessory Claims to Non-Sentient Physical Objects

The baseline possessory rules provide robust protection for people's claims to the physical objects they have justly acquired. But the Principle of Fairness, the Principle of Respect, and the desiderata that underlie the baseline rules offer little support for the possibility of possessory claims that do not involve non-sentient physical objects. Enslaving other persons necessarily involves the enslaver in violating the Principle of Respect and the Principle of Fairness, and the desiderata underlying the baseline possessory rules provide little support for asserting possessory claims to the bodies or labor of others. Once the injustice of purposeful attacks on nonhuman sentients and of unfairly disregarding their interests is acknowledged, it should be clear that treating them as justly acquired possessions is indefensible for reasons similar to those that render enslaving persons unwarranted. The Principle of Fairness and the desiderata that ground the baseline rules offer little reason to license possessory claims in abstract patterns and, indeed, in things of any sort other than actual physical objects. It is reasonable to conclude that just possessory claims may only be asserted with respect to physical objects.

[131] It is therefore not quite right to say (*cf.* Demsetz, *supra* note 3, at 348) that the point of the baseline rules is to facilitate the internalization of what would otherwise be externalities, since what (at least as regards the legal regime envisioned here) *counts* as an externality can only be determined once the question of justice in possessory claims has been sorted out.

VI. ARGUMENTS FOR EXCEPTIONLESS POSSESSORY CLAIMS SEEM UNPERSUASIVE

A. Reasonable Moral Rules Protecting People's Justly Acquired Possessions Would Not Feature Absolute Prohibitions on Interference with Those Possessions, though Such Prohibitions Might Reasonably Be Embodied in Legal Rules

While the Principle of Fairness, together with the various desiderata, generates robust protections for just possessory interests, it does not require, and is likely inconsistent with, *exceptionless* protections for such interests; and alternate groundings for exceptionless rules protecting possessory interests do not seem readily available. The natural-law tradition itself treats some exceptions as reasonable And while the notion that there were justifiable exceptions to reasonable possessory rules might be hard to defend if possession itself were a basic aspect of well-being—in which case purposeful interference with it would be ruled out by the Principle of Respect—it doesn't seem in fact to be a fundamental dimension of welfare (Section B). It is not possible to argue that all attacks on possessions are also, at the same time, attacks on basic aspects of welfare, and so ruled out by the Principle of Respect, though the Principle of Respect obviously *does* rule out some kinds of interference with others' possessory interests (Section C). Interfering with another's possessions is not morally equivalent to enslaving her (Section D). But the baseline rules yield different consequences for personal decisions and legal rules (Section E); thus, while exceptions may be permissible for particular moral agents to make occasionally, interference with others' possessions can be ruled out exceptionlessly from the standpoint of legal institutions (Section F).

B. Possession Is Not a Basic Aspect of Well-Being Safeguarded by the Principle of Respect

1. *Neither Any Particular Possession nor the Capacity to Possess Seems Obviously Like an Authentic Dimension of Welfare*

While they are strongly protected by the Principle of Fairness, just possessory claims do not deserve the unqualified respect to which basic aspects of welfare are entitled.

If controlling the disposition of (justly acquired) possessions were itself a basic aspect of well-being, any purposeful or instrumental attack on a just possessory claim would be unreasonable. Perhaps, the argument might run, a person's possessory claims to material realities external to her person should be treated as equivalent to her person, as an extension of her body. Just as it would be wrong to attack a person's body, on this view, it would be equally wrong, and wrong for the same basic reason, to attack her possessions. But there is little reason to believe that possession is a basic dimension of flourishing or well-being.

Possessions themselves are at least ordinarily instrumentally rather than intrinsically valuable (Subsection 2). Possessing something does not appear to be a basic reason for action (Subsection 3). Interference with possessory interests is, indeed, sometimes experienced as an injury without the need to refer to any other aspect of well-being (Subsection 4). But other approaches to identifying basic dimensions of welfare don't seem to suggest that possession is such a dimension. There does not seem to be anything self-contradictory about denying that possession is a basic aspect of welfare (Subsection 5). Possessory interests enjoy respect cross-culturally, but not necessarily in a way that shows that they are treated as basic (Subsection 6). It's not clear that reflective equilibrium grounds support for treating them as such, either (Subsection 7). There does not seem to be any justification for treating attacks on possessory interests as attacks on basic aspects of well-being, and so on the self, at least in general (Subsection 8). And even if possession *were* a basic aspect of well-being, the Principle of Fairness, rather than the Principle of Respect, would still typically be the norm that determined whether a given interference with another's possessions was or wasn't just (Subsection 9). Exceptionless protections for possessory claims probably cannot be grounded in the Principle of Respect (Subsection 10).

2. *Possessions Themselves Seem to Be Instrumentally Rather than Intrinsically Valuable*

There is good reason to understand the value of possessions as instrumental. For "anything human persons make, or have, considered as distinct from persons ... cannot be basic. It is always for ... reasons which culminate within persons ... that individuals and communities are concerned with such goods."[132] We acquire a physical object because it is beautiful, because it will provide space for a family to flourish, because it will promote bodily well-being—because it will enable us to achieve other goals. Even if we don't know just what we will want to do with money we acquire, we understand that we acquire it to achieve other ends. We can and do explain our acquisition of particular possessions in terms of the ways in which we're able to flourish in virtue of having those possessions. In short: we ordinarily pursue the acquisition of particular things as an instrumental rather than as an intrinsic good, and I think we would be inclined to regard the pursuit of material objects, or of material wealth more broadly, as fetishistic unless undertaken for some ulterior

[132] FINNIS ET AL., *supra* note 1, at 178.

purpose. (We might have good reason to regard the attempt to obtain or retain a just possessory claim with respect to some specific, identity-constitutive possession—understood as inherently valuable—as a different matter. But such claims should not, I have argued, receive particular protection from the legal system.)

Doubtless the lines are not absolutely clear. My hand is part of me, and so intrinsically valuable; by contrast, an object I control with my hand is not. But of course some things that are external to me may be identity-constitutive in ways that some aspects of my body—the tips of my hair or of my fingernails, say—are not. And of course a prosthesis would seem to have a more intimate relationship to my identity than a purely external object (a tool, for instance), but less so than, say, a flesh-and-blood hand. (Would it matter whether the hand was grafted on, regrown, or an original part of my body?) So it might seem reasonable to talk here about a difference in degree rather than in kind. It seems to me, though, that (*i*) we *do* characteristically treat the relationship between our identities and parts of our bodies as a different kind from at least most of the relationships between our identities and physical realities external to our bodies. Further, (*ii*) even if the difference is judged to be a difference in degree rather than in kind, the difference in degree seems to be substantial. And (*iii*) the difference between the bodily and the nonbodily can thus conveniently serve, for legal purposes, as marking a bright-line distinction in many cases.[133]

3. *We Don't Characteristically Treat Possession as a Basic Reason for Action*

Of course, it does not follow from the fact that this or that possession is instrumental that possession *itself* is instrumental. Perhaps one pathway or another to the identification of other aspects of human well-being as basic might also justify characterizing control over the use and disposition of justly acquired possessions as a basic aspect of welfare. It may be that we value possession itself—control over aspects of the non-sentient world that have come legitimately to be ours—intrinsically. The question, then, is: *do* we treat possession as a reason-terminator? Do we regard possessions justly. or maintaining control over the use and dispossession of justly acquired possessions as itself an exhaustive explanation of or justification for an action?[134] And it seems, in general, that we do not: rather, we reason in terms of the instrumental value of particular possessions.

To be sure, we extend ourselves into the physical world when we come to possess things, and the capacity to possess things in at least relatively undisturbed fashion would seem to be a constitutive component of personal autonomy. But autonomy

[133] Thanks to an anonymous reader for emphasizing the need to clarify this point.

[134] *Cf.* FINNIS, ETHICS, *supra* note 57, at 51–52; FINNIS, *supra* note 7, at 51–99; CHAPPELL, *supra* note 57, at 35).

is not itself a basic aspect of well-being—rather, it is a precondition for flourishing that is safeguarded in virtue *both* of the value of those aspects of well-being *and* of the requirements that flow from the requirements of practical reasonableness. (Anyone who is unwilling to accept infringements on her own autonomy in a given set of circumstances will act unreasonably if she infringes on another's in similar circumstances. The protection of autonomy is also a by-product of the protection of other interests of which we must reasonably take account in accordance with the Principle of Fairness. And it is difficult to avoid violating the Principle of Respect when infringing on another's autonomy.) Interference with people's justly acquired possessions will be unreasonable insofar as they are assaults on basic aspects of well-being or violations of the Principle of Fairness. But it does not seem as if any and all interferences with people's just possessor claims will be either attacks on basic aspects of welfare or instances of unfairness.

4. *We Sometimes Regard Deprivation of Possessions as a Harm*

A basic aspect of well-being just *is* what has been (ultimately) damaged any time one has suffered a recognized harm or loss. Certainly, when something has been stolen from me, I am inclined to see the wrong done not only as instrumental—so that theft, say, is objectionable just because it keeps me from enjoying some future benefit—but also as a violation of a protected sphere of my existence. When you take something that is legitimately mine, I will be inclined to experience this as a violation quite apart from its obvious instrumental undesirability.

Consider an analogy with *liberty*. Someone might argue that "[p]eople want liberty in order to pursue the truth, to worship as they think right, to participate in the responsible play of political decision-making, to live in friendship, and so on."[135] In fact, however, people often seem to seek liberty because they do not wish to be dominated, subordinated, pushed around; they appear to value liberty *for its own sake*. Similarly, while it might at first be thought that possession mattered only instrumentally, we *do* seem sometimes to regard an attack on a moral patient's possession of something as a harm in its own right, apart from any particular instrumental loss resulting from the attack.[136]

It might be possible to explain this phenomenon, first of all, by adverting to the Principle of Fairness. Intrusion into someone's protected sphere understandably provokes resentment because the intruder treats her victim in a way she would be unwilling to be treated herself or to see her loved ones treated. Given that one's

[135] FINNIS ET AL., *supra* note 1, at 278).

[136] Our concern in these cases may be seen as with the attacker's *attitude*—her disrespect for our just possessory claims—as well as with her *violation* of our *autonomy*, along with our related right to *control* our possessions.

possessory claims are rightly protected in accordance with the Principle of Fairness, one might reasonably treat the violation of those claims as problematic because unfair, quite apart from the specific losses suffered as a result of the violation (to seek and value fairness is itself an aspect of practical reasonableness). And this might be enough to explain someone's characteristic reaction to interference with her possessions as undesirable apart from specific instrumental consequences; there would be no need to invoke the notion that possession itself, or any possession, should be seen as a basic aspect of well-being. (This kind of analysis probably works for liberty as well, given that violations of liberty are often, ultimately, violations of the Principle of Respect—not because liberty itself is a basic aspect of well-being, but because attacks on liberty are frequently at the same time attacks on various aspects of well-being, notably bodily well-being, peace of mind, and practical reasonableness—and the Principle of Fairness.)

Of course, thieves with no claim at all to possessions they have stolen may be angry when those possessions are reclaimed—even (perhaps sometimes especially) by the just possessors. While the recognition of harm in the case of theft does highlight something of moral importance, any account of possession would be deficient to the extent that it failed to give adequate attention to the distinction between *justly* and *unjustly acquired* possessions. That this is so highlights the dependence of any account of possession as a fundamental dimension of flourishing on independently specified rules governing the acquisition, retention, and extent of possessory claims. Even, therefore, if possession were a basic aspect of well-being, the Principle of Fairness would still (as I will argue in more detail below) play a crucial role in determining its contours.

5. *It Is Not Obvious That Denying the Possibility of Just Possessory Claims Would Ensnare One in Self-Contradiction*

Perhaps it might be argued that denying the inherent value of possession involves one in self-contradiction. One might maintain, for instance, that one cannot adopt a purpose as one's own without valuing autonomy, and that one cannot value autonomy without valuing the just possessory claims that make it possible to be autonomous, so that anyone who attempts to achieve a purpose while denying the value of just possessory claims is implicitly contradicting herself.[137] This sort of argument would not settle which claims were just, however. And even if the argument were persuasive, it would not follow that one would thus be treating possession *itself* as a

[137] *See, e.g.*, HANS-HERMANN HOPPE, THE ECONOMICS AND ETHICS OF PRIVATE PROPERTY (2006); *cf.* David D. Friedman, *The Trouble with Hoppe*, LIBERTY, Nov. 1988, at 4, *available at* http://www.daviddfriedman.com/Libertarian/On_Hoppe.html.

basic aspect of well-being. Rather, it seems as if one could just as well be understood to be affirming its undoubted instrumental value, its integral connection with the pursuit of inherently valuable aspects of welfare.

6. *There Is Clear Cross-Cultural Support for the Protection of Possessory Interests, But Not Necessarily for Identifying Possession Itself as a Basic Aspect of Welfare*

While cross-cultural support for the identification of something as a basic aspect of welfare is a pointer to—not constitutive of—its status,[138] cultural variation in this area is enormous. Some control over resources has been seen as crucial, but whether that control should be vested in particular persons or in groups, whether it should be viewed instrumentally, how far it should extend, and how it might appropriately be established have been viewed quite differently. That doesn't mean that some culture-specific possessory patterns aren't preferable to others, that some cultures aren't more insightful than others as regards possessory issues, but it does mean that it's hard to ground the claim that possession as such is a basic aspect of well-being in cross-cultural consensus.

7. *Reflective Equilibrium Provides Little Support for the Notion That Possession Is a Basic Aspect of Welfare*

It seems likely that recognition of just possessory claims of some sort will form part of a system of beliefs in reflective equilibrium, but it is unclear that a reflective-equilibrium-based approach would be sufficient to justify the claim that possession was a *basic* aspect of welfare. That is because it will be possible to cash almost any argument for the *value* of possession as an argument for its *instrumental* value.

8. *There Isn't Much in the Way of Convergent Support for the Notion That Possession Is a Basic Aspect of Well-Being*

We appear to value possessions instrumentally. Asking whether the claim justly to possess some particular thing serves as the terminus in a plausible chain of practical reasoning seems to lead to a negative answer, even if possession itself might seem a more likely candidate for status as a fundamental aspect of flourishing. The approach by way of privation suggests, albeit not definitively, that we may see, at least, control over what is already legitimately ours as intrinsically important, but this may be because others' respect for one's possessions is an aspect of their

[138] *See* FINNIS, *supra* note 7, at 83–85, 97.

treating one in accordance with the requirements of practical reasonableness, and not because possession itself is a basic aspect of well-being. There is little reason to think that *either* the claim that a given possession was a basic aspect of well-being *or* the claim that possession itself was an aspect of well-being could be denied without self-contradiction. Cross-cultural evidence and reflective equilibrium alike might provide some general support for the value of possession, but certainly quite little support for treating it as an intrinsic good. There is little in the way of convergent support from these various approaches for the notion that possession itself is an intrinsic, rather than instrumental, aspect of well-being. I think it likely makes more sense to read evidence that might be adduced in support of the view that an attack on a just possessory claim is an injury in its own right as supporting the view that just possessory claims, though instrumental, play vital roles in securing autonomy, in protecting our *capacity* to flourish, and in fostering our flourishing (particularly given that respecting just possessory claims is a way of treating us in accordance with the Principle of Fairness), and should therefore be regarded as very robust indeed.

9. *Even if Possession Were a Basic Aspect of Well-Being, the Principle of Fairness, Rather than the Principle of Respect, Would Still Be Decisive as Regards Most Instances of Interference with Others' Possessions*

There might be some limited reason to think of possession as a basic aspect of welfare. But it will often be the case that an infringements on a possessory claim cannot plausibly be understood as a purposeful or instrumental *attack* on a just possessor's claim to possess (whatever she possesses) without interference. Actions which cause harm to possessions or impede a just possessor's control over her possessions may be incidental rather than purposeful or instrumental. Thus, even if possession were a basic aspect of well-being, it would not rule out these incidental harms. Instead, the appropriateness of causing them would need to be assessed using the Principle of Fairness.

A further, related, problem is that acknowledging the intrinsic value of possession wouldn't answer the question of what scheme or schemes of possessory rules should be understood as just. Treating possession as intrinsically valuable provides no particular basis for defining just what claims ought to be secure against interference and how these claims ought to be acquired.

The definition of just possessory claims—including both their acquisition and their extent—seems unavoidably dependent on the Principle of Fairness. But if this is the case, then, even if possession *were* a basic aspect of well-being, the actual contours of just possessory claims would be little different from what they would be if they had been defined in light of the Principle of Fairness *without* any reference to possession as a basic aspect of well-being. If exceptions to general possessory rules were consistent with the Principle of Fairness, it is not clear why such exceptions would not be reasonable even if possession were understood to be a fundamental dimension of flourishing. It's just that the Principle of Fairness would lead to the prior definition of the relevant boundaries.

Suppose someone took another's possessions under circumstances in which doing so would be justifiable if possessory rules were simply determined in accordance with the Principle of Fairness: it seems as if taking another's possession would similarly be justified if possession were a basic aspect of well-being—provided the contours of possession were shaped by the Principle of Fairness. Thus, it is unclear that treating possession as a basic aspect of well-being, even were it defensible, would yield moral conclusions different from those that would result if possessory rules (and so possessory claims) were seen as derivative from the Principle of Fairness.

10. *Exceptionless Protections for Possessory Claims Cannot Plausibly Be Rooted in the Principle of Respect*

If the good of possession were understood as involving the baseline possessory rules without exception, the Principle of Respect might generate exceptionless prohibitions on interfering with others' possessions. But it is difficult to see how the view that possession should be seen as a basic aspect of well-being, or the claim that, if it were, this would lead to the conclusion that possessory rules should never admit of exceptions permissible in accordance with the Principle of Fairness, could be defensibly grounded.

C. Possessory Interests May Coincide with Basic Aspects of Welfare, But Attacks on Possessions Are Not Always Attacks on Basic Aspects of Welfare

1. *Attacks on Possessions Need Not Be Attacks on Basic Aspects of Welfare*

Attacking another's possessions need not simultaneously amount to attacking a basic aspect of her well-being.

Specific possessions clearly function instrumentally to foster various sorts of flourishing. Thus, it might be argued that, because of this instrumental relationship, any attempt to damage a person's possessions or deprive her of them will also, at the same time, be an attack on one or more basic aspects of well-being and so be precluded by the Principle of Respect. In fact, however, this will not always be the case, both because attacking another's possessions may not harm any basic component of her welfare (Section 2) and because, even if it does, it may not involve doing so purposefully or instrumentally (Section 3). Except when it does, its wrongness will be a function of the Principle of Fairness (Section 4).

2. *Harms to Possessions May Not Be Harms to Basic Aspects of Well-Being*

Not every attack on another's possessory claims will cause or constitute harm to a basic aspect of well-being. Because people's possessions are, at least ordinarily, external to their identities, a possession isn't itself an instance of a fundamental kind of welfare. Neither taking someone's money nor destroying her car involves, as such, any harm to a basic aspect of her well-being.

3. *Harms to Possessions That Are Harms to Basic Aspects of Well-Being May Be neither Purposeful nor Instrumental*

An attack on a possession may be, at the same time, an instance or cause of harm to a basic aspect of the possessor's well-being. But this sort of attack will frequently not be a *purposeful* or *instrumental* assault on her well-being. Very frequently, interference with another's possessions in a manner consistent with the Principle of Fairness will qualify as a foreseen but unintended interference, undertaken neither for the purpose of harming a basic aspect of well-being nor in a manner that involves harm to a basic aspect of well-being as a means to some other end. While there are many cases in which assaults on possessions will be assaults on basic aspects of well-being (a hostile attack on a painting may be *both* an attack on someone's justly acquired possession *and* a purposeful assault on an æsthetic experience) it is hard to see that this will be true in every case.

Using a computer to embezzle money could be an attack on some basic aspect of well-being if its *purpose* were to keep someone from realizing that aspect of well-being (the thief might want the victim not to be able to pay medical bills and so to die; this would surely count as an attack on the good of life and bodily well-being), but harm to a basic aspect of well-being might well be neither the thief's purpose nor an accepted means to some other end embraced by the thief. And it would be easy to identify a range of other cases in which an attack on someone's possessions did not count as an attack on any basic aspect of well-being.

4. *The Principle of Respect Will Not Likely Be the Standard That Rules Out Most Instances of Interference with Others' Possessory Claims*

Attacks on people's possessions are not so predictably coincident with attacks on basic aspects of their well-being as to be ruled out by the Principle of Respect. Attacks on possessions may not affect basic aspects of welfare at all, and, when they do, they may cause or constitute harm neither purposefully nor instrumentally. The

Principle of Respect will, of course, rule out attacks on people's possessions that *do* amount to attacks on basic aspects of well-being. And it will also preclude attacks on possessions that, even if they do not constitute attacks on basic aspects of well-being, are *motivated* by hostility toward authentic dimensions of people's welfare. In general, however, the Principle of Respect itself will not rule out attacks on people's possessions. These attacks may well be unreasonable, but, when they are, this will be in virtue of the Principle of Fairness.

D. Not Every Nonconsensual Use of People's Possessions Is Tantamount to Enslavement

Interfering with another's justly acquired possessions cannot be treated as in principle wrong on the basis that it is an instance of enslavement.

A justly acquired and maintained possessory claim is acquired either through the labor of the possessor, through the labor of someone cooperating voluntarily with the possessor (since the establishment of effective possession, required to establish a just possessory claim, necessarily involves some form of labor), or in transfer from someone with just possessory claims rooted in acquisition through labor. Thus, it might be thought, to commandeer someone's possessions is in effect to commandeer her labor, and thus to make her a slave.[139] The argument can be spelled out in something like the following manner:

VI.1. Slavery is wrong.
VI.2. To enslave another is to treat her as my possession.
VI.3. An aspect of treating another as my possession is treating not only her body but also her labor as at my disposal.
VI.4. All justly acquired possessions are products of labor.
VI.5. Treating another's justly acquired possessions as mine rather than hers is an instance of treating a product of her labor as mine rather than hers.[140]
VI.6. To treat a product of her labor as mine rather than hers is to treat her labor itself as if at my disposal.
VI.7. To treat a product of her labor as mine rather than hers is to treat her as my possession.
VI.8. To treat another as my possession is to enslave her.
VI.9. Treating a product of another's labor as mine rather than hers is wrong, because enslavement is wrong.
VI.10. Treating another's justly acquired possessions as mine is wrong.

[139] A standard version of this argument can be found in ROBERT NOZICK, ANARCHY, STATE, AND UTOPIA (1974).
[140] Or to treat someone else's labor in this way, if she received the possession through voluntary transfer.

The crucial element of the argument is (VI.6). It is not clear that this claim is fully defensible. That is, what is wrong with enslavement, as I have already argued, is the particular, unreasonable choices that render another a slave or keep her enslaved. These choices will either be unreasonable because—in virtue of denying the basic moral equality of putative slave and would-be slave-master—they violate the Principle of Fairness or because they involve unjustified actual or threatened attacks on the putative slave's body, which violate the Principle of Respect.

Thus, it is doubtless correct that it would be unfair to compel another to build a wagon for me: to use or threaten force to ensure that she labored to construct it. The Principle of Fairness and the Principle of Respect would both preclude my doing so. But it is not equally obvious that taking the wagon after its construction would—at least necessarily—fall foul of the Principle of Respect, for doing so need not involve actual or threatened attacks on the builder's body for incentival or deterrent purposes. Clearly, it might involve such attacks, and so violate the Principle of Respect. But it might also simply involve the use of force to defend the taker against the builder. And whether *this* use of force was just would depend on whether the taking itself was just, which would have to be determined in light of the Principle of Fairness. The justice of the taking cannot be determined in light of the justice of the use of defensive force—rather, the justice of the taking itself would have to be determined in advance; only then could the justice of the use of force be assessed.

In any case, if the use of force against the builder's body weren't at issue, the Principle of Respect wouldn't likely be relevant, for the reasons I've already discussed: the basic disanalogy between the body on the one hand and physical objects external to the body on the other is morally significant. Of course, enslavement is also unjust as a violation of the Principle of Fairness. And the Principle of Fairness—both in virtue of its role as the ground of the baseline rules and as a constraint on particular interactions between particular persons—can be expected to rule out the theft of the wagon. But it need not (though it might) do so for just the same reason it rules out enslavement—viz., that asserting domination over another's life and labor is unreasonable because one would not want to be dominated in this way oneself. It is perfectly possible to explain the wrongness of interference with another's possessions without collapsing the distinction between theft and enslavement.

E. The Baseline Rules Have Different Implications for Personal Choices and Legal Institutions

1. *Personal Moral Choices and Systemic Legal Standards Flow in Different Ways from the Baseline Possessory Rules*

The baseline rules constrain particular people's choices with respect to others' possessions, but exceptions to the rules in some cases may be consistent with the Principle of Fairness and the Principle of Respect, and so may be morally permissible (Section 2). Just legal rules will nonetheless require compensation even in cases in which violations are morally acceptable (Section 3), even as they will embody strict limitations on the use of force to defend even justly acquired possessions (Section 4). Legal rules will not treat the use of force to defend possessions lightly, though they may sometimes tolerate it even in cases in which it is rightly condemned by nonlegal social institutions (Section 5). In short, the baseline rules will play different roles in relation to particular moral decisions on the one hand and to legal rules on the other (Section 6).

2. *The Principle of Fairness May License Some Ad Hoc Exceptions to the Baseline Rules at the Level of Personal Choice*

Just legal rules will provide robust protection for just possessory claims. At the same time, some personal choices that interfere with such claims may be consistent with the Principle of Fairness.[141]

The baseline possessory rules provide particular persons with good reasons to respect others' possessions. They flow from the Principle of Fairness, which is a norm of personal choice, and from the various desiderata, which ought to be relevant in most circumstances to most people, and about which the Principle of Fairness gives each of us reason to be concerned—because of their significance for others—even when we're not directly affected ourselves. Simply in virtue of the Principle of Fairness, it will ordinarily be unreasonable to interfere with others' possessions, and a number of the relevant truisms—notably, that respect for others' possessions further autonomy, which each person has some reason to prize—can be seen as quite directly relevant to personal choice in particular cases, quite apart from their systemic context.

In addition, of course, the desiderata support the existence and operation of a robust *system* of possessory rules. Those who would be adversely affected by choices reducing the effectiveness of the system of rules protecting their possessions and the possessions of those near and dear to them will have good reason to be unwilling to accept those choices. This means that the Principle of Fairness provides further reason for most people generally to support legal requirements implementing the baseline rules, quite apart from the reasons for respecting others' possessions it offers in particular cases in which systemic effects are ignored. In addition, someone might explicitly consent to the possessory rules upheld by a particular legal regime (or to the authority of the mechanisms generating these rules), and will thus be prima facie

[141] David Gordon has persuaded me that Rothbard deserves more credit than I previously gave him, *see* CHARTIER, JUSTICE, *supra* note 8, at 87 n.25, for acknowledging the potential moral appropriateness of interference with otherwise just possessory interests. *See, e.g.*, ROTHBARD, *supra* note 124, at 151–52.

obligated to uphold these rules.[142] To the extent that applicable regime-specific rules track the baseline rules, these people will thus have additional reasons to uphold the baseline rules.

Nonetheless, even when taking systemic effects into account, someone (perhaps in some cases even someone who has consented to the authority of a legal regime implementing the baseline rules or to the rules themselves as embraced by a given regime) might on occasion reasonably conclude that it was just for her to interfere with another's possessions—as in an emergency, or in a case in which infringement was de minimis or in which it was needed to prevent, end, or remedy aggression.

As regards emergencies: consider the case in which you opt to break into my unoccupied mountain cottage to escape an avalanche, or to take a rifle belonging to a misanthrope I know would be unwilling to part with it in order to stop a mass murderer.[143] Though it would be important to have more situation-specific information in order to be sure, both actions seem likely to be entirely consistent with the Principle of Fairness.

Both Thomas Aquinas and John Locke explicitly acknowledged that emergencies justified interference with otherwise stable, reliable protections for people's just possessory claims. St. Thomas maintains that when a need is "so manifest and urgent, that it is evident that the present need must be remedied by whatever means be at hand (for instance when a person is in some imminent danger, and there is no other possible remedy), then it is lawful for a man to succor his own need by means of another's property, by taking it either openly or secretly: nor is this properly speaking theft or robbery."[144] Locke's position seems to be, if anything more expansive. He writes: "charity gives every man a title to so much out of another's plenty, as will keep him from extreme want, where he has no means to subsist otherwise."[145]

The positions of such earlier natural-law thinkers as Aquinas and Locke point to an awareness that possessory claims, though important, should not be treated as absolute, and might reasonably be limited, at least in emergencies. The question in such cases will be whether interference with another's just possessory claims is consistent with the Principle of Fairness, both in the instance immediately under consideration and in light of relevant systemic effects—as well as, where applicable, obligations assumed by consent.

The Principle of Fairness might sometimes license not only emergency violations of but also de minimis infringements on others' just possessory claims. These will

[142] *See* Chapter 4, *infra*.

[143] *Cf.* David D. Friedman, The Machinery of Freedom: Guide to a Radical Capitalism 168–76 (2d ed., 1989).

[144] Thomas Aquinas, Summa Theologiæ II-II q. 94 a. 7c (Fathers of the English Dominican Province trans., 2d ed., 1920).

[145] John Locke, First Treatise of Government ch. IV, §42 (1689).

sometimes be ruled out, of course, on situation-specific or systemic grounds. But it is hard to imagine that, for instance, cutting across a small corner of a neighbor's field to avoid a much longer walk, without causing any damage to her fence or grass or crops, would consistently be ruled out by the Principle of Fairness.

And of course it may be reasonable to violate otherwise just claims to possessions to the extent needed to prevent, end, or remedy aggression. It will be entirely reasonable, for instance, to enter someone's home in order to rescue a kidnapping victim or to disable a sniper (even if the just possessor is not responsible for the presence in her home of the victim or the sniper). In the same way, it will be appropriate to claim another's possessions in order to provide compensation for harm she has caused to the body or possessions of another.

3. *Legal Rules Will Require Compensation even for Morally Acceptable Interference with Others' Possessions*

Even where someone's choice to interfere with another's justly acquired possessions is reasonable, the Principle of Fairness dictates that just legal rules require full compensation for the costs associated with the interference.

People determining whether particular interferences with others' possessions ought to take the systemic effects of their particular choices into account. But these effects are likely to be relatively limited, and this fact can reasonably influence their choices. By contrast, of course, actors playing official roles in just legal institutions cannot but be concerned quite directly and centrally with systemic consequences. It is their responsibility to ensure that the baseline possessory rules (and any rules consistent with them that are also enforced by the relevant institutions) function effectively. Acting in accordance with the Principle of Fairness will necessarily mean, for them, taking full account of the tendencies of their actions and fostering the reliability of just possessory claims. Thus, they will have every reason to treat even a reasonable interference with a just possessory claim as a compensable harm.[146] Doing this is a vital way of emphasizing the importance of robust possessory claims, discouraging people from ignoring those claims frivolously, and ensuring that injuries to people's possessions are remedied.

This is true despite the fact that people sometimes make foolish or morally objectionable, even if nonaggressive, choices about how to use their possessions. In view

[146] The position I defend here might seem to amount to the claim that, per the scheme elaborated in Guido Calabresi & A. Douglas Melamed, *Property Rules, Liability Rules and Inalienability: One View of the Cathedral*, 85 HARV. L. REV. 1089 (1972), the law should recognize only liability rules and not property rules. However, this analysis is perhaps complicated by the fact that, on my view, the legitimacy of the use of force to protect bodies and justly acquired possessions against unjust attack, when it obtains, is triggered by the unwarranted crossing of predefined boundaries.

of the importance of the various desiderata, in recognition of the value of autonomous decision making, and in full view of institutions' frequent and unavoidable ignorance of people's purposes, legal institutions should operate as if people are using their goods to pursue genuinely valuable aspects of well-being in reasonable ways, whether they are or not. Thus, it would be reasonable for just legal regimes to be willing to defend against all attacks on participants' justly acquired possessions, to treat participants' reasonable acts undertaken in defense of any of their own justly acquired possessions as legitimate, and to require compensation for all instances of interference with such possessions—except those being used unjustly to attack others' bodies or possessions or justly claimed to secure restitution for prior unjust attacks.[147]

The requirement of compensation is not merely a product of the need to maintain the operation of just legal institutions, of course: it reflects the fact that, ex hypothesi, interference with just possessory interests has taken place. And there is surely no reason the just possessor should be expected to bear the cost. Most of us would typically be unwilling to accept a refusal on the part of someone who caused us harm to take responsibility for remedying it, so the Principle of Fairness suggests as a plausible remedial rule that someone who damages or misappropriates another's possessions should, in fact, be expected to provide the just possessor with appropriate compensation. Appropriate compensation surely ought to include not only the immediate cost of repairing or replacing a damaged possession and the costs associated with not having access to it, but also the various reasonable costs of recovery—the costs associated with identifying the person responsible for causing the harm and with securing legal redress from her. In the absence of these costs of recovery, the just possessor would be worse off than she was before the harm occurred even with the possession repaired or replaced.

It may reasonably be assumed that someone interfering with another's justly acquired possessions is *either* responding to an emergency or an act of aggression or proceeding de minimis, intending to use or interfere with the possessions to an appropriately limited degree, *or* is acting in bad faith, attempting to misappropriate another's possessions in violation of the Principle of Fairness and the baseline possessory rules. In neither case would the baseline rules permit the interferer to come to have any just claim to the relevant possession as against the just possessor or someone to whom the just possessor has transferred her own claim. To deprive the just possessor of her claim would be to treat her unfairly in the particular case in question, to undermine the effectiveness of the baseline rules, and to incentivize

[147] That others have the right to restrain me in cases in which I am engaging in aggression does not imply that they also have the right permanently to deprive me of any possessions I am using to facilitate my aggression. Thanks to Roman Pearah for emphasizing the need to clarify this point.

the interferer and others similarly situated to treat others' justly acquired possessions as fair game.

An obvious risk associated with a model of just possessory claims in accordance with which people may sometimes—when they judge their actions to be consistent with the Principle of Fairness, even after taking into account systemic effects—regard themselves as entitled to interfere with others' justly acquired possessions is that a culture of "take and pay" will develop. People might find it overly tempting to interfere with others' possessions. In some cases, they might do so in good faith; but, even so, widespread interference would obviously reduce the effectiveness of the baseline rules. In other cases, doubting that they will be identified and expected to compensate those they have harmed, people may simply act in bad faith.

While the monetary compensation someone may reasonably demand from someone else for interfering with her justly acquired possession is the economic cost of replacing or repairing the possession and the cost associated with its absence, together with the reasonable costs of recovery, additional mechanisms may reasonably be employed to reduce the likelihood both of widespread interference with others' possessions in general and of repeated attacks on others' possessions by specific people in particular. The determination of motivation is irrelevant to the need for compensation: even someone who interferes with another's justly acquired possessions from the best of motives still owes the just possessor appropriate compensation, in accordance with the Principle of Fairness. But it is certainly relevant to the moral assessment of the interferer by her peers and to their judgments regarding the risks she might pose in the future. The broad dissemination of information regarding the determinations by relevant social institutions of the circumstances surrounding and the motives underlying someone's interference with another's justly acquired possessions can make it possible for irresponsible or dangerous interferers to be shunned or to be denied opportunities they might otherwise enjoy to interfere with others' possessions.

Just legal rules will provide for the provision of compensation by whoever is ultimately *causally responsible* (subjecting someone to duress would presumably make one responsible for injuries she caused while under duress) for causing harm to someone's justly acquired possessions (*ultimately* because principals ought to be responsible for the actions of agents acting within the scope of their agency): it is unreasonable to ask that the risk of loss here fall on the possessor, and a rule requiring compensation from the person responsible for the harm is both simplest and most obviously in accord with the Principle of Fairness. Compensation should include both immediate losses and reasonable costs of recovery. Appropriate mechanisms for social norm maintenance can ensure that no one takes for granted the option of simply interfering with another's possessions and then providing compensation.[148]

4. *The Extent to Which It Is Reasonable to Use Force to Stop Interference with One's Justly Acquired Possessions Will Vary from Situation to Situation*

Force may reasonably be employed to defend against unjust attacks, but the Principle of Fairness will constrain its use, especially in cases in which it is not being used to defend against threatened or actual bodily harm.

It is in principle consistent with the Principle of Respect to use force to resist force, and it will likely be reasonable to use potentially lethal force to resist an attack that threatens to cause death or serious bodily injury to oneself or another. Most people would use force in such cases themselves, and so have no basis for objecting if others do so when responding to their aggressive attacks.

Most people would likely be willing to use force in response to some kinds of attacks on possessions, and so could not reasonably object if others used force against them to stop these kinds of attacks, either. Consider, for instance, someone who has taken or is seeking to take all of the water possessed by someone else who is stranded in the desert—intending, perhaps, to hold the water for ransom. Given that the stranded person needs to possess the water in order to preserve her life, it might be reasonable for her to use considerable force to keep it from being taken (or to recover it). As in the simpler case of defense against a bodily attack, harm to the would-be appropriator of the water need be no part of the proposal the stranded person adopts when attempting to stop the aggressor from taking the water or from using force to keep it from being retaken by its just possessor, even if the attempt involves the use of force that in fact causes great bodily harm or death.

It will often be unclear whether an attack on someone's possessions is also intended as, or is likely to be accompanied by, an attack on her person. A mugging in a secluded place or the attempted robbery of an occupied home at night might easily turn into physical attacks. Though sometimes there will be clear and convincing evidence to the contrary, it will on occasion be reasonable for someone whose possessions are being attacked in such a situation to assume that her person is under threat and to use force accordingly. And a just possessor may sometimes

[148] Jonathan Crowe asks (in a prepublication review) whether *A* should be required to compensate *B* for the use of *B*'s justly acquired possessions in an emergency when *A* "has a just claim to assistance from *B*." Requiring compensation, he suggests, seems unreasonable, "given that *B* had a duty to assist *A* in the first place." I am inclined to think that Crowe is largely correct if *A*'s claim on *B* is a legally enforceable one, for the relevant claim will either involve (*i*) the transfer of a just claim to the possessions in question from *B* to *A*, in which case no compensation will be due, or (*ii*) the forfeiture of some bond or other payment on *B*'s part, which could be expected to offset any required damages in whole or in part.

employ minimal force in an attempt to restrain someone seeking to interfere with her possessions—only to be met by an aggressive response. It is surely reasonable for the just possessor to defend herself in this case using an appropriate level of force.

Sometimes, it will be clear that only one's possessions are under direct attack, that the loss of the possessions will pose no serious harm to one's person, and that the would-be taker poses no reasonable threat to one's person. It will still be true in this case that one might use significant force to protect control over a justly acquired possession without adopting any proposal to which harm to any basic aspect of the aggressor's well-being is integral. But the Principle of Fairness will often militate against the use of substantial force in such a case.

(*i*) It will not be reasonable to employ more force than is needed to prevent one's possession from being taken or, alternately, to stop the unjust taker from preventing one from retaking it. Using more force than is intelligible only if one is seeking to harm the other purposefully (perhaps as an act of vengeance) or instrumentally (perhaps to make her an example), and seeking to cause harm in either of these ways is inconsistent with the Principle of Respect. (It may also be that one is simply careless; if one is, this evinces an unreasonable lack of concern for another's welfare, a lack of concern that is itself inconsistent with the Principle of Fairness, since one presumably would be unwilling to accept a similar lack of concern in one's own case.)

(*ii*) Even someone who might regretfully accept the use of force against, say, a loved one who posed a serious threat to another's life might be unwilling to accept the use of considerable force against the same loved one in an otherwise similar situation if she posed a threat only to a recoverable possession not needed for immediate life support—especially if limited force would clearly be quite sufficient to recover the possession subsequent to its misappropriation or to prevent its misappropriation in the first place. Someone who would be unwilling to accept the use of force in this kind of situation could not reasonably employ comparable force herself under similar circumstances.

It is consistent with the Principle of Fairness and the Principle of Respect to use force to defend one's body (or another's) against direct attack, to stop or remedy an attack on one's possessions with serious consequences, or to defend against someone threatening one's possessions (or another's) who might also threaten one's own (or another's) person. It may be consistent with the Principle of Respect to use force against someone who only threatens one's possessions, but the extent to which it will be reasonable to do so will be limited by the Principle of Fairness, which will likely mandate the use of relatively minimal nondefensive force against attackers' bodies in such cases.

5. *Just Legal Rules Should Protect Those Who Use Force to Defend against Physical Aggression, But Not Those Who Use Excessive Force to Defend Possessions against Interference*

Force may reasonably be used to protect oneself and one's possessions against attackers. But one may only use force when one's purpose is not to cause injury and when one's choice to use force is consistent with the Principle of Fairness. However, the application of this standard by a just legal system might reasonably embody presumptions, in cases of genuine unclarity, that deny liability for some injuries for which liability might be appropriate were circumstances clearer.

Law is unavoidably a blunt instrument. It will be difficult for courts to articulate or apply rules as nuanced as those we can and should employ in evaluating our own or others' conduct. The use of legal rules as useful guides to conduct requires that such rules be clear, simple, easy to follow, general, and consistently applied. Thus, generally just legal rules may sometimes err by being overinclusive or underinclusive, treating as illegitimate conduct that is actually reasonable or treating as reasonable conduct that in fact is not. In light of the Principle of Fairness and the desiderata that motivate the baseline rules, it is obviously important that legal rules and institutions treat people's just possessory claims with respect. So there is perhaps reason on occasion for just legal rules and institutions to give the benefit of the doubt to someone who uses what might, in fact, be excessive force in defense of her justly acquired possessions. When, and only when, there is genuine doubt, it should presumably be resolved in favor of someone who is *defending* a legitimate claim rather than someone who seeks to *violate* such a claim.

From the standpoint of the agent here, it may clearly be wrong to use force with the potential to kill or maim, as it surely will be in many cases in which the defense of purely possessory interests is at stake. And when it is clear what has occurred, a just legal institution may reasonably treat a just possessor who uses force against someone seeking to interfere with her possessions as acting unreasonably, and bound to compensate the interferer or the interferer's heirs or assigns for harm to the interferer—and as behaving in a way that may, indeed, merit the use of defensive force.[149] This

[149] Because the use of force to defend threatened possessions can clearly be unreasonable, it may sometimes be reasonable for someone engaged in unjust conduct to use force to defend herself against someone who is using unjust force in response to her conduct. Someone whose life is threatened because she has stolen a stick of gum, for instance, might reasonably respond with defensive force in a case in which returning the gum, or otherwise avoiding confrontation, failed to eliminate the risk that she might be killed.

The same sort of analysis would presumably apply in case of at least some justifiable emergency infringements on others' possessions. For instance: consider again the mountain cabin/avalanche example. Suppose Max, a decided misanthrope, is the just possessor of two cabins located on the peaks of two adjoining mountains. Max is sitting on the porch of one cabin just as an avalanche gets under way. Max witnesses Chris, who's been mountain-climbing, trying to break into the other cabin

will be true in any of several kinds of cases: (*i*) when no threat was posed to anyone's physical well-being, (*ii*) when more force was employed than was needed to prevent misappropriation, (*iii*) when a misappropriated item could have been recovered (or replaced at the misappropriator's expense) with limited use of force, or (*iv*) when a reasonable person would be unwilling to accept the level of force employed if a loved one were the target in a similar situation. The presumption in favor of the just possessor should only operate, it seems to me, when there really is genuine lack of clarity about whether the just possessor was acting to protect herself against bodily harm or acted reasonably in using significant force to protect herself against dispossession.

The kinds of norm-maintenance mechanisms sensible people could and should employ to reduce the risks to others posed by those who high-handedly interfere with others' possessions while offering compensation could and should be used to help people understand and respond to cases in which just possessors used potentially unreasonable force to defend their possessions. (Unreasonable but nonactionable conduct in either sort of case might be dealt with using boycotts and blacklists, for instance; these might continue until an unreasonable injurer participated in some appropriate kind of reconciliation process.) While simple, bright-line legal rules cannot always make relevant moral distinctions, social institutions can provide people with the information they need to determine whether they judge someone who has used force to defend her possessions as worthy of acclaim or reprobation, whether such a person should be embraced or feared. Nonlegal institutions complement legal ones and perform work it is not reasonable to use force, legal institutions' stock-in-trade, to attempt.

6. *Just Legal Rules Provide General, But Not Exceptionless, Protections for Possessory Claims and Seek to Minimize the Use of Force*

The baseline rules provide very good reason for particular persons as well as legal institutions to respect others' justly acquired possessions. There is no reason the baseline rules should be understood to incorporate systematic permissions for interference with anyone's possessions: such permissions would compromise their simplicity, their autonomy-protecting function, and their potential to incentivize economic productivity, among other things. But particular people, not acting as occupants of particular institutional roles, might sometimes reasonably judge that

to escape the avalanche. Max begins to fire a rifle at Chris to stop Chris from breaking into the cabin. Chris, who expects to be killed by the avalanche if she is unable to find shelter in the cabin (and who knows herself, we may assume, perfectly willing to compensate Max for damage to the cabin—indeed, without any involvement by the legal system), would, it seems to me, be justified in using force to defend herself against Max's attack.

it was consistent with the Principle of Fairness, including systemic responsibilities flowing from the Principle, to interfere with others' justly acquired possessions. Even if they did so judge in good conscience, however, this would not absolve them from legal responsibility for compensating just possessors for damage to their possessions, and their misappropriation could not itself reasonably lead in any circumstances to their acquiring just claims to misappropriated possessions. It will often be reasonable for just possessors to use force to prevent or end interference with their justly acquired possessions, to recover misappropriated possessions, and to secure compensation for misappropriated possessions that cannot be returned. But only in limited cases will it be reasonable for them to cause death or great bodily harm in the course of so doing. And, while just legal rules and institutions will sometimes give just possessors the benefit of the doubt, they will not treat the use of evidently excessive force as legitimate. With respect to both interference with justly acquired possessions and the use of force in response to such interference, appropriate social institutions can often make and communicate moral distinctions finer than those legal rules and institutions can articulate.

F. Just Possessory Claims, though Not Exceptionless, Are Robust

The Principle of Fairness itself is, like the Principle of Respect, absolute: disregarding it is always unreasonable. But what the Principle of Fairness requires would seem to vary far more with circumstance than what the Principle of Respect requires. Thus, mid-level general norms that flow from the Principle of Fairness –*Keep promises*, for example, or *Avoid rudeness*—may admit of a variety of exceptions, just as Aquinas and Locke supposed. By contrast, there are no exceptions to, for instance, the prohibition, derived from the Principle of Respect, against purposeful or instrumental killing.

Attempts to ground possessory claims *apart* from the Principle of Fairness—attempts to demonstrate that possession is a basic aspect of well-being, or that particular possessions are instances of fundamental kinds of flourishing or that attacks on possessions are always, at the same time, purposeful or instrumental attacks on well-being, so that interference with others' possessions is always wrong because always inconsistent with the Principle of Respect or that interference with possessory claims amounts to enslavement—are unsuccessful. At the same time, however, there is good reason for a general system of reliable protections for people's just possessory claims that uniformly upholds the baseline rules, and for particular people reliably to respect others' justly acquired possessions. For instance:

- Whatever judgments people tend to make about their own possessory claims will be judgments fairness will demand that they accept when reaching conclusions about others'.

- More generally, Principle of Fairness, in tandem with the desiderata, can be seen as providing strong justification for (*i*) legal institutions to treat the baseline rules as exceptionless and to treat violations as always triggering compensation requirements and (*ii*) particular persons to treat others' just possessory claims as largely inviolable.
- Consequentialism is indefensible and incoherent. That doesn't mean, of course, that expected consequences are never relevant to deliberation about reasonable action, but their reasonableness is to be gauged in light of the Principle of Fairness rather than in terms of a putatively objective metric that allows a "best overall state of affairs" to be identified. Multiple options are consistent with the demands of reason. So, while pragmatic considerations can certainly enter into moral deliberation, *global consequentialism* can't justify any sort of attack on someone's person, and can't be invoked in support of any infringement of someone's possessory claims.
- Our flourishing, and our attempts to flourish, will characteristically involve the use of possessions. Attacks on someone's possessions might sometimes be unreasonable precisely because they are also purposeful or instrumental attacks on basic aspects of well-being.
- Similarly, people often protect their possessions using their bodies, and an attack on someone's possessions will thus sometimes be inappropriate precisely because it involves using force purposefully or instrumentally in ways that harm her body.
- Acting out of hostility toward someone by harming him or his possessions will always be inconsistent with the Principle of Respect.
- Further, someone who may quite reasonably be willing to accept one sort of imposition on her possessions may well be quite *unwilling* to accept another, and so be precluded from engaging in or supporting a similar sort of imposition on someone else's.

There might still be circumstances in which people could reasonably violate others' just possessory claims on an ad hoc basis. However, in so doing they would accept responsibility to provide compensation for the harms they caused and any reasonable costs of recovery, while not acquiring any sort of title to the possessions with which they interfered. And they would remain liable not only for damages but potentially also to public shaming and shunning.

VII. KEY REQUIREMENTS OF PRACTICAL REASONABLENESS CAN BE ENCAPSULATED IN THE NONAGGRESSION MAXIM

Although the Principle of Respect and the Principle of Fairness have significant implications for nonviolent conduct, as regards the use of force they ground a requirement that may be summed up in the nonaggression maxim:[150] *avoid aggression against others and their just possessory interests*. This phrase summarizes a set of interrelated moral prohibitions on aggression—that is, on (*i*) purposefully or instrumentally attacking others' bodies; (*ii*) causing harm unfairly to others' bodies or interfering unfairly with their just possessory interests; and, derivatively, (*iii*) declining to provide compensation for injuries, both reasonable and unreasonable, deliberate and unintentional, for which one is causally responsible. The NAM offers robust safeguards for peaceful, voluntary cooperation and creates spaces for the exercise of creative self-determination.

What counts as a justly acquired possession is determined primarily by the Principle of Fairness. In tandem with this principle, various truisms about human behavior and the human condition ground overlapping, mutually reinforcing desiderata for a robust scheme of requirements I call the *baseline possessory rules*, protecting initial acquisition of physical objects through effective possession and entitling just possessors to control and transfer their possessions. These rules do not protect possessory claims on persons, on nonhuman animals, or on physical embodiments of abstract patterns as such, but only on non-sentient physical things. There is good reason for just legal rules and institutions not only to enforce the baseline rules but also to treat them as exceptionless, and for moral agents to regard the possessory claims they ground as generally inviolable. But it may also sometimes be consistent with the requirements of practical reasonableness for moral agents to infringe on these claims, as in emergency and de minimis situations, with the recognition that in so doing they accept responsibility to provide compensation for any harms they cause.

In accordance with the NAM, the circumstances under which force can be used in response to moral wrongdoing are limited to those in which force is necessary to stop harm to bodies and (sometimes, though not necessarily) interference with just possessory claims. That is because, while just legal rules flow from the requirements of practical reasonableness, those principles themselves generate limits on their immediate applicability. In particular, when they are applied in the context of legal institutions, they generate limits on the goals those with official roles within

[150] This maxim is similar to, but not identical with, the Non-Aggression Principle defended by Murray Rothbard. As Rothbard outlines this principle: "no one may threaten or commit violence ('aggress') against another man's person or property. Violence may be employed only against the man who commits such violence; that is, only defensively against the aggressive violence of another. In short, no violence may be employed against a nonaggressor." Murray N. Rothbard, *War, Peace, and the State*, *in* THE MYTH OF NATIONAL DEFENSE: ESSAYS ON THE THEORY AND HISTORY OF SECURITY PRODUCTION 66 (Hans-Hermann Hoppe ed., 2003). I refer to the nonaggression maxim, rather than the nonaggression principle, because of the limited qualifications I note in Chapter 2.V, *supra*. I do not mean to imply (*see* n.141, *supra*) that Rothbard, at any rate, would have disagreed regarding many of the situations to which I mean my qualifications to apply.

those institutions can pursue and the means they can justly employ in pursuit of those goals in their official capacities—and thus, in short, the legal rules reasonable people can uphold.[151]

The NAM does not comprehend all moral requirements, of course. It is concerned "with violence and non-violence as modes of interpersonal relations."[152] Its narrow purpose is to ground legal rights. To say that a given interest is safeguarded by a right is to say that the interest may not be "interfered with by violence," and that it may be vindicated using force, not to deny that there may be "immoral ways of exercising that right."[153] Many actions are wrong but not *aggressive*. But only (aggressive) force may be met with (defensive and remedial) force. Conduct may thus be inconsistent with the requirements of practical reasonableness *even though* one or more of these principles might *also* preclude *forcible interference* by others with that conduct. The NAM therefore enshrines, in an important sense, a "right to do wrong."

Despite initial appearances, the recognition of such a right is in no sense paradoxical once it is clearly understood. The recognition of a right to do wrong in the sense in which such a right ought to be acknowledged by a just legal system is not premised on the assumption that it is right—morally appropriate—to do wrong, or on the curious notion that a choice can simultaneously be morally right and morally wrong in complementary senses. Rather, a just legal order will safeguard a right to do wrong only in that it will license the use of force only to prevent, end, or remedy aggression.[154] The NAM, the ground of a just legal order, does not itself resolve a broad range of moral problems, the province of those requirements of practical reasonableness that underlie it. But it is nonetheless exceedingly important, since it provides a framework for peaceful, voluntary cooperation.

I have not attempted to defend or elaborate the NAM by treating, say, *self-ownership* as a premise. This notion is sufficiently contentious that it does not make an appealing starting-point for legal or political theory.[155] Self-ownership is arguably better understood as a conclusion than as a starting-point, a *consequence* of accepting the principles of practical reasonableness. Instead of saying that someone should embrace the NAM because she believes in self-ownership, it would make more sense to say that she should affirm self-ownership because she endorses the NAM.

[151] While I would hope successfully to avoid Hume's subjectivism and consequentialism, the kind of approach he wants to take seems to me, if nothing else, a useful model for the way in which the transition from the interpersonal to the institutional might be made.

[152] ROTHBARD, *supra* note 124, at 25.

[153] *Id.* at 24.

[154] With the qualifiers noted in Chapter 2.VI, *supra*.

[155] *Cf.* Carole Pateman, *Self-Ownership and Property in the Person: Democratization and a Tale of Two Concepts*, 10 J. POL. PHIL. 20 (2002).

It is frequently supposed that the operation of a society in which the NAM is consistently respected—a society organized on the basis of peaceful, voluntary cooperation—depends on the existence and operation of the state. In fact, however, the state is *both* unnecessary to the maintenance of the social order needed for cooperation to flourish *and* inimical to this kind of order, given its persistent engagement in aggression and its support for the aggression-based privileges of elite groups. The state is aggression writ large. It is an enemy of the NAM and so of just social order. In Chapter 3, I seek to explain why the state is unnecessary, dangerous, and deeply compromised by its ongoing involvement with injustice.

3

Safeguarding Cooperation

I. THE STATE IS INIMICAL TO PEACEFUL, VOLUNTARY COOPERATION

The state is not needed to foster or safeguard peaceful, voluntary cooperation, to which it has, in fact, been persistently hostile.

Peaceful, voluntary cooperation is protected by the nonaggression maxim (NAM) and is a vital constituent of and contributor to flourishing (Part II). The state's claim to authority is an implicit denial of the bedrock importance of social cooperation (Part III). Despite the claim that the state plays a vital role in preserving and fostering social cooperation, it is in fact not needed to resolve disputes and to offer protection against aggression (Part IV), or to provide vital public goods (Part V).

Not only is the state unconcerned with and unnecessary to peaceful, voluntary cooperation: in fact, it has undermined and attacked social cooperation in the interest of the ruling class and its cronies (Part VI). If peaceful, voluntary cooperation is a bedrock value, there is no need for the state, and good reason to reject it (Part VIII). And the putative value of the public good of general preemptive defense is insufficient to render the state necessary (Appendix).

II. PEACEFUL, VOLUNTARY COOPERATION IS AN ASPECT OF AND A CRUCIAL PRECONDITION FOR A FLOURISHING LIFE

Peaceful, voluntary cooperation is simply the kind of interaction—with friends and strangers, face-to-face and at great distances—that occurs in the general absence of aggression. It is not, of course, the sum total of any and all aspects of flourishing. Rather, it provides preconditions for the realization of well-being in all its varieties while incorporating important aspects of flourishing.

Although it might sometimes in principle be possible to flourish in isolation, it is far easier to do so while cooperating peacefully and voluntarily with others—realizing inherently worthwhile relationships and pursuing flourishing in innumerable further ways.

For instance: in a society marked by peaceful, voluntary cooperation, strangers can interact confidently and trustingly. This means that they can work together, without knowing each other personally, to support valued institutions and activities. And their myriad encounters can help to shape decisions about the goods and services worth producing; the levels at which each should be produced; and who should produce, distribute, and consume them. This kind of social cooperation is instrumentally valuable, since it makes various kinds of flourishing possible: almost everyone benefits from the greater accessibility of desired goods and services. In some cases, consuming these goods and services will itself be a matter of flourishing; in others, doing so will facilitate, even though it does not constitute, people's well-being. Either way, peaceful, voluntary cooperation can play a vital role in making flourishing possible.

At the same time, simply participating in widespread social cooperation helps to bridge gaps, build bridges, and foster friendship, and therefore contributes instrumentally to flourishing and fulfillment quite apart from its contribution to the production of valuable goods and services. And of course social cooperation need not only *foster* positive relationships: it can directly involve *participating* in such relationships. These relationships may be of many different kinds—from ones with intimates to ones with strangers. Some of these relationships will be, in various ways, friendships that are intrinsically valuable. And of course one can also rightly value the more attenuated but still positive relationships with the near and the distant that are significant aspects of the process of social cooperation.

Peaceful, voluntary cooperation is also important for another reason: when people are able to make significant choices voluntarily, they help to create their own identities and to nourish themselves as morally and spiritually mature agents. In an environment in which people's choices are constrained by the threat of aggression, they will have difficulty making genuinely responsible choices about who and what they will be, since it will be hard for them not to choose based on what those with the capacity to threaten them want them to do. And in such an environment, marked by a great deal of background unpredictability, it will be particularly difficult for them to make long-term plans and commitments. In a society rooted in peaceful, voluntary cooperation, by contrast, people can effectively take responsibility for their own lives. (Doing this is, of course, a basic aspect of well-being: exercising practical reasonableness.)

In addition, the social and legal order that connects actors with both friends and strangers while fostering peaceful, voluntary cooperation can *itself* be seen as embodying various aspects of flourishing. When it functions well, it can be beautiful and elegant, constituted by many valuable skills, relationships and capacities.

And its operation can involve the pursuit of knowledge, the exercise of practical reasonableness, engagement in a kind of play, and perhaps an attenuated form of friendship.

Peaceful, voluntary cooperation matters. It fosters flourishing. Participating in social cooperation is a matter of participating in friendship and community. And acting without compulsion means taking responsibility for one's own life. In addition, the formal and informal structures that preserve peaceful, voluntary cooperation are marked by, even as they encourage, diverse aspects of flourishing.

III. STATE ACTORS' REFUSAL TO COOPERATE WITH OTHERS ON A PEACEFUL, VOLUNTARY BASIS IS HIGHLY PROBLEMATIC

A. Because State Actors Frequently Fail to Cooperate with Others on a Peaceful, Voluntary Basis, Their Official Actions and Claims to Authority Require Justification

The things state actors do and their demands that others comply with their orders are very much in need of warrant. They insist on obedience (and so demand involuntary cooperation), and they both attack people's bodies and interfere with their possessions (and so decline to be peaceful and, because of their use of aggressive force, render cooperation with them involuntary) (Section B). Their demands for involuntary cooperation fly in the face of the fact that there is no natural right to rule, that no one is the state's slave, and that state authority is not grounded in consent (Section C). Their taking of others' possessions could only be justified if the presumption, rooted in the Principle of Fairness and embodied in the baseline rules, against unjust acquisition and interference with just possessory claims were overturned, and could command assent only if their authority claims were upheld (Section D). And their anything-but-peaceful attacks on people's bodies too often flout the Principle of Respect and seem, especially given the validity of the baseline rules, to be inconsistent with the Principle of Fairness (Section E). Absent special justification, state actors' authority claims and their invasive actions—their unwillingness to cooperate on a peaceful, voluntary basis—seem clearly unwarranted (Section F).

B. State Actors Behave in Ways, and Make Claims, That Ordinary People Do Not

State actors claim that they are entitled to *command*—that they *deserve* their subjects' obedience. They also maintain that, if their subjects decline to obey, they are entitled to *use force against their subjects' bodies* to punish them for not doing so and to incentivize them to comply and to *use force to take their possessions* to punish them for disobedience and to support the state's various activities.

C. State Actors' Claims to Deserve Obedience Require Justification

1. *The Character of State Actors' Claims to Exercise Legitimate Authority Makes These Claims Problematic*

State actors' claims to authority—to be able to make it the case that others have decisive reasons for obeying them simply in virtue of their positions—need some sort of warrant. People's essential equality in authority means that no one is naturally entitled to dominate anyone else (Subsection 2). Given the wrongness of slavery, the state is not entitled to treat anyone like a slave (Subsection 3). And, while fairness seems to require that demands for obedience at least ordinarily be rooted in consent, the state's subjects cannot reasonably be said to have consented to its authority (Subsection 4). It is thus difficult to see on what basis the state's claim to authority might be defended (Subsection 5).

2. *The Principle of Fairness Suggests That People Should Be Seen as Fundamentally Equal in Authority*

If state actors' claims are defensible, they must be grounded in something other than the status or ancestry of those making them: there is no natural right to rule.[1] This is another way of saying that the Principle of Fairness implies a basic equality between one person's inherent authority and anyone else's.[2] Of course it is true that people who don't want to be dominated (violently or nonviolently) act unreasonably if *they* seek to dominate others; this is an obvious *application* of the Principle of Fairness. More than this, however, the idea that *grounds* the Principle of Fairness, and that is presupposed by the Principle of Respect, would seem to be that there is no essential difference among moral patients (including the moral patients who are also moral agents) where moral considerability is concerned. Thus, for instance, everyone's interests deserve to be taken into account—no one can be arbitrarily discounted. Everyone is entitled to use limited force to defend herself or others against unjust attack. And so forth. This idea, the idea of basic equality, renders

[1] *Cf.* JOHN FINNIS, AQUINAS: MORAL, POLITICAL, AND LEGAL THEORY 264 (1998); GERMAIN GRISEZ & JOSEPH M. BOYLE, JR., LIFE AND DEATH WITH LIBERTY AND JUSTICE: A CONTRIBUTION TO THE EUTHANASIA DEBATE 26–27 (1979).

[2] *Cf.* Roderick T. Long, *Liberty: The Other Equality*, THE FREEMAN: IDEAS ON LIBERTY, Oct., 2005, at 17, http://www.fee.org/pdf/the-freeman/0510Long.pdf; Roderick T. Long, *Equality: The Unknown Ideal*, MISES DAILY, Oct. 16, 2001, http:www.mises.org/story/804.

inherent distinctions in authority untenable. It also creates a strong presumption against derived distinctions in authority. Such distinctions, if they are to qualify as reasonable, must be *justified* in accordance with the Principle of Fairness. Thus, if the authority of state actors, in particular, is to be legitimate at all, it must be derivative—and clearly warranted.

3. *No One Is the State's Slave*

A corollary of the notion that people are morally equal is that no one is anyone's slave—and so that no one is the state's slave, or the slave of any state actor. Many defenses of state authority seem to treat the state's subjects effectively as slaves (to democratic parliaments and executives if not to kings).[3] On this view, the state's subjects' bodies and possessions are at the state's disposal, to be employed only at the state's sufferance. It should be clear that defenses of state authority and of state actors' attacks on other people's bodies and possessions that presume that those over whom the state claims authority, or those whom state actors attack, are—in effect if not in name—slaves will be unsuccessful to the extent that it can be shown, as I have sought to argue, that slavery is morally indefensible.[4] Claims that the state owns its subjects will not provide the needed warrants for state action and authority.

4. *There Is Ordinarily Good Reason to Treat Nonconsensual Authority as Illegitimate, and State Authority Is Nonconsensual*

The behavior of state actors, rooted in a rejection of peaceful, voluntary cooperation, requires some justification if it is to be legitimate. A common justification trades on the notion that people have consented, or should be treated as having consented, to obey the state. It is understandable that this justification focuses on consent, since there are good reasons to treat consent as a crucial condition for the appropriate exercise of authority.

(*i*) The notion of essential moral equality embodied in the Principle of Fairness is incompatible with anyone's possessing authority over others naturally or inherently. When authority is justified, therefore, it is always in order to ask what justifies it. *Consent* is an obvious and, given respect for others' autonomy rooted in moral equality and the importance of the free exercise of practical reasonableness as a basic aspect of welfare, ordinarily irrebuttable answer. It is obviously at least, therefore, a sufficient condition for the reasonable exercise of authority.

[3] *Cf.* Robert Nozick, Anarchy, State, and Utopia 290–92 (1974).

[4] *See* Chapter 2.V.B, *supra*.

(*ii*) Most of us would be unwilling as a general matter that things be done to us without our consent. It is thus unreasonable for us to do things to others without their consent.

(*iii*) Requiring consent as a condition of the legitimacy of the exercise of authority ensures that people will have options, since they will be able to withhold or withdraw consent from unsatisfactory regimes and choose alternatives that seem more appealing. The availability of options means, in turn, that alternatives that attract support will be able to flourish, while those that are not able to do so will, rightly, perish. A political–legal ecosystem that features consent, and therefore choice, will feature greater diversity and greater opportunities for worthwhile institutional possibilities to emerge.

(*iv*) The violation of consent in the imposition of authority will often, as with enslavement (a particularly extreme case of the imposition of nonconsensual authority), involve specific violations of the NAM.

These considerations do not suggest that *majority* consent is required, but that *each person's* consent is presumptively required if the exercise of authority over her is to be just. I do not claim to have shown that an absolute requirement of personal consent flows from the principles of practical reasonableness. I believe, however, that these principles do establish a presumption in favor of such a requirement.

While consent ought to be treated as a crucial condition for the exercise of authority, the claim that the state's subjects actually *have* consented in a verifiable way that might entitle the state to exercise authority over them is indefensible. There is no reason to suppose that anyone *could* give active, verifiable consent to the state's authority (consent under threat of violence is obviously suspect). And, even if one supposes that people *could* do so, there is no reason to believe that people in general have, in fact, done so.[5]

[5] I will not rehearse here the arguments others have offered, and I have summarized, elsewhere in support of this contention; *see, e.g.*, 1 LYSANDER SPOONER, NO TREASON (1867), *available at* http://lysanderspooner.org/node/44; 2 LYSANDER SPOONER, NO TREASON: THE CONSTITUTION (1867), *available at* http://lysanderspooner.org/node/63; 6 LYSANDER SPOONER, NO TREASON: THE CONSTITUTION OF NO AUTHORITY (1870), *available at* http://lysanderspooner.org/node/64; STEPHEN R.L. CLARK, CIVIL PEACE AND SACRED ORDER 71–92 (1988); STEPHEN R.L. CLARK, THE POLITICAL ANIMAL: BIOLOGY, ETHICS, AND POLITICS 23–39 (1999); LESLIE GREEN, THE AUTHORITY OF THE STATE (1990); JOSEPH RAZ, THE AUTHORITY OF LAW: ESSAYS ON LAW AND MORALITY (1979); A. JOHN SIMMONS, MORAL PRINCIPLES AND POLITICAL OBLIGATIONS (1981); M.B.E. Smith, *Is There a Prima Facie Obligation to Obey the Law?*, 82 YALE L.J. 950 (1973); Charles W. Johnson, *Can Anybody Ever Consent to the State?*, RAD GEEK PEOPLE'S DAILY, Jan. 8, 2009, http://radgeek.com/gt/2009/01/08/can_anybody; GARY CHARTIER, THE CONSCIENCE OF AN ANARCHIST: WHY IT'S TIME TO SAY GOOD-BYE TO THE STATE AND BUILD A FREE SOCIETY 5–10 (2011); CRISPIN SARTWELL, AGAINST THE STATE: AN INTRODUCTION TO ANARCHIST POLITICAL THEORY (2008); JAN NARVESON, YOU AND THE STATE: A SHORT INTRODUCTION TO POLITICAL PHILOSOPHY 183–201 (2008); AEON SKOBLE, DELETING THE STATE: AN ARGUMENT ABOUT GOVERNMENT (2008); CAROLE PATEMAN, THE PROBLEM OF

5. *The Idea That State Actors Are Entitled to Demand Obedience Is, at Minimum, Hard to Defend*

State actors characteristically regard themselves, and expect others to regard them, as legitimate sources of authority, able to insist on compliance with their demands *for moral reasons*. But some sort of defense is needed if this seemingly problematic claim is to be credible. The claim is problematic because there is no natural right to rule; because, if no one is a slave, then it follows by implication that no one can be the state's slave; and because there is little reason to believe that states enjoy their authority in virtue of the consent of their subjects. There is thus, at minimum, a very serious question about the viability of state claims to legitimacy.

D. State Actors' Interference with Other People's Possessions Needs to Be Warranted because of Their Inconsistency with the Baseline Rules

The baseline rules specify that a physical object may justly be possessed by someone when she (*i*) takes effective possession of it at a time when it is not justly claimed by anyone or (*ii*) receives it voluntarily from a just possessor. The rules entitle a just possessor to use her possessions at her discretion (except, of course, in cases in which she uses them to attack others' bodies or possessions). The state does not acquire possessions in either of these ways. Instead, it takes possessions either (*i*) by demanding that just possessors give it their possessions when it tells them to do so, while maintaining that they are obligated to obey it or (*ii*) threatening just possessors that it will use force against them if they do not surrender these possessions, in either case denying their exclusive control over their justly acquired possessions. Unless state actors are morally entitled to demand others' possessions, their demanding or forcible taking of these possessions renders them thugs, bandits, social parasites.

And, of course, even if someone *were* morally required to obey a given demand from a given state actor, it would not follow that the state actor was necessarily entitled to use *force* to secure compliance with the demand. As a general matter, this obviously is not the case: someone may be morally required to maintain a sexually

POLITICAL OBLIGATION: A CRITICAL ANALYSIS OF LIBERAL THEORY (1985). There is a particularly rich discussion of multiple theories of state legitimation in MICHAEL HUEMER, THE PROBLEM OF POLITICAL AUTHORITY: AN EXAMINATION OF THE RIGHT TO COERCE AND THE DUTY TO OBEY (2013). For an alternate view, *see* GRISEZ & BOYLE, *supra* note 1, at 25–34. I believe Charles Johnson is right that there is a serious problem with the claim that people could, in principle, consent to the authority of a monopolistic state, given the threat the state poses to those who don't consent; but even if the question of consent were an empirical one, the state would be in trouble: *see* Scott Rasmussen, *New Low: 17% Say U.S. Government Has Consent of the Governed*, RASMUSSEN REPORTS, Aug. 7, 2011, http://www.rasmussenreports.com/public_content/politics/general_politics/august_2011/new_low_17_say_u_s_government_has_consent_of_the_governed.

exclusive relationship with his partner, but this does not mean that his partner may forcibly drag him away from a liaison with someone else. Whether it's appropriate to use force will depend on the relevant moral constraints. And the baseline rules seem to yield quite substantial constraints on anyone's forcible taking of someone else's possessions.

Thus, if state actors were justified in taking other people's possessions without their consent, it would need to be the case either (*i*) that they deserved obedience when they commanded people to surrender their possessions *and* were entitled to use force to compel obedience (since it is not the case that force may be used to compel performance of every moral duty), or (*ii*) that they were entitled to take people's possessions even when not owed obedience. To ground the first sort of claim, it would be necessary to show that state actors were owed duties of obedience (since, again, there is no natural right to rule), and to ground *either* sort, it would be necessary to show that the baseline rules ought to be altered to permit state actors' interference with people's possessions.

E. State Actors' Attacks on People's Bodies Require Justification in Virtue of the Principle of Respect and the Principle of Fairness

State actors regularly attack people's bodies. Some kinds of attacks are ruled out *tout court* by the Principle of Respect. Others would be permissible only if they were consistent with the Principle of Fairness, which it seems likely they would be only if state actors' interference with people's possessions were justified.

State actors could not reasonably use force against people's bodies to subject them to retributive punishment or to deter them from engaging in future conduct the state actors regarded as undesirable. That's because neither retribution nor deterrence provides any independent justification for anyone's use of force against people's bodies.[6] The Principle of Respect unequivocally rules out these justifications for the use of force.

State actors *could* obviously use force to defend themselves when engaged in otherwise legitimate activities. If, for instance, they were entitled to take other people's possessions under some circumstances, they *might* be justified in using force to repel attempts to keep them from doing so (though of course they might not be). But *whether* they were entitled to take people's possessions would depend on whether the baseline rules should be altered to permit them to do so, and perhaps also on whether they were entitled to people's obedience. And, if they weren't, they obviously wouldn't be entitled to use force in the course of what would be, in effect, theft, though there might be other circumstances in which they might use force legitimately.

[6] *See* Chapter 5.II.C, *infra*.

F. The Things State Actors Do, and Their Expectation That Other People Will Comply with Their Orders, Are Presumptively Unreasonable

State actors frequently do not seem committed to peaceful, voluntary cooperation. They demand that others cooperate with them unwillingly, and they use force to compel acquiescence in their demands or to take resources they cannot obtain peacefully. Their claims to enjoy legitimate authority appear problematic. No one is born with spurs on her heels, just as no one is born with a saddle on her back. People are inherently equal, as in their (limited, defensive) right to use force against each other. No one is a slave—so no one is the state's slave. And if putative slaves have no duties to their putative masters, it is hard to see how, in general, people could have duties to obey the state without consenting to its authority. However, people haven't, in general, even professed to consent to the state's authority, and it is not clear they *could* do so, given the alternatives the state presents to those who challenge its rule.

The problematic character of state actors' claims to legitimacy is shared by their forcible interference with people's bodies and possessions. The Principle of Respect precludes retributive or deterrent attacks on people's bodies, and the Principle of Fairness rules out the taking of possessions by state actors (with the effect that state actors cannot reasonably claim, at least in ordinary circumstances, that they are entitled to use force to defend themselves in the course of this kind of taking). It seems clear that state actors' claims to authority and attacks on other people's bodies and possessions—their uncooperative, non-peaceful behavior, their refusal to allow others to cooperate peacefully and voluntarily—could be legitimate, if at all, only with some special, and substantial, justification.

In short: there is good reason to regard the exercise of nonconsensual authority as unreasonable—sufficiently good reason that a strong presumption against the exercise of this kind of authority can reasonably be said to have been established. Similarly, there is good reason to regard the state's violation of the baseline rules as in need of a very robust justification if it is to be reasonable.

IV. THE STATE IS NOT NEEDED TO ENSURE PEACEFUL, VOLUNTARY COOPERATION

A. Peaceful, Voluntary Cooperation Can Happen without the State's Assistance

People can and do cooperate peacefully and voluntarily in the absence of the state.[7] In order to overcome the strong presumption against nonconsensual rule, attacks on

[7] As Matt Zwolinski reminds me, a pessimistic induction seems to be waiting in the wings: if stateless societies are viable, we would expect to see some in existence; since we don't, we might conclude

people's bodies, and systematic interference with people's possessions, an argument for the state would need to show that the state offered people something important that they couldn't provide for themselves—that, say, peaceful, voluntary cooperation couldn't be anticipated in the state's absence (Section B). But in fact it can. People might reasonably be expected to cooperate peacefully and (in general) voluntarily for several mutually reinforcing reasons: because engaging in some kinds of peaceful cooperation has immediate positive consequences and because declining to engage in some other varieties has immediate negative ones (Section C); because they are concerned about their reputations and the likelihood that they will be able to interact fruitfully with others in the future (Section D); because they want to avoid various sorts of nonviolent social sanctions (Section E); because there may be biological predispositions to engage in cooperative behavior (Section F); because of social norms they have internalized, habits they have adopted, and social conventions they have embraced (Section G); because they have personally accepted relevant moral requirements mandating peaceful cooperation (Section H); because they accept legal requirements mandating peaceful cooperation as legitimately meriting their support (Section I); or because they do not wish to engage in aggressive conduct that will be restrained by force (Section J). And state actors are unlikely to be untrustworthy sources of social order (Section K). In short: the social order that

that stateless societies aren't viable. But of course it is possible to challenge this argument on at least two grounds: one might argue that we *have*, in fact, seen examples of stable stateless social orders, *or* one might argue (whether as a complement or as an alternative) that significant factors which render a stateless society potentially viable did not obtain in the past. Certainly, while the facts to which this pessimistic induction alludes could reasonably be seen as troubling to overly facile defenders of anarchism, appealing to any or all of several relevant factors might serve to undermine the threat it could seem to pose to anarchism. (*i*) There do, in fact, seem to have been multiple complex societies that have been either entirely or almost stateless, *see* CHARTIER, *supra* note 5, at 19–24; the truth of the argument's initial premise is not, at any rate, quite so obvious as it might first appear to be. (*ii*) Ideological mystification—of which the divine right of kings is a good, but hardly the only, example—helps to keep people from resisting state power. (*iii*) Lack of awareness, understanding, or appreciation of practical alternatives to top-down social organization tends to limit people's willingness to resist or opt out of the state. (*iv*) The viability of a stateless society depends on the existence and wide dissemination of social norms calling for peaceful, voluntary cooperation, and not all societies have embraced such norms. (*v*) To the extent that stateless societies *are* absent from the scene, this may be a comment on the ability of states to snap up such societies, not on those societies' inherent instability. We've never had the opportunity to observe a confrontation between a developed, sophisticated stateless society and a state; rather, states tend to pounce on disorganized and chaotic stateless regions, rather than organized and otherwise stable societies. *These* sorts of societies, if they could survive past state depredation, might prove thoroughly viable. For some general theoretical treatments of social order without the state, on which I rely in the remainder of this Section, *see, e.g.*, ANARCHY, STATE, AND PUBLIC CHOICE (Edward P. Stringham ed., 2005) [*hereinafter* CHOICE]; ANTHONY DE JASAY, THE STATE 35–52 (1998); MICHAEL TAYLOR, COMMUNITY, ANARCHY, AND LIBERTY (1982) [hereinafter TAYLOR, COMMUNITY]; MICHAEL TAYLOR, THE POSSIBILITY OF COOPERATION (1987) [hereinafter TAYLOR, COOPERATION].

safeguards peaceful, voluntary cooperation can and should be fostered in multiple, complementary ways without the state's involvement (Section L).[8]

That the state is not necessary for the occurrence of peaceful, voluntary cooperation is a reflection of the sort of verdict a sensible anarchism must render on the question of human nature. The sort of anarchism I seek to defend here seeks to take people as it finds them. It does not begin with a cynical picture of persons as exclusively concerned with their own well-being and incapable of respecting the rights or caring for the interests of others (though it does not assume that everyone is equally virtuous or that people in positions of power and influence are similar in character to randomly selected members of the population). Nor does it endorse a romantic view of persons as essentially good or of human nature as dramatically malleable and capable of being remade by politics. Instead, it treats persons as the mixtures of generosity and greed, openness and bigotry, benevolence and detachment, decency and malice, respect and aggressiveness, that we know from our encounters with others and our reflection on our own characters.[9] Building on its realistic conception of human nature, it maintains that a combination of factors can ground a consistent and predictable pattern of peaceful, voluntary cooperation. At the same time, it seeks to foster the maintenance of institutions that will minimize the ability of the minority of agents who are inclined to behave unreasonably to harm others.

B. The Strong Presumption against Nonconsensual Rule and Noninterference with People's Justly Acquired Possessions Cannot Be Overcome by the Claim That the State Is Needed to Safeguard Cooperation

Even if the authority of the state can be shown to be distinguishable in morally relevant ways from that of a slave-master, the strong presumption against nonconsensual rule must be overcome if state authority is to be legitimate. And it would need to be shown that the baseline rules ought to be altered to permit the state's systematic

[8] The viability of a legal regime depends on the more basic viability of the social norms and practices and structures that are quite distinct from the law and that may help to maintain order quite apart from the operation of legal institutions. The laws upheld by a just legal regime are among the sources of peaceful, voluntary cooperation, but they are hardly the only sources.

[9] *Cf.* Yochai Benkler, The Penguin and the Leviathan: How Cooperation Triumphs over Self-Interest (2011); Matt Ridley, The Origins of Virtue: Human Instincts and the Evolution of Cooperation (1996); Alfie Kohn, The Brighter Side of Human Nature: Altruism and Empathy in Everyday Life (1992); Kristen Renwick Monroe, The Heart of Altruism: Perceptions of a Common Humanity (1996); Frans B.M. de Waal, Good Natured: The Origins of Right and Wrong in Humans and Other Animals (1997); Elliott Sober & David Sloan Wilson, Unto Others: The Evolution and Psychology of Unselfish Behavior (1997); Robert Wright, The Moral Animal: Why We Are the Way We Are (1995); Samuel Bowles, A Cooperative Species: Human Reciprocity and Its Evolution (2011).

interference with possessions justly acquired in accordance with the rules and its attacks on people's bodies to foster this interference.

There is good reason to accept several propositions that seem to render state authority and state actors' characteristic behaviors deeply problematic.

(*i*) Authority, to be legitimate, must be consensual.

(*ii*) Every actor should conform her conduct to the baseline possessory rules. Systematic interference with people's justly acquired possessions could be appropriate only if it were reasonable for the baseline rules to take a form significantly different from the one I've outlined here, one that allowed for the taking of justly acquired possessions by state actors.

(*iii*) No one should use force for retributive or deterrent purposes. She should not use force for defensive purposes except to protect herself against an unjust attack. She should thus defend herself by force against someone trying to stop her from taking his possessions only if she really is justified in interfering with the possessions (so that her target's use of force against her really counts as an unjust attack).

It is difficult to see how the cluster of presumptions against nonconsensual rule and in favor of the baseline rules in the form in which I have defended them here could be overcome apart from showing that the state was necessary to the achievement of some significant good. It is arguable that the most obvious candidate would be the good of safeguarding peaceful, voluntary cooperation, given its status as an aspect of human fulfillment and its role as a precondition and facilitator of diverse ways of flourishing.[10]

Perhaps someone might value the safeguards for peaceful, voluntary cooperation she regarded the state as essential to delivering *so* highly that, because the state was (ex hypothesi) necessary to the provision of these safeguards, she would be willing to accept the state's authority in order to ensure their availability. If she were willing to do this, she would be warranted in concluding, it would not be unfair of her to

[10] I focus on the task of safeguarding peaceful, voluntary cooperation because it makes the achievement of other valuable goals possible, and because it has been the focus of state apologists from Hobbes to the present. The other obvious candidates for the putatively essential state function justifying nonconsensual rule and interference with people's justly acquired possessions might be (*i*) providing vital public goods and (*ii*) responding to the challenge of economic deprivation and insecurity. But once it is apparent that, as I argue in Part IV, people can reasonably be expected to cooperate peacefully and voluntarily in the state's absence, neither the problem of public goods nor the problem of poverty looks especially daunting. I argue in Part V, *infra*, that there will be good reason to expect people to provide public goods in the state's absence. I maintain in Part VI.C.9–10, *infra*, that the state plays a key role in *causing* the problem of poverty and the marginalization of the economically vulnerable. And I suggest in Chapter 6.III, *infra*, that non-state legal institutions could foster the redistribution of wealth and make possible the alleviation of poverty in the state's absence.

subject *others* to the state's authority. And someone else, disinclined to accept the state's authority, might regard himself as required to do so because he judged that it really was necessary as a means of safeguarding peaceful, voluntary cooperation. The occurrence of this kind of cooperation is obviously beneficial to (almost) everyone. So accepting state authority might be morally required as a matter of fairness to those—almost everyone—who could be expected to benefit were peaceful, voluntary cooperation safeguarded.

Thus, in short, if state action were an essential means of safeguarding peaceful, voluntary cooperation, state actors might behave reasonably when they demanded obedience, interfered with others' justly acquired possessions, and used force to defend themselves against those seeking to impede the performance of state functions that were, ex hypothesi, legitimate (i.e., necessary to safeguarding peaceful, voluntary cooperation). In this case, the Principle of Respect would not preclude the use of force to defend those maintaining the state (since those attacking them to prevent them from performing state functions would be doing so unjustly). And it might be consistent with the Principle of Fairness to understand the baseline rules as permitting whatever interference with people's just possessory claims could be shown to be necessary to maintain the state.

But of course opting to accept state authority or impose it on others could not be simply a matter of arbitrary preference on the part of someone supporting the creation and maintenance of the state. Her underlying belief in the state's necessity as a protector of peaceful, voluntary cooperation would need to be *reasonable*. The problem, however, is that there is good reason to believe that peaceful, voluntary cooperation could occur in the state's absence. This kind of cooperation has been evident at various points in history. Further, of course, it characterizes the relationship of states (and of people subject to different states) in today's world, since no super-state exists to regulate their interactions.[11] And this kind of cooperation appears probable

[11] *See, e.g.*, CHARTIER, *supra* note 5, at 19–24; TAYLOR, COOPERATION, *supra* note 7, at 166; Jeffrey Rogers Hummel, *Tullock on Anarchy*, *in* CHOICE, *supra* note 7, at 200, 202 (noting the non-state organization of Native American tribes); Peter T. Leeson, *One More Time with Feeling: The Law Merchant, Arbitration, and International Trade*, INDIAN J. INT'L TRADE, special issue, Sept., 2007, at 29; Y Paul Milgrom, Douglas North & Barry Weingast, *The Role of Institutions in the Revival of Trade: The Law Merchant, Private Judges, and the Champagne Fairs*, 2 ECON. & POL. 1 (1990); David D. Friedman, *Private Creation and Enforcement of Law: A Historical Case*, 8 J. LEG. STUD. 399 (1979); Joseph R. Peden, *Property Rights in Celtic Irish Law*, *in* ANARCHY AND THE LAW: THE POLITICAL ECONOMY OF CHOICE 565 (Edward P. Stringham ed., 2007) [*hereinafter* ANARCHY AND THE LAW]; ROBERT ELLICKSON, ORDER WITHOUT LAW: HOW NEIGHBORS SETTLE DISPUTES (1994); TERRY L. ANDERSON & PETER J. HILL, THE NOT SO WILD, WILD WEST: PROPERTY RIGHTS ON THE FRONTIER (2003); PETER T. LEESON, THE INVISIBLE HOOK: THE HIDDEN ECONOMICS OF PIRATES (2009); Peter T. Leeson, *Better off Stateless: Somalia before and after Government Collapse*, 35 J. COMP. ECON. 689 (2007); Benjamin Powell, Ryan Ford & Alex Nowrasteh, *Somalia after State Collapse: Chaos of Improvement?*, 67 J. ECON. BEH. & ORG. 657 (2008). *Cf.* Stephen Edward Sachs,

for a range of additional, more general, reasons, in virtue of which the claim that state authority is necessary for its occurrence appears thoroughly implausible.

C. Concern with Immediate Consequences Can Readily Motivate Cooperative Behavior

Peaceful, voluntary cooperation can frequently be expected even on the part of agents utterly unconcerned with others or with the long-term consequences of their actions. Any peaceful, voluntary exchange (direct or indirect) confers some desired benefit on each party, so cooperating in such an exchange is of immediate benefit to each participant. And cooperation can also enable rational actors to avoid immediate harms: to take the most obvious example, a rational agent could be expected to drive on the same side of the street as others simply to avoid injury. When cooperating with others yields immediate positive consequences, or when failing to cooperate yields immediate negative consequences, cooperation on the part of even minimally rational agents is easy to predict.

D. People Can Be Expected to Cooperate to Protect Their Opportunities for Future Interaction

If I expect to interact repeatedly with a given person, I have good reason to want her to trust me, and so to perform reliably in relation to her. And even if I do not intend to interact with her again, I still have good reason not to want to acquire the reputation of someone who is untrustworthy, since others will be disinclined to engage in future transactions with me. Further, the best way to acquire a reputation as a reliable person may be to *be* a reliable person: to develop habits that render one trustworthy; and, if this is so, the economic pressure to be reliable, to acquire a good reputation, will have positive spillover effects on people's behavior even when their reputations are not at stake.[12] And the same general principles will apply not only to cases in which the question is whether I will keep an agreement but also to cases

From St. Ives to Cyberspace: The Modern Distortion of the Medieval Law Merchant, 21 AM. U. L. REV. 685 (2006) (challenging the view expressed in the Milgrom et al. article); BRUCE BENSON, THE ENTERPRISE OF LAW: JUSTICE WITHOUT THE STATE (2011) (discussing a variety of non-state order-maintenance strategies from an economic perspective); Benjamin Powell & Edward Stringham, *Public Choice and the Economic Analysis of Anarchy: A Survey*, 140 PUB. CHOICE 503 (2009) (noting a variety of historical examples of non-state governance); HAROLD J. BERMAN, LAW AND REVOLUTION: THE FORMATION OF THE WESTERN LEGAL TRADITION (1983) (offering valuable insights into the diversity of legal institutions operating in medieval Europe). Thanks to Tom Palmer for emphasizing the significance of a number of these sources.

[12] *Cf.* REPUTATION: STUDIES IN THE VOLUNTARY ELICITATION OF GOOD CONDUCT (Daniel B. Klein ed., 1997).

in which the question is whether I can be counted on to avoid causing harm or whether I will take reasonable responsibility for harm I have caused.[13]

These kinds of mechanisms are especially effective, of course, in small communities in which people have regular face-to-face contact with each other—in which norms can be reinforced, conventional behavior observed and copied, and misdeeds sanctioned. But there is no reason to think that only in tiny, geographically self-contained communities could people be expected to take reputation into account when deciding how to interact with others.[14] Technology, in particular, makes it increasingly possible to assess and act on the past performance of people in different geographic regions from one's own and also of people currently in one's own region but without significant local records of performance. Further, in a setting in which past performance is rightly seen as crucial, mechanisms for evaluating reputations and enforcing reputation- or past-performance-based sanctions (say, by denying membership in an organized group of potential exchange partners) without the aid of high technology could be expected to emerge.[15] It is thus reasonable to anticipate that concerns with reputation and with continued access to groups with whose members they might want to engage would dispose people to engage in a range of cooperative behaviors (and perhaps to internalize motives that might render those behaviors instinctive).

E. People Can Be Expected to Cooperate to Avoid Nonviolent Social Sanctions

Acquiring a bad reputation will obviously be undesirable because it will limit opportunities for future interaction with others who will avoid someone with such a reputation because they have been or do not wish to be victimized by her. But someone will also have good reason to avoid acquiring such a reputation because others may take active steps to sanction her quite apart from avoiding her as a means of ensuring that they are not harmed by her. Not only those injured by bad behavior but also others acting in solidarity with them may protest, picket, strike, boycott, ostracize, or publicly shame in order to prevent, end, or remedy what they judge to be unfair or otherwise injurious conduct. And the awareness that they are likely to do so can effectively motivate someone to avoid or end such conduct and to compensate

[13] *Cf.* Peter Leeson, *Do Contracts Require Formal Enforcement?*, *in* CHOICE, *supra* note 7, at 67, 68–70.

[14] *See* ANTHONY DE JASAY, AGAINST POLITICS: ON GOVERNMENT, ANARCHY, AND ORDER 206–08 (1997); Christopher Coyne, *Social Interaction without the State*, *in* CHOICE, *supra* note 7, at 49, 54–56; Leeson, *supra* note 13, at 70–73.

[15] *See, e.g.*, Lisa Bernstein, *Opting out of the Legal System: Extralegal Contractual Relations in the Diamond Industry*, 21 J. LEG. STUD. 145 (1992); Edward P. Stringham, *The Extralegal Development of Securities Trading in Seventeenth-Century Amsterdam*, 43 Q. REV. ECON. & FIN. 521 (2003).

others when she is perceived to have engaged in it, since these nonviolent sanctions can result in both economic and social losses most people would very much prefer to avoid.

F. Biological Dispositions May Foster Cooperative Behavior

Given the advantages of cooperative behavior, there is good reason to think that genes which increase the likelihood that organisms will engage in this kind of behavior will be transmitted intergenerationally. A genetic inheritance predisposing people to engage in cooperative behavior will provide a useful foundation for spontaneous cooperation.[16]

G. People Can Be Expected to Cooperate in Virtue of Social Norms, Habits, and Conventions

People characteristically learn that others expect them to cooperate peacefully, and to interact in accordance with a variety of other more specific expectations. They characteristically follow conventions and internalize norms calling for peaceful cooperation (as well, of course, as norms of other sorts), so that these norms come to be accepted and acted on not as means of achieving goals external to them but as inherently worthwhile. The same is frequently true of habits acquired in homes, schools, and places of worship. Deeply ingrained ways of thinking and acting can dispose most people to avoid considering aggression as a live option in most situations.[17]

H. Morality Is a Crucial Source of Peaceful Cooperation

Behaving in a peaceful, cooperative fashion is frequently a function of people's compliance with what they take to be reasonable moral requirements. People support

[16] *See, e.g.*, PAUL J. ZAK, THE MORAL MOLECULE: THE SOURCE OF LOVE AND PROSPERITY (2012); ROBERT AXELROD, THE EVOLUTION OF COOPERATION (rev. ed., 2006); Stephen Jay Gould, *Kropotkin Was No Crackpot*, 106 NATURAL HIST. 12 (1997). *Cf.* Jason Osborne, *Jungle or Just Bush? Anarchy and the Evolution of Cooperation*, *in* CHOICE, *supra* note 7, at 24; AEON SKOBLE, DELETING THE STATE: AN ARGUMENT ABOUT GOVERNMENT (2008); MICHAEL SHERMER, THE MIND OF THE MARKET: COMPASSIONATE APES, COMPETITIVE HUMANS, AND OTHER TALES FROM EVOLUTIONARY ECONOMICS (2008). *Cf.* STEPHEN R.L. CLARK, THE NATURE OF THE BEAST: ARE ANIMALS MORAL? (1982).

[17] On forming and following norms and conventions, *see, e.g.*, CHRISTINA BICCHIERI, THE GRAMMAR OF SOCIETY: THE NATURE AND DYNAMICS OF SOCIAL NORMS (2005); ERIC POSNER, LAW AND SOCIAL NORMS (2002); ELLICKSON, *supra* note 11; ELINOR OSTROM, GOVERNING THE COMMONS: THE EVOLUTION OF INSTITUTIONS FOR COLLECTIVE ACTION (1990); DAVID LEWIS, CONVENTION: A PHILOSOPHICAL STUDY (1969).

norms, rules, and institutions they take to be substantively appropriate on moral grounds. Neither concern about the nonviolent reactions of others nor fear of retaliatory aggression is needed to prompt respectful, fair, or compassionate behavior much of the time. This is especially true when moral principles track stable social conventions, which I have already suggested that they should in the case of the baseline possessory rules. The state isn't needed to prompt social order when people follow internalized moral principles, as they frequently do.[18]

Accepting moral requirements could also dispose people to conform their behavior to some legal requirements. As I argue in Chapter 5, formal legal regimes could perfectly well operate without the state. People who accept particular moral requirements would presumably be especially inclined to accept legal requirements promulgated by such regimes if the legal requirements tracked the moral requirements they accepted—if they regarded the legal requirements as substantively legitimate.

Obviously, conformity with moral requirements will ensure respect for social norms and legal rules in a stateless society only, in general, to the extent that they do tend to track the demands of morality. The state's use of force is most needed to prompt conformity with its demands when those demands seem least consistent with the requirements of morality or of prudentially beneficial social conventions. And it is precisely this distance between the moral and the prudential on the one hand and what is required by the state on the other that raises serious questions about the desirability of the state in the first place. The state may, indeed, be needed to ensure that people obey the state's own commands when these commands don't flow from moral requirements, but this is an argument *against* the state: it certainly doesn't count in favor of the state to maintain that only the state can ensure conformity with demands by the state that wouldn't be made in the state's absence. Unlike the sort of social order created and maintained by the state, a society rooted in peaceful, voluntary cooperation would not depend on the state's activity, in part precisely because legal rules could be expected to

[18] *Cf.* MORAL MARKETS: THE CRITICAL ROLE OF VALUES IN THE ECONOMY (Paul J. Zak ed., 2008); Edward P. Stringham, *Embracing Morals in Economics: The Role of Internal Moral Constraints in a Market Economy*, 78 J. ECON. BEH. & ORG. 98 (2011). It may plausibly be argued that the prevalence of some deeply internalized moral requirements (calling for trust and trustworthiness) within a society, and the recognition by the society's members that they can count on each other to adhere to these requirements, plays a crucial role in fostering the society's economic development; *see* DAVID C. ROSE, THE MORAL FOUNDATION OF ECONOMIC BEHAVIOR (2011). There is thus a case to be made that there will be ongoing sociocultural pressure in favor of embracing these requirements throughout a society, and the fact that there is suggests that we have some reason to expect adherence to moral requirements that foster peaceful, voluntary cooperation. (Rose's point is that culture is an important variable here, but I'm suggesting that we might expect a long-term convergence on prosperity-producing cultural values.)

coincide more closely with social expectations and moral norms absent the state's coercive interference.

I. People Can Be Expected to Cooperate because They Accept Legal Requirements Mandating Cooperation as Legitimate

Even when people might not be inclined to accept particular legal requirements on substantive grounds, they may be expected to support these requirements if they judge them to emerge from proper *procedures*. People are inclined to uphold norms, rules, and institutions that they believe to be legitimate, that have suitable origins, even when their substance may not necessarily seem appealing.[19] If someone believes that a particular rule emerges from a procedure or mechanism she views as legitimate because she has consented to it (or because she regards it as legitimate for some other reason), she may be inclined to support the rule's enforcement, even if she might have some disagreement with the substance of the rule. Thus, people can be expected to comply with what they regard as legitimate rules fostering social order, and the fact that legal rules in a stateless society would, as I argue in Chapter 6, be rooted in actual consent could be expected to render compliance especially likely, given the predictable link between the consensual nature of a legal regime and the perceived legitimacy of its enactments.

There's also an indirect argument here: defenders of the state often suppose that constitutional constraints will keep state actors from engaging in predatory behavior. But anyone who expects state actors to adhere to constitutional requirements should surely expect ordinary people (who can, for multiple reasons, be expected to be better-behaved on average than state officials) to respect what they regard as legitimate legal constraints on their behavior. The sorts of reasons defenders of constitutions offer in support of the conviction that state power can be appropriately cabined should provide them with reason to acknowledge that ordinary people don't need the threat of Leviathan hanging over their heads in order to uphold what they take to be legitimate rules. So it's reasonable to expect people in a stateless society to cooperate peacefully and voluntarily in virtue of (among other things) what they take to be legitimate rules.

[19] *Cf.* Tom R. Tyler, Why People Obey the Law (2d ed., 2006). Of course, that people regard a procedure as a source of legitimation does not show that it is, in fact, a reasonable source of legitimation. Someone might regard a particular mechanism as legitimating out of habit, or because she believes incorrectly that it has been endorsed by God, or because she accepts some false story about the mechanism, or because she accepts a true story about that mechanism along with the false belief that stories of the relevant kind are reasonably understood as legitimating.

J. Legitimate Force Can Be Used to Safeguard Cooperation

1. *Appropriately Cabined Force Could Help to Promote Peaceful, Voluntary Cooperation*

The actual or threatened use of force could serve to restrain predatory behavior in a stateless society. It could be deployed effectively by non-state legal regimes (Section 2). Legal regimes using force in a stateless society would not, contrary to a common objection, be more dangerous than the state itself (Section 3). Thus, such regimes could be counted on to contribute to the prevention of predation through the use of force (Section 4).

2. *Non-State Legal Regimes Could Use Force to Prevent, End, or Remedy Predatory Behavior*

Force is sometimes needed to prevent, end, or remedy aggression, and some people may cooperate peacefully with others only because they fear being restrained by force. The threat of force is not, in general, primarily responsible for disposing people to cooperate peacefully, but it can obviously contribute to restraining those who might otherwise engage in aggressive conduct. People will predictably and (to the extent that they conform their requirements to the NAM) reasonably employ self-help against those they perceive to have engaged, or to be poised to engage, in aggression against them. And of course, within the limits set by the NAM, they may appropriately ask others to use force with them or on their behalf to prevent, end, or remedy aggression.[20] Where force in such cases is used in a manner consistent with the NAM, it can be a reasonable means of fostering and safeguarding peaceful cooperation. Because legal regimes in a stateless society could be expected to employ reasonable force to prevent, end, and remedy aggression, people in such a

[20] *See* Leeson, *supra* note 13, at 73–74. Non-state legal regimes (*see* Chapter 4) would obviously not be entitled to do anything their participants and workers were not themselves entitled to do. Such regimes could be expected to enforce standards to which people had actually consented, or which emerged from processes to which they had actually consented, and so would involve the exercise of no more authority than people would enjoy on their own. This would simultaneously ensure procedural and substantive legitimacy and minimize the number of legal requirements thus enforced. The use of force would be far less needed for ordinary order-maintenance without the state because of the contents and sources of the rules enforced in a stateless society. The state must rely on force as a primary source of the social order it seeks to maintain precisely because that order is very frequently *not* the kind of order people would choose for themselves. Because the requirements a non-state legal regime enforced would be rooted in consent, and because the interests protected using self-help would reflect simple and widely shared moral convictions, the appeal to force would be considerably less significant as a source of social order in a stateless society.

society likely to engage in aggression absent the threat of force can be expected (in general) to avoid aggressive behavior and so to cooperate with others peacefully. Legal regimes in a stateless society can promote peaceful cooperation using force just as the state's defenders suppose that it can do.

3. *A Society Filled with Non-State Legal Regimes Need Not Be Riven with Endless Violent Conflict*

i. Non-state legal regimes need not be expected to be predators

Defenders of the state might argue that if multiple legal regimes in a given region could engage in or license legitimate force, these regimes could be expected to engage in violence against each other or to back participants in violent conflicts. But while there is no way to guarantee that a legal regime in a stateless society wouldn't be a rogue (just as there's no effective mechanism for ensuring that states will avoid engaging in inter-state violence), regimes need not be *expected* to be violent or to license violence by participants. Factors that dispose people in general to engage in peaceful, voluntary cooperation could be expected to lead to positive behavior on the part of many regime officials (Subsubsection ii). Concerns about prompting participants to exit would discourage regime officials from engaging in or encouraging predatory behavior (Subsubsection iii). Regimes could be expected to want to avoid the costs associated with predatory violence (Subsubsection iv). And it's worth emphasizing that states are more likely to engage in predatory behavior because of special characteristics that non-state legal regimes wouldn't exhibit (Subsubsection v) and that special temptations to engage in predatory behavior are associated with being a state official, whether acting officially or unofficially (Subsubsection vi). Non-state actors can be trusted to keep the peace, which state actors too often cannot (Subsubsection vii).

ii. The kinds of restraints that encourage cooperation generally would tend to dispose the officials of non-state legal regimes to behave peaceably

Proponents of the view that legal regimes in a stateless society would engage in or encourage violence have to assume, very implausibly, that only the perceived legitimacy of laws and constitutions keeps state officials in check and that, because overarching legal rules wouldn't bind non-state legal regimes, such regimes, unrestrained by a territorial monopolist, would all be rogues. However, formal legal constraints aren't the only sources of good behavior by state actors just as they aren't the only sources of good behavior by other people. The other factors I identify in this part as likely to lead to peaceful, voluntary cooperation in the state's absence can reasonably be expected to constrain the use of force by functionaries of legal regimes. In particular, there would be good moral and prudential reasons for regime participants to support and for regimes to adopt specific prohibitions on predatory behavior, and for regime officials to regard these prohibitions as procedurally legitimate and so to adhere to them. Given that these officials wouldn't enjoy any special legal rights not possessed by others, they could be expected not to exhibit the full range of negative characteristics typical of untrustworthy, power-hungry state officials, which likely flow in significant part from their special legal status.

iii. Non-state legal regimes would tend to be deterred from engaging in predatory behavior by the possibility of a range of costs

If regimes were consensual, people would be free to leave them, and participants could often be expected to leave a regime that engaged in predation against nonparticipants (*i*) to avoid bearing the extra costs directed associated with aggression; (*ii*) to avoid social sanctions imposed on those seen to be associated with a rogue regime; (*iii*) to distance themselves from the regime in order to avoid being, or to avoid being misperceived as being, involved in or supportive of its predatory behavior; and (*iv*) to reduce the likelihood that the regime would engage in predatory behavior against *them*. The threat that people would likely abandon predatory regimes would at least to some degree restrain regimes *ex ante*, and the fact that they *had* done so could weaken predatory regimes *ex post*.

iv. The threat of force might restrain rogue regimes

The threat of force by other regimes and by people engaged in self-help would tend to deter rogue regimes, and other regimes, in particular, would have good reason to take action to stop a regime engaged in predatory violence. Thus, one could argue that, while a stateless society would lack a dictator who qualified as a Hobbesian Leviathan, the entire network of social institutions engaged in dispute resolution and peacekeeping in a stateless society, provided it was viewed as legitimate, would qualify as a kind of Leviathan. (Contrary to appearances, even in Hobbes, Leviathan's efficacy, especially if Leviathan is a parliament and not a single ruler, is hard to understand or justify absent perceived legitimacy.)

v. States are more dangerous than non-state legal regimes would be because of the special temptations they confront

The state, as a monopolist, engages in all sorts of unaccountable violent acts, from wars to police raids on nonviolent people. States capitalize on their perceived legitimacy to enable them to engage in these kinds of acts with impunity. They are able to do so because they exclude alternatives, because they draw on forcible funding, because people tend to treat their violent acts as legitimate, and because they are not held legally accountable even for what are agreed to be abuses. In all these ways, states are clearly more dangerous than non-monopolistic legal regimes in a stateless society—which would lack forcible funding, which participants would be free to exit, which would be subject to legal liability for abuses (given inter-regime liability agreements), and which would enjoy only consent-based legitimacy, not the kind of all-encompassing sovereign power states (implausibly) claim.

vi. State officials are more liable to engage in predatory behavior than their counterparts in non-state legal regimes would be

State officials can be expected to engage in predatory behavior more frequently than agents of legal regimes in a stateless society.[21] A key reason is that state officials enjoy privileges and immunities that wouldn't be available to people acting without the cover of state authority. Free from the mystique and the state-made legal rules that protect state actors, agents of non-state legal regimes would not be viewed as immune to liability and could thus expect, for instance, to be held personally accountable for violating their regimes' rules. (Regimes that did not provide for this kind of liability could be expected to lose participants.) And regimes that allowed or encouraged their agents to engage in aggressive conduct could expect to be held accountable in multiple ways (via legal liability—in virtue of cross-regime dispute-resolution agreements—and perhaps also via the use of defensive force if they seemed unconcerned about acknowledging just legal limits on their actions), while also losing participants (because participants wouldn't likely want to be victimized by the regimes, because they wouldn't want to bear the extra costs associated with the regimes' abusive conduct, and because they wouldn't want to be associated in others' minds with abusive regimes). Regimes would thus have incentives to rein in rogue behavior. State officials, by contrast, frequently operate with impunity because their offices enable them to engage in aggressive acts, whether on behalf of the states for which they work or in their own immediate interests and those of their cronies. Any claim that state officials can be trusted to keep the peace as well as or better than workers in non-state legal regimes needs to be made in light of the recognition that states create distinctive opportunities for aggression.

vii. There is no reason either to expect non-state legal regimes to be aggressors or to ignore the risks that states and state officials will be aggressive in ways these regimes would not

In general, the same factors that can be expected to restrain predatory violence by states can be expected to restrain such violence by consensual legal regimes. Officials of non-state legal regimes, not possessed of the same privileges as state officials, could be expected to cooperate peacefully and voluntarily for the same reasons that people in general in a stateless society could be counted on to do so. Ease

[21] *Cf.* Section K, *infra*.

of exit, lack of compulsory funding, and the absence of the sense of moral entitlement that often affects state actors with special legal privileges could be expected to further reduce the likelihood that consensual legal regimes would engage in predatory violence. Non-state actors in a stateless society using force to restrain predatory behavior can be expected to adhere to what they regard as legitimate limits on their use of force. And not only can agents of non-state legal regimes reasonably be expected to avoid persistently engaging in predatory behavior—it is also important to emphasize that state actors often engage in this kind of behavior, both in the state's interest and in their own.

While defenders of the state frequently suppose that the threat of state force will keep ordinary people from engaging in predatory behavior, they may doubt that legal regimes in a stateless society could be trusted to use force responsibly. But consider the possibilities. (*i*) Suppose state actors have good motives and respond to social and moral constraints on their behavior. In this case, legal regime workers (who shouldn't be expected to operate with less admirable motivations than state actors) can be expected to do so as well. (*ii*) Suppose that state actors have bad motives but are nonetheless trustworthy for prudential reasons. In this case, non-state legal regime workers with bad motives can similarly be expected to be trustworthy. (*iii*) Perhaps state actors have bad motives and are untrustworthy, and thus can't be trusted. It might be the case that, in virtue of being selected and incentivized in different ways, non-state legal regime actors could be expected to be more trustworthy than state actors.[22] At worst, however, they could be expected to be untrustworthy just like state actors—but with less power. And this would hardly give anyone reason to prefer the state as a source of social order.

4. *Force Could Be among the Factors Used to Address the Problem of Predatory Behavior in a Stateless Society*

While people could be expected to cooperate peacefully and voluntarily for multiple reasons in a stateless society, legal regimes in such a society could threaten or use force to help prevent, end, or remedy predation just as proponents of the state expect it to do. The state's defenders might maintain that such regimes would themselves be dangerous sources of violence, but this expectation fails to take into account the factors that could be expected to restrain their misbehavior—both the same kinds of legitimacy-based constraints that defenders of the state must suppose keep state actors in line and a range of external incentives that non-state legal regimes, unlike states, are likely to confront—as well as the penchant for mischief on the part of state officials. Non-state legal regimes can use force to deal with predation without themselves

[22] *See* Chapter 2.IV.K, *infra*.

becoming predators or sources of chaos. And this means that force—defensive and remedial, not punitive or retaliatory or predatory—could reasonably be an effective means of ensuring peaceful, voluntary cooperation in a stateless society.

K. It Would Be Unwise to Trust State Officials to Foster Peaceful, Voluntary Cooperation

Whatever reasonable questions there might be about people's ability to cooperate peacefully and voluntarily in the state's absence, it is still worth emphasizing that state actors are insufficiently trustworthy to render them reliable defenders of peaceful, voluntary cooperation.[23]

Those who occupy significant decision-making positions in any state apparatus, whether they are elected or appointed, do not check their personal motivations at the door when they take up their offices. They are more likely than the average person to be ambitious and power-hungry, since being so increases the likelihood that one will want a powerful position and that one will succeed in securing it—in virtue both of drive and of the willingness. The sheer possession of organizational (and so, surely, political) power tends to bring out narcissistic and egotistical character traits and to dispose the powerful to ignore important facts and to misinterpret others' behavior. And coming to occupy a position of power over others can tend to incline someone to want to exercise the power her position affords and to maintain the institutional setting in virtue of which her position exists and she possesses power.[24]

The funds required to enable one to gain public prominence and to secure elected and appointed offices will often be used by donors to curry favor and manipulate, and those who do not need to depend on the provision of such funds by others may themselves be wealthy persons with quite specific ends to be served through the occupancy of this or that state office. Those who come to occupy state offices, even if, improbably, their intentions are good initially, will find themselves confronted both by the inherent temptations of power, since they can now do things they could not previously accomplish, and by the increased attention of those interested in suborning them and securing their loyalty. Government officials who leave office

[23] *See, e.g.*, F.A. Hayek, The Road to Serfdom 157–70 (Bruce Caldwell ed., 2007) (discussing the plausible notion that "the worst get on top"). *Cf.* William C. Mitchell & Randy T. Simmons, Beyond Politics: Markets, Welfare, and the Failure of Bureaucracy (1994); Benjamin Powell, *Public Choice and Leviathan*, *in* Choice, *supra* note 7, at 88, 91–95. *But cf.* Robert Higgs, *Public Choice and Political Leadership*, *in* Against Leviathan 41–44 (2004), *available at* http://www.independent.org/pdf/tir/tir_01_3_etc.pdf (noting that public choice analysis may make overly rosy assumptions about politicians' motivations); Frederick G. Bailey, Humbuggery and Manipulation: The Art of Leadership (1988).

[24] *Cf.* Philip Zimbardo, The Lucifer Effect: Understanding How Good People Turn Evil (2007).

can be expected to use their contacts to lobby on behalf of corporate clients—and to allow the knowledge that they will be able to do this to influence their behavior while in office; and those in office can be expected to be particularly responsive to the lobbying of former colleagues. And regulators can often be expected to enact policies that confer privileges on the industries they are expected to regulate simply in virtue of the fact that industry groups' expertise and focused interest allow them to shape regulators' decisions in the groups' own interests.

For all these reasons, state officials do not seem especially well positioned to promote peaceful, voluntary cooperation. They may, of course, seek to mask their pursuit of private goals as the promotion of peaceful, voluntary cooperation. But, whatever their rhetoric, there is little reason to give it any credit—both because, a priori, they can be expected to serve themselves and the wealthy and well-connected at the public's expense, and because considerable evidence suggests that this is precisely what they in fact do.

Constitutional constraints seem ill-designed to restrain the rapacity of state actors. State officials can be expected to parade their enthusiasm for such constraints while persistently seeking opportunities to violate them. While people in general are not inherently vicious, the proportion of the vicious among state actors is likely to be significantly greater than among members of the general population. So it makes little sense to look to state actors to protect ordinary people from those who wish to interfere with peaceful, voluntary cooperation: state actors themselves impede social cooperation with disturbing frequency.

This claim does not depend on a generally pessimistic view of human nature. My argument, instead, is that the people who exercise significant state power can't be trusted, not that people in general can't be. Those who exercise state power in a given population aren't likely to be just like randomly selected members of that population, both because of the traits that dispose and equip them to acquire state power and because of the influences that come to bear on them when they do acquire it.

L. The State Is Not Needed to Protect or Promote Peaceful, Voluntary Cooperation

It's certainly possible to imagine an argument for the conclusion that it would be reasonable for people to accept state authority, and that the baseline rules should be understood to permit the systematic taking by the state of people's justly acquired possessions, in order to ensure the protection of peaceful, voluntary cooperation. Such an argument might maintain that the presumption against consent as a precondition for legitimate authority, and in favor of the baseline rules in their undiluted form, could be overcome because a reliably peaceful, voluntary, cooperative social order could only be secured by the action of the state. It is notoriously difficult, if not impossible, to cabin the state's activities in such a way that it limits itself to safeguarding and fostering peaceful, voluntary cooperation. Even were it possible to do this, however, the state's authority would still not be justified. Peaceful, voluntary cooperation can clearly occur in the state's absence.[25]

Without the overhanging shadow of Leviathan, people could be expected to cooperate in support of peaceful, voluntary cooperation for purely prudential reasons—because cooperating seemed likely to yield immediate benefits or because noncooperation seemed immediately harmful or likely to hamper their chances to participate in mutually beneficial activities in the future or subject them to social sanctions of various sorts. They might cooperate because they were disposed to do so by their genes or by social norms, habits, and conventions. They might cooperate in fulfillment of specific moral requirements, in support of laws implementing such requirements, or in support of laws they take to have emerged from what they view as legitimate procedures. Indeed, since the state tends to impede the formation and expression of cooperative motives, by seeming to obviate them and by modeling anti-cooperative behavior, people could be *more* inclined to cooperate in its absence. And, of course, they might do so because they feared that they would be forced to cooperate—by a legal regime or by those injured by aggression resorting to self-help—if they do not do so in the absence of coercion. The various factors promoting peaceful (and, in general, voluntary) cooperation will tend to reinforce and sustain each other. Thus, peaceful, voluntary cooperation need not depend upon the existence and operation of the state. And, indeed, this is hardly surprising given that state actors are likely to be inclined to pursue their own ends and those of their cronies in ways that are likely to violate the norm of peaceful, voluntary cooperation and to interfere with the cooperative activities of others. People need not depend on the state to safeguard peaceful, voluntary cooperation, and they have little reason to trust it to do so.

An objector might seek to show that this conclusion was unlikely to be correct, arguing that, historically speaking, the state *has* been necessary to the occurrence of peace and prosperity, and that we know this because of the perceived correlation between the emergence of the state on the one hand and, on the other, the rise of complex civilizations and the decline in rates of violence. But other explanations for this observed relationship are available.[26]

It certainly seems quite possible that state formation is correlated with increasing peace and economic development because states are parasitic on these developments in the worst sense, rather than responsible for them. On this view, it would likely become profitable to establish a state ruling a given society only when the

[25] *See* CHARTIER, *supra* note 5, at 11–19.

[26] Thanks to Brian Doherty for a useful exchange related to this question.

society began to generate enough resources—in the state's absence—to render the extraction of a significant portion of those resources by a state apparatus worthwhile. And only when a society was sufficiently well developed that, even after the extraction of resources, people could be expected to enjoy enough material well-being not to respond with violence to the state's exaction of tribute would it be safe or economical to establish a state. In addition, even if it could be shown definitively that state action *did* bring about the occurrence of peaceful, voluntary cooperation in particular cases, it wouldn't follow that non-state institutions couldn't have achieved similar outcomes in similar cases.

The objector might maintain that the absence of such alternate institutions from the historical record was good evidence that similar outcomes couldn't have been achieved without the state. However, the state tends (often, though not always, forcibly) to crowd out alternatives, so it's hardly surprising that they might not be evident. And strategies designed to legitimate state power (mythological claims about the divine right of kings or the necessity of a Hobbesian Leviathan) might simultaneously boost the credibility of states as sources of social order and undermine the perceived appeal of alternatives to the state. Nonetheless, as I've already noted, there *have* been non-state sources of the order needed for peaceful, voluntary cooperation in various epochs and cultures.

Cooperating peacefully and voluntarily—including cooperating to prevent, end, or remedy attacks on bodies and justly acquired possessions—is ordinarily a matter of conferring particular benefits on particular people. When it is, the people who provide these benefits are supplying what are, in the economist's sense, *private goods* (albeit ones with positive externalities). A private good is one that can be supplied to some consumers and not others at the provider's discretion. Private goods can be supplied without essential difficulty by people cooperating peacefully and voluntarily, whether as gifts or as paid-for services. [27] Sometimes, however, cooperating peacefully and voluntarily involves or depends on people's supplying *public goods*. A public good is one that is unavoidably available to all members of a given public if it is available to any. It is often supposed that the state is essential to the production of vital public goods because these goods will be undersupplied unless provided on the basis of forcible funding. Ex hypothesi, they will be undersupplied because—since they will

[27] They can therefore be funded on a pay-as-you go basis, in accordance with the *cost principle* that legal structures ought to ensure that people internalize the costs of their own choices. It might seem reasonable to respond to advocates of the cost principle that expecting people to pay for the services they receive will place the poor at a significant disadvantage. But I am inclined to think that the right way to address this risk is to eliminate structural poverty and to reduce the risk of (and, through appropriate social norms, the risks associated with) accidental poverty (*see* Chapter 6.III), and so to facilitate access by everyone to the relevant goods and services by increasing the wealth of the worst-off, rather than, as a structural matter, severing the link between payment and services rendered, which would run the risk of increasing inefficiency in the pricing and delivery of the relevant goods and services.

necessarily be available to all the members of a relevant public if available to any—absent coercion, people can be expected to contribute little, if at all, to their provision. In fact, however, peaceful, voluntary cooperation can supply these goods, too.

V. THE STATE IS NOT NEEDED TO ENSURE PEACEFUL, VOLUNTARY COOPERATION IN THE PRODUCTION OF CRUCIAL PUBLIC GOODS

A. The Putative Need for Public Goods Does Not Justify the State's Existence and Operation

The need to produce public goods does not justify the existence and operation of the state. A public good is available to every member of a given group if it is available to any member (Section B). While there are genuine public goods, many goods that might initially be thought to be public are in fact not (Section C). The Public Goods Argument holds that the existence and operation of the state are justified because important public goods cannot be produced at optimal levels in its absence (Section D). But this argument is unpersuasive. There is no credible way of giving objective content to the notion of an optimal supply level for a public good (Section E). Even if there were, however, public goods can, in fact, be supplied voluntarily without the state's involvement (Section F). The claim that a given public good is very important is insufficient to justify its being provided forcibly (Section G). It is not clear that the forcible provision of public goods by the state would be effective (Section H). And even if it could be shown that it was quite important to provide a given public good forcibly, it might still be reasonable to decline to understand the baseline rules as permitting the state's institutionalized use of force to provide the good (Section I). The putative value of public goods does not justify abandoning the principle that social life should be organized on the basis of peaceful, voluntary cooperation (Section J).

B. A Public Good Is Available to All When Available to Any

A good is public with respect to a given population if someone in the population can obtain it just as long as it is provided to any other member of the population.[28] The

[28] Anthony de Jasay has argued that perhaps *no* good is ultimately a public good—that it is simply more costly to exclude free riders from enjoying some goods. *See, e.g.*, ANTHONY DE JASAY, SOCIAL CONTRACT, FREE RIDE: A STUDY OF THE PUBLIC GOODS PROBLEM 66–67 (1989). But whether this is so obviously depends on background entitlements. It seems as if someone justly possessing land in a given geographically localized community could be excluded from enjoying the benefits of a preemptive strike on a gang of thugs who had already targeted the entire region in which the community was located for attack only by being excluded from the region itself and so deprived of access to the land. It seems that the kind of exclusion required to convert some public goods into private ones would be possible only given the absence of stable, legally protected possessory claims.

easier it is to free ride on others' provision of a given good, the more publicness the good tends to exhibit.

It is important to stress that calling something a public good says nothing about its importance or value. I might develop the capacity to change the color of the sky over a large region of the earth. Everyone in the relevant region might be able to see the resulting changes in the sky's colors, and many might find these changes attractive. The changed color of the sky might well qualify as a public good. But it would hardly be important under realistically conceivable circumstances.

C. Many Putatively Public Goods Are Not Genuinely Public, though Some Are

1. *Most Goods Are, in the Economic Sense, Private*

There are fewer authentic public goods than is frequently thought. Rectification of many environmentally mediated injuries to sentients' bodies and to possessions is a private good (Subsection 2). The same is true of what I will call *ordinary defense* against aggression (Subsection 3). The provision of some private goods does generate some positive externalities, but this doesn't render these goods public (Subsection 4), though subsets of the broader sets of environmentally rectificatory and defense-related goods *do* count as public, along, perhaps, with some kinds of social sanctions (Subsection 5). The range of private goods is thus broader than might initially be supposed (Subsection 6).

2. *The Good of Preventing, Ending, or Remedying Environmentally Mediated Injuries Is Often Private*

Specifying just possessory claims and identifying causal responsibility can ensure that particular persons and groups can take responsibility for preventing, ending, or remedying environmentally mediated injuries they undergo or cause. Clearly identifying just possessors of particular objects and protecting bodies and just possessory claims creates opportunities and incentives for people to take action to deal with, for instance, pollution. Whenever someone's actions threaten or cause harms to particular bodies or possessions, providing compensation for these injuries, as by means of a well-functioning tort law system, is a matter of providing clearly private goods; and, depending on the circumstances, preventing or ending them *directly* (as by injunction) may be as well. (The possibility that compensation may be required can obviously lead *indirectly* to preventing or ending the injuries; pursuing compensation is thus, in effect, a matter of providing a private good with positive externalities).

3. *The Good of Ordinary Defense against Aggression Is Private*

Ordinary defense against aggression seems to be a private good.[29]

By *ordinary defense*, I mean the defense of identifiable people or possessions against attacks targeting them. The provision of ordinary defense is a private good, and so one that can in principle be provided on a non-compulsory basis.[30] Ordinary defense is, after all, widely available *already* without forcible funding. Security services of all kinds are currently volunteered, self-provided, bought, and sold (as by private detectives and security guards) on a widespread basis. And, indeed, there is good reason to believe that effective resistance even to large-scale violence can be mounted on a grass-roots basis without the involvement of a territorial monopolist.[31]

In a stateless society, some person or group of people will be responsible for each possession which some defense provider is tasked with protecting. This follows simply from the fact that there will be no state to claim any possession in such a way that no person or group is responsible for it, and that any possession could thus be homesteaded by the person or group. Thus, ordinary defense would be the actual defense of particular people's bodies and possessions—an activity with specifiable beneficiaries. People protecting themselves or their loved ones, volunteers, or security workers could defend a particular body or possession against aggression even if they did not defend others. No matter how many bodies or possessions are being defended simultaneously, as long as specific defense providers focus on repelling attacks directed at particular bodies or possessions, so that there will be little reason to be a free rider, the defense of any one of these bodies or possessions will be a private good.[32]

[29] *But cf.* MITCHELL & SIMMONS, *supra* note 23, at 93; DAVID SCHMIDTZ, THE LIMITS OF GOVERNMENT: AN ESSAY ON THE PUBLIC GOODS ARGUMENT 56 (1991); DAVID GAUTHIER, MORALS BY AGREEMENT 271 (1986); TAYLOR, COMMUNITY, *supra* note 7, at 44–65; DAVID D. FRIEDMAN, THE MACHINERY OF FREEDOM: GUIDE TO A RADICAL CAPITALISM 135 (2d ed., 1989).

[30] *Cf.* Jeffrey Rogers Hummel & Don Lavoie, *National Defense and the Public Goods Problem*, *in* ARMS, POLITICS, AND THE ECONOMY 37 (Robert Higgs ed., 1990); Roderick T. Long, *Defending a Free Nation*, *in* ANARCHY AND THE LAW, *supra* note 11, at 149.

[31] *See* GENE SHARP & BRUCE JENKINS, CIVILIAN-BASED DEFENSE: A POST-MILITARY WEAPONS SYSTEM (1990); GENE SHARP & JOSHUA PAULSON, WAGING NONVIOLENT STRUGGLE: TWENTIETH CENTURY PRACTICE AND TWENTY-FIRST CENTURY POTENTIAL (2005); GENE SHARP, THE POLITICS OF NONVIOLENT ACTION (3 vols., 1973–85); ANDERS BOSERUP, WAR WITHOUT WEAPONS: NONVIOLENCE IN NATIONAL DEFENCE (1974). A strategy of nonviolent resistance to invaders can be defended on practical rather than narrowly moral grounds; I have nothing in particular to say about the practicality of such a strategy, except that (*i*) if it really is as effective as or more effective than strategies of forcible resistance to invasion, this fact would certainly have implications for the value of defensive strategies involving the state. Further (*ii*) there is doubtless something important to be learned from analyses of such strategies even if one judges some forms of forcible resistance to be at least sometimes just and efficacious.

[32] An organized aggressor with a technologically advanced military capability could seek to deploy overwhelming force against the residents of a stateless society, conquering them, as it were, from house

4. The Fact That a Private Good Generates Positive Externalities Does Not Make It a Public Good

Seeking compensation for an environmentally mediated injury that has already occurred, or seeking an injunction to prevent or end such an injury, obviously has the potential to yield benefits for people other than the one seeking compensation or injunctive relief. Seeking compensation in one case will send a message to those potentially responsible for environmentally mediated injuries in the future that they can expect to be required to provide compensation if they do so, and the prospect of having to pay compensation will tend to deter them from causing these injuries. In the nature of the case, an injunction preventing an environmentally mediated injury to one person's body or possessions from occurring or continuing will very often have the same effect on injuries to other people's bodies or possessions.

Similarly, the defense of any particular body or possession would doubtless generate some positive externalities.[33] It will frequently stop aggressors who would otherwise attack other bodies and possessions or reduce the likelihood that they will attack other bodies and possessions either by depleting their resources or creating a reasonable apprehension of harm. When an act of aggression is believed to be prevented or remedied, others contemplating the possibility of engaging in aggressive conduct may be deterred from doing so. Deterrence with respect to future harms committed specifically against those directly benefiting from order-maintenance activities—as harms against them are prevented, ended, or remedied—will be private goods. But potential aggressors will be deterred to some degree from engaging in harms against those who have not directly benefited from a particular instance of order-maintenance as well.

This does not seem likely to lead to an undersupply of the relevant goods, however (even assuming, *arguendo*, that it is possible to define optimal supply objectively, as I argue below that it is not). Among other things, it would seem to be a very risky proposition to decline to take steps to protect oneself against aggression (whether environmentally mediated or engaged in by violent people) on the grounds that those who might aggress against one would be deterred from doing so by efforts that effective prevented, ended, or remedied aggression against others. If one doesn't take steps to secure compensation for an environmentally mediated injury, one won't be compensated. If one waits to seek injunctive relief from an actual or potential environmentally mediated injury in the hope that someone else

to house. But defense against this kind of attack, despite its scale, would still constitute a private good because particular people were being targeted. Repelling this kind of attack in advance would not, of course, constitute a private good since doing so would benefit even free riders. Thanks to an anonymous reader for highlighting the need to make this point.

[33] *Cf.* TAYLOR, COMMUNITY, *supra* note 7, at 59–65.

will do so first, one runs the risk of suffering serious harm or seeing such harm befall one's friends and family members. And if one has not taken steps to protect oneself against interpersonal violence by associating with an appropriate defense provider, then, presuming self-help won't be adequate, the fact that someone else has been protected by her own defense provider will be largely irrelevant to one's safety. One may well benefit from the deterrent effect of a given potential attacker's having been immobilized in one way or another, but it will hardly be reasonable to *count* on benefiting from this sort of immobilization when deciding whether to seek protection against aggression.

The benefits to people in general associated with the deterrence of violence and environmentally mediated injury are spillover effects of self-protection against, or the pursuit of compensation for, these kinds of harms by particular people. The benefits to people in general gained when particular people secure injunctive relief from anticipated or continuing environmental harms can be seen in the same way. The value to particular persons of seeking compensation for or injunctive relief from environmentally mediated injuries or defending themselves against violence would be great enough that the temptation to free ride could be expected to be limited. And the relevant sorts of compensation, injunctive relief, and defense are not automatically provided to everyone when provided to someone in particular. It's not reasonable, therefore, to regard them as public goods.

5. *Some Goods Are Public*

i. *A limited range of goods may exhibit publicness*

Ordinary defense and the rectification of many environmentally mediated injuries are private goods. But of course this doesn't show that there are no public goods. Consider, for example, the rectification of some environmentally mediated injuries (Subsubsection ii), what I call generalized preemptive defense (Subsubsection iii), and the provision of some kinds of social sanctions for bad behavior (Subsubsection iv). Some goods do qualify as public (Subsubsection v).

ii. *Environmental goods with distinctive characteristics qualify as public*

Some environmentally rectificatory goods seem to be public. The good of preventing, ending, or remedying natural disasters which do not appear to result from the choice of any person but which pose widespread risks (for instance, the risk that a meteorite will strike the earth and cause massive harm) is surely public. So, too, would be the good of preventing or ending injury mediated through an environmental resource (air, for instance) enjoyed by everyone in a particular region. (The provision of restitution to someone who has suffered this latter sort of injury would, by contrast, be a private good.) It wouldn't be possible to provide this kind of good to specific people in the benefited population and not to others.

iii. General preemptive defense is a public good

Ordinary defense against aggression is not, as I have already suggested, a public good. But at least one defense-related good *would* seem to be public—what I call *general preemptive defense*.

General preemptive defense is defense that is in some way proactive or preventive, involving attacks on prospective aggressors as they begin large-scale aggressive actions or on weapons of mass destruction maintained by aggressors before they are employed.[34] If aggressors are known to be planning an attack on a given region, for instance, all of the region's residents would likely benefit if the aggressors or their weapons were preemptively disabled. No resident of the region could be excluded from the benefit provided by the preemptive disabling of the aggressors.[35] Lacking excludable beneficiaries, preemptive action against an aggressor targeting an entire group or region could thus amount to the provision of a public good.[36]

[34] By considering this possibility, I do not intend to imply that the preventive use of force, forced deployed against nonbelligerents on the theory that they will at some point become belligerents, is morally appropriate. Only when an aggressor has clearly committed to an aggressive course of action—as when a hostile army is poised for attack, or a hostile navy is sailing toward the site of an obviously planned invasion—is the use of force likely to be justified; *cf.* Germain Grisez, *Toward a Consistent Natural-Law Ethics of Killing*, 15 AM. J. JURIS 64 (1970).

[35] Walter Block offers an attempted *reductio ad absurdum* of a public goods argument focused on general preemptive defense. He notes that, if residents of one community can finance a defense system capable of specifically targeting distant aggressors, those in surrounding communities can easily choose to free ride by declining to contribute to covering the cost of the system. But if the public goods problem justifies the existence and authority of at least a minimal state, does this not mean that not only the residents of immediately surrounding communities but, indeed, the residents of the entire world should be required to fund defensive services, since others benefit from the existence of the defensive system? It seems, then, that "what we have here is an argument for a world government, encompassing all of the peoples of the earth" (*National Defense and the Theory of Externalities, Public Goods, and Clubs*, THE MYTH OF NATIONAL DEFENSE: ESSAYS ON THE THEORY AND HISTORY OF SECURITY PRODUCTION 301, 324 (Hans-Hermann Hoppe ed., 2005). It is not clear what this argument establishes. No doubt the defender of the Public Goods Argument could without self-contradiction concede that everyone was obligated to support the establishment of a world government. But, in any event, the envisioned precision defense system only needs to be used when its actual possessors are threatened or attacked; as he describes it, it is best understood as the source of a private good for its possessors. Block approaches the problem *ex post*, while my focus here has been *ex ante*: the question is whether defensive mechanisms with the potential to benefit significant numbers of free riders would be put in place at all, and whether the concern that they might not be would justify those seeking to put them in place in a stateless society to opt for the creation of a state.

[36] MURRAY ROTHBARD, FOR A NEW LIBERTY 250 (1973) seems to elide the aspect of defense that is a private good with the aspect of defense that is a public good. Rothbard refers to people "subscrib[ing]" and "invest[ing]" in defensive services without any indication that there might be a free-rider problem in the case of general preemptive defense.

iv. Socially sanctioning a wrongdoer may count as the supply of a public good
Boycotting, protesting, shaming, and shunning may be useful nonviolent strategies for promoting good behavior and discouraging bad behavior. In some cases, at least, engaging in one or more of these activities may qualify as providing a public good, at least when it is difficult or impossible to segregate beneficiaries from non-beneficiaries. The effectiveness of these norm-maintenance strategies will depend on widespread participation, but because they are likely to be effective even if some people don't participate, there will always be the temptation to be a free rider.

v. Some goods may reasonably count as public
Although the range of public goods is narrower than is sometimes supposed, some goods are, indeed, public. These include environmentally rectificatory goods that must be provided to everyone if provided to anyone; general preemptive defense, which can protect even free riders against aggression; and perhaps some kinds of social sanctions for wrongdoing. The existence of a narrow range of clearly public goods does not, of course, undermine the general point that most goods are, in the economic sense, private.

6. *Public Goods Are Features of the Economic Landscape, though They Are Arguably Less Common than Is Sometimes Supposed*

Public goods occur in a relatively narrow range of cases, and some goods which might initially be thought to be public are, in fact, private. The rectification of many environmentally mediated injuries is a private good: it can be provided by means of a well-functioning legal system that protects people's bodies and just possessory claims (whether held by particular persons or by groups). The same is true of ordinary defense, which can be supplied to specific persons without being automatically offered to everyone. Ordinary defense and environmental rectification do, of course, yield positive externalities, but this does not somehow convert either into a public good: in particular, the likelihood that these externalities will occur does not mean that people will be able to free ride successfully on the provision of the relevant goods. A few goods are public, including the provision of remedies for a limited class of environmental goods, the supply of general preemptive defense, and the imposition of some kinds of social sanctions. Most, however, are economically private.

D. The Public Goods Argument Holds That the Need for Public Goods Entails the Creation of the State

The Public Goods Argument is the claim that vital public goods cannot be provided at a satisfactory level except by the state, and that, because the provision of these goods is so important, the existence of a state, with the ability to provide them forcibly, is justified. The argument rests on the assumption that, absent state action, public goods for which the benefits exceed the costs will fail to be produced—that some mutually beneficial exchanges will not take place when people can't be forced to shoulder the costs of the benefits they receive.[37]

The proponent of the Public Goods Argument seeks to show that important public goods can't be provided voluntarily, so that people in a stateless society would be unreasonable if they declined to create an institution that would be able to provide these goods by force—by requiring everyone to contribute to their provision or by providing them through the imposition of across-the-board *ex ante* regulations or *ex ante* liability requirements (an activity which would itself presumably need to be forcibly funded); that they would thus have no choice to establish what was, in effect, a (minimal) state; and so (implicitly) that critiques of state authority are finally unreasonable.[38]

The argument can be envisioned as taking something like the following form for any public good Γ:

VII.1. The supply of Γ to the members of a given public P will not be optimal unless the members of P contribute to its provision at a given level.
VII.2. The members of P will not contribute voluntarily to the provision of Γ at the relevant level.
VII.3. It is very important that the supply of Γ be optimal.
VII.4. If Γ is provided forcibly to the members of P, its supply (and the supplies of goods affected by the process of supplying it) will be optimal.
VII.5. Γ may justifiably be forcibly provided to the members of P.
VII.6. An entity that justifiably uses force to fund its activities or regulate economic activity qualifies as at least a minimal state.
VII.7. At least a minimal state is justified.

E. There Is No Objective Measure of the Optimal Level of Public Goods Provision

1. *The Quest for an Optimal Level of Public Goods Provision Is a Will-O'-the-Wisp*

Forcible provision of putative public goods cannot be justified on the basis that non-forcible provision would lead to the provision of the relevant services at

[37] Thanks to an anonymous reader for prompting me to clarify this point.

[38] My goal here is to defend anarchism against the Public Goods Argument. It is not to argue for or against particular varieties of anarchism. I intend my arguments to apply to genuinely stateless societies of all kinds and to be compatible with support for a wide range of anarchist tendencies.

suboptimal levels. There is no objective way of determining just what an optimal level of provision might mean in this context.

No objective standard for determining whether public goods are being provided at an optimal level is available, even in principle. The values instantiated in various states of affairs can't be meaningfully aggregated and compared (Subsection 2). It's possible to talk about a state of affairs as optimal if it emerges from acts of peaceful, voluntary cooperation, but this sort of optimality won't help the defenders of the Public Goods Argument (Subsection 3). An account of an optimal level of public provision as what people *would* choose under specified conditions is problematic for multiple reasons (Subsection 4). The kind of optimality needed to ground the Public Goods Argument simply isn't available (Subsection 5).

2. *The Impossibility of Aggregating Incommensurable and Non-Fungible Aspects of Different People's Well-Being Ordinarily Renders Claims about the Optimality of an Overall State of Affairs Incoherent*

The Public Goods Argument seems to assume that there is an objective measure of optimality against which the level of public goods production absent the state can be judged and found wanting. However, if what I've already said about the in-principle impossibility of consequentialist reasoning is correct, then it will not be possible to make any sort of objective claim about aggregated welfare. The claim that a given overall state of affairs is superior to another is simply incoherent. And so the attempt to characterize a given level of public goods production as superior to any other will ordinarily be a nonstarter.

3. *A Transactional Conception of Optimality Is Defensible, but Provides No Support for the Public Goods Argument*

An alternate conception of optimality might focus, not on the objective superiority of the outcome, but on the justice of any constraints affecting the transactions leading to the outcome. A proponent of this sort of conception might say that a good has been produced at an optimal level if it has been produced in accordance with the preferences people have revealed through their actual decisions, given that the voluntary character of those decisions has not been vitiated by force or fraud or impaired by background conditions marred by serious injustice. A given level of public goods provision might be thought to be optimal, at least presumptively, if it reflects the preferences people actually express under these conditions.[39] But this account would provide no reason to question the optimality of the level of public goods provision in

[39] For a similar argument, see SCHMIDTZ, *supra* note 29, at 180–81 n.15.

a stateless society, given that the transactions resulting in that level were voluntary. It therefore provides no basis for a defense of state authority.

4. *A Counterfactual Payment Account of Optimality Is Implausible on Multiple Grounds*

i. The public goods argument cannot be rescued by defining optimality in terms of people's choices in an imagined situation

A proponent of the Public Goods Argument might also seek to defend the argument by suggesting that we could judge the level of public goods provision absent forcible provision to be suboptimal were it less than the level everyone would be willing to purchase if most or all other people paid comparable or proportionate amounts for the same level. But this seems unsatisfactory. It is not clear that anyone could *know* what this level might be, because knowledge of a large population's preferences absent their expression of those preferences in the course of peaceful, voluntary exchange is necessarily limited (Subsubsection ii); because the only preferences that finally matter are those revealed in people's actual interactions, which may be different from those they might express with nothing at stake (Subsubsection iii); because people's preferences vary (so that there is no one level that would be acceptable to everyone) (Subsubsection iv); and because there is good reason to regard counterfactual claims regarding free choices as either without truth-values or as false (Subsubsection v). The envisioned reply is therefore unsuccessful (Subsubsection vi).

ii. Compulsory provision limits access to knowledge regarding people's subjective preferences

When people are able to cooperate by peacefully and voluntarily exchanging goods and services against a background of just, reliable rules, information regarding their preferences can affect production levels and distribution patterns and they can obtain services at the levels they prefer. But the compulsory provision of public goods necessarily involves the supply of such goods at levels *not set* through this kind of cooperative process. And this obviously limits anyone's ability to determine what levels of public goods provision people might prefer.

iii. Revealed preferences are, in any case, decisive measures of subjective valuation in ways that unexpressed ones are not—even if they could be identified

People are likely to want all sorts of goods provided at very high levels if the resources needed to provide these goods are infinite—or, at any rate, if they themselves will not be required to provide the resources. But this tells us very little about what level of any good people would actually want if they had to bear the costs of providing the good. In the absence of *revealed* preferences, it is unclear just what kinds of public goods people really want, and preferences expressed through, for instance, surveys don't provide satisfactory substitutes because selecting a given option as part of a survey doesn't involve bearing any personal cost. In addition, there may be incentives for people to provide inaccurate responses to survey questions, given that service levels, and so compelled contributions, will be set in light of these responses.[40] Recall that the Public Goods Argument holds that people should be forced to fund the provision of public goods that will, ex hypothesi, be insufficiently supplied in the absence of forcible funding. Survey data cannot tell us at what level people would be willing to pay for a particular public good given everyone else's willingness to join them in paying for it; only real choices by people with actual stakes in the outcomes of their choices seem likely to do so.

An alternative to the use of surveys might be the employment of deliberative democratic procedures to determine an optimum level of provision for a given public good. But the use of deliberative democracy to answer this kind of question seems likely to be problematic (*i*) because of the risks associated with creating a collective decision-making entity with the power to compel support for a public goods project; (*ii*) because deliberative democracy unnecessarily privileges the articulate; (*iii*) because, as when responding to surveys, people can express positions in the course of democratic deliberation with little personal cost; and (*iv*) because deliberative democratic procedures are likely to be very time-consuming.[41] Obviously, if an emergency procedure for forcible public goods production were required in a particular case,[42] as it might well not be, it would be preferable that it feature some mechanism for taking everyone's interests into account (though an emergency might not allow time for this). But this is no reason to suppose that such a procedure would, in fact, be necessary or, even if it were, to put public goods *in general* in the hands of deliberative assemblies.

iv. It is improbable that there is one quantity of any public good which everyone would have reason to prefer prospectively under ordinary circumstances

People's preferences vary, and it is thus not clear that there is a single level at which it would be rational for everyone, even in principle, to prefer that a given public good were provided, even if all the members of a given public were forced to help fund its provision.[43] A decision is rational in a narrowly economic sense to the extent

[40] ANTHONY DE JASAY, JUSTICE AND ITS SURROUNDINGS 21–22 (2002).

[41] On deliberative democracy as an alternative to distributed decision making, *see* MARK PENNINGTON, ROBUST POLITICAL ECONOMY: CLASSICAL LIBERALISM AND THE FUTURE OF PUBLIC POLICY 53–55, 65–71, 75–79, 126, 215–17 (2011).

[42] *See* Part V.G.3, *infra*.

[43] *Cf.* MITCHELL & SIMMONS, *supra* note 23, at 93; JASAY, *supra* note 14, at 39–40. Pareto-optimality does not provide a satisfactory criterion here, since some people would doubtless be worse off, as judged by

that it efficiently achieves the goals the actor actually has. Different people have different levels of risk tolerance and different preferences regarding various public goods, so it will be rational for different people to prefer different levels of public goods provision. And it is not obvious that someone who prefers a high level of some public good should rationally prefer to pay for a low level even if everyone else is paying for that level, too, since she may not regard being compelled to pay for a low level of the relevant good as preferable to not being compelled at all. She may regard it as wasteful to pay for a low level of the good, since she may not believe that her expenditure will be worth anything (perhaps she supposes that the good needs to be provided at a level beyond a certain threshold or it will be relatively valueless, and judges that a given low level of service falls below that threshold).

Similarly, it is not obvious that someone who prefers a low level of the relevant public good should rationally prefer to pay for a high level rather than to pay for none at all. She might prefer to pay at a given low level *if* everyone else paid at that level, but to pay at a level that was higher, but still not as high as some proposed high level favored by others, even if others did *not* have to pay, *rather than* to be forced to pay at the proposed high level.[44] (Perhaps she might be able to provide the good herself at a cost higher than her preferred low level but lower than the proposed high level.)

v. Counterfactuals of freedom are likely to lack truth-values or to be false

A focus on revealed preferences is a focus on people's publicly accessible *choices*. Choices are actions. And, on the assumption that people's choices are free in a reasonably robust sense,[45] there is no sense in talking about what they *would* do under counterfactual circumstances. Probabilistic judgments may sometimes be feasible and useful in such cases. But because there is no presently existing truth-maker for claims about free choices under counterfactual conditions (if there were, the

their own lights, if required to pay for any defensive services at all, and others will be worse off, on the same criterion, if required to pay for the particular services they will in fact be forced to fund.

[44] A Lindahl tax scheme might be designed that would require someone to pay just for the benefit from a given defense scheme she herself received. However, it seems impossible accurately to measure this benefit. Even were it possible to do so, and even if the optimal level of general preemptive defense provision were a matter of fact, there is no reason to think that politically driven processes would yield provision at this level. Also problematic about a Lindahl tax approach would be the potential abuses of a monopolistic state, once it was created to implement the tax and administer programs under the tax, as well as the aggression involved in collecting the tax in the first place. Thanks to an anonymous reader for emphasizing the need to make this point.

[45] *See, e.g.*, JOSEPH BOYLE, JR., GERMAIN GRISEZ & OLAF TOLLEFSEN, FREE CHOICE: A SELF-REFERENTIAL ARGUMENT (1976); CARL GINET, ON ACTION (1989); DAVID RAY GRIFFIN, UNSNARLING THE WORLD-KNOT: CONSCIOUSNESS, FREEDOM, AND THE MIND-BODY PROBLEM (1998); ROBERT KANE, THE SIGNIFICANCE OF FREE WILL (1998); JOHN THORP, FREE WILL: A DEFENSE AGAINST NEUROPHYSIOLOGICAL DETERMINISM (1980); AUSTIN FARRER, THE FREEDOM OF THE WILL (1957). *Cf.* BENJAMIN LIBET, MIND TIME: THE TEMPORAL FACTOR IN CONSCIOUSNESS 123–56 (2004).

choices wouldn't be free), it is impossible for such claims to be true. (Whether they are false—because they entail the existence of nonexistent truth-makers—or simply lacking in truth-values is not relevant here.)

vi. A counterfactual account of optimality is unsupportable

Information about the preferences of large groups of people can be reliably obtained by attending to those preferences as they are revealed through the information people themselves distribute in the course of peaceful, voluntary, cooperative activities. Compulsory provision precludes access to this information. Information obtained through surveys is an inadequate substitute. There almost certainly isn't a consistently preferred level of public goods provision, in any case. And the envisioned argument rests on the possibility that there are true counterfactual propositions about free choices, which seems unlikely. The counterfactual analysis of optimality is unsustainable.

5. *Objective Claims about Optimality of the Kind Needed to Ground the Public Goods Argument Are Unsupportable*

There is no single rational level of preference for public goods. The global comparison of states of affairs in terms of some metric that allows them to be rank-ordered is generally impossible in principle because of the incommensurability of the various aspects of human welfare. A transactional account of optimality wouldn't provide any support for the Public Goods Argument. And it is not clear that there is a rationally defensible mechanism for specifying an optimal level of public goods provision under the hypothetical condition that most or all of the people receiving the services are bearing the costs of providing them. But since the claim that the nonforcible provision of public goods is suboptimal *depends* on the ability to highlight a difference between the level that would be provided without forced participation by all and the level to which all would agree if all were forced to participate, there seems to be no meaningful way of making out that claim at all. Thus, (VII.1) proves to be indefensible.

F. Public Goods Could Be Provided on a Peaceful, Voluntary Basis despite the Free-Rider Problem

1. *There Are Multiple Paths to the Voluntary Provision of Public Goods*

There are multiple factors that might lead to the provision of public goods despite the threat of free riding. These include rational actors' penchants for risk-management (Subsection 2); the use of assurance agreements (Subsection 3); the bundling of public and private goods (Subsection 4); and a combination of social norms, moral duties, and concern with reputation and social pressure similar to that responsible for peaceful, cooperative behavior generally (Subsection 5).[46] The provision of public goods on a bottom-up basis is a viable possibility (Subsection 6).

2. *Rational Actors Will Often Contribute to the Provision of Public Goods to Avoid Suffering Various Risks to Themselves*

People who interact repeatedly may be able to count on each other to produce public goods,[47] because each knows that the others will be more likely to provide the relevant goods in tandem with her if she shows herself willing to cooperate in providing them, so that the desired good will be more forthcoming and because those who interact with her on a repeated basis may stop doing so if she does not contribute to providing the goods.

It will also sometimes make sense to someone to provide, or help provide, public goods herself even if most others *don't* participate in doing so.[48] This will be so, at minimum, when a public benefactor prefers the benefit she expects to realize from bearing the cost of providing a public good—either alone or with a subset of other members of the benefited public—to whatever she must contribute toward the production of the good. This is a state of affairs that is perfectly possible even when the proportion of contributors is small.

Even in cases in which the relevant costs are *not* small, there will still be reasons for people to be public benefactors. When the probability that a public good will be made available as a result of the contribution made by a given potential benefactor is relatively low, she may *still* have reason to contribute to its provision. This will be so, at any rate, if she prefers the benefit she will reap if the public good is produced—even in view of the probability of its being produced given the likelihood that a given fraction of the relevant public will opt to ride free—to whatever she might lose by contributing to its production. When the benefit resulting from a project designed to provide a public good is more substantial, there is obviously, as a general rule, a higher chance that the benefits someone stands to realize from contributing to the project will be such that she will support it.

[46] FRIEDMAN, *supra* note 29, at 139–42, canvasses some of these possibilities.

[47] *Cf.* ANTHONY DE JASAY, POLITICAL PHILOSOPHY, CLEARLY: ESSAYS ON FREEDOM AND FAIRNESS, PROPERTY AND EQUALITIES 291 (2010).

[48] *Cf.* JASAY, *supra* note 28, at 133–218; JASAY, *supra* note 47, at 288–98. I am happy to acknowledge my dependence on Jasay's arguments throughout my discussion of the merits of being a public benefactor. Thanks to Jonathan Crowe for suggesting that it might be more helpful to refer to "public benefactors" than to "suckers" in this context.

This will likely be true when the issue is the production of a public good which can be delivered in proportion to the contributions made in its support.[49] But it will certainly true in a case in which there is a possibility that failing to contribute will keep the level of the good being produced from crossing a relevant threshold, with the result that *much* less of the good is produced. In this case, it will make sense to take into account the possibility that contributing may exert a substantial effect, rather than a narrowly proportional one, on the quantity of the good produced. (In the limit case, the failure to cross the relevant threshold will mean that the good, at least in a useable form, is not produced at all.)

In a situation in which a given, generally desired public good will only be produced if contributions to its delivery are made at a certain level, everyone may for simplicity's sake be expected to want to make the minimum contribution necessary to ensure the delivery of the good. In deciding whether to contribute, therefore, each member of the public needs to take into account the possibility that others' contributions will not be calculated to bring the total contribution level any farther beyond the threshold that must be crossed if the good is to be produced than is necessary to ensure its delivery (allowing, of course, for difficulties in predicting the total needed amount and gauging the behavior of others, and thus for bet-hedging strategies designed to allow for these uncertainties).[50] And this means, in turn, that the total amount contributed might be expected to linger near the threshold level, and that an actor can reasonably regard herself as confronting the non-trivial probability that the good may not be produced at all without her involvement. This should clearly affect the rationality of her participation in the process of delivering the good.

Imagine, for instance, that an armed satellite orbits above a particular territory, equipped to cause targeted destruction anywhere in the territory; everyone is required to pay tribute to the satellite's operator—the failure to pay will result in violent retaliation. (Assume perfect targeting; with less precise targeting, of course, the incentive for widespread participation increases.) Suppose an anti-satellite missile or laser system can be secretly built and deployed for $20 million. And suppose that someone with an annual income of $5 million stands to lose $2 million per year to

[49] It may often be the case that "the effect of a marginal contribution to total cost is a marginal increase in total benefit; this is heavily diluted among all members of the public, most of it accruing as an externality to its other members, the part accruing to the individual contributor being (except in freak cases) imperceptibly small." JASAY, *supra* note 47, at 296 (the source of much of the analysis offered in this subsection). However, the proportionately small increments produced in such cases may still be large enough in some instances, not necessarily freakish, that some people will choose to contribute.

[50] If a typical member of the relevant public assumes that far more or far less than the needed number of contributors will contribute, she will then be less likely (on austere assumptions) to contribute herself. In the former case, her contribution would be unnecessary, while in the latter it would be pointless. *See* JASAY, *supra* note 28, at 183–86.

the satellite-wielding terrorists in perpetuity. She might be willing to pay the entire $20 million needed to fund the anti-satellite system's construction and use if no one else can be persuaded to assist her, since she likely stands to lose more by letting the satellite continue in operation than by fronting the cost of downing it. Obviously, in the real world, probabilities related to the involvement of others, the potential detection of the anti-satellite efforts, and so forth would need to be taken into account, but it still seems plausible that the outcome I've anticipated here would result.

The need for public goods is frequently viewed as the single most important source of justification for the state. This perception reflects the sense that these goods are tremendously important. If this belief is inaccurate, then there may be relatively little reason to be concerned about the provision of public goods, and so little reason to seek to see them supplied by force. But if it *is* accurate, in which case it can reasonably be expected that the belief that these services are tremendously important will be widely shared, it is especially likely that people will be inclined to support provision of these services. And, indeed, people seem unlikely to withhold support from public goods they view as extremely worthwhile.[51]

Evidently valuable public goods can be expected to be provided voluntarily in significant quantities. People can be expected to help produce public goods to encourage others to do so and to avoid the negative consequences of others' disapproval, and because they prefer that the goods be available even if others do not choose to supply them, and thus to act accordingly to ensure that the goods are available.

3. *Assurance Agreements Can Sometimes Facilitate the Provision of Public Goods*

Assurance agreements can help to guarantee that some public goods are provided.[52] Someone who belongs to a particular group makes an assurance agreement with other members of the group when she agrees to be bound by the agreement—and so, for instance, to contribute to the funding of services to be provided under the agreement—if, but only if, a specified fraction of the group's other members agree to accept comparable obligations under the agreement, or only if the obligations assumed under the agreement by others reaches a certain minimum. So, if my city is about to be attacked, I might agree to purchase a $1,000 bond designed to help defray the cost of a preemptive strike against the prospective attacker, but only if, say, 70 percent of the other adults resident in the city do so as well, or only if the total

[51] See SCHMIDTZ, *supra* note 29, at 135. In support of this contention, Schmidtz cites R. Mark Isaac and James M. Walker, *Group Size Effects in Public Goods Provision: The Voluntary Contribution Mechanism*, 103 Q.J. ECON. 179 (1988).

[52] On assurance agreements, see, *e.g.*, SCHMIDTZ, *supra* note 29, at 66–78; FRIEDMAN, *supra* note 29, at 136–37.

value of bonds purchased by others reaches $70,000,000. Similarly, the members of a cooperative might agree to address some negative environmental consequence of a policy pursued by the cooperative, but only if some appropriate fraction of other organizations generating comparable negative consequences did the same thing. Making and acting on an assurance agreement might make sense in a case in which action seemed to be pointless absent the involvement of others.[53]

Making assurance agreements is not a device to overcome the free rider's disposition to avoid contributing to the support of a public good.[54] But, as the argument in Subsection 2 suggests, where the good to be provided through an assurance agreement is one of enormous value, people may well be willing to commit themselves by means of such an agreement to supporting the good's provision even if they know that some others will opt to be free riders.

4. *In Limited Cases, Bundling Can Facilitate the Provision of Public Goods*

It would sometimes be possible to secure funding for public goods by bundling them with other goods.

One option would be to charge high prices for the other, consistently desired, services and then to use the resulting revenues to pay for one or more public goods. It is regularly objected that schemes of this kind would prove nonviable because other suppliers would offer the other services without bundling them with public goods and would thus be able to provide them less expensively, with the result that no one would willingly buy the bundled services.

As a general rule, this objection seems obviously correct. Arguably, however, there might be instances in which the cost a consumer could be charged for the unbundled services equaled or exceeded the cost she was being charged for the bundled services. Suppose, for instance, that a producer cooperative operated a road system in a densely populated community[55]; the cooperative might decide to bundle some public good with its road-related services. In principle, its decision to do so could create an opportunity for another group to construct an alternate road network. However, the cost of doing so might be quite high, given the need to acquire land currently in use for residential or industrial purposes. It might, indeed, be high

[53] See Friedman, *supra* note 29, at 134–37; Hummel & Lavoie, *supra* note 30; Jasay, *supra* note 40, at 22–23. Taylor, Community, *supra* note 7, at 60, expresses the suspicion that assurance agreement schemes "are likely to work only in very small publics." But this objection seems to me perhaps to underestimate the ability of both interlocking personal networks and impersonal legal and exchange systems—facilitated by developments in information technology—to extend the information needed to ground personal trust and mistrust beyond people's immediate social circles or local communities.

[54] *See* Schmidtz, *supra* note 29, at 57.

[55] On such arrangements, *see, e.g.*, Walter Block, Privatization of Roads and Highways (2009).

enough that, if the existing road cooperative's delivery of public goods proved highly efficient and inexpensive, it would be prohibitively costly to establish an alternative road system. In this case, bundling might be a successful strategy for the provision of one or more public goods.

Similarly, it would be possible to bundle public goods with those provided by institutions offering basic social services, including income support in the event of illness, lack of work, or retirement. To the extent that these were geographically based (albeit non-monopolistic), there might be social pressure from friends and neighbors to participate in supporting the social service provider, and so, indirectly, to support its provision of public goods. Here, the idea would not be that social pressure would lead to direct support of public goods provision but rather that it would lead to participation in the support of a provider of more comprehensive services that most people might have good reason to want to see maintained in operation. Obviously, a lower-cost source of some private good or goods could seek to supplant this provider. But a combination of local loyalty and path-dependence could potentially preserve the viability of the comprehensive provider of bundled public and private goods.[56]

5. *Moral Duties, Social Norms, and Concern with Reputation and Social Pressure Can All Facilitate the Voluntary Provision of Public Goods*

Multiple factors can help to ensure that peaceful, voluntary cooperation occurs in the absence of a territorial monopolist. Many of these factors can be expected to foster the non-forcible production of public goods. For instance: providing public goods can be a source of desirable reputational effects. The awareness of the benefits associated with being identified by others as a cooperator and the costs associated with being labeled a free rider can cause people to be concerned about establishing and maintaining good reputations as benefactors—reputations that they may expect to aid them in a variety of contexts.[57] People who fail to contribute to the provision of public goods when others expect them to do so may be subjected to nonviolent social sanctions. Biologically encoded dispositions to cooperate seem likely to foster cooperation in the provision of public goods; social norms and habits can be expected to do so as well because there may be biological predispositions to engage in cooperative behavior. Someone's belief that she has a moral obligation to help defray the costs of providing public goods from which she herself has benefited or expects to benefit—whether the contribution is framed as a donation or as a purchase—may be sufficient to prompt her to contribute to covering the costs of

[56] Thanks to Kevin Carson for elaborating this option.

[57] *See, e.g.*, TAYLOR, COOPERATION, *supra* note 7.

these services. All of these factors can help to ensure the provision of public goods in the absence of forcible funding.

6. *Public Goods Could Be Provided Satisfactorily in a Stateless Society through a Mix of Non-Forcible Mechanisms*

Public goods could be supplied voluntarily at significant levels in various ways. People might choose voluntarily to facilitate the provision of public goods as a result of many of the same factors that dispose them to cooperate peacefully and voluntarily (or to support institutions that facilitate cooperation) in the state's absence, including social norms, moral requirements, cooperative impulses, responsiveness to social pressure, and a recognition of the importance of reputation. Assurance agreements might sometimes prompt widespread participation in public goods provision, and bundling public and private goods together might help as well. And the simple desire to realize benefits or avoid harms by producing public goods might well lead rational actors to contribute to their provision in the absence of coercion, even while they were aware that others might free ride on their contributions.

Thus, (VII.2) is almost certainly false. There is no way of specifying an optimal level or variety of public goods provision (except, of course, that voluntary provision is better than involuntary provision). But it is clear that public goods could be produced at *significant* levels on a voluntary basis.

G. The Putative Importance of Public Goods Does Not Justify Their Forcible Provision

1. *There Is No Clear Path from the Importance of a Public Good to Its Putatively Necessary Provision by the State*

Even were it possible to render coherent and successfully defend the claim that public goods would be provided sub-optimally absent the state, it would not be obvious that public goods should be forcibly supplied. The attempt to justify forcible provision of public goods in light of their putative importance is unsuccessful if importance is understood in consequentialist terms (Subsection 2), but also if importance is understood with reference to the putative preconditions for peaceful, voluntary cooperation (Subsection 3). While forcibly providing public goods might realize certain values, it also seems likely to carry significant risks of great harm (Subsection 4). Thus, appeals to the putative worth of public goods need not be seen as justifying their forcible provision (Subsection 5).

2. *The Claim That the Value of Public Goods Justifies Their Forcible Provision Is Unjustifiable if It Depends on a Questionable Consequentialist Calculus*

The claim that the forcible provision of public goods facilitated the realization of a state of affairs of sufficient value to justify the use of force to make it possible is most plausibly understood as depending on the viability of weighing the goods realized in large-scale states of affairs. But there is good reason to think that quantification of the required sort is impossible in principle. Different states of affairs seem to embody different, incommensurable aspects of welfare; and, if they do, there is no way to compare them and conclude that one embodies more overall good than another.[58] In addition, even if there were not objectively valuable aspects of fulfillment, welfare, well-being, or flourishing, and all preferences were equally worth satisfying, the problem of making interpersonal utility comparisons would remain. And, absent such comparisons, it is unclear how the great value arguably produced by some public good could be judged to be worth achieving by means of forcible provision.

3. *A Non-Consequentialist Reading of the Importance Claim Fails to Justify the Creation and Maintenance of the State*

An alternative reading of the claim that the provision of a given public good in a given way or at a given level was so important that supplying the good by force was reasonable might avoid the difficulties associated with the consequentialist interpretation. The alternative might run as follows: if the existence of a social order rooted in peaceful, voluntary cooperation is under threat, and if an effective response to the relevant threat is the provision of a public good, then it might be reasonable to use force to compel people to contribute to the cost of providing that good. And to treat the use in such a case of what would otherwise count as aggressive force as legitimate, would be to endorse, in effect, an understanding of the baseline rules as permitting the forcible funding of at least a minimal state.[59] (Presumably one could go on to argue for the legitimacy of those institutions needed to ensure the effective but appropriately constrained operation of the state thus justified.)

Given that the existence of a particular social order is unlikely to be under threat most of the time, this argument really justifies only an authority that either exists temporarily or, if more permanent, is ordinarily dormant. The need for it might be invoked in response to grave military or environmental threats, but hardly at other

[58] For this cluster of objections to consequentialism, see Chapter 1, *supra*, n. 50.

[59] *Cf.* SCHMIDTZ, *supra* note 29, at 157.

times. In view of the strong presumption in favor of leaving the baseline rules undisturbed and the great likelihood that, once invested with coercive power, people would be unlikely to surrender it, this approach to justifying even a temporary minimal state seems to face an enormous justificatory burden. In addition, even if the functions of the authority were narrowly cabined on its establishment, its officials could reasonably be expected to seek to expand these functions in the interests of their own power, their own goals, and their own interests and those of their cronies.

Obviously, whether such a state could ever even in principle be justified in this way would be an empirical question.[60] This argument, if it succeeded, would depend on its being the case that (*i*) the relevant threat really existed—the putative emergency the coercion was designed to deal with really existed and was really likely to have the effects purportedly justifying the coercion; (*ii*) the projected, forcible response would deal effectively with the emergency; (*iii*) this projected response would actually occur if the mechanism for forcible provision were in place; (*iv*) an alternative featuring non-forcible provision was unlikely to be available, or, if likely to be available, then unlikely to be effective; and (*v*) the reach of the envisioned coercive public good provider could be effectively cabined, so that it dealt only with the provision of essential public goods that would not otherwise be produced and did not stray into other terrain, with its functionaries returning, like Cincinnatus, to the plow after resolving the emergency that putatively justified their assumption of coercive powers.

Given that it is likely that the relevant public goods *could* be provided noncoercively, there seems little reason to take the risk involved in creating a state, even one of this kind. The underlying force of the considerations that warrant the baseline rules in their undiluted form would of course have to be taken very seriously. And it would still need to be ascertained just how severe the relevant threat to peaceful, voluntary cooperation really was. That is, for instance, if the threat were military, one would need to know whether the threat encompassed the obliteration of everyone in the relevant region, or simply the exaction of tribute from them. In the latter case, one might reasonably conclude that although there was a good chance that a forcibly supplied response might stand a better chance of dealing with the threat, it would be more reasonable to opt for a noncoercive solution than to allow either (*i*) the short-term interference with otherwise just possessory claims which a coercive solution would necessarily involve, or (*ii*) the risks of long-term predation associated with the creation of a coercive institution whose functionaries would almost certainly be tempted to keep it in place after the end of the emergency putatively justifying its creation.

[60] *See id.* at 158–60.

Some violations of the baseline rules in emergencies might be morally permissible, though the permissibility of these violations would not remove the need to compensate those violated. (And of course the Principle of Respect would still obtain, emergency or no emergency, with the result that the use of force would be strictly limited in ways that would substantially inhibit the behavior of any would-be emergency public goods provider.) In theory, then, it might be reasonable to infringe on people's just possessory claims to meet a public good–related emergency if one were willing to compensate particular persons for the resulting losses. But whether this proved justifiable would depend on the probabilities I have already discussed, and these probabilities would certainly be affected by the considerations I adduce regarding the noncoercive provision of public goods. Even if it *did* prove justifiable in a particular emergency case, however, it could hardly be thought to justify the creation of even a minimal state, rather than a temporary emergency-oriented structure. Ordinary people would have every reason to resist vigorously the establishment, even in response to an emergency, of anything with the potential to function as the nucleus of a state.[61]

[61] There is one further wrinkle, however. The take-and-pay rule may be seen as providing an incentive to those from whom resources are taken in a public goods–related emergency to free ride. After all, I will often have not only moral but prudential reasons to devote my own resources to responding to the need to create a public good. In this case, I will bear part of the cost of helping to produce the good. But I may reason that, if I do nothing, others may claim resources from me to help produce the good, but that they will then be required to compensate me. If I act voluntarily to help produce the public good, I will need to draw on my own resources to do so; but if others take resources from me to do so, I will lose nothing, since I will be compensated for the resources they have taken. Thus, I have a strong incentive not to contribute and to wait for others to take my resources.

The take-and-pay rule makes perfect sense in cases in which private goods are being produced, since there is no incentive to free ride in such cases. While the rule works to ensure accountability when someone acts to prevent an emergency by creating a private good, it may discourage accountability when the issue is the production of a public good. There does not seem to be an obvious way to draw the kind of line between the two cases of which the law could readily take account. There is not a legal solution.

Those interested in producing public goods in emergency situations would often be well-advised to avoid commandeering the resources of others in such situations; a combination of benevolence, fellow-feeling, and self-interest, supplemented by public pressure, can be expected to dispose people to contribute on their own to the emergency production of public goods. If people do seek sometimes to resolve an emergency public goods problem by taking the resources of others, expecting to compensate them, legal rules or public pressure might enable them to pay back someone from whom they've taken the resources under the take-and-pay rule while deducting (a proportionate share of) their costs, reflective of the benefit they have conferred on her. If the take-and-pay rule is not to become a source of incentives to interfere with others' justly acquired possessions, the option of deducting these expenses would need to be tightly cabined—perhaps protected by social pressure rather than by the legal system, and thus allowing for greater flexibility and less opportunity for abuse. But the most effective way to avoid promoting free riding seems likely to be to decline to put any sort of coercive public-goods provider in place.

4. *The Forcible Provision of Public Goods Might Yield Significant Disvalues*

Any entity with the capacity to provide public goods by force would be dangerously powerful. Given the temptations associated with power, those directing such an entity can hardly be trusted to avoid benefiting themselves and their cronies at the public's expense and amassing more power in the course of—putatively—providing public goods. And centralized decision making is likely to have significant unanticipated consequences with much greater potential for harm than mistakes made by non-state actors with considerably less power; the general informational and incentival problems that beset attempts to direct the production of goods and services on a centralized basis could be expected to affect centralized efforts to manage the production of public goods in particular. If there were an objective measure of the optimal supply of a given public good, it might reasonably be suspected that state actors responsible for forcibly supplying the good would be perfectly capable of undersupplying or oversupplying it,[62] in either case perhaps at great cost, whether out of a desire to benefit themselves and their cronies or because of a severe good-faith miscalculation. (If there is not, as I maintain, any such objective measure, then the basic argument that state actors must supply public goods forcibly to prevent their undersupply obviously collapses.)

5. *The Putative Value of a Public Good Doesn't Justify Providing It Forcibly*

Perhaps it is the case that some public good is very valuable. But there is less reason to think that its putative value would justify anyone's use of force to ensure that it was provided. This might be so because the kind of weighing of values required to justify the use of force to supply it proved incoherent or because the sort of prediction required to anticipate the consequences of providing it proved impossible. There is thus good reason to doubt the correctness of (VII.3). There is the bare possibility that forcible provision consistent with the principles of practical reasonableness might be acceptable in some emergency situations, but while (if so) this might leave (VII.3) intact, it would not provide any justification for the creation of a state, even a minimal one.

H. It Is Not Obvious That Forcible Provision of a Public Good Would Be Effective

The forcible provision of a public good would be subject to the range of epistemic and incentival problems that complicate state action generally. If state actors lack

[62] *Cf.* SCHMIDTZ, *supra* note 29, at 104.

the knowledge needed to make good choices about the production and distribution of goods and services generally, there is no reason to expect them to know more that is relevant to the production and distribution of public goods. And reasonable doubts about the benevolence and fair-mindedness of state actors certainly ought to affect expectations about their behavior as overseers of the supply of any public good. Thus, even if my earlier objections were overcome and voluntary provision of a public good could be shown to be objectively suboptimal, it would not follow that forcible provision of the good by the state would be superior. Further, even if the relevant public good were supplied by the state at what would otherwise be an objectively optimal level, forcible provision of the good by the state might mean that the supplies of *other* goods, public or private, were rendered nonoptimal by state action associated with the provision of the relevant good (again, assuming, dubiously, that the notion of objective optimality is coherent). The correctness of (VII.4) may thus be questioned with some confidence.

I. There Might Be Reason to Avoid Diluting the Baseline Rules even if the Forcible Provision of an Important Public Good Were Necessary to Its Optimal Supply

Even if it could be shown that the supply of a public good would be optimal (in some coherent sense) only if the good were provided by force and that the good was very important, it still would not follow that the baseline rules should be understood to permit the forcible provision of the good. (There would still, of course, be the likely inconsistency between some actions of even a minimal state and the Principle of Respect.) It might be that full consideration of the requirements of practical reasonableness and the desiderata rendered it unreasonable for those considering the possibility of providing some public good by force to read the baseline rules as permitting this dramatic, systematic infringement on the interests the rules would otherwise serve to protect. Taking the desiderata and the requirements of practical reasonableness seriously might mean saying "no" even to an emergency-basis minimal state. The outcome to which the deliberation of reasonable people reflecting on this possibility might be expected to lead is not, at any rate, certain (and might, of course, vary with the underlying preferences of the people involved). While the recognition that this is the case need not lead to a wholesale rejection of (VII.5), it provides some reason to question this premise of the Public Goods Argument.

J. The Public Goods Argument Does Not Offer a Plausible Justification for State Authority

The first three premises of the Public Goods Argument can be confidently rejected. The fourth is subject to serious question. And it is not, at any rate, obvious that the fifth is correct. The argument fails to defeat the strong presumption against nonconsensual authority or to provide good reason to read the baseline rules as permitting forcible interference with bodies and justly acquired possessions. Thus, it does not succeed as a demonstration that the state is necessary.

Most goods are, economically speaking, private: they can be provided in a manner that prevents free riders from taking advantage of their availability. A limited number of goods are doubtless public. But there are multiple ways of supplying these goods without forcible provision, and it is unclear that there is any objective meaning to the claim that the level at which any of them would be supplied absent forcible provision would prove suboptimal. It doesn't necessarily follow from the supposed importance of any given public good that it may justifiably be provided by force, and the state might, in any event, prove an ineffective provider of any public good it sought to supply. And it might make sense to retain the baseline rules in unqualified form, and so to reject the state, even if multiple premises of the Public Goods Argument weren't rejected. The state's putative value as a source of public goods does not justify its existence and operation.

VI. THE STATE IS DANGEROUS

A. The State Is a Tool of Domination

The state declines to act peacefully to elicit or foster voluntary cooperation and repeatedly interferes with peaceful, voluntary cooperation among ordinary people. It undermines social order and harms particular people in persistent and predictable ways, especially in order to create, preserve, and defend the influence and wealth of the ruling class.[63] It is ill-suited to be an agent of peaceful, voluntary cooperation: its past history and present dynamics are those of an entity designed for and repeatedly recalled to the task of benefiting privileged interests at the expense of ordinary people. It imposes a range of unjust laws, limits people's opportunities to care for themselves, and engages in large-scale aggression (Section B). Its destructiveness is both a product and source of its role as a means of class rule (Section C). Not only is its *existence* rooted in aggression; it has *perpetrated* large-scale aggression—including dispossession and enslavement—at multiple points in its history, aggression without which the existing distribution of wealth and power would be incomprehensible (Section D). And not only past acts of aggression committed or sanctioned by the state but also ongoing privileges secured by the state serve to limit ordinary people's economic opportunities while enriching the ruling class and its cronies (Section E). The state is dangerous and destructive (Section F).

[63] *See* CHARTIER, *supra* note 5, at 25–86.

B. The State Is an Instrument and Product of Aggression and Domination

1. *Aggression Helps to Explain the Origin of the Ruling Class, Its Continuing Power, and the Dynamics of Its Actions*

The state is inimical to peaceful, voluntary cooperation because it is an agency of class dominance. This is not an accident, but rather a function of the kind of entity the state *is*. Concentrated state power is a product of aggression; in turn, aggression reinforces and preserves the strength of the ruling class—those who direct the state and their intimate allies. In addition, its availability for capture serves as an incentive to the formation of organized class groupings and the pursuit of class interests through aggression.[64]

The state's origins may plausibly be reconstructed as lying in aggression (Subsection 2), and past and ongoing state-tolerated or state-perpetrated aggression are essential to explaining the composition, nature, and power of the ruling class (Subsection 3). The ruling class comprises elites inside and outside the formal state apparatus (Subsection 4); wealth enables some of its members to rule, while rulership enables some of its members to acquire wealth (Subsection 5). It is reasonably understood as divided into diverse, sometimes conflicting, sectors and factions (Subsection 6). Even as the ruling class pursues its own interests, it seeks to justify its aggressive behavior through appeals to the public weal (Subsection 7). State power can benefit not only members of the ruling class but also other privileged but less influential beneficiaries of state action (Subsection 8). Aggression and the power of the ruling class are persistently intermingled (Subsection 9).

2. *The State Is Reasonably Seen as a Creation of Aggression*

The state is rooted in predatory violence. On a hypothetical but plausible reconstruction of the state's historical origins, the state emerged from the successful efforts of

[64] *See, e.g.*, Roderick T. Long, *Toward a Libertarian Theory of Class*, 15 Soc. Phil. & Pol'y 303 (1998); Tom G. Palmer, *Classical Liberalism, Marxism, and the Conflict of Classes: The Classical Liberal Theory of Class Conflict*, *in* Realizing Freedom: Libertarian Theory, History, and Practice 255 (2009); Walter E. Grinder & John Hagel, *Toward a Theory of State Capitalism: Ultimate Decision Making and Class Structure*, 1 J. Libertarian Stud. 59 (1977); David M. Hart, The Radical Liberalism of Charles Comte and Charles Dunoyer (1994) (unpublished PhD dissertation, University of Cambridge); Hans-Hermann Hoppe, *Marxist and Austrian Class Analysis*, 9 J. Libertarian Stud. 79 (1990); Wally Conger, Agorist Class Theory: A Left Libertarian Approach to Class Conflict Analysis (n.d.), http://www.agorism.info/AgoristClassTheory.pdf; Albert Jay Nock, Our Enemy the State (1935); Kevin A. Carson, *Another Free-for-All: Libertarian Class Analysis, Organized Labor, Etc.*, Mutualist Blog: Free Market Anti-Capitalism, Jan. 26, 2006, http://mutualist.blogspot.com/2006/01/another-free-for-all-libertarian-class.html; Sheldon Richman, *Class Struggle Rightly Conceived*, The Freeman: Ideas on Liberty, July 13, 2007, http://www.thefreemanonline.org/columns/tgif/class-struggle-rightly-conceived.

marauders to establish their authority over the territories in which they had engaged in aggression.[65] Over time, the rule of the thugs responsible for the state's creation, and their successors, came to appear natural, normal, and legitimate. Recognizing the state's roots in conquest leads to an appealing analysis of the ongoing dynamics of power politics under state rule.[66] In brief: those who occupy positions of power in the state apparatus use aggressive force to acquire and maintain their positions and to enrich themselves and their allies. And, very often, their wealth and power are rooted precisely in the aggression of their ancestors or institutional predecessors.[67]

3. *Aggression—of Which State Action Is a Paradigm Case—Is a Constitutive Characteristic of Class Rule*

Threatened and actual aggression against persons and their justly acquired possessions constitutes and maintains class divisions. Because it is the agency of deliberate aggression par excellence, the state is the source of the ruling class's power.[68]

Threatened or actual aggression, especially aggression by the state, is the operative mechanism responsible for (actively or passively) enabling the ruling class to acquire and maintain its prerogatives. The ruling class can be said to be *defined* by its use of deliberate aggression, of the "political" or "military" means of gaining possessions, as opposed to the ruled class, which employs the "economic," "social," or "civil" means.[69] Some class theories see class stratification and power as rooted in the impersonal operation of economic exchange: on this view, the accidents of history will lead to a concentration of wealth and social influence irreversible except through the use of aggressive force. But it may plausibly be maintained that this sort of concentration occurs only when people engage in aggression in their own interests or when they capture a state apparatus whose métier is aggression. Absent the use of aggression to steal resources and to create and maintain privileges for favored groups, especially the ruling class itself, the irresistible "creative destruction"

[65] *See* Franz Oppenheimer, The State (1997).

[66] *Cf.* Stephen R.L. Clark, The Political Animal: Biology, Ethics, and Politics 34 (1999); Jasay, *supra* note 14, at 16–21.

[67] *See* Kevin A. Carson, The Iron Fist behind the Invisible Hand: Corporate Capitalism as a State-Guaranteed System of Privilege (2002).

[68] One cannot claim that this or that element of someone's identity, including an element that renders her a member of a particular class, *exhaustively determines* her perspective or her behavior. But one can perfectly well acknowledge that shared characteristics (including, for instance, shared kinds of relationships with state power) influence people's behavior, and that people engage in predictably patterned interactions in ways that admit of interesting and illuminating theoretical analysis.

[69] *See, e.g.*, Oppenheimer, *supra* note 65; Clark, *supra* note 66. "Military" emphasizes the centrality of conquest and other forms of aggression to the status of the power elite. The use of "civil" or "social" stresses that what matters about the alternative to the use of aggression is not that it is specifically commercial but rather that it is peaceful and voluntary.

generated by the continuing process of peaceful, voluntary exchange would tend to erode privilege.

It is not possible to *rule*—to compel obedience—without violence, so in the absence of the systematic violence of the state (or some appropriately state-like entity or activity), no one could be said to rule, so there could be no ruling class. (The kind of violence required to rule and to be in any sense a class must be systematic and persistent, rather than ad hoc.) Thus, ruling class identity is *constituted*, albeit not *exhausted*, by relationships with the state.

4. *The Ruling Class Is Plausibly Understood as Comprising Both State Actors and People without Formal State Power*

The ruling class can be seen as fluid, and as including both people who occupy the highest-level positions of decision making within the state and people outside the state apparatus.

Although ruling means being associated with the state, it does not follow that the members of the ruling class, the "power elite,"[70] are simply *identical* with the top-level functionaries of the state. Lines of influence are fluid, as are the memberships of influential groups. Given the fluidity of the ruling class's boundaries and the different purposes for which one might want to discuss this class, it will be a matter of convenience just how one attempts to mark those boundaries. On balance, though, I think it will generally be most illuminating if we say that the ruling class comprises (*i*) those who are (*a*) currently holding the reins of state power or (*b*) substantially influencing those who are (many business elites, especially those in the finance capital sector, are likely to fall in this category);[71] (*ii*) those who have held office or substantially influence officeholders in the past and seem likely to do so again; and (*iii*) those who are closely linked, socially or organizationally, to those in the first two categories—linked intimately enough to be able to influence those who influence state actors or to benefit directly from the exercise of such influence.

5. *Wealth and Social Prominence Are Related to Membership in the Ruling Class in More than One Way*

Being wealthy and socially prominent does not make one a member of the power elite. But there are likely to be connections between wealth and social prominence and membership in the ruling class: being wealthy obviously *does* make it easier to

[70] *Cf.* C. Wright Mills, The Power Elite (1956); G. William Domhoff, Who Rules America? Challenges to Corporate and Class Dominance (6th ed., 2009).

[71] *Cf.* Murray N. Rothbard, Wall Street, Banks, and American Foreign Policy (2011); Anthony C. Sutton, Wall Street and FDR (2007).

shape the ways in which state power is used, and exercising state power makes it easier to become wealthy.

Some wealthy people become elected or appointed officials. Wealthy people may sponsor candidates for elective or appointive office and so promote the selection of persons who are either wealthy themselves or else agents of people who are wealthy. Once in office, elected or appointed officials not already committed to the agenda of elite groups predictably become the foci of efforts to suborn or manipulate them. And, of course, the nature of both campaigning for elective or appointed offices and of exercising the power associated with such offices means that those who successfully seek them are likely, on average, to be significantly more ambitious, power-hungry, and adept at acquiring and keeping power than typical members of the population. Thus, even if previously relatively distant from those with wealth and power, they may be more susceptible to influence by elite groups that offer them security, opportunities for greater power, and chances for financial rewards. And, in any event, they can be expected—presuming they are not already wealthy and socially influential—to employ their offices to secure status, power, and wealth, whether or not by directly serving the interests of the already wealthy.

State functionaries enjoy multiple opportunities to benefit cronies who are not state actors and to obtain benefits conveyed by such cronies. In a state-dominated economy, opportunities for acquiring resources will therefore be greatest, often enough, for those with access to state power. So it is not entirely unlikely that those with access to the wealth needed to offer valuable favors to state actors are people who have already benefited from intimate relationships with the state; and those who may not have had such relationships already but who are able to initiate them can gain more wealth. Thus, in a state-dominated economy, there is good reason to expect both that many of the wealthy will be linked with the state and that people linked intimately with the state will be wealthy. Some members of the ruling class doubtless are not wealthy, but most can be expected to be.

6. *The Ruling Class Need Not Be Thought of as Monolithic*

The state actors and wealthy people who make up the ruling class have overlapping but diverse interests.

Economic and political elites can be seen as entering into shifting alliances of various sorts, in which different factions of the ruling class's complementary sectors—political and economic—are sometimes dominant within their respective sectors, and in which one sector sometimes exercises more, and sometimes less, influence when compared with the other. Regional, cultural, or industrial connections might lead to the creation of factions within the ruling class, factions which might, indeed, be actively at odds with each other.[72]

Just as wealthy people who influence the state from outside may be expected to have diverse and sometimes conflicting goals, state actors, too, have their own commitments and concerns, and can be expected to act accordingly even if these commitments and concerns are at odds with those of this or that wealthy elite. Some state actors will focus directly on enlarging and exercising state power. They may see the expansion of state power as a means of achieving personal goals or perhaps as a way in which such goals might be achieved. That is, they might seek to expand the state's power in order to use that expanded power to confer independent benefits on themselves or their cronies; they might do so because they find the experience of exercising power itself ego-gratifying, even if they are not unilaterally responsible for setting the state's goals, and of course they might pursue ideologically driven goals as well.

On the other hand, however, while the independent concerns of state actors may sometimes explain their actions, political elites will often serve the interests of the ruling class as a whole, or of factions of the ruling class that incorporate both economic and political elites. In particular, when an ideology of support for the interests of the ruling class is widely embraced, and when economic theories that support its goals are conventionally embraced, it may often seem perfectly natural for state functionaries to act in ways that serve the ruling class's overall objectives even in conflict with the preferences of some significant portion of the ruling class's members. And once it is recognized that different sectors of the economic elite do not have perfectly aligned interests, and often compete with each other to capture and deploy state power, it should be apparent that, when political and economic elites are in conflict, state actors are sometimes not directly concerned with promoting their own interests as members of an independent segment of the elite, though they *may* be doing so indirectly. Rather, it will often be the case that they are serving the interests of one elite faction (to which they may belong or with which they may be affiliated) against another.

7. *Elites Justify the Actual or Threatened Use of Aggression through Appeals to Public Well-Being*

Aggressive dispossession is certainly an element of the political means of acquiring wealth. But elites don't characteristically frame their actions as rapacious. Changes in legal rules and institutions designed to benefit privileged elites are often framed

[72] *Cf.* CARL OGLESBY, THE YANKEE AND COWBOY WAR (1977).

as efforts to protect the public. In recent American history, for instance, efforts to reduce pressure on large corporations from upstart alternatives and to enable major industry players to promote cartels were predictably characterized as efforts to protect consumers,[73] even though they often ensured that consumers would pay higher prices or confront fewer options than they otherwise would have. Elites characteristically prefer to promote their own interests under the guise of promoting those of ordinary people.

8. *Spillover Effects of State Policies Designed to Benefit Elites Can Have Favored Consequences for Other Privileged Groups*

Elite groups that belong to the ruling class are not the only beneficiaries of state action. Politically influential, well-favored groups, many of whose members are not part of the ruling class, may nonetheless gain privileges from the state in virtue of the fact that some of their members do belong to the power elite, or simply from the fact that they are able to lobby successfully. These privileged nonelite groups derive some wealth from the political means but no doubt frequently generate wealth using the economic means, as well. Whether the members of such intermediate groups should be seen as primarily identified with the ruling class or whether they are only incidentally associated with it will ordinarily be a matter of degree.

To the extent that such groups exist on the periphery of the power elite, it is because they actively seek privileges from the state and use their influence with economic or political elites to secure rents to which they would not be able to obtain through peaceful, voluntary cooperation. Thus, it is possible clearly to distinguish between these groups and economically vulnerable recipients of state-provided social services. Poor people lack the political influence to shape state policy: they are not responsible for the existence and operation of state programs from which they benefit. These programs are much more likely to be the products of decisions by elite actors, whether undertaken to reduce social conflict, to express compassion, or to bolster their reputations. And, while it is hard to be sure, it is not unreasonable to suspect that poor people are generally net losers, receiving less from the state than they lose to it as a result of opportunities they are prevented from realizing and taxes they are forced to pay.[74]

[73] *See* Gabriel Kolko, The Triumph of Conservatism: A Reinterpretation of American History, 1900–1916 (1963); Butler Shaffer, In Restraint of Trade: The Business Campaign against Competition, 1918–38 (1998). *Cf.* James Weinstein, The Corporate Ideal in the Liberal State, 1900–1918 (1968); Gabriel Kolko, Railroads and Regulation, 1877–1916 (1977); Paul H. Weaver, The Suicidal Corporation: How Big Business Fails America (1989).

[74] *Cf.* Friedman, *supra* note 29, at 135.

9. *The Aggression-Based Dominance of the Ruling Class Lies at the Heart of the State*

Rooted in aggression, the state serves to secure and reinforce the power of the ruling class and to channel resources to the various elite groups that make up this class. While superficially diverse, these groups are linked by their dependence on state power, which they deploy in ways that they seek to persuade others, and perhaps themselves, serve the flourishing of all. In fact, however, as a tool of predatory elites, the state is the enemy of peaceful, voluntary cooperation.

C. The State Persistently Threatens Peaceful, Voluntary Cooperation

1. *The State Serves Particular Interests while Interfering with Peaceful, Voluntary Cooperation*

The state undermines peaceful, voluntary cooperation by interfering with just rules and general order-maintenance strategies and by engaging in constant injustice in relation to particular people. It engages in aggression on a grand scale (Subsection 2), enforces unjust rules that restrict personal freedom (Subsection 3), interferes with people's discretionary control of their possessions and disrupts bottom-up social self-organization by attempting to engage in large-scale planning of which it is in principle incapable (Subsection 4), undermines alternatives to itself (Subsection 5), empowers political elites and their subordinates to pursue their own interests and those of their cronies at the public's expense (Subsection 6), and discourages the formation and expression of caring motives (Subsection 7). Its very existence impedes fruitful legal experimentation and flexibility (Subsection 8). It has perpetrated and continues to ratify large-scale theft in the interest of elites (Subsection 9). It maintains systems of privilege that benefit the well-connected while increasing poverty and economic vulnerability (Subsection 10), and it has proven dangerous not only to the economically vulnerable but also to those marginalized in other ways (Subsection 11). It persistently impedes peaceful, voluntary cooperation (Subsection 12).

2. *The State Engages in and Sanctions Large-Scale Aggression*

The state promotes and engages in war.[75] Its ability to secure funding forcibly, borrow, and (over the short term) create money enables it to maintain and deploy

[75] *See* CHARTIER, *supra* note 5, at 53–68; RUDOLPH JOSEPH RUMMEL, STATISTICS OF DEMOCIDE: GENOCIDE AND MASS MURDER SINCE 1900 (1997); [Matthew White] *Source List and Detailed Death Tolls for the Twentieth Century Hemoclysm*, HISTORICAL ATLAS OF THE TWENTIETH CENTURY, http://www.erols.com/mwhite28/warstat1.htm.

military forces. It can maintain standing military forces, and thus deploy them with little popular oversight. It goes to war for unjust reasons—to increase its own power or to enrich its cronies. When it engages in war, it consistently fails to discriminate between combatants and noncombatants. And it uses warfare as an excuse for domestic authoritarianism. In addition, preparing for large-scale aggression has the perverse effect of prompting potential victims to prepare for and engage in war; and this can add to the illusion of the state's own indispensability, since it can position itself as the only entity capable of protecting people from the threat of violence perpetrated by others—violence which it has itself helped to render more likely.[76]

3. *The State Restricts Personal Freedom*

The state uses force to prevent, end, or remedy conduct that is not precluded by the NAM. In particular, it unjustly implements a system of criminal law.[77] A crime is an offense against the state, rather than against any particular sentient. The criminal law allows the state to impose penalties, up to and including life imprisonment and death, in the absence of actual injury, evidence of the *extent* of putative injury, or the desire of a victim to seek redress, and without providing compensation to actual victims. The criminal law gives the state an open-ended license to regulate, regiment, prohibit, and punish peaceful, voluntary conduct. State-maintained police forces act with impunity as they enforce the criminal law, operating without the constraints and risks of liability that would be confronted by non-state actors; thus, they consistently engage in brutal aggression with minimal consequences. And the state uses its authority to regulate personal conduct—involving everything from the voluntary use of chemical substances to consensual sexual behavior—in ways that constrain people's freedom and increase and perpetuate serious social problems (as with the "War on [some] Drugs"). While it does this especially through the criminal law, it also creates tort law remedies for conduct that does not violate the NAM, again interfering with peaceful, voluntary conduct by introducing force into disputes that ought to be resolved nonviolently.

4. *The State Seeks to Manage or Plan the Economy at the Micro and Macro Levels*

The state consistently violates the NAM by interfering with people's just possessory claims. It does so through regulatory schemes that constrain people's use of their

[76] *See* TAYLOR, COOPERATION, *supra* note 7, at 165–66.

[77] *See* CHARTIER, *supra* note 5, at 69–86. On the injustice of the criminal law and the institutions that implement it, *see, e.g.*, CLARENCE DARROW, RESIST NOT EVIL (1902); Chapter 5.II, *infra*.

possessions and through various activities that actually deprive people of their possessions. These interventions create and maintain monopolies over the provision of various goods and services—with all the difficulties predictably associated with monopolies, including unresponsiveness, inefficiency, inflexibility, inadequate provision levels, and high cost. The state also seeks to offer macro-level direction to the economy despite the fact that it lacks, in principle, the information needed to do so—and, given its illegitimacy, lacks the authority to do so as well. Thus, it promotes chaos and inefficiency.[78] It sometimes does this because of the delusion that it can, in fact, provide effective direction regarding production and distribution, and sometimes simply to benefit various well-connected groups. Its attempts at macro-level management, both those rooted in overweening confidence in expertise and those reflective of venality, disrupt economic life, foster over- and underproduction, and redistribute wealth upward to favored groups.

5. *The State Weakens or Eliminates Non-State Institutions*

The state renders social order less robust by colonizing multiple areas of social life and displacing people's attempts to maintain order without its interference. By seeking to create alternatives to the institutions communities can create on their own, the state reduces the likelihood that people will persist in maintaining order or in caring for each other absent its involvement.[79]

6. *The State Empowers Actors Who Can Be Counted on to Pursue Their Own Interests and Those of Their Cronies and Who Are in Large Part Unaccountable*

The state creates repeated opportunities for harmful conduct on the part of those who occupy official positions. The opportunity to use force to control others' lives attracts the venal and the power-hungry, and even decent persons who assume government positions are often corrupted. By giving distinctive opportunities for the ambitious and greedy to exercise power, the state puts everyone else at risk.

The opportunities the state affords those with power are particularly dangerous because influencing state actors and holding them accountable is enormously difficult and costly. Given the unavoidable institutional limitations of state decision-making entities and the complexity of the decisions made by state actors, with their vast ramifications, it is not overly surprising that most people lack good information

[78] *See, e.g.*, F.A. Hayek, Individualism and Economic Order 33–56, 77–91 (1948); Ludwig von Mises, Socialism: An Economic and Sociological Analysis 97–105, 112–23 (1981).

[79] *See* Taylor, Cooperation, *supra* note 7, at 166–68.

regarding policies the state is considering and those it has chosen to implement and good theoretical frameworks within which to interpret these policies.[80] Most people also, unavoidably, lack good information about the actual positions (as opposed to the public postures) of state decision makers and about the implications of moves made by politicians in complex chess games that may be completely opaque when viewed only in part, as well as the ability to effectively influence these decision makers.[81]

7. *The State Reduces the Likelihood of Peaceful, Voluntary Cooperation by Altering Ordinary People's Incentives and Motivations*

State action tends to discourage the formation and propagation of altruistic motivations and behaviors, with the result that people are less likely than they would be in its absence to care for each other on a personal basis or to help craft and maintain institutions that benefit others—whether by promoting peaceful, voluntary exchange, fostering mutual aid, or acting caringly in other ways.[82]

8. *The State Retards Legal Experimentation and Flexibility*

An entity with a monopoly of force in a given geographic area reduces the opportunities available to its subjects to experiment with alternate legal standards and procedures. It is costly, in both monetary and non-monetary terms, to uproot oneself and relocate in search of alternate legal institutions. But the only way to create or support alternate institutions, when one lives under the rule of a state, is to relocate geographically—to vote with one's feet. Legal experimentation leads to the development of new and better rules and institutions and encourages their adoption by others, but it is much more difficult for this kind of experimentation to take place and to be effective when states exercise geographic monopolies of force. When legal regimes are entirely deterritorialized, or when, though territorial, they do not monopolize the process of creating and enforcing legal rules within their territories, experimentation can take place with far less cost, so that rules and institutions can be refined through ongoing experimental processes. By contrast, states inhibit experimentation and limit the discovery and adoption of fruitful, emulable legal rules and institutions.[83] As geographic monopolists, they offer one-size-fits-all

[80] *Cf.* Mancur Olson, The Logic of Collective Action: Public Goods and the Theory of Groups (1971); Bryan Caplan, The Myth of the Rational Voter: Why Democracies Choose Bad Policies (2007).

[81] *Cf.* Charlotte A. Twight, Dependent on D.C.: The Rise of Federal Control over the Lives of Ordinary Americans (2003). Thanks to Sheldon Richman for this reference.

[82] *See* Taylor, Cooperation, *supra* note 7, at 168–79.

[83] Paul Roemer's proposals regarding "charter cities" capture some of the concerns I note in this section, not least because the cost of exiting a typical city is far smaller than the cost of exiting a typical

solutions to societal problems, minimizing opportunities for choice and for flexible, particularized responses to complex challenges.[84]

9. *The State Underwrites the Aggression That Lies behind the Contemporary Distribution of Wealth*

i. State-sanctioned or state-perpetrated theft, engrossment, and enslavement have created elites and boosted their wealth and power

Occurring at the state's hands, with its blessing, or as aspects of its origin, land theft and land engrossment have taken place on an enormous scale in the history of multiple societies around the world, as have enslavement and serfdom, consistently giving rise to dominator and dominated classes. The large-scale theft involved in the "primitive accumulation" of resources impoverished peasants and enriched aristocrats (Subsubsection ii). Later land theft, the engrossment of land to which no one had a just claim, and other sorts of aggression further enhanced the wealth of the ruling classes and their cronies (Subsubsection iii). Past injustice lies at the root of ruling class power (Subsubsection iv).

ii. Primitive accumulation led to widespread reductions in economic well-being, social influence, and freedom for many people

Members of the peasant class have been repeatedly subjected to a series of legally effected or legally tolerated dispossessions that constrained their access to resources and that continue to affect their descendants' economic positions.[85] These dispossessions were responsible for the creation of enormous agricultural estates and the concentration of land in the hands of the agricultural aristocracy. "Nowhere and at no time has the large scale ownership of land come into being through the working of economic forces.... It is the result of military and political effort. Founded by violence, it has been upheld by violence and by that alone."[86]

Consider the English experience. Feudal land tenure arrangements, in which smallholders became serfs, came into being in multiple ways. Frequently, however,

state. Still, Roemer's charter cities would be, at best, geographic monopolists with small territories (and sometimes not even that, since charter cities could frequently be expected to operate within the confines of rules established by the states claiming the territory in which the charter cities operated). For ongoing discussion of Roemer's ideas, see the blog CHARTER CITIES, http://chartercities.org/.

[84] *See* FRIEDMAN, *supra* note 29, at 156–59.

[85] I draw throughout this historical discussion on the work of Kevin Carson; *see, e.g.*, KEVIN A. CARSON, STUDIES IN MUTUALIST POLITICAL ECONOMY (2007). *Cf.* J.L. & BARBARA HAMMOND, THE VILLAGE LABOURER, 1760–1832: A STUDY IN THE GOVERNMENT OF ENGLAND BEFORE THE REFORM BILL (1913); CHRISTOPHER HILL, THE CENTURY OF REVOLUTION: 1603–1714 (1961); CHRISTOPHER HILL, REFORMATION TO THE INDUSTRIAL REVOLUTION, 1603–1714 (1967). Thanks to Carson for these sources and for providing further insights in an exchange regarding the contents of Chapter 3.

[86] LUDWIG VON MISES, SOCIALISM: AN ECONOMIC AND SOCIOLOGICAL ANALYSIS 335 (1981).

violent usurpation was used to create the peasant class. When people in undisputed possession of land were converted by force in early mediæval England from independent smallholders to tenants, their incomes were reduced and their independence constrained; they became serfs subject to the authority of feudal overlords. Without land of their own, peasants had no choice but to accept work on the landlords' terms and to devote labor to paying rent on what should have been their own land, thus diverting resources from their own consumption and from productive, rather than parasitic, exchanges with others.

The dissolution of the monasteries and the disbursement of their land to the state's cronies further increased peasants' economic insecurity. Many of the monasteries' tenants were further impoverished by being evicted from their land, and income the monasteries had previously used to provide poor relief—especially important to peasants paying high rents, or with no access to land at all—was no longer available, because the monasteries no longer operated and new claimants had no great interest in aiding the poor. Those who continued as tenants when land formerly held by monasteries was distributed to the wealthy and well-connected enjoyed reduced security and less favorable terms.

Subsequently, successive waves of enclosures—converting fields that belonged to groups of peasants into the possessions of aristocrats—limited access to land used for grazing and the cultivation of crops. The remaining entitlements of peasants, unjustly treated as tenants on what should have been their own land, were increasingly reduced in ways that made it easier for wealthy landlords to evict them. The few remaining legal safeguards from which they might have benefited were relentlessly pruned away, as feudal landlords came increasingly to be treated as just possessors and peasants as mere renters. And laws against hunting further affected the independence of most people, accustomed to eating meat. Without land to raise their own animals and without the ability to hunt on land engrossed by the Crown and the aristocracy, people often had no choice but to accept paid work on unattractive terms; and, of course, those in a position to offer paid work on these terms were not infrequently also those responsible for the enclosures and the preclusion of hunting.

By the eighteenth century, the second great wave of enclosures had begun, with the wealthy and well-connected seizing cottagers' land and, significantly, ensuring—quite deliberately—that many ordinary people would have few options other than paid employment. And again, not surprisingly, such employment was often provided by the same people who had enthusiastically promoted the measures that had eliminated other means of subsistence. In addition, an internal passport system effectively limited people's ability to seek employment outside their home parishes and required them to accept work on whatever terms were locally available: they were denied the benefits the availability of alternatives and opportunities to travel freely in search of work might otherwise have afforded them.

iii. Past and present land theft and engrossment and other forms of aggression continue to drive wealth concentration

The use of state-secured privilege to acquire land did not stop with the enclosures nor was it limited to Europe. It has been a central aspect of the colonial experience as well.

In colonial North America and the early United States, politicians used violence to evict American Indians from land they occupied and used. And the British government handed out enormous parcels of land—land stolen from the Indians and land arbitrarily claimed by the Crown—to colonial aristocrats and other cronies. The same practice continued after independence, as politicians enriched themselves and their cronies by stealing Indian land and by engrossing unoccupied land to which no one had a just claim and creating title to it out of thin air.[87] Land engrossment simultaneously decreased the options available to already economically vulnerable people and increased the relative power of the politically privileged elites who benefited from it.

The creation of the *latifundia* of Latin America by means of the forcible conversion of customary possessors of agricultural land into serfs and tenants led to the impoverishment of many people and the enrichment of the elite. And other kinds of aggression have also served to deprive ordinary people of resources and opportunities while funneling both to politically privileged groups, which have enjoyed a thoroughgoing "subsidy of history."[88] Obvious examples include conquest and enslavement, which helped dramatically to reduce the economic prospects of racialized groups in the Americas and in the South Pacific.

iv. Theft, engrossment, and enslavement underlie the power of the rulers and the liabilities experienced by the ruled

Class dynamics emerge from aggression, including theft, engrossment, and enslavement—beginning with feudal land theft, continuing with enclosure, and including such later developments as vast North American landgrabs and the rise of the global slave trade. All of these developments help to provide the background to much of the distribution of wealth and social and political influence in contemporary society.

Feudal dispossession, enclosure, and other sorts of dispossession still profoundly affect the distribution of wealth and social influence. This would be true even in an economic environment unfettered by subsequently instituted varieties of

87 *See, e.g.*, A.M. Sakolski, The Great American Land Bubble: The Amazing Story of Land Grabbing, Speculations, and Booms from Colonial Days to the Present Time (1932); Joseph Stromberg, *The American Land Question*, *in* Markets Not Capitalism: Individualist Anarchism against Bosses, Inequality, Corporate Power, and Structural Poverty 335 (Gary Chartier & Charles W. Johnson eds., 2011) [*hereinafter* Markets Not Capitalism].

88 *See* Kevin A. Carson, *The Subsidy of History*, The Freeman: Ideas on Liberty, June 2008, at 33, *available at* http://www.thefreemanonline.org/featured/the-subsidy-of-history.

privilege—people's starting points can and do affect their abilities to take risks and survive downturns—but it is doubly true given that the shape of contemporary society continues to be distorted by privilege and the maldistribution of power. Land is still the foundation of much wealth, and those who hold unjustly acquired land titles are as able to use their possessions to buffer them against the effects of ineptitude and ill-fortune as are those with justly gained titles. The consequences of past land theft reverberate across successive generations. The same is obviously true of enslavement, which can dramatically affect people's life-chances and those of their descendants.

Land theft, land engrossment, conquest, and slavery can be seen as legally sanctioned in two senses. First, when they occurred, they characteristically took place with the authority or tolerance of the state. Second, systematic legal remedies have not been provided to their victims. The beneficiaries of this legally sanctioned aggression have varied to some extent, but they have consistently belonged to politically favored groups—they've been either members of the power elite or their associates. These groups have also benefited, not only from specific acts of large-scale, legally sanctioned injustice, but also from injustices embodied in statist legal systems themselves in the form of structural privileges.

10. *Continuing State-Secured Privileges Enrich the Wealthy and Well-Connected while Making and Keeping Many People Poor*

i. The state benefits the wealthy and harms the poor

The state preserves the power of the ruling at the expense of ordinary people. This is true not only when the state is monarchical, aristocratic, or dictatorial, but also when it is democratic: democratic political institutions and processes simply serve as new sources of legitimation for elite rule, arguably more effective than ones that highlight, rather than appearing to collapse, the distinction between the rulers and the ruled. A broad range of legal rules and institutions create wealth for privileged elites (Subsubsection ii) while making or keeping other people poor (Subsubsection iii).[89] The state is an agency of entrenched privilege and deprivation (Subsubsection iv).

[89] *Cf.* Kevin A. Carson, Organization Theory 381–426 (2008), for a discussion of many of these privileges. Which rules regarding the just possession of land count as privileges secured by the state to the benefit of economic elites is a matter of considerable debate. For Georgists, *see, e.g.*, Henry George, Progress and Poverty (4th ed., 1912), people may justly become entitled to possess land and to generate income from improvements to land, but some or all of the unimproved value of land may justly be claimed by community institutions. For contemporary mutualists, *see, e.g.*, Carson, *supra* note 85, someone must personally occupy and use land in order to maintain a claim to own it. By contrast, for Lockeans, *see, e.g.*, Murray N. Rothbard, The Ethics of Liberty (1982), absentee land claims are perfectly acceptable, and the unimproved as much as the improved value of land rightly belongs to the absentee possessor. The gaps between these positions can be narrowed in various ways. For instance, in a community with Lockean legal rules regarding land, nonviolent

ii. State regulations boost the wealth of the wealthy and well-connected
Laws repeatedly transfer resources from ordinary people to the ruling class and other groups able to extract privileges from the state.[90]

- Land-use regulations and building codes, whatever the intentions of some who support them, tend generally to redistribute wealth to those with land by reducing the alternatives available to those without land who wish to acquire it or use it temporarily, and thus raising the cost of rental or purchase.[91] They also increase the profits of the politically well-connected construction industry.
- Currency monopolies are not necessary as sources of financial stability or monetary integrity;[92] while justified as if they were, their effective function is in fact to allow states to create money that is disproportionately bestowed on privileged interests before its value is decreased by inflationary pressures. The initial recipients—as of bailout funds in the United States—benefit while subsequent recipients often suffer because of inflation. These monopolies enable states to impose what amount to hidden taxes by inflating the currency at will and thus

social pressure can be used to ensure payment of what would be a Georgist land value tax if extracted by force (thanks to Less Antman for this example). Similarly, adverse possession standards in a community with Lockean legal rules regarding land that treated fully unoccupied land as abandoned after a relatively limited period could function much like occupancy-and-use standards in a mutualist community (albeit without the requirement of personal occupancy). And mutualist communities might have varying views about just how absent an absentee would have to be to abandon land, and how to understand the difference between agents on the one hand and co-possessors on the other.

[90] These privileges persistently redistribute wealth from ordinary people to the wealthy and well-connected and ought—as it will be obvious I am arguing—to be eliminated. Thus, a scheme of legal protection for just possessory claims would certainly affect the availability of rent and profit because it would involve the elimination of privilege. However, (*i*) I do not wish to maintain that land and capital would earn no return in an economic environment free from privilege, though it does seems to me that the returns earned by both are inexplicable apart from the labor that underlies capital and cultivates land, making each available for use. (*ii*) I would not argue that interest and rent are *as such* monopolistic, and I certainly do not believe they ought to be legally precluded. But it also seems plausible to me that, absent state-secured privilege, interest rates and rental costs could be expected to be lower than at present. The current levels of interest and rent *do*, I think, reflect the effects of privilege (whether or not it makes sense to talk about this privilege as monopolistic). (*iii*) Without state-facilitated land engrossment and land theft, state-mandated building codes, zoning regulations, and so forth, the cost of access to land would be far lower than at present; the practical result, it seems to me, in a privilege-free environment marked by ease of entry, would be that rental costs were driven down significantly. (*iv*) Without restraints on banking, mutual banking schemes might sometimes be able to provide capital at lower rates than those otherwise on offer; the availability of such schemes, if they proved viable, could drive down interest rates offered by conventional banks. Although returns not dependent on privilege could be expected to persist, the effect of eliminating all privileges, while enforcing the baseline rules, could be significantly to lower returns.

[91] On the impact of these kinds of regulations on access to housing, *see* WILLIAM TUCKER, THE EXCLUDED AMERICANS: HOMELESSNESS AND HOUSING POLICIES (1990).

[92] *See* GEORGE A. SELGIN, THE THEORY OF FREE BANKING: MONEY SUPPLY UNDER COMPETITIVE NOTE ISSUE (1988); LAWRENCE H. WHITE, THE THEORY OF MONETARY INSTITUTIONS (1999).

to fund costly, destructive projects—notably large-scale wars—while encountering relatively little political opposition (given that the link between purchasing power reductions and inflation is less obvious than the link between income reductions and taxation—the other likely source of revenue for these projects).

- Capitalization requirements and other regulations on banking tend to benefit established industry players and to limit opportunities to engage in banking and thus the availability of capital—in particular, by preventing people from pooling their resources to create low-capital alternatives to conventional banking arrangements. Thus, they increase the cost of capital and the profits of bankers.[93]
- Subsidies to transportation—as, for instance, investments in roads the costs of which are not fully internalized by frequent, heavy users—heighten the profits of large firms dependent on the long-distance movement of goods at the expense of other firms not dependent in this way and of the members of the public required to pay for the subsidies.[94]
- Rules allowing for compulsory purchase are used by the state to acquire land at rates lower than those people would be willing voluntarily to accept and to transfer it to private developers—a practice that spares developers the expense of acquiring the land on terms satisfactory to the just claimants and thus amounts to an involuntary transfer to the developers.
- Professional licensing and accreditation rules help to create transactional environments distorted by oligopolistic privilege and so to shift wealth to politically well-connected groups at the expense of consumers. Business and professional licensing drives up the profits of those with licenses—from physicians and lawyers to beauticians[95]—while unnecessarily reducing the options and the resources of those who take advantage of their services.[96]
- Accreditation and need-certification requirements for hospitals and similar facilities reduce supply, thus increasing the costs of health care and increasing the profits of established players.
- Zoning and similar regulations increase the costs associated with starting small firms and thus force many people who would prefer to work for themselves into paid employment.

[93] *See* William Batchelder Greene, Mutual Banking (1850).

[94] *See* Kevin A. Carson, *The Distorting Effects of Transportation Subsidies*, The Freeman: Ideas on Liberty, Nov. 2010, at 17, *available at* http://www.thefreemanonline.org/featured/the-distorting-effects-of-transportation-subsidies.

[95] Mechanisms for certifying the quality of providers of professional and other services would remain vital in any conceivable society; such mechanisms could and would readily emerge without the state's involvement. Thanks to Stephen Clark for reminding me of the importance of making this point explicitly.

[96] *See* Milton Friedman, Capitalism and Freedom 137–60 (1962).

- Regulations sold to the public as designed to benefit consumers or small producers are much more likely, in general, to solidify the positions of large established businesses and to enable them to profit at consumers' expense by insulating them from the pressure to serve consumers that is created by the existence of alternatives.[97]
- Monopolistic PP privileges offer arbitrary protection to artificial possessory claims that foster inefficient litigation, allow their holders to infringe on the justly acquired possessions of others, reduce innovation, concentrate wealth, enhance corporate power, and fail to spur the productivity their defenders adduce in support of their continued availability.[98]
- Tariffs help to maintain and enhance the wealth of well-connected firms. They boost the profits of domestic producers at the expense of consumers and foreign producers and make it easier for domestic producers to cartelize by insulating them from the pressures generated by the presence of genuine options for consumers. Tariffs also hurt poor people in developed societies by significantly increasing the costs they need to pay for imported goods (including, often enough, food needed for good health that would be less expensive than domestic alternatives absent import duties) and reduce the incomes of producers in less-developed ones. Though often touted as propping up poor workers' incomes, they serve primarily to increase the profits of poorly performing domestic producers at the expense of both domestic consumers (especially poor ones) and foreign producers.[99]

[97] *See* the sources cited in note 73, *supra*.

[98] *Cf.* KEVIN A. CARSON, "INTELLECTUAL PROPERTY": A LIBERTARIAN CRITIQUE 19 (2009), http://c4ss.org/wp-content/uploads/2009/05/intellectual-property-a-libertarian-critique.pdf; STEPHAN KINSELLA, AGAINST INTELLECTUAL PROPERTY (2008); MICHELE BOLDRIN & DAVID K. LEVINE, AGAINST INTELLECTUAL MONOPOLY (2008); Chapter 2.V.D, *supra*.

[99] *See* JAY R. MANDLE, GLOBALIZATION AND THE POOR (2003); Elaine Maag, *How Tariff Policy Can Hurt the Poor*, CHRISTIAN SCI. MONITOR, June 14, 2011, http://www.csmonitor.com/Business/Tax-VOX/2011/0614/How-tariff-policy-can-hurt-the-poor; Matthew Franklin, *Julia Gillard Throws Open Market to World's Poor*, AUSTRALIAN, Oct. 26, 2011, http://www.theaustralian.com.au/national-affairs/gillard-throws-open-market-to-worlds-poor/story-fnapmixa-1226176658147; DANIEL GRISWOLD, MAD ABOUT TRADE: WHY MAIN STREET AMERICA SHOULD EMBRACE GLOBALIZATION (2009); Daniel Griswold, *Obama's Protectionist Policies Hurting Low-Income Americans*, CATO INSTITUTE, Sept. 29, 2009, http://www.cato.org/pub_display.php?pub_id=10590; Al From, *America by the Numbers: How Tariffs Hurt the Working Poor*, DLC, Jan. 25, 2002, http://www.dlc.org/ndol_ci.cfm?kaid=127&subid=305&contentid=250141; EDWARD GRESSER, FREEDOM FROM WANT: AMERICAN LIBERALISM AND THE GLOBAL ECONOMY (2007); Edward Gresser, *The Rebirth of Pro-Shopper Populism: Affordable Shoes, Outdoor Apparel, and the Case for Tariff Reform*, June 2011, http://www.outdoorindustry.org/pdf/Tariffs_Taxation.pdf. The link between tariffs and economic vulnerability was particularly apparent during the nineteenth-century English dispute over the Corn Laws. *See, e.g.*, PAUL A. PICKERING & ALEX TYRRELL, THE PEOPLE'S BREAD: A HISTORY OF THE ANTI-CORN LAW LEAGUE (2000); FRANK TRENTMANN, FREE TRADE NATION: COMMERCE, CONSUMPTION, AND CIVIL SOCIETY IN MODERN BRITAIN (2009).

- The provision of subsidies to state-favored corporations and nongovernmental organizations simultaneously impoverishes ordinary people—who are required to pay for these subsidies—and boosts the influence of the favored organizations, which are thus able to gain further wealth and power.
- Politically guaranteed privileges are responsible in multiple ways for many corporate profits. In an environment in which this is so, unionization can help to improve workers' economic positions. Legally imposed limitations on union activity can tend to reduce unions' influence, and so to reduce the incomes of workers who might make more were they free to engage in more radical (nonaggressive) bargaining tactics.[100] These limits thus amount to privileges conferred on employers.

Multiple privileges, often sold as somehow designed to benefit ordinary people at the expense of the wealthy and well-connected, frequently serve, in fact, precisely to secure the economic positions of the favored at the expense of others. As Adam Smith observed, "People of the same trade seldom meet together, even for merriment and diversion, but the conversation ends in a conspiracy against the public, or in some contrivance to raise prices."[101] The state is the agency through which they do this.

iii. Regulations help to make and keep people poor

Privileges conferred on the wealthy and well-connected are, simultaneously, serious burdens on the poor.

- The requirement that one obtain a business license, or some other sort of permission from local authorities, in order to open a business limits the ability of people with little start-up capital to start new firms, thus constraining their income-earning opportunities and propelling them into paid employment, even at terms they find thoroughly undesirable.
- Specific occupational licensing requirements are obviously even more burdensome, especially when they require costly and dispensable equipment or unnecessary certification. Rules that necessitate enormous up-front expenditures to work in particular fields—say, those needed to obtain New York taxicab medallions—obviously limit poor people's access to income and productive work as well.
- Immigration restrictions keep poor people from seeking work legally. These restrictions thus prevent those who are subjected to them from bettering their economic positions. They also ensure that poor immigrants who work illegally

[100] *See* Kevin A. Carson, Labor Struggle: A Free Market Model (Center for a Stateless Society, Paper 10, 2010), http://c4ss.org/wp-content/uploads/2010/09/C4SS-Labor.pdf.

[101] Adam Smith, An Inquiry into the Nature and Cause of the Wealth of Nations 1.10.2 (1776).

may accept low wages and poor working conditions without protest in order to avoid exposure and deportation.

- Zoning and similar requirements keep people from using the low-cost facilities that are their own homes to produce goods and services or make them available to others, thus imposing the heavy burden of working elsewhere.
- The burden on the poor is only increased when certain kinds of jobs are denied to people entirely—as, for instance, selling medications in locations other than legally approved pharmacies supervised by licensed pharmacists.[102]
- Building regulations and land-use requirements affect the ability of poor people in developed societies to find housing: housing that doesn't meet someone else's standards of middle-class acceptability is denied to poor people who could pay for it, but who might be unable to pay for anything else.
- Minimum wage requirements reduce work opportunities for poor people.[103] They have also served, and have been intended precisely to serve, to exclude the putatively unfit and undesirable, including women and members of ethnic minority groups, from the workforce.[104]

In addition to sanctioning theft, dispossession, and slavery and safeguarding the privileges of the wealthy and well-connected, the state enacts regulations that, in effect, impose particular liabilities on the poor—together constituting, in effect, a hidden tax on poverty.

iv. The state is a persistent source of privilege for the favored and of liability for the disfavored

The state is frequently justified as a source of "countervailing power" capable of balancing the influence and potential for mischief of economic elites. The "countervailing power" thesis reflects a view of state power that seems unwarrantedly benign. State actors cannot be counted on to exert countervailing power to restrain or counter elites; it is much more sensible to expect them frequently either to use

[102] *Cf.* Charles W. Johnson, *Scratching By: How Government Creates Poverty as We Know It*, *in* MARKETS NOT CAPITALISM, *supra* note 87, at 377, http://www.thefreemanonline.org/featured/scratching-by-how-government-creates-poverty-as-we-know-it. While licensing laws of all kinds are deeply problematic, this obviously does not mean that we would be without reliable means of determining the qualifications of professionals absent the state.

[103] *Cf.* Daniel Shaviro, *The Minimum Wage, the Earned Income Tax Credit, and Optimal Subsidy Policy*, 64 U. CHI. L. Rev. 405 (1997); James R. Kearl et al., *A Confusion of Economists?*, 69 AM. ECON. REV. 28 (1979); Bruno Frey *et al.*, *Consensus and Dissension among Economists: An Empirical Inquiry*, 74 AM. ECON. REV. 986 (1984). Thanks to Shaviro for the subsequent references. Obviously, while lack of the kinds of work opportunities minimum wage laws reduce is undesirable, work for oneself or as part of a partnership or cooperative is surely preferable in most cases to paid employment.

[104] *See, e.g.*, Thomas C. Leonard, *Protecting Family and Race: The Progressive Case for Regulating Women's Work*, 64 AM. J. ECON. & SOCIOLOGY 757 (2005); Thomas C. Leonard, *Eugenics and Economics in the Progressive Era*, 19 J. ECON. PERSPECTIVES 207 (2005).

their power to promote their own, independent, interests, or to partner with other members of the ruling class to abuse ordinary people (or perhaps to promote the interests of particular elite factions). The privileges state actors secure for members of the ruling class and their cronies often serve to redistribute wealth upward—to increase the wealth and power of the well-connected while directly and indirectly limiting the opportunities of ordinary people, often consigning them to poverty and forcing them to accept work on employers' terms.

11. *The State Fosters Oppression on the Basis of Ethnicity, Gender, and Sexual Identity*

I have focused primarily on the use of state power to maintain the wealth and position of elite groups defined in economic terms. And it is clear that socioeconomic, ethnic, cultural, and gender-based violence and social dominance intersect in multiple ways, with members of disfavored groups likely to suffer from the problems attendant on poverty and economic vulnerability generally. But it is obvious that not all inequities are narrowly economic in nature. The state's violence targets women, sexual minorities, and members of disfavored ethnic,[105] cultural, and religious groups in differential ways, both reflecting and strengthening patterns of violent abuse and nonviolent subordination. Thus, for instance:

- States have imposed legal disabilities on women—including paternalistic labor legislation and limits on work—while legitimizing the use of violence against women (as in rape inside and outside marriage) to compel their submission to men.[106]
- States have been key enablers and proponents of genocide.[107]
- State power was used to steal land from American Indians and to subject them to violent repression when they resisted.[108]
- Indigenous Australians were evicted from their land and killed with disturbing frequently in connection with the settlement of Australia by Europeans, too often with state connivance or support.[109]

[105] *See, e.g.*, WALTER WILLIAMS, THE STATE AGAINST BLACKS (1984).

[106] *See, e.g.*, Sharon Presley, *Government Is Women's Enemy—Part 1*, FREE VOICES, Jan.–Feb. 2012, at 6; FREEDOM, FEMINISM, AND THE STATE (Wendy McElroy ed., 1991).

[107] *See, e.g.*, ADAM JONES, GENOCIDE: A COMPREHENSIVE INTRODUCTION (2006).

[108] *See* Carl Watner, *Libertarians and Indians: Proprietary Justice and Aboriginal Land Rights*, 7 J. LIBERTARIAN STUD. 147 (1983). *Cf.* GLORIA JAHODA, TRAIL OF TEARS: THE STORY OF THE AMERICAN INDIAN REMOVALS 1813–1855 (1975); FRANCIS PRUCHA, THE GREAT FATHER: THE UNITED STATES GOVERNMENT AND THE AMERICAN INDIANS (1984); DEE BROWN, BURY MY HEART AT WOUNDED KNEE: AN INDIAN HISTORY OF THE AMERICAN WEST (2007).

[109] *See, e.g.*, A. DIRK MOSES, GENOCIDE AND SETTLER SOCIETY: FRONTIER VIOLENCE AND STOLEN INDIGENOUS CHILDREN IN AUSTRALIAN HISTORY (2004).

- While slavery in other societies has not necessarily been racialized, and so can be seen as an egregious abuse occurring primarily in the economic realm, as an expropriation of labor, an ideology of racial subordination emerged to rationalize chattel slavery in the United States, with black people enslaved in vast numbers—a matter of private violence carried on with the sanction of the state's legal system—and picked out for legal disabilities even when they were not slaves.[110]
- In the post-slavery "Jim Crow" era, state power—used in tandem with state-tolerated private violence—was used to limit black Americans' work options,[111] economic opportunities, and access to private facilities that would otherwise have been made available to them. In many cases, legal rules effectively recreated slavery for putatively free people.[112]
- The American state's "War on Drugs" has been fed by images of black perversity and delinquency and has been consistently applied in racialized ways, with different penalties for the consumption of substances preferred by different ethnic groups and with members of ethnic minorities more likely to suffer severe consequences for consuming illegal substances than whites.[113]
- In South Africa, the state brutally imposed a system of racial segregation on an often unwilling population, using violence to maintain it.[114]
- State-imposed barriers to immigration into the United States seem fairly clearly to be driven in significant part by racist suspicion of poor, nonwhite Latin Americans (who serve, of course, as convenient targets for fears derived from economic insecurities for which they bear no responsibility).[115]

[110] *See, e.g.*, Ira Berlin, Generations of Captivity: A History of African American Slaves (2003); Orlando Patterson, Slavery and Social Death (1982); Orlando Patterson, Rituals of Blood: Consequences of Slavery in Two American Centuries (1999); David Brion Davis, Inhuman Bondage: The Rise and Fall of Slavery in the New World (2006); A. Leon Higginbotham, Jr., In the Matter of Color: Race and the American Legal Process: The Colonial Period (1978).

[111] *See, e.g.*, David E. Bernstein, Only One Place of Redress: African Americans, Labor Regulations, and the Courts from Reconstruction to the New Deal (2001).

[112] *See, e.g.*, Douglas A. Blackmon, Slavery by Another Name: The Re-Enslavement of Blacks from the Civil War to World War II (2008).

[113] *See, e.g.*, Michelle Alexander, The New Jim Crow: Mass Incarceration in the Age of Colorblindness (2010); Doris Marie Provine, Unequal under Law: Race in the War on Drugs (2007); Clarence Lusane, Pipe Dream Blues: Racism and the War on Drugs (1999).

[114] *Cf.* P. Eric Louw, The Rise, Fall and Legacy of Apartheid (2004); William H. Hutt, The Economics of the Colour Bar (1964); Martin Meredith, In the Name of Apartheid: South Africa in the Postwar Period (1988); Dan O'Meara, Forty Lost Years: The National Party and the Politics of the South African State, 1948–1994 (1996).

[115] *See, e.g.*, Justin Akers Chacon & Mike Davis, No One Is Illegal: Fighting Racism and State Violence on the U.S.–Mexico Border (2006); Immigrants Out!: The New Nativism and the Anti-Immigrant Impulse in the United States (Juan Perea ed., 1996); Mae M. Ngai, Impossible Subjects: Illegal Aliens and the Making of Modern America (2004); Peter Schrag, Not Fit for Our Society: Immigration and Nativism in America (2011); Tunde

- States have frequently singled out lesbians, gays, bisexuals, and transgendered people not only for special legal disabilities but, indeed, for violence, threatening people with imprisonment and even death for harmless sexual behavior.[116]
- State power was responsible for the murder of vast numbers of Jews, Romani, gays, and others targeted on the basis simply of group membership during the Holocaust.[117]

The state is particularly dangerous to members of marginalized groups subjected to irrational prejudice and discrimination. It can license, legitimate, and, indeed, organize violence against such groups. It can impose constraints on their members that its victims can escape only by leaving its territory. It can distort the shapes of social institutions and cooperative relationships—enabling bigots to impose the costs of conforming to their prejudices on all those subject to its rule who have no interest in acting on prejudiced attitudes (just as it does when implementing criminal statutes that reflect pressure group prejudices) and maintaining cartel-like arrangements that reduce the economic penalties for bigotry while preventing those who want to be inclusive from doing so. (Arrangements of this sort are crucial for the maintenance of discriminatory behavior patterns, since these would otherwise prove economically unsustainable.[118]) And it can effectively scapegoat members of marginalized groups in times of crisis. States often foster the subordination of members of marginalized groups so that those the ruling class demeans and excludes

Obadina, *Anti-Globalisation, Nativism and Racism*, Africa Economic Analysis, May 23, 2008, http://www.africaeconomicanalysis.org/articles/73/1/Anti-globalisation-nativism-and-racism/Page1.html.

[116] *See, e.g.*, Richard Plant, The Pink Triangle: The Nazi War against Homosexuals (1988); Naomi Abraham, *Gay Africans Flee Persecution*, Salon, Oct. 29, 2011, http://www.salon.com/2011/10/29/gay_africans_flee_persecution/; James Peron, The State against Gays (forthcoming); Rafael Ocasio, Cuba's Political and Sexual Outlaw: Reinaldo Arenas (2003); Joey L. Mogul, Andrea J. Ritchie & Kay Whitlock, Queer (In)Justice: The Criminalization of LGBT People in the United States (2011). *Cf.* Demetrios Simopoulos, John Dececco & Lawrence Murphy, Perverts by Official Order: The Campaign against Homosexuality by the United States Navy (1988); David K. Johnson, The Lavender Scare: The Cold War Persecution of Gays and Lesbians in the Federal Government (2006).

[117] *See, e.g.*, Michael Berenbaum, A Mosaic of Victims: Non-Jews Persecuted and Murdered by the Nazis (1990); Michael Burleigh & Wolfgang Wippermann, The Racial State: Germany 1933–1945 (1991); Suzanne Evans, Forgotten Crimes: The Holocaust and People with Disabilities (2004); Saul Friedländer, Nazi Germany and the Jews (2 vols., 1998–2007); Raul Hilberg, Perpetrators, Victims, Bystanders: The Jewish Catastrophe 1933–1945 (1992); Raul Hilberg, The Destruction of the European Jews (1985); Clarence Lusane, Hitler's Black Victims: The Historical Experience of Afro-Germans, European Blacks, Africans and African Americans in the Nazi Era (2002); Timothy Snyder, Bloodlands: Europe between Hitler and Stalin (2010); Radu Ioanid, The Holocaust in Romania: The Destruction of Jews and Gypsies under the Antonescu Regime, 1940–1944 (2001).

[118] *See, e.g.*, Gary S. Becker, The Economics of Discrimination (1957); Thomas Sowell, Markets and Minorities 19–33 (1981).

from influence will see themselves as having a stake in the status quo because of their supposed social superiority to the members of these groups—a superiority they count on the state to help preserve. The state is hardly the only source of bigotry and prejudice, but its scale and its ability to externalize costs and exclude alternatives make it particularly dangerous to those who belong to disfavored groups.

12. *The State Is Inimical to Peaceful, Voluntary Cooperation*

State actors decline to engage in peaceful, voluntary cooperation with their putative subjects (at least in their official capacities), and they regularly interfere with the peaceful, voluntary interactions of others. The state attacks social order and fosters injustice—enacting laws and regulations that fly in the face of the requirements of practical reasonableness; perpetrating and legitimating aggression; attempting an impossible oversight of people's use of their possessions, their transactions, and the economy as a whole; colonizing all areas of social life; undermining cooperative behaviors and dispositions; reducing opportunities for the exploration of alternative patterns of institutional design; creating and maintaining the power of the ruling class and its cronies and increasing poverty and economic vulnerability; and underwriting, extending, and utilizing prejudice and bigotry. Its defenders may respond that these are problems with this or that state, but not with *the state as such*, and that the state is necessary to restrain economic elites. But they are mistaken. The power of the state makes it inherently dangerous, and state actors are considerably more likely to be allies of economic elites than of ordinary people. The state is morally problematic, of course, simply because of its inefficiency and its infringement on people's freedom. And it is doubly problematic because it is, as a result, an agency of unjust class dominance.

D. Its Involvement in Aggression and Its Role as a Tool of Class Rule Make the State an Enemy of Peaceful, Voluntary Cooperation

By serving the interests of elites—financiers, military contractors, land speculators—and other well-connected groups seeking privileges, the state attacks peaceful, voluntary cooperation. This is hardly surprising, since the roots of states can often be seen to lie in conquest and domination, and state power has persistently been used to bolster the positions of those with access to it at the expense of many or most others. It ignores and violates the baseline rules, undermines alternatives to itself, and practices killing and theft on a grand scale. As an instrumentality of class oppression, it has actively impoverished vast numbers of people and destroyed their lives; and, in less dramatic ways, it upholds privileges that consistently exclude and impoverish. The state and peaceful, voluntary cooperation are almost inevitably at odds.[119]

VII. EMBRACING PEACEFUL, VOLUNTARY COOPERATION MEANS REJECTING THE STATE

A just society is a society whose institutions characteristically safeguard peaceful, voluntary cooperation—one in which people can expect not to be subjected to actual or threatened aggression and in which they can care for others and for themselves and pursue opportunities for flourishing.

The state is the enemy of peaceful, voluntary cooperation, both because it uses actual or threatened aggression to compel cooperation with its demands and because it impedes ordinary people's efforts to cooperate peacefully and voluntarily.[120] It appeals to the consent of its subjects in an attempt to legitimate its authority, even though this consent is entirely lacking. While its authority is sometimes claimed to be necessary on the basis that it is needed to secure peaceful, voluntary cooperation, theoretical argument and historical evidence suggest that people can organize their lives cooperatively and peacefully, providing each other both private and public goods, without the aid of a territorial monopolist.[121] Peaceful, voluntary cooperation

[119] This does not mean, of course, that the state *never* does things that foster peaceful, voluntary cooperation or that otherwise contribute to ordinary people's well-being. Clearly, after all, some state actors purposefully act in constructive ways; and it is, in any case, important for the ruling class to ensure that order is maintained to further its control of the populace and its exaction of tribute (bandits challenge the state's monopolistic control over the use of violence and limit its revenues, both by taking what the state could otherwise claim and by contributing to a climate of uncertainty that reduces productivity). Rulers must also avoid prompting popular discontent and must therefore sometimes respond to public pressure in ways they might prefer to avoid doing. Obviously, too, the claim that state actors tend to be rapacious hardly means that all are and that none have decent motives. Thanks to Kevin Carson for discussion of this point.

[120] While it is important to emphasize the illegitimacy of the state's dependence on forcible funding, even if it could be shown that state action could be consistent with a just scheme of possessory rules, with the result that some state interference with people's possessions proved justified, little in the way of actual or threatened harm to their bodies would be morally acceptable. Given the unjustifiability of purposeful or instrumental harm to people's bodies (a clear and indubitable mandate of the Principle of Respect), and given the indefensibility of retributive or deterrent punishment (*see* Chapter 5.II.C), there would be no justification for state actors to use force against anyone's body for punitive or incentival purposes—only purely defensive state force would be warranted. Thus, crucial mechanisms of state control would be ruled out whether or not the baseline rules as I have defended them here survived criticism.

[121] Suppose it is true that, say, Americans' "common political purposes" include, in addition to "protection against overt violence and security in possessions," a variety of "wider purposes": "a set of goods which Americans do in fact reasonably care about and do not believe capable of being promoted effectively except by means of the apparatus of the state, under direct control of the government." GRISEZ & BOYLE, *supra* note 1, at 35. This underlying justification for state authority will be unpersuasive to the extent that these purposes can be pursued in the state's absence. If people can, indeed,

is both possible and likely without the state—and, indeed, it is in an important sense *more* likely without the state because the state tends to undermine peaceful, voluntary cooperation and the well-being to which such cooperation tends to lead. The state persistently and predictably acts to *undermine* both social cooperation and the well-being of particular people; indeed, because the state is necessarily the agent and enabler of a ruling class whose interests are inimical to those of others, state action is a very poor means of ensuring social cooperation. The state rapaciously claims people's possessions, makes war, privileges economic elites and their cronies, violently subordinates members of outsider groups, and represses freedom. It is neither necessary nor desirable as a protector of peaceful, voluntary cooperation.

In light of these considerations, it's possible to augment my earlier observations regarding the state's claim that its authority rests on the consent of the governed. There is good reason to think that state actors could never be entitled to regard anyone as having consented to their authority. However, it can reasonably be argued that, even if verifiable consent to state authority were possible, it would be wrong for anyone to give it. We don't ordinarily need the state, or anything resembling it, to preserve social order; thus, in light of the state's dangerous and destructive character, consenting to its authority might typically not only not be required by the Principle of Fairness but also, in fact, actually *violate* the Principle of Fairness, at least if one's consent to the state's authority involved empowering it to act in relation to anyone other than oneself.[122]

The state is illegitimate, aggressive, unnecessary, and dangerous. People can cooperate peacefully and voluntarily in its absence. So there is good reason to consider an alternative rooted in peaceful, voluntary cooperation.[123] Accepting such an alternative means accepting a fully consensual legal order, one in which it is the case not only that legal rules protect peaceful, voluntary cooperation but also that accepting the authority of a legal regime is itself a matter of peaceful, voluntary cooperation. In such a legal order, no one would be subject to an obligation—including the obligation to support a particular legal regime or any other institution—that did not flow directly from the NAM unless she had actually consented to accept the obligation or the procedure giving rise to it.

The NAM constrains the content of just law. But a stateless society could nonetheless be expected to feature multiple consensual legal systems, for several reasons:

cooperate peacefully and voluntarily to produce both private and public goods, it seems as if the relevant goods could be promoted effectively through means having nothing to do with the apparatus of the state and that the state will therefore be unnecessary.

[122] Thus, if morally justified consent to the state requires the assumption that the state is necessary to serve the common good, *see id.* at 28–29, consent to the state will not be morally justified.

[123] Mark Murphy has argued that most people in developed contemporary societies are obligated to obey the state and that standard anarchist criticisms should not be seen as undermining their duty to do so. I seek to respond to Murphy in Gary Chartier, *In Defence of the Anarchist*, 29 O.J.L.S. 115 (2009).

(*i*) the NAM does not *determine* the contents of all legal rules, so that sets of legal rules consistent with it might nonetheless differ in important ways; (*ii*) people would obviously be free to consent to the authority of legal regimes as members of which they subjected themselves voluntarily to rules inconsistent with the NAM; (*iii*) there is no guarantee, obviously, that everyone would support legal rules consistent with the NAM—there would, ex hypothesi, be no central authority mandating legal uniformity, though there would be internal pressures that would likely lead to standardization, and, precisely in virtue of the NAM, there would be good reason, in general, to avoid interventionist attempts to alter communities' institutions by force; and (*iv*) even people who did accept the NAM might still value the existence of alternative *mechanisms* designed to safeguard peaceful, voluntary cooperation.[124] In Chapter 4, I examine the nature of a stateless society's consensual legal institutions and explain why they would reasonably be regarded *as* peaceful and voluntary and *not* as imposing their authority on the unwilling in imitation of the state.

APPENDIX
THE FACT THAT GENERAL PREEMPTIVE DEFENSE IS A PUBLIC GOOD DOES NOT SERVE AS A PLAUSIBLE JUSTIFICATION FOR THE STATE

A. The Difficulties Associated with the Provision of the Putative Good of General Preemptive Defense Do Not Justify the Existence of a Monopolistic State

The state is not needed to provide the public good of general preemptive defense.

The putative need to supply various public goods is insufficient to justify the existence and operation of the state. In virtue of its general conceptual features, the Public Goods Argument is unsuccessful as a defense of the state. But particular factors related to the appeal to the public good of general preemptive defense to justify the state deserve more focused attention.

There are multiple ways in which defense against aggression might be provided in a stateless society without forcible funding (Section B). The provision of defensive services, however delivered, ought to be somewhat less expensive in the state's absence (Section C). Whatever the costs of non-state defense, there are particularly serious risks associated with the operation of a forcibly maintained military establishment for the purpose of providing the public good of general preemptive

[124] It seems wildly unlikely that one model of economic relations would prevail after the state's collapse or dissolution, at least not initially. But communities opting for collective possession could allow space for idiosyncratic individualists, and communities with individualistic possessory norms would surely need to permit those who wanted to explore group possessory options to do so.

defense, risks that might provide good reason to regard other means of doing so as vastly preferable (Section D). The importance of general preemptive defense does not suggest the need for a state any more than the putative need for any other public good does so (Section E).

B. Defense Services in a Stateless Society Could Presumably Be Delivered in Multiple, Complementary Ways

In a stateless society, defense against aggression—whether against the small-scale aggression of muggers and robbers, the medium-scale aggression of terrorists, or the large-scale aggression of marauding would-be conquerors—might be provided by:

- volunteers aiding their neighbors or others in need of defense;
- charities providing defense services for free or selling them at deliberately low rates;
- cooperatives providing defense services to their members;
- people defending themselves;
- cooperatives, partnerships, or other organizations providing defense services to nonmembers and receiving compensation for their work.[125]

As I have already done in this chapter, I refer to these as defense providers.[126] They might, though they need not, be components of, or associated with, the legal regimes that would seek to resolve disputes in a stateless society.

Volunteer and charitable defense both involve people circumventing the public goods problem. If it is acknowledged that defense can be provided in these ways at significant levels, it is also acknowledged that the public goods problem need not be overwhelming. And of course no public goods problem seems to attend on people's engaging in self-defense. Thus, my primary concern will be with the viability of defense providers that are not charities, that are not volunteer-based, and that provide defense services to nonmembers at non-charitable rates.[127]

[125] On several such varieties, *see* Philip E. Jacobson, *Three Voluntary Economies*, FORMULATIONS, Sum. 1995, http://www.libertariannation.org/a/f24j1.html. Thanks to Roderick T. Long for this reference.

[126] *See, e.g.*, Joseph R. Stromberg, *Mercenaries, Guerillas, Militias, and the Defense of Minimal States and Free Societies*, *in* THE MYTH OF NATIONAL DEFENSE: ESSAYS ON THE THEORY AND HISTORY OF SECURITY PRODUCTION 215 (Hans-Hermann Hoppe ed., 2005) [*hereinafter* MYTH]; Larry J. Sechrest, *Privateering and National Defense: Naval Warfare for Private Profit*, *in* MYTH at 239; Jeffrey Rogers Hummel, *The Will to Be Free: The Role of Ideology in National Defense*, *in* MYTH at 275.

[127] Presumably, some communities in a stateless society would feature gift economies or similar arrangements. If the members of a community are predictably disposed to participate in a gift economy, the community might not confront public goods problems. Stateless communities that did not feature exchange-based economies but that did need to deal with possible free riders would obviously need to find noncommercial solutions to free-rider problems.

C. The Difficulty of Funding Defensive Services in the State's Absence Could Be Less Than at Present

1. *Defense Costs Could Be Relatively Low in a Stateless Society*

There is no optimal level of provision for the public good of general preemptive defense, any more than there is for any other public good. But it is nonetheless, of course, good news that general preemptive defense services might be demanded rather less frequently in a stateless society than they are in a world overrun by states, with the result that the task of delivering these services should prove less challenging than it otherwise could be. Defensive services would likely be offered at significantly lower costs (Subsection 2). Defense providers in a stateless society could be counted on to avoid aggressive behavior more frequently than states (Subsection 3), so that the stateless societies they defended would likely be subject much less frequently to attacks (Subsection 4). When residents of these societies were attacked, it would thus be less likely that they would be collectively targeted; it would thus be more likely that they wouldn't *need* general preemptive defense in the first place, and that defense providers would be responsible for relatively small areas (Subsection 5). And they could be expected to prepare, in general, for conventional attacks—for which general preemptive defense would be unnecessary—rather than ones using weapons of mass destruction (Subsection 6). While costs could well be lower for a particular stateless society in a world otherwise full of states than they would be for a state in such a world, they would of course be even lower in a world entirely free of states and similar entities (Subsection 7). The demands of funding general preemptive defense services in a stateless society could well be less daunting than they are at present (Subsection 8).

2. *Defense Providers in a Stateless Society Could Be Expected to Hold Their Costs under Control*

State military forces, funded by blank checks from legislators and willing to pay crony contractors on cost-plus bases, rack up costs for reasons quite unrelated to the actual demand for their services.[128] Because people would be free, ex hypothesi, to select from among various defense providers in a stateless society, providers would have good reason to deliver their services inexpensively.

[128] *Cf.* Robert Higgs, Depression, War, and Cold War (2006).

3. Defense Providers in a Stateless Society Would Find It Rational to Avoid Aggression

A state often maintains a military apparatus for aggressive purposes. It can afford to do so because it funds its military forces aggressively, through the tax system or by creating money while monopolizing currency production. In a stateless society, those actually interested in promoting aggression would need to pay for aggressive military action themselves or (in the case of volunteers or cooperative members) persuade others to take the risks associated with engagement in aggression. If they needed to persuade participants, they would likely be less able to appeal to nationalistic fervor and patriotic sentiment absent a nation-state to serve as the focus of such enthusiasm and a governmental apparatus engaged in propaganda designed to stir up martial sentiments. Given the difficulty of maintaining a military force intended for aggressive purposes, it seems relatively unlikely that such a force would be funded and operative in a stateless society. Thus, people would likely need to bear the costs of genuine defense only.

4. That Defense Providers in a Given Region Were Unlikely to Engage in Aggression Would Reduce the Likelihood of an Attack on the Region

If defense services in a given region were delivered by providers genuinely prepared for and likely to engage exclusively in *defensive* action, the region would be much less likely than many modern states to be subjected to attack in the first place.[129] It would not be attacked as a way of retaliating for military aggression, since its defense providers would not, ex hypothesi, be engaged in such aggression. And it would not for similar reasons be attacked preemptively to prevent planned future aggression. My point is not, of course, that it therefore wouldn't be attacked at all, since it might be targeted by aggressors, but there would, at any rate, be fewer reasons to attack it than there are to attack many states today. This fact might be expected to reduce the demand for, and thus expenditures on, defensive services to some degree.

5. The Absence of a State or State-Like Entity in a Region Reduces the Likelihood of Collective Targeting of Those Residing in the Region

While military aggression in relation to those in another region is the kind of negative behavior most likely to provoke the responsive use of force, it seems less likely than at present that the residents of a given stateless community would be targeted

[129] *Cf.* Murray Rothbard, For a New Liberty 248 (1973).

qua residents for *retaliation* for *any* reason, military or otherwise. The subjects of a state may be targeted for retaliation because they are treated as somehow responsible for the state's actions or because, even if they are not, the attackers may assume that harming or threatening to harm its subjects may encourage the state to behave in what the attackers regard as a desirable way. In the absence of a state, however, attacks for either sort of reason seem less probable.

In a stateless society, there will be no governmental apparatus in a given region for the misdeeds of which residents of the region could be held responsible. And there would be no such apparatus attackers might reasonable expect to influence by attacking residents qua residents. This would be a further reason not to expect anyone (whether marauder or retaliator), in the absence of the state, to attack any region, group, or person other than the attacker's actual target.

In a stateless society occupying something like contemporary North America, for instance, no one could threaten Los Angeles by proposing to bomb New York any more than someone could threaten Los Angeles by proposing to bomb Paris or Jakarta or Canberra. At present, an attack on any portion of a state's territory is characteristically understood as an attack on the state itself, a threat to its human and material resources. Absent the state, however, an attack on a given person or location would not ordinarily be an effective means of attacking another person or institution. It would not be a reasonable way of taking revenge on others (if troops from San Diego are occupying Ottawa, people from Ottawa have no reason, even as a matter of retaliatory retribution, to attack people in Sacramento). And such an attack could deter defensive action only by serving as a demonstration of raw power, not by functioning as a means of punishment directly affecting those not targeted. (I don't mean to minimize the likelihood that demonstrations of raw power could occur; but there would be multiple costs associated with such demonstrations that might be expected to discourage them.)

This does not mean, of course, that people would not, could not, or should not care about each other's fates in a stateless society. Far from it. It does mean, however, that people in one geographic region would not be available, as they are now, to serve as hostages who could readily be threatened to gain leverage against people in another region. Defense in a stateless society would thus involve resisting aggression against those purposefully or instrumentally targeted by the aggressors—those the aggressors wished to conquer or despoil. If no state ruled a given state-sized region, people living in the region wouldn't be required to support the defense of the entire region.[130] In the absence of collective targeting, defense against marauding hordes in a stateless society could be expected to be focused on regions much smaller than most contemporary states.[131]

[130] *Cf.* FRIEDMAN, *supra* note 29, at 137–38.

[131] *Cf.* ROTHBARD, *supra* note 5, at 249.

6. *It Is Not Obvious That a Provider of General Preemptive Defense in a Stateless Society Would Need to Be Seriously Concerned with the Risk of an Attack Using a Weapon of Mass Destruction and Designed as a Demonstration of Raw Power*

Perhaps an aggressor might be willing to annihilate a particular community in a stateless society in order to make clear its ruthlessness and so to subjugate other communities without attacking them.[132] But I think there is reason to regard this possibility as providing little comfort to the defender of the state. A would-be conqueror's use, for instance, of nuclear weapons, or of biological agents without *very* short half-lives, against a particular community would pose the obvious difficulty that it would render both that community's territory and adjacent regions uninhabitable, and therefore of limited value either for economic exploitation or for colonization by the aggressor. In addition, actually making good on a threat to use weapons of mass destruction *pour encourager les autres* seems likely to deprive the attacker of moral legitimacy and to promote intense, violent, resistance.

If a nuclear attack, for instance, appeared realistically possible, repelling it would require only a purely defensive system. However expensive it turned out to be, such a system would surely be considerably less costly than a putatively deterrent system with retaliatory-cum-offensive capability.[133] The use of a deterrent system would, in any event, be (I believe) indefensible from a moral standpoint.[134] And if this is so, the fact that maintaining a deterrent would be very costly is irrelevant, since no one could reasonably employ it.

7. *The Costs of Defending a Stateless Society Would Be even Lower if the World Were Entirely Free of States and State-Like Entities*

People seeking to establish a stateless society in a world otherwise full of states need not be deterred by worries about the costs of general preemptive defense. But in a world without any states, it seems as if the need for this kind of defense would be even less pronounced. The direct and indirect costs associated with creating and maintaining military forces without the option of funding them forcibly would mean that most people in a stateless society would be inclined to seek the services of genuine *defense* providers rather than military forces with offensive capabilities. And the absence of many offensive military forces in their environs would obviously make the economical provision of defense services more reasonable and, given the limited risks of large-scale attacks, render the delivery of such services less costly.

[132] *Cf.* FRIEDMAN, *supra* note 6, at 135.
[133] *Cf. id.* at 138.
[134] *See* JOHN FINNIS, JOSEPH BOYLE & GERMAIN GRISEZ, NUCLEAR DETERRENCE, MORALITY AND REALISM (1987).

8. *It Could Be Easier to Deliver General Preemptive Defense Services without the State because of the Reduced Cost of These Services*

It could be less costly than at present to provide even the public good of general preemptive defense in a stateless society. Defense providers in stateless societies would be cost-conscious—or else cease to exist. They would be unlikely to engage in aggressive behavior, even if they were otherwise inclined to do so, given the costs of aggression, so aggression would likely be absent as a trigger for attack by others. Collective targeting would be less likely because it would generally not make sense. Costs would also be lower because defensive services could generally be provided for relatively small areas. Preemptive defense of large areas by, say, antimissile systems, might be necessary but need not be prohibitively costly in the same way that the deployment of offensive antipopulation weapons would be. And, in any case, there would be reasons not to expect weapons of mass destruction not to be used against population centers. These cost savings would, of course, be even greater in the complete absence of states. Thus, the task of funding general preemptive defense services in a stateless society wouldn't have to be overwhelming.

Given that the state retards the economic health of a society, its absence would likely lead to increased prosperity. And this, in turn, means that a stateless society might be subjected to more threats of invasion and pillage than it would if it were (mis)ruled by a state. This increased risk could obviously increase the relative need for defensive services in one sense.[135] However, given the multiple, reinforcing factors likely to reduce the costs of providing defensive services in a stateless society, it still seems plausible, even if not certain, that the overall cost of delivering these services would be significantly lower than at present, and that the challenge of providing general preemptive defense, in particular, need not be overwhelming.

D. The Forcible Provision of General Preemptive Defense Would Be Associated with Great Dangers

It is all too likely that a forcibly maintained apparatus designed to provide general preemptive defense would, if established, yield significant disvalues. It would be naïve to suppose that such an apparatus would be employed only to provide generalized preemptive defense or any other good. There is a considerable risk that, once in place, a military establishment could and would be used to engage in aggression and suppress dissent. People given responsibility for directing such a forcibly funded apparatus could easily use military force to pursue their own political or economic ends. A forcibly funded military could be put to uses for which a non-

[135] Thanks to an anonymous reader for highlighting the need to address this point.

forcibly funded defense provider, dependent on attracting and maintaining consumer support, could not be employed. And once the possibility of forcible funding was established, mechanisms designed aggressively to obtain funding for military affairs could obviously be used to secure funds for other purposes.[136] There are thus excellent reasons to avoid creating a forcibly maintained military establishment to provide the public good of general preemptive defense.

E. The Value of General Preemptive Defense Does Not Provide Any Special Basis for the Claim That the State Is Necessary

While general preemptive defense is important, its importance does not warrant the creation of anything like a state to supply it in a stateless society. Any mechanism likely to facilitate the production of public goods in general in the state's absence would seem to be especially likely to foster the production of general preemptive defense in light of its apparent significance, especially given that people seem particularly prone to contribute to the support of public goods they regard as very important.[137] Several factors make the task of providing this public good seem less daunting than it otherwise might be. It ought to be considerably less difficult to fund the provision—by any of the various sources of defensive services that would likely operate in a stateless society—of general preemptive defense without the state's involvement. Supplying this good could be less necessary in a stateless society than it tends to be for a state because of the kinds of threats such a society might be expected to encounter. And, given the dangers posed by even a putatively minimal state with military capabilities, there is good reason to regard almost any alternative to the state provision of general preemptive defense as preferable. Like other public goods, general preemptive defense can and should be provided without the state.

[136] For some cautionary tales, *see* RALPH RAICO, GREAT WARS AND GREAT LEADERS (2010).

[137] *See* R. Mark Isaac & James M. Walker, *Group Size Effects in Public Goods Provision: The Voluntary Contribution Mechanism*, 103 Q.J. ECON. 179 (1988). Thanks to David Schmidtz for this reference.

4

Enforcing Law

I. FORCIBLY IMPOSING LEGAL REQUIREMENTS IN A STATELESS SOCIETY IS NOT OBJECTIONABLE ON THE SAME GROUNDS AS AGGRESSION BY THE STATE

Diverse legal regimes could resolve disputes and maintain order in a society rooted in peaceful, voluntary cooperation. Someone could be morally obligated to obey a rule upheld by a given regime under at least two circumstances: (*i*) she gave her actual consent to the requirement or to a mechanism responsible for generating it, *or* (*ii*) the legal requirement was also an enforceable moral requirement. It could thus be consistent with the NAM to enforce a narrow range of legal requirements even against people who had not consented to them (call them, without prejudice, "outlaws"). Law enforcement need not render the enforcer the moral equivalent of the state.

Legal authority would be vital to the maintenance of order in a stateless society. But it is easy to see why there might seem to be tension between endorsing (some variety of) legal authority and embracing anarchy (Part II). Unlike states, however, the diverse regimes making up a stateless society's polycentric legal order would be fully consensual;[1] though the NAM places limits on the contents of just legal rules, regimes would in fact likely uphold varying rules, though multiple pressures might lead them to converge on common legal requirements (Part III). The potentially forcible resolution of conflicts between participants in the same regime would not qualify as state-like aggression, and the same would be true of the forcible resolution of conflicts between participants in different regimes that were parties to agreements governing cross-regime disputes (Part IV). The existence of pre-legal rights, embodied in the NAM, helps to provide the notion of voluntary consent with determinate content; but while there are limits on the rules legal regimes could justly enforce, recognizing these limits would be quite compatible with embracing the notion of polycentric law (Part V). A regime's

[1] *Cf.* Peter T. Leeson, *Government, Clubs, and Constitutions*, 80 J. ECON. BEHAV. & ORG. 301 (2011).

use of force against an outlaw need not be state-like (Part VI), and a consensual legal regime in a stateless society would not be the moral equivalent of a state (Part VII).

II. THERE MIGHT SEEM TO BE A TENSION BETWEEN OPPOSING THE STATE AND SUPPORTING THE IDEA OF LAW

The use of force to prevent, end, or remedy unjust actions might seem to make a legal regime in a stateless society uncomfortably state-like.

Opposition to the state does not entail pacifism (though pacifism *does* fairly obviously entail opposition to the state). There are occasions when using force is consistent with the requirements of practical reasonableness—most commonly, to protect oneself or another against unjust attack or to secure compensation for such an attack. If I may justly use force on such occasions, then others may reasonably do so on my behalf. And they may do so not only on an ad hoc basis but systematically, institutionally, as a matter of enforcing *law*.[2] By enforcing law, people help to make possible orderly, predictable, nonaggressive interactions among strangers—a vital service to everyone. The operation of law can thus be seen as very desirable in any society, including a stateless one.

It might also appear, however, that supporting the existence of legal institutions in a stateless society creates a contradiction. The fact that the state's purported authority does not rest on the actual, clearly conveyed consent of its subjects is deeply problematic.[3] The Principle of Fairness grounds a strong presumption against exercising authority over people, and thus against demanding their obedience or using force against them, without their agreement. And at first glance, a person or group using force to secure compliance with a legal requirement in a stateless society appears to

[2] On the general idea of law without the state, *see, e.g.*, LAW AND ANARCHISM (Thom Holterman & Henc van Maarseveen eds., 1982); ANARCHY AND THE LAW: THE POLITICAL ECONOMY OF CHOICE (Edward P. Stringham ed., 2007).

[3] *See, e.g.*, 1 LYSANDER SPOONER, NO TREASON (1867), *available at* http://lysanderspooner.org/node/44; 2 LYSANDER SPOONER, NO TREASON: THE CONSTITUTION (1867), *available at* http://lysanderspooner.org/node/63; 6 LYSANDER SPOONER, NO TREASON: THE CONSTITUTION OF NO AUTHORITY (1870), *available at* http://lysanderspooner.org/node/64; STEPHEN R.L. CLARK, CIVIL PEACE AND SACRED ORDER 71–92 (1988); STEPHEN R.L. CLARK, THE POLITICAL ANIMAL: BIOLOGY, ETHICS, AND POLITICS 23–39 (1999); LESLIE GREEN, THE AUTHORITY OF THE STATE (1990); JOSEPH RAZ, THE AUTHORITY OF LAW: ESSAYS ON LAW AND MORALITY (1979); A. JOHN SIMMONS, MORAL PRINCIPLES AND POLITICAL OBLIGATIONS (1981); M.B.E. Smith, *Is There a Prima Facie Obligation to Obey the Law?*, 82 YALE L.J. 950 (1973); Charles W. Johnson, *Can Anybody Ever Consent to the State?*, RAD GEEK PEOPLE'S DAILY, Jan. 8, 2009, http://radgeek.com/gt/2009/01/08/can_anybody; GARY CHARTIER, THE CONSCIENCE OF AN ANARCHIST: WHY IT'S TIME TO SAY GOOD-BYE TO THE STATE AND BUILD A FREE SOCIETY 5–10 (2011); CRISPIN SARTWELL, AGAINST THE STATE: AN INTRODUCTION TO ANARCHIST POLITICAL THEORY (2008); JAN NARVESON, YOU AND THE STATE: A SHORT INTRODUCTION TO POLITICAL PHILOSOPHY 183–201 (2008); AEON SKOBLE, DELETING THE STATE: AN ARGUMENT ABOUT GOVERNMENT (2008). *Cf.* CAROLE PATEMAN, THE PROBLEM OF POLITICAL OBLIGATION: A CRITICAL ANALYSIS OF LIBERAL THEORY (1985).

be acting very much like a state, and in a manner that is morally objectionable for the same reason the state's conduct is morally objectionable. For it is almost certainly the case that not everyone in a stateless society will have consented to the same laws or law-generating mechanisms, and that some outlaws will have consented to none at all. In enforcing its rules against nonparticipants, including outlaws, something it would doubtless sometimes need to do, a legal regime in a stateless society would seem to be acting recognizably like a state, and to be criticizable for the same reasons. The belief that a stateless society should feature functioning legal institutions might thus appear to entail *support* for institutions that are clearly unjust. In fact, however, it does not.

III. LEGAL CODES IN A STATELESS SOCIETY WOULD HAVE VARIED SOURCES AND CONTENTS, BUT MIGHT EXHIBIT COMMON FEATURES

A. For Multiple Reasons, Legal Diversity, Whether Limited or Radical, Would Be Evident in a Stateless Society

It is unrealistic to suppose that everyone in a given society could or would consent to a detailed legal code. While just legal rules are those consistent with the NAM, there is no reason to imagine that everyone in a stateless society would automatically embrace such rules.

A genuinely stateless society would feature a variety of legal regimes—often non-territorial (Section B). These regimes could not all be expected to enforce identical legal standards: uniform consent to a given legal code seems most unlikely to emerge voluntarily, at least not all at once and not for an extended period, and the sort of consent needed to secure immediate, universal adoption of such a code could be obtained only through the actual or threatened use of aggressive procedures—procedures that would seem to be objectionably state-like (Section C). At the same time, however, a variety of factors might lead different regimes to converge on similar, perhaps antiauthoritarian, standards (Section D). There would thus be no guarantee of uniformity, but some reason to expect similarity, in the codes upheld by legal regimes in a stateless society (Section E).

B. A Polycentric Legal Order Would Feature Considerable Institutional Diversity

A stateless society's legal order would likely be *polycentric*.[4] Legal rules (whether in the form of judge-made common law, legislation, or something else entirely) in such a society might be generated by several different kinds of legal regimes:

[4] *See, e.g.*, Tom W. Bell, *Polycentric Law in a New Century*, POLICY, Autumn 1999, at 34. John Hasnas has offered a conception of polycentric law as evolved customary law, a conception drawing on the

- the *territorially localized, consensus-based legal regime*, made up of the majority of people (surely not all) in a given geographic area, people who voluntarily accept a given set of legal rules and law-generation and law-enforcement mechanisms. The regime might often be maintained by mutualized institutions formerly part of a state apparatus. The difference between this sort of regime and a state would be that no one in the relevant geographic area would be treated as having accepted the regime's authority without her *actual consent*, so that some people in the territory doubtless would be participants in other regimes.
- the *non-territorial, agreement-based legal regime*, made up of people, not necessarily occupying geographically contiguous territory, who have opted for the services of the same dispute resolution entity—whether a cooperative serving members or a partnership, association, or other organization serving nonmembers—and who thus accept the legal rules developed and the law-generation and law-enforcement mechanisms employed by the regime.
- the *non-territorial, communal legal regime*, made up of people, not necessarily occupying geographically contiguous territory, who opt for the dispute resolution services, as well as the legal rules and law-generation and law-enforcement mechanisms, of a religious or cultural community.

These sorts of legal regimes could provide dispute resolution services tailored to the particular concerns of diverse people and groups in a stateless society.

C. The Idea of a Uniform Legal Code in a Stateless Society Is Implausible

i. Complete legal uniformity should not be expected in a stateless society

It is unrealistic to suppose that legal regimes in a stateless society would all enforce identical legal standards. Consent-based and aggression-based mechanisms for ensuring a uniform legal code in a stateless society are unsatisfactory. Consent-based mechanisms are unlikely to be successful (Subsubsection ii), and the use of aggression-based mechanisms would convert the entity using them into something like a state (Subsubsection iii). Despite its desirability, unequivocal legal uniformity is not a reasonable goal for a stateless society (Subsubsection iv).

model of early English common law. Hasnas suggests that evolved, customary law should be welcomed because it is *depoliticized*—it does not involve "the command of any identifiable person and [is] not an embodiment of anyone's will. Therefore, one can be bound by depoliticized law without thereby being rendered subject to the will of another." John Hasnas, *The Depoliticization of Law*, 9 Theoretical Inquiries in Law 529, 545 (2008). Hasnas grants that systems of depoliticized law of this sort need not all be just, *id.* at 545, but the procedures that generate them will ensure that they are more likely to be, on average, than sets of legal rules crafted by monopolistic states.

ii. Consent-based mechanisms would be unlikely to bring about legal uniformity

The NAM constrains what will count as a set of just legal rules. But it seems unlikely that argumentation and debate, at least, would lead to anything like the uniform adoption of any set of legal rules on a consensual basis throughout an entire population. Given people's differing circumstances, preferences, and backgrounds, different residents of a stateless society are unlikely to adopt the same standards at the same time.

iii. Actual or threatened aggression is not a satisfactory means of ensuring legal uniformity in a stateless society

A regime could seek to secure society-wide consent to a uniform legal code by engaging in or threatening to engage in aggression, but of course aggression by a legal regime in a stateless society, for this or any other purpose, would render the regime morally indistinguishable from a state.

A regime might seek to secure uniform consent by the members of a given society to a particular legal code in at least two ways. (*i*) It might seek to limit admission to the society to those agreeing to support the code. Alternatively, (*ii*) it might forcibly evict those who declined to consent to the code after arrival.

The first option would be viable if, and only if, the territory (whether or not contiguous) occupied by the society were held before widespread occupancy by an entity which was committed to the relevant set of principles and which allowed people to enter and live in the territory only if they pledged to uphold the principles. Perhaps the members of a small, cohesive community could come unanimously to adopt a legal code in this way on a peaceful, voluntary basis. But it does not seem realistically conceivable that an entity wishing to secure consent to a legal code could acquire enough territory to accommodate an entire society (before conditioning entry into the territory on the basis of agreement to the code) without engaging in aggression. The putative possession of by a single person or an ideologically cohesive group of enough territory to accommodate an entire society seems likely to be explicable only with reference to just the kind of unjust dispossession and engrossment that lie at the root of the state. Consent to a legal code secured in virtue of an unjust claim would be of dubious validity.

The second option, the exclusion of everyone unwilling to embrace a given legal code *after* the emergence of a peaceful, voluntary society, seems equally difficult to envision as a viable means of securing uniform consent to such a code. Suppose people have come to live in a particular region without having agreed to adopt a particular code. In this case, it would be reasonable to compel them to accept the code on pain of exclusion from the region only if the entity excluding were already entitled to exercise authority over them. The Principle of Fairness suggests that the entity wouldn't ordinarily be entitled to do so without their consent, and it seems most unlikely that all the members of a society would consent to the authority of an entity with the capacity to expel them from their homes. It's very unlikely that any entity could legitimately acquire consent-based authority to exclude those who declined to accept a given legal code, and excluding people *without* their consent would render the excluding entity an institutionalized aggressor, a kind of state, and so illegitimate.

iv. A truly uniform legal code for a stateless society isn't realistically conceivable
Everyone in a stateless society could be expected to consent to the same set of specific legal rules in a relatively brief period only on the basis of miraculous consensus or forcible exclusion. The former possibility seems too unlikely to justify treating it as a live option. The latter would probably involve objectionably state-like behavior. If a stateless society were conceivable only if it operated in accordance with a universally shared code, then, given that such a code is only realistically imaginable if imposed by force, the society would, indeed, be indistinguishable in important respects from a state.

D. Multiple Pressures Could Lead to Convergence on Legal Rules across Regimes

The sources of legal rules in a stateless society would unavoidably be diverse. And consensus could not be mandated and would be most unlikely to emerge from simultaneous particular agreements. But it is perfectly possible that legal regimes in a stateless society might converge over time on particular legal standards. Multiple factors could lead to this sort of convergence. These factors might include

(*i*) increased common understanding of social-scientific and natural-scientific findings related to the nature and dynamics of human organisms and societies;
(*ii*) active, persuasive advocacy of common standards by lawyers, academics, and actual and potential litigants;
(*iii*) the practical benefits of legal uniformity (quite apart from the *content* of the relevant standards) from the standpoint of the various regimes—in particular, the role of standardization in facilitating conflict resolution and reducing costs;[5]

[5] Regimes with similar rules would presumably find it easier, on average, to resolve disputes between their members than ones with different rules: (*a*) there would be less confusion among members about which rules were applicable in particular cases, and so fewer confusion-related conflicts; (*b*) litigation-related expenses occasioned by choice-of-law disputes would be reduced; *and* (*c*) there would be fewer situations in which courts had to expend the time and energy required to understand and apply unfamiliar legal principles. Within regimes, rules that were costly to interpret, apply, or obey would tend to be abandoned in favor of simpler rules. And insofar as the range of realistically employable simple rules governing possessions, agreements, and injuries is, at any rate, significantly narrower than the range of possible complex rules, the choice of simple over complex rules would probably lead to some convergence among regimes. (Since simplicity is a defining characteristic of

(*iv*) the practical benefits of adopting standards *substantively* similar to the baseline rules, together with the inherent appeal of such standards;

(*v*) economic pressure derived from the ease of exit from legal regimes (obviously from deterritorialized ones, but also from geographically localized ones, given the relatively small sizes of the likely territories served by such regimes, and their non-monopolistic status even within such territories), which could be expected to encourage regimes to adopt antiauthoritarian standards;

(*vi*) the need for those seeking the enforcement of particular legal rules to internalize the costs of enforcing these rules—which would obviously discourage the enforcement of meddlesome rules concerned with the nonaggressive behavior of others and which could thus lead to convergence on less rather than more authoritarian standards;

(*vii*) the difficulties local authoritarians would confront in excluding antiauthoritarian ideas from other communities and, in extreme cases, outsiders interested in assisting the authoritarians' victims—which might be expected (in virtue of costly conflict, social unrest, and institutional pressure) to increase pressure for the adoption of antiauthoritarian standards.

Thus, the emergence of significant common ground among legal regimes in a polycentric legal order—absent both miraculous consensus and involuntary consent—could be reasonably expected.[6]

E. Moral and Institutional Diversity Would Likely Generate at Least Some Legal Diversity

Legal rules in a stateless society would be *just* to the extent that they were consistent with the NAM. However, there would be no direct, nonaggressive way of compelling uniform consent to any set of just legal rules. A polycentric legal order would feature multiple legal regimes, both territorial and non-territorial. No regime or combination of regimes could compel unanimous consent to any particular set of legal rules, and genuinely voluntary but unanimous consent to such rules seems thoroughly improbable. However, economic, social, and cultural pressures could be expected to lead to a measure of convergence.

the baseline possessory rules I defend here, there is further reason to expect convergence on rules like these, in particular.)

[6] Thanks to Kevin Carson for these points. Jonathan Crowe has also emphasized the importance of stressing the evolutionary pressures that could be expected to lead to the adoption of similar standards and has noted the importance to the issue of the evolutionary convergence of legal systems of Friedrich Hayek, Garrett Barden, and Tim Murphy. *See* 1 FRIEDRICH A. HAYEK, LAW, LEGISLATION, AND LIBERTY: RULES AND ORDER (1973); 3 FRIEDRICH A. HAYEK, LAW, LEGISLATION, AND LIBERTY: THE POLITICAL ORDER OF A FREE PEOPLE 155–76 (1979); F.A. HAYEK, THE FATAL CONCEIT (W.W. Bartley III ed., 1988); GARRETT BARDEN & TIMOTHY MURPHY, LAW AND JUSTICE IN COMMUNITY (2010).

IV. RESOLVING DISPUTES BETWEEN PARTICIPANTS IN STRUCTURED LEGAL REGIMES NEED NOT INVOLVE STATE-LIKE INJUSTICE

A. Legal Disputes in a Stateless Society Could Have Multiple Loci, None of Which Need Be Such as to Require the Use of Force against Unconsenting Persons

A legal dispute in a stateless society could in principle occur between:

- two (personal or organizational) participants in the same legal regime;
- two participants in different legal regimes;
- a participant in a legal regime and an outlaw (again, personal or organizational) not affiliated with any regime.

Forcibly resolving a dispute between participants in the same legal regime need not involve aggression (Section B). The same is true of a dispute between participants in different regimes, provided the regimes are linked by relevant agreements (Section C). Using force to secure compliance with a regime's rules in order to end such conflicts need not be state-like (Section D).

B. Disputes between Participants in the Same Regime Could Be Resolved on a Fully Consensual Basis

When a legal dispute occurs between two participants in the same legal regime, it is clear that—presuming the regime is genuinely consensual, featuring full exit rights—the participants will *either* have agreed directly to the rules governing their conflict *or* have agreed to standards governing the determination of such rules in the awareness that such rules would, in fact, be determined. In either case, they will voluntarily have accepted the jurisdiction of the relevant legal regime—and, in the prior case, the specific applicable rules as well. The regime's use of force to resolve the participants' dispute—say, by determining that one of them has a just possessory claim to some object and forcibly protecting the claim against attack by the other—in accordance with rules the participants have directly or indirectly accepted is clearly not on all fours with using force to impose state dictates on people who have not actually consented to them.

C. Disputes between Participants in Different Regimes Linked by Appropriate Agreements Could also Be Resolved Consensually

Different legal regimes may feature the same rules relevant to a particular conflict, or different ones. Cross-regime disputes involving either kind of rule can be resolved—if necessary, by force—without aggression.

When a dispute occurs between participants in different consensual legal regimes with the same relevant rules, the participants will have consented voluntarily to the norms or to standards governing their generation. Thus, again, using force to ensure their cooperation will be justified given their prior consent to the applicable norms.

If different regimes ordinarily enforce different rules applicable to a particular kind of dispute, then it will obviously be in the best interests of each regime to establish guidelines—choice-of-law and conflict-of-law rules, primarily—for resolving cross-regime disagreements about the resolution of disputes of this kind (typically, though not necessarily, embodied in agreements with other regimes). If a given regime is fully consensual, then a participant in that regime will have accepted these second-order rules directly or will, again, have consented in one way or another to procedures for their determination. A participant in a legal regime will thus have consented to the employment by the regime of such second-order rules to reach a conclusion regarding the substantive principles to be applied in resolving a dispute and then to use force, if need be, to resolve the dispute. So, again, the use of force here will be legitimate.

D. Legal Regimes Could Often Resolve Disputes Peacefully without Compelling the Unconsenting to Comply

Two disputants who are participants in the same regime have, ex hypothesi, given actual consent either to particular rules applicable to their case or to the regime's rule-making procedures. Enforcing the regime's rules with respect to them is therefore presumptively just. Disputants who are participants in different regimes are in the same position, provided their regimes are linked by agreements that govern the resolution of cross-regime legal conflicts. In both kinds of cases, because a regime's use of force would be fully consensual, it would not be subject to the same objections as the use of force by the state.

V. THE REALITY OF MORAL CONSTRAINTS ON LEGAL RULES WOULD RENDER THE NOTION OF CONSENT NONCIRCULAR AND WOULD BE COMPATIBLE WITH LEGAL POLYCENTRICITY

A. Moral Rights That Are Logically Prior to Legal Ones Would Limit Just Options within a Polycentric, Consent-Based Legal Order

Rooting justice in consent only makes sense given a logically prior definition of aggression. However, it might be argued, aggression can only be defined by a legal regime, so that no one could be said to consent to a legal regime. But a pre-legal account of the moral limits on legal rights is, as I have already argued, perfectly defensible (Section B). Still, it might seem in turn that acknowledging pre-legal rights might be incompatible with supporting the existence of a truly polycentric legal order. In fact, though, it is possible both to support polycentricity and to endorse the existence of pre-legal rights (Section C). The reality of pre-legal moral constraints on legal rights can make the idea of consent credible and need not undermine legal polycentricity (Section D).

B. Defining Rights and Aggression Pre-Legally Makes Possible a Non-Question Begging Understanding of Consent

1. *A Credible Understanding of Aggression Requires a Substantive Account of Pre-Legal Rights*

The idea of voluntary consent to a legal regime's authority makes sense only on the assumption that there are pre-legal rights, but this idea need not be troubling.

The recognition that legal regimes could sometimes rightly opt for different legal rules might seem to suggest that all legal rights are conventional, that there is no objective moral standard on the basis of which a regime's decision to treat a certain interest as a protectable right could be judged reasonable or not. This denial that there are any pre-legal rights would seem, if correct, to vitiate the notion of voluntary consent to any legal regime (Subsection 2). However, there are multiple ways of thinking about the moral status of legal rights in a stateless society in general, and two of these are consistent with the existence of pre-legal rights (Subsection 3). Two further moves related specifically to rights to possess things, in particular, might also undermine the possibility of voluntary consent, but neither is plausible (Subsection 4). A credible view of the relationship between moral requirements and legal rights need not render the idea of voluntary consent to a regime vacuous (Subsection 5).

2. *If Most or All Significant Rights Were Fully Dependent on Action by a Legal Regime, It Is Unclear That There Could Be a Way of Giving Content to the Idea of Voluntary Consent to the Regime's Rules*

Consent to the jurisdiction of a given legal regime might take multiple forms: formally joining a particular religious community (and so explicitly accepting, say, some version of the Code of Canon Law as governing disputes to which one is a party)[7] or agreeing to draw on the services and abide by the decisions of a dispute

[7] Someone might opt to have legal disputes resolved by a religious community to which she *didn't* belong, but it seems more likely that people would opt for full-scale involvement in a community and *then* employ its legal institutions as an incident of membership.

resolution cooperative. In each case, we can reasonably ask whether the participant's consent was voluntary. And it seems clear that whether someone's decision to consent to a regime's jurisdiction was voluntary would depend on how her rights were defined prior to membership.

At least, this seems clear if we understand a voluntary act, as I do here, as one in which the actor is not compelled to engage by actual or threatened aggression. (Otherwise, nothing would stop a regime from maintaining that someone's consent to its authority was voluntary, even though she had consented in face of, say, the threat that the regime would take her home and give it to someone else while imprisoning her.) But what counts as aggression is obviously dependent on what rights someone is judged to have.[8] Thus, for the notion of free consent to the jurisdiction of a given legal regime to have any meaningful content, it must be possible to specify a core of relevant rights that obtain independently of the determinations made by the regime (or, probably, any regime).

However, the notion of a polycentric legal order presupposes the existence of multiple legal regimes, specifying different legally recognized rights. It might seem as if the reasonableness of a polycentric legal order implied that all rights were legal rights, dependent on the existence and operation of some legal regime or other. If this were so, then there would be no pre-legal rights. And so, in turn, there would be no way of specifying content for the notion of voluntary consent to a legal regime. And this would suggest that the notion of a consensual legal order, fundamental to the concept of a stateless society, was unsustainable and perhaps incoherent.

3. *There Are Multiple Possible Moral Positions regarding the Status of Legal Rights in a Stateless Society*

We can imagine at least three possible general moral positions regarding the status of legal rights: (*i*) there is one just set of legal rights, (*ii*) there are several just sets of legal rights, or (*iii*) there are no legal rights because there are no true moral claims at all.

If (*i*) is correct, then there will be an unequivocal standard against which it will be possible to measure the freedom of consent. An act will be free in the relevant sense just insofar as someone is not compelled to engage in it by aggression or the threat of aggression. I have argued, in effect, that this position is correct *as regards the most central elements* of a just legal system: the rules enforced by such a system must be consistent with the NAM. At the same time, I have also argued, the NAM is consistent with a range of possible legal rules.

[8] For a similar conclusion in the context of a discussion of the idea of *duress*, *see* Charles M. Fried, Contract as Promise: A Theory of Contractual Obligation 94–103 (1981).

Thus, the position I have defended here is, arguably, a version of (*ii*). While on this view there is not a single set of legal rights that can serve as a standard against which it will be possible to measure the freedom of consent, there are, ex hypothesi, moral constraints on what a just set of legal rights can be like. So although (given this position) different legal rules might define legal rights in different ways, the choice among just norms would be significantly constrained. For instance: a legal rule that required or permitted the systematic violation of the baseline rules as best understood would clearly be unjust; by contrast, different rules that provided for different periods or processes for the abandonment of a piece of land justly claimed under the baseline rules could both be just, even though they might yield different conclusions in similar cases. So, again, if (*ii*) were correct, the notion of aggression would have determinate content, even though some issues could reasonably be resolved in different ways.

It is certainly possible that (*iii*) might be correct (though the very notion of correctness here is, of course, a normative one, and it would be difficult to affirm the validity of an epistemic norm while accepting the sorts of arguments likely to lead to skepticism about moral norms). Accepting (*iii*) as true would mean denying any moral difference between self-defense and state aggression. But it would also deny anyone who accepted it any basis for engaging in intelligible moral criticism of anyone else. In any event, generalized moral skepticism cannot simply be asserted; it has to be defended in one way or another. Until it is, we need not be overly troubled by it;[9] and, if its validity is ultimately established, there will be more serious problems to resolve than the best way to talk about legal rights in a stateless society.

It seems likely that any reasonable legal regime would treat killing or battering people or threatening to kill or batter them as illegitimate. And the fact that consent to participation in a regime secured by a threat of battery or murder obviously would not count as voluntary would go a long way toward ensuring that the notion of voluntary consent to a regime had meaningful content. A just legal regime, I believe, would also regard torture and interference with people's possessions in a manner inconsistent with the baseline rules as unacceptable, and so as improper means of securing consent. But even if the general account of what just legal rules involve that I am defending in this book is incorrect, consent to a legal regime in a stateless society can be genuinely voluntary as long as there is *some* substantial pre-legal moral constraint on the contents of legal rules.

[9] *See, e.g.*, Terence Cuneo, The Normative Web (2007); Michael Huemer, Ethical Intuitionism (2005); Russ Shafer-Landau, Moral Realism: A Defence (2004); Nathan Nobis, Truth in Ethics and Epistemology: A Defense of Normative Realism (2004) (unpublished PhD dissertation, University of Rochester).

4. *There Are Multiple Possible Moral Positions regarding the Status of Legal Rights Related to Possession, in Particular*

Possessory claims raise interesting questions of their own. With respect to these sorts of rights, in particular, it is possible that (*iv*) there are no just possessory claims, because it is wrong for anyone to claim to control any part of the material world or (*v*) there are no just claims because, for one reason or another, while there are true moral claims about other matters, there are no true moral claims about our possessions in the material world apart from the determination of some particular legal regime.[10] I have offered substantive reasons to reject both of these views, of course, in connection with my defense of the baseline rules.[11] But it is worth considering their implications in this context.

Of course, if (*iv*) were correct, this would indeed establish a moral equivalence between actions with respect to legal claims in a stateless society and actions with respect to such claims by a state. But it would do so at the cost of rendering orderly, purposeful action in the world impossible. There would be little reason for anyone to endorse (*iv*).

If (*v*) were correct, so that there were no moral constraints on specifically possessory rules in the absence of legal institutions, if a legal regime could create just any legal rules regarding possession, then the range of putatively aggressive conduct would be significantly narrower than we often imagine. Suppose there were no pre-legal rights with respect to possessions. Suppose, too, that a regime dramatically constrained someone's freedom of action (indeed, her freedom to remain alive) by appropriating or destroying her possessions, or limiting her access to them, or that it threatened to do so—in order to secure her agreement to participate in it. If there were no pre-legal constraints on people's behavior with respect to other's possessions, it seems as if we would be required to judge that consent to the regime by the imagined person in these circumstances was voluntary, as long as the regime declined to threaten to attack her body.

But the notion that there are no pre-legal rights (or, at any rate, no *significant* pre-legal rights) with respect to possessions is difficult to defend. My arguments for the baseline rules are, I hope, persuasive. But if they are not, other alternative groundings for distinctions between just and unjust possession are available.[12] This is hardly

[10] I ignore the possibility that pre-legal social consensus might play the same role, because, since consensus need not be imposed or maintained by force, this option can be handled under (*ii*), above.

[11] *See* Chapter 2.IV, *supra*.

[12] *See, e.g.*, David Hume, A Treatise of Human Nature 3.1.2 (2d ed., 1749); David Hume, An Enquiry Concerning the Principles of Morals 3.1–2 (1751), 3.1–2; Anthony de Jasay, Political Philosophy, Clearly: Essays on Freedom and Fairness, Property and Equalities 141–51 (2010); David D. Friedman, The Machinery of Freedom: Guide to a Radical Capitalism 3–11 (2d ed., 1989); John Finnis, Natural Law and Natural Rights 168–73 (1980).

surprising. It would be bizarre to suppose that a morality appropriate for embodied persons in a world remotely like ours would lack implications regarding the just treatment of their possessions. I believe we can safely proceed on the assumption that no approach to morality that denied the reality of pre-legal moral constraints on legal rules related to possession would be credible absent substantial counter-arguments, whatever degree of variety in such rules might be permissible. A regime that sought to secure participation by threatening people's just possessory claims, whether my account of such claims is correct or not, could not be said to have secured genuinely voluntary consent to its authority.

5. *Reasonable Claims regarding the Relationship between Morality and Legal Rights Need Not Render the Notion of Voluntary Consent to a Legal Regime Meaningless*

The idea of consent to a legal regime would, indeed, be meaningless, because compatible with almost any conceivable decision by such a regime, if there really were no pre-legal rights. The reality of such rights can reasonably be affirmed; I've sought to defend them in this book. But even if I am mistaken about the details of these rights, as long as there are genuine constraints what a regime may legitimately offer or threaten to do to secure consent, the notion of voluntary consent has genuine content. Even if, *contra* my contention in Chapter 2, sets of just possessory rules can differ from each other on truly central points, there are not infinitely many such sets, and a regime is not free to treat just any possessory rules as reasonable. A robust conception of consent, in accordance with which consent is voluntary when it is given in the absence of actual or threatened aggression, is therefore defensible.

C. A Legal Order Can Reasonably Be Polycentric even if There Are Objective, Pre-Legal Rights

It is perfectly possible to affirm that some schemes of legal rights are just and some are not while still supporting the existence of a polycentric legal order featuring multiple legal rights, including multiple possessory rules.

It is reasonable to assume that there are constraints on actions with respect to others' bodies and possessions sufficient to give the notion of aggression, and so of voluntary consent, determinate content (I have, after all, sought to elaborate and defend such constraints). But it might be thought that the existence of these constraints was incompatible with the existence of a genuinely polycentric legal order. In the absence of an overarching authority ensuring the operation of a consistent set of legal rules, some of the legal rules enforced by some regimes in a polycentric legal order will doubtless be unjust. Since no one can reasonably want unjust norms to obtain, the argument might run, we must all be obligated to oppose the existence of a polycentric legal order and to favor the establishment and enforcement of a uniform set of legal rules.

A stateless society could, in principle, feature such a uniform set of norms. I think it is clear, though, as I have suggested, that the voluntary adoption of a uniform code enshrining consistent legal rules would require far more consensus than is likely to be evident in the foreseeable future. In a society without the state, there would undoubtedly be multiple sets of legal rules, though various factors would be likely to prompt a meaningful consensus on multiple issues.

It will certainly be possible to object on moral or prudential grounds to some of these rules. Different legal regimes will doubtless make mistakes, perhaps sometimes very serious ones. And a stateless society's equivalents of the Abraham Lincoln Brigade may sometimes have reason to become involved in remedying clear injustices perpetrated by some legal regimes. But belief in objective constraints on legal rules is quite compatible with supporting, rather than opposing, legal polycentricity.

(*i*) That there is a fact of the matter about which legal rules are just does not mean that everyone, or anyone, has infallible knowledge of those rules. Polycentricity creates room for experimentation and discovery. Different legal regimes can thus serve as laboratories of liberation in which different options are explored and put on display for others to observe and evaluate.

(*ii*) Some just rules may be appropriate for people with particular characteristics—histories, personalities, and so forth—and communities of such people may tend to opt for those rules. It does not follow that other just rules won't be appropriate for people with other characteristics. (Obviously, as long as people consent voluntarily to particular rules and retain exit rights, it will not be reasonable to interfere forcibly with a regime enforcing those rules, even if, were the rules enforced nonconsensually, interference would be justified.)

(*iii*) Even if it a given regime's rules are thoroughly wrongheaded, people can quite reasonably welcome a system that allows participants in that regime, always with consistent exit rights, to adopt those rules voluntarily. It can be reasonable to welcome a system that permits the adoption of such rules because of the obvious risks associated with alternatives that allowed for the imposition of legal rules on the unconsenting by a top-down authority or by would-be crusaders.

Legal polycentricity is quite compatible with the existence of substantial pre-legal moral constraints on the content of legal rights. Nonetheless, the importance of experimentation, the value of diversity, and the undesirability of the use of force to compel conformity all militate in favor of supporting opportunities for diverse legal institutions to exist and for diverse legal rules to be enforced, even though it would likely be preferable (certainly in light of the considerations I have adduced here) for the range of enforced rules to be quite narrow.

D. The Notion of Substantive Pre-Legal Rights Can Give Content to the Notion of Aggression and Constrain What Does and Does Not Count as Voluntary Consent to a Legal Regime's Authority

The idea of aggression acquires content only in relation to a correlative understanding of rights and duties. If the judgment that a legal regime is not aggressive is to be non-vacuous, there must thus obviously be significant pre-legal moral requirements with regard to bodies and possessions. I have sought to argue for the existence of a set of such requirements; and if I am correct, or if some other account that does comparable work turns out to be accurate, it will be possible to give objective content to the notion of someone's having voluntarily consented to the authority of a given legal regime. Of course, while there are, I believe, substantial pre-legal moral constraints on legal rights, it hardly follows that they will be uniformly acknowledged. It's hardly certain that divergent legal regimes might converge on the same legal rules, though there are certainly pressures that might dispose them to do so. And there will be reasons to favor legal polycentricity even if one believes, as I do, that moral constraints significantly limit the range of possibly just legal rights.

VI. A REGIME COULD FORCIBLY RESOLVE CONFLICTS WITH OUTLAWS WITHOUT BECOMING MORALLY INDISTINGUISHABLE FROM A STATE

A. Using Force against Outlaws Could Be Justified in Limited Circumstances

A regime responding to the behavior of outlaws need not be regarded as behaving in a state-like manner. The outlaw might be thought to pose a problem for the clear delineation of the difference between a consensual legal regime and a state (Section B). However, a regime can largely avoid the risk of engaging in state-like behavior by avoiding contact with outlaws absent specific agreements (Section C). A regime responding to simple aggression by outlaws by forcibly upholding what are clearly just claims need not be seen as engaging in objectionably state-like behavior (Section D). The possibility of the outlaw need not pose an insuperable problem for the attempt to articulate a viable conception of a legal regime in a stateless society as fundamentally different from a state (Section E).

B. The Outlaw Is Arguably a Problem because She Has Not Consented to a Legal Regime's Authority

A given legal regime will have various occasions to interact with outlaws. It's easy to envision a legal dispute between the outlaw and a participant in the regime—perhaps the regime endorses one set of land tenure rules, and the outlaw prefers another. Because she's an outlaw, she's not a participant in any legal regime other than her own (by definition), and it's likely that she doesn't have any preexisting agreement with the relevant regime about legal disputes (if she does, her case raises no special concerns and can be ignored). Thus, there's no basis for saying she's consented either to the substantive legal rules enforced by the regime or to any second-order choice-of-law rules. However, in defending what it takes to be a just claim against the outlaw, a regime may use force against her without her consent. And this might seem to render the regime morally indistinguishable from a state.

C. Regimes Can Often Avoid State-Like Behavior in Part by Avoiding Contact with Outlaws That Is Not Regulated by Clear Agreement

In some cases, of course, a regime could secure an outlaw's consent to its authority.

If an outlaw sought to involve the regime in a dispute regarding an agreement between her and one of its participants, the regime could obviously decline to become involved absent the outlaw's consent to the legal principles or institutional mechanisms the regime proposed to use to resolve the dispute (or both). The regime could similarly decline to become involved when one of its participants asked it to resolve a dispute with an outlaw using its preferred legal rules rather than the outlaw's unless the outlaw consented to the regime's authority in the matter (though, to anticipate, it would only *need* to do this when the outlaw's conduct didn't clearly violate the NAM).[13]

This need not be a serious barrier to orderly interaction. An outlaw would obviously have good reason to want to agree to the regime's involvement to facilitate orderly dispute resolution. And the regime could obviously instruct participants that, when concluding agreements with outlaws, they should incorporate provisions

[13] A regime participant might, of course, specify in some appropriately public way that entering land or a space under her control constituted consent to her regime's rules, or some relevant subset of these rules. But whether entering the land or space *would* constitute consent would obviously depend on the validity of the participant's claim to it, since she would not, in fact, be entitled to exclude those declining to consent unless her claim was valid. Pre-legal moral constraints on applicable legal rules might not resolve the question of the claim's validity. If her claim depended on the rules in question, then, since these rules would be binding only on the consenting, and since the validity of her demand for consent as a condition of entry would depend on the binding nature of the rules, it's not clear that she could rightly exclude others who declined to consent to the regime's rules.

specifying that legal conflicts regarding the agreements be settled by the regime if they expect the regime to become involved.

D. A Regime Can Defend Participants against Aggressive Outlaws and Demand Compensation from Them without Engaging in State-Like Aggression

Following a policy combining the making of preemptive agreements with a refusal in general to become involved with participants' voluntary relationships with unconsenting outlaws would make it relatively easy for a regime to avoid state-like behavior. This does not mean, of course, that a regime would always be able to avoid using force against outlaws. It could reasonably limit the situations in which it did so, however, to ones in which outlaws clearly violated, or were poised to violate, the NAM.

Some outlaws may engage in what may reasonably be regarded as simple aggression against a regime's participants, aggression they would not be prepared to defend on moral grounds. Some disputes, by contrast, may involve good-faith disagreements. But enforcing genuinely just rules against those who don't, in good faith, agree with them is not necessarily immoral or state-like. Whether a moral constraint binds someone obviously doesn't depend on whether she acknowledges it or consents to it: no one needs to endorse the requirement that she not murder or to consent to be bound by that requirement for it to be binding on her. And when violating a moral constraint involves what can objectively be regarded as aggression, preventing or ending that aggression and remedying it will be permitted or required by the principles of practical reasonableness. Without securing her consent, a regime could justly use force to stop an outlaw's aggressive conduct and to secure compensation for any harm she might have done.

For a regime to avoid engaging in state-like aggression, it would need to limit itself in this sort of case to using force only when the participant whose claim it was seeking to defend would be justified in doing so whether the regime's legal rules had been enacted or not. That's because, again, the regime would be entitled to no authority not possessed by its particular participants, who could confer on it only rights they already had. Pre-legal moral requirements bind quite apart from the regime's decisions about which legal rules to enact and uphold; as moral requirements, they apply to everyone.[14] By contrast, a regime's own positive legal requirements would bind only the participants in the regime themselves when they imposed limits on their own actions more extensive than those imposed by pre-legal

[14] I leave to one side here a range of interesting questions about obligations derived solely from pre-legal moral principles but reflective of "facts on the ground" brought into being by the actions of a regime.

moral requirements. Thus, a regime could reasonably use force against outlaws without even ad hoc relationships with the regime only when they violated pre-legal moral requirements.

To the extent that the legal rules enforced by the regime track pre-legal moral requirements, the regime would be entitled legitimately to implement its substantive rules using force. That, of course, is because particular participants would be acting in a manner consistent with the NAM if they did so themselves. Nonetheless, while a regime would act justly in enforcing pre-legal rights, it might expect to encounter less resistance when doing so if those rights were widely acknowledged, despite the fact that the legitimacy of their enforcement would not depend in principle on their widespread recognition. It might be hoped that the kinds of evolutionary pressures I noted earlier would lead progressively to the recognition of the NAM as a sort of *ius gentium* endorsed by most legal regimes.[15] Of course, when a rule upheld by a regime reflected only one of several options compatible with the NAM, it would not be reasonable for the regime to enforce it against unconsenting outlaws whose conduct was consistent with the NAM but not the rule. Different legal rules can be just, for instance, while providing for different abandonment periods for land: a hundred years and ninety days might both be unreasonable, but two years and four years might both be reasonable.

Practically speaking, in any case, it would often not be necessary to sort out disagreements between different theories regarding such contested matters as the extent of just possessory claims in order to determine whether a regime participant or an outlaw was in the right. The same claim might be defensible on a number of different theories. Respect for people's expectations and the need for the general reliability and consistency of legal rules could also establish (defeasible) presumptions a regime might tend to apply when it became involved in a particular kind of dispute with an outlaw.

Further, even where a dispute implicated contingent, regime-specific rules, a regime could certainly defend a participant against an outlaw using force when doing so was necessary to protect the participant's undisputed entitlements—to be free from aggression against her body, for instance. And even where rules about claims to land were in dispute, the regime could presumably defend a participant's land when doing so was an integral and unavoidable aspect of defending her body.[16]

[15] Thanks to Jonathan Crowe for emphasizing the need to make this point.

[16] The same kinds of considerations would obviously apply if the aggression involved were undertaken not by outlaws but by another regime that simply refused to negotiate a choice-of-law agreement. Such a regime could reasonably be treated as a collection of outlaws—not in order to justify hunting and killing its participants, but to ensure that they were treated with the wary respect due dangerous and uncivil predators.

E. When a Regime Must Interact with Outlaws, It May Sometimes Justifiably Use Force against Them without Becoming a State-Like Entity

The possibility that a legal regime might need to use force against outlaws need not call into question the status of a polycentric legal order comprising an array of legal regimes as a genuine alternative to a statist legal system. While an outlaw may not be a participant in a legal regime, her specific interactions with members of the regime may often be governed by rules to which she has actually consented. And, when she has not, a regime need not engage in state-like aggression if it protects its participants against her aggressive conduct or requires that she compensate them for harms she has committed, provided it uses force only when any participant it defends would be entitled to do so in accordance with the NAM.

VII. A LEGAL REGIME IN A STATELESS SOCIETY WOULD BE MORALLY DISTINGUISHABLE FROM A STATE IN IMPORTANT WAYS

Legal authority in a stateless society would rest on actual consent. Thus, forcibly resolving disputes regarding legal rights need not make a legal regime in a stateless society state-like. The legal rules applicable to most disputes would be fully consensual, either (*i*) because the participants both belonged to the same regime and had consented to its rules; (*ii*) because the participants belonged to different regimes, had consented to these regimes' rules, and had thus consented to the regimes' rules regulating conflict between participants in different regimes; or (*iii*) because the participants were bound by situation-specific agreements specifying the rules applicable to their dispute. With regard to someone to whom its rules were not applicable on any of these grounds, a regime could justly use force only when doing so was consistent with the NAM.

Consensual rules accepted by regime participants and consensual agreements between regimes could resolve most legal disputes. Because they were consensual, enforcing them would not need to be state-like. The NAM imposes robust constraints on the range of possibly just schemes of rights, and the existence of such constraints makes it possible for talk about voluntary consent—as to a regime's authority—to be meaningful. Nonetheless, a polycentric legal order might feature multiple consensual regimes enforcing multiple schemes of legal rights—rooted in custom, tradition, legislation, or precedent (the roots don't matter as long as people have full exit rights). And there would still be good reason to support the existence of a polycentric legal order as a whole, even though it made room for the maintenance of some undesirable, even clearly unjust, regimes. (Particular people and groups could obviously challenge regimes that systematically violated the NAM or infringed on freedom or dignity in other ways, and might in some cases even be morally obligated to do so.)

Whatever the legal rules upheld by a just regime, the existence of outlaws need not compel it to behave like a state. In large part, a regime could avoid nonconsensual relationships with them, and when it had no choice but to engage with them, it would not act unjustly if it used force only to stop aggressive conduct on their part or to require redress for such conduct.

There would obviously be considerable economic and social pressure on outlaws in a stateless society to affiliate with legal regimes and on regimes to standardize mechanisms for resolving cross-regime disputes. There would also be real, if less intense, economic and ideological pressures for regimes to adopt similar rules. Though the injustice of state-like conduct does not depend on its extent—subjecting anyone to aggression is wrong—there need be relatively few pressures on a regime to engage in such conduct. It could, in any case, avoid aggression by ensuring that its internal rules rested on the consent of its participants, by ordering its relationships with other regimes consensually (and in ways that merited the consensual self-obligation of its members), by avoiding nonconsensual contacts with outlaws where possible, and by using force against outlaws only in a manner consistent with the NAM.

The substantive rules enforced by particular legal regimes in a stateless society might vary. But members of a stateless society would have good reason, while respecting the variety of the rules enforced by their various legal regimes, to continue to seek to ensure that the rules safeguarded and fostered peaceful, voluntary cooperation. The NAM entails a variety of constraints on the contents of legal regimes' substantive rules, particularly as regards what is arguably the most important aspect of legal rule-making: defining and remedying injury. I laid the groundwork for a discussion of injuries and remedies in Chapter 2, by noting limits on just possessory claims. I seek in Chapter 5 to lay out a more detailed and general account, noting especially the absence of the category of *crime* from the rules that would be enforced by just legal regimes in a society rooted in peaceful, voluntary cooperation.

5

Rectifying Injury

I. JUST LEGAL REGIMES IN A STATELESS SOCIETY CAN EFFECTIVELY PREVENT, END, AND REMEDY INJURIES

Just legal regimes could safeguard peaceful, voluntary cooperation by ensuring that people and their possessions were protected from aggression, that aggression already underway was stopped, and that remedies were provided for injuries resulting from aggression. Such regimes would not address these injuries using the essentially statist category of *crime*, but would instead feature remedies offering *restitution* for all kinds of injuries caused by aggression, supplemented by mechanisms for the restraint of the persistently aggressive (Part II). A just legal regime could deal appropriately with environmentally mediated injuries and with harms to vulnerable persons and nonhuman sentients (Part III). Just legal regimes in a stateless society could respond effectively and appropriately to injuries to bodies and possessions alike (Part IV).

II. JUST LEGAL REGIMES WOULD USE CIVIL RATHER THAN CRIMINAL JUSTICE MECHANISMS TO RECTIFY INJURIES

A. A Stateless Society Would Be Crime-Free

A just legal regime would address injuries using civil rather than criminal laws. The category of *crime* is essentially statist (Section B). Seeking the distinctive objectives often proposed as warranting a system of criminal law is inconsistent with the requirements of practical reasonableness (Section C), and there is good reason to see the maintenance of such a system as dangerous (Section D). While talk about the absence of crime for a stateless society's legal system is first of all a way of emphasizing that such a system wouldn't feature the *category* of crime, the absence of the state could, indeed, be expected to reduce occasions for conflict and diminish the frequency of crime in the sense of aggressive violence (Section E). The fact that legal regimes in a stateless society needn't feature systems of criminal law should be no cause for concern (Section F).

B. "Crime" Is a Statist Category

The notion of *crime* is incomprehensible without the notion of the state, so the idea of crime would have no obvious place in the rules enforced by just legal regimes in a society without the state.

The contemporary legal category of *crime* concerns what are now frequently characterized as assaults on "the public" or "the body politic" or "the state." In a putatively democratic polity, the state will be rhetorically (mis)identified with the entire population. But of course the habit of characterizing the state as the object of crime grew out of the identification of the state with the sovereign in a monarchy.

A crime was an act that was understood to be against the king for multiple reasons: because it violated the king's law, and so challenged the king's authority; because the king feared spillover effects from some acts of great violence—particularly, no doubt, from tit-for-tat acts of retaliation with the potential to involve whole clans in blood feuds; because declaring something an act against the king meant requiring use of the king's courts, and so the payment of court fees to the king; and because putatively criminal acts might reduce the king's tax revenues.[1] In addition, of course, some offenses would only, could only, *be* offenses given the existence of the king. Insults to the king, perhaps assaults on the church established by the king, certainly attempts to overthrow the king—a separate category was purportedly needed for these, in part because they would be inconceivable without the king, and so would not figure in a system of law oriented toward the resolution of disputes among legally equal persons, and partly because there would be every reason for the king to want to underscore their great significance.

The rulers and rhetorical enablers of the democratic state have sought to characterize it as, effectively, stepping into the place of the king. What were once offenses against the king now become offenses against the democratic state and so, purportedly, against all of its people. Heads of state and heads of government in democratic states frequently enjoy something like the legal status of monarchs, despite the use of

[1] *See* Richard A. Posner, The Economics of Justice 204 (1981) (identifying the impact on tax revenue as a likely rationale for the emergence of criminal law systems and noting that "citizens are already protected—not badly on the evidence of prepolitical societies—by the compensation system" predating the creation of the criminal law). Posner notes that, even before the emergence of the state, legal liability may sometimes have been imposed for conduct, such as incest, believed to have negative consequences for an entire community, even though the serious injuries that are seen today as paradigmatic crimes would have been dealt with via compensation; the broad-stroke story I've told here would obviously need to be significantly nuanced were this an essay in legal history.

egalitarian rhetoric,[2] and offenses against such states are greeted with the same lack of amusement with which a king would have reacted to a treasonous conspiracy.

A crime is an offense against the king or, latterly, the state. So it is difficult to see why people in a society free of kings and states should employ the separate category of crime to characterize certain offenses. In such a society, it would be clear that all harms to bodies and instances of interference with just possessory claims had identifiable victims—victims who were neither monarchs pretending to stand in for their subjects nor such abstractions as "the state." And it therefore seems as if there would be a strong presumption in favor of eliminating the category of *crime* entirely and rectifying all injuries using what we might think of as a purely civil justice system.

C. Reasonable Justifications for Legal Liability for Aggressive Injuries Leave No Room for a Separate Criminal Justice System

1. *Warrants for the Use of Force against Those Who Harm Others Aggressively Are Limited*

There are multiple goals a legal regime might be thought to serve when responding to aggressive harm; but most of these goals do not, in fact, provide independent justification for the use of force against those who harm others, and those that do provide this kind of justification offer no rationale for a system of criminal law distinct from the ordinary system of civil law.

Among the distinguishable potential objectives of a legal response to injury caused by aggression are:

- *deterrence*: discouraging the wrongdoer herself and others similarly situated from causing injury in the future by harming her in a way that effectively threatens harm for causing injury in the future;
- *restitution*: restoring to the victim the possession of which she has been deprived by the injury, or the equivalent (together with the reasonable costs of recovery and the reasonable costs associated with acquiring a temporary replacement before full restitution is available)[3];
- *retribution*: harming the wrongdoer in order to give her what she purportedly deserves;
- *restraint*: limiting the wrongdoer's capacity to cause future harm in virtue of the recognition, triggered by the fact that she has caused harm in a particular case, that she poses a serious risk to others;

[2] Consider the dismay and media hand-wringing that so often follow what are seen as affronts to the imperial dignity of the president of the United States.

[3] Legal fees would ordinarily qualify as reasonable costs of recovery. But some limits on legal fee awards might be appropriate in order to discourage frivolous suits and to prevent the imposition of the requirement to pay legal fees from being used as a hidden means of exacting punitive damages.

- *reconciliation*: fostering the reconstruction of personal relationships broken by wrongful harm;
- *reintegration*: fostering someone's reconnection with a community after she's become alienated from it by causing serious injury to another member or members;
- *rejection*: expressing a community's moral revulsion at the wrongdoer's actions by excluding her from continuing membership; *and*
- *rehabilitation*: changing the wrongdoer's character so that she rejects wrongdoing and is likely to behave responsibly in the future.

The category of crime is often defended on the grounds that one or more of these goals justifies imposing the kinds of penalties that are today unique to the criminal law—especially confinement and execution. However, rationales characteristically advanced for the existence of a separate system of criminal law are frequently unappealing. The need for restitution provides consistent, independent justification for the use of force against people's possessions (Subsection 2). Deterrence may be welcomed as a side effect of otherwise reasonable choices, but provides no independent justification for the use of force against bodies or possessions (Subsection 3). Retribution is a deeply problematic notion, and may neither be sought as a goal nor welcomed as a side effect of reasonable action (Subsection 4). Defending oneself or others by posing a threat to use force against someone effectively committed to a program of ongoing aggression may only involve restraining her if no other option is available (Subsection 5). Reconciliation and reintegration are generally valuable goals but may not be sought using force against bodies or possessions (Subsection 6). Rejection is a morally troubling goal for action and is not as such a reasonable objective or justification for the use of force against anyone's body or possessions (Subsection 7). And rehabilitation, while it may be welcomed as a side effect of reasonable action against someone's body or possessions, does not provide any independent justification for the use force, particularly given the potential of a rehabilitation-based rationale for the use of force to excuse autonomy-denying manipulation and control (Subsection 8). Because there is no warrant for executions or punitive fines, and no warrant for restraint (which need not involve imprisonment) except as a matter of self-defense and the defense of others, there is no need for the distinctive institutions and practices of the criminal law (Subsection 9).

2. *Just Legal Rules and Institutions Can and Should Require Restitution for Aggressive Harms and at Least Some of Their Consequences*

i. Restitution is a vital means of rectification

Providing monetary restitution for the harms one causes is a key duty that flows from the Principle of Fairness, and one that is entirely consistent with the baseline possessory rules (Subsubsection ii).[4] Liability ought not to vary with moral culpability, since its purpose is to rectify injury (Subsubsection iii). The requirement of compensation for injury to bodies and possessions provides the basis for an account of liability for failure to perform agreements that cabins this liability and doesn't risk making promises in general legally enforceable (Subsubsection iv). The account of compensation provided here also helps to explain why compensation should not be available for expressive acts (Subsubsection v), and so for libel, slander, or defamation (Subsubsection vi), why paternalistic attempts to sanction people for nonaggressive behavior would have no place in a just legal system (Subsubsection vii), and why positive moral duties to others should not be enforced by a legal regime when not embodied in enforceable agreements (Subsubsection viii). Institutions not employing force against persons or their possessions can help to resolve problems resulting from injuries that cannot be suitably addressed by a legal regime (Subsubsection ix), and such institutions, as well as informal norms and practices, can reasonably be expected to address non-compensable wrongdoing and to supplement legal liability for harms rooted in malice (Subsubsection x). A well-functioning system of justice requiring compensation for injuries is preferable on multiple levels to a system of state-mandated regulation (Subsubsection xi). A just legal regime's focus on providing restitution would enable it to respond effectively to injuries of all sorts (Subsubsection xii).

ii. The baseline possessory rules and the principle of fairness require economic compensation for unjustified injuries to others' bodies and possessions that can be understood in economic terms

The baseline rules permit—indeed, require—monetary restitution for (the economic aspects of) unjustified harms to bodies and possessions. I owe restitution at least because (*i*) *I* have *caused* an injury; (*ii*) I would not want a similar injury which *I* suffered to be ignored; (*iii*) I would likely expect the person responsible for an injury to my body or possessions to remedy it, so it's reasonable for me to accept responsibility when *I* cause such an injury; (*iv*) the Principle of Fairness would at least ordinarily rule out holding *someone else* responsible for harm that I have caused (I would not be willing to be held responsible for an injury caused by someone else); (*v*) I am better positioned to avoid harms I cause than anyone else, and knowing that I likely will be held responsible will dispose me to use my knowledge and control over my own behavior and immediate circumstances to avoid causing injuries; *and*

[4] Randy E. Barnett has systematically explored and defended this idea. *See, e.g.*, Randy E. Barnett, The Structure of Liberty: Justice and the Rule of Law 158–60, 176–84 (1998); Randy E. Barnett, *The Justice of Restitution*, 25 Am. J. Juris. 117 (1980); Randy E. Barnett, *Restitution: A New Paradigm of Criminal Justice*, 87 Ethics 279 (1977).

(*vi*) actually holding me responsible will dispose me to avoid causing harms in the future.

The restitution I owe for harming another's possessions will include the costs of restoring misappropriated possessions or their monetary equivalents and the reasonable costs of recovering damages (including, ordinarily, attorneys' fees, court costs, investigative fees, and so forth). The compensation I owe for harming another's body will include medical and recovery costs.

Because many wrongs do not involve injuries to others' bodies or just possessory claims (even though they may involve injuries to basic aspects of well-being), using force against bodies or justly acquired possessions to prevent, end, or remedy these wrongs (much less for acts that are not harmful at all, including the mere *possession* of anything not used against another) would be consistent with the NAM. In particular, therefore, it would be unreasonable to use force to secure restitution for these wrongs.[5]

Money damages are rightly available for the monetizable harms to bodies and possessions that result from aggression. To make them available for other kinds of injuries would be to deny the validity of the baseline rules, since providing monetary remedies for such harms would license interference with just possessory claims. It would make little sense to understand the baseline rules as permitting damage awards in such cases—doing so would not only allow interference with otherwise just possessory claims but also render the baseline rules less simple and more reliability- and autonomy-infringing than the rules as I have sought to spell them out. There is a strong presumption in favor of the rules in their clearest and simplest form, and there is little reason to favor altering them to allow for compensation for nonaggressive harms.

If I misappropriate someone's justly acquired possession, I am obligated to return that possession, and I can reasonably be regarded as having acquired a debt in the amount of the reasonable costs my victim has borne in the course of recovering her misappropriated possession (and of temporarily replacing it before recovery). Something similar may be said as regards bodily harm: by harming your body, I compel you to bear various costs associated with repairing the damage I have done

[5] It will be apparent from what I have said here and in Chapter 1, for instance, why conduct causing *emotional distress* would not yield legally enforceable restitution claims under the rules I am envisioning. (*i*) It would frequently be a stretch to describe causing emotional distress as injuring someone's body. (*ii*) I experience emotional distress precisely because something important to me has been adversely affected or is being threatened (or because I take this to be the case). If what occasions the distress is an injury to my body or involves interference with a just possessory interest, then the injury itself will be an appropriate predicate for liability; on the other hand, if it isn't, then the fact that it occasions distress doesn't change the fact that it's non-compensable because nonaggressive. Distress is a (fallible) pointer to actual or threatened harm, and the nature of the harm to which it points, rather than the distress itself, should be what determines whether liability is appropriate.

simply in order to restore your body to its condition before my action, and I can reasonably be said to have acquired a corresponding debt to you for these costs and the associated costs of recovering the debt.

By contrast, if I cause an injury to you that does not involve aggression against your body or a just possessory claim on your part, I have not assumed a monetary debt to you. Money damages are available for physical injuries because money enables the replacement of a damaged or misappropriated physical object or the repair of a bodily injury; it is, in effect, the best available substitute for an intact physical possession, organ, or limb. To maintain that I have assumed an injury-based debt to you is to maintain that I owe you compensation for some injury to a legally protected interest. It's easy to see why compensation is appropriate when I damage your body or possessions.

Maintaining that you have some enforceable obligation to compensate me when you have *not* damaged my body or possessions will ultimately amount to asserting that you've adversely affected some other legally protected interest of mine—otherwise, what would be the basis for the claim that you owe me anything? But this assertion will thus *either* mean that you have affected another's body or possessions in some way that I don't like *or* that you have affected something that is *no one's* body or possession in a way I don't like. In neither case do I, ex hypothesi, have a just claim on whatever it is that you're supposed to have affected, since it is either another's or no one's, so there's no reason to suppose that you owe me damages for whatever I allege that you've done to it. To say otherwise would be to imply that I had legally protected interests in others' bodies or possessions (or, paradoxically, in something to which no one had any justly protected interest); but to enforce the claim that I had this sort of interest would, absent some specific agreement, involve aggression against those others—since they would be entitled in accordance with the NAM to noninterference on my part with their bodies and possessions—and would thus be unjustified and illegitimate. In short, the underlying logic of the compensation requirement is that economic damages are due for physical harms to people's bodies or possessions and that force can reasonably be used only in response to force.

In addition to this basic moral justification for the limits on compensation I have defended, there are additional rationales. Clearly limiting legal redress to those cases in which physical harm has occurred minimizes the potentially costly use of the judicial system. And accepting a clearly delimited range of instances in which the use of force against others' possessions may be justified obviously places a clear and convenient boundary on the use of force, and so on the use of its substitute, the law. The existence of such a boundary could be expected to minimize conflict and to render social life reliable and predictable. Considerations of reliability and simplicity, which help to constrain the range of possibly reasonable baseline rules, also rightly enter into determinations of the right second-order rules and procedures that safeguard the interests protected by the baseline rules themselves.

But none of this means that proponents of just legal rules can or should regard wrongs that don't involve compensable attacks on others' bodies or just possessory claims as anything but wrongs. It is an entirely unwarranted non sequitur to conclude from the fact that just legal rules preclude the use of force to prevent, end, or remedy certain kinds of immoral conduct that support for such a legal order entails or implies endorsement or trivialization of the immoral conduct. For instance: legal rules that permit people to exclude others from access to their justly acquired possessions will, by implication, permit them to do this for morally objectionable reasons; but it will be reasonable to support the baseline rules, which allow for this sort of unreasonable exclusion, in spite of, rather than because of, the immoral reasons for which people might take advantage of the opportunities afforded them by the rules. It is perfectly consistent to affirm that just legal rules leave no room for the imposition of monetary sanctions on or the use of physical force against people because they violate binding commitments to sexual exclusivity, for instance, while unequivocally rejecting sexual betrayal. Just legal rules will protect a "right to do wrong" only in the narrow sense that they will not license the use of force to prevent, end, or remedy nonaggressive wrongdoing.

iii. Liability to compensate others for aggressive harms one has caused ought to be strict

The requirement of restitution is not rooted in any sort of judgment about moral culpability on the part of the defendant (though the plaintiff's contribution to the injury or her culpability with respect to its occurrence ought to affect the defendant's liability—there should, for instance, be no liability to provide restitution to someone for injuries caused by the reasonable use of force against her in the course of defending against an unjust attack in which she is engaged).[6] The point, rather, is that the plaintiff has been harmed through, ex hypothesi, no fault of her own. It will be more fair to ask the person or persons responsible for the harm to compensate the victim than to ask others to do so, and the responsible parties will be, in any event, better equipped to avoid harm resulting from their actions than anyone else, so that holding them responsible is both a matter of fairness with respect to past acts and of incentivization with respect to potential future acts. Holding people strictly liable for harms they actually cause, and so holding them responsible for compensating their victims for these harms, ensures that injuries are actually remedied—that the injured receive compensation and the injurers bear the costs of remediation.

Strict liability is, in principle, liability for whatever harm one has actually caused—with the understanding that (*i*) someone who uses actual or threatened aggression

[6] *Cf.* Chapter 2.III, *supra*. On the economic logic of strict liability claims, *see* POSNER, *supra* note 1, at 199–200 (concluding that strict liability rules should be seen as economically rational in "primitive" societies).

to coerce someone to do something (or who deceives another into doing her will) ordinarily bears responsibility for any harm the person thus coerced performs under compulsion (though an aggressor's threat to harm her or someone else if she does not do so provides no excuse for someone to cause death or great bodily injury to a third party) and that (*ii*) an unjust attacker is not entitled to compensation if she is injured by someone defending himself or another against her attack. If multiple actors are responsible for a harm, their moral responsibility to the victim is proportional to their causal responsibility for the harm. When responsibility can be readily apportioned, it would be unfair for a court not to apportion it. However, when questions about causal responsibility are murky, there may be no choice but to assign liability jointly and severally, leaving responsible parties to litigate how much responsibility each actually has for the harm—or, when responsibility is uncertain, *whether* a plausibly responsible party is actually responsible.

iv. Compensation for damage to or loss of possessions should be the remedy for violations of enforceable agreements

Violations of prior agreements should be remedied through the provision of compensation for misappropriated or damaged possessions.[7] Specific performance will never be a remedy except when it involves the transfer of a particular possession when the transfer of title to the possession has already been completed but the physical transfer has not taken place, or the return of particular possessions secured fraudulently or on the basis of a conditional agreement that is violated.

The baseline rules entitle people freely to transfer their possessions to others. Violating an agreement justly triggers compensation to the extent, and only to the extent, that it involves damage to or loss of what should be regarded as someone's

[7] Grant Gilmore famously argued that a distinct law of agreements was in the process of vanishing, with a more inclusive law of civil obligation coming increasingly to replace sharply differentiated sets of legal rules related to personal injuries and agreements; *see* GRANT GILMORE, THE DEATH OF CONTRACT (2d ed., 1995). Gilmore's suggestion may be seen as involving the claim that principles focused on binding promises linking the parties, *see* CHARLES M. FRIED, CONTRACT AS PROMISE: A THEORY OF CONTRACTUAL OBLIGATION (1981), are perhaps being, perhaps should be, replaced with broader, societally focused principles that could be used to invalidate agreements on various sorts of consequentialist grounds. While my concern here is quite specifically with a narrowly transactional model of the enforceability of agreements, one that does not allow for the introduction of external factors into the determination of an agreement's enforceability, there is a sense in which I am proposing something quite similar to what Gilmore seems to have had in mind. That is, I am arguing that promises should be legally enforceable precisely when the failure to enforce a promise would be to fail to provide a remedy for unjust harm to another's possessions. Obviously, the difference between my proposal and Gilmore's is that, while arguing, in effect, for the collapsing of the law of agreements into the law of injuries, my conception of tort law is narrower than Gilmore's, since it drastically cabins the use of consequentialist considerations in the determination of liability for individual injuries.

justly acquired possessions.[8] Thus, to take the simplest case, if A makes an agreement with *B* regarding some possession, *P*, that licenses *B* in taking possession of *P*, *P* is now *B*'s justly acquired possession. If A then denies *B* access to *P*, A has violated *B*'s just possessory claim to *P* and owes *B* compensation, ideally by delivering *P* or, if this is for some reason impossible, by compensating *B* for the loss of *P* just as if A had misappropriated *P* were it already in *B*'s possession.

A promise by A to *B* that does not involve any sort of transfer will doubtless very often be morally binding. But there is no basis for a just legal regime to provide any sort of *forcible compensation* for its violation. For restitution involves the appropriation of someone else's possessions, and this appropriation is justifiable only as a means of rectifying the loss resulting from the misappropriation of or damage to someone else's possessions. If there has been no actual transfer by A to *B* of a just claim to some possession, then either A has done some agreement-independent damage to some possession of *B*'s, in which case reference to any agreement is irrelevant, or A has done no damage to any justly acquired possession of *B*'s, in which case no compensation from A to *B* would be due. Limiting damages in this way makes sense given the underlying character of the compensation requirement. It is also appropriate because it effectively cabins the use of force, providing a bright-line distinction between moral and legal obligation (while also reducing the risk that some onerous promissory burdens will be legally enforceable).

Thus, for instance, violation of a personal service agreement of some kind could not reasonably trigger an enforceable requirement to pay compensation. A person's services are not possessions that can be conveyed to others. The failure to provide a personal service is not an interference with anyone's justly acquired possessions, and cannot be a predicate for compensation (though of course someone who accepted payment in advance for services she did not perform could obviously

[8] *Cf.* MURRAY N. ROTHBARD, THE ETHICS OF LIBERTY 133–48 (1982); Williamson M. Evers, *Toward a Reformulation of the Law of Contracts*, 1 J. LIBERTARIAN STUD. 3 (1977); LYSANDER SPOONER, POVERTY: ITS ILLEGAL CAUSES AND LEGAL CURE 65–108 (1846). *But cf.* Frank Menetrez, Comment, *Consequentialism, Promissory Obligation, and the Theory of Efficient Breach*, 47 UCLA L. REV. 859 (2000) (arguing for the legal enforcement of at least some promissory obligations through specific performance requirements).

One consequence of adopting this approach would presumably be substantial limits on the enforceability of some agreements providing for the payment of interest on loaned money. While the return of the principal and reasonable costs of recovery could be required, along, presumably, with some sort of payment for the temporary unavailability of the principal (compare: if I steal your car and return it a year later, I presumably owe you some compensation for your inability to use the car), it is not clear that the payment of interest itself could be enforced simply in virtue of an agreement to pay it, though perhaps some more complex mechanism could yield enforceable obligations to pay interest in some cases; and, of course, there would be quite substantial reasons for firms and particular people to comply with many interest agreements even when they were not enforceable. *Cf.* Roderick T. Long, *The Enforceability of Interest under a Title-Transfer Theory of Contract*, PRAXEOLOGY.NET, http://praxeology.net/title-transfer.pdf. Thanks to David Gordon for discussing the issue with me.

be required to return the payment for work not done).[9] Someone wishing to ensure compensation for the failure to provide a personal service would need to arrange for some sort of bonding, risk management, or liquidated damages arrangement that would be enforceable in a manner consistent with the requirements of practical reasonableness. Clearly, people could decline to work or exchange with those who failed to perform personal service agreements, and other kinds of nonaggressive sanctions for unreasonable failure to perform such agreements would be possible, but providing monetary compensation would be inconsistent with the baseline rules.

This kind of limit on the availability of damages for failures to fulfill agreements has obvious implications for any agreement regarding land that is said to "run with the land"—to be binding on successive just possessors of the land. The failure to fulfill such an agreement could trigger payment of liquidated damages or a bond forfeiture, for instance. But it would be difficult in many cases to justify the loss of the land itself, or of certain otherwise just claims on the land. This is particularly true given that such agreements are ordinarily thought to confer claims on land to entities not parties to the transaction involving the transfer of the land, and the mechanisms needed to confer these kinds of claims on them would seem to be highly complex. Obviously, people interested in imposing certain kinds of restrictions on land could make agreements that created associations and vested just claims to land in those associations, rendering the associations the just possessors of the land and particular persons, in effect, their tenants. This cession of control seems likely, however, to reduce the attractiveness of the land to those who might wish to acquire it.

An example: suppose Alix, Barbara, Chris, Dani, Em, and Fred are already just possessors of various parcels of land. Each one agrees with every one of the others that she will never transfer her land to any member of the Jones family. At some point, however, Fred opts to transfer her parcel to Georgina, who turns out to be a Jones. Alix, Barbara, Chris, Dani, and Em haven't transferred any land to Fred, ex hypothesi, so she hasn't misappropriated anything of theirs. If the remedy for breach of an agreement is the return of misappropriated possessions or their monetary equivalent, the five would seem to have no remedy. Absent an actual or attempted unjust taking by Fred of something belonging to them, Fred has simply made a bare promise, the violation of which can't rightly trigger economic damages (even if it may in some cases—probably not in this one—be morally objectionable and subject to various sorts of nonviolent social sanctions). Of course, the others might receive payments under enforceable bonding or liquidated damages agreements. But they

[9] An agreement to be a slave—to provide personal services indefinitely—is thus unenforceable, though someone could be required to return payment made in anticipation of her fulfillment of such an agreement, complete the conditional transfer embodied in a liquidated damages agreement, or forfeit a bond posted in anticipation of possible breach. *Cf.* Chapter 2.V.B, *supra*.

would not be entitled to legal damages, and they certainly would not be entitled to void the transfer to Georgina.[10]

The situation would seem to be different if the six first formed an association, Anti-Jones Holdings, transferred their possessions to it, and then reacquired what had been their possessions from AJH. In this case, violating an agreement with AJH might at least in some cases trigger return of the possessions to the association. However, it would seem practically important to treat AJH's claims as having lapsed after a certain period unless formally reestablished, so that current claimants could rest secure in their claims. And it would be increasingly difficult to enforce the no-sale-to-Joneses requirement as possessions were transferred from possessor to possessor, even if each subsequent possessor had to include the requirement in a transfer agreement on pain of forfeiture. Of course it might be possible to structure things in such a way that, each time land was to be transferred, it would first be claimed by AJH and only then transferred to a new just possessor, so that she did have a direct relationship with AJH (and would presumably become a participant in the association herself). However, the transaction costs and the loss of control associated with this sort of awkward arrangement would presumably make it unattractive to many people.[11]

v. Compensation should not ordinarily be available for purely communicative acts

Requiring compensation for putatively problematic instances of expression in virtue of their communicative content is objectionable for multiple reasons.[12]

[10] *Cf.* Sheldon Richman, *Restrictive Covenants: Rule by the Dead Hand of the Past*, CATO UNBOUND, June 29, 2010, http://www.cato-unbound.org/2010/06/29/sheldon-richman/restrictive-covenants-rule-by-the-dead-hand-of-the-past/. Bryan Caplan floats the idea of an association of roughly the kind I consider here in the course of responding to Richman; *see* Bryan Caplan, *Restrictive Covenants, HOAs, and Libertarian Legal Theory*, LIBRARY OF ECONOMICS AND LIBERTY, http://econlog.econlib.org/archives/2010/06/restrictive_cov.html.

[11] A further wrinkle: a legal regime might simply decline in advance to enforce anti-Jones agreements of this kind. It's easy to imagine that it might take this sort of stance for both moral and prudential reasons. No regime is, of course, morally obligated, nor could it justly be legally obligated, to provide all services to all actual or potential participants absent specific agreements.

[12] My focus here is on what amounts to restitution for expressive acts imposed *ex post*. *Ex ante* forcible interference with communicative acts—prior restraint—will be objectionable because it will involve infringement on the just possessory claims of the communicator or of anyone whose justly acquired possessions are being used (with the just possessor's permission) by the communicator in the course of communicating. This kind of interference will obviously be inconsistent with the baseline rules. Preemptive interference with people's possessions is, of course, justifiable to prevent immediate legally cognizable harm (I can enter your home to stop you from firing a gun out the window at me). But since the putative harms arguably resulting from speech are not legally cognizable, for the reasons indicated in the text, preventing or ending these putative harms can't provide a justification for preemptive interference with anyone's communicative acts in virtue of the anticipated communicative content of those acts.

(*i*) Expressive acts obviously do not *constitute* harms to bodies or physical objects. No one's body or possessions can be said to be harmed just insofar as someone else communicates something, anything. A legally cognizable, because compensable, harm to me is a harm to my body or my just possessory claims. But to count as a harm to a body or a physical object, something must *be* a change in the body of the physical object. And *your* communicative act can't be a change in *my* body or any of my justly acquired possessions.[13]

Communicative acts convey feelings or sounds, depict narratives or images, or express attitudes or propositions. The mere fact that A strongly, viscerally, irrationally detests *B*, for instance, does not in any way constitute an injury to *B*'s body or possessions. Nor does *A*'s *expression* of her hatred for *B*, for such an expression can only make *B* aware of A's attitude. And if the attitude itself does not amount to harming *B*, then being aware of it cannot harm, either.

It can, to be sure, create *apprehension* of harm. Perhaps A is plotting violence against *B*, and A's expression of hatred makes this clear (and this may rightly affect not only *B*'s view of A but also the appropriateness of *B*'s behavior—say, *B*'s use of what she intends as defensive force—in response to ambiguous actions on A's part). But awareness of possible harm isn't itself an injury. The same is true of speech conveying a proposition. Here, as with the expression of an attitude, speech does not *constitute* a harm. If endorsing the proposition does not constitute a harm—and how could it?—neither does expressing it. Transmitting a sound or image or conveying a narrative, similarly, can't be an instance of harming in the relevant sense because doing something of this sort doesn't amount to changes in bodies or possessions.

(*ii*) Expressive acts also cannot be said to *cause* harms to bodies or physical objects. Any harms associated with communicative acts will be the responsibility of those who perform them. Expressing attitudes and propositions may, of course, *affect* other people's behavior (and affecting someone's behavior may be morally objectionable in ways that rightly trigger guilt and social sanctions). But that's not the same thing as *causing* a harm. If *C* and *D* behave unjustly toward *B* as a result of A's words, then it is *C* and *D* who have harmed *B*, and who therefore owe *B* compensation, not A. (The situation will be different if A, *C*, and *D* are engaged in some

It is also worth emphasizing that my concern is with liability in cases in which specific agreements are irrelevant. There might in principle be cases in which the communicative content of someone's expressive act triggered some consequence or other under an otherwise enforceable *agreement*.

[13] There are exceptions: (*i*) I enslave you and use your body in the course of some kind of communicative act; or (*ii*) I misappropriate one of your possessions and use it in the course of a communicative act. But here the legally compensable injury would be the enslavement or the misappropriation and wouldn't be dependent either on the fact that my unjust act was communicative in nature or on the specific communicative *content* of the act.

sort of clearly cooperative venture. And, even if they are not, A might owe *C* and *D* some sort of indemnification if such indemnification could be required under an otherwise enforceable agreement.) A's choice to communicate with them in particular ways may be morally abhorrent (since it may have been motivated by the desire to persuade them to harm *B*), and it may have *influenced* their behavior, but it did not *cause* their actions, given the intervening reality of their own free choices. Because, ex hypothesi, they acted freely, they are responsible for their own choices. If they acted in violation of the NAM, they should have known that doing so was unreasonable; and, whether they did or not, they are responsible for rectifying harms created by their aggressive conduct. (Of course, if they have not violated the NAM, they are not liable for damages to *B* in any case.)

The issue here is not *culpability*: *C* and *D* are liable because their actions caused the injury to *B*, while nothing in turn physically necessitated that they would perform these actions, and A did not use force to *compel* them to harm *B*. (It would, of course, be wrong for *C* and *D* to, say, maim or kill *B* even under threat of physical violence from A, since these actions are always wrong because inconsistent with the Principle of Respect; but it would not seem ordinarily to be inconsistent with the Principle of Fairness for them to steal from *B* under threat of violence from A. Of course, that's not the kind of case under consideration here.) In any case, what matters is that *B* be compensated for injuries resulting from aggressive conduct, and this can happen provided *C* and *D* are liable for their acts of aggression. Whether A, who bears some *moral* responsibility, is also *legally* liable need not affect the availability of compensation for *B*.

People are not, it is safe to assume, passive recipients of communications from others. Rather, they decide what to do with these communications—whether to ignore them or to act on them and, if they do decide to act on them, how they will do so, and *they* must therefore be treated as responsible for their harmful (and other) actions. (Further, it would obviously be unwise to treat anyone as a passive recipient overmastered by someone else's communication, since the incentive to deny responsibility would be enormous.)

In addition, (*iii*) even if there were, as I deny, good reason to require restitution from people in virtue of the communicative contents of their expressive acts in particular cases, it seems likely to be very difficult indeed to cabin legal sanctions for such acts. Once the principle of interference with communication is allowed, anyone with the ability to influence a legal system might be able to see to it that the range of predicates for putatively acceptable communicative liability was expanded. To treat any institution as legitimately able to sanction communication is to treat it as possessing substantial and dangerous power. To do so is also problematic because, once the principle that liabilities should be limited to tangible harms to tangible possessions (or bodies) has been attenuated, there might be expected to be institutional pressures to allow for liability in other kinds of cases, with predictable violations of the NAM. Because of the systemic risks—of dramatic reach as regards communicative acts beyond those originally thought worth sanctioning as well as noncommunicative acts not involving or causing physical harm—there is good reason to ensure that a legal system designed to implement the NAM does not offer opportunities for people to be sanctioned for the communicative contents of their expressive acts.

Attempts to restrain speech are problematic for other reasons, which provide redundant support for the view that a just legal system should not impose constraints on expression.[14]

(*iv*) Restraining expressive acts interferes with the communicators' autonomy; since most people would not wish their autonomy infringed, it will be unreasonable for them to infringe on the autonomy of others.

(*v*) Interference with expression represents an attack on a centrally important human capacity—the capacity to communicate—and on relationships rooted in this capacity, and thus might be seen as particularly troubling.

(*vi*) Interference with expressive acts impedes the self-disclosure that is necessary for the achievement of relationship and community.

(*vii*) Interference with communication impedes the quest for truth and understanding, which are best fostered as ideas are exposed to public scrutiny and winnowed by criticism—and which cannot be promoted at all if ideas are suppressed. In the same way, it impedes the discovery and evaluation of alternative ways of being human: attitudes and lifestyles can be considered for adoption only if they are put on display and offered for assessment. Thus, it constrains social and intellectual experimentation.

[14] These additional reasons are redundant *as regards* the use of force to require compensation for expressive acts or to subject such acts to prior restraint. They are *not*, of course, redundant when the issue is the use of social or economic *influence*, rather than force, to punish people for past expressive acts or to prevent such acts from occurring in the future. These further rationales provide people with reasons to avoid imposing non-forcible restraints on communication as well as forcible ones. Because of these factors (as well as those identified earlier in this subsubsection: the causal break between an expressive act and any harm putatively resulting from it will still be relevant as regards contemplated non-forcible restraints on communication, as will the fact that expression does not constitute harm and the merits of not encouraging or empowering institutions to interfere with communication), it will frequently be unreasonable for people to seek to restrain or sanction expression non-forcibly, and such restraints will therefore count as violations of what I have identified as *social freedom*, though of course some kinds of communication may well warrant nonviolent protest. (To be sure, when the issue is the non-forcible restraint of, or the imposition of non-forcible sanctions for, expressive acts, the range of wrongful harms for which these non-forcible responses are appropriate may reasonably be wider than would be the case where the use of force was concerned.)

(*viii*) Interference with expressive acts impedes the autonomy of *recipients* of communications as well as the originators, since they are denied the opportunity to undergo experiences and evaluate ideas, attitudes, and factual proposals.

(*ix*) Interference with expressive acts in the putative interests of listeners treats them as being incapable of forming rational judgments and acting on such judgments. Thus, it infantilizes them and encourages them to avoid accepting responsibility for what they do with the ideas and images and sounds they encounter.

(*x*) Restraints on communicative acts prompted by the communicative contents of these acts seem especially likely to suppress minority attitudes, and so to reinforce majoritarian social dominance.[15]

The point, obviously, is not that communicative acts never involve wrongdoing or lead to serious harms. It is rather that there is (as it seems to me) decisive reason not to use force to suppress communicative acts or to require communicators to provide compensation for harms with which their communicative acts are associated. There is often also decisive reason not to interfere nonviolently with communicative acts in virtue of their communicative content, though various forms of nonviolent protest—itself, of course, in part a kind of communication—may be entirely fitting as responses to some wrongful communicative acts.

vi. Compensation should not ordinarily be available for the non-fraudulent dissemination of false information

Similar considerations help to explain why libel, slander, and defamation claims are unjustifiable. Suppose you publicly distribute some sort of false claim about me that embarrasses me and, in an extreme case, prompts others to avoid interacting with me, perhaps with some sort of resultant economic loss. You have obviously done something wrong: you have acted out of hostility toward me, and you have acted unfairly toward me and toward others (in the case of the others, by deceiving them). But it does not follow that the remedy for your wrongdoing should take the form of restitution required by law. For, as a general rule (absent specific enforceable agreements), others have no enforceable duty to interact with me, whether or not their interacting with me confers some economic benefit on me. So I cannot reasonably claim compensation from *them* (even if there are cases in which *they* might reasonably be entitled to compensation from *you*). But you have not deprived me of any justly acquired possession. Rather, you have affected the availability to me of certain relationships which are most assuredly *not* possessions (you cannot be said to have *deprived* me of them, since the participants in those relationships were, ex hypothesi, free to decide whether they did or did not wish to continue participating in the

[15] *But cf.* Rae Langton, *Speech Acts and Unspeakable Acts*, 22 PHIL. & PUB. AFF. 293 (1993). Thanks to an anonymous reader for noting the significance of Langton's critique.

relationships). Since they were not my possessions, I can claim no compensation for their loss.

Falsehood used to obtain the transfer of A's justly acquired possession to *B* is another matter, of course, since the falsehood will ordinarily have vitiated A's free consent. This kind of falsehood—fraud—is remediable like any other misappropriation of someone's possessions. And specific agreements might, of course, allow for compensation to be claimed for economic losses resulting from libel or slander.

vii. Just legal rules will not provide for the imposition of liability on people for injuries they have putatively done to themselves

Among the obvious advantages of thinking about legal liability in the way I have suggested here—as imposed by civil justice institutions unified around principles requiring compensation for harm to bodies and physical possessions—is that it offers no obvious opportunity for the imposition of liability for actual or prospective harms to oneself. This kind of liability is often justified on either retributive or deterrent grounds, neither of which, as I argue below, can provide any independent justification for the imposition of legal liability. By requiring that there be a plaintiff who can show that her body, her possessions, or both have actually suffered harm; that she be able to clearly specify the extent of the harm; and that she make clear how a proposed economic remedy can deal appropriately with the harm, a just legal system would make it impossible for people to sanction others for behavior that didn't harm the bodies or possessions of people prepared to seek liability. Because busybodies hadn't themselves been harmed, they would have no basis for demanding restitution.

This is an advantage of the model I have defended here for several reasons. (*i*) Even when those who seek paternalistically to manage others' lives or punish them for what the would-be punishers regard as self-harm are correct about the needs of their prospective targets, the use of force against the targets' bodies and possessions is objectionable for the reasons all violations of the NAM are objectionable. (*ii*) In addition, to the extent that the purpose of the paternalists' interventions is the moral reformation of their targets, they seem likely to be unsuccessful, at least to the extent that their targets are likely to change their behavior, if at all, for the wrong reasons and to experience a diminution in their capacity for independent moral judgment (presuming that they learn to make choices based, to a greater degree than before, on their fear of punishment). (*iii*) Would-be paternalists will often *not* be correct about the circumstances of their targets' lives, the nature of flourishing, and the demands of morality. To the extent that they are not, it is to everyone's advantage that they be unable to use force to implement mistaken beliefs. Requiring identifiable victims who are willing to take the initiative to seek compensation because they have suffered identifiable harms to a narrow range of interests to specifiable degrees places a substantial limit on the use of force. If minimizing the use of force is a source of greater civility and security in a society, it would be advantageous to deny would-be paternalists opportunities to attack others for behavior that doesn't violate the NAM.

viii. Economic liability should not be imposed for failures to fulfill positive duties not grounded in enforceable agreements

The Principle of Fairness is a source of positive obligations in a variety of cases.[16] While it will be difficult to spell out in advance what these cases will look like in detail, it is clear that it will sometimes be unfair not to be benevolent, not to render aid. This may be a matter of helping specific, identifiable others—rescuing a drowning child,[17] or a drowning dog, for instance. And it may also be a matter of selecting any of several, perhaps many, recipients of financial assistance: in this case, it might be, say, that no particular organization could object if one failed to provide *it*, in particular, with assistance, and that no precise amount of assistance was required by the Principle of Fairness, but that choosing to benefit none of the potential recipients, or to give a very tiny amount to one, would be unreasonable.[18] Inaction may sometimes be perfectly reasonable, but it may sometimes be anything but morally trivial; under some circumstances, a failure of benevolence may be far more objectionable morally than a minor act of aggression.

Whether this is so in any particular case obviously requires careful moral analysis. However, this is an entirely separate question from whether a just *legal regime* could require compensation from someone who failed to perform a duty of benevolence or confiscate her possessions to ensure her fulfillment of such a duty. Unless positive duties were embodied in enforceable agreements, there would be no just predicate for forcibly compelling the provision of compensation for failure to fulfill such duties. Failure to assist another in the absence of enforceable agreement does not constitute aggression against her body or her justly acquired possessions and thus cannot trigger a requirement to compensate.

Enforceable agreements need not be formal, written documents, of course. Persistently engaging in a given pattern of behavior without qualifying one's actions in relevant ways may amount to agreeing to accept certain duties in certain circumstances. And social conventions may reasonably lead to the assumption that duties are being undertaken in particular cases unless specifically disavowed. At the same time, though, the general limits on the enforceability of agreements remain.

[16] *See* John Finnis, Natural Law and Natural Rights 107 (180).

[17] *See* Robert P. George, In Defense of Natural Law 95 (2001).

[18] *Cf.* Chapter 6.III.C, *infra*.

Where restitution could not appropriately be required for an unreasonable failure of benevolence—because of the absence of an enforceable agreement, whether explicit or implicit—a range of nonaggressive sanctions could, should, and doubtless would be available in a stateless society. While requiring restitution for such a failure of benevolence would be inconsistent with the underlying logic of the restitution requirement, various social mechanisms could be used to underscore its moral significance.

ix. While compensation should be required only for monetizable harms caused by aggressive injuries, nonlegal social institutions can and should deal with other kinds of harms

Not all losses and harms are monetary or monetizable, and many do not result from aggression. This means that monetary compensation may not be sufficient fully to rectify every loss associated with a given harm. It may be not only impossible but insulting to attempt to place a monetary value on a ruptured interpersonal relationship, for instance. Rather than pretending that all losses are monetarily compensable losses, it will make the most sense for a just legal regime to offer the kind of relief it may reasonably offer, while leaving other kinds of communal institutions, with the capacity to influence behavior and express convictions in a variety of nonforcible ways, to address nonmonetary losses resulting from aggressive harms, as well as the various sorts of losses resulting from nonaggressive harms. Ostracism, public shaming, boycotts, nonviolent protests, peaceful strikes and work slowdowns, the use of various institutional and personal bully pulpits, and other nonaggressive mechanisms can reasonably be used to address harms of this kind.

x. Liability for restitution cannot be expected to be the only consequence of wrongdoing

The degree of moral culpability for particular actions, compensable and noncompensable, will vary quite widely, and it will obviously be relevant in multiple contexts. If someone consistently acts in a manner that undermines the well-being of others, or declines to assist them when the Principle of Fairness requires that she do so, people may be disinclined to deal with her (even when they would be quite willing to deal with someone else who has caused similar sorts of harms, but has done so inadvertently). People would doubtless be deterred from various kinds of actions that might not justly trigger forced compensation not only by their own consciences but also by concern about possible nonaggressive sanctions.

xi. A legal regime that requires restitution for injuries to bodies or possessions is preferable to a state regulatory apparatus

Requiring complete restitution for harms to bodies and harm to or interference with justly acquired possessions is superior to using state regulation to prevent, end, or remedy these harms.

State regulation deprives people of the opportunity to make their own judgments about risk and risk tolerance—to use the best information available to them to judge whether harms are likely and how willing they are, in principle, to suffer these harms. Similarly, state regulations make implicit judgments about just how worthwhile avoiding various harms ought to be. By contrast, people anticipating possible harms and aware of the potential for litigation can craft agreements designed to manage risk that reflect their particular risk-related preferences and judgments and to take realistic account of available resources in determining just how high a priority ought to be placed on suppressing certain risks.

In addition, state regulation is often designed to benefit favored corporations and other well-connected groups—who are either exempted from liability or otherwise advantaged in relation to other persons and organizations. Simple liability rules, by contrast, ensure an even playing field.

Further, state regulators are likely to use limited or otherwise inadequate information to make regulatory decisions. By contrast, people crafting agreements designed to manage risks and people involved in litigation after those risks have materialized can and will use not only general but local knowledge to reach desirable solutions. Potential tortfeasors aware of the risk of liability will take serious account of their local knowledge to keep the possibility of harm appropriately low. Litigation-based approaches can be appropriately flexible and fact-sensitive.

xii. Restitution can and should play a crucial role in rectifying injuries

The duty to compensate others when one has harmed them flows from the requirements of practical reasonableness. This duty is *strict*—when one is actually responsible for an injury, one ordinarily owes compensation proportionate to one's responsibility (and one may sometimes reasonably need to resolve the question of proportionality with other tortfeasors even as one is fully liable to the victim). And it extends to some, but not all, harms related to violations of agreements—those harms that also involve, in effect, the misappropriation of possessions. It does not include a responsibility to provide compensation for any purely expressive act. It does not extend to harms resulting from the choices of people not specifically obligated by enforceable agreement not to interact with others, to harms done by agents to themselves, *or* to harms resulting from inaction, except as provided by specific, enforceable agreements, but this is not because these harms are morally insignificant. While injuries to bodies and possessions that are economically compensable are real and important, they are hardly the only sorts of harms people suffer (and of course that the injuries are compensable does not mean that the losses resulting from the injuries are only economic in nature), but the use of force is not appropriate, and legal institutions are not well suited, to address wrongful injuries that aren't economic in nature and economic losses that don't result from aggression.

These sorts of injuries and losses can reasonably be dealt with by social institutions outside the legal arena. Similarly, compensation is owed for aggression quite apart from moral culpability—the negligent person is no less liable than the person who causes harm purposefully—but culpable action or inaction may result in a variety of nonaggressive social consequences, the possibility of which may serve as a deterrent to wrongdoing that may not as such trigger legal liability. A system of compensation requiring restitution can achieve the legitimate goals of a system of state regulation without many of the attendant problems. Compensation can and should play the central role in the legal system's response to injuries to bodies and possessions.

3. *Deterrence Provides No Independent Justification for the Use of Force against Anyone*

i. Deterrence is unjustifiable

The putative desirability of deterrence does not warrant the implementation of distinctive criminal penalties. The notion of deterrence is the notion of harming someone to increase the likelihood of improved future behavior (Subsubsection ii). Some deterrent choices violate the Principle of Respect (Subsubsection iii). Others would seem to be in tension with the baseline possessory rules (Subsubsection iv). And support for a general system of deterrence seems to run the risk of disconnecting legal responsibility from actual injury and to invest decision makers with excessive power (Subsubsection v). There is thus little justification for treating deterrence as legitimate (Subsubsection vi).

ii. Deterrence involves harming for putatively good ends

The idea of deterrence is fairly straightforward: harm is caused to someone who has engaged in legally cognizable wrongdoing, *for the purpose* of discouraging her from engaging in future wrongdoing ("specific deterrence") or discouraging others from engaging in future wrongdoing ("general deterrence"), in either case out of fear of experiencing harm in the future for relevantly similar conduct. Such harm can effectively take two forms: harm to some basic aspect of the injurer's well-being, or harm to her possessions. Direct attacks on bodies for deterrent purposes are always wrong, and there are very good reasons consistently to preclude deterrent attacks on people's possessions.

iii. Purposefully harming a basic aspect of well-being violates the principle of respect

Harm to someone's body *for the purpose* of bringing some future event about will obviously violate the Principle of Respect. It will thus in principle be wrong, whatever other factors are involved. (Harm to other aspects of someone's well-being for this purpose will also be immoral, of course, though they will not be legally cognizable unless they involve harms to bodies or possessions.)

iv. Deterrent attacks on people's possessions are hard to square with the baseline possessory rules

a. Deterrent attacks on people's possessions are unjustifiable for the same reason other misappropriations of people's possessions are unjustifiable

Deterrent harm to someone's possessions is likely to be inconsistent with the baseline possessory rules.

Fairness dictates that people take responsibility for the harms they have caused and thus that they owe victims compensation for these harms. The victims have, ex hypothesi, been harmed; it would be unreasonable to assign third parties rather than those responsible the duty to provide restitution to the victims; and those responsible are better able than third parties to prevent the harms they cause and can thus reduce the risk that they will have to provide compensation. The amount of compensation due follows from the damages and the reasonable costs of recovery.

A compensation requirement seems perfectly consistent with the baseline rules. If people's just possessory claims are to be safeguarded, then when justly acquired possessions are misappropriated, they ought to be returned. If a misappropriated possession can't be returned, monetary compensation provides a reasonable second-best alternative. While bodies are not possessions in the same sense that physical objects external to bodies are, injuries to bodies can be addressed in the same general way as harms to just possessory interests, since remedying them costs money.

But while interference with people's justly acquired possessions as a way of enforcing restitution requirements is perfectly reasonable, interference that doesn't involve stopping them from harming others or securing compensation for aggressive harms will be inconsistent with the NAM. This sort of interference, including interference with others' possessions for deterrent purposes, is just the sort of thing a just legal regime is designed to protect people *against*.

Deterrent interference might take either of two forms: (*i*) some possession or possessions belonging to someone who's engaged in some sort of aggression might simply be destroyed in order to send the message that engaging in the relevant sort of aggression will yield this undesirable outcome; (*ii*) in addition to the full compensation due the plaintiff for the harm she's caused, someone might be deprived of some additional sum of money (presumably, though not necessarily, payable to the plaintiff) for what are often called "exemplary" purposes. Simple destruction of people's possessions violates the Principle of Fairness (Subsubsubsection b), while awarding punitive or exemplary damages is inconsistent with the values underlying the baseline rules and seems to treat people who have caused legally cognizable harms as somehow also responsible for harms they have not caused (Subsubsubsection c). Deterrent takings are likely to be unwarranted (Subsubsubsection d).

b. Destroying others' possessions for deterrent purposes is unjustifiable
Sheer destruction of others' possessions for exemplary purposes is clearly not defensible. It would seem to be inconsistent with the baseline rules, and it is hard to see why the rules should be altered to permit it. Even if an injurer were responsible for exemplary as well as compensatory damages, others who might have received the possessions were they taken from her could reasonably object that destroying them had wasted them. And simple destruction is likely to breed anger and aggression at higher levels than will awards of exemplary damages for deterrent purposes. Only the latter option seems even potentially reasonable.

c. Taking others' possessions for deterrent purposes is unjustifiable
Deterrent takings would appear to be unjustifiable. Allowing them would likely be inconsistent with the desiderata underlying baseline rules. Legitimate deterrent effects are exerted by the simple fact of legal liability. But imposing additional penalties for deterrent purposes would seem to make sense only if the person being asked to pay them were being held responsible for harms she had not caused and could not reasonably be expected to cause.

The baseline rules themselves can only be maintained if people are unable to violate others' just possessory claims with impunity and are instead required to compensate those whose just possessory claims they violate. And regard for economically compensable harms to bodies similarly requires compensation. But it is unclear what would justify altering the baseline rules to allow what would otherwise be misappropriation in the interests of deterrence.

Clearly, people's ability to plan requires predictability. And this means that allowing open-ended awards of exemplary damages should not be permissible. It is entirely possible to manage the risk of causing harm to others *ex ante*, but it is far more difficult to anticipate the amount of an open-ended exemplary damage award resulting from such harm.

Further, allowing open-ended awards for putatively deterrent purposes would leave open the possibility that judges and juries would in fact use them as a covert means of exacting retribution in some cases—something I argue below they should not be permitted or encouraged to do. This sort of action is problematic, surely, because of its inconsistency with the Principle of Respect—which precludes acting out of hostility, and there is thus reason not to encourage it institutionally. In addition, permitting exemplary damages is likely to encourage plaintiffs and defendants alike to spend money on litigation rather than on productive activity.

These considerations on their own might be thought to leave open the possibility that exemplary damages might reasonably be awarded if the relevant rules rendered exemplary damage awards highly structured and thoroughly predictable by potential defendants. But there is good reason not to permit them at all.

The sheer fact that an injurer would be required to compensate her victim, together with the associated reputational and related losses, would be sufficient to exert significant deterrent effects. Actual and potential injurers would obviously take into account the likelihood that a just legal regime would reliably require compensation for injuries—along with the probability that other community members would take into account someone's responsibility for an injury, together with her moral culpability, if any, in deciding whether, and, if so, how, to deal with her in the future—in ways that would surely affect future behavior. But the proponent of exemplary damages wishes to maintain that a *further* payment should be required for deterrent purposes. If this is so, however, it is unclear why the person who's caused a given injury should be responsible for such a payment. Could other, future victims reasonably will that she pay exemplary damages at a level sufficient to deter those responsible for harming *them*? If there is a robust causal link between the action of the person who's caused the injury in question and the harms to these later victims, then it seems reasonable to expect that she compensate them. But it is unclear why she should be responsible when *others* injure them—and doubly so since she is not being asked to compensate them, but her own victim.

To be sure, an injurer's behavior might increase the likelihood of future harms if she *avoided* legal liability; but, of course, if she did, no court would be considering the extent to which she owed damages. Given that she *has* been found liable, she has already played an exemplary role, signaling others that there will be consequences if they cause injuries. There is, in any event, nothing about the *possibility* that people will be injured in the future that entitles a current plaintiff to greater compensation, any more than later plaintiffs would be entitled to such compensation absent a clear and substantial causal connection between the actions of the person responsible for the injury in the present and *their* injuries (supposing, for instance, that exemplary damages, instead of being paid to the initial plaintiff, were held in trust for future plaintiffs).

Holding people responsible for future injuries similar to ones they've caused is obviously also problematic because the injuries are *future*. There is no guarantee that they will occur, and their causal links to present-day defendants' actions are unknown because, in the nature of the case, they do not exist. In brief: to the extent that someone is not responsible for future harms, it is not reasonable to hold her responsible for preventing them, which is precisely what exemplary damage awards effectively do.

Awarding exemplary damages—even rigidly predictable ones—would seem, in short, to be unfair. And it would also seem to be inconsistent with the desiderata underlying the baseline rules. It will, for instance, reduce autonomy. It will divert resources from productive use and so reduce the accessibility of genuinely desired goods and services. It will require the adoption and enforcement of more complex rules than would otherwise be the case. It will discourage people from taking what might in many cases be quite beneficial risks by imposing on the taking of those risks a further penalty in addition to responsibility to any harm that might result from risky action. It will limit opportunities for generosity. It will, in short, be difficult to defend.

d. Interfering with people's justly acquired possessory interests for deterrent purposes is unlikely to be justifiable

Exemplary damages unfairly hold people responsible for injuries they have not caused. And it would make little sense to understand the baseline rules as, despite appearances, allowing for such damages. Economic deterrence, just like deterrence effected through attacks on basic aspects of well-being, is unreasonable.

v. A deterrence-based system can feature legal liability for victimless conduct and vest dangerous authority in legal decision makers

A legal system that allows deterrence to serve as an independent justification for legal liability could encounter a further problem. A compensation-based system ensures a fit between conduct and liability—there can only be compensation if an identifiable victim or group of victims can be shown to have suffered a measurable injury, with the result that liability will never be imposed absent such an injury and that the amount of compensation will reflect the severity of the injury: such a system features built-in limits on the severity of the liability it imposes and, indeed, on whether this liability is imposed at all. By contrast, a deterrence-based system requires some independent determination that conduct is to be deterred, with liability for engaging in the conduct reflecting the potentially arbitrary judgment of the entity determining the extent of liability regarding the conduct's seriousness. Supporting a deterrence-based system therefore opens the door to the imposition of liability for victimless conduct and invests the sanction-determining entity with considerable power, with the potential to be exercised dangerously. Both features of a deterrence-based system provide good reason not to support it.

vi. Imposing deterrent penalties is probably inconsistent with the requirements of practical reasonableness

Attacking a basic aspect of anyone's well-being for deterrent purposes would violate the Principle of Respect. Attacking someone's possessions would be inconsistent with the baseline rules, and there is little reason to amend the rules to permit deterrent attacks on people's possessions, especially given that legal liability is itself a source of deterrent effects, that awarding punitive or exemplary damages would seem to involve holding people responsible for effects they have not and will not cause, and that a deterrence-based system has the potential to cut the link between legal liability and actual harm and offer excessive discretion to those determining legal sanctions. In short, deterrence is a deeply problematic justification for legal liability.[19]

[19] I have argued strenuously against deterrence as an independent justification for any legal penalty—not only against deterrent attacks on people's bodies but also against deterrent attacks on their possessions. Such attacks, I maintain, unfairly make people responsible for outcomes over which they have little or no control and which there is no good reason to task them with preventing. At the same time, however, I argue *for* the use of incentives in at least three contexts: (*i*) with regard to the baseline rules, I suggest that one reason to accept these rules is that they incentivize productivity; (*ii*) with regard to the provision of legal remedies for injury, I argue that requiring compensation for harm is important because, for example, it conveys the message that the misappropriation of others' possessions will not prove a successful way of enriching oneself; and (*iii*) with regard to the provision of remedies for non-aggressive injuries, I have defended the use of boycotts, shunning, and similar strategies to encourage people to take appropriate responsibility for such injuries. The cases I affirm and those I reject can be differentiated in several ways:

(*i*) Putatively deterrent sanctions deprive people of what are acknowledged to be their justly acquired possessions. By contrast, the baseline rules' potential to incentivize enters into the determination of what counts as a just possessory interest in the first place. Deterrent sanctions are applied to possessions which it is presupposed are justly claimed by those upon whom the sanctions are imposed, if for no other reason than that sanctions applied to other people's possessions rarely move us as much as ones that affect our own. So a rule permitting such sanctions would be inconsistent with the baseline rules. But the determination that the baseline rules are defensible in part because they incentivize could hardly be inconsistent with the rules themselves, since it is a consideration entering into their justification

(*ii*) Incentival considerations *reinforce* the other considerations that support the baseline rules, rather than undermining them. By contrast, applying deterrent sanctions *reduces* the ability of the baseline rules to achieve their desired effects.

(*iii*) With regard to compensation for harms: incentival considerations don't affect *how much* compensation is owed. Rather, they serve simply to support, in tandem with considerations rooted in the importance of desert, the claim that requiring compensation makes sense. By contrast, deterrent sanctions do require people to pay more than they would need to pay were responsibility for the actual harms they have caused the only issue.

(*iv*) As regards the baseline rules: the rules incentivize by conferring (or, better, by allowing for the conferral of) benefits, not by imposing harms. Deterrent sanctions, on the other hand, necessarily involve what those to whom they are applied are expected to regard as harms.

(*v*) As far as nonviolent norm-maintenance is concerned: boycotts, shunning, etc., may be undertaken, not to make anyone an example, but rather, to persuade someone to take responsibility for remedying a nonaggressive harm; thus, they need not be ways of imposing any sort of open-ended responsibility for future harms. And of course they do not involve unjust injury to anyone's body or unjust injury to or interference with anyone's justly acquired possessions.

(*vi*) Systemically, allowing for deterrent penalties creates an opportunity for people to engage in retribution under the guise of deterrence. Implementing the baseline rules doesn't create such an opportunity in any obvious way, and while requiring compensation for injustices that occurred in the distant past may create opportunities for people to act with retributive *motives*, by limiting the amount required from perpetrators' successors-in-interest to actual damages plus recovery costs, retributive *sanctions* are largely precluded.

(*vii*) The baseline rules incentivize people by allowing them to reap *benefits* for *their own* productive choices. Deterrent sanctions incentivize people by *harming*—and by harming *other* people.

(*viii*) Those who are harmed by deterrent sanctions are arguably *instrumentalized* to a degree that those who are encouraged to be productive by the baseline rules and those who are required to

4. Harming Others to Exact Retribution Is Indefensible

i. The idea of retribution seems to rest on a set of mistakes

The idea of retribution is deeply problematic. It reflects one or more mistakes—that a harm to an injurer could constitute a benefit to the person's she's injured, the order of justice, or herself (Subsubsection ii); that accountability requires retribution (Subsubsection iii); that the Principle of Fairness requires retribution (Subsubsection iv); that a victim's improved feelings attendant on harm to the person who's injured could represent a benefit to the victim justifying retributive punishment (Subsubsection v); or that the supposed goodness of retributive balancing constitutes a logical primitive (Subsubsection vi). The appeal of retribution seems to be rooted in a mistaken application of economic logic (Subsubsection vii). The notion of retribution is finally indefensible (Subsubsection viii).

ii. Retributive punishment could be justified, if at all, because it constituted a benefit to someone, which it does not

a. The notion of retribution would seem to be sensible only if harming one person could benefit anyone

Because the Principle of Respect rules out causing harm to a basic aspect of well-being as a means to bringing about any sort of good, there will be no justification for causing harm in order to effect a logically subsequent good. So the only justification for causing harm to an injurer (except when harm is caused in the course of defending against an unjust attack) will be that causing the harm *constitutes*, just *is*, a benefit. It is unclear just what this benefit could be, and more unclear how something undergone by one person could *constitute* a benefit to another (Subsubsubsection b). It is even more unclear how an abstract "order of justice" might be benefited by retributive punishment, or why anyone ought to care if it were (Subsubsubsection c). And it is unclear that retributive punishment can plausibly be said to benefit the injurer herself (Subsubsubsection d). Retribution therefore seems to lack any justification consistent with the Principle of Respect (Subsubsubsection e).

provide restitution by the legal system are not. The use of nonviolent norm-maintenance strategies against a nonaggressive injurer need not instrumentalize her in the way general deterrence might seem to do (since her suffering adverse consequences is not being used to encourage others to behave differently) nor in the way specific deterrence might be thought to do (since her suffering adverse consequences is not designed to deter her from future wrongdoing). Asking her to take responsibility for her own conduct seems less instrumentalizing than using her as an example for others or trying to prevent the occurrence of potential future conduct. And some limited instrumentalization consistent with the Principle of Respect and the Principle of Fairness need not be seen as troubling.

b. It is unclear how a harm to one person could constitute a benefit to another

It is difficult to see just what the benefit putatively conferred by retribution might be. It is not even obvious in most cases that a *benefit* to one person *constitutes* a benefit to another. We may reasonably judge that this is sometimes true—as in the case of parents and children, friends, and lovers. But in such cases a benefit to one constitutes a benefit to the other precisely because the two parties are in some important sense identified with each other, so that something that affects one in a given way can be seen to affect the other in a comparable way. But of course no such identification obtains in the case of an injurer and the person she's injured; while their fates may in some sense be linked, although each may be deeply invested emotionally in what happens to the other, the one who's been injured simply does not identify with the person who's injured her in a way such that what happens to the person causing the injury happens to her as well. And, of course, not only is this sort of identification not a feature of the relationship between the person causing and the person undergoing an injury; it is also obviously the case that, if the one injured *did* identify in this way with the person who had injured her, harm to the person causing the injury would constitute further harm to the one injured, not any sort of benefit to her.

To be sure, a harm to one person may be a cause of or a precondition for another's benefit, but that's a different matter. The sadist may, indeed, take pleasure precisely in harm to someone else, and *Schadenfreude* is an all-too-common social phenomenon. But there is no reason to think that the benefit here is real: a harm to you is not an aspect of my well-being, even if it is something I desire or welcome.

c. It is also difficult to see what it might mean to confer a benefit on "the order of justice"

An alternative approach is to argue that it is not the victim per se, but rather "the order of justice" that is benefited by retribution. But if this is to be more than metaphorical mystification, "the order of justice" must be understood to refer to patterns of relationships among real people. Abstractions don't benefit from anything in particular, and there is no obligation to treat them with fairness or respect. So retributive punishment must constitute a benefit to some real person or people if it is to be justified. And if the one injured does not herself benefit from retribution, then who does? It will be just as difficult to explain how anyone other than the one injured benefits when the injurer is harmed as it will be to explain how harming the injurer constitutes a benefit to the victim herself. By contrast, if the order of justice is seen as having independent existence, it is unclear why anyone should have any particular reason to confer a benefit on it, given that it is not a sentient.[20]

[20] I prescind from the possibility that the order of justice *is* sentient—as, for instance, God. This is not the place to untangle the relevant logical knots, except to say that, insofar as God is personal,

d. Retributive punishment does not benefit the punished person

Being subjected to retribution is, under any definition, a bad thing. Something will not constitute retributive punishment unless it is reasonably regarded by the person being punished as an attack on some aspect of her well-being, whether intrinsic or instrumental. So the case that retribution benefits its object is, at minimum, difficult. But perhaps the defender of retribution could argue that retribution simultaneously harmed and benefited its object. Such an argument seems unlikely to be persuasive. On the one hand, the argument could amount to the claim that being treated justly *just is* a benefit. But this argument would be successful only if there were some independent reason to believe that being subjected to retributive punishment constituted being treated justly; it could not on its own suffice to show that it did. On the other hand, the argument could amount to the claim that being punished will bring about some future benefit, such as moral reformation, but in this case the good is not constituted by, but rather flows from, the retributive act. In neither case does retribution seem to be justified as constituting a benefit to its object.

e. Retributive punishment does not, as such, constitute a benefit

The retributive punishment of an injurer does not constitute a benefit to her victim or anyone else. Any argument for it will thus need to involve the claim that it brings about some future benefit, but to cause harm in order to bring about a future benefit isn't retributive at all, but deterrent (or something similar). Retributive punishment seems finally to involve causing harm for no good reason.

iii. Accountability does not require retribution

Charles Barton argues that "[t]o hold persons responsible and accountable for wrongs to fellow members [of their community] and to the common good is to consider them liable for blame and punishment for such wrongs. . . ."[21] But while holding people responsible for wrongs *just is* holding them liable for blame—presuming that blame is equivalent to attributing responsibility—I confess that I cannot see why holding people responsible for wrongs means considering them liable for retributive punishment. This seems to presuppose just the point at issue. And even if the focus

(*i*) God would not benefit from any event in the creaturely world except, in general (the exceptions—involving, say, divine appreciation of inanimate beauty—wouldn't alter the conclusion here), if some creature benefited from it; (*ii*) an injury to a creature would no more constitute a benefit to God than it would constitute a benefit to any creature; and (*iii*) if the order of justice were an aspect of the divine being, it would be necessary, eternal, and in an important sense impersonal, and thus not capable of being the recipient of a benefit or of adjusting in accordance with events in the creaturely world. *Cf.* David Ray Griffin, Reenchantment without Supernaturalism: A Process Philosophy of Religion (2000).

21 Charles K.B. Barton, Getting Even: Revenge as a Form of Justice 93 (1999). While I had purchased this book before communicating with him about it, I thank Stephan Kinsella for reminding me of its existence and leading me to rediscover it in my library.

is on accountability rather than responsibility, the same difficulty seems to persist. Unless liability to retributive punishment is built into the very notion of accountability (and why should it be?), accepting accountability could at least as readily be understood to mean accepting a duty to provide restitution as needed—with the added advantage that conferring restitution on a victim actually addresses the wrong one has committed, while accepting retributive punishment does not.

iv. The principle of fairness does not require retribution

It is true that something not unlike retribution is involved in the idea that "one good turn deserves another": the Principle of Fairness requires us to return good for good, and returning good for good can be seen as an instance of acting in accordance with the requirements of practical reasonableness. If acting reasonably is an instance of flourishing, a kind of well-being, then doing good to one who has done good to me will, like engaging in any other reasonable act, constitute a benefit for me as well as for her. But this provides no justification for retributive punishment.

The Principle of Fairness requires us to compensate those we have harmed, just as we would expect compensation from those who have harmed us (we likely wouldn't be willing to take responsibility for harms caused by others, and those who cause harms are best situated to prevent them and so to reduce the burdens associated with providing compensation for them). But it can't require that we undergo harms (under that description) because we've harmed others unless, at minimum, our being harmed benefits them (provided we don't expect those who have subjected us to injuries to undergo corresponding injuries).

It is obvious that conferring a good on someone (as when I return a favor) benefits her, and that compensating her when I have harmed her does so as well. Returning a favor and compensating someone I have injured are both required by the Principle of Fairness. But this principle need not be not invoked here to explain that conferring compensation or returning a favor constitutes a benefit (it may be relevant, of course, in the determination of whether compensation or an act meant to return a favor is reasonable), but only to make clear that it is required. By contrast, if the Principle of Fairness were invoked to justify retributive punishment, it would need to be used, in effect, to explain what (supposedly) *constituted* the benefit.

Ordinarily, when I understand someone to have treated me fairly, I do so in view of the impact of the other's behavior on some independently specifiable aspect of my well-being. In such a case, the Principle of Fairness explains why the other is responsible for affecting (or not affecting) the relevant aspect of my well-being in a particular way, but the value of that aspect of my well-being is presupposed. In the case of retributive punishment, by contrast, the purported good *just is* an injurer's being harmed, and the status of someone's being retributively punished *as a good* is supposedly explained as a matter of what the Principle of Fairness requires. But while in other cases the Principle of Fairness is drawn upon to explain who should receive some good, in this case it is purportedly used to identify something as good in the first place. However, absent a logically prior argument that harming an injurer constitutes a benefit to her victim or someone else, it is not clear how the Principle of Fairness can be understood to require it.

v. That improved feelings might follow retributive punishment does not justify retribution

A defender of retribution could seek to justify it by maintaining that harm to the injurer might make the one injured *feel* better. But there are at least two problems with this sort of justification for retribution.

A feeling presents itself either as a bare sensation or as a component of an emotion, and so as associated with a cognition in one way or another. If it is a bare sensation, it might be an instance of physical pleasure, a genuine aspect of flourishing. But, if it were, this would not justify causing harm to the injurer to produce it; the Principle of Respect rules out attacking one instance of flourishing to bring about another, or acting out of hostility. In any case, however, the "feeling good" on the part of a victim (or someone else) that might be brought about by causing harm to an injurer does seem to be an emotion, rather than a bare sensation; it presents itself as reflective of or as embodying or pointing to a judgment that the harm to the injurer either causes or constitutes a benefit to someone.[22] It is not ordinarily reasonable to seek an emotion for its own sake.[23] So there will be no justification for bringing about some emotion by causing harm to the injurer unless, at minimum, harm to the injurer does, indeed, constitute an actual benefit to someone. Since it does not, as I have already argued, positive feelings will not reasonably figure in any justification offered for the imposition of retributive punishment.

vi. There is little reason to regard the putative goodness of retributive balancing as logically primitive

The defender of retribution might suggest that we should view the goodness of the sort of retributive balancing for which she argues as logically primitive, not capable of being explained in terms of any other sort of benefit or in need of any sort of justification. The idea here would be that it is a basic aspect of my well-being that injurers (whether their actions affect me or someone else) are retributively punished. But

[22] I suggest, without attempting to argue the point, that the persistence of retributive feelings, which present themselves in such a way that retribution is *experienced* as inherently valuable, can be explained in sociobiological terms with reference to the predictable survival value of playing tit-for-tat.

[23] If there are exceptions, these will not involve attempts to come to believe or not believe propositions or to accept or not accept judgments when one is not entitled to regard oneself as objectively warranted in doing so.

it is hard to see how this notion could be rendered intelligible. Perhaps retribution against an injurer constitutes a benefit to me; perhaps, too, I benefit when a flightless biped with vestigial wings on Betelgeuse IV loses a feather—but why should I think this is the case? When it is utterly unclear why something might count as an aspect of my well-being, I suggest, the burden of proof rests with the person who wants to maintain that it is, in fact, an aspect of my well-being.

vii. The idea of retribution seems to involve a mistaken application of economic thinking

The notion of retribution appears to trade on an illusion. It assumes that, in economistic fashion, a harm to an injurer can somehow balance or compensate for the harm done to her victim.[24]

Of course, when one person causes a monetizable harm to another, she can compensate her victim by transferring to the victim a sum equal to the monetary value of the harm she has caused. Similarly, if she has taken someone's justly acquired possession, she owes the other the return of the possession (in addition, presumably, to the reasonable costs of recovery and perhaps other associated damages). And of course the money payment in the first case and the return of the misappropriated item in the second amount to losses—in some sense, to harms—to the injurer. But it is not under *this* description that they are justly required. What the injurer owes her victim is not that she undergo some harm or loss but that she *compensate* the victim. She will suffer a material loss in virtue of providing compensation, but it is providing compensation, not undergoing harm or loss, for which she is responsible.

The idea of retribution seems to be the product of an attempt to generalize from the duty to compensate, an attempt rooted in a faulty assumption about the moral principle revealed by and reflected in endorsement of this duty. At any rate, it is clear that retribution does *not* compensate: harm to the injurer does not, as such, make the victim or anyone else better off.[25]

viii. The notion of retribution is implausible

It seems clear that that appeal of retribution as a moral concept is not rooted in its intellectual plausibility. Arguments for retribution are terribly strained. Retribution does not benefit those injured, injurers, or the order of justice. It is not necessary to achieve accountability. It is warranted neither by the Principle of Fairness nor by the purported value of the good feelings it may produce. It is not a logical primitive. Rather, it seems to be a misapplication of economic logic. The attraction of

[24] The analysis is more complicated, but not essentially different, if the victim *is* the injurer—if the injurer is thought to have wronged herself in some way. Much statist paternalism might be justified in retributive terms if retribution were legitimate.

[25] I bracket here the question of potential *instrumental* benefit resulting from harm to the injurer; see the earlier discussion of deterrence.

retributive acts and institutions reflects the appeal of (*i*) emotional responses which, since they admit of no obvious reasonable justification, can safely be explained away in light of their evident sociobiological function; and (*ii*) metaphors which make it unduly easy to transplant the idea of compensation outside the economic realm in which it is meaningful.

5. *The Need to Restrain Those Committed to Ongoing Programs of Aggression May Sometimes Justify Confinement*

While restraint for purposes of deterrence or retribution is not justifiable, restraint for the purpose of protecting people against the habitually aggressive may be legitimate when no less restrictive alternative exists. The restriction on their movements may be justified, if at all, along the same lines as threatening the use of force to stop continued combat activity by a combatant.

To begin with, consider the use of force in the context of armed conflict. Given that it is objectively unreasonable for a combatant to use force against me or others, it can be quite compatible with the Principle of Respect and the Principle of Fairness to use force against her, provided I use no more force than necessary to stop aggression on her part and provided I impose no unfair risk of collateral harm on any noncombatant.

A combatant, I take it, is someone who is engaged directly or indirectly in an ongoing program of using force against others. A combatant may be someone actually using a weapon; someone who is part of a military unit that is using force on a continuing basis, even though currently inactive (because bivouacked, say); or a military officer or politician actually involved in directing combat operations. The use of force against a combatant is permissible because it need not (of course, in a particular case it may) involve causing harm purposefully or instrumentally.

Thus, for instance, because he was actively involved in overseeing operations involving the unjust use of force, and because there was no effective means of immobilizing or capturing him without using lethal force against him, assassinating Adolf Hitler could—at least assuming that collateral harm was reasonably minimized—have been morally appropriate. By contrast, the U.S. military's reported decision to kill Osama bin Laden rather than capturing him was not, given that, on the U.S. government's own account, he could have been prevented from engaging personally in aggression or overseeing others' aggression without killing him.

If it is appropriate to use force to stop aggression, it is surely also appropriate to make an aggressive person aware that one will do so if need be. To alert her to the risk that one will use force to stop her may be sufficient to lead her to discontinue aggressive action or to decline to commence it. It may thus be reasonable to keep her under guard as long as she is an ongoing combatant. Obviously, this does not mean that she may be abused, tortured, or humiliated. It would not, however, be consistent with the Principle of Fairness for her to expect extensive accommodation if the need to hold her, say, at gunpoint were a function of her continued involvement in a program of aggression suspended only in virtue of the presence of people capable of defending themselves and others against her attacks. There may be in principle no need to confine her; but confinement may be the most efficient way to ensure that she is prevented from engaging in continuing aggression. Given that she cannot reasonably object to the use of efficient measures designed to prevent her from engaging in aggressive harms, she cannot reasonably reject confinement, provided no less restrictive alternative is realistically available, as long as she remains a combatant.

Most people who harm others unjustly by attacking their bodies are not engaged in ongoing programs of aggression. It is not realistic to regard such people as ongoing threats, any more than one might so regard a soldier who has credibly surrendered and abandoned participation in combat. There is, in general, no nonpunitive reason (and therefore no reason) to hold such a person at gunpoint, since threatening to use force against a combatant is appropriate simply as a way of signaling to her that potential victims or their allies are prepared to defend themselves against, and so to stop, unjust attacks on her part and are willing to use force to do so. There is no reason to convey this message to someone who is not a combatant, who has clearly laid down her arms or otherwise to restrain her movement. She poses no ongoing danger. Because she does not, she need not be confined or confronted with the threat that defensive force might be used against her.

Some people who harm others unjustly by engaging in aggression outside a setting of armed conflict can perhaps be understood to be committed, like combatants who have not surrendered, to ongoing programs of aggression. Absent credible indications of surrender, they may reasonably be treated as combatants. Thus, it is conceivable that such people need to be restrained or threatened with the continued possibility that they will be subjected to defensive force to protect others from their attacks. If this is so, they, like military combatants, might sometimes justly be confined.

As with military combatants, however, this is so only if less restrictive alternatives are not available. It is conceivable, for instance, that robust mechanisms for risk-management and the protection of people's possessions might ensure that the persistently aggressive were denied opportunities to harm others without being confined, or were denied such opportunities by quasi-confinement arrangements recognizably very different from existing prisons.[26] Such less restrictive alternatives are to be preferred given that they allow for the restraint of those effectively committed to ongoing programs of aggression while involving as little infringement on their dignity and autonomy as possible.

[26] *Cf.* Robert P. Murphy, Chaos Theory: Two Essays on Market Anarchy 17–18, 31–32 (2002).

6. *Reconciliation and Reintegration Are Desirable Goals, but Not Reasonably Achievable by Force*

Reconciliation and reintegration are standard goals of the "restorative justice" movement.[27] Both are obviously desirable. Causing harm to others ruptures interpersonal relationships and disconnects people from their communities. Given the importance, both intrinsic and instrumental, of interpersonal relationships and communal connections, the Principle of Fairness might seem to suggest that those who value these relationships and connections for themselves ought to foster opportunities for others to reestablish them.

There is a limited sense in which this is doubtless true. A legal framework consistent with the requirements of practical reasonableness would leave essentially unlimited space for freedom of association, and the Principle of Fairness would make promoting certain kinds of association within the terms of that framework desirable in some cases and perhaps even required in others. But there are at least two important qualifiers. (*i*) The value of promoting reconciliation and reintegration does not offer any special justification for the use of aggressive force against injurers' bodies or their possessions to foster altered relationships—as, for instance, by confining them until they agree to participate in reconciliation or reintegration efforts. (*ii*) Those whom well-meaning third parties might seek to see reconciled with injurers might have legitimate concerns about potential risks to the safety of their bodies or possessions that might be posed by engagement with injurers. In part because of these sorts of risks, promoting reconciliation and reintegration cannot be anything like a universal imperative.

It is entirely appropriate, and it may even in some cases be required, for some people to employ nonviolent means—perhaps on a consistent, public, widely recognized basis through various sorts of nonlegal institutions—to foster reconciliation and reintegration. But it is not appropriate to do so using force. Reconciliation and reintegration provide no independent justification for anything like a criminal justice system.

7. *Rejection Is Morally Problematic*

Precisely because of the underlying importance of connection and relationship reflected in the importance of reconciliation and reintegration, rejection is a deeply problematic justification for any sort of legal standard or procedure. The proponent of rejection understands it as a means either of *expressing* disapproval for an injurer's misbehavior or of actually expelling the injurer, viewed as a toxin or germ, from the body politic.

[27] *See, e.g.*, JOHN BRAITHWAITE, CRIME, SHAME AND REINTEGRATION (1989).

The injurer is a moral patient. As an attenuated kind of friendship, communal connection may be seen as a basic aspect of her well-being. The Principle of Respect precludes directly targeting this aspect of well-being—purposefully harming it for the purpose of, say, conveying a particular message. And the Principle of Fairness dictates that those who would not want to be rejected in particular circumstances decline to reject others in comparable circumstances. Further, to the extent that it is important to express disapproval of an injurer's conduct, this can be done directly through the imposition of legal judgments requiring compensation for the harm she has caused. And to the extent that rejection treats an injurer not as a moral patient, much less as a person, a moral agent, but as filth to be expelled, it rests on a false belief and is thus unreasonable.

If rejection is undertaken through the confinement of an injurer, it is subject to the basic objections to routine confinement already noted. And if it is undertaken by means of an attempt to banish the injurer entirely from a given community, it is obviously problematic because it interferes with the associational freedom of those in the community who *do* wish to associate with the injurer and with their right to use their possessions, including physical spaces over which they exercise legitimate control, as they see fit.[28] To banish an injurer from such physical spaces would clearly be impermissible because it would violate the baseline rules, denying people control over their own possessions.

The baseline rules obviously leave people free to decline to associate with injurers, both for sensible reasons (to protect their safety and the safety of their possessions) and for indefensible ones (to reject them as unworthy or unclean, or to punish them for their misdeeds). Legal rules consistent with the requirements of practical reasonableness obviously create space for people to make both reasonable and unreasonable decisions about association with others. But there is no room for anyone justifiably to use force to prevent an injurer from interacting with those who are willing to associate with her in their own physical spaces or to confine her as a means of expressing disapproval of her or her conduct.

8. *Rehabilitation Is Desirable but Cannot Be Achieved Using Force*

Some people who injure others do so accidentally, or in light of character flaws that are really quite minor. Some, however, do act in virtue of deep-seated habits, attitudes, beliefs, and values that are seriously distorted. And some proponents of the state's criminal "justice" system see that system as justified precisely as a mechanism

[28] The one exception here would obviously be a case in which every one of the members of a specific group has voluntarily consented to some sort of collective decision-making mechanism that would allow some members to decide that none of them could use their possessions in certain ways. Most people would, I suspect, strongly resist the creation of such mechanisms.

for altering these personal qualities. But rehabilitation does not provide any sort of independent justification for the use of force.

Rehabilitation as a justification for the use of force is problematic in part because the use of force undermines the autonomy that is essential to the development of flourishing personhood. Force can certainly be used to foster a minimal sort of good behavior—to keep people from engaging in aggression and to secure compensation when they do so. But it is much more problematic when it is employed in an attempt to *make people good*—to create good characters. Such characters have to be chosen, and chosen for the right reasons, and the use of force minimizes the capacity for choice and creates inapposite incentives for making good choices.

In addition, rehabilitation as a justification for the use of force confers a frightening amount of power on those who are expected to foster it.[29] Those who are authorized to rehabilitate others are, in effect, licensed to manipulate them at will to achieve desired ends. Further, those desired ends themselves are unavoidably ill-defined. Wide-ranging disagreements about what constitutes moral goodness render it particularly troubling to authorize some people to use force against others for the purpose of making them morally good. And the goal of rehabilitation is sufficiently open-ended that it seems to leave people who are to be rehabilitated under the control of their would-be rehabilitators indefinitely.

Rehabilitation as an independent justification for the use of force is fundamentally problematic because it simply licenses too much infringement on injurers' bodies, possessions, and freedom. The requirement of restitution is easy to defend because it rectifies an injury the injurer has actually caused. But it is hard to see what would obligate the injurer to submit to the ministrations of the rehabilitator or what would license the rehabilitator or others in using force against her person or possessions to make her to do so. The general strictures on confinement would seem to apply here as well.

Rehabilitation is obviously a good thing. Injurers with seriously flawed characters, as well as those whose persons or possessions they might otherwise harm, will be better off if they develop better habits, values, character traits, beliefs, and so forth. And reasonable people may quite appropriately welcome any rehabilitative consequences that happen to flow from an injurer's contact with a just legal regime, as also to support nonaggressive mechanisms designed to foster rehabilitation. But the level of power required to rehabilitate the unwilling and the absence of clear bounds on a program of rehabilitation render it an unacceptable justification for the use of force against injurers.

[29] A locus classicus for this view is C.S. Lewis, *The Humanitarian Theory of Punishment*, 6 RES JUDICATÆ 224 (1953). It will be clear that I have no burden to defend the retributivist alternative Lewis advocates in tandem with his plausible critique of rehabilitation as an independent justification for the use of force.

9. *Justifications for Using Force against Those Who Unjustly Harm Others Do Not Warrant a Separate Criminal Justice System*

Restitution, the heart of a reasonable system of interpersonal justice, is entirely appropriate as a warrant for the use of force. And forcible restraint may occasionally be unavoidable. But other rationales for a distinct scheme of criminal law—deterrence, retribution, reconciliation, reintegration, rejection, and rehabilitations—are either undesirable or else incapable of providing independent warrant for such a system.

The primary purpose of the kind of system I have defended would thus be to ensure compensation for harms. And it is no criticism of a restitution-based system to say that it compensates rather than punishing or deterring. At the same time, however, while retributive punishment is, I believe, morally illegitimate, deterrence would surely often be a welcome side effect of the operation of a compensation-based system (in tandem with the existence of mechanisms for restraining the habitually violent, the possibility of potentially lethal self-defense, and the operation of various nonviolent mechanisms for responding to harm outside the ambit of the court system).

It is clear that frequently advanced rationales for the institution of the criminal law tend to presuppose the validity of the criminal law's familiar features—the category of crime, loss of liberty, prison, execution—while seeking to produce some sort of post hoc justification for them. My view, by contrast, is that the criminal law is a dubious institution, and that moving beyond the state should also coincide with the project of moving beyond the criminal law.

D. The Category of "Crime" Is Dangerous

Criminal penalties often attach to serious acts of aggression, but the structure of the criminal law seems to render the link between aggression and criminal penalty contingent. The defining feature of "crime" is punishment—the infliction of some harm supposedly merited by the wrongness or dangerousness of the act being punished—untethered from any restitution requirement. Thus, the availability of the criminal law as a tool of state power means (*i*) that someone's body or possessions or both can be subjected to the use of force in response to the reality or possibility of conduct without any demonstration that the conduct has harmed anyone, (*ii*) that someone can be penalized for her conduct without any serious attempt to determine the *magnitude* of any harm for which she might be supposed to be responsible, and (*iii*) that someone can be penalized for her conduct without any attempt to see to it that the penalty rectifies any injustice created or constituted by the conduct. These dubious features reflect the mistaken attempt to short-circuit legal deliberation by treating some acts as harmful per se, and by treating others as harmful, not to any identifiable person, but to the body politic—which can apparently be injured even when no one's body or possessions can be seen to suffer any demonstrable injury.

Because of the disconnection between harm and consequence that is a predictable result of the structure of the criminal law, its existence and operation leave open the possibility that someone will be penalized, not because she has engaged in aggression, but because she has violated the interests of the criminal gang that is the state or because she has acted contrary to some precept the violation of which does not, in fact, involve tangible harm to the body or possessions of any moral patient.

It is clear, then, that the category of crime confers enormous—and dangerous—power on at least two groups. It empowers state authorities to protect their class interests and to require conformity with their own personal preferences with very little cost to themselves. And it indirectly empowers those capable of lobbying for the imposition of legal prohibitions on conduct they find repugnant but which does not cause or constitute compensable harm to anyone—again, at very little cost to themselves.

Both sorts of empowerment are obviously dangerous to those victimized by the use of the state's power as it is embodied in the criminal law. The dangers they pose help to explain why, quite apart from the general points I've already made about appropriate legal remedies, the criminal law would not figure in the rules and institutions of a just legal regime in a stateless society.

E. "Crime" Rates Might Be Expected to Fall in the State's Absence

The absence of the state would mean a reduction in crime in at least two senses.

First, the state is itself an aggressive gang of thugs. It engages in large-scale aggression. This is especially true in the context of war, but it is also true with respect to a wide range of additional activities in which the state engages, since it forces people to pay for services they may not want, or may not want at the levels or in the forms in which it provides them. And it engages in aggression against people for engaging in a range of peaceful activities, including gambling, prostitution, the violation of state-imposed monopolies, and the production and consumption of chemicals over which the state seeks to exert control. The end of the state would mean the end of this sort of aggression.

Second, the state's prohibitions on various peaceful activities pushes these activities underground and makes aggression related to them more likely. This is so, first of all, because, since they are illegal, the barriers to entry faced by those who wish to engage in them are high, and this means, in turn, that people can generate substantial revenue by engaging in them. This prospect makes engaging in aggression more attractive than it would otherwise be. And the likelihood of aggression is further increased because both consumers and producers of illegal products and services cannot rely on the state to protect them when they are robbed or defrauded: thus, they may be disinclined to report aggression against them to the state authorities and quite inclined to engage in aggression both to despoil others and to remedy wrongs committed against themselves. Eliminating the state would eliminate underground-economy-related encouragements to engage in aggression.

Ultimately, of course, eliminating the state would eliminate crime entirely, not because state aggression is the only source of incentives to engage in aggressive behavior—clearly it is not—but because the elimination of the state ought to lead to the elimination of the *category* of crime itself, understood as an offense against the state. Criminal justice would thus be absorbed into civil justice and the dangerous and unjustified criminal justice system would vanish.

F. A Stateless Society Could and Should Do without the Criminal Law

The notion of *crime* originated as the idea of an assault directly against the king. Ultimately, the modern, impersonal state took the king's place, but the idea of crime as a harm to no one in particular other than the state itself persisted. Absent the state, there would be no justification for the continued use of the idea of crime. The standard justifications for doing the things the criminal law does—taking people's lives and freedom and possessions—do not stand up under scrutiny in most cases; the instances in which restraining people or taking their possessions *are* warranted could be justified under a civil justice system without recourse to the category of crime, with its disconnection of legal consequences from actual harm to identifiable persons. This disconnection is a primary source of the statist criminal law's extreme dangerousness, and a strong reason for the criminal law's absence from the set of rules that could reasonably be enforced by a just legal regime. Such a set of rules would not feature the category of crime and would give rise to far less conduct of the sort currently deemed seriously criminal than contemporary statist legal codes (quite apart from the fact that it would not require compensation for conduct that didn't harm actual people in tangible ways, since there would be no one to be compensated). A stateless society would be well rid of the criminal law.

III. A JUST LEGAL REGIME IN A STATELESS SOCIETY COULD RECTIFY ENVIRONMENTALLY MEDIATED INJURIES AS WELL AS INJURIES TO NONHUMAN ANIMALS AND VULNERABLE HUMAN PERSONS

A. Legal Institutions in a Stateless Society Could Offer Remedies for Environmentally Mediated Injuries and Injuries to Sentient Nonhuman Animals and to Human Persons Incapable of Protecting Themselves

One last-ditch argument for maintaining the criminal law and its cousin, state regulation of economic activity, is that some kinds of injuries cannot be satisfactorily rectified without these varieties of "public law"; this argument is unpersuasive. Injuries to sentients' bodies and to possessions mediated through environmental degradation and injuries to both sentient nonhuman animals, on the one hand, and, on the other, infant members of personal species and persons with limited capacities (as in Chapter 2, I'll call such individuals "vulnerable persons") could also be dealt with in the state's absence. Some, even if not all, environmentally mediated injuries can be addressed by assigning responsibility for particular aspects of the natural world to identifiable people or groups; risk-management strategies can also form part of the institutional infrastructure needed to deal with such harms; and the viability of public goods provision without the state suggests that further strategies for preventing, ending, or remedying environmentally mediated injuries could emerge in a stateless society (Section B). Sentient nonhuman animals and vulnerable persons can be protected by appropriately incentivized proxies—an imperfect arrangement, but one that is surely no worse than, and likely superior to, entrusting care for them to the state (Section C). Legal arrangements in accordance with which litigants act on their own behalf or through proxies can address injuries the criminal law and state economic regulation are designed to rectify without the risks and abuses likely under a statist legal system (Section D).

B. Compensation-Based Rectificatory Legal Rules Could Successfully Rectify Environmentally Mediated Injuries

1. *A Stateless Society Could Deal Successfully with the Problem of Environmentally Mediated Injuries*

Preventing, ending, or remedying environmentally mediated injuries—injuries to bodies or justly acquired possessions effected by pollution or other forms of environmental degradation—does not require the involvement of the state. Absent criminal law and state regulation, central varieties of environmentally mediated injury could be satisfactorily prevented, ended, or remedied. Safeguarding just possessory claims to those aspects of the non-sentient world that mediate harms to sentients is crucial (Subsection 2). In tandem with the protection of such claims, a reliable system ensuring compensation for injuries would keep people from externalizing the costs of environmentally mediated injuries (Subsection 3). Such a system, when linked with suitable risk-management techniques and norm-maintenance mechanisms, could deal not only with harms with easily identifiable causes but also with cases in which causation was unclear (Subsection 4). A state-managed approach to the rectification of environmentally mediated injuries is not preferable to one rooted in the consensual law of a stateless legal regime (Subsection 5), and state regulation does not enjoy clear advantages over a stateless legal order as a means of preventing, ending, or remedying environmentally mediated injuries (Subsection 6). State force is not needed to secure cooperation in response to actual or threatened environmentally mediated injuries (Subsection 7). While the failure to conserve wild places would not ordinarily be a compensable injury, legal arrangements that protected just possessory claims could facilitate conservation (Subsection 8). Just legal regimes in a stateless society could prevent, end, or remedy environmentally mediated injuries or facilitate their rectification (Subsection 9).

2. *Preventing, Ending, or Remedying Many Environmentally Mediated Injuries Will Be Easier When Identifiable Persons or Groups Are Responsible for Particular Things*

Preventing, ending, or remedying injuries to bodies and possessions effected by pollution, other forms of environmental degradation, or climate change can often be facilitated if identifiable groups or people are responsible for particular aspects of the non-sentient world. This kind of responsibility will offer both the incentive and the opportunity for them to care for the elements of the world entrusted to them. And it will enable them to take appropriate legal action to prevent, end, or achieve recompense for environmentally mediated injuries that affect them. In brief: provided there is an effective, just legal system in place—provided the safeguards for bodies and possessory interests for which I have already argued are available—then people will be able to protect themselves and others against obvious forms of pollution and similar environmentally mediated injuries.[30]

If a place, a region, an ecosystem, an aspect of the non-sentient world is the responsibility of some person or group, the person or group will have the desire and the capacity to care for it. The person or group might claim the possession in order to develop it for economic reasons, but might just as well be interested in preserving it, or planning to limit or entirely prohibit economic development. Whatever the projected use, a person, cooperative, partnership, charity, or other entity with just possessory claims can be expected to care for what it claims.

This sort of approach is often taken to presuppose a naïve individualism and rationalism and a simplistic, maximizing approach to efficiency. Instead, however, it can be seen as entirely consistent with a sense of agents as socially situated, of knowledge as dispersed in ways that constrain the effectiveness of deliberate planning, and of environmentally mediated injuries and environmental solutions as systemic rather than personal. It need not be understood as in any way anti-communitarian,

[30] *Cf.* Murray N. Rothbard, *Law, Property Rights, and Air Pollution*, 2 Cato J. 55 (1982); Richard Stroup, Eco-Nomics: What Everyone Should Know about Economics and the Environment (2003); Terry L. Anderson & Donald R. Leal, Free Market Environmentalism (2001); David D. Friedman, The Machinery of Freedom: Guide to a Radical Capitalism 102–03 (2d ed., 1989).

as long as communitarianism can be understood to be compatible with distributed problem-solving and emergent rule-formation rather than top-down or collective decision making.[31]

If people enjoy a relevant range of just possessory claims, they can use legal dispute resolution mechanisms and their pre-legal entitlement to self-defense to protect possessions against pollution and other forms of environmental degradation and against the negative consequences of climate change. They can reach reasonable conclusions about risks and harms, acting proactively or responsively, as circumstances permit, to protect themselves and others.

Consider a paradigmatic environmentally mediated injury: an instance of aggression—the pollution of a stream, say—committed by an identifiable person or organization.[32] Where this sort of harm is concerned, a robust system of just possessory claims should be more than sufficient to ensure that pollution levels are kept at levels satisfactory to those subjected to them. That's true when environmentally mediated injuries are direct—when an immediately proximate polluter, say, harms the land or airspace justly possessed by a given group or person. It's also true when there are intermediaries—when, say, pollutants affect the land, air, or water of multiple groups or persons before reaching their final destination; in this case, at least sometimes, not only the polluter but, at least potentially, others who failed to take reasonable steps to prevent harm to others might be liable. Similarly, injuries to bodies and possessions caused by increasing water levels resulting from anthropogenic climate change clearly ought to qualify as compensable injuries.[33]

3. A *Just Legal System Offering Compensation for Injuries Could Prevent the Externalization of the Costs of Harms to Bodies and Possessions*

Pollution is an obvious instance of *externalization*: polluters externalize their costs onto others, seeking to make others bear the burdens associated with the achievement of the polluters' goals (say, the production and distribution of goods and services). Externalization simultaneously imposes burdens unjustly on others while allowing polluters' costs to be kept artificially low and thus further incentivizing their engagement in potentially destructive behavior. If polluters had no choice but

[31] *See* Mark Pennington, *Liberty, Markets, and Environmental Values: A Hayekian Defense of Free-Market Environmentalism*, 10 INDEP. REV. 39 (2005), *available at* http://www.independent.org/pdf/tir/tir_10_1_2_pennington.pdf.

[32] Pollution is best conceptualized as an instance of aggression against bodies (human and otherwise) and possessions; *cf.* Roy Cordato, *Toward an Austrian Theory of Environmental Economics*, 7 Q.J. AUSTRIAN ECON. 3, 7–13 (2004), *available at* http://beepdf.com/doc/146097/toward_an_austrian_theory_of_environmental_economics.html.

[33] *See, e.g.*, Jonathan H. Adler, *Taking Property Rights Seriously: The Case of Climate Change*, 26 SOC. PHIL. & POL'Y 296 (2009).

to internalize their costs, they would be considerably less likely to impose harms on the unwilling, and the costs of their activities would reflect the costs of avoiding injuries to others. When potential polluters sold products and services to others, and when the prices of these products and services reflected the costs of avoiding pollution, consumers would ultimately need to bear these costs if they acquired the products and services—which would thus likely be significantly less popular than they would otherwise be. It is obviously not possible to ensure that costs are internalized in the case of every environmentally mediated injury, but robust enforcement of legal rules embodying the NAM can prevent or minimize cost-externalization in many instances.

Consider air pollution, for instance: given that a person or community is the just possessor of a given unpolluted airspace, the introduction of pollutants into this airspace will constitute a compensable injury. Similarly for water pollution: the introduction of toxins into a body of water will trigger liability to the just possessor or possessors of the body of water. (Legal action in such cases will obviously be a realistic option here only when pollution levels are non-trivial, since it will not be economical to file a suit to prevent the introduction of the occasional, harmless microparticle.) Polluters will need either to stop polluting or to agree with just possessors to limit pollution levels—or else face continuing, potentially devastating, liability.

The same, again, is true of various other sorts of environmental degradation. To the extent that they are caused by human action and result in injuries to bodies or possessions, they amount, in effect, to the externalization of the costs of the actions that lead to their occurrence. A legal system providing compensation for injuries to bodies and possessions can require those responsible to internalize these costs.

4. A *Just Legal Regime in a Stateless Society Could Deal Satisfactorily with Cases in Which Causal Responsibility for Environmentally Mediated Injuries Was Unclear*

Difficulties arise, of course, when causal connections cannot be definitely identified. Consider a case, for instance, in which one, but only one, of several polluters must be responsible for a given harm, but in which it is unclear *which one* is responsible. In some cases, scientific or historical analysis, or some combination, will enable a difficult question of this sort to be answered. But perhaps, in a given case, they will not. In such a case, however, a legal regime could reasonably resolve the issue of liability as a court might in the case of, say, an accident in which someone is unjustifiably injured by a single bullet fired by a given shooter but in which it cannot be determined which of several shooters fired the bullet. In this sort of accident case, under current law, the hunters can be held jointly and severally liable to the victim while left with the responsibility for litigating the issue of proportionate responsibility for the harm among themselves. The same kind of response would presumably be available to a just legal regime in a stateless society in the case of environmentally mediated injuries.

Risk-management schemes involving widespread risk pooling could obviously provide compensation for people affected by large-scale environmentally mediated injuries resulting from actions with unclear causal links to particular losses.[34] But organizations and associations providing these risk-management services could also take responsibility—as they surely would—for large-scale litigation related to such harms (and, of course, the prospect of such litigation could reduce the injuries' occurrence in the first place).[35] They might also in some cases be able to seek injunctive relief against conduct likely to result in environmentally mediated injuries. While particular persons and loosely affiliated groups might find it difficult to pursue complex litigation related to cases in which vast numbers of defendants might share responsibility for particular environmentally mediated injuries, risk pooling associations or organizations would have the resources and the incentives to pursue such litigation in many cases, and thus to require those responsible for environmentally mediated injuries to internalize the costs of these harms. There will obviously be considerable incentives for such organizations or associations, which could be authorized to act directly on behalf of their members or clients, to obtain the best possible information regarding environmental risks and to take these into account both in determining costs and structuring compensatory arrangements and in litigating to secure injunctive relief designed to prevent various environmentally mediated injuries from occurring in the first place.

5. *The State Is Ill-Suited to Deal with Environmentally Mediated Injuries*

i. The state is not always the friend of the environment

Dealing with environmentally mediated injuries is sometimes thought to be an area in which the state has a comparative advantage. Given the perceived importance of these injuries, the state's potential as a means of addressing them is thus seen as strongly weighing in favor of the continued existence and operation of the state. There are several reasons to doubt that this is the case. The state is often *responsible* for environmentally mediated injuries (Subsubsection ii). The state gets in the way

[34] *Cf.* Gene Callahan, *How a Free Society Could Solve Global Warming: The Advantages of Unfettered Markets Offer the Best Way to Manage Climate Change*, THE FREEMAN: IDEAS ON LIBERTY, Oct. 2007, at 8, *available at* http://www.thefreemanonline.org/featured/how-a-free-society-could-solve-global-warming; Sheldon Richman, *Fixing Global Warming for Fun if Not Profit: Free Rider Problem Overcome*, THE FREEMAN: IDEAS ON LIBERTY, June 4, 2010, http://www.thefreemanonline.org/columns/tgif/fixing-global-warming-for-fun-if-not-for-profit.

[35] *See* Graham Dawson, *Free Markets, Property Rights and Climate Change: How to Privatize Climate Policy*, LIBERTARIAN PAPERS, 2011, at 18–25, http://libertarianpapers.org/articles/2011/lp-3-10.pdf.

of attempts to secure remedies for such injuries (Subsubsection iii). And the state sometimes limits opportunities for people to take responsibility for particular aspects of the non-sentient world in ways that limit their incentives and opportunities for stewardship (Subsubsection iv). It is thus not clear that the state is better positioned to prevent, end, or remedy environmentally mediated injuries than the institutions of a stateless society would be (Subsubsection v).

ii. The state causes many environmentally mediated injuries

The state has been a serious polluter and a major source of environmentally mediated injuries, as the fate of Eastern Europe in the second half of the twentieth century seems to show fairly clearly. The state's record does not suggest that it is especially expert at the task of environmental stewardship or especially likely to undertake the task benevolently. And this is not especially surprising, since state decision makers (who can be expected to be less altruistic than the average person) lack both (*i*) the capacity to benefit in systematic, above-board ways from aspects of the non-sentient world over which they are able to exercise authority; and (*ii*) personal responsibility for harms to these aspects of the non-sentient world they may cause. This lack of responsibility reflects, in turn, both (*i*) the absence of mechanisms capable of holding state officials personally responsible for specific harms; and (*ii*) the collective structure of much state decision making, which makes it difficult or impossible to regard someone as personally responsible for a given outcome or to identify those who are rightly regarded as responsible. And the state's problematic environmental record reflects not only its inability to exercise sensible environmental stewardship but also its active encouragement of inefficient behavior with negative environmental consequences through subsidies, land-use regulations, and similar policies.[36]

iii. The state has limited the availability of remedies for environmentally mediated injuries

The state, predictably allied with wealthy corporations that are happy to externalize their costs on others, has frequently limited people's ability to hold polluters liable for the harms they have caused. In the United States, the doctrine of federal preemption limits the use of ordinary tort lawsuits against polluters whose actions cross state lines, and particular state governments often block suits against polluters. And polluters are often allowed by courts to acquire what amount to easements that enable them to keep polluting—with the cost determined by the courts rather than through any sort of peaceful, voluntary process.[37] In a stateless society, by contrast,

[36] *Cf.* Charles W. Johnson, comment under Charles W. Johnson, *The Many Monopolies*, The Freeman: Ideas on Liberty, Sept. 2011, at 35, http://www.thefreemanonline.org/featured/the-many-monopolies/comment-page-1/#comment-45875, Aug. 26, 2011.

[37] *See* Jonathan H. Adler et al., *Global Warming: A Dialogue*, PERC Reports, Spring 2005, http://www.perc.org/articles/article532.php?view=print.

the state would not be available to shield polluters, and just legal regimes in such a society would not offer protection to polluters.

iv. The state limits particularized responsibility for elements of the non-sentient world

The state can deny particular persons and groups the opportunity to take untrammelled possessory responsibility for given aspects of the non-sentient world, even as it fails to take responsibility for them itself. In so doing, it obviously reduces the likelihood that these aspects of the world will be well cared for.

v. The state's environmental track record is poor

The state sometimes actively harms the non-sentient world. It limits attempts to secure compensation for harms by its corporate cronies. And it limits attempts by people to take responsibility for particular elements of the non-sentient world in ways that might make for effective stewardship. There is thus little reason to think a stateless society would be at an environmental disadvantage when compared to a state.

6. *State Environmental Regulation Is Not Superior to a Robust Compensation Law System as a Means of Preventing and Ending Environmentally Mediated Injuries or Securing Compensation for Them*

i. Regulation is not superior to a compensation-focused system of preventing, ending, or remedying environmentally mediated injuries

It is unwise to contrast an idealized version of state action with the messy and doubtless imperfect reality of bottom-up, distributed decision making. The mistake is clearly evident where environmental regulation is concerned.

I have already noted the general problem faced by the use of *ex ante* regulation rather than *ex post* litigation to deal with a variety of harms to bodies and justly acquired possessions. In addition, when the state attempts to frame environmental regulations, it will be subjected to a variety of political pressures that will likely distort these regulations. Political pressure groups, particularly those serving wealthy and well-connected corporate interests, can be expected to press for regulations that further the objectives of those who fund them, and that therefore disregard the best available evidence regarding harms and their causes and often force members of the public to, in effect, subsidize politically favored interest groups.

The purported advantages of state regulation in the environmental context might be argued to be three: (*i*) the state can take advantage of the best available information in framing regulations, (*ii*) the state can require collective involvement in addressing environmental risks without the need to assign particularized liability in cases in which causal responsibility is unclear, and (*iii*) the state can prevent grievous harms before they occur. None of these considerations provides significant support for the existence and operation of the state as environmental regulator. The state needn't have better information than others (Subsubsection ii). A just legal regime in a stateless society can deal with cases of causal unclarity (Subsubsection iii). And legal and risk-management institutions in a stateless society can encourage people to deal with harms proactively (Subsubsection iv). The purported advantages of state regulation as a means of dealing with environmentally mediated injury do not justify opting for the state over a stateless society (Subsubsection v).

ii. Expert information possessed by the state need not be superior to the information available to non-state actors and need not be expected to be used in ways superior to the ways in which non-state actors could be expected to use the information available to them

Risk-management organizations and associations would have every reason to find and employ the best available information, including the best available environmental science. So, too, would those anticipating potential liability and interested in avoiding it, given the existence and operation of a legal regime capable efficiently of holding them responsible for environmentally mediated injuries. There's no reason to regard the scientific information available to either group as likely to be deficient when compared to the scientific information available to state officials framing and implementing regulations. Further, neither would confront the incentive state actors face to use scientific arguments to justify privileges for elite corporations and other well-connected players.

Statists often think the state has information that ordinary people lack. But to the extent that this information concerns optimal production levels and distribution patterns for goods and services, we know as confidently as we know anything about economics that more information is distributed throughout a given economic environment, possessed by various actors as a matter of "local knowledge," than state actors do or could in principle possess. Polycentric processes that mobilize this local knowledge will ultimately prove more effective at aggregating relevant information than top-down, hierarchical ones.

Statists might suggest that the state had an important role to play, not so much because it possessed information relevant to consumption and production, but because it possessed access to expert information about scientific matters. The assumption here seems to be that experts know just what needs to be done about a given problem but, because ordinary people aren't convinced, the options are either to let nothing be done about a serious problem or to impose the will of the experts.

Clearly, there are problems with this sort approach related to the ignorance of experts: it is not obvious why the state's experts should have better technical and scientific information than people in the trenches—both those with the potential to cause environmentally mediated injuries, who would obviously have incentives to avoid choices that could lead to liability, and those seeking to prevent, end, or remedy such injuries, who would obviously have incentives to learn as much about potential sources of injury as possible. It is also important to ask how information comes to be classified as expert, and how it is likely to be used by the state. Political processes clearly affect the selection of experts and the assessment of the information they provide. Further, given both the potential abuse of expertise as a rationalization for authoritarianism, and the inherent value of personal autonomy, it does not seem as if the conclusions of particular experts ought to be imposed on people without their consent. There are, it seems, side constraints on the use of expert authority, whatever its potential value. Finally, if expert claims are accurate, why can they not be winnowed by public evaluation—in the course of conversations in which experts from outside the political process, as well as ordinary people able to employ their common sense, are free to participate—without being imposed nonconsensually, on a top-down basis?

iii. Collective liability need not be the province exclusively of the state

One purported advantage of state-based environmental regulation is rooted in the difficulty of identifying relevant causal connections between particular actions and environmentally mediated injuries. If legal rules protecting bodies and possessions are to be used to ensure compensation for victims of such injuries and if the prospect of compensation is expected to play a key role in deterring violators, but if there is no clear way of identifying the actual cause of an injury, it might seem that numerous harms would go uncompensated.

Risk-management organizations and associations and persons who are plaintiffs can perfectly well seek collective liability in some cases. Legal rules treating environmental pollution and similar phenomena as, or like, injuries to possessions ordinarily actionable at common law, combined with specific possessory claims in particular regions and ecosystems now claimed en masse by the state, could perfectly well make possible a thoroughgoing system of restraints on environmentally mediated injuries, restraints imposed by possessors or risk-management associations and organizations acting on behalf of their members or clients. They could, that is, insist on joint and several liability for those responsible for particular harms when specific liability was not determinable.[38] So here, too, there is no particular advantage enjoyed by state regulators. Of course, it won't always be consistent with the evidence or the demands of justice for stateless legal regimes' courts to impose collective liability. But the state's capacity to assign collective liability in similar circumstances, when doing so would be equally unreasonable, hardly counts in the state's favor.

[38] *Cf.* FRIEDMAN, *supra* note 30, at 103.

iv. Non-state institutions can prompt preventive as well as remedial action

To the extent that reliable scientific information is available in advance of an environmental problem, risk-management organizations and associations, people anticipating potential liability for the problem, and potential victims will all have access to it just as the state would, and so will all be able to act to address the problem. If risk-management organizations possess this information and fail to act, it can only be because they anticipate that they will not face claims, which will only be the case if agreements with members or clients don't cover the relevant harms (a fact that ought to dispose people to seek alternate risk-management mechanisms) or if they believe they won't be held legally responsible for paying these claims (a remediable problem, and one that would presumably have parallels in a state-governed society). Similarly, if people who might be held liable for particular environmentally mediated injuries possess this information and fail to act, their failure will most likely result from the expectation that they can cause injuries with impunity. The state, of course, often ensures that they can do so, by capping liability for environmentally mediated injuries or by ruling it out altogether. But a just legal regime in a stateless society could and would hold them accountable. On the other hand, if the available scientific information is not decisive, it is not obviously advantageous to anyone if the state acts on this information in framing environmental regulations any more than it would be for a non-state legal regime to do so.

v. Environmentally mediated injuries can be addressed absent state action

We can be confident that ordinary people can respond to environmentally mediated injuries with information as good as or better than that possessed by the state, especially given the state's in-principle inability to amass and utilize *distributed, local* knowledge. Legal regimes in a stateless society could provide remedies for actual or potential environmentally mediated injuries even when issues of causation could not readily be resolved,[39] and the institutions of a stateless society could function in ways that prompted potential sources of environmentally mediated injury to avoid causing it or to reduce it. People don't need the state to make them cooperate in dealing with environmentally mediated injuries.

Further, if particularized responsibility, social norms, and agreements still leave some problems unresolved, it is still the case, I believe, that the difficulties associated with state-based alternatives mean that there's no good reason to prefer such solutions to non-state ones. For if worthwhile cooperation is not forthcoming in some cases in which we wish it might be, we must still recall that the state is not,

[39] These legal rules may not lead to the internalization of *all* costs by those causing environmentally mediated injuries. But even ensuring payment of a significant portion of the costs polluters impose on others would lead to substantial improvements in their behavior. Thanks to Kevin Carson for this point.

never has been, and never will be directed by angels and that instituting an organization with monopolistic control over the use of force in a given region opens up enormous possibilities not only for well-intentioned but serious errors but also for aggression (including unjust dispossession, grants of privilege, and so forth). In short, while there may be failures of cooperation, the costs associated with these failures must be compared to the costs associated with failures on the part of monopolistic states.

Any good thing the state can do, we—peaceful people in a stateless society—can do better. What we do will be done more *efficiently*, because we can draw on bottom-up knowledge and avoid politicized determinations of liability or politicized distortions of expert opinion, and more *peacefully*, because we can avoid the use of aggressive force.

7. *Collective Action in Support of Efforts Designed to Rectify Environmentally Mediated Injuries Is Possible in a Stateless Society*

Just legal regimes in a stateless society could play a crucial role in preventing, ending, and remedying environmentally mediated injuries. Voluntary collective institutions could do so as well. The factors that ordinarily enable people to cooperate in the state's absence—if necessary, to produce public goods—could be expected in many cases to foster collective action in the absence of threatened force.

People might seek to act collectively for multiple reasons. There might be considerable economic advantage, for instance, for groups of people to opt to share possessory claims on the airspace immediately over, or bodies of water under, or serving, their residences and workplaces, thus creating institutions that could act to control pollution by members and litigate on their behalf against nonmember polluters.[40] While the number of participants in a given first-level network would probably need to be relatively limited, smaller networks could effectively be nested within larger, more inclusive ones, with nesting occurring at four or five levels.[41] Nesting can obviously help people overcome problems that arise when communication is difficult and trust can't be readily established;[42] so, too, can a legal system that safeguards

[40] *Cf.* Mark Pennington, Robust Political Economy: Classical Liberalism and the Future of Public Policy 233–35 (2011) (discussing land-use planning by proprietary communities). The model on which Pennington focuses features extensive, possession-based involvement by residential communities in development planning and management; in view of the petty authoritarianism to which proprietary communities are prone, I believe there's some reason to favor cooperative ventures that share narrower ranges of just possessory claims than do such communities.

[41] *See* Elinor Ostrom, Governing the Commons: The Evolution of Institutions for Collective Action 101–02, 189–90 (1990); *cf.* Pennington, Economy, *supra* note 40, at 234.

[42] *Cf.* Elinor Ostrom, Understanding Institutional Diversity 254 (2005).

people's personal and shared possessory claims and makes it easy for those claims to be vindicated and injuries to be remedied.

8. *The Mechanisms That Enable People to Rectify Environmentally Mediated Injuries Will also Permit Them to Engage in Conservation*

Changes to particular aspects of the non-sentient world won't be compensable injuries, provided that just possessory claims are respected. But distributed responsibility for the varied aspects of the non-sentient world can allow people to conserve places of natural beauty and scientific significance.[43]

There's no *guarantee*, of course, that the allocation of just possessory claims on the basis of the baseline rules will result in a possession's being put to the predetermined use preferred by any particular group. There is good reason to believe that, as a general rule, if people have just possessory claims to things, they will care for those things, but their objectives may vary (though of course there may be a general consensus that can be sustained through ordinary social norm-maintenance mechanisms).

Just as groups such as the Nature Conservancy currently acquire land, similar associations in a stateless society could acquire or homestead land or other aspects of the non-sentient world to limit human interference with it. Homesteading with economic objectives certainly could and would occur, too. A stateless society would doubtless feature a mixture of both. But, in any case, if there were specific possessors to whom liability would be owed in the case of harm, rather than politicians often indebted precisely to the entities doing the harming, the non-sentient world could be conserved and nurtured effectively, whatever the precise character of the possessors' interests in their possessions.

These possessors might not want to preserve their possessions in pristine condition, but they would have good reason to want them to flourish. If they allowed development, there would be incentives for them to take a range of protective measures, including prohibiting some kinds of activity entirely, requiring performance bonds, requiring on-site inspections, and so forth. They might, of course, fail to do this, but, if they did, they would suffer the resulting economic consequences, and quite possibly find retaining their possessions too costly. They might well also suffer from serious public disapproval. The recognition that this could happen could dispose even those with limited concern for environmental protection as intrinsically important to engage in intelligent stewardship.

[43] *See, e.g.*, STROUP, *supra* note 30, at 21–23; Robert J. Smith, *Special Report: The Public Benefits of Private Conservation*, *in* ENVIRONMENTAL QUALITY: THE 15TH ANNUAL REPORT OF THE COUNCIL ON ENVIRONMENTAL QUALITY 363–429 (Executive Office of the President, Council on Environmental Quality, 1984).

9. *The Institutions of a Stateless Society Could Address Environmental Problems with No Need for the State*

Addressing environmentally mediated injuries in a stateless society is not, need not be, a matter of law alone, but also of the network of institutions just legal regimes would help to make possible—in particular, systems of just possessory claims that ensure particularized responsibility for the various aspects of the non-sentient world, rules safeguarding such claims, dispute resolution fora of various sorts, and associations and organizations facilitating the reasonable management of risk. Such institutions can prevent, end, or remedy environmentally mediated injuries in the state's absence by ensuring liability for those who cause such injuries and ensuring compensation when they occur, both when causal responsibility is clear and when it's not. The kind of protection they afford is not obviously inferior to that provided by the state, particularly given the state's own dismal environmental track record, and the claimed superiority of regulation over NAM-rooted ordinary law as a means of dealing with environmental problems is, at any rate, not immediately evident.

A state-like institution capable of forcibly implementing *ex ante* environmental regulations as an alternative to ensuring the rectification of environmentally mediated injuries by means of the bottom-up activities of people and groups would seem to be unjust and, because of its power, highly dangerous (especially if global in extent).[44] We have no good reason to want anything like a state, and a regime of voluntary cooperation in which people use their personal or group possessory interests to protect ecosystems seems perfectly workable. Environmental challenges can be satisfactorily addressed by a combination of voluntary, peaceful cooperation (including various complex but emergent possessory structures) and robust legal liability. Statist alternatives are neither necessary nor appealing. Without the state, it's perfectly possible for people to deal with environmentally mediated injuries and to conserve wild places.

C. Just Legal Regimes in a Stateless Society Could Provide Appropriate Protections for Vulnerable Persons and Sentient Nonhuman Animals

A non-state legal system could offer effective protection to nonhuman animals and vulnerable persons. Given that it's wrong to use force against at least some animals for the same general reasons it's wrong to use force against people, these animals, like

[44] Stephen Clark offers a variety of dystopian observations about the possibility of a "Global Ecological Authority" (naturally referred to as "GEA"); *see* STEPHEN R.L. CLARK, HOW TO THINK ABOUT THE EARTH: PHILOSOPHICAL AND THEOLOGICAL MODELS FOR ECOLOGY 49–51, 108–09, 153–54 (1993). *Cf.* PENNINGTON, ECONOMY, *supra* note 40, at 241–43 (dissecting the potential merits of a "global minimal state" charged specifically with addressing ecological problems).

vulnerable persons, would seem to deserve legal protection (though that doesn't, of course, that any legal regime would be obligated to provide such protection except by specific agreement). They're no one's just possessions.[45]

Nonhuman sentients are in some important sense capable of agency. But of course, with the exception of some higher mammals, they are not able, as far as we can tell, to communicate verbally or symbolically and, like vulnerable persons, they do not seem equipped to make effective use of the legal system to vindicate their right not to be subjected to aggressive force. That sentient nonhuman animals and vulnerable persons are unable to vindicate their own claims in the courts of any legal regime means that others will need to act on their behalf if those claims are to be protected.

At present, the state plays the role of halfhearted trustee on behalf of some vulnerable persons and some sentient nonhuman animals. Obviously, its doing so involves the same sorts of risks that are involved in any purportedly protective action by the state. The state can arrogate power to itself using any excuse, and state functionaries are apt to use this power not only to promote the state as over against society but also to promote their own personal interests and agendas and those of their cronies. In addition, state actors purportedly defending the interests of one group of vulnerable persons, children, often intervene in families in ways that children find no more appealing than do their parents. In a stateless society, it will be important to avoid not only the aggressive monopolization of the role of caretaker of animals or vulnerable persons in which the state currently engages but also the other problematic features of the state's intermittent—and hardly always benevolent—trusteeship.

While parents might reasonably be regarded as children's presumptive legal representatives, it is obvious that the interests of children and parents diverge too frequently for the presumption in parents' favor not to be rebuttable. Some alternative is clearly desirable. Parents might be treated as the default legal agents for vulnerable children of whatever age, but there must be straightforward mechanisms for replacing them when their interests and those of the people they purport to represent are clearly at variance—and, of course, for establishing that those they seek to represent don't need representing at all but are perfectly capable of acting for themselves (as will presumptively come more and more to be the case as children age).

Like parents, those who act on behalf of sentient nonhuman animals cannot, ex hypothesi, be the just possessors of those they represent. While establishing possessory claims over aspects of the non-sentient world ensures, in general, that they will be well cared for, non-sentient realities do not have interests independent of those

[45] The position for which I argue here is thus more radical than that defended in a number of the essays in a recent collection: *see* ANIMAL RIGHTS: CURRENT DEBATES AND NEW DIRECTIONS (Cass R. Sunstein & Martha C. Nussbaum eds., 2004). That does not mean, of course, that Sunstein, Nussbaum, et al. haven't offered useful suggestions related to the legal protection of nonhuman animals' interests.

who possess them. Sentient nonhuman animals *do* have such interests. They may not, as I have argued, reasonably be regarded as anyone's just possession. Allowing people to possess animals would certainly ensure that some aspects of animals' well-being will be served, but it seems likely to ensure that others would not be—especially given that the capacity for self-direction is itself deeply important.

There are at least two obvious alternative sets of arrangements that might deal with the problem of ensuring representation for vulnerable persons and for sentient nonhuman animals. In some (territorial or virtual) communities, someone might enjoy a recognized social role as a trustee for vulnerable persons or sentient nonhuman animals (or both). Alternatively, when someone became aware of a potential opportunity to vindicate the legal interests of a vulnerable person or a sentient nonhuman animal, perhaps she could simply homestead the right to represent the vulnerable person or the animal (though her entitlement itself might need to be tested in court if part of her claim was that an existing putative representative other than herself was neglectful or engaged in self-dealing and should not be entitled to continue acting for the vulnerable person or animal). The trustee or freelance advocate who took on a case for a vulnerable person or a sentient nonhuman animal, functioning as something like what is today called a "private attorney general," should be able to recoup salary and expenses when successful in court. The ability to do so would presumably incentivize people to represent vulnerable people and animals; social expectations and the inherent rewards associated with assisting the vulnerable could surely be effective motivators as well.

The trustee and freelance advocate options both leave open familiar principal–agent problems. Trustees' interests would not, after all, be automatically aligned with those of the vulnerable persons or sentient nonhuman animals they were expected to serve. It is indeed possible to imagine someone homesteading the opportunity to represent a vulnerable person or an animal precisely in order to prevent a legitimate claim from being asserted on the human's or animal's behalf, and a trustee could abuse her position in a similar way. Also problematic is the possibility that someone might use her role as a putative protector of one or more vulnerable persons or animals to advance a personal agenda unrelated to the well-being of her putative clients. Courts would obviously need to be attentive to such possibilities, and systems would need to be put in place that incentivized others to keep people purporting to represent vulnerable persons or sentient nonhuman animals honest and focused on the needs of those they purportedly represented.

Providing suitable representation for those who cannot represent themselves is always potentially challenging, and any system that allows for such representation has the potential to give rise to various abuses. But there is no reason to think that the state does or would do a better job securing the interests of vulnerable persons or sentient nonhuman animals than someone tasked with doing so by conscience, community-sanctioned role, or personal self-interest. Trustees and freelance advocates can be expected to contribute meaningfully, even if imperfectly, to safeguarding vulnerable persons' and sentient nonhuman animals' interests.

D. Just Legal Regimes in a Stateless Society Could Prevent, End, or Remedy Injuries of Diverse Kinds

Environmentally mediated injuries and harms to vulnerable persons and sentient nonhuman animals might be thought to create significant difficulties for a non-state system of justice—a system featuring neither *ex ante* state regulation nor the criminal law. But the kinds of legal regimes I envision here can, in fact, deal with both. Stewardship happens when people are responsible for particular things, spaces, and elements of the non-sentient world; a comprehensive system of robust possessory claims would ensure that the non-sentient world was cared for and that pollution and other environmentally mediated injuries were prevented. And those—human and nonhuman—who are unable to take action to safeguard their own legal interests can be represented by trustees or freelance advocates. Just legal regimes in a stateless society can provide adequate, even if doubtless sometimes flawed, remedies for harms the state's supporters sometimes argue it is needed to address.

IV. JUST LEGAL REGIMES CAN RECTIFY INJURIES WITHOUT THE INVOLVEMENT OF THE STATE

Legal rights count as rights precisely because they can be vindicated by legal regimes and so, if necessary, by force. Because legal regimes deploy force against bodies and possessions, there are limits to the kinds of remedies they can offer. A broad range of moral wrongs do not themselves involve the use of force against bodies or possessions, and thus do not admit of legal remedies. This is true even when legally cognizable wrongs are associated with other wrongs that can't be rectified by a just legal regime. Legal regimes can offer people money damages. And they may also, when no other options are available, use actual or threatened force to restrain those committed to programs of aggression. It is the task of other social institutions that do not use force to deal with a broad range of wrongs legal regimes are not competent to address.

Just legal regimes in a stateless society need not treat as legitimate the category of *crime*, with its essentially statist character and justifications and its potential for tremendous abuse. Instead, their focus should be on restitution. A restitution-based model can deal not just with ordinary interpersonal wrongs, but with environmentally mediated injuries and harms to vulnerable persons and sentient nonhuman animals.

Rectifying injury by means of legal rules and institutions is often thought of as a matter of vindicating preexisting claims between persons. By contrast, many people, not all of them among the state's defenders, often suppose that social problems—especially *large-scale* problems, or ones that seriously affect people's welfare or their social freedom but not their freedom from aggression (including wealth disparities, workplace inequities, deep-seated prejudices, and stultifying constraints on personal development)—can be resolved only through state action or other conduct inconsistent with the NAM.

There's something ironic about this, of course, since a number of these problems, at least in anything like their current forms, would be unimaginable without the state's action. At any rate, positive social change can be achieved without violating the NAM, and so without the existence and activity of the state. The legal institutions of a society rooted in peaceful, voluntary cooperation can address some of the social problems that are often seen as requiring state action. And others can be resolved effectively without the use of force but within the space created and protected by just legal rules and institutions. Solving these problems does not require anyone to engage in aggression. I seek in Chapter 6 to explain why, by explaining how the politics of social change might look in a society rooted in peaceful, voluntary cooperation.

6

Liberating Society

I. JUST LEGAL RULES AND INSTITUTIONS IN A STATELESS SOCIETY COULD FACILITATE LIBERATING SOCIAL CHANGE USING NONAGGRESSIVE MEANS

Just legal rules and institutions in a society rooted in peaceful, voluntary cooperation can make it possible, without aggression, to end structural poverty and to undermine hierarchy, structural racism and sexism, and stultifying constraints on personal self-development and expression.[1] Strategies for fostering positive social change can include rectifying injury, eliminating privilege, and engaging in coordinated, nonaggressive action (Part II). Just legal rules and institutions in a stateless could effect and promote the redistribution of wealth through the remediation of large-scale and structural injustices and acts of solidarity and peaceful exchange (Part III). Eliminating these injustices would also conduce to the creation of humane workplaces in which dignity and autonomy were much more likely to be respected than at present (Part IV). The end of the state and the existence and operation of just non-state legal regimes would liberate people to explore a cornucopia of approaches to humanness, even as it also ensured that they could nonaggressively oppose ways of life that—whether violently or nonviolently—promoted subordination, exclusion, and deprivation. (Part V). The occurrence of radical social change isn't dependent on the state (Part VI).

[1] *See generally* MARKETS NOT CAPITALISM: INDIVIDUALIST ANARCHISM AGAINST BOSSES, INEQUALITY, CORPORATE POWER, AND STRUCTURAL POVERTY 391 (Gary Chartier & Charles W. Johnson eds., 2011) [*hereinafter* MARKETS NOT CAPITALISM]. Thanks to Charles Johnson for highlighting for me the liberating potential of non-state social action and for emphasizing the aptness of the metaphor of "space" in this context.

II. TECHNIQUES FOR FOSTERING SOCIAL CHANGE NEED NOT BE AGGRESSIVE

A. Nonaggressive Strategies Can Lead to Social Transformation

Embracing the kinds of just legal rules I seek to defend here would eliminate multiple kinds of aggression and pave the way for the eradication of others. But the emergence of a healthy society would require changes that, while facilitated by the operation of just legal regimes, would need to extend beyond the realm of law, and which could reasonably be pursued in nonaggressive ways. Politics under the rule of the state predictably involve aggression—some action in pursuit of social and political goals is directly aggressive, and much political activism seems directed at persuading the state to engage in aggression (Section B), and the state tends to reduce the likelihood that community action and efforts designed to foster social change through nonaggressive mechanisms will occur (Section C). A stateless society's legal and social institutions would create opportunities for the practice of a stateless politics (Section D), which could foster positive social change nonaggressively in accordance with alternative strategies I call *political anarchism* and *cultural anarchism* (Section E). Some paths to change would focus primarily on the use of legal strategies, some primarily on approaches to activism taking place outside the courts (Section F). Just legal regimes in a stateless society would give political activists a panoply of options for fostering a free culture without engaging in aggression (Section G).

B. Aggression Is Central to Statist Politics

Political action within the ambit of the state involves, as much as anything, the attempt to influence executives to adopt particular policy positions and legislators and regulators to adopt particular rules, whether those on whom the rules will be imposed, or those whom the policy choices will affect, consent or not. Thus, attempts to foster positive social change under the state's putatively benevolent rule often involve the use of the political process to *force* people to live in what *others* regard as more free or fair or responsible ways. Under the state's dominion, legal rules—civil and criminal—may frequently infringe on bodies and just possessory claims in ways that would be precluded by legal rules embodying the NAM. The state uses aggressive force to achieve putatively desirable cultural goals, to promote what it characterizes as morally responsible behavior, and to fund its operations. Even presuming, for the moment, that the state's objectives were desirable, the use of aggressive force to achieve those objectives would still be objectionable.

C. The State Undermines the Appeal and Effectiveness of Nonaggressive Political Strategies

The existence and operation of the state tend in a variety of ways to crowd out fruitful forms of politics that might otherwise flourish.[2]

(*i*) The power of the state makes capturing the state apparatus a sufficiently attractive goal that attempts to work for social change outside the state are frequently dismissed as idealistic and utopian. Thus, associations not devoted to working through the state to effect social change may often have difficulty attracting members and resources.

(*ii*) The state colonizes various aspects of social life that might initially not seem to be politically significant. Non-state institutions that could offer mutual aid, provide dispute resolution services, and foster labor solidarity are reduced in importance, or eliminated altogether, when the state begins to occupy the spheres in which they would otherwise operate. The practical effect: these organizations not only cease to perform the tasks to which, were they functioning vibrantly and effectively, they would be committed—they also stop serving as loci of community organization and social pressure, and so as potential sites of political action outside the state apparatus.

As a result, the state political apparatus is too often seen to be essential to politics and to social problem-solving, so that people find it difficult to envision alternatives. And people reasonably fear the dissolution of the state because of the absence of alternative institutions. State action is thus all too frequently self-perpetuating.

D. Political Action Could and Would Take Place in a Stateless Society

In a stateless society, a society in which aggression was no longer normalized, politics would certainly take place. Politics in a stateless society obviously wouldn't involve lobbying the legislators or executives of aggressive territorial monopolists, since state functionaries wouldn't, ex hypothesi, exist in such a society. And it definitely wouldn't involve pressing for or engaging in aggression, even in the interest of positive social change. But that doesn't mean that people couldn't engage in politics in the state's absence.

Political action in the state's absence might involve anything from litigating to secure return of stolen land, to encouraging a given legal regime to retain a particular rule, to urging a cooperative to drop a supplier that used slave labor, to pressuring a segregated school to admit students on an inclusive basis, to persuading an organization to concede more decision-making authority to its workers, to campaigning for

[2] Thanks to Jonathan Crowe for emphasizing the need to make this point.

office in an association, to engaging in public debate about some matter of moral, economic, social, or cultural importance.[3]

E. Political Action in a Stateless Society Might Be an Expression of Political or Cultural Anarchism

We can reasonably distinguish between kinds of broadly political stances people might adopt in a stateless society consistent with general support for the institutions of such a society. They might opt for *political* anarchism, opposing aggression, including aggression undertaken under the color of law, but otherwise (at least outside of their own immediate circles), opting for a live-and-let-live attitude. Or they might opt for *cultural* anarchism, opposing aggression but also seeking peacefully to undermine hierarchies in workplaces, neighborhoods, families, worshiping communities, and other social institutions; to promote personal freedom of self-development, self-definition, and self-expression; and to foster an ethos of openness, dialogue, and critical reflection on social norms.

People obviously have wildly divergent desires regarding the ways in which they would like to live their lives. A narrowly political anarchism would not deprive anyone of the opportunity to adopt any lifestyle—unless, of course, doing so entailed using force against others—and would doubtless contribute to the flourishing of a significant number. Though it would not, of course, embrace forcible interference with any nonviolent lifestyle, cultural anarchism might involve active, nonviolent opposition to some of these ways of being human, even as it left many undisturbed.

Cultural anarchism could be expected to flow from the respect for the essential equality of moral patients that underlies opposition to aggression and to the state. The same facts about moral patients that make it unjust for anyone to rule another using force can also be seen—certainly, the Principle of Fairness suggests that they *should* be seen—as rendering it unreasonable for anyone to dominate or manipulate another, to exercise positional authority over her, even nonviolently. Cultural anarchism would likely be sustained by multiple convictions: not only that the assumptions grounding some cultural arrangements were inconsistent with those grounding the NAM, but also that people who were not consistently skeptical about positional authority would find it difficult to sustain a free society; and that aggression frequently made possible the maintenance of hierarchical social arrangements, even if those arrangements were not themselves aggressive.[4]

[3] *Cf.* Geoffrey Allan Plauché, *Immanent Politics, Participatory Democracy, and the Pursuit of Eudaimonia*, LIBERTARIAN PAPERS, 2011, http://libertarianpapers.org/articles/2011/lp-3–16.pdf.

[4] Thanks to Charles W. Johnson for these points; *see* Charles W. Johnson, *Libertarianism through Thick and Thin*, *in* MARKETS NOT CAPITALISM, *supra* note 1, at 131 http://radgeek.com/gt/2008/10/03/libertarianism_through.

F. Political Action in a Stateless Society Might Take Place Inside or Outside the Legal Arena, but in Neither Case Would It Need to Involve Aggression

1. *The Legal Arena Would Provide One, but Only One, Context for Political Activism in a Stateless Society*

In a stateless society, political action on behalf of positive social change could and would take two forms: intra-legal action (Subsection 2) and extralegal action (Subsection 3).[5] Though very different from statist politics, politics in a stateless society would play an important social role (Subsection 4).

2. *The Legal Arena Would Be an Important Site for Political Action in a Stateless Society*

In a stateless society, political objectives could and would be achieved by *ending* and *remedying* aggression and state-secured privilege, in tandem with a range of cooperative efforts designed to organize mutual aid schemes, change attitudes, and alter behaviors. Legal rules and institutions in a stateless society would thus foster the birth of a culture of freedom, not by using force to stop people from engaging in morally objectionable but nonviolent behavior, but by eliminating support for privilege, ending the legitimation of past acts of aggression, laying the groundwork for the provision of remedies for past aggression, and creating the conditions in which people could act freely and cooperatively to exchange goods and services, exhibit solidarity with each other, and discourage nonviolent behavior that constrained freedom.[6] *Structural change*, rather than the direct pursuit of good consequences in specific cases and without regard for side-constraints, could facilitate the emergence of a genuinely free culture without involving self-defeating, inconsistent, and counterproductive attempts, like those prevalent under the state, to achieve freedom by violating freedom.

Nonviolent social pressure could also affect the legal arena in at least one other way: it could be used to discourage a legal regime from making agreements to enforce unfair policies of various kinds. Nothing would require a regime to provide across-the-board services to all clients under all circumstances. While it would often be unreasonable to ask regimes to violate prior agreements, it would be entirely appropriate for people to urge regimes prospectively not to *make* certain kinds of

[5] The term "extralegal" is frequently employed to mean "outside the law" in the sense of "not in conformity with the law." I refer to action as "extralegal" here if it does not depend on litigation or otherwise involve the courts.

[6] *See* Parts III–V, *infra*.

agreements. And regimes' unwillingness to make such agreements would obviously increase the costs borne by those who wished to engage in unfair practices. For instance, if regimes were unwilling to make agreements requiring them to evict, or support the eviction of, people of the wrong ethnicity from segregated facilities, the costs to the operators of discriminating unfairly (already likely to be higher than those borne by operators with inclusive policies) would obviously increase in ways that would surely discourage them from indulging their own prejudices or others'. (This kind of discrimination is often, of course, a product not only of operators' own tastes for discrimination, but also of violence regimes would be equipped to prevent.) The kinds of agreements made by legal regimes could thus be significant foci for political action in a stateless society.

3. *Political Action Outside the Legal Arena Could Take a Variety of Forms*

It is not reasonable to respond to wrongdoing that doesn't involve aggression with acts that interfere with the wrongdoers' bodies or their justly acquired possessions, but people in a stateless society could deal effectively with this kind of wrongdoing using a variety of techniques that didn't involve unjust interference.[7]

Many sorts of nonviolent actions not involving the legal enforcement of rights could be used to promote social change. These might include public shaming, use of certification systems, personal boycotts, encouraged group boycotts, coordinated boycotts, and norm-maintenance mechanisms.[8]

Public shaming has the potential to be an effective means of influencing others' behavior. Identification in a newspaper, or on a website devoted to "the Workplace Hall of Shame,"[9] can certainly exert significant pressure, especially in a smaller, more self-contained community, on someone who has violated others' dignity or social freedom.

Certification systems are less flashy, but surely also useful. Perhaps only positive options would be available, and people would draw conclusions based on the absence of a positive certification of, say, a cooperative's treatment of its members. But I think there would be considerable demand for negative information. And if large numbers of (again, in this case, say) cooperatives bet that their own ratings

[7] On the dynamics and effectiveness of nonviolent strategies for social change, *see* Gene Sharp & Bruce Jenkins, Civilian-Based Defense: A Post-Military Weapons System (1990); Gene Sharp & Joshua Paulson, Waging Nonviolent Struggle: Twentieth Century Practice and Twenty-First Century Potential (2005); Gene Sharp, The Politics of Nonviolent Action (3 vols., 1973–85); Anders Boserup, War without Weapons: Nonviolence in National Defence (1974).

[8] *See* Charles W. Johnson, *We Are Market Forces*, *in* Markets Not Capitalism, *supra* note 1, at 391, http://radgeek.com/gt/2009/06/12/freed-market-regulation.

[9] For more discussion of work-related issues, *see* Part IV, *infra*.

would be positive, they might be willing to participate in a system that gave some organizations quite negative ratings.

Personal boycotts of those who treat others poorly are always possible, of course. And perhaps in relatively small, self-contained communities, such boycotts might exert some meaningful influence, though it's easy to be doubtful.

What might be called *encouraged multi-person boycotts* could be more effective. A encouraged boycott might take place when, say, a pressure group made some kind of general announcement urging people to join a campaign by not dealing with a particular person or entity. The effectiveness of this strategy would obviously depend on the influence of the pressure group. Absent credible commitment and extensive coordination, this sort of boycott, too, might not be overly effective.[10]

Coordinated boycotts could be a good deal more successful. Membership organizations might organize boycotts, plan for alternatives to transacting with those being boycotted, and keep up pressure on identifiable members to participate in the boycotts. Agreements might also prove useful here: people might agree among themselves that circumstances of some specifiable kind would trigger a boycott and that violating the boycott would subject the violator to damages (though whether such agreements would be enforceable in court would depend on whether they were structured in such a way that failing to pay damages would amount to misappropriation of someone's justly acquired possessions). Even if relatively small, boycotts of this kind could be reasonably effective, though it's unclear how many people would be comfortable belonging to organizations likely to pressure them in the way I'm envisioning (especially if they feared that ignoring the boycotts could subject *them* to boycotting).

Among the various sorts of agreement-based or otherwise coordinated boycotts might be one in which a group of people agreed that, if an arbitrator's decision could not justly be implemented using force, they would encourage acceptance of the decision by boycotting someone who failed to respect it. Even if an arbitrator declines to employ force to implement it, a decision in favor of one party can confer legitimacy on the party. And, although, ex hypothesi, the loser (the party seeking to ignore the unenforceable agreement) could turn to another arbitrator in search of relief (if there were no enforceable agreement-based obligation to use the court in question), there might be tangible and intangible costs associated with doing so. Doing so might cast doubt on the loser's credibility; initiating a new case could impose financial burdens; others might be less likely to transact with the loser in the future, especially if the court were clearly identified with the local community and depends upon local support.[11] The possibility of a boycott could obviously provide further reason to accept the arbitrator's decision.

[10] On the moral status of these kinds of boycotts, *see* GARY CHARTIER, ECONOMIC JUSTICE AND NATURAL LAW 176–82 (2009).

[11] Thanks to Kevin Carson for insights related to this point.

The problems the loser in such a case might confront can be seen to highlight the general importance of *norm maintenance* in furthering a cultural-anarchist agenda. It's easy to imagine a (geographic or virtual) community's maintaining a norm such as, *These work-related practices should be avoided* or *Adhere to the decisions of such-and-such a dispute resolution organization even when they will not be implemented by force*. A wide range of subtle mechanisms for maintaining these sorts of norms exists beyond the relatively blunt ones I've considered here. Even in an environment with diverse alternative institutions, a community's norms could clearly confer greater legitimacy on one or more of these institutions. And even in an environment in which it was agreed that, say, certain kinds of agreements couldn't be implemented using force, a community's norms could certainly remind someone that "we don't do that sort of thing here."

To be sure, nonviolent norm-maintenance mechanisms can be used to uphold thoroughly illiberal norms. But to the extent that they are nonviolent, they leave open extensive possibilities for dissent. And, of course, the nonviolent strategies I have considered can be used effectively to undermine mechanisms used to support illiberal norms and the institutions that uphold them.

All of these sorts of social action are responses to nonviolent wrongdoing. But other kinds of activism clearly count as instances of politics as well. Cooperative efforts designed to organize mutual aid schemes, create new social institutions, change attitudes, and alter behaviors can obviously qualify as political, too. And it is important to stress the importance of these *positive* varieties of political activism—facilitated in various ways by just legal regimes in a stateless society—as well as the negative varieties directed at preventing, restraining, ending, and remedying aggression and unfair but nonaggressive behavior.

4. *Extralegal as well as Legal Strategies will be Effective Means of Political Action in a Stateless Society*

Political action in the legal arena in a stateless society would likely be necessary to effect the remediation of past injustices and the elimination of structural privileges—both central to the promotion of positive social change. But various nonaggressive extralegal strategies could play vital complementary roles in addressing wrongs that could not reasonably be dealt with using aggression.

G. Stateless Politics Could Lead Effectively to Positive Change Using Complementary Legal and Extralegal Strategies

Politics in a state-dominated society too often seems to mean, for practical purposes, the attempt to persuade the state to engage in aggression to achieve some desired end. And the state discourages social action that occurs outside the realm of statist politics. So it's easy, perhaps, to identify action designed to influence the state to solve social problems with politics, per se. In reality, though, the absence of the state would not preclude the practice of politics, and people could reasonably be expected to take more than one sort of broadly political position in light of basic anarchist values in a stateless society—with the difference that, in the state's absence, politics need not focus on or involve aggression. Recognizably political action could be expected to take a variety of forms in a stateless society. Such action could reflect either a commitment to a narrowly *political* anarchism or to a broader *cultural* anarchism. Nonaggressive politics—engaging in aggression-free activism *outside* the legal arena, and protecting against aggression, undermining privilege, and rectifying injury *within* it—could help to create a culture that was free of institutionalized aggression and in which violations of social freedom were persistently challenged and undermined, and in which it was thus possible to explore an enormous array of peaceful human possibilities.

III. JUST LEGAL RULES AND INSTITUTIONS IN A STATELESS SOCIETY WOULD FURTHER WEALTH REDISTRIBUTION

A. Upholding Just Legal Rules Would Lead to the Redistribution of Wealth from the Privileged to the Victims of State-Perpetrated and State-Sanctioned Aggression

Just legal rules and institutions in a stateless society would foster the redistribution of wealth through the elimination of privilege; the rectification of injustice; the redemption of assets stolen by the state and its cronies; acts of solidarity; and peaceful, voluntary exchange.

Alternative statist and stateless approaches to wealth redistribution can be helpfully contrasted (Section B). The stateless approach can be understood as featuring several mutually reinforcing elements. Structural changes—changes in institutions and legal rules—that eliminate privilege would redistribute wealth from those who have enjoyed statist privileges to those who have been disadvantaged in virtue of those privileges (Section C). The rectification of massive, systematic injustices, both past and ongoing, would require large-scale redistribution—but not at the hands of the state or in state-like fashion (Section D); this kind of rectification should include the radical homesteading of assets stolen or engrossed by the state or acquired using stolen or engrossed assets (Section E). Solidaristic redistribution can be seen as warranted in light of an overlapping consensus supported by moral views embraced by many antistatists (Section F). Peaceful, voluntary exchanges of goods and services could reduce wealth disparities and promote greater economic security (Section G). Redistributive mechanisms in a stateless society could deal effectively with the challenge of poverty and economic vulnerability (Section H). A stateless society's institutions could foster and effect the redistribution of wealth in ways that served a variety of useful objectives (Section I).

B. Statist and Stateless Redistribution Serve Many of the Same Goals, but Involve Radically Different Means

1. *It Is Useful to Contrast Statist and Stateless Models of Wealth Redistribution*

Statism and anarchism feature alternate conceptions of resource redistribution. On the statist model, the state responds to inequality and deprivation resulting from bad luck by acquiring wealth by force and redistributing it using social programs (Subsection 2). The stateless alternative I defend here, by contrast, involves redistribution through a combination of legal change; rectification of specific injustices; solidarity; and peaceful, voluntary cooperation through exchange (Subsection 3). The goals of stateless redistribution overlap significantly with those of statist redistribution, but the means differ substantially (Subsection 4).

2. *The Statist Model Focuses on Using State Power to Redistribute Wealth in the Interests of Remedying the Effects of Bad Luck*

A typical statist understanding of redistribution can be articulated as a set of theses:

1. *The Statist Explanation Thesis*: Poverty and inequality result primarily from bad luck.[12]
2. *The Statist Remedy Thesis*: Poverty and inequality should be remedied through the redistribution of wealth from the well-off to the economically vulnerable.
3. *The Statist Means Thesis*: Redistribution should be effected using tax-funded services and programs.
4. *The Statist Agents Thesis*: Redistribution should be effected by legislators and bureaucrats.
5. *The Statist Goal Thesis*: The purpose of redistribution should be substantially to reduce inequality—thus making society more inclusive and less hierarchical—and poverty, if not to eliminate them entirely.
6. *The Statist Justification Thesis*. The redistribution of wealth through social programs is justified because it is likely to achieve a putatively desirable goal.

[12] The language in the text is intended to capture the "luck-egalitarianism" that one might associate in different ways with the thought of John Rawls and Ronald Dworkin. More radical statist leftists would obviously be much more inclined to endorse the notion that systemic injustice is responsible for deprivation, and would therefore be more inclined to share (in this respect) the alternative view I defend.

3. *The Stateless Model of Redistribution Focuses on Using a Variety of Nonaggressive Means, Notably Actions by Just Legal Regimes, to Remedy Not only the Results of Ill-Fortune but also, More Important, the Results of Injustice*

An alternative approach to redistribution is implicit in the account of a stateless society's legal order, an approach which overlaps significantly with—even as it also differs radically from—the Statist Model. The elements of this approach can be summed up this way:

1. *The Stateless Explanation Thesis*: Poverty and inequality may derive to some degree from bad luck, but result primarily from past and ongoing force and fraud, particularly force and fraud engaged in or tolerated by the state.
2. *The Stateless Remedy Thesis*: Poverty and inequality should be remedied (*i*) through the redistribution of wealth from aggressors to victims and others through the rectification of past wrongs; the elimination of privileges; and processes of peaceful, voluntary cooperation in exchange; and (*ii*) solidaristically, from the well-off to the economically vulnerable.
3. *The Stateless Means Thesis*: Redistribution should be effected through changes in legal rules affecting economic life, through the return or reallocation of stolen possessions; through the fulfillment of personal imperfect duties to share resources; and through peaceful, voluntary cooperation in exchange.
4. *The Stateless Agents Thesis*: Redistribution should be effected by ordinary people, personally and in cooperation—by participants in the shaping of legal rules; by workers; by dispossessed people; by people fulfilling duties of beneficence; and by participants in peaceful, voluntary exchanges.
5. *The Stateless Goal Thesis*: The purpose of redistribution should be to rectify injustice, improve productivity, reduce inequality, end structural poverty, and deal effectively with accidental or emergency poverty.
6. *The Stateless Justification Thesis*. Different kinds of redistribution can be justified in virtue of the injustice of state-secured privileges, the appropriateness of rectifying injustice, people's personal redistributive duties, people's rights to use their justly acquired possessions without aggressive interference, and the value of freedom.

4. *The Stateless Model Could Achieve Many of the Goals of the Statist Model, but Using Different Means and for Somewhat Different Reasons*

The statist model of wealth redistribution focuses on the exaction of tribute, borrowing, and spending by the state to reduce poverty and inequality. It presupposes that the state is ultimately entitled to the resources generated within its subject territory and that it thus has the duty to allocate them in accordance with an overall distributional pattern. And it largely ignores the role of the state in creating and perpetuating poverty, and the character of the state as rapacious and untrustworthy.

The stateless model, by contrast, features a cluster of complementary approaches to ending structural poverty, reducing subordination and accidental and emergency poverty, and fostering inclusion while also encouraging economic productivity and providing remedies for past injustice. Redistribution without the state can take place in multiple ways: through structural change; rectification; homesteading; solidarity; and peaceful, voluntary cooperation in exchange. Stateless redistribution can achieve many of the goals of statist redistribution without the use of aggression.

C. Addressing Persistent Injustices That Pervade Capitalist Economies through Structural Change Would Be a Vital State-Free Mechanism for Redistributing Wealth

1. *Eliminating Privilege Would Redistribute Wealth from the Privileged to the Ruling Class's Victims*

Enforcing standards embodying the baseline possessory rules, which leave no room for state-secured or similar privileges, would undermine the maldistribution of wealth brought about by such privileges.[13] It would reduce living costs (Subsection 2), empower workers (Subsection 3), minimize poverty (Subsection 4), and significantly limit elite power (Subsection 5)—in short, redistributing wealth from the privileged to those subordinated by the state (Subsection 6).

2. *Eliminating Privilege Would Help to Reduce Ordinary People's Living Costs*

In virtue of this kind of redistribution, people with limited incomes would be able to live less expensively, since many of the relevant state-secured privileges raise the cost of work, housing, eating, and other basic activities. Whether or not their money incomes increased, their living costs would be significantly reduced.

3. *Eliminating Privilege Would Help to Improve the Lives of Workers*

The absence of various corporate privileges would make it easier for workers to pursue options other than paid employment. Large, hierarchical corporations would be less likely to exist in an economy organized on the basis of peaceful, voluntary

[13] State-secured privileges increase the resources available to the wealthy and well-connected while limiting economic opportunities for ordinary people and increasing their expenses; *see* Chapter 3.VI.E, *supra*.

cooperation than they are at present. Absent subsidies to corporate size and hierarchy, people would find it easier to work in cooperatives or partnerships or to work for themselves.[14] Unions could ultimately be more effective without statist restrictions, so those workers remaining in paid employment might be more likely to enjoy union protections or the equivalent. And with living costs lower, people would be freer to risk striking out on their own and would also thus be better positioned to bargain—collectively or individually—with corporate employers for preferable work terms. Making options available to workers other than subjection to the authority of bosses would effectively represent a redistribution of resources from those benefiting from the operation of corporate hierarchies *to* workers, whether reflected in incomes, working conditions, or both.[15]

4. *Eliminating Privilege Would Help Substantially to Reduce Poverty*

State action plays an absolutely vital role in creating and maintaining poverty.[16] Ending licensing and zoning requirements, building codes, minimum wages, and similar restrictions would represent a shift of income to poor people, whose costs of living would be reduced and whose economic positions would be improved because they would be able either to work for organizations that wouldn't otherwise exist or wouldn't be able to provide them with work *or* to work for themselves when they otherwise couldn't. Ending privilege would thus redistribute resources to poor people from those now benefiting from unjust legal rules.

5. *Ending Privilege Could Help to Reduce Rent-Seeking, Poverty, and Elite Power*

Elite power is rooted in legal entitlement. In a statist society, the ability to secure the relevant legal entitlements is due in large part to elite groups' wealth. And that

[14] *See* KEVIN A. CARSON, ORGANIZATION THEORY: A LIBERTARIAN PERSPECTIVE (2008). *Cf.* RICHARD C. CORNUELLE, DE-MANAGING AMERICA: THE FINAL REVOLUTION (1976).

[15] "Boss" is not, of course, a precise moral or metaphysical category. Ignoring cases when people use violence to maintain influence over others, I suggest that the difference between a boss and a client is quantitative rather than qualitative—but that the quantitative distinction matters a great deal. Bosses and clients differ along several axes: (*i*) *process/outcome*: a boss is more likely to be concerned with *how* work is done rather than just with the fact that it *is* done—with process as well as outcome; (*ii*) *frequent contact/infrequent contact*: contact with a boss is likely to be more frequent; (*iii*) *concentrated risk/dispersed risk*: one is likely to have more clients than bosses, so that a tiff with one needn't have catastrophic consequences. A boss's violation of what I have called *social freedom* (*see* Introduction, note 9, *supra*) is likely to leave one significantly less socially free than a client's, and bosses are more likely to violate social freedom in the first place than are clients.

[16] *See* Charles W. Johnson, *Scratching By: How Government Creates Poverty as We Know It*, *in* MARKETS NOT CAPITALISM, *supra* note 1, at 377, http://www.thefreemanonline.org/featured/scratching-by-how-government-creates-poverty-as-we-know-it.

wealth, in turn, would be inexplicable apart from legally secured privilege: legal entitlements bestowed on the wealthy and well-connected enable them to reap monopoly profits at the expense of those without privilege. Ending privilege would end those monopoly profits. It would also reduce the wealth available for use in attempts to subvert social institutions for the purpose of acquiring privilege. (Of course, absent a state apparatus to capture, people would find it harder in any case to secure privileges—a polycentric legal system would be much harder to game.) Ending privilege would thus amount to a redistribution of wealth from effective rent-seekers to workers whose capacity to serve others effectively would yield advantages to them in an economy rooted in peaceful, voluntary cooperation.

6. *Redistributing Wealth by Ending Unjust Privilege Could Help to Disperse Social Power and Minimize Economic Insecurity*

There is good reason to support robust protections for just possessory claims. But there is none at all to support state-secured privileges for the ruling class and other favored groups. Economic and political elites use state power to secure, maintain, and extend such privileges. Eliminating these privileges, and so fostering inexpensive living and workplace empowerment, while reducing poverty and the ongoing acquisition of privilege by the elite, would represent a substantial redistribution of wealth from elites to ordinary people.

D. Rectifying Past Injustices Is an Indispensable Means of Stateless Redistribution

1. *Rectification Addresses the Problem of Past Injustice by Returning Assets to Those from Whom They Have Been Stolen*

By enforcing just remedies for violations of the baseline possessory rules, just legal institutions in a stateless society would foster the redistribution of wealth from victimizers to victims. Rooted in aggression, many large-scale possessory claims are invalid (Subsection 2). It might be possible in many cases to identify just claimants to stolen assets and return these assets to them (Subsection 3)—not through mob violence or actions emulating the behavior of the state, but through the mechanisms provided by just legal regimes (Subsection 4). Rectification would be a crucial means of redistribution in a stateless society (Subsection 5).

2. *Existing Possessory Claims Are Often Illegitimate*

Decisions by state authorities to seize unoccupied land, to take land from those entitled to possession by custom, or to tolerate the aggressive seizure of people's justly acquired possessions by favored elites do not erase existing titles or create legitimate new ones.[17] A satisfactory understanding of just possession makes it possible to see both theft and various sorts of political decisions regarding land, in particular, as unjust and therefore invalid.

> Much … [land] is stolen. Much is of dubious title. All of it is deeply intertwined with an immoral, coercive state system which has condoned, built on, and profited from slavery; has expanded through and exploited a brutal and aggressive imperial and colonial foreign policy, and continues to hold the people in a roughly serf-master relationship to political-economic power concentrations.[18]

3. *Many Specific Past Injustices Could Be Corrected*

It is obviously not possible to correct all historical injustices. But to the extent that victims and perpetrators of injustice or their successors-in-interest could be identified, victims could reasonably be provided with just compensation for the losses they have suffered from those who are responsible for these losses or from *their* (identifiable) successors-in-interest.[19]

Thus, for instance, serfs working on *latifundia* cultivating land that would be theirs had it not been forcibly retitled deserve to receive title, while those responsible for stealing their titles or perpetuating the thefts do not seem to deserve compensation for the loss of land that has been, in effect, stolen from the original just possessors.[20]

Similarly, it can reasonably be argued that slaves should have been understood to be entitled to the plantation land on which they worked: their putative "owners" had frequently not used their own labor, or the labor of free people cooperating with them, to cultivate the land; rather, those who cultivated it for the members of the plantocracy did so at gunpoint. Thus, the land, which might sometimes reasonably have been regarded as not subject to any just claim prior to the cultivating work of the slaves, should have been treated as, in effect, homesteaded by the slaves—who also clearly merited compensation for their enslavement by their "owners."[21]

[17] *See* Murray Rothbard, The Ethics of Liberty 62–76 (1982); Roy A. Childs, Jr., *Land Reform and the Entitlement Theory of Justice, in* Liberty against Power: Essays by Roy A. Childs, Jr. 185 (Joan Kennedy Taylor ed., 1994).

[18] Karl Hess, *Letter from Washington: What Are the Specifics?*, Libertarian Forum, June 15, 1969, at 2.

[19] While it is not a source of independent justification for reallocating possessory claims, the greater dispersion of wealth this kind of redistribution effects can be welcomed by anarchists both in virtue of the benefits it confers on economically vulnerable people and because of its contribution to greater social stability.

[20] *Cf.* Rothbard, *supra* note 17; Childs, *supra* note 17.

[21] Rothbard, *supra* note 17, at 74.

Even when those responsible for providing compensation could not be identified, other mechanisms enabling people "to participate in the communities of the land, finally, as equals and not wards,"[22] could effectively be employed; for instance, state-engrossed lands should obviously be made available for homesteading (though of course they should be accessible not only to the descendants of the enslaved, but also to everyone else). Comparable compensation is obviously due the successors-in-interest of the victims of the enclosures when they can be reliably identified.

4. *Rectification Should be Pursued in the Legal Arena by Those with Specific, Defensible Claims*

Just what form the rectification of injustices like land theft and enslavement ought to take is a complex practical question which I will not attempt to answer here. What is clear, however, is that once the principle has been granted that the thief or slaver is not entitled to what she has stolen and that, where possible, victims of theft or enslavement deserve to be compensated, ideally by the return of what has been stolen from them, a stateless society's legal order must provide for some sort of redistribution of demonstrably stolen assets. The agents of redistribution should not, of course, be representatives of this or that legal regime arrogating state-like powers to themselves, but rather the people who justly claim land or other possessions unjustly taken from or denied to them or their predecessors in interest.

Where there has been no realistic legal recourse for an act of aggressive dispossession under statist law—because the act took place with state sanction, or because the violator has acted effectively to prevent the victim from taking advantage of available legal remedies—there seems no good reason for a statute of limitations to preclude recovery until there's been opportunity for redress. To say otherwise would be inconsistent with the Principle of Fairness, since it would compel a victim (or her successor-in-interest) to bear the cost of the violator's wrongdoing.

5. *Compensating People for Past Injustices Could Involve the Redistribution of Significant Amounts of Wealth in a Stateless Society*

The state has been the protector of the wealthy and well-connected, and it has thus provided cover for a broad range of aggressive acts of dispossession and enslavement—clearly inconsistent with the NAM. Where victims or their successors-in-

[22] Hess, *supra* note 18, at 2. Obviously, Hess's argument assumes the legitimacy of some variety of inheritance or succession in interest: otherwise, slaves' descendants could not reasonably be said to merit compensation for harms done their ancestors. Thanks to Stephen Clark for underscoring the need to make this point.

interest could be identified, they should be entitled to restitution, and should be able to obtain it by means of just legal regimes.

E. The Radical Homesteading of Directly or Indirectly Stolen Resources Could Be an Appropriate Means of Redistribution

At least three other kinds of redistribution that could be expected to be facilitated by just legal regimes in a stateless society are similar to, but meaningfully different from, the kind of redistribution that would be effected when assets stolen with state sanction were returned to specific, identifiable just claimants or slaves, or their successors-in-interest: (*i*) claiming state-engrossed land, (*ii*) claiming stolen assets when victims or their successors-in-interest could not be identified, and (*iii*) claiming assets acquired indirectly using resources stolen by the state.

The state has frequently engrossed unclaimed land. In colonial North America, as also in the newly minted United States, political authorities arbitrarily claimed vast tracts of land and proceeded to parcel it out to their cronies. They clearly were not entitled to do so, since the land had not been claimed in accordance with the first baseline rule. And where engrossed land that has been claimed by the state is still held by the state, it is ripe for homesteading.

Where once-engrossed land has not been distributed to non-culpable claimants but is instead still held by people or organizations responsible for using political connections or otherwise employing violence to secure their claims, it is, again, ripe for homesteading. Neither the state nor its cronies should be entitled to profit from the use of force to exclude peaceful people from earlier opportunities to homestead.

When assets have clearly been stolen and are still in possession of the thief or the thief's heirs, then, even if no specific victim can be identified, there is good reason to treat them as ripe for homesteading for the same reason. And assets acquired *on the basis* of large-scale theft can reasonably be treated as themselves stolen, and thus currently not subject to just claim and therefore ripe for homesteading.

Even when it doesn't steal identifiable possessions and pieces of land from particular people, the state uses its power to take resources that don't belong to it—and goes on to use stolen resources to fund its own activities and those of its cronies. To take an obvious example: the state funnels huge sums of money to corporations, think tanks, and universities that maintain cozy relationships with the "defense" establishment. No one in particular can rightly claim the resources unjustly taken by the state to fund favored institutions connected with the war machine (it would be impossible logistically to trace the funds, and impossible conceptually to attribute them). But the assets of entities that receive most of their funds from the state can reasonably be regarded as not justly possessed by anyone, and so ripe for homesteading.[23] These assets can be redistributed by being claimed by ordinary people willing to occupy them, people whose just claims others should be quite willing to support. Those who work for the state-enmeshed institutions may (presuming they are not responsible for state-linked mischief) enjoy some sort of presumptive claim to their assets in virtue of their sweat equity, but others would surely be entitled to stake claims as well.

Just legal rules in a stateless society would allow people to homestead land and assets unjustly claimed by the state and its cronies. This kind of redistribution, potentially effective on a large scale, would not require any sort of top-down implementation or oversight, but could reasonably be effected by the courts.

F. Solidarity Grounds a Key Variety of Stateless Redistribution

1. *Solidaristic Action Could Play a Key Role in Effective Non-State Responses to Poverty and Economic Insecurity*

By enforcing the baseline possessory rules, just legal institutions in a stateless society would free and encourage people to engage in multiple acts of solidarity.

Redistributing wealth can be an exercise in solidarity, linking economically secure and economically vulnerable people.[24] Solidarity would be a crucial practice in any healthy stateless society.[25] Solidaristic redistribution can take multiple forms, including both gifts to economically vulnerable people and to organizations serving such people, and the creation and support of mutual aid networks helping to provide ongoing security against risk (Subsection 2). The responsibility to engage in solidaristic redistribution can be seen to flow from whatever underlying moral principles ground a commitment to anarchism (Subsection 3). Solidaristic redistribution can help to promote the value of freedom (Subsection 4) and challenge aggression (Subsection 5). Compulsory redistribution of the kind in which the state tends to engage is not an appropriate alternative to solidaristic redistribution (Subsection 6). Solidaristic

[23] *Cf. id.*; Murray N. Rothbard, *Confiscation and the Homestead Principle*, LIBERTARIAN FORUM, June 15, 1969, at 3.

[24] Solidaristic redistribution is my focus here, but redistribution is not, of course, the only reasonable expression of solidarity. Mutual aid networks might be funded in part redistributively. But the kinds of structural changes envisioned in (especially) Part V could and would enable people who are currently economically vulnerable to organize social services—including the provision of health care, risk-management services, and pensions—in solidarity *with each other*.

[25] For multiple categories of reasons for solidaristic redistribution, *see* Johnson, *supra* note 4; Charles W. Johnson, *Liberty, Equality, Solidarity: Toward a Dialectical Anarchism*, *in* ANARCHISM/MINARCHISM: IS A GOVERNMENT PART OF A FREE COUNTRY? 155, 179–83 (Roderick T. Long & Tibor Machan eds., 2008), http://radgeek.com/gt/2010/03/02/liberty-equality-solidarity-toward-a-dialectical-anarchism/.

redistribution could be an effective response to economic vulnerability in tandem with other varieties of stateless redistribution (Subsection 7).

2. *Solidarity Could Lead to Both Need-Focused Redistribution and to the Creation of Mutual Aid Networks*

Solidaristic redistribution could take place in at least two different ways. People could contribute money, material goods, expertise, and labor directly to others who were poor, economically vulnerable, victimized by accident or disaster, or otherwise in need of assistance. Similarly, they could contribute to institutions aiding others on an ongoing basis. They could also contribute to ongoing redistribution by participating in mutual aid networks designed to provide support to those dealing with lack of work, disability, dramatically reduced circumstances, health-care challenges, retirement, and other sources of insecurity.[26] In such networks, some would likely gain only peace of mind, while others would acquire much-needed, tangible support; the networks therefore amount, effectively to devices for redistributing from the former to the latter—though of course the donors and the beneficiaries often wouldn't be identifiable in advance. Need-focused solidaristic redistribution and mutual aid networks could foster the emergence of what can reasonably be termed a "welfare society."

3. *Solidaristic Action Could Flow from Sensitivity to Multiple, Compatible Reasons for Anarchism*

Anarchist legal theory is concerned primarily "with violence and non-violence as modes of interpersonal relations," rather than with "the moral or immoral ways

[26] *Cf.* David T. Beito, From Mutual Aid to the Welfare State: Fraternal Societies and Social Services, 1890–1967 (1999); Johnston Birchall, Co-Op: The People's Business (1994); Roderick Moore, Self-Help in the Past, the Present and the Future (1995); J.C. Herbert Emery, *The Rise and Fall of Fraternal Methods of Social Insurance: A Case Study of the Independent Order of Oddfellows of British Columbia Sickness Insurance, 1874–1951*, 23 Bus. & Econ. Hist. 10 (1994); C.R. Fay, Co-Operation at Home and Abroad (2 vols., 1948); Peter H.J.H. Gosden, The Friendly Societies in England, 1815–1875 (1961); Peter H.J.H. Gosden, Self-Help: Voluntary Associations in the Nineteenth Century (1973); David G. Green, Reinventing Civil Society: The Rediscovery of Welfare without Politics (1993); David Green, Working-Class Patients and the Medical Establishment (1985); David G. Green & Lawrence G. Cromwell, Mutual Aid or Welfare State: Australia's Friendly Societies (1984); Roderick T. Long, *Who's the Scrooge? Libertarians and Compassion*, Formulations, Winter 1993–94, http://www.http://freenation.org/a/f12l1.html; Stephen Pollard, Terry Liddle & Bill Thompson, Toward a More Cooperative Society (1994); David Schmidtz, *Taking Responsibility*, *in* David Schmidtz & Robert E. Goodin, Social Welfare and Individual Responsibility: For and Against 3–96 (1998); Robert L. Woodson, Breaking the Poverty Cycle (1989); Richard C. Cornuelle, Reclaiming the American Dream: The Role of Private Individuals and Voluntary Associations (1993). Thanks to Roderick T. Long and Roderick Moore for many of these references.

of exercising" the freedom secured by the right not to be a victim of aggression.[27] I have argued for a version of anarchism rooted in a more comprehensive natural law position, and natural law theory certainly provides support for a robust duty of beneficence.[28] But a wide range of moral theories can doubtless ground versions of anarchism. These moral theories often feature duties of beneficence, or requirements that could reasonably be extrapolated to ground such duties.[29] Anyone who embraced anarchism in virtue of an underlying commitment to a view that explicitly or implicitly grounds a duty of beneficence would also be committed to acknowledging such a duty (as, of course, would anyone committed to anarchism who was also, *independently*, committed to such a view). Either way, solidaristic redistribution would be a natural fit with any of several diverse varieties of anarchism.

4. *Solidarity Would Be a Useful Means of Promoting Freedom*

Economic vulnerability makes it easier for one to find oneself in circumstances in which other people are able to make important decisions affecting one's life. Being poor may make one more willing than one might otherwise be, for instance, to accept a job at a hierarchical firm at which one is subjected to arbitrary rule by petty tyrants.[30] There is good reason to value not only freedom from aggression but also social and other kinds of freedom,[31] and so to work to see that people are not pushed around—even nonviolently. Given the recognition that everyone is fundamentally equal in moral authority,[32] it makes sense the establishment and maintenance of hierarchies that implicitly deny this equality of authority (albeit without using aggressive force). Solidarity can help in multiple ways to foster social freedom; and given the value of the various kinds of freedom, there is thus good reason to provide assistance that makes freedom more likely and domination less so.

[27] *See* Rothbard, *supra* note 17, at 24.

[28] *See, e.g.*, John Finnis, Natural Law and Natural Rights 107, 298–304 (1980).

[29] *See, e.g.*, Liam Murphy, Moral Demands in Non-Ideal Theory (2000); Thomas M. Scanlon, What We Owe to Each Other 295–317 (1998); Onora O'Neill, Towards Justice and Virtue: A Constructive Account of Practical Reason 196–200 (1996); Tibor Machan, Generosity: Virtue in Civil Society (1998); David Kelley, Unrugged Individualism: The Selfish Basis of Benevolence (2003). *Cf.* David Schmidtz, *Separateness, Suffering, and Moral Theory*, *in* Person, Polis, Planet: Essays in Applied Philosophy 145 (2008).

[30] *Cf.* Johnson, *supra* note 25.

[31] *See* Kerry Howley, *We're All Cultural Libertarians*, Reason, Nov. 2009, *available at* http://reason.com/archives/2009/10/20/are-property-rights-enough.

[32] *See* Johnson, *supra* note 25, at 179–83; Roderick T. Long, *Liberty: The Other Equality*, The Freeman: Ideas on Liberty, Oct. 2005, at 17, http://www.fee.org/pdf/the-freeman/0510Long.pdf; Roderick T. Long, *Equality: The Unknown Ideal*, Mises Daily, Oct. 16, 2001, http:www.mises.org/story/804.

5. *Solidaristic Redistribution Challenges Aggression*

A great deal of poverty and economic insecurity can reasonably be seen as rooted in aggression. There is very good reason to condemn, challenge, and eliminate institutionalized aggression and to demand satisfactory remedies for specific acts of unjust dispossession. But seeing economically vulnerable people as victims of aggression may reasonably prompt not only opposition to the underlying conditions responsible for their vulnerability but also assistance in meeting the particular challenges posed by that vulnerability.[33]

6. *It Is Not Reasonable to Use Force to Effect Solidaristic Redistribution*

While force may reasonably be employed to redistribute wealth by rectifying past and ongoing injustice and safeguarding peaceful, voluntary cooperation, there are multiple reasons not to use force to redistribute wealth solidaristically.

It is important to distinguish between what it is reasonable and unreasonable for a given person to do, and what it is reasonable and unreasonable for someone else to use force to *compel* her to do. There is good reason for people to engage in the solidaristic redistribution of their own resources by contributing to charities, communal projects, and other worthwhile endeavors. But even though there is good reason for them to do so, this is not, at the same time, an argument for the existence of an administrative apparatus with the capacity to force them to do this.

Systematic interference with people's control over their justly acquired possessions would be inconsistent with the baseline rules as I've stated and defended them. And it is not clear that it would be reasonable to endorse a revised version of the rules that allowed for such interference in the interest of ensuring the fulfillment of people's duties to engage in solidaristic redistribution. To alter the rules in the requisite way would arguably be inconsistent with appropriate regard for the desiderata that underlie the baseline rules and for the Principle of Fairness. It's not obvious that the importance of duties of beneficence somehow alters the desiderata or the way in which they ought to figure in reasonable decisions in light of the Principle of Fairness. Arguments in favor of revising the rules to allow the use of force to effect solidaristic redistribution would thus need to be especially strong. And it is unclear that these arguments would be strong enough to justify discounting the various considerations that weigh directly against revising the baseline rules to permit *forcing* people to fulfill what would otherwise be solidaristic duties.

(*i*) Duties of beneficence are imperfect duties. While it would be unreasonable not to be beneficent, there are ordinarily multiple ways *in* which and degrees *to* which duties of beneficence can appropriately be fulfilled. One

[33] *Cf.* Johnson, *supra* note 25; Johnson, *supra* note 4.

might contribute to worthwhile projects, provide work, make various kinds of productive investments, or give directly to economically vulnerable people. Because there are multiple kinds of choices someone can reasonably make in fulfillment of a duty of beneficence, other people cannot reasonably be regarded as entitled to determine which of these choices she should be expected to make (all are presumptively appropriate). Further, since someone would not seem in virtue of a duty of beneficence to owe anything in particular to any specific person, duties of beneficence are duties without correlative claims for others to seek to vindicate (much less enforceable rights).[34] If other people can't reasonably determine how someone *should* fulfill a duty of beneficence, it will be hard to defend the claim that they should be able to force her to do so in one way rather than another.

(*ii*) Other people frequently lack information regarding particular people's needs, circumstances, and obligations. Because they may thus be quite unlikely to know what ways of fulfilling a given person's duty of beneficence are and are not reasonable for her, it will be unreasonable for them to use force to compel her to be beneficent in particular ways. Even though someone might know in a specific case that another's choice was inconsistent with her duties of beneficence, the *general* fact of ignorance regarding such choices would warrant institutional limits on acts interfering with others' bodies and justly acquired possessions undertaken to ensure that they fulfilled their duties of beneficence.

(*iii*) Similarly, this sort of ignorance would tend to create serious risks that community-wide compulsory programs of organized beneficence would be inefficient—providing people with goods and services they did not necessarily want, at levels they did not want, and at excessively high costs. (Guaranteed provision of health care, say, or education, at a specific level seems all too likely to encourage overconsumption by beneficiaries, inefficiently high pricing by providers, and an inefficiently extensive range of services.)[35]

(*iv*) To treat a person or organization as entitled to make someone fulfill a duty of beneficence, or some other imperfect duty (even when she really is failing to

[34] Obviously, there may be moral duties to provide specific assistance to particular, identifiable persons. In which even of these cases, if any, such duties ought to be enforceable by law is obviously a distinct issue, with which I am not concerned here.

[35] This problem in particular could be remedied by replacing diverse social welfare programs offering services of various sorts with a basic income grant that allowed recipients to set their own priorities and negotiate with service providers; *see, e.g.*, HORIZONS OF REFORM: BASIC INCOME AROUND THE WORLD (Carole Pateman & Matthew Murray eds., 2012); Carole Pateman, *Another Way Forward: Welfare, Social Reproduction, and a Basic Income*, *in* WELFARE REFORM AND POLITICAL THEORY 34 (Lawrence M. Mead & Christopher Beem eds., 2005); Carole Pateman, *Democratizing Citizenship: Some Advantages of a Basic Income*, 3 POL. & SOC'Y 89 (2004); Carole Pateman, *Freedom and Democratization: Why Basic Income Is to Be Preferred to Basic Capital*, *in* THE ETHICS OF

fulfill the duty, and so acting wrongly) is to equip the person or organization with substantial power. This kind of power is far too likely to be used abusively. It is likely to be used abusively when employed in good faith to require people to fulfill their duties of beneficence—because of (*a*) informational deficits and (*b*) problems related to people's overconfidence in (*1*) their own virtue and capacity for moral judgment and (*2*) the importance of what they are doing. But it is also likely to be used abusively when those with power yield to the temptation to employ their power to reach goals unrelated to ensuring that others fulfill their duties of beneficence, as, for instance, to benefit their cronies or to punish or reward favored ethnic, cultural, or religious groups.

(*v*) People work less energetically and enthusiastically when they know that some of what they produce will, in effect, be taken from them forcibly. Thus, taking resources from people as a way of enforcing solidaristic redistribution can function as a drag on overall economic productivity. By contrast, when people give willingly as a matter of solidaristic redistribution, their own objectives are not being thwarted; if they wish to support these efforts, then they will be willing to work hard to do so. Thus, the existence of even quite substantial redistributive efforts in a stateless society need not conflict with people's working enthusiastically to earn wealth and thus with overall economic productivity as state-enforced redistributive efforts might.

(*vi*) Even when it is undertaken in the interests of beneficence, the operation of systematic, impersonal institutions—the sort likely to be put in place to distribute resources acquired through large-scale compulsory extraction—runs the risk of creating perverse incentives both for those who manage the institutions and for those they are designed to benefit, with the practical effect that poverty levels may be maintained or increased.

(*vii*) The operation of such institutions also runs the risk of undermining and displacing beneficent relationships, practices, and structures which are valuable in their own right and which may play important social roles that impersonal, compulsory institutions do not.

(*viii*) Forcible redistribution is not, finally, solidaristic, since it is not undertaken out of solidarity. And, indeed, it runs the risk of undermining solidarity insofar as it produces resentment directed at recipients.[36]

STAKEHOLDING 130 (Keith Dowding, Jurgen De Wispelaere & Stuart White eds., 2003); PHILLIPE VAN PARIJS, REAL FREEDOM FOR ALL: WHAT (IF ANYTHING) CAN JUSTIFY CAPITALISM? (1995); FRIEDRICH A. HAYEK, THE CONSTITUTION OF LIBERTY 257–59 (1960); 3 FRIEDRICH A. HAYEK, LAW, LEGISLATION, AND LIBERTY: THE POLITICAL ORDER OF A FREE PEOPLE 54–56 (1979); MILTON FRIEDMAN, CAPITALISM AND FREEDOM 190–95 (1962).

[36] *Cf.* ROBERT HIGGS, AGAINST LEVIATHAN 21–30 (2004). It will be apparent in this Subsection that I have learned from Higgs at various points.

7. *Solidaristic Redistribution Can Be an Effective Response to Economic Insecurity*

Redistribution undertaken in solidarity with victims of aggression and victims of circumstance is a general moral responsibility, supported by a broad range of moral theories. Solidaristic redistribution can not only address particular needs but also help to create networks and institutions that can reduce economic insecurity and vulnerability. This kind of redistribution can also assist in fostering freedom and challenging aggression. There are good reasons for people to engage in solidaristic redistribution, but there is not, by contrast, good reason for states or other entities to use force to compel people to do so.

G. Peaceful, Voluntary Cooperation through Exchange Is a Crucial Means of Redistributing Wealth

By enforcing standards embodying the baseline possessory rules, just legal institutions in a stateless society would make voluntary, peaceful cooperation through exchange possible; and this kind of cooperation would effect an ongoing redistribution of resources with the tendency to undermine the concentration of wealth and social influence.[37]

While peaceful, voluntary cooperation through exchange would not create mathematical equality, it would make it difficult for vast disparities of wealth to persist. The enforcement of standards embodying the baseline rules would redistribute resources away from people who were wealthy because of one sort of privilege or another. The extant economic system is profoundly distorted by privilege;[38] if standards embodying the baseline rules were enforced, those who had benefited from state-secured privilege, forced to participate along with everyone else in the process of peaceful, voluntary cooperation, would tend to lose ill-gotten gains.[39] The tendency of a system of cooperation through peaceful, voluntary exchange would be to eliminate every variety of economic rent. At the same time, it would also, relatedly, redistribute wealth away *from* people who were *not* serving others effectively and *to* people who *did* serve others effectively. Such a system would effectively *socialize the benefits of productivity*.[40]

[37] Obviously, this is only one of several complementary strategies. Exchange on its own, even when subject to just rules, cannot eliminate the effects of large-scale past injustice. Structural change of the kind for which I argue here is vital.

[38] *See* KEVIN. A. CARSON, NOTHING LIKE A FREE MARKET: CORPORATE CAPITALISM IN THE USA (2006).

[39] *Cf.* Jeremy Weiland, *Let the Free Market Eat the Rich*, *in* MARKETS NOT CAPITALISM, *supra* note 1, at 301, http://anarchywithoutbombs.com/2010/03/13/let-the-free-market-eat-the-rich.

[40] Thanks for Kevin Carson and Anna Morgenstern for the points made in the final two sentences of this paragraph. The italicized phrase is Carson's paraphrase of the view of Benjamin R. Tucker.

Enforcing standards embodying the baseline rules, and therefore facilitating peaceful, voluntary exchange, would also contribute to the redistribution of resources because this kind of exchange tends to make goods and services more affordable than they would otherwise be, and thus more accessible. The end result would be that someone who didn't necessarily achieve a higher money income could nonetheless over time come to enjoy a higher standard of living.

H. The Kind of Redistribution Effected and Facilitated by Just Legal Rules and Institutions in a Stateless Society Could Deal Effectively with the Problem of Poverty

1. *Stateless Redistribution Could Undermine Deprivation and Economic Insecurity*

Redistribution in multiple forms—the elimination of privilege; rectification; the creation of opportunities for radical homesteading; solidarity; and peaceful, voluntary cooperation through exchange—could play a key role in the process of addressing the problem of deprivation in a stateless society. Deprivation matters (Subsection 2), but that hardly means that remedies for deprivation need to be provided by the state or any state-like entity. State antipoverty programs can be problematic because they provide excuses for the mistreatment of aid recipients (Subsection 3), but, in any case, the state itself actively impoverishes people in a range of mutually reinforcing ways (Subsection 4). The various, complementary varieties of stateless redistribution could all help to address the challenge of poverty in a stateless society (Subsection 5). Eliminating the state would reduce the frequency of poverty, reduce the liabilities associated with being poor, and increase the resources that could be solidaristically redistributed (Subsection 6).[41] Solidaristic redistribution could be effective without any sort of forcible backing from the state or any state-like entity (Subsection 6). Eliminating the state and engaging in stateless redistribution could enable people in a stateless society to end structural poverty and deal successfully with poverty caused by accident and emergency (Subsection 7).

2. *Deprivation Is a Crucial Concern for Multiple Reasons*

Deprivation ought to matter to everyone. Those who suffer from deprivation are equal in moral worth to others, so that the Principle of Fairness precludes trivializing their vulnerability and loss. Deprivation frequently results from injustice, and the requirements of practical reasonableness dictate that those who have engaged

[41] *Cf.* Thomas E. Woods, Meltdown (2011).

in injustice remedy it. And the risk of deprivation confronts many people who are not currently deprived, so that prudence entails concern on the part of those not deprived with the kinds of risks that might lead to their own deprivation. But any of a wide range of responses to deprivation might be reasonable, provided that they were consistent with the demands of prudence or fairness and that they could reasonably be regarded as likely to be effective.

3. *States Treat Those Receiving Aid Poorly*

States don't treat recipients of their aid well. States routinely intrude into the lives of recipients of state assistance, violating people's privacy and seeking to regulate their behavior. People pay a high price for aid provided by the state.[42]

4. *The State Actively Redistributes Wealth away from Economically Vulnerable People*

State policies deprive people unjustly of wealth, make them economically vulnerable, and intensify the risks associated with their vulnerability.

States actively make and keep people poor. Licensing laws, zoning regulations, and similar restrictions make it hard for poor people to seek particular kinds of work in cooperation with others and to work for themselves out of their own homes. Without the state to put these kinds of restrictions in place, people would be less likely to be poor, since they would have more opportunities for work. And states sanction massive injustice, depriving people of liberty and of land and other resources and thus impoverishing them and their descendants, with long-term consequences for societal wealth distribution.

States also raise the cost of being poor. Building codes and zoning regulations in developed societies raise the cost of housing, and so make it harder for people to find inexpensive homes. Some people are forced to live without permanent housing at all, while others must spend much larger fractions of their incomes on housing than they otherwise would. Agricultural tariffs raise the cost of food, arguably the most important portion of anyone's budget. Without the state to make meeting their basic needs unnecessarily expensive, poor people would have more disposable income and would be more economically secure.[43]

And *states actively take money from poor people*. Many poor people pay more to the state than they get back in services under the state's rule. These people would have more resources, net, in the absence of the state's demand for tribute.

[42] *Cf.* Higgs, *supra* note 36.
[43] *See* Chapter 2.VI.C.10, *supra*.

In addition, many people are poor, or poorer, today because the state has actively stolen land and other resources from them or their ancestors or has sanctioned such thefts committed by the wealthy and well-connected. This is true not only because people have been directly impoverished by this kind of theft but also because reductions in available options effected by this kind of theft channel people into settings in which they can be counted on to accept low-wage employment on dismal terms. Inflationary money creation by state central banks further reduces poor people's real wealth.[44]

The state deprives poor people of money and of money-generating opportunities while making it more costly to be poor because it *raises the cost of obtaining key services*. The state does a range of things (notably requiring professional licenses, hospital accreditation, and prescriptions and enforcing drug and medical device patents, and other restraints on peaceful, voluntary cooperation) to make particular services, such as those related to health care, especially expensive.[45]

The various state actions and policies that make and keep people poor tend to reinforce each other, each one making people's conditions worse than they'd otherwise be and making the effects of the other factors more severe. People often start out with less money because of large-scale past injustices. They have less money now because of government limitations on the kind of work they can do and where they can do it. Their ability to provide decent lives for themselves and their families is further limited because the government raises the cost of housing and various important goods and services. And state manipulation drives down the overall level of productivity even further in ways that obviously have economy-wide effects but that hurt the poor the most.

5. *A Range of Redistributive Strategies Could Combine to Enable People to Deal Effectively with the Problem of Poverty in a Stateless Society.*

The problem of deprivation could be dealt with quite satisfactorily in the state's absence, notably through the redistribution of resources. Multiple kinds of redistribution—rectification for specific past injustices; the homesteading of engrossed or stolen assets; the termination of state-secured privilege; solidarity; and peaceful, voluntary cooperation through exchange—could contribute to reducing poverty. Each of the varieties of redistribution I've already canvassed could help to make the challenge of poverty manageable in a stateless society.

[44] Thanks to Steve Horwitz for this point.

[45] For an anarchist approach to the problem of health care, *see* GARY CHARTIER, *State Socialism and Anarchism: How Far They Agree and Wherein They Differ Regarding Health-Care Reform*, *in* SOCIALIST ENDS, MARKET MEANS: FIVE ESSAYS 12 (Tulsa Alliance of the Libertarian Left, 2009).

6. *Eliminating State Inefficiency and State-Secured Privilege Could Reduce Economic Insecurity while also Increasing the Funds Available for Solidaristic Redistribution*

Ending the state would make dealing with the problem of poverty more manageable in multiple ways.

Structural changes would make poverty less likely in a stateless society. Rules that made it harder for absentee proprietors to sit on effectively unclaimed or abandoned land would open up this land for homesteading by people with limited resources and thus help them achieve greater economic security. Eliminating props for hierarchical corporations would increase the likelihood that people could enjoy the job security associated with working for themselves (with less risk than accompanies doing so in a less healthy economy) or in partnerships or cooperatives and that, when they did work for others, they could bargain successfully for better compensation. And the elimination of rules requiring occupational licensure, constraining land-use, governing construction patterns, and affecting similar matters would increase poor people's opportunities to create wealth through peaceful, voluntary cooperation in exchange while reducing their living costs.

Without state interference, *basic services would be less expensive* and more available. Without the state, these services would be provided non-monopolistically by ordinary people rather than by the state or state-privileged monopolists—and thus in most cases less expensively. In addition, some services (think a bloated military with an offensive capacity) wouldn't be part of the picture at all. Because they would pay less for needed services than they do under the state's rule, people would have more disposable income than at present. This means *both* that people with limited incomes would be better off, since they would spend less on basic services while not being taxed to support the wealthy and well-connected, *and* that people with more money would have bigger disposable incomes from which to give to support good causes.

The problem of poverty would be less severe in the state's absence, and more resources would be available to deal with it when it did occur, because *the absence of the state would make almost everyone richer*. The state hamstrings innovation and hampers productivity by privileging some at the expense of others and seeking, impossibly, to manage the economy on a top-down basis. State subsidies and regulations drive down the overall productivity of a society's economy when compared with what could be expected in an otherwise similar society operating in accordance with the baseline rules. So there's good reason to believe that, in its absence, people, including poor people, would be wealthier on average than they are today. Poor people would thus have more money, and those in a position to help them would, too.

7. *Solidaristic Redistribution Could Be Effective in a Stateless Society without Backing by the State*

Solidaristic redistribution is likely to be more effective as a response to some aspects of the problem of poverty in a stateless society than it appears to be in state-dominated environments.

The existence of state antipoverty programs minimizes the apparent effectiveness of alternative antipoverty efforts because *the state crowds out alternatives*. It's easy to view these alternatives as essentially ineffectual and anemic because they're not more vibrant today. But of course a crucial reason they're not is that state action persistently attracts money and attention that might otherwise be directed to these alternatives, creating the illusion that, in the state's absence, they couldn't be much more effective.

Support for poverty relief doesn't just come from state funds now, and there's no reason to think people wouldn't support poverty relief efforts absent the state.[46] People give money to charitable causes over and above their tax bills today, despite the huge sums the state claims. It's reasonable to expect that they would do so in a stateless society. It is naïve to suppose that the wealthy and powerful are opposed to state funding for services to the poor at present; the poor have far less clout than do the wealthy and powerful, and yet the state provides minimal services for poor people. There is no reason to suppose that wealthy and well-connected people willing to see the state spend their tax money to support services for the poor would be dramatically less willing to contribute to the support of such services without the state. (Of course, in the absence of state-secured privilege, one might expect the relative wealth of these people would be reduced—but this needn't be relevant to the problem of poverty relief in a stateless society, since the effect of eliminating privilege would be to boost opportunities for economic well-being for many of those currently less well-off.) Why do people give money to good causes, including voluntary programs that help the poor? Why do wealthy and well-connected people endorse state spending on programs that provide services to poor people (which they must if these programs are to persist, since recipients of state poverty-relief funds do not constitute a powerful lobbying group)?[47] Presumably for a combination of reasons, including (in no particular order) compassion, social norms, the desire for good reputations, the desire to avoid bad reputations, and the desire to avoid social disorder. All of these factors would be operative in a stateless society.

[46] This assumes that poverty relief is not, in the economist's sense, a public good (though even if it were, this would not rule out its effective provision in the state's absence; *see* Chapter 3.V.F, *supra*). For an argument that it is not, *see* Mark Pennington, Robust Political Economy: Classical Liberalism and the Future of Public Policy 163–65 (2011).

[47] Thanks to Kevin Carson for this point.

Mutual aid networks could provide many of the services well-intentioned statists want the state to offer. Societies in which people pooled risk and provided pensions, health care, and other services functioned effectively before the rise of state social services, and there's no reason to think they couldn't do so again without the state. Indeed, there's no reason to think they wouldn't function much better, given that people would have access to more resources and that the state wasn't on-hand to regulate them out of existence.

Mutual aid and other kinds of solidarity are more viable, more able to help economically vulnerable people efficiently, than state-administered programs precisely because those programs feature *high administrative costs*. Programs supported freely by people in a stateless society would not feature such high administrative costs: because donors could support multiple programs, there would be persistent pressure for administrative costs to be reduced.

In addition, *social norms could ensure predictable, consistent support of community-wide aid programs without taxation*. General acceptance of a social norm entailing regular contributions to a community income support fund could ensure that poor people who needed it could rely on community assistance. (Other institutions are possible, too, of course. A norm, as in Leviticus, requiring that the edges of fields be available for gleaning provides a homely example.)

Statists sometimes worry that the absence of the state would mean a return to the misery and squalor typical of many people's lives in the eighteenth- or nineteenth-century; too often, they attribute these conditions to the absence of state regulation and antipoverty programs. But *these conditions reflected the much lower overall levels of societal wealth* that obtained in the eighteenth and nineteenth centuries. People weren't poor because of the absence of state regulations and antipoverty programs; they were poor *both* because of persistent—remediable—injustice on the part of elites and their political cronies *and* because there was very little wealth overall (often as the result of state mischief) and thus less for those who did seek to help the poor to use to do so.[48]

8. *Stateless Redistribution Could Help to Meet the Challenge of Poverty*

Poverty is a serious problem, but the state is hardly necessary or desirable as the agent to be charged with responding to this problem. The state makes and keeps people poor, not only through unjust policies but also through its efforts to help. The state plays a direct role in creating and perpetuating poverty. Thus, a crucial variety of redistribution—eliminating the state and state-secured privilege, the causes of *structural* poverty—could play a crucial role in dramatically reducing the

[48] *Cf.* Kevin A. Carson, Studies in Mutualist Political Economy (2007).

incidence of poverty. But of course that doesn't mean that, absent the state, people wouldn't have accidents, confront disasters, and make unwise choices. With costs of living reduced, as they would be in a stateless society, people would find it easier to deal with these challenges. They would still need each other's help. But people and institutions could respond effectively to deprivation and economic insecurity in the state's absence by employing a variety of mutually reinforcing redistributive strategies.[49] Redistribution can play a crucial role in helping people in a stateless society to meet the challenge of poverty.

I. Just Legal Rules and Institutions in a Stateless Society Would both Foster and Effect Redistribution

Just legal rules and institutions in a stateless society would *foster* redistribution by making solidaristic redistribution and peaceful, voluntary economic transactions possible. They would *effect* redistribution by eliminating privilege, providing for restitution, and legitimating radical homesteading.

Statist redistribution is unjust because it employs aggressive means, because it is undertaken by an aggressive monopolist, and because it unreasonably serves the interests of the ruling class and its cronies at the expense of ordinary people. Stateless redistribution would be designed to move beyond injustice, create new wealth, and meet the challenge of poverty. Thus it would involve the elimination of state-secured privilege; the provision of remedies for past injustice; the homesteading of assets stolen and engrossed by the state and its cronies; acts of solidarity; and peaceful, voluntary cooperation through exchange—which could simultaneously boost the economic well-being of ordinary people and disperse the ill-gotten gains of

[49] My focus here has been on the challenge of dealing with the problem of poverty in an economically developed society in the state's absence. The issue of what to do about the global problem of poverty is obviously more complex. What I've said here obviously applies, in multiple ways, but there's obviously more to be said about global poverty. Global poverty is doubtless exacerbated by geographic and cultural factors, but at present it is a deeply *political* problem, driven by abuses within both developed societies and poor ones. It seems as if (*i*) developed societies could deal with the structural problems underlying the problem by (*a*) eliminating import duties and other barriers to the movement of goods and services that privilege domestic producers over ones in poor countries; (*b*) ending restrictions on immigration, since immigration both allows people currently in poor countries to better their conditions and enables them to help support friends and family members at home with remittances; (*c*) ending military aid to poor-country governments; (*d*) ending attempts to manipulate poor-country political systems; and (*e*) discontinuing legal and political support for abusive behavior by developed-country multinationals operating in poor countries. At the same time, (*ii*) governments of poor countries could contribute to addressing the problem of poverty by (*a*) removing restrictions on economic initiative by the people in their societies; (*b*) ending restrictions on foreign direct investment; (*c*) ending restrictions on civil liberties; (*d*) facilitating restitution for the theft of stolen land and other assets; and (*e*) refusing to impede homesteading of engrossed and abandoned land. It is obvious in many cases that simply ending state abuses would effect the needed changes.

the privileged. This multipronged approach to redistribution could eliminate structural poverty and respond powerfully to accidental poverty.

IV. RECTIFYING INJUSTICE COULD HELP TO CREATE ALTERNATIVES TO WORKPLACE HIERARCHIES

A. A Nonaggressive Politics Could Lead to Workplace Freedom

Remedying injustice could play a crucial role in fostering liberating workplaces in a stateless society. Large, hierarchical firms confront challenges created by various diseconomies of scale (Section B). The existence of such firms and their dominance by investors may seem inevitable. But much wealth concentration is rooted in large-scale, often systemic, injustice perpetrated or tolerated by the state (Section C), which also places roadblocks in the way of the creation of alternatives (Section D). Structures offering workers greater opportunities for control of or participation in decisions regarding firms would offer distinct advantages (Section E). Because firms with these kinds of structures could be expected to flourish in the absence of state support for hierarchical corporations and state-created impediments to the creation of alternatives, workplace freedom could be effectively fostered by just legal regimes in a stateless society when the regimes invalidated or declined to enforce unjust claims and refused to preserve unjust privileges (Section F).

B. Large, Hierarchical Firms Are Inefficient for Multiple Reasons

1. *Corporate Hierarchies Suffer because of Diseconomies of Scale*

Large, hierarchical firms are plagued by serious problems that are inherent consequences of their sizes and structures. Managers in such firms lack access to the knowledge they need to make good decisions (Subsection 2). And investors, managers, and ordinary workers in these firms confront persistent challenges related to the divergence of interests between principals and agents (Subsection 3). While such firms are often said to enjoy economies of scale, it is important to emphasize that their effectiveness is hampered by *diseconomies* of scale (Subsection 4).

2. *Corporate Central Planners Face Serious Knowledge Problems*

Acquiring and deploying information within and on behalf of a firm is increasingly difficult as the firm's size increases.[50] The sheer volume of information is

[50] *See* CARSON, *supra* note 14, at 153–70, 197–224.

enormous.[51] And the internal politics of firms make it easy for information to be distorted, as people seek to block the transmission of, or simply to ignore, data that might be seen as justifying interference with their pet projects or as supporting efforts to undermine their positions.[52]

Corporate central planners confront the same kinds of broad challenges as state central planners.[53] State central planners lack information about opportunities, supplies, and consumer preferences that is dispersed widely throughout an entire economy.[54] They lack the information about priorities, preference strengths, and resource availability provided by prices arrived at through ongoing processes of peaceful, voluntary cooperation in exchange, particularly as regards, not just consumer goods, but also the means of production.[55] It is only by accident, if at all, that their decisions are able to effect the internalization of costs or benefits, with the result that actors in the economies over which they preside often lack incentives to behave responsibly and productively. And central planners will frequently be affected by political considerations, which can lead them to confer benefits on the influential and well-connected. Thus, they consistently mandate production levels and distribution patterns inadequately reflective of people's actual desires.

Similarly, corporate central planners lack the information about divisional or departmental needs often possessed by those on the ground. It is often difficult for them to take advantage of the local knowledge of frontline workers. They are frequently unable to make rational decisions about capital goods because those goods are artificially priced. Budget allocations need not reflect economic realities because internal subsidies can keep inefficiencies from becoming apparent, and internal corporate politics can effect significant distortions in economic judgment. The alignment between productivity and performance is often tenuous. Like state central planners, corporate central planners frequently allocate resources inappropriately.[56]

Large firms' internal operations are isolated from the feedback they could be expected to gain through transactions with others if they acquired goods and services from others rather than doing so internally. And the internal transfer pricing on which they depend is relatively arbitrary. Thus, large firms might be expected in principle to face significant problems in virtue of size.

[51] *See id.* at 153–57.

[52] *See id.* at 157–66.

[53] *See id.* at 197–224.

[54] *See* Friedrich A. Hayek, *The Use of Knowledge in Society*, 35 AM. ECON. REV. 519 (1945).

[55] *See* Ludwig von Mises, *Economic Calculation in the Socialist Commonwealth*, *in* COLLECTIVIST ECONOMIC PLANNING 87 (F. A. Hayek ed., 1935).

[56] *See* CARSON, *supra* note 14, at 197–224.

3. *Investors and Corporate Executives Face Serious Principal–Agent Problems*

The interests of investors, executives, mid-level managers, and ordinary workers diverge persistently.[57] Investors provide capital to conventional corporate firms. But senior executives, rather than investors, characteristically make top-level decisions and find it relatively easy to evade investor scrutiny in most cases. In turn, it is difficult for executives to monitor the behavior of lower-level managers and other workers. And the problems at all levels are not simply informational—it's not just that it's difficult for putative superiors to know what putative subordinates are doing, but that the various groups have unavoidably disparate interests and may often be expected, especially when agreement-based obligations are open-ended, effectively unenforceable, or both, to pursue those interests actively. Monitoring and supervision costs grow, and authoritarianism, with predictably negative consequences, becomes increasingly common. The structure of the large, hierarchical firm makes it effectively impossible to ensure that most or all firm actors internalize most of the costs and benefits of their firm-related choices.[58] The result is that firm efficiency is undermined by low-level, ongoing internal conflict.

4. *Large, Hierarchical Firms Exhibit Inherent Operational Inefficiencies*

The large, hierarchical firm enjoys some advantages because of its size. But it also confronts a variety of disadvantages. There are, for instance, serious informational problems involved in attempting to plan and manage the activities of such a firm. And the divergent interests of the multiple participants in this kind of firm's operations create friction and increase monitoring and supervision costs. Left to its own devices, the large, hierarchical firm might be expected to experience serious difficulties surviving.

C. State Action Has Subsidized the Existing Corporate Form

1. *The State Contributes Significantly to the Creation and Maintenance of Large, Hierarchical Firms*

State action has encouraged the emergence and continued existence of what would otherwise be inefficiently large and hierarchical firms in at least two ways: by increasing the wealth of the members of ruling class and their cronies (Subsection 2) and

[57] *See id.* at 171–95.
[58] *See id.* at 193.

by conferring privileges and imposing regulations that make large firms more economical than they would otherwise be (Subsection 3). State action thus increases the odds that firms will be large and hierarchical (Subsection 4).

2. *The State Has Helped to Funnel Wealth to Members of the Ruling Class and Their Cronies, Who Might Be Expected to Prefer Hierarchical Firms*

Wealth concentration is hardly inevitable: it is much more likely in a society shaped by unjust political choices carried out over many centuries. State-secured privilege and state-sanctioned and state-perpetrated violence have made and continue to make and keep many people poor or economically insecure even while fostering the concentration of wealth and social influence in the hands of the members of the ruling class and their cronies.[59]

Members of the ruling class and their cronies may prefer and promote hierarchically structured firms for several reasons.

(*i*) They are often investors (since those with investable wealth may be more likely than the average person to be beneficiaries of state-secured privilege). And this, in turn, may mean that they favor hierarchical firms because they (*a*) believe it will be easier to control such firms by installing individual executives who can be held accountable for firm performance; (*b*) find it easy to identify with the perspectives and favor the interests of executives, who are more likely than frontline workers to resemble these investors socially and culturally; and (*c*) view the dominance within firms of executives who are generally like themselves as inescapable and obviously appropriate.

(*ii*) They may occupy or desire executive or managerial positions in such firms themselves, and therefore not want to see such positions rendered superfluous.

[59] *See* Chapter 3.VI.C-E, *supra*. On primitive accumulation and subsequent instances of systemic theft in Europe, North America, and elsewhere, *see* Michael Perelman, The Invention of Capitalism: Classical Political Economy and the Secret History of Primitive Accumulation (2000); William Blum, Killing Hope: U.S. Military and CIA Interventions since World War II (1995); Chakravarthi Raghavan, Recolonization: GATT, the Uruguay Round and the Third World (1990); Martin Sklar, The Corporate Reconstruction of American Capitalism, 1890–1916: The Market, the Law, and Politics (1988); Gabriel Kolko, Confronting the Third World: United States Foreign Policy 1945–1980 (1988); Michael Perelman, Classical Political Economy: Primitive Accumulation and the Social Division of Labour (1984); Cheryl Payer, The Debt Trap: The International Monetary Fund and the Third World (1974); 1 Immanuel Wallerstein, The Modern World System (1974); George Beckford, Persistent Poverty: Development in Plantation Economies of the Third World (1972); Eric Hobsbawm & George Rudé, Captain Swing (1968); Paul Baran & Paul Sweezy, Monopoly Capitalism: An Essay in the American Economic and Social Order (1966); E.P. Thompson, The Making of the English Working Class (1963); Maurice

The governance structures of conventional firms are hierarchical in significant part because the resources used to fund the development and operation of these firms are available to investors because of past and ongoing injustice. As long as the state operates to increase and protect the wealth of the ruling class and its cronies, who may be expected to prefer hierarchical firms, firms can be expected to tend disproportionately to be hierarchical.

3. *State Action Has also Helped to Make and Keep Firms Large*

The state has effectively promoted the creation and maintenance of large, hierarchical firms in a variety of ways. For instance:

- The adoption of the corporate form itself is encouraged by state action, since, even if something like corporate entity status could be created by agreement, the transaction costs associated with formulating and negotiating the relevant agreements would be greater than the costs of adopting a uniform, state-created status.[60] And perhaps the corporate form in some ways makes the creation of larger and more hierarchical firms easier than would otherwise be the case.
- State funding of transportation and communication infrastructure—from railroads to highway systems to civil aviation systems to telegraph and telephone systems to the Internet—has reduced the cost to big businesses of expanding their operations, insulating them against the effects of increasing size.[61]
- Patents and copyrights foster the low-cost concentration of wealth, discouraging innovation, posing barriers to entry, cartelizing industries, encouraging firms to take high-cost product development paths with the potential to lead to patent or copyright privileges, and monopolizing control over thus helping to make the large firms that hold these state-created privileges economical,[62] while concentrating wealth in the hands of elite investors.
- The state subsidizes much of the research and development that grounds firms' wealth-concentrating, size-fostering patent claims.[63]

DOBB, STUDIES IN THE DEVELOPMENT OF CAPITALISM (1963); WILLIAM APPLEMAN WILLIAMS, THE TRAGEDY OF AMERICAN DIPLOMACY (1959); FRANZ OPPENHEIMER, THE STATE (1914). Thanks to Kevin Carson for identifying most of these sources. The overall level of economic productivity in modern Western economies is immeasurably greater than that in, say, eighteenth-century England, so the effects of past and ongoing injustice are less obvious. Nonetheless, such injustices clearly help to constrain the shapes of contemporary workplaces.

60 *See* CARSON, *supra* note 14, at 58–60.

61 *See id.* at 65–72; Kevin A. Carson, *The Distorting Effects of Transportation Subsidies*, THE FREEMAN: IDEAS ON LIBERTY, Nov. 2010, at 17, *available at* http://www.thefreemanonline.org/featured/the-distorting-effects-of-transportation-subsidies.

62 *See* CARSON, *supra* note 14, at 72–76.

63 *See id.* at 74.

- Tariffs facilitate cartelization and otherwise reduce the impact of the pressure on firms that would otherwise be exerted by the availability of alternatives to consumers and thus make it easier to maintain large firms.[64]
- A broad range of regulations sold to the public as designed to protect consumers' health or pocketbooks seem in fact to have proved especially attractive to big businesses as mechanisms for cartelization, insulating established players from challenges by upstarts and reducing pressures to respond more flexibly to consumer demand, and so creating secure and comfortable environments for large firms.[65]
- Sales taxes encourage firm growth because internal transactions aren't taxed, while external ones are—thus, firms are incentivized to create structures large enough for them to do as much as possible without having to acquire goods and services elsewhere and pay taxes as a result.[66]
- Tax law encourages the reinvestment of corporate earnings rather than their distribution in the form of dividends. If a given firm's shareholders received dividends, they might be inclined to invest what they'd received in other firms if the alternatives seemed more productive; instead, however, money that might have been used for dividend payments is spent on the firm's expansion, and wealth that might have been dispersed is concentrated.[67]
- Other tax rules also prompt firms to become and remain large, including ones that promote investment in high-cost technology, permit capital depreciation, implicitly favor mergers and acquisitions, and provide for the deductibility of interest on corporate debt.[68]
- "Accredited investor" requirements effectively channel most people's investments into publicly traded, and so large, firms.[69]
- State funding of education—especially higher education and technical education—reduces the cost to big business of securing corporate bureaucrats and other workers whose involvement is essential to the operation of large (but not necessarily of small) firms. And state educational institutions often encourage the docility and organizational consciousness required to adjust successfully to corporate employment.[70]
- Nationalization of health insurance, in one form or another, removes health coverage from the list of factors firms need to use to attract workers, thus leveling

[64] *See id.* at 77.
[65] *See id.* at 79–83
[66] *See id.* at 83; in support of this contention, Carson cites Ronald H. Coase, *The Nature of the Firm*, 4 ECONOMICA 386, 393 (1937).
[67] *See* CARSON, *supra* note 14, at 83.
[68] *See id.*
[69] *See id.* at 84.
[70] *See, e.g.*, *id.* at 87, 88–89.

the playing field among firms. Nationalizing health insurance via mandates on employers, in particular, could be expected to work to the advantage of big businesses, which might find it easier than smaller firms to cover the costs of providing mandated coverage.[71]

- Spending in support of the military-industrial complex amounts, effectively, to a vast subsidy to technological research and development efforts by big businesses, simultaneously encouraging the growth of military contractors and reducing the growth costs borne by other firms that benefit from militarily driven technological advances.[72]
- The state successfully absorbs many of the products of various inefficient industries, thus masking their inefficiency and allowing them to remain large and bloated.[73]

Large firms unavoidably confront serious efficiency problems. But when they operate within an environment misshaped by state action that benefits them disproportionately, hierarchical behemoths are better able to persist.

4. *The State Underwrites the Existing Pattern of Firm Structure, Control, and Investment*

The success and persistence of large, hierarchical firms is significantly dependent on state-secured privilege and the wealth concentration resulting from past acts of dispossession.

Unjustly gained wealth and state-secured privilege can help to insulate such firms against the effects of economic forces that would tend to compel the replacement of corporate divisions and departments by small, nimble organizations related by agreement. The members of the ruling class and its cronies might be expected to prefer these kinds of firms. And a range of state policies makes it easier for favored firms to become and remain large. (Naturally, of course, as they increase in size and wealth, firms will increasingly have access to resources they can use to seek more state-secured privileges, and thus more size and wealth. Privilege feeds itself, and the existence of the state apparatus serves as a persistent temptation to would-be rent-seekers.)

In addition, when, as a result in significant part of state action, firms are large and hierarchical, senior (and often mid-level) managers frequently enjoy higher salaries, more bountiful perquisites of employment, and greater status. They are thus incentivized to oppose reductions in firm size and hierarchical structure, and are typically

[71] *See id.* at 88.
[72] *See id.* at 90.
[73] *See id.* at 92–93.

in a position to see their preferences implemented (especially since ordinary investors can be expected to see those preferences as entirely natural). Thus, size and hierarchy naturally generate powerfully supportive internal constituencies.

Investors' wealth and social attitudes and the various factors that insulate large, hierarchical firms against pressures that might lead them to change form and size reflect the past and ongoing behavior of the state. State-perpetrated and state-tolerated dispossession and state-secured privilege are important drivers of the size and structure of the modern corporate firm.

D. The State Places Roadblocks in the Way of Creating Alternatives to Large, Hierarchical Corporations

Current work environments feature a persistent separation among investors, managers, and workers.[74] But it is not an immutable law of nature that workers are poor and unable to start or acquire firms or to exert leverage within firms in which they are employed by others. The most fundamental problem here is, of course, the impact of state-secured privilege and state-perpetrated or state-tolerated dispossession on the resources and opportunities available to workers. But the state impedes workers' efforts to create their own firms in other ways, too.[75]

(*i*) The state increases firm start-up and operating costs. For instance: it requires licenses—sometimes very expensive ones—to engage in various kinds of work. And it imposes land-use regulations and building codes that limit people's use of available land and, perhaps especially, their own homes to start firms.

(*ii*) The state limits access to capital. It reduces alternatives in the banking industry, makes it unnecessarily hard for people to capitalize their own assets, and reduces opportunities for small firms to attract investors.

(*iii*) State action also raises workers' living costs—as, for instance, through building codes and land-use regulations, which limit their abilities to live where and how they like. There are multiple ways in which these increased living costs impact workers' abilities to start their own firms. If living costs were reduced, workers would have more money to invest in start-ups. In addition, if living costs were reduced, the risks associated with starting new firms would also be reduced: it would cost less to maintain oneself if a start-up in which one was involved failed. Thus, reduced living costs, together with

[74] It can be argued that treating absentee investors as just possessors often serves primarily as a source of legitimation of what is in fact simply control by managers. Thanks to Kevin Carson for helping me to see this point. *Cf.* Harold Demsetz, *Toward a Theory of Property Rights*, 57 AM. ECON. REV. 347, 358–59 (1967).

[75] *Cf.* CARSON, *supra* note 14, at 400–21.

> reduced start-up initiation costs, would also mean greater bargaining leverage for workers seeking positions in corporate firms as well. That's because it would be easier for such workers to insist on better terms of employment and more opportunities to participate in decision making if they knew it was realistically possible for them to start their own firms and to maintain themselves successfully during periods of unemployment.

Most people, it is safe to assume, would prefer workplaces in which they can participate in the formulation of decisions that affect their work-lives, are well compensated with their work, are treated respectfully, and can use their expertise to perform their jobs efficiently and effectively. If people had multiple options—if it were easy to survive for a meaningful period without work, easy to work for oneself, easy to acquire the resources needed to begin working for oneself or with others—they might, of course, decide not to work in corporate firms at all. If they did choose to work for others, they could be expected to bargain confidently and energetically and persistently (personally or collectively) for better compensation, greater dignity and security, and greater involvement in decision making. By raising start-up and operating costs and living costs and constraining access to capital, the state makes it easy for larger, more established firms to avoid confronting the challenges posed by start-ups, including worker-organized start-ups, and ensures that the start-ups that do emerge are much more likely than would otherwise be the case to be created by people who already have significant resources.

E. Worker Control and Worker Participation Are Accompanied by Significant Economic Advantages

There is good reason to believe that small firms are frequently more efficient than larger ones.[76] And such firms would be easier than large ones for workers to manage without the putative aid of specialist executives. Not all small firms should be expected to be worker-controlled, and not all worker-controlled firms should be expected to be small. However, factors tending to make it easier for worker control to occur will also tend to facilitate the emergence of small firms, and vice versa. It will thus make sense to assume that worker-controlled firms will typically be small and that a greater percentage of small firms than large ones will be worker-controlled.

Worker control and worker self-management allow workers to make effective use of their local knowledge regarding production processes, resource options, and customer needs. Without needing to secure approval from relatively detached managers, they can make decisions rapidly and flexibly.

[76] A small firm, as I envision it here, might be a cooperative, a partnership, a single-person organization, or something else.

A worker-controlled firm can avoid the principal–agent problem that besets the typical corporate firm. Difficulties associated with knowing what others were doing would obviously be reduced in a smaller firm. More than that, however, in a firm controlled by workers able to reap the rewards of their own productivity, most workers would be principals, rather than agents, with the result that there would be built-in incentives for workers to cooperate with each other in boosting firm performance and to encourage each other to behave productively. This could be expected to increase productivity and economic viability directly, while also dramatically reducing expenses on monitoring and supervision and the conflict associated with these activities.[77]

Because reductions in firm size in tandem with authentic worker empowerment would make it much more likely that key decisions could be made in real time by workers, the need for workers to play managerial roles or appoint managers would be significantly reduced as well. Decreased expenses on management would minimize bureaucratic meddling with and second-guessing of workers' decisions, reduce occasions for management-related workplace conflict, and free up more resources for investment in productive firm activities.

Participatory structures in firms of all sizes enhance performance.[78] But small work associations, related by agreement, seem especially likely to be able more efficiently

[77] On problems associated with monitoring and supervision, *see, e.g.*, Lawrence E. Mitchell, *Trust and Team Production in Post-Capitalist Society*, 24 Iowa J. Corp. L. 869, 883–87 (1999); Kent Greenfield, *Using Behavioral Economics to Show the Power and Efficiency of Corporate Law as Regulatory Tool*, 35 U.C. Davis L. Rev. 581, 618–22 (2002); Samuel Bowles & Herbert Gintis, *The Democratic Firm: An Agency-Theoretic Evaluation*, *in* Markets and Democracy: Participation, Accountability, and Efficiency 13 (Samuel Bowles, Herbert Gintis & Bo Gustafsson eds., 1993).

[78] *See generally* Thomas Ahrens & Christopher Chapman, *Accounting for Flexibility and Efficiency: A Field Study of Management Control Systems in a Restaurant Chain*, 21 Contemp. Acct. Research 271 (2004); Vanessa Urch Druskat & Jane V. Wheeler, *How to Lead a Self-Managing Team*, 45 MIT Sloan Mgmt. Rev. 65 (2004) (noting the effectiveness of self-managed teams); Ismail Bakan *et al.*, *The Influence of Financial Participation and Participation in Decision-Making on Employee Job Attitudes*, 15 Int'l. J. Hum. Resource Mgmt. 587 (2004) (pointing to the importance of participation in decision making as a predictor of job satisfaction); George K.Y. Tseo *et al.*, *Employee Ownership and Profit Sharing as Positive Factors in the Reform of Chinese State-Owned Enterprises*, 25 Econ. & Ind. Democracy 147 (2004) (suggesting that worker ownership and participation in decision making at the level of the shop floor contributed to productivity, but that worker participation in governance exerted a negative effect on productivity); Virginie Perotin & Andrew Robinson, *Employee Participation and Equal Opportunities Practices: Productivity Effect and Potential Complementarities*, 38 Brit. J. Ind. Rel. 557 (2000) (highlighting a complex interaction between participation and equal-opportunity policies vis-à-vis productivity); Robert McNabb & Keith Whitfield, *The Impact of Financial Participation and Employee Involvement on Financial Performance*, 45 Scottish J. Pol. Econ. 171 (1998); Casey Ichniowski & Kathryn Shaw, *The Effects of Human Resource Management Systems on Economic Performance*, 45 Mgmt. Sci. 704 (1999); Richard B. Freeman & Morris M. Kleiner, *Who Benefits Most from Employee Involvement: Firms or Workers?*, http://www.nber.org/sloan/freeman.html; Social Development Canada, The Influence of Employee Involvement on Productivity: A Review of Research—June 2000, http://www11.sdc.gc.ca/en/cs/sp/arb/publications/research/2000–002584/

to perform the same tasks as corporate divisions or departments. They could do so because of their greater capacity for responsiveness to information about supplies, needs, preferences and so forth that would be available to them because of the ways in which they would acquire goods and services, set prices, and engage in similar activities. And they could do so because, to the extent that they were worker-owned, they wouldn't be hobbled by principal–agent problems and worker–management conflicts in the same ways as large, hierarchical firms.

F. Structural Changes Could Foster the Emergence of Democratic and Participatory Workplaces

While, in a given case, a specific worker's inability to acquire the resources needed to start or purchase a firm may not result from anyone's treating her unjustly, past injustice and ongoing privilege do lie behind workers' general lack of the resources needed to initiate or acquire their own firms. State-secured privilege and state-perpetrated and state-tolerated dispossession simultaneously boost the wealth of the ruling class and its cronies and reduce the resources and options available to ordinary people. Thus, they dramatically impact the structure of work-life, fostering hierarchy and wealth concentration, in at least three interlocking ways: (*i*) by minimizing pressures to reduce corporate size and replace divisions and departments within large organizations with small firms related by agreement, firms in which it would be easier for workers to manage themselves; (*ii*) by dramatically limiting the bargaining leverage of ordinary workers and thus their ability to secure opportunities

page07.shtml; YI NGAN, ESTIMATING THE POTENTIAL PRODUCTIVITY AND REAL WAGE EFFECTS OF EMPLOYEE INVOLVEMENT (1996); Derek C. Jones & Takao Kato, *The Effects of Employee Involvement on Firm Performance: Evidence from an Econometric Case Study*, William Davidson Institute Working Paper 612 (2003); ADBI INSTITUTE, EMPLOYEES IN ASIAN ENTERPRISES: THEIR POTENTIAL ROLE IN CORPORATE GOVERNANCE, http://www.adbi.org/articles/38.Employees.in.Asian.Enterprises/4.2.Employee.Involvement.on.the.Shop-Floor/Page1.php (citing sources including Sandra E. Black and Lisa Lynch, *What's Driving the New Economy: The Benefits of Workplace Innovation*, Working Paper 7479, National Bureau of Economic Research (2000); Chris Doucouliagos, *Worker Participation and Productivity in Labor-Managed and Participatory Capitalist Firms: A Meta-Analysis*, 49 IND. & LAB. REL. REV. 58 (1995); Mark Huselid & Brian E. Becker, *Methodological Issues in Cross-Sectional and Panel Estimates of the Human Resource-Firm Performance Link*, 35 IND. REL. 400 (1996); Bradley Kirkman & Benson Rosen, *Beyond Self-Management: Antecedents and Consequences of Team Empowerment*, 42 ACAD. MGMT. J. 59 (1999); Richard B. Freeman, Morris M. Kleiner & Cheri Ostroff, *The Anatomy of Employee Involvement and Its Effects on Firms and Workers*, Working Paper 8050, National Bureau of Economic Research (2000); Jeffrey M. Hirsch, *Labor Law Obstacles to the Collective Negotiation and Implementation of Employee Stock Ownership Plans: A Response to Henry Hansmann and Other Survivalists*, 67 FORDHAM L. REV. 957, 971 (1998) (citing Joseph Blasi *et al.*, *Employee Stock Ownership and Corporate Performance among Public Companies*, 50 INDUS. & LAB. REL. REV. 60, 62 [1996]; Henry Hansmann, *When Does Worker Ownership Work? ESOPs, Law Firms, Codetermination, and Economic Democracy*, 99 YALE L.J. 1749, 1768 [1990]).

to participate in workplace governance; and (*iii*) by increasing the costs to people of working for themselves and of creating partnerships and cooperatives, and ensuring that, when they do choose to work for others, they have little opportunity to work for smaller, more nimble, more human-scale, more participatory firms.

There are excellent moral and prudential reasons for those able to shape firms' governance structures to seek to organize them democratically.[79] But whether or not they do so, a just legal regime in a stateless society could help to foster workplace democracy and worker participation in decision making by remedying the past injustices and eliminating the persisting privileges responsible for concentrating wealth, boosting firm size, and making it hard for workers to subsist without wage employment and to pursue alternate work options.[80]

V. A STATELESS SOCIETY'S LEGAL ORDER WOULD FOSTER THE EMERGENCE OF A FREE CULTURE

A. Legal Rules That Safeguard Autonomy Make It Possible for People to Opt for Diverse Lifestyles and to Promote Fairness and Inclusion

A stateless society's legal order would offer space for people to explore a dizzying variety of ways of being human; at the same time, it would also leave room for

[79] The moral reasons include the equal dignity of all workers, the character of the firm as a community, the absence of a natural right to govern on the part of investors or executives, the unfairness of subordination imposed by those who wish not to be subordinated themselves, the capacity of democratic governance structures to protect workers' well-being, the potential of such structures to enhance firm efficiency and productivity, and the principle of subsidiarity. *See* CHARTIER, *supra* note 10, at 89–107. The prudential reasons (discussed in this part) include the capacity of worker-owned firms to overcome the principal–agent problem that besets firms managed by investor-appointed executives and to mobilize local knowledge more effectively than hierarchical firms.

[80] On the provision of these sorts of remedies for past and ongoing injustice, *see* Part IV.C–E, *supra*. Radical remediation could be expected to foster democratic and worker-owned firms. But a stateless legal regime should not directly mandate the creation of democratic workplace governance structures. Doing so would violate the baseline possessory rules, by interfering with people's decisions about how justly acquired possessions, including places of work, could be used. And there is little justification for altering the baseline possessory rules so that they permitted the forcible interference with the internal operations of firms that would be required were the moral requirement of democratic firm governance to be implemented by law. (This would not be true, of course, in the case of fully consensual law—law produced by the courts or other institutions of a non-monopolistic, consensual legal regime from which voluntary exit was possible, law to which each of the members of such a regime gave actual consent; *see* Chapter 4, *supra*. My treatment of workplace-related legal rules in CHARTIER, *supra* note 10, at 89–107 is unclear on this point; I'd want it to be read as concerned exclusively with rules adopted as part of a fully consensual legal order—to enforce these rules nonconsensually would be to violate the NAM.) A further problem would obviously be the mischief likely to be perpetrated by the people responsible for the relevant legal mandates, who would be unlikely to craft standards genuinely beneficial to workers and who could be expected often to use their power to benefit themselves and the wealthy and well-connected and, even when well intentioned, to make errors with wide-ranging consequences.

people to seek to embody the values underlying a commitment to anarchism by enabling others to experience this opportunity for exploration as an occasion for greater freedom rather than subjection to local tyranny.

The proscription of aggression by just legal regimes in a stateless society would leave room for the expression of multiple lifestyle preferences (Section B). But the rules enforced by such regimes would leave space for those committed to a culture of freedom, not only from aggression but also from hierarchies and stultifying mores, to promote their goals actively (Section C). An anarchist legal order would be thoroughly hospitable to diverse kinds of personal self-expression, both by preventing aggressive restrictions on self-expression and by offering a legal framework within which nonviolent advocacy on behalf of diverse kinds of self-expression could take place (Section D).

B. Just Legal Rules and Institutions in a Stateless Society Would Leave Room for the Development and Expression of Diverse Ways of Being Human

1. *Without Compelling People to Adopt Particular Options, Just Legal Rules Would Safeguard Their Lifestyle Decisions*

Just legal rules and institutions in a stateless society would leave people free to form whatever nonaggressive social arrangements they might like and to remember and celebrate whatever narrative sources of cultural identity they might opt to embrace. Do you claim the story of the Israelites following Moses through the wilderness as your own? Are the Cluniac monks your spiritual ancestors? Do you see the Boxer Rebels as your forebears? Anarchist law of the sort I have envisioned here would leave you free to identify with them, to celebrate what you judge to be their accomplishments, to treat them as central to your own heritage—in short, to organize your life as you see fit. Just legal rules and institutions in a stateless society would leave everyone free to explore alternative lifestyles and cultural possibilities (Subsection 2), though not to use aggression to impose a lifestyle or culture on anyone else (Subsection 3). A stateless society would be a fertile environment for the discovery and display of ways of being human (Subsection 4).

2. *A Stateless Society's Legal Rules Would Create Space for Exploration*

i. People could explore varied lifestyle and cultural options in a stateless society without engaging in the kinds of conflicts over these issues that seem very typical in a statist society

Just legal rules and institutions in a stateless society would not feature the kinds of difficulties that generate perpetual conflict over lifestyle issues under the state's rule.

The existence and operation of the state provide repeated occasions for passionate disputes over spaces, artifacts, and resources (Subsubsection ii). A stateless society's legal institutions would make it possible for people to pursue alternate lifestyles and explore diverse cultural identities without the same sorts of conflicts (Subsubsection iii). These institutions could render cultural and lifestyle-related conflict in a stateless society more manageable than it might otherwise be (Subsubsection iv).

ii. The state's existence leads to unavoidable conflicts over different ways of being human

It seems clear that, in some important respects, people would be more able to preserve and share cherished lifestyles in a stateless society than they are at present.[81]

By demanding tribute from people, for instance, states claim resources their subjects could have used to preserve identity-constitutive places, objects, and traditions. But the state poses more serious problems for those who want to nourish particular ways of being.

The state's haphazard identity-preserving projects are funded in part by people—for instance, members of outsider cultural groups—who may have little interest in preserving the artifacts or lifeways on which the state focuses the resources it has acquired. In addition, even putatively liberal states frequently suppress or relocate cultural minorities, and state media and schools can operate to erase regional dialects and other signs of subcultural distinctiveness. At the same time, because governments overseeing increasingly diverse societies frequently wish to treat all cultural groups inclusively, those creating state-funded cultural projects may be pressured to create works with little or no capacity to contribute to the transmission of *any* particular cultural identity. Further, when the state claims the authority to safeguard a majority culture, it almost unavoidably also claims a hegemonic role as *interpreter* of that culture—often distorting or reconstructing it in perverse ways, or co-opting its values and symbols as sources of legitimation for state policies.

The existence of state-controlled land and other possessions and the opportunities for work with state agencies create endless occasions for conflict over cultural matters in statist societies. Which religious symbols may be displayed on public land? Will officially led prayers be permitted in state schools? Which holidays will be officially recognized? Which culturally significant dress codes will teachers, soldiers, judges, or nurses be allowed to follow? Different interest-groups with the

[81] I deliberately use the term "lifestyle" for its open-endedness. Some lifestyles will be understood by people who embrace them as inescapable, natural, and necessary components of their identities, others as quite contingent and as reflectively and deliberately adopted. By employing "lifestyles" to refer to a broad range of ways of being human, I do not intend to prejudge questions about the nature and validity of these patterns of existence.

ability to influence the state can engage in repeated contests over such matters, each seeking to ensure that the state works to preserve particular identity markers. The end result is that cultural, religious, and ethnic communities come repeatedly into conflict with each other, and that pressure to avoid any expression of distinctiveness increases.

The problem is only exacerbated when the state opts to use force not only to manage affairs on the land it claims for itself but also to constrain people's freedom with respect to admittedly *non-state* possessions in the interests of preserving or suppressing particular cultural identities. The French government's bans on the public wearing of the *burqa* and on the wearing of the *hijab* in state schools are obvious examples—they prevent people from using their own possessions in relation to their own bodies.[82] So are efforts in New York and elsewhere in the United States to use the state's claimed power to regulate land-use to prevent the construction of religious structures. In statist societies, people's peaceable attempts to express their identities and nourish their traditions can be opposed by actual or threatened state aggression. And people who have no interest in telling others how to dress or what symbols to display can be required to fund acts of cultural oppression and exclusion when authoritarians and bigots succeed in using the state apparatus to implement their preferences.

iii. A stateless society's institutions would allow people to avoid conflicts over lifestyles and cultural markers that are endemic to life under the state's rule

In a stateless society, people would obviously be free to spend their money as they chose. They would not be required to subsidize others' lifestyle preferences. They could erect monuments and houses of worship, and put iconic images on display, at their own discretion on their own possessions. They could invest in efforts designed to preserve objects and practices and memories they cherished. They could operate schools that transmitted their beliefs and habits.

[82] The motivations underlying the bans are surely complex. Some supporters doubtless favor a liberal society and see the bans as helping to protect women from confining, restrictive social mores and to foster a more open, sexually free environment. Others presumably want public space as secularized as much as possible. Others surely favor the suppression of the visible otherness of Muslim women. The point is not that the motives of those in the first category aren't generally laudable (the other two sets of motives strike me as deeply problematic); the point, rather, is that it is the presence and activity of the state, as the controller of public space, as the operator of state schools, that makes conflicts over these matters inevitable. Disputes over public apparel don't need a uniform, forcibly imposed solution, and people's decisions about their own bodies wouldn't be loci of public contestation in the same way or to the same degree if the state were out of the picture. And authorizing institutions to use force to deal with the problem of inequitable cultural forms by compelling women to remove the *burqa* or the *hijab* creates opportunities for, and tends to legitimate, extensive control over women's bodies by the legal system. It's also worth noting that feminist activists with no time for cultural repression have nonetheless rejected the bans as instances of intrusive state interference with women's bodies.

Obviously, conflicts over the proper uses of places and things with multiple cultural meanings wouldn't go away in a stateless society. However, by assigning responsibility for contested sites or objects to particular people or organizations in accordance with fair, outcome-independent rules, just legal rules and institutions in a stateless society could in some ways localize their intensity, reducing the likelihood of spillover clashes, and render them more manageable.

While people in a stateless society might still have quite decided preferences with respect to others' nonviolent actions, they would not be free to mobilize state aggression to prevent or end behavior they didn't like, nor would they be able to compel others to pay the costs of imposing their preferences on others. The absence of legal authority to (*i*) regulate behavior that isn't aggressive and (*ii*) force others to pay the cost of one's attempts to affect such behavior would likely effect a dramatic reduction in attempts to constrain others' lifestyle choices.

iv. A stateless society's legal institutions could serve to minimize culture- and lifestyle-related conflicts

Conflict over scarce state resources and state-controlled spaces makes disputes over cultural differences under the state's rule inevitable. Further conflict is likely to result whenever some people try to commandeer state resources to limit other people's lifestyle choices. By eliminating state resources and spaces as sites of conflict and denying people the opportunity to use the state to enforce their preferences regarding others' behavior, a stateless society could allow for diverse forms of cultural expression and lifestyle without occasioning the same sorts of conflicts as those to which the state's existence and operation tend to give rise.

3. *Aggression Could Not Reasonably Be Used to Promote Particular Lifestyle Options*

In a stateless society, people would be free to explore a broad range of lifestyles—and unlikely to confront many of the conflicts over convictions, values, and ways of being that the state unavoidably creates. Such a society would thus not only be free from state-related tensions that often prompt the suppression of personal and subcultural particularity but also provide more room for personal expression than a statist society. At the same time, however, it would not and could not make room for any and all practices designed, even in good faith, to preserve deeply valued mores. For a stateless society would be one in which rejecting aggression was rightly understood as a necessary prerequisite to social peace and to both personal and cultural flourishing.

In such a society, the claim that a given practice somehow supported the preservation of this or that lifestyle would obviously be insufficient to justify the practice if it involved aggressive attacks on persons or their justly claimed possessions. To take obvious examples, clitoridectomy, infibulation, and foot-binding could not be regarded simply as expressions of particular preferences, to be treated with the same deference as habits of dress and efforts directed at the preservation of historically significant monuments. As instances of aggressive force, they would clearly fall beyond the pale in a stateless society.[83] So, too, would the use of physical force to exclude people from voluntary transactional relationships, to prevent people of the purportedly wrong sort from living in particular neighborhoods, or to keep people from destroying or altering their own possessions in ways likely to eliminate or distort objects of cultural significance.

Some ways of being might not survive if those who valued them could not use aggressive force to preserve them. So be it. The institutions of a stateless society would leave room for many lifestyles and cultural patterns, but such a society obviously could not be equally welcoming to all. Only those that didn't involve aggression would be acceptable. Of course this would remove one means of preserving and transmitting some ways of being. At the same time, however, it would ensure that those embracing particular lifestyles did so voluntarily and were thus more personally invested in them—and so more likely to preserve and transmit them—than might be the case in a society in which they were maintained by force.

4. *Law Could Create the Context for the Pursuit of a Culture of Freedom in a Stateless Society*

Just legal rules and institutions would not be the mechanisms by which all social goals were directly *achieved* in a stateless society. Rather, legal rules and institutions would play crucial roles in restraining and remedying aggression, but they would therefore also create space in which people could make an enormous variety of nonaggressive choices. The freedom thus secured would enable people to develop diverse patterns of living, provided they avoided aggression against others.

While just legal rules and institutions would offer protection against the use of aggressive means to prevent someone from exploring a given lifestyle, people would be quite free to object on moral grounds to choices others made—as the underlying moral foundations of the kinds of legal rules I have defended here, in particular, should sometimes encourage them to do. And they would also be free to employ a range of nonaggressive strategies to address unfair, exclusionary, subordinative, or depriving behavior on the part of others.

[83] I prescind from those cases in which those who would otherwise clearly qualify as the victims of these aggressive acts indisputably render free and informed consent to them.

C. Just Legal Rules Would Make Possible the Promotion of Liberating Cultural Values

1. *A Stateless Society's Legal Order Would Give Cultural Anarchists Multiple Opportunities to Oppose Ways of Being That Sapped Vitality and Undermined Freedom*

While just legal rules and institutions in a stateless society would create space for the exploration of diverse ways of being human, the *values underlying* a commitment to anarchism might be friendly to a narrower range of lifestyles, subcultures, and practices. Cultural anarchism would certainly not be inhospitable to community as such (Subsection 2), but it would unequivocally reject authoritarian, racist, nativist, nationalist, sexist, heterosexist, and other unreasonable ways of structuring communities, even when they were nonviolent (Subsection 3). Cultural anarchists would obviously challenge some kinds of family practices, but not others (Subsection 4). Cultural anarchism's opposition to subordination, deprivation, and exclusion would lead it to oppose a variety of lifestyles, but many different ways of being (some unchanged, some transformed) would surely persist in a stateless society, even one suffused with cultural-anarchist values (Subsection 5). Cultural anarchists, operating within the constraints of the just legal rules of a stateless society, could foster the emergence of a culture of freedom creatively and nonaggressively (Subsection 6).

2. *Affirming Individuality Is Quite Compatible with Affirming Non-Oppressive Community and Relationship*

Cultural anarchism is rooted in a recognition of the distinctive and irreplaceable value of particular persons. But this grounding need not entail any deep-seated conflict with the affirmation of ways of being involving densely textured cultural identities. It is quite possible to value the dignity and rights of particular persons and to decline to be subsumed by any group to which one belongs while cherishing a sense of place, treasuring the contributions historical predecessors have made to one's identity, and recognizing the importance—indeed, the inescapability—of learning about the world and one's place in it from one's traditions. Cultural anarchism need involve no commitment to a Promethean view of autonomy, an existentialist vision of self-creation, or a naïvely foundationalist rejection of tradition. One can be a cultural anarchist without aspiring to be the deracinated individual of philosophical fantasy.

Cultural anarchism is animated first and foremost by a desire, positively, to see the full range of human possibilities explored and put on display and, negatively, to avoid the suppression of dignity, freedom, creativity, and uniqueness that occurs when people are subjected to the whims of hierarchs, experts, bluenoses, busybodies, and paternalists. In short, cultural anarchists "don't want to push other people around ... and ... don't want to be pushed around themselves."[84] Seeking neither to push nor to be pushed is quite compatible with commitment to a wide range of specific lifestyles. And it is quite compatible with identifying with a particular tradition or community or embracing a distinctive way of life, provided one can do so without pushing or being pushed around.

3. A *Cultural-Anarchist Politics Would Reject Nonviolent as well as Aggressive Authoritarianism*

i. Cultural anarchists would act within just legal constraints to oppose lifestyles that subordinate, exclude, and impoverish

If support for cultural anarchism need not mean opposition to collective identity in principle, it is still certainly the case that it *would* mean rejection of particular *sorts* of lifestyles. Cultural anarchism will certainly prompt rejection, for instance, of *racism, sexism, heterosexism*,[85] and multiple varieties of *nationalism* (Subsubsection ii).[86] Cultural anarchists would obviously welcome the fact that simply enforcing a consistent requirement of nonaggression would ensure that ways of engaging in economic activity misshapen by ethnic, gender-based, nationality-based, and other forms of prejudice tended to wither on the vine (Subsubsection iii), but they would also take full advantage of the options afforded by just legal rules to engage in nonviolent protests of various kinds designed to challenge discriminatory practices (Subsubsection iv). The adoption of cultural-anarchist values would tend to undermine statist and racist varieties of nationalism (Subsubsection v) and both in-group and out-group mistreatment (Subsubsection vi). Cultural anarchism would be perfectly hospitable to cultural variety, but strongly opposed to authoritarian or exclusionary lifestyles (Subsubsection vii).

ii. The cultural anarchist should and could effectively oppose arbitrary discrimination

Racialized distributions of wealth and social influence are often rooted in past acts of aggression—enslavement and dispossession are particularly clear instances. Inequities related to gender, sexual orientation, and geographic origin are maintained

[84] Letter from Murray N. Rothbard to David Bergland (June 5, 1986), *quoted in* Justin Raimondo, An Enemy of the State: The Life of Murray N. Rothbard 263–64 (2000).

[85] *Cf.* Gary Chartier, Comment, *Natural Law, Same-Sex Marriage, and the Politics of Virtue*, 48 UCLA L. Rev. 1593 (2001).

[86] These are illustrative examples: similar considerations would obviously apply in relation to discussion of other forms of irrational prejudice.

and replicated both by legal privilege—a kind of institutionalized aggression—and by repeated individual acts of aggression. A narrowly political anarchism will have good reason to want to see such acts of aggression remedied. But it is quite possible to be a racist, a sexist, a nativist, or a heterosexist without engaging in ongoing acts of aggression—to avoid aggressive violence while nourishing prejudice and fostering and engaging in bias-based discrimination. One may quite nonaggressively develop and cling to a sense of oneself defined by identification with one group of people on the basis of their race, gender, sexual orientation, or geographic origin and rejection of others on the basis of theirs. A narrowly political anarchism may have nothing in particular to say about this sort of nonviolent stance. But it would fall foul of a more broad cultural anarchism.

The underlying sense of the moral equality of persons that is a central justification for anarchism's rejection of statism seems presumptively inconsistent with prejudice rooted in ethnicity, gender, or sexual orientation. This sort of bias is also inconsistent with the appreciation for human particularity and diversity that cultural anarchism embraces, since it is rooted in the unwillingness to see others as the specific persons they are. And, of course, even if it is itself expressed nonviolently, racism, sexism, nativism, and heterosexism can all clearly prompt aggression.

None of this means that the cultural anarchist would judge it appropriate to use *force* to punish the prejudiced person for thinking bad thoughts, to make the racist associate with those toward whom she is bigoted, or to prevent anyone from catering nonviolently to racist, sexist, nativist, or heterosexist tastes. *Legal requirements* that people make unbiased decisions about whether to transact with others would be inconsistent with the baseline rules (except when imposed only on the consenting, and doubtless those inclined to consent to such requirements, or to procedures and institutions generating such requirements, would be unlikely to engage in arbitrary discrimination in the first place). But just legal rules in a stateless society would both encourage an end to discrimination and facilitate efforts to undermine and oppose it.

iii. Just legal rules and institutions in a stateless society would reduce the likelihood of discrimination without interfering with freedom of association

Legal standards embodying the baseline rules themselves would tend directly to undermine discriminatory behavior by compelling would-be discriminators to internalize the cost of acting on their biases.[87] Irrational prejudice is costly: the refusal to work with, offer work to, or otherwise transact with others based on such irrelevant characteristics as ethnicity, gender, geographic origin, and sexual orientation is likely to reduce the discriminator's income—unless, of course, legal requirements or threats of

[87] *Cf.* Gary S. Becker, The Economics of Discrimination (1957); Thomas Sowell, Markets and Minorities 19–33 (1981).

extralegal violence *mandate* discrimination (nonviolent pressure to engage in irrational discrimination is likely to be unsuccessful both because of responsive nonviolent protest and because voluntary cartels are unsustainable over the long term, especially when there are consistent countervailing economic pressures to be rational).

Such unjust legal requirements have in fact—in the Jim Crow South and apartheid-era South Africa, for instance—played crucial roles in ensuring the persistence of discriminatory regimes, given the incentives that would otherwise dispose people to defect from discriminatory agreements (implicit or explicit). Such requirements are, of course, themselves inconsistent with the baseline rules, and would thus not be upheld by any just legal regime in a stateless society. As a result, those who sought to discriminate would consistently suffer losses that would discourage them from continuing to discriminate and that would lead to the discontinuation of firms that persisted in acting on the basis of prejudice.

Enforcing legal standards embodying the baseline rules would also mean the elimination of a broad range of privileges upheld by the state. Such privileges tend to make and keep people poor. They are often in fact, whether or not in intention, discriminatory, falling especially heavily on members of outsider groups, so that removing them would itself be an instance of moving beyond discrimination. And they tend to reinforce the subordination, in workplaces and elsewhere, of people who are predictably subjected to prejudice-based discrimination. Removing them would foster greater economic empowerment on the part of such people. It would thus reduce the *impact* of ongoing discrimination—since potential victims would be less vulnerable to the economic consequences of discrimination if they had more resources—and to reduce the *frequency* of ongoing discrimination—since the increased resources available to potential victims would make discriminating against them more costly.

Remedying past and continuing aggression would also play a key role in addressing the problem of discrimination, to the extent that those subjected to large-scale injustice, or their successors-in-interest, were potential targets of irrational prejudice. And, given the extent of systemic aggression and individual acts of aggression rooted in racism, sexism, nativism, and heterosexism, the provision of remedies for these kinds of aggression could have quite substantial consequences.[88] It could be expected to affect both the immediate well-being of those subjected to aggression and the economic environment within which ongoing efforts to preserve racism,

[88] *Cf.* ROTHBARD, *supra* note 17, at 73–74 (1982) (arguing that freed slaves should have received "forty acres and a mule," taken from former slave masters, to compensate them for the unjust expropriation of their labor) (citing CLAUDE F. OUBRE, FORTY ACRES AND A MULE: THE FREEDMAN'S BUREAU AND BLACK LAND OWNERSHIP (1970)); Roderick T. Long, *Comment*, AUSTRO-ATHENIAN EMPIRE, May 19, 2010, http://aaeblog.com/2010/05/19/electoral-race/comment-page-1/#comment-356413 (arguing that "[t]he distribution of property in, *e.g.*, North Carolina was the result of systematic government intervention on behalf of whites at the expense of blacks—not just during slavery but for a hundred years thereafter. I'd say this left blacks with some credible claims against white property.").

patriarchy, national superiority, and heteronormativity took place—and so the frequency of ongoing discriminatory conduct.

iv. Just legal rules and institutions in a stateless society would facilitate effective nonviolent responses to discriminatory conduct

At the same time as just legal rules and institutions in a stateless society directly undermined discrimination, such rules and institutions would also create a framework for further action designed to prevent, end, or remedy discriminatory conduct. These rules and institutions would make it possible for cultural anarchists to use multiple nonaggressive forms of social pressure—shunning, public shaming, peaceful boycotts, nonviolent sit-ins,[89] and peaceful protests and strikes—to undermine unfair, bias-motivated conduct.

v. Cultural-anarchist values would be inconsistent with statist nationalism, but not necessarily with localism

While some kinds of group bias are obvious morally objectionable and inconsistent with cultural-anarchist values, there is no obvious incompatibility between embracing cultural anarchism and identifying with a particular place—provided one simply values its treasures for their own sake, or prizes its contribution to making one who one is, rather than judging other places to be objectively inferior. G. K. Chesterton and Bill Kauffman provide obvious and appealing models for an admirable localism. Conventional nationalism is another sort of creature altogether, however.

For those whose identities aren't constituted by relationships with particular places, nationalism even of the most benign variety may seem quite arbitrary. But nationalism characteristically involves loyalty, not to a revered place as such, but rather to the nation-state. The anarchist can hardly welcome a willingness to cheer for "my country, right or wrong," not only because to support wrongdoing is to risk moral corruption but also because "my country" really means, not people and places dear to my heart, but rather the implacable apparatus of the state.

Nationalism too often finds expression in aggression, especially militaristic aggression—whether of an irredentist variety or in support of state expansion. Of course it need not. But cultural anarchists will be wary of its capacity to underwrite violence.

They will also look askance at nationalism's frequent valorization of state boundaries, which often fail to track culture or geography meaningfully. There may be little connection between the actual people and places on which one's loyalty

[89] Some critics will maintain that sit-ins are inherently aggressive. Charles Johnson has responded effectively to the charge of trespassing against sit-in protestors. *See, e.g.*, Charles W. Johnson, *Opposing the Civil Rights Act Means Opposing Civil Rights? It Just Ain't So*, The Freeman: Ideas on Liberty, Sept. 2010, at 4, *available at* http://www.thefreemanonline.org/departments/it-just-aint-so/opposing-the-civil-rights-act-means-opposing-civil-rights; Charles W. Johnson, *Comment*, Austro-Athenian Empire, May 19, 2010, http://aaeblog.com/2010/05/19/electoral-race/comment-page-1/#comment-356416.

focuses and the borders of one's state. Similarly: sensitive to particularity and diversity, cultural anarchists will also recognize that the geographic territory claimed by nation-states is characteristically home to people with varied identities. Loyalty to the nation often seems to mean loyalty to the majority in a particular region, or perhaps to a minority that holds the reins of state power. Nationalism too frequently seems to involve the erasure of the particularity of those who don't identify with the majority's culture—including members of minority cultures, people who identify with multiple cultures, people linked with cultures embraced primarily by others outside the nation's boundaries, and people in some sense within the majority culture who seek in one way or another to transform it.

The territory claimed by a large nation-state may arguably be not only too arbitrarily demarcated but also too extensive to provide a manageable focus for personal loyalty. A genuinely local perspective may often prove more compatible with human-scale attachments. This does not mean, of course, that one can or should ignore the role of others who are not local in shaping one's identity and experience. The Loiner may recognize London as a world quite different from his or her own while still acknowledging that Trafalgar Square memorializes events without which life in Leeds might be very different indeed. But this need not provide an opportunity to smuggle nationalism in through the proverbial backdoor, for we can reasonably treasure our connections with geographically dispersed people and places—ones it would never occur to anyone to link with us under the same national umbrella—that have helped to make us who we are.

vi. Cultural anarchism could be expected to address in-group as well as out-group mistreatment

A just system of law in a stateless society will leave space for the cultural anarchist to challenge not only mistreatment of those outside a given group but also mistreatment of a group's own members. This sort of mistreatment is especially likely, of course, to be focused on members of particularly vulnerable subgroups—women, children, the elderly. When people within a group are subjected to physical aggression and are unable to seek legal redress, proxies could, as I suggested earlier, act for them (though there would obviously have to be safeguards here designed to prevent opportunism and genuinely unwanted representation). But even when repression is nonviolent, the broad range of nonviolent responses a just legal system could and would leave open to cultural anarchists would be available to foster liberalization and the decent treatment of the vulnerable.

vii. Cultural anarchism would lead people to oppose those lifestyles and cultural forms that are destructive or that involve systematic unfairness

Its regard for individuality and moral equality need not dispose cultural anarchism to oppose all organized traditions and ways of life, but only ones that deny individuality and fail to treat people with respect. Racism, nationalism, sexism, and heterosexism, for instance, are ways of being, and of understanding oneself, that are not only limiting to those who embrace them but potentially very harmful to others—perhaps leading to aggression and certainly leading to conduct that is patently unfair.

Cultural anarchists would actively discourage racism, nationalism, sexism, and heterosexism. And, more fundamentally, the widespread adoption of freedom-oriented cultural values would make it difficult for anyone to sustain a sense of self rooted in illusions of group superiority or sustained by exclusivity and rejection. Thus, just legal rules and cultural change would work hand in hand both to undermine discriminatory attitudes and to facilitate nonaggressive challenges to discriminatory practices. Cultural-anarchist values would lead people to oppose discriminatory ways of life nonaggressively, both through various sorts of protest and through the maintenance of counter-aggressive legal standards that would keep prejudiced people from being insulated against the effects of acting on their prejudices.

4. *Whether Cultural Anarchists Challenged Intra-Familial Dynamics Would Depend on How Families Embodied and Transmitted Their Values*

Whatever the fate of nationalist, racist, patriarchal, and similar lifestyles in a stateless society, tensions surrounding families would doubtless be unavoidable. A society that tolerated aggression against children would hardly count as anarchist (insofar as even narrowly political anarchism rejects aggression). And legal mechanisms could readily be developed that would make it possible for people to protect children from aggression within their families and communities.

But of course families unavoidably shape children in innumerable nonviolent ways, and there would surely be those of a culturally anarchist bent who would challenge what they (perhaps rightly) saw as illiberal indoctrination of children by parents. In a stateless society, not only particular persons but also families and other groups in search of mutually reinforcing support for their distinctive worldviews and lifeways could obviously craft communities, territorial or virtual, in which their critical mass could allow them to counter the effects on each other of what they saw as objectionable elements of the wider culture. At the same time, it is easy to see that a society that created space for diversity would, indeed, render it difficult for any subcultural group to ensure wholesale identification with its traditions by all of its members.

Without state force at its disposal, a subcultural group that sought to shield its children from wider cultural influences would obviously find it very difficult to do so. And those who sought to counter illiberal indoctrination would have multiple mechanisms at their disposal to undermine clannish exclusion and foster awareness of the wider cultural world.

5. *Cultural Anarchism Would Unavoidably Undermine Some Ways of Life, but It Would Leave Many Intact and Transform Others*

Cultural anarchism would tend to militate against a range of habits and practices that might be seen by some people as integral to their collective identities. Identities of some sorts—I have already instanced racism, sexism, heterosexism, and many sorts of nationalism, but there are obviously others—would not be likely to survive in an anarchist culture, in which they could not depend on state subsidies and other kinds of state violence. Others would persist, and perhaps even thrive, while being transformed by anarchist attitudes that undermine subordination and exclusion. And it would be unfair to deny that the loss of some cultural forms would be a genuine loss, in the sense that it would deprive people of patterns of existence and ways of understanding themselves and others that offered meaning and order to their lives, even if those forms could not be expected to persist without state support. Those committed not only to political but also to cultural anarchism must remember that there are costs associated with the embrace of freedom.

But this is hardly reason to treat cultural anarchism as promoting cultural decline. No more than political anarchism need cultural anarchism be seen as requiring or promoting the abandonment of all sources of identity. Those that respect freedom and personal particularity can thrive in an anarchist culture. To be sure, the very capacity of some lifeways to foster meaningfulness and order may be seen as depending on their immunity to criticism and their appearance of inevitability, and they would lack both in a culture of freedom. But an awareness of possibilities for improvement and a denial of uncritical regard to previously established cultural authorities can be quite compatible with continued esteem for and identification with traditions and communities and ways of life that offer people meaning and identity.

6. *Cultural Anarchism Would Seek Ways of Opposing Nonviolent Subordination, Exclusion, and Deprivation within the Framework Provided by the Rules Enforced by Just Legal Regimes*

At least as I've framed it here, anarchism makes sense in light of a commitment to moral equality and an opposition to ruling and being ruled, as well as a rejection of aggression. While these values issue first of all in opposition to aggression, an opposition that would be embodied in just legal rules and institutions in a stateless society, they are also reasonably expressed in opposition to destructive cultural patterns—notably subordination, exclusion, and deprivation.

Anarchist opposition to these patterns—cultural anarchism—wouldn't lead to the rejection or undermining of community, but it *would* prompt efforts to craft healthy communities, in which individuality was respected, and in which such denials of individuality as racism, nationalism, sexism, heterosexism, and paternalism were rejected—and challenged in appropriately nonaggressive ways. Despite cultural anarchism's challenge to undesirable cultural patterns, a society in which cultural-anarchist values were widely embraced would surely still be home to many different ways of being human.

D. An Anarchist Legal Order Would Encourage the Expression of Human Variety

A stateless society's legal order would create space for many different kinds of identity-maintaining ways of being human—more, in general, than a society in which aggression was legitimized and force used to exclude, to discriminate, and to force disfavored lifestyles and cultural identities underground. Only those identities maintained through the use of force would be excluded from such a society, and we would be, I believe, well rid of them. A stateless society infused with culturally anarchist values would likely be free of such sources of identity as racism, sexism, heterosexism, and nationalism. But this kind of society could still welcome local loyalty, and any number of other distinctive ways of being human compatible with regard for personal dignity and freedom and the diverse forms of human flourishing.

VI. JUST LEGAL RULES IN A STATELESS SOCIETY WOULD CONDUCE TO POSITIVE BUT NONAGGRESSIVE SOCIAL CHANGE

Defenders of the state often suppose that the occurrence of positive social change depends on the state's capacity to use aggressive force against people—to punish them retributively and deterrently, to compel them to cooperate even when they're not being aggressive, to invade their homes and places of work and voluntary associations. The underlying values reflected in the kinds of legal rules I've attempted to describe and defend here, especially such values as the essential equality of moral patients, militates against deprivation, subordination, and exclusion. But these vices can be confronted effectively without the use of aggressive force—through securing restitution for unjust harms to bodies and possessions, ensuring that everyone's legal authority is equal, and engaging in nonviolent activism. The result: workplaces can be rendered more humane, wealth redistributed, deprivation minimized, and diversity provided substantial opportunities to flourish. A stateless society may not qualify as perfect, as a full-blown utopia, but it can be an exciting, thriving place in which people, working peacefully and cooperatively, can continue to make positive social change happen.

This positive vision of a society rooted in peaceful, voluntary cooperation, a vision marked by rejection of exclusion, subordination, and deprivation, helps to highlight the consonance of the vision of anarchism I've outlined here with the traditional concerns of the Left. In Chapter 7, I will explain why the account of stateless law and politics I have offered here can reasonably be seen as idiosyncratically, but authentically, leftist, anti-capitalist, and socialist.

7

Situating Liberation

I. JUST LEGAL RULES AND INSTITUTIONS IN A STATELESS SOCIETY WOULD EMBODY LEFTIST, ANTICAPITALIST, AND SOCIALIST VALUES

The legal and political project I have sought to advance here—the project of fostering a society rooted in peaceful, voluntary cooperation—is leftist, anticapitalist, and socialist. It is leftist because it is motivated by the crucial leftist concerns of opposition to subordination, exclusion, deprivation, and war (Part II). It is anticapitalist because just legal rules and institutions in a stateless society would eliminate the privileges and undermine the social dominance of capitalists (Part III). It can be seen as socialist because of its continuities with the commitments of those antistatist socialists who sought to address "the social question" and to foster genuinely social cooperation decisively and radically (Part IV). By combining distinctive versions of leftism, anticapitalism, and socialism with radical antistatism, it represents a pronounced challenge to the political and legal status quo (Part V).

II. THE PROJECT OF CREATING A STATELESS SOCIETY WITH JUST LEGAL RULES AND INSTITUTIONS IS A LEFTIST PROJECT

A. A Stateless Society's Legal Order Can Embody Leftist Concerns without the Need for an Aggressive State Apparatus

The vision of an anarchist legal and political order I've been developing is authentically leftist. At least as a first pass (and painfully aware that "leftist" is an essentially contested concept), I suggest that an authentically leftist position might be thought to be marked by a variety of features that also characterize the account of anarchism on offer in this book, including opposition to subordination (Section B), to exclusion (Section C), and to deprivation (Section D), whether or not these inequities are rooted in aggression, as well as to aggression itself, particularly the aggression of war

(Section E).[1] The program for law and politics in a stateless society I have sketched here is thus recognizably leftist (Section F).

B. Concern with Subordination Helps to Render the Position I Defend Here Leftist

Subordination may involve one person's persistent (frequently, though not necessarily, institutional) domination of another through actual or threatened infringement on any of the varieties of freedom—through actual or threatened force in the case of freedom from aggression, or through any conduct inconsistent with the principles of practical reasonableness in the case of social freedom. The position I defend here offers a plausible explanation of subordination's morally objectionable character: it is inconsistent with the Principle of Fairness, since most of us would prefer not to be subordinated, and also, at least if it involves bodily aggression, with the Principle of Respect.

Note that the question, *Is there a relationship of subordination in a given case?* doesn't determine the answer to the question, *If there is subordination in this case, what is the appropriate remedy?* I emphasize this because the NAM constrains the *kinds* of remedies that might be appropriate for unreasonable subordination.

Someone who endorses the NAM may be nervous about the notion that subordination (or domination, or hierarchy—not all hierarchies are subordinative, but hierarchy and subordination are frequently entangled) might be exercised economically or psychically. Clearly delimiting subordination, so that it's clearly understood as physical in nature, provides a check on the use of physical force. By contrast, appearing to conflate different kinds of subordination might be thought to run the risk of justifying the use of force to respond to non-forcible exercises of influence.

But this worry is ill-founded, for several reasons.

[1] A not-dissimilar analysis of the heart of leftist values is provided by Jesse Graham, Jonathan Haidt & Brian A. Nosek, *Liberals and Conservatives Rely on Different Sets of Moral Foundations*, 96 J. PERS. & SOC. PSYC. 1029 (2009); *cf.* JONATHAN HAIDT, THE RIGHTEOUS MIND (2012). The concern with deprivation tracks liberals' tendency to focus on care/harm (because the deprived are vulnerable), fairness/unfairness (because deprivation often results from unfair behavior), and liberty/oppression (because deprivation often leads to violations of social freedom). The concern with subordination tracks the same concerns: subordination evokes care because the dignity of those who are subordinated is often violated; it's a fairness-related concern because people often treat subordinates in ways they wouldn't want to be treated themselves, and subordination clearly depends on and (as regards social freedom) involves oppression. The dignity of the excluded is similarly adversely affected in ways that understandably evoke care; exclusion often seems to depend on arbitrary factors on which it would arguably be unfair to focus; and exclusion is often a predicate for subordination, and therefore occasions concern about oppression (understood, again, as a denial of social freedom). Concern with aggression fairly readily emerges from a commitment to care (aggression is hugely harmful). To the extent that it's an exercise in bullying, it also likely triggers concerns with fairness and oppression.

(*i*) Legally remediable aggression can be seen to underlie many other forms of domination that do not themselves involve physical force. Persistent aggression against women in a given social environment may lead to a climate of fear and submission on the part of many women, even in relationships with men who have not themselves behaved aggressively and might not threaten to do so or be inclined to do so. The knowledge that a strike might be broken through the use of aggression might dispose workers in a morally objectionable work setting to avoid initiating the strike in the first place. And so on. An important aspect of the objectionable nature of the subordination in these cases will be, precisely, the existence of this background of aggression.

(*ii*) Someone who acknowledges that subordination comes in different forms need not maintain that all of these forms merit the same kind of remediation. Being on the left means being opposed to subordination, but it needn't mean supposing that all sorts of subordination should be dealt with in the same way. There is nothing inconsistent about holding both that workers in a given firm are dominated in a morally objectionable way by managers and that this morally objectionable domination does not on its own in any way justify the use of physical force against the managers. Acknowledging the reality of subordination as morally objectionable need not involve erasing moral differences among kinds of subordination or responses to them.

Just legal institutions in a stateless society would, as I have already noted, undermine subordination in several complementary ways. They would ensure that violence was not available as a tool of subordination. They would remove the support for hierarchy provided by privilege, thus making it easier for people to craft and sustain nonauthoritarian forms of association. And they would make it easier for people to use nonaggressive social pressure to resist and challenge hierarchies of all sorts.

C. The Position I Defend Here Is Leftist in Virtue of Its Opposition to Exclusion

A position would not be recognizably leftist if it were unconcerned about exclusion, which can be clearly and helpfully addressed by the anarchist legal and political position I have sought to defend here.

Some person, A, is excluded from a group when it is made clear that she does not belong to the group, that she is entitled neither to the material incidents of membership nor to the recognition, regard, and respect associated with belonging. Anyone who is not willing as a general rule to be excluded arbitrarily—which is to say, almost anyone—will be precluded by the Principle of Fairness, again as a general rule, from excluding others in this way. And the Principle of Fairness will provide further reason to avoid arbitrary exclusion because of its effects on third parties. (Regarding this latter point: suppose, for instance, that a hospital excludes an excellent surgeon from its staff because of her religion. Patients who might otherwise have benefited from the surgeon's services, and receive a noticeably lower quality of care because of her absence from the staff, will have good reason to reject the hospital's exclusionary action, and hospital decision makers will act unreasonably if they do not take the interests of these patients into account.)

Unavoidably, some intimate relationships exclude: close friendships and monogamous partnerships are obvious examples. This kind of exclusion is consistent with the Principle of Fairness, and no credible leftist position will seek to eradicate the particularity of these relationships. While it will be difficult to articulate any bright-line rule regarding reasonable and unreasonable exclusion, apart from the general one that exclusion is permissible only when consistent with the Principle of Fairness, at least two kinds of limits on morally permissible exclusion can reasonably be defended.

(*i*) Even when particular intimate subcommunities justly exclude someone—for the simple reason that they would cease to be the kinds of communities they are if they weren't strictly limited in size—there should clearly be room for her in the broader community of which they are components. She should clearly be welcome there, clearly included there.

(*ii*) When justifiable exclusion occurs, it ought not to reflect false beliefs about or unreasonable reactions to some group to which the excluded person belongs. Perhaps A acts reasonably in declining to marry *B* because of, say, important differences in the ways in which *B* and A understand the nature of marriage, differences which might emerge from *B*'s membership in a particular group with a tradition of viewing marital relationships in a certain way. But surely this is quite different from A's declining to marry B either because of (*a*) the fact that certain visible members of *B*'s group hold beliefs about marriage, even if (1) A does not know that *B* holds these beliefs or (2) *B* credibly denies holding these beliefs, or (*b*) A holds to a visceral prejudice against members of *B*'s group, believing, say, that cohabitation with a member of this group would render A unclean.

A credibly leftist position, then, will oppose exclusion-in-general, treating exceptions as reasonable only (roughly) when they don't involve exclusion from more comprehensive communities and relationships and only when they are not rooted in false beliefs or unreasonable reactions. Because the Principle of Fairness grounds clear moral opposition to exclusion, the position I defend here should be seen, again, as recognizably leftist.

As with subordination, it is important to emphasize that treating exclusion as morally objectionable does not determine what counts as an appropriate remedy for morally unjustifiable exclusion. It is not necessary to justify exclusion as reasonable or morally appropriate, all things considered, to object to the use of physical force as a remedy for exclusion. A broad range of nonaggressive strategies can be effective and appropriate in particular cases. Thus, just institutions in a stateless society would not compel people to associate involuntarily. However, they would protect people against violent barriers to association; eliminate the privileges that reduce the costs of exclusion to the excluders; and create safe, free spaces in which people could undermine the perceived legitimacy of exclusion by creating inclusive social forms and putting them on display and in which they could challenge the unreasonableness of exclusionary practices through multiple forms of nonviolent protest, while exploring diverse ways of being human and embracing varied group identities (provided they were not aggressive).

D. The Antistatist Position I Defend Here Is Leftist because It Is Concerned with Deprivation

A recognizably leftist position must be concerned with deprivation, as is the view I advocate here.

Someone can be said to suffer from deprivation if she lacks the resources needed for health, personal dignity, and participation in the life of her society. Deprivation in this sense has been a persistent concern of the modern political left—a concern clearly given robust support by the moral position I have defended here and thus one integral to the legal and political position that flows from it.

In virtue of the Principle of Fairness, there will obviously be reason to be concerned about deprivation to the extent that it is a product of unjust dispossession, engrossment, or privilege: people fully capable in principle of providing for themselves are persistently subjected to deprivation when the products of their labor are expropriated and redistributed to the wealthy and well-connected, frequently by the state. But the Principle of Fairness also suggests that someone's economic insecurity, whatever its source, is a consideration counting independently in favor of providing her with assistance.[2]

The rules enforced by just legal regimes in a stateless society would foster effective responses to deprivation. The dramatic reduction or elimination of economic insecurity and vulnerability could be achieved by means of the redistribution of

[2] Just how much it counts will vary from situation to situation, of course. Duties of benevolence are imperfect duties without specifiable recipients, and some people's choices may on occasion mitigate, even if they do not eliminate, their claims on others.

wealth, achieved not through top-down mandates aiming at predefined end-states, but rather through the provision of remedies for past injustice; the eradication of ongoing legally embodied privilege; solidaristic giving; and peaceful, voluntary exchange. A history of aggression and collusion with (or sponsorship of) tyranny on the part of economically influential people vitiates the legitimacy of the titles to land and to other assets conferred on these people by the state. And this means, in turn, that the homesteading of these assets by workers and others, an effective remedy for deprivation in some cases, can be entirely appropriate. Deprivation can also be challenged by eliminating expensive licensing requirements that enhance the economic well- being of well-connected groups while harming both the public and poor people who don't belong to the privileged groups. A just legal order would help in multiple ways to create institutional environments conducive both to the relief of particular instances of deprivation and to the minimization of future deprivation.[3]

E. The Antistatist Position I Defend Here Is Leftist because of Its Opposition to War and War-Like Aggression

Credibly leftist positions have consistently been concerned with war. Even if not pacifist, they have treated war as a great and terrible disaster and the initiation of war, and other kinds of war-like aggression, as a great wrong. The anarchist position I have outlined here squarely embraces this leftist commitment.

(*i*) It does so, fundamentally, because the NAM rules out aggressive warfare, which necessarily violates the prohibition on purposefully and instrumentally causing harm. The prohibition is not limited to warfare by the state, of course: it would be wrong on the same basis for people acting under the umbrellas of associations and communities in a stateless society to engage in war-like aggression.

(*ii*) More broadly, the position I am seeking to defend embraces and supports the leftist opposition to war because it is antistatist, whether the NAM alone is sufficient to rule out the state or not. The state's war-making efforts depend on its ability to exact tribute, conscript, misdirect research funding, borrow at will, and create fiat money to facilitate its war-making efforts, and to eliminate this ability is in large measure to eliminate the state itself.

State actors pass on the costs of their aggressive choices to the ordinary people who will pay for those choices in money and in blood. And war is, in turn, as Randolph Bourne famously said, the health of the state: in war-time, states aggregate power to themselves with abandon and find excuses to ride roughshod over dissenters,

[3] *See* Chapter 6.III, *supra*.

and they decline to give up this power even after a return to peace. Thus, anyone opposed to war ought to be opposed to the state, just as anyone opposed to the state ought to be opposed to war. (The evil of war-making doesn't justify the use of aggressive force against the state; the way to end its wars is to defund it, delegitimize it, and refuse to participate in its military.)

Because opposition to aggressive war is a defining leftist commitment, and because anarchism is deeply consonant with that commitment, the constraints on militarism implied by acceptance of the NAM provide further reason to see the account of stateless law I have offered here as promoting a clearly leftist project (of course, the opposition to imperial ambition and concern for the vulnerable that mark opposition to war are also pretty clearly leftist positions).[4] By ruling out aggression, the requirements of practical reasonableness deny moral legitimacy to war and war-like violence. And by ruling out the state, just legal rules in a stateless society, rooted in these requirements, would reduce the risk of war and other forms of systematic aggression. In both ways, then, the position I seek to defend here can be seen as responsive to a central leftist concern.

F. The Anarchist Vision Delineated Here Is Recognizably Leftist

The familiar left–right distinction began in pre-Revolutionary France, with parliamentary supporters of the king sitting on the right in the National Assembly and his opponents on the left. It seems reasonable to say, in continuity with initial usage, that a position recognizably leftist is fundamentally concerned with the protection of the weak against the strong, the marginalized against the established, victims against aggressors, the unprivileged against the privileged.

More specifically, we might say that a position qualifies credibly as a leftist position if it (*i*) involves clear moral objection to subordinating others, to excluding them from community membership, to tolerating their deprivation, and to subjecting them to aggressive violence and (*ii*) grounds morally appropriate institutional responses to these sorts of wrongs. The position I have sought to defend here does both. It explains why subordination, exclusion, deprivation, and martial aggression are wrong. And it explains why institutions grounded in the principles in virtue of which these social phenomena are wrong could preclude some of their manifestations in principle and effectively undermine others. Thus, it's reasonable to regard this position as located on the political Left.

To be sure, not all those who might self-identify as leftists would acknowledge just the commitments I have identified as characteristic of the Left. And many of those

[4] This is not, obviously, to deny that there have been lots of principled opponents of war who have been in some sense conservatives; *cf.* BILL KAUFFMANN, AIN'T MY AMERICA: THE LONG, NOBLE HISTORY OF ANTIWAR CONSERVATISM AND MIDDLE-AMERICAN ANTI-IMPERIALISM (2008).

associated with the Left might go on to hold particular positions about the most effective or just ways of achieving leftist goals quite inconsistent with those I have defended here. Some might argue, for instance, that a position was not authentically leftist if it failed to involve recourse to the state or the use of physical force to prevent subordination, exclusion, or deprivation. This seems to me to be a *possible* development of leftism, but not a necessary one. One could surely embrace key leftist values while rejecting aggression (as I understand it) and denying legitimacy to the state.

One reason it might seem especially appropriate to do so is the degree to which the state is deeply implicated in the structures of subordination, impoverishment, and aggression antistate and pro-state leftists both reject. State-secured privileges and state-sanctioned dispossession play an enormous role in underwriting the various social inequities leftists rightly protest. The elimination of state-secured privilege, the removal of the threat of state aggression as a backstop for privilege, and the rectification of state-tolerated and state-perpetrated abuses would play an enormous role in effecting liberation.

Opposing subordination, exclusion, deprivation, and war means opposing what the state is doing at present. But it also means opposing the characteristic tendency of state action for millennia. It would seem, at minimum, enormously difficult to cabin the options available to state actors in ways that would prevent them from seeking and conferring the privileges leftists should oppose and engaging in the dispossession and other kinds of violence leftists should reject. Thus, the simplest way to eliminate the privileges and to minimize the likelihood of systematic dispossession and war is to eliminate the state apparatus itself: embracing anarchism is an effective means of realizing key leftist goals.

Another source of consonance between leftism and anarchism: the same moral principles that drive opposition to the state's oppressive power can provide good reason for challenging social inequities. The idea of *equality of authority*—the idea that no one has any inherent or natural right to govern anyone else—provides a particularly good example.[5] This idea is simultaneously a source of support for anarchism and for leftism. It is a source of support for anarchism because it undermines the claims of state actors to rights others lack. And it is a source of support for leftism because it would seem oddly inconsistent for someone who supported equality of authority to be concerned about subordination, exclusion, and deprivation when they result from aggression while treating them as unworthy of concern when they resulted from arbitrary, unfair, but nonaggressive conduct.[6]

[5] *See* Roderick T. Long, *Equality: The Unknown Ideal*, MISES DAILY, Oct. 16, 2001, http://www.mises.org/story/804.

[6] *See* Charles W. Johnson, *Libertarianism through Thick and Thin, in* MARKETS NOT CAPITALISM: INDIVIDUALIST ANARCHISM AGAINST BOSSES, INEQUALITY, CORPORATE POWER, AND STRUCTURAL POVERTY 131 (Gary Chartier & Charles W. Johnson eds., 2011) [*hereinafter* MARKETS NOT CAPITALISM].

A related link between leftism and the kind of anarchist project made possible by the kind of legal order I have defended here is anarchism's radically decentralist character, its support for grassroots institutions and its opposition to top-down control. Links with the social vision of New Left should be obvious. New Left decentralism naturally militates against centralized political authority—and thus, ultimately against political authority of any sort.

Class analysis is the source of an especially important connection between leftist politics and the kind of anarchist project I have sketched here. Since the kind of class analysis I have offered here tends to focus on the creation of the state through conquest and the use of the state apparatus to subordinate, exclude, and deprive, there is a deep-seated connection between the kind of leftism I embrace a suspicious view of the state that certainly might tend to dispose someone toward anarchism.

The kind of anarchism I wish to defend is committed to eliminating the privileges that make it viable for people to unreasonably subordinate, exclude, and deprive others and to engage in aggression against them. These fundamentally unreasonable choices are costly. But the state persistently confers privileges that force the unwilling to bear the costs of these wrongs and that actively prevent people from seeking or realizing remedies for them. Just legal rules in a society rooted in peaceful, voluntary cooperation will eliminate these privileges and actively preclude attempts to reestablish them using aggressive force. While it is frequently supposed that the state is needed to achieve leftist goals, especially to serve as a counterweight to the strength of putatively non-state actors, it is finally more reasonable to suppose *both* that the state is itself a persistent source of exclusion, deprivation, subordination, and aggression *and* that the supposedly private centers of influence to which state power is often seen as counterpoised are in fact dependent on the state. Thus, the elimination of the state, and with it state-secured privilege, has the potential to level the social playing field dramatically. In addition, underlying anarchist values—equality of authority, opposition to aggression—and concerns—with decentralization, with class analysis—motivate principled anarchist support for traditional leftist causes. The tie between anarchism and leftist politics is thus integral, not accidental.

III. THE PROJECT OF BUILDING A STATELESS SOCIETY WITH JUST LEGAL RULES AND INSTITUTIONS IS AN ANTICAPITALIST PROJECT

A. The Anarchist Vision Outlined Here Is Anticapitalist

The model of peaceful, voluntary cooperation—a pattern of interaction that would be fostered by the rules enforced by just legal regimes in a stateless society—reflects values that are clearly anticapitalist.[7] There are at least five potential

[7] *Cf.* William Gillis, *The Freed Market*, *in* MARKETS NOT CAPITALISM, *supra* note 6, at 19, http://williamgillis.blogspot.com/2007/07/freed-market-one-of-tactics-ive-taken.html.

meanings of "capitalism" (Section B); the moral, legal, and political vision I have sought to defend challenges capitalism in my second, third, fourth, and fifth senses (Section C). There are, in turn, good reasons to use "capitalism" to tag some of the social arrangements which just legal rules in a stateless society could be expected to undermine (Section D). Thus, the emergence of a polycentric legal order in which the kinds of legal rules for which I have argued here were consistently enforced would reasonably be described as a move beyond capitalism (Section E).

B. There Are at Least Five Senses of "Capitalism"

There are at least five distinguishable senses of "capitalism":[8]

$capitalism_1$	an economic system that features protections for people's just possessory claims and their voluntary exchanges of goods and services
$capitalism_2$	an economic system that features a symbiotic relationship between big business and government
$capitalism_3$	an economic system that features dominance—over workplaces, society, and (if there is one) the state—by *capitalists* (that is, by a relatively small number of people who control investable wealth and the means of production)[9]
$capitalism_4$	the economic system currently prevalent in the developed world and, increasingly, in less-developed communities
$capitalism_5$	a social system in which narrowly commercial motives, interactions, and institutions predominate over or even crowd out noncommercial ones

[8] *Cf.* Charles W. Johnson, *Anarquistas por La Causa*, RAD GEEK PEOPLE'S DAILY, Mar. 31, 2005, http://radgeek.com/gt/2005/03/31/anarquistas_por; Charles W. Johnson, *Libertarian Anticapitalism*, BLEEDING HEART LIBERTARIANS, Aug. 18, 2011, http://bleedingheartlibertarians.com/2011/08/libertarian-anticapitalism/; Roderick T. Long, *POOTMOP Redux*, AUSTRO-ATHENIAN EMPIRE, June 22, 2009, http://aaeblog.com/2009/06/22/pootmop-redux; Fred Foldvary, *When Will Michael Moore Nail Land Speculators?*, THE PROGRESS REPORT, Oct. 19, 2009, http://www.progress.org/2009/fold635.htm. "Capitalism" in Johnson's third sense refers to "boss-directed labor" (in the first article) or "the wage-labor system" (in the second), while Long's parallel expression, "capitalism-2," denotes "control of the means of production by someone other than the workers—i.e., by capitalist owners." Foldvary's parallel proposal is "exploitation of labor by the big owners of capital." I am inclined to think that many of those who employ "capitalism" in the pejorative sense intend it to encompass the dominance by capitalists of all social institutions, and not just workplaces, though they doubtless see societal dominance and workplace dominance as connected. At any rate, supposing that they do may provide a slender justification for distinguishing my typology from the ones offered by Johnson, Long, and Foldvary. My fifth proposed meaning reflects Johnson's suggestion, in the second article, that "capitalism" might also refer to a pattern of social organization that is not only commercial but *commercialized*. For an earlier discussion of the inherently ambiguous character of "capitalism," see Clarence B. Carson, *Capitalism: Yes and No*, THE FREEMAN: IDEAS ON LIBERTY, Feb. 1985, at 75, http://www.thefreemanonline.org/columns/capitalism-yes-and-no; thanks to Sheldon Richman for bringing this article to my attention.

[9] While $capitalism_2$ obtains whenever business and the state are in bed together, under $capitalism_3$ and $capitalism_4$, business is clearly on top.

Capitalism$_1$ just *is* a set of arrangements allowing for peaceful, voluntary exchange; so if "anticapitalism" meant opposition to captalism$_1$, it would amount, unreasonably, to opposition to that kind of exchange. But what's worth objecting to isn't captalism$_1$ but rather capitalism$_2$, capitalism$_3$, capitalism$_4$, and capitalism$_5$.[10] The first three of these would be undermined by the kinds of legal rules for which I have been arguing here, while these rules would in no way promote or require the last and would certainly protect space within which alternatives to it could be developed and practiced.

Many people seem to employ definitions that combine elements from these distinct senses of "capitalism." For instance: enthusiasts for and critics of capitalism seem too often to mean by the word something like "an economic system that features protections for people's just possessory claims and their voluntary exchanges of goods and services—and *therefore, predictably,* also rule by capitalists."[11] But there's good reason to challenge the assumption that dominance by a small number of wealthy people (a central characteristic of the economic system we have now, capitalism$_4$) is in any sense a likely feature of an economy marked by peaceful, voluntary cooperation. Such dominance, I suggest, is probable only when force and fraud *impede* peaceful, voluntary cooperation through exchange.

C. The Legal order Envisioned Here Would Preclude Capitalism$_2$ and Capitalism$_4$ while Undermining Capitalism$_3$

1. *Capitalism in the Objectionable Senses either Involves Aggression Directly or Depends on Aggression*

Capitalism$_2$, capitalism$_3$, and capitalism$_4$ are all in tension with the baseline possessory rules and the other standards that would be enforced by just legal regimes in a stateless society: capitalism$_2$ because it involves direct interference with people's peaceful, voluntary exchanges (Subsection 2); capitalism$_3$ to the extent that it

[10] It is unclear when the English word "capitalism" was first employed. William Makepeace Thackeray was arguably the earliest user of the term: *see* 2 The Newcomes: Memoirs of a Most Respectable Family 75 (1854–55), *quoted in* Oxford English Dictionary (here, the term is used in a relatively neutral sense). By contrast, "capitalist" as a pejorative has an older history, appearing at least as early as 1792, and figuring repeatedly in the work of Thomas Hodgskin: *see, e.g.*, Thomas Hodgskin, Popular Political Economy: Four Lectures Delivered at the London Mechanics Institution 5, 51–52, 120, 121, 126, 138, 171 ("greedy capitalists"!), 238–40, 243, 245–49, 253–57, 265 (1827); Thomas Hodgskin, The Natural and Artificial Right of Property Contrasted: A Series of Letters, Addressed without Permission to H. Brougham, Esq. M.P. F.R.S. 15, 44, 53, 54, 67, 87, 97–101, 134–5, 150, 155, 180 (1832). The pejorative use occurs nearly eighty times throughout the thirty-odd pages of Thomas Hodgskin, Labour Defended against the Claims of Capital, or, The Unproductiveness of Capital Proved (1825). It is also possible to find "capitalist" employed in less-than-flattering ways by another social theorist in the same period; *see* John Taylor, Tyranny Unmasked (1822).

[11] *Cf.* Roderick T. Long, *Rothbard's "Left and Right": Forty Years Later*, Mises Daily, April 8, 2006, http://mises.org/daily/2099 (discussing this sort of use of "capitalism" and the parallel word "zaxlebax").

depends on such interference—both past and ongoing (Subsection 3)—and because it flies in the face of the general commitment to freedom that underlies support for peaceful, voluntary exchange in particular (Section 4); and capitalism$_4$ because it embodies the central elements of both capitalism$_2$ and capitalism$_3$ (Subsection 5). Capitalism$_5$ is not a necessary product of the kinds of institutions I have defended and could effectively be challenged in a stateless society in multiple ways (Subsection 6). Just legal rules and institutions in a stateless society would undermine the viability of capitalism in all of these senses (Subsection 7).

2. *Capitalism$_2$ Would Be Inconsistent with Just Legal Rules in a Stateless Society because It Involves Direct Interference with Peaceful, Voluntary Exchange*

Capitalism$_2$ is clearly inconsistent with rules fostering peaceful, voluntary exchange. Under capitalism$_2$, some people interfere with other people's just possessory claims and their voluntary exchanges of goods and services in order to enrich themselves and their allies (political, economic, or both). Such interference would obviously be inconsistent with the NAM.

3. *Capitalism$_3$ Would Be Undermined by Just Legal Rules in a Stateless Society because It Is Fostered by Past and Ongoing Interference with Peaceful, Voluntary Exchange*

Just legal rules in a stateless society would impede the occurrence and persistence of capitalism$_3$ in multiple ways. (*i*) In a society featuring peaceful, voluntary exchange, the kinds of privileges afforded the (usually well-connected) beneficiaries of state power under capitalism$_2$ would be absent. Thus, wealth would be widely distributed and large, hierarchical businesses would prove less efficient and less likely to survive than at present. (*ii*) At the same time, people would find it much easier to work in partnerships or cooperatives or for themselves, particularly given the absence of the various sorts of privileges for the politically well-connected that tend to make and keep people poor.[12] (*iii*) In the state's absence, people wouldn't be able, as under capitalism$_3$, to manipulate politicians to gain and maintain wealth and social influence. (*iv*) Further, vast acts of past injustice would as far as realistically possible be remedied.[13] For all these reasons, it would be difficult for a few people to

[12] For a devastating critique of rules—often supported by politicians beholden to wealthy and well-connected people who expect to benefit from them—that systematically make and keep people poor, *see* Charles W. Johnson, *Scratching By: How Government Creates Poverty as We Know It*, *in* MARKETS NOT CAPITALISM, *supra* note 6, at 377, http://www.thefreemanonline.org/featured/scratching-by-how-government-creates-poverty-as-we-know-it.

[13] *Cf.* Chapter 3.IV, *supra*.

control wealth and exercise vastly disproportionate social influence in a society that embraced the kinds of legal rules for which I have argued here.[14]

4. *The Rules Enforced by Just Legal Regimes in a Stateless Society Would Ensure Space for People Nonaggressively to Oppose Capitalism$_3$, Which Is Plausibly Seen as Inconsistent with Support for the Underlying Logic of Anarchism*

The style of anarchist politics I have termed *cultural anarchism*,[15] rooted in the logic underlying support for anarchism more generally, leads fairly clearly to opposition to the exercise of arbitrary authority in the workplace. And the operation of just legal regimes in a stateless society would facilitate the embodiment of cultural anarchism.

Valuing different kinds of freedom emphatically isn't the same as approving the same kinds of remedies for assaults on these different kinds of freedom. Cultural anarchism needn't involve the view that petty indignities warrant aggressive responses. But support for cultural anarchism should be seen as reflecting the plausible conviction that it makes no sense to favor freedom as a general value while treating nonviolent assaults on people's freedom as trivial. The cultural-anarchist understanding of freedom as a multi-dimensional value that can be subject to injuries both aggressive and nonaggressive would provide cultural anarchists with good reason to oppose capitalism$_3$ even if—as is most unlikely—it were to occur in complete isolation from capitalism$_2$. Thus, cultural anarchism can be seen as underwriting nonaggressive responses to, for instance, workplace authoritarianism, including public shaming, blacklisting, striking peacefully, engaging in work slowdowns, protesting, withholding voluntary certifications, and boycotting.[16]

A just legal order in a stateless society would not require such responses. But it *would* provide protection for them, and thus further facilitate efforts to undermine capitalism$_3$ in ways that would increase the likelihood of its absence from such a society.

5. *Capitalism$_4$ Would Be Inconsistent with Rules Protecting Peaceful, Voluntary Cooperation because Capitalism$_2$ and Capitalism$_3$ Would Be as Well*

Capitalism$_4$, the economic system we have now, features both corporate privilege and social dominance by capitalists. Thus, the features of a just legal order that

[14] On the issues addressed in this paragraph, *see* Chapter 3.VI and Chapter 6, *supra*.

[15] *See* Chapter 6.V, *supra*.

[16] *Cf.* Johnson, *supra* note 6; Kerry Howley, *We're All Cultural Libertarians*, REASON, Nov. 2009, http://reason.com/archives/2009/10/20/are-property-rights-enough.

would preclude capitalism$_2$ and undermine the viability of capitalism$_3$ would necessarily militate against the occurrence of capitalism$_4$ in a just stateless society.

6. *Capitalism$_5$ Need Not Emerge because Just Legal Rules Were in Place, and Features of a Just Legal Order Could Undermine the Dominance of Commercialized Motives and Interactions*

Capitalism$_5$, a not merely commercial but thoroughly commercial*ized* social system, reflects an impoverishment of people's motives and attitudes and interactions. There is reason to object to such a society—because it fails to take full advantage, or encourage the full expression, of the wide range of positive human potentialities—but none to think that the kind of impoverishment it involves would flow necessarily or predictably from the establishment of a just stateless society's institutions. These institutions would not depend on commercial motives to operate effectively; rather, they would leave space for interactions of many different kinds.

In addition, these institutions would create opportunities for people to undermine the dominance of commercialized motives and interactions by choosing alternatives to them. Gift-economies, noncommercial creativity, and solidaristic networks and actions could be expected to flourish in such a society. They could be expected to flourish because they are very much in evidence in our society—there is thus no doubt that they're perfectly possible—but also for other reasons. (*i*) The state tends to crowd out alternatives to itself, making it inefficient or even illegal for people to explore non-state alternatives to service provision and cooperative action. Thus, such institutions as mutual aid societies vanished under various kinds of state pressure. The elimination of the state would end statist crowding-out, and thus open up new possibilities for solidaristic motives to find full expression. And, with the overall level of productivity much higher than in the past, the potential of solidaristic institutions to do exciting and transformative things would be greater than their predecessors'. (*ii*) Past solidaristic and other sorts of noncommercial institutions and movements were hampered by the prevalence and aftereffects of state-sanctioned and state-committed aggression, which impoverished people, raised the minimum work requirements for living a decent life, and limited the resources available for investment in noncommercial social structures. In the absence of these kinds of aggression, and with past instances remedied where possible, people would be freer to engage in noncommercial activity. Given that there's good evidence that they would often like to do so, the creation of a stateless society would increase the likelihood that they *would* do so.

The value of goods and services to consumers is, in general, unaffected by the motives of those who provide them. And a system of peaceful, voluntary social cooperation within a framework provided by the baseline rules is to be prized in significant part precisely because it fosters fruitful but arms-length relationships with strangers. However, such a system doesn't depend in any sense for its existence or viability on the rejection of interdependence or the denial that cooperative relationships are valuable for their own sake. Prizing this kind of cooperation does not in any way require disregard for the recognition that many relationships would be diminished were they brought within the cash nexus or if they functioned on a quid pro quo basis. Exchange relationships are valuable, but they are hardly the whole of life; no one wants all interactions to be strategic. And the model of social and economic life operating within the framework of stateless law defended here is not committed to obscuring this vital point in any way. Impersonal exchange relationships can help to support personal, solidaristic ones. And interactions initially rooted in exchange can come increasingly to be personal relationships valued for themselves. But direct cooperation—an aspect or form of friendship (itself, of course, an independently valuable aspect of flourishing)—can and should be treasured as intrinsically and not just instrumentally valuable, and just legal rules in a stateless society will encourage and facilitate this kind of cooperation. Embracing a just legal order need not mean embracing capitalism$_5$, and can clearly, indeed, mean embracing a set of social arrangements with the capacity to undermine capitalism$_5$.[17]

7. *Anarchist Values and Just Legal Rules in a Stateless Society Would Not Require (and Could Help to Undermine) Capitalism in Multiple Senses*

Capitalism$_2$ and capitalism$_3$ are both at odds with the baseline rules: capitalism$_2$ because it involves direct interference with just possessory claims consistent with those rules, capitalism$_3$ because it depends on such interference—both past and ongoing—and because it flies in the face of the general commitment to freedom that underlies support for peaceful, voluntary exchange in particular. Capitalism$_4$ just is a synthesis of capitalism$_2$ and capitalism$_3$, so it is problematic for the same reasons. Capitalism$_5$, a style of social interaction, is not inconsistent with the NAM, but the effective operation of a society structured by the NAM hardly requires capitalism$_5$, and the adoption of legal rules embodying the NAM could contribute in more than one way to undermining this style of social interaction.

D. The Arrangements Precluded or Undermined by Just Legal Rules in a Stateless Society Could Reasonably Be Referred to as "Capitalist"

1. *Anarchists Should Not Shy away from "Anticapitalist" Language*

It makes sense to describe the arrangements ruled out by just legal rules in a stateless society as "capitalist." Doing so makes clear why capitalism$_3$, in particular, is

[17] Thanks to Shawn Wilbur for underscoring the need to make these points.

problematic (Subsection 2). It makes clear that anarchists are not apologists for the status quo (Subsection 3). It highlights the gap between present reality and the social arrangements that would be fostered by just legal rules in a stateless society (Subsection 4). It emphasizes the importance of labor as a factor of production (Subsection 5) and highlights the emphasis cultural anarchists will rightly place on solidarity with workers struggling with bosses (Subsection 6). It also emphasizes the consonance between the project of implementing the kind of legal order for which I have argued here on the one hand and the concerns of the global anticapitalist movement on the other (Subsection 7). Given the contradictory meanings of "capitalism," perhaps sensible people should avoid using it at all. But "words are known by the company they keep."[18] Thus, while anarchists certainly shouldn't use "capitalism" as a tag for the system they favor, there *is* good reason to employ it as a label for the system or systems precluded or undermined by just legal rules in a stateless society (Subsection 8).[19]

2. *This Language Helps to Emphasize the Specific Undesirability of Capitalism$_3$.*

Labels such as "state capitalism" and "corporatism" capture what is wrong with capitalism$_2$, but they don't quite get at the problem with capitalism$_3$ or capitalism$_4$. Even if, as seems plausible, rule by capitalists requires a political explanation—an explanation in terms of the independent misbehavior of politicians and of the manipulation of politicians by business leaders[20]—it is worth objecting specifically to social

[18] I became acquainted with this phrase thanks to NICHOLAS LASH, BELIEVING THREE WAYS IN ONE GOD: A READING OF THE APOSTLES' CREED (1992). But it appears, I have subsequently discovered, to have a legal provenance and to be a rough translation of the Latin phrase *noscitur a sociis*.

[19] To be sure, proponents of peaceful, voluntary exchange could obviously refer to capitalism$_2$, at least, as "state capitalism," "corporate capitalism," "actually existing capitalism," or "corporatism." But doing so wouldn't make clear their opposition to capitalism$_3$.

[20] *See, e.g.*, Kevin A. Carson, *Another Free-for-All: Libertarian Class Analysis, Organized Labor, Etc.*, MUTUALIST BLOG: FREE MARKET ANTI-CAPITALISM, Jan. 26, 2006, http://mutualist.blogspot.com/2006/01/another-free-for-all-libertarian-class.html; Wally Conger, AGORIST CLASS THEORY: A LEFT LIBERTARIAN APPROACH TO CLASS CONFLICT ANALYSIS (n.d.), http://www.agorism.info/AgoristClassTheory.pdf; Walter E. Grinder & John Hagel, *Toward a Theory of State Capitalism: Ultimate Decision Making and Class Structure* 1 J. LIBERTARIAN STUD. 59 (1977); David M. Hart, The Radical Liberalism of Charles Comte and Charles Dunoyer (1994) (unpublished PhD dissertation, University of Cambridge); Hans-Hermann Hoppe, *Marxist and Austrian Class Analysis*, 9 J. LIBERTARIAN STUD. 79 (1990); Roderick T. Long, *Toward a Libertarian Theory of Class*, 15. SOC. PHIL. & POL'Y 303 (1998); ALBERT JAY NOCK, OUR ENEMY THE STATE (1935); CARL OGLESBY, THE YANKEE AND COWBOY WAR (1977); FRANZ OPPENHEIMER, THE STATE (1997); TOM G. PALMER, *Classical Liberalism, Marxism, and the Conflict of Classes: The Classical Liberal Theory of Class Conflict*, *in* REALIZING FREEDOM: LIBERTARIAN THEORY, HISTORY, AND PRACTICE 255–76 (2009); Sheldon Richman, *Class Struggle Rightly Conceived*, THE FREEMAN: IDEAS ON LIBERTY, July 13, 2007, http://www.thefreemanonline.org/columns/tgif/class-struggle-rightly-conceived. *Cf.* C. WRIGHT MILLS, THE POWER ELITE (1956); G. WILLIAM DOMHOFF, WHO RULES AMERICA? CHALLENGES TO CORPORATE AND CLASS DOMINANCE (6th ed., 2009).

dominance by big business in addition to challenging business–government symbiosis. To the extent that those who own and lead big businesses are often labeled "capitalists," identifying what proponents of freedom oppose as "capitalism" helps appropriately to highlight their critique of capitalism$_3$ and capitalism$_4$.

3. *This Language Helps to Differentiate Anarchists from People Who Defend the Status Quo as if Contemporary Society Had Been Liberated from Systemic Aggression*

The "capitalist" banner is often waved enthusiastically by people who seem inclined to confuse support for freedom with support for capitalism$_2$, capitalism$_3$, and capitalism$_4$—perhaps ignoring the reality or the problematic nature of these social phenomena, perhaps even celebrating the social dominance of capitalists as appropriate in light of the purportedly admirable characters of business titans. Opposing "capitalism" helps to ensure that advocates of the baseline rules, of peaceful, voluntary exchange, are not confused with these vulgar proponents of freedom-for-the-power-elite.

4. *This Usage Helps to Emphasize That Genuinely Peaceful, Voluntary Cooperation Is Very Much an Unknown Ideal*

Given the frequency with which the contemporary economic order in Western societies is labeled "capitalism," anyone who acknowledges the vast gap between ideals of freedom and an economic reality distorted by privilege and misshapen by past acts of aggression will have good reason to oppose what is commonly called "capitalism" rather than embracing it.

5. *This Usage Helps to Challenge the Assumption That Capital Is More Economically Fundamental than Labor*

Multiple factors of production—notably including labor—contribute to the operation of a complex economy. To refer to such an economy as "capitalist" is to imply, incorrectly, that capital plays the most central role in the economy, and that the "capitalist," the absentee possessor of investable wealth, is ultimately more important than the people who are the sources of labor. Advocates of peaceful, voluntary cooperation should reject this inaccurate view.[21]

[21] *See* Kevin A. Carson, *Capitalism: A Good Word for a Bad Thing*, CENTER FOR A STATELESS SOCIETY, Mar. 6, 2010, http://c4ss.org/content/1992.

6. *This Usage Helps to Emphasize Solidarity with Workers*

The ability of big business to maximize the satisfaction of its preferences more fully than workers are able to maximize the satisfaction of theirs is significantly enhanced by a business–state symbiosis that is inconsistent with the NAM. And if, as I believe, cultural anarchism is correct, there is often further reason to side with workers when they are being pushed around, even nonaggressively. To the extent that the bosses workers oppose are often called "capital*ists*," so that "anticapital*ism*" seems like a natural tag for their opposition to these bosses, and to the extent that an economic system structured by the NAM and offering social freedom—by contrast with capitalism$_2$, capitalism$_3$, and capitalism$_4$—would dramatically increase the opportunities for workers to shape the contours of their own lives and to experience significantly greater prosperity and economic security, embracing "anticapitalism" is a way of clearly signaling solidarity with workers.[22]

7. *This Usage Explicitly Links Anarchists with the Global Anticapitalist Movement*

Owning "anticapitalism" is also a way, more broadly, of identifying with ordinary people around the world who express their opposition to imperialism, the increasing influence on their lives of multinational corporations, and their own growing economic vulnerability by naming their enemy as "capitalism." Perhaps some of them endorse inaccurate theoretical accounts of their circumstances in accordance with which it really is a system of peaceful, voluntary exchange structured by the NAM that should be understood as lying behind what they oppose. But for many of them, objecting to "capitalism" is wildly unlikely to mean opposing peaceful, voluntary exchange; instead, it's likely to be a matter of using a convenient label to name the forces that seem bent on misshaping their lives and those of others.[23]

[22] *Cf.* Sheldon Richman, *Workers of the World Unite for a Free Market*, THE FREEMAN: IDEAS ON LIBERTY, Dec. 18, 2009, http://www.thefreemanonline.org/tgif/workers-of-the-world-unite.

[23] "'If you were to ask, "What is anarchism?" we would all disagree,' said Vlad Bliffet, a member of the collective that organized the ... [2010 Los Angeles Anarchist Bookfair]. While most anarchists agree on the basic principle that the world would be better without hierarchy and without capitalism, he said, they have competing theories on how to achieve that change"; Kate Linthicum, *Book Fair Draws an Array of Anarchists*, L.A. TIMES, Jan. 25, 2010, *available at* http://www.latimes.com/news/local/la-me-anarchists25-2010jan25,0,3735605.story?track=rss. Given the focus on opposition to real-world hierarchy, I suspect, without evidence, that Bliffet's primary objection was not to capitalism as a system of personal possession and exchange in the abstract—capitalism$_1$—but rather to social dominance by capitalists—capitalism$_3$ (and to the politico-economic status quo in general—capitalism$_4$—and so, by implication, to state–corporate partnership—capitalism$_2$). The failure to see this point will tend to impede otherwise natural alliances focused on issues ranging from war to torture to surveil-

8. *It Is Reasonable to Label the Project of Promoting the Adoption of Just Legal Rules in a Stateless Society an Anticapitalist Project*

Capitalism—whether understood as state–corporate partnership, social dominance by bosses, or the deeply fractured economic order we have now—is practically and morally problematic. So it is reasonable for anarchists to own the "anticapitalist" label as a means of highlighting the specific problems with rules by bosses, differentiating anarchism from corporate apologetics, making clear the difference between extant neoliberalism and the kind of society an anarchist legal order would help to cultivate, underscoring the significance of labor and the value of labor solidarity (both in the present and in the anarchist future), and linking anarchism with the global anticapitalist movement. The kind of project proposed and defended here should thus be forthrightly characterized as inimical to capitalism.

E. The Anarchist Legal Order Envisioned Here Would Undermine Capitalism

Almost four decades ago, anarchist Karl Hess wrote: "I have lost my faith in capitalism" and "I resist this capitalist nation-state," observing that he had "turn[ed] from the religion of capitalism."[24] Distinguishing five senses of "capitalism"—voluntary cooperation, business-government partnership, rule by capitalists, the politico-economic status quo, and hyper-commercialization—helps to make clear the various possible links between commitment to freedom and passionate opposition to something called "capitalism," both values that would be served by the kind of legal order I have sought to explain and defend here.

A credible anarchist project would involve an attack on capitalism in multiple senses—state-secured privilege, social dominance by elites, the worship of commerce, and, thus, the economic arrangements prevalent in our world. And it makes sense to *name* what an anarchist law and politics would undermine "capitalism." Doing so calls attention to the radical nature of the anarchist legal project outlined here; highlights the difference between the ideal of peaceful, voluntary cooperation and the present reality of state-secured privilege; underscores the fact that anarchists

lance to drugs to freedom of speech to corporatism to bailouts to decentralization to the reach of the administrative state.

[24] Karl Hess, Dear America 3, 5 (1975). Even more bluntly, Hess writes: "What I have learned about corporate capitalism, roughly, is that it is an act of theft, by and large, through which a very few live very high off the work, invention, and creativity of very many others. It is the Grand Larceny of our particular time in history, the Grand Larceny in which a future of freedom which could have followed the collapse of feudalism was stolen from under our noses by a new bunch of bosses doing the same old things." *Id.* at 1. (Complicating the story is the fact that Hess subsequently wrote Capitalism for Kids: Growing up to Be Your Own Boss (1987). But I think it is clear that by "capitalism," Hess meant $capitalism_1$; he was certainly no fan of the other four varieties.)

rightly object to nonviolent as well as aggressive restraints on freedom; ensures that anarchists aren't confused with people who use the rhetoric of freedom to prop up an unjust status quo; and expresses solidarity between opponents of the state and workers—as well as ordinary people around the world who use "capitalism" as a shorthand label for the world-system that constrains their freedom and stunts their lives. Identifying the anarchist project I defend here as an instance of "anti-capitalism" encapsulates and highlights its support for a full-blown commitment to freedom and its opposition to alternatives that use talk of freedom to conceal acquiescence in exclusion, subordination, deprivation, and aggression.[25]

IV. THE PROJECT OF FOSTERING A STATELESS SOCIETY WITH JUST LEGAL RULES CAN REASONABLY BE DESCRIBED AS SOCIALIST

A. The Anarchist Legal Project Outlined Here Can Be Seen as Socialist

The goal of fostering the emergence of a stateless society with just legal rules is plausibly understood as *socialist*. A key reason this is so is that it is perfectly possible to see the proposal I offer here for a stateless legal order as continuous with others emanating from within the socialist tradition. Two thinkers often identified with that tradition who embraced antistatist values of the general sort I defend here can serve as useful examples. Thomas Hodgskin, frequently labeled a "Ricardian socialist," articulated an account of justice that parallels the one I defend (Section B). Similarly, Benjamin Tucker, who explicitly identified himself as a socialist, defended a variant of anarchism similar to the one I embrace here, calling for the abolition of state-secured privilege as the key to ending the inequities of capitalism (Section C). A minority position within the broader socialist tradition can thus be seen as identified by its emphasis on peaceful, voluntary cooperation (including cooperation in exchange) and the elimination of privilege, rather than by any sort of commitment to statism or to collective possession or control, as grounding radical emancipation (Section D). Its roots in this minority tradition can justify labeling the radical position I seek to defend as a variant of socialism (Section E).

B. Thomas Hodgskin Took a Position That in Important Respects Anticipated the One I Defend

Thomas Hodgskin—political economist, pamphleteer, and sometime editor of *The Economist*—was a leading light among the thinkers and activists sometimes referred

[25] *But cf.* Brian Doherty, *Ayn Rand: Radical for Something Other than Capitalism?*, HIT AND RUN: REASON MAG., Jan, 20, 2010, http://reason.com/blog/2010/01/20/ayn-rand-radical-for-something.

to as "Ricardian" or "Smithian" socialists.[26] Hodgskin challenged the social dominance of capitalists and aristocrats by calling for an economic environment radically liberated from the effects of pervasive privilege.[27] He delivered an impassioned critique of unequal exchange—that is, exchange distorted by privilege—as the source of economic injustice. His moral critique of capitalism emphasized the distinction between "natural" and "artificial" possessory claims—those to which people are entitled in justice on the one hand and those created by state-secured privilege on the other. Abolishing protection for artificial possessory claims would ensure that workers could receive the just product of their labor.

J. E. King suggests a broad definition of what united the Ricardian socialists—ideologically, they were, he maintains, "hostile to capitalism … [and] sympathetic to the working class."[28] King maintains that the Ricardian socialists "were 'Socialists' only on a very loose usage of the term, and … Hodgskin not even then." He goes on to concede, however, that "[t]he label has stuck, … and it seems unnecessary to invent a new one…."[29]

King offers no justification for his bald assertion that Hodgskin should not be identified as a socialist. The definition he proposes as a means of picking out the Ricardian socialists from their contemporaries seems perfectly sensible, and he does not seek to defend the implicit claim that it is not really a suitable definition of socialism. Words are known by the company they keep, and the fact that Hodgskin has been identified for decades as part of the socialist tradition suggests that it would be fruitless and quixotic to treat him as if he were not.

In a standard discussion of the Ricardian socialists, which features a chapter devoted to Hodgskin, Esther Lowenthal, too, resists characterizing Hodgskin as a socialist. Lowenthal's argument against viewing Hodgskin as a socialist begins from the premise that socialism involves not only a critique of capitalism or support for the labor theory of value, but also "a constructive philosophy of social control."[30] Since Hodgskin's institutional proposals involve the elimination of privilege as the mechanism to be used to dispel injustice, rather than the creation of any new system of control to replace the corrupt network of institutions that sustain capitalism, Lowenthal doubts that he can reasonably be thought of as a socialist.

[26] *Cf.* NOEL W. THOMPSON, THE PEOPLE'S SCIENCE: THE POPULAR POLITICAL ECONOMY OF EXPLOITATION AND CRISIS 1816–34 (2002); John Edward King, *Utopian or Scientific? A Reconsideration of the Ricardian Socialists*, 15 HIST. POL. ECON. 345 (1983); ESTHER LOWENTHAL, THE RICARDIAN SOCIALISTS (1911). Hodgskin did not label himself a "socialist."

[27] *See generally* HODGSKIN, POPULAR POLITICAL ECONOMY, *supra* note 10; HODGSKIN, THE NATURAL AND ARTIFICIAL RIGHT OF PROPERTY CONTRASTED, *supra* note 10; HODGSKIN, LABOUR DEFENDED, SUPRA note 4.

[28] King, *supra* note 26, at 345.

[29] *Id.* at 346.

[30] LOWENTHAL, *supra* note 26, at 81.

Whether Lowenthal is right depends, of course, on whether socialism should be understood as concerned primarily with ends or with means. A credibly socialist program must be concerned with social institutions that conduce to the public benefit, but it is an entirely different question whether these institutions must involve centralized, forcible control of economic activity (which is what I take it Lowenthal means when she talks about "a constructive philosophy of social control"). If the genus *socialism* is, roughly, about emancipation from the ill effects of capitalism (understood in any or all of my second, third, fourth, or fifth senses), then Hodgskin's species can be seen as concerned with achieving this emancipatory goal through the elimination of privilege. Were socialism necessarily a position committed to the use of statist means as well as to the pursuit of emancipatory ends, then the use of the label "Ricardian socialist" for Hodgskin would be inapposite; but given that socialism is rather a matter of ends—of fostering the emergence of institutions that undermine subordination and deprivation—then there is no reason not to continue referring to Hodgskin as a socialist, and to recognize the practice of identifying him as such as a clue to the semantic range of "socialist."

C. Benjamin Tucker Defended as Socialist a Position Featuring both Peaceful, Voluntary Cooperation through Exchange and the End of State-Secured Privilege

The American anarchist Benjamin Tucker provides a clear instance of the links between the elements of the socialist and anarchist traditions from which the anarchist model I defend here emerges. Present at the creation of the modern socialist movement,[31] Tucker was one of a number of contemporaries who rallied under the socialist banner because of a shared concern with "the social question"—in a broad sense, the cluster of problems posed by evident class distinctions that seemed to be sources of persistent misery and conflict. Tucker explicitly embraced "anarchistic socialism." Thus, he rejected the state, and so the use of statist means to achieve socialist ends. And he similarly denied the importance, necessity, or desirability of mandatory collectivization without the state as an element of the socialist agenda.

Tucker experimented with various definitions of socialism, but one that he offered in multiple forms was this: "Socialism is the belief that the next important step in progress is a change in man's environment of an economic character

[31] Tucker welcomed the Socialistic-Revolutionary Congress, held in Chicago in 1881, and commissioned a representative. Evidence of the fluidity of the early socialist movement's self-definition: the Congress offered a "cordial reception" to "Josiah Warren's American socialism" and chose Tucker's *Liberty* as its "English language organ." *See* James J. Martin, Men against the State: The Expositors of Individualist Anarchism in America, 1827–1908 at 214–15 (1953). Thanks to Kevin Carson for this reference.

that shall include the abolition of every privilege whereby the holder of wealth acquires an anti-social power to compel tribute."[32] Socialism, he suggested, "properly includes all plans for the furtherance of human welfare which satisfy the two following conditions: 1. that of acting, not directly upon the nature of individuals, but upon their relations and environment; 2. that of acting upon relations and environment with a view to preventing possession of wealth from being a means of levying on the product of labor. Under this definition, an Anarchist may be a Socialist, and, as a matter of fact, almost all Anarchists are Socialists."[33] While Marx famously embraced "scientific socialism," Tucker used this phrase in an interestingly different way:

> Now, so far from not offering anything in the place of what is now false called government, we have something very tangible to offer,—something very rational, practical, and easy of application. We offer cooperation. We offer non-compulsive organization. We offer associative combination. We offer every possible method of voluntary social union by which men and women may act together for the furtherance of well-being. In short, we offer voluntary scientific socialism in the place of the present compulsory unscientific organization which characterizes the State and all of its ramifications. . . .[34]

In effect, a program that allowed for the ongoing experimentation that a scheme of genuinely voluntary cooperation would make possible was a truly *scientific* socialism.

For Tucker, socialism was rooted in the abolition of unjust privilege.

> Socialism says that what's one man's meat must no longer be another's poison; that no man shall be able to add to his riches except by labor; that in adding to his riches by labor alone no man makes another man poorer; that on the contrary every man thus adding to his riches makes every other man richer; that increase and concentration of wealth through labor tend to increase, cheapen, and vary production; that every increase of capital in the hands of the laborer tends, in the absence of legal monopoly, to put more products, better products, cheaper products, and a greater variety of products within the reach of every man who works; and that this fact means the physical, mental, and moral perfecting of mankind, and the realization of human fraternity. . . . Socialism does not order; it prophesies. It does not say: Thou shalt not steal! It says: When all men have Liberty, thou wilt not steal.[35]

[32] Benjamin R. Tucker, *Armies That Overlap*, Liberty, Mar. 8, 1890, at 4, *available at* http://fair-use.org/benjamin-tucker/instead-of-a-book/armies-that-overlap.

[33] Benjamin R. Tucker, untitled comment following D., *The Palmer-Carnegie Incident*, Liberty, Jan. 14, 1888, at 7.

[34] Benjamin R. Tucker, *Liberty the Mother of Order*, Liberty, Oct. 14, 1882, at 2.

[35] Benjamin R. Tucker, *Socialism: What It Is*, Liberty, May 17. 1884, at 4, *available at* http://fair-use.org/benjamin-tucker/instead-of-a-book/socialism-what-it-is.

Tucker makes clear why he sees Josiah Warren, P. J. Proudhon, and Karl Marx as socialists sharing a commitment to the liberation of labor. Anarchists and state-socialists, Tucker maintains, are like participants in a broader socialist tradition, devoted to comparable goals but embracing very different means of achieving those goals. The key socialist idea, he avers in this context, is that "labor is the true measure of price." According to Tucker,

> the natural wage of labor is its product; that this wage, or product, is the only just source of income (leaving out, of course, gift, inheritance, etc.); that all who derive income from any other source abstract it directly or indirectly from the natural and just wage of labor; that this abstracting process generally takes one of three forms,—interest, rent, and profit; that these three constitute the trinity of usury, and are simply different methods of levying tribute for the use of capital; that, capital being simply stored-up labor which has already received its pay in full, its use ought to be gratuitous, on the principle that labor is the only basis of price; that the lender of capital is entitled to its return intact, and nothing more; that the only reason why the banker, the stockholder, the landlord, the manufacturer, and the merchant are able to exact usury from labor lies in the fact that they are backed by legal privilege, or monopoly; and that the only way to secure labor the enjoyment of its entire product, or natural wage, is to strike down monopoly.[36]
>
> While Warren and Proudhon were opposed to socializing the ownership of capital, they aimed nevertheless to socialize its effects by making its use beneficial to all instead of a means of impoverishing the many to enrich the few. And when the light burst in upon them, they saw that this could be done by subjecting capital to the natural law of competition, thus bringing the price of its own use down to cost,—that is, to nothing beyond the expenses incidental to handling and transferring it.[37]

Tucker's understanding of socialism is rooted, as he emphasizes, in the idea of privilege. The way to solve the social question, for Tucker, is not to vest all authority in the state and trust that it will achieve socialism's goals; rather, it is to remove all privileges—that is, restraints on bodies and possessions rooted in actual or threatened aggression. With privileges eliminated, disparities in wealth will be reduced, the risk of serious deprivation will be minimized, and workers' control over their workplaces will be enhanced. A just price is thus one that emerges in the absence of privilege, in a context of genuinely voluntary exchange. On Tucker's view, labor gets, as it were, its just deserts in a truly free(d) exchange, because privileges—restraints on peaceful, voluntary exchange imposed by actual or threatened aggression—are absent. A

[36] Benjamin R. Tucker, *State Socialism and Anarchism: How Far They Agree, and Wherein They Differ*, *in* Markets Not Capitalism, *supra* note 6, at 21, 24, *available at* http://fair-use.org/benjamin-tucker/instead-of-a-book/state-socialism-and-anarchism.

[37] *Id.* at 27–28.

legal order that makes this kind of exchange the norm is therefore, in Tucker's terms, a socialist order.

While Tucker is aware that other privileges obtain, he focuses on four: the state's control over banking and the issuance of money, the state's interference with exchange and support for established corporations at the expense of consumers through tariffs, the state's conferral of monopolistic patents and copyrights, and the state's engrossment of land and its protection of unjust land titles.[38] The elimination of these privileges would have a variety of predictable effects, Tucker believed. It would lead to the abolition of (*i*) wage labor as the primary mode of economic activity; (*ii*) the dominance of society by (*a*) the people who regularly employ significant numbers of wage laborers and (*b*) the people who own large quantities of wealth and capital goods; and (*iii*) persistent, systemic, exclusionary poverty. And it would foster (*i*) wide dispersal of control over the means of production and (*ii*) increased opportunities for worker self-management. Eliminating privilege would thus lead to the achievement of a range of goals consistently identified as central to the socialist tradition. For Tucker, then, socialism might be understood as emancipation through the elimination of privilege.

D. The Work of Hodgskin and Tucker Suggests How the Legal and Political Project I Have Outlined Might Be Understood as Socialist

Hodgskin and Tucker can both be seen as exemplifying an idiosyncratic strand within the socialist tradition that seeks to pursue the socialist goal of abolishing capitalism—in my second, third, fourth, and fifth senses—by eliminating privilege. Hodgskin framed his critique of existing conditions, a critique reasonably understood as a contribution to the socialist tradition, as an attack on artificial possessory claims—on those that would not exist without state-secured privilege. Tucker focused on a similar problem, but used the language of "monopoly" to capture what the state did to prop up economic elites. Neither would have agreed with some of the details of the proposal I have offered here.[39] But both were convinced that ending special privileges for the wealthy and well-connected would lead to radical social transformation. While their rejection of statist means and their failure to embrace mandatory collective possession or control certainly marks them as representatives of a minority position within the broader socialist tradition, the frequent identification of Hodgskin as a "Ricardian socialist" and Tucker's self-description as a socialist,

[38] *Cf.* Charles W. Johnson, *Markets Freed from Capitalism*, *in* MARKETS NOT CAPITALISM, *supra* note 6, at 59.

[39] *See, e.g.*, Eric Mack, *Lysander Spooner: Nineteenth-Century America's Last Natural Rights Theorist*, 29 SOC. PHIL. & POL'Y 139, 146–47 (2012) (arguing that Hodgskin held, like Tucker, that land should be viewed as abandoned by a would-be just possessor who ceased personally to occupy and use it).

together with his engagement with the wider socialist movement, makes it difficult to deny that both were socialists. The socialist position I defend here is in deliberate continuity with theirs.

The work of Hodgskin and Tucker suggests a distinctive understanding of "socialism"—roughly, as radical emancipation, the satisfactory resolution of "the social question" (appropriately accomplished, on their view, through the elimination of privilege). That these antistate radicals have been historically identified as socialists suggests that the socialist tradition may be capacious enough to include the variety of anarchism I have sought to defend here.[40]

The legal and political project I have defended here is socialist in the same basic sense as those of Hodgskin and Tucker: it involves unequivocal opposition to privilege, and so to capitalism$_2$, capitalism$_3$, and capitalism$_4$. And it also merits the "socialist" label because it is rooted in the recognition that society—people cooperating freely and voluntarily—rather than the state should be seen as the source of solutions to human problems; in this sense, *social*ism can be seen not as a kind of, but as an alternative to, *stat*ism.[41] Abolishing privilege and fostering peaceful, voluntary cooperation offer a way of achieving socialist goals—fostering the empowerment of workers and the wider dispersion of possession *of* and control *over* the means of production while eliminating the principal causes of structural poverty—by encouraging the emergence of a system of cooperation through peaceful, voluntary cooperation, rather than state action.[42]

Like all interesting and important words, "socialism" has an extensive semantic range. Clearly, other users might not employ it as inclusively as Tucker, for instance, did. If it is understood to mean (*i*) control of the major means of production by conventional modern states or (*ii*) control of the major means of production by small-scale microstates, then the legal rules defended here would not qualify as socialist: obviously, a genuinely stateless society won't feature the control of anything by the state. Even if socialism were understood as involving (*iii*) some non-state variety of mandatory collective possession or control, the stateless legal

[40] *See id. Cf.* Kevin A. Carson, *Socialist Definitional Free-for-All: Part II*, MUTUALIST BLOG: FREE MARKET ANTI-CAPITALISM, Dec. 8, 2005, http://mutualist.blogspot.com/2005/12/socialist-definitional-free-for-all_08.html; Brad Spangler, *Market Anarchism as Stigmergic Socialism*, *in* MARKETS NOT CAPITALISM, *supra* note 6, at 85.

[41] Thanks to Sheldon Richman for helping me to see this point.

[42] *Cf.* Alex Tabarrok, *Rename Capitalism Socialism?*, MARGINAL REVOLUTION, Jan. 25, 2010, http://www.marginalrevolution.com/marginalrevolution/2010/01/rename-capitalism-socialism.html. Tabarrok maintains: "capitalism is a truly *social* system, a system that unites the world in cooperation, peace and trade. Thus, if all were tabula rasa socialism might be a good name for capitalism. But that boat has sailed." It seems to me that Tabarrok misses the point of the argument about "capitalism," which is precisely whether what is regularly labeled "capitalism" by the majority of the people in the world really is "a truly social system . . . that unites the world in cooperation, peace and trade."

order I have envisioned here clearly wouldn't seem particularly socialist, though it certainly would leave room for the just acquisition of possessions by groups, and though it would pose no barrier at all to the creation of voluntary communities featuring collective control or of gift-economies of whatever scale. But "socialism" need not name a project of any of these sorts. Instead, socialism can be understood as a project of radical liberation committed to empowering people and combating deprivation by eliminating unjust privilege.

Using the "socialist" label for the kind of legal model I defend here provides the occasion for a clear distinction between the genus "socialism" and the species "state-socialism." Thus, it offers a convenient opportunity to highlight the statist assumptions many people reflexively make (assumptions that make it all-too-easy for political theory to take as given the presupposition that its subject matter is the question, "What should the state do?"). Various schemes for state control (or for collective possession or control by some state-like entity) should not be seen as being essential to socialism; rather they are ways of achieving the underlying *goal* of socialism—emancipation, an end to subordination and to widespread deprivation. But they are both unjust and ineffective means of achieving this goal.

For the proponent of the kind of anarchism I defend here, there is an inconsistency between the state-socialist's emancipatory goals and the statist means she professes to prefer. Purported statist responses to bossism, for instance, create more, and more influential and dominant, bosses, and the state is much better at causing deprivation than curing it. The socialist's ultimate attachment, I suggest, need not be to statist means, but instead to an appealing end, the achievement of human emancipation, which can be realized without statism or mandatory collectivization.

Rather than realizing socialist goals through the operation of structures of top-down control that pursue specified end-states and interfere with people's peaceful, voluntary interactions in order to do so, institutions operating in accordance with the principles I defend here would foster the achievement of these goals by ending privileges that confer more legal rights on some people than on others and that thus enable some people to use force to dominate others. If social institutions are not distorted by aggression, interactions within the terms of those institutions will be peaceful and voluntary, free from domination; prosperity will be widely shared; and social oppression will be minimized. The program for stateless law I have defended here is a program for the creation and maintenance of such institutions, and so for the establishment of socialism in an idiosyncratic but defensible sense.

E. Socialism and Anarchism as I Have Understood Them May Be Seen as Consonant

Widely characterized as a "Ricardian socialist," Thomas Hodgskin called for the abolition of artificial possessory claims rooted in state-secured privilege. Propounding what he termed "anarchistic socialism," Benjamin Tucker identified the path to emancipation as the elimination of state-created monopolies. The kind of legal and political project I have defended here can be seen as socialist in the sense that Hodgskin and Tucker may be seen as members in good standing of the socialist tradition. Despite some differences with them, I join them in arguing for the achievement of socialist ends through the elimination of privilege and the establishment of a society rooted in peaceful, voluntary cooperation (including cooperation in and through exchange).

V. THE MODEL OF STATELESS LAW OUTLINED HERE EMBODIES A DISTINCTIVELY LEFTIST, ANTICAPITALIST, AND SOCIALIST ANTISTATISM

Contemporary projects that identify themselves as leftist, anticapitalist, and socialist are characteristically either (*i*) statist or (*ii*) committed to collective control over people's possessions or to gift-economies as alternatives to cooperation in and through exchange. The proposal for an anarchist legal order I have developed here is neither. But I believe it no less leftist, anticapitalist, or socialist for this reason.

Leftist political projects are frequently rooted in the assumption that opposition to exclusion, subordination, and deprivation means support for state action targeting these ills. But all are, in fact, created or exacerbated by the state, can be remedied without the state, and would be easier to address were it not for the state's actions. Leftist politics are also characteristically antimilitarist and anti-imperialist, but it is hard to see how advocating the continued existence or, indeed, the augmentation of the state could be consistent with opposition to war and empire, which feed and are fed by state power. Being an authentic leftist—being motivated by genuine concern with exclusion, subordination, deprivation, and aggression—does not require anyone to be a statist, and provides good reason not to be a statist. The anarchist project defended here, with the potential to undermine exclusion, subordination, deprivation, and aggression, can thus be characterized with confidence as a leftist project.

It is also, more specifically, an anticapitalist project. At least, this is the case if capitalism is understood as a system of special privilege for economic elites secured by the state, as social dominance by those elites, as the hyper-commercialization of society, or, most broadly, as the economic system we (in the West and in regions significantly influenced by the West) have now. By eliminating ongoing privileges, by fostering remedies for past acts of deprivation by elites, and by creating space for acts of solidarity and peaceful action that undermine elite dominance and reduce the risk of its recurrence, the kind of stateless legal order envisioned here would clearly qualify as anticapitalist.

Thus it would also qualify, in particular, as socialist. It is rooted in an early strand of socialism, articulated with particular force by such figures as Benjamin Tucker and Thomas Hodgskin, that emphasizes the role of privilege as the defining characteristic of the unjust order to be opposed and the elimination of privilege as the essential feature of the establishment of socialism. The elimination of privilege has the potential to effect a substantial reordering of social influence—to empower workers, undermine workplace hierarchies, end structural poverty, and foster the wider dispersion of wealth. The kind of socialism promoted by Hodgskin and Tucker is not state-socialism, nor does it involve the enforcement of collective possession or worker self-management by law. What it does instead is to create the *institutional preconditions* that offer new opportunities for people to develop and implement various models of possession and work-life that reflect their preferences and meet their needs.

It's useful clearly to distinguish goals and methods. Efforts to achieve particular goals directly by state action frequently founder—because of the informational limitations state actors confront, the (at best) mixed motives that drive them, and the risks of abuse that unavoidably attend the enhancement of state power even for putatively good ends. State action to achieve even desirable goals is not only unwise but also frequently unjust for various reasons. But rejecting state action as a means of achieving particular goals is hardly the same as rejecting the goals in toto.

Leftism, anticapitalism, and socialism are best understood as traditions (in some broad sense) that are ultimately concerned with goals, not with the use of statist means to achieve those goals. As long as that distinction is acknowledged, a legal order featuring rules that encourage peaceful, voluntary cooperation; eliminate privilege; allow the constrained use of force to prevent, end, or remedy acts of aggression; and create space within which nonviolent social pressure can be employed to address nonviolent wrongs can rightly be seen as leftist, anticapitalist, and socialist.

Conclusion

Ordering Anarchy

A popular stereotype has it that anarchy is chaos. So the idea of anarchy as lawful, of anarchy as occurring in tandem with legal order, may initially seem almost oxymoronic. I hope I have made clear why it need not be, and why the constraints on just legal rules that render state authority indefensible simultaneously lay the groundwork for a stateless society's legal order.

A credible account of anarchy as peaceful, voluntary cooperation will see it not only as grounded in practical reasonableness but also as embodying plausible legal principles that themselves count decisively against the authority and legitimacy of the state. While each moral agent is certainly free to impose on herself whatever obligations she chooses by making accepted commitments to others, there are clear limits to the obligations that can be *enforced*, especially against the unconsenting. These limits—the baseline possessory rules, along with basic prohibition on harming moral patients' bodies (including those of nonhuman sentients) purposefully or instrumentally—flow from the requirements of practical reasonableness. They can be summed up in the nonaggression maxim, which safeguards the space needed for peaceful, voluntary cooperation.

Peaceful, voluntary cooperation can be protected and fostered without the state. People can even manage to provide themselves with vital public goods without the state's purported aid. It is obvious, in addition, that entrusting the state with responsibility for safeguarding cooperation is unreasonable because states actively *undermine* just social order. They engage in aggression in multiple ways—by making war, restricting personal freedom, engaging in or sanctioning dispossession in the interests of the ruling class and its cronies, and conferring privileges on the well-connected. The state is illegitimate, it isn't necessary, and it's dangerous.

The authority of state-made law purportedly rests on the consent of those subjected to it. Clearly, it doesn't. But law in a stateless society could, in large measure, *be* authoritative only when it was consensual. Thus, such a society could feature a broad range of legal regimes, each rooted in revocable, voluntary consent, overlapping geographically and cooperating with each other to resolve disputes on both moral and prudential grounds. Only in the case of outlaws need laws be enforced against the unconsenting. But enforcing those laws simply embodying the NAM would not be an injustice against anyone: providing restitution- and restraint-based remedies for aggression is not an instance of aggression.

Although a stateless society would almost certainly feature multiple legal regimes, the need to cooperate would lead to a measure of convergence in legal standards. And though it can hardly be assumed that the requirements of justice as reflected in the NAM would be embraced by all regimes, the NAM does tightly constrain the kinds of rules just regimes could enforce. Under the rule of the state, many injuries are dealt with using the category of *crime*, the persistence of which creates innumerable opportunities for aggression. Just legal regimes in a stateless society would do without this category, focusing instead on providing remedies for (economically compensable) injuries and ensuring the restraint of those reasonably regarded as committed to programs of ongoing aggression. Just legal regimes in a stateless society could deal effectively not only with ordinary interpersonal injuries but also with harms to sentient nonhuman animals and vulnerable persons and with substantial environmentally mediated injuries.

Just legal rules in a stateless society could not license the use of force against bodies or justly acquired possessions except to prevent, end, or remedy aggression. Recognizing this limit might seem to mean declining to deal with large-scale social inequities, including poverty, workplace authoritarianism, and persistent (nonviolent) racism, sexism, and heterosexism.[1] But it need not mean this at all. The patterns of behavior and distorted social institutions responsible for deprivation, exclusion, and subordination very often flow directly from remediable injustice. Ending systematic aggression will increase the costs and decrease the frequency of social inequities. And just legal rules and institutions in a stateless society can and should create opportunities for concerted nonviolent actions—protests, boycotts, and the like—designed to challenge nonviolent institutional, cultural, and social wrongs. Thus, through the maintenance of the kinds of rules that would be upheld by just legal regimes, the incidence not only of aggression but also of nonviolent authoritarianism and restraint could be reduced in a stateless society, leaving considerable room for the development of multiple liberated lifestyles and diverse modes of non-oppressive self-expression.

The anarchist legal order I have defended here is recognizably *leftist* because of its capacity to undermine subordination, exclusion, deprivation, and aggressive warfare.

[1] Obviously, racism, sexism, heterosexism, religious bigotry, speciesism, etc., can issue in, and be reinforced by, brutal violence, which can be dealt quite straightforwardly using ordinary mechanisms for preventing, ending, and remedying aggression.

The project of implementing this kind of legal order would, in effect, be *anticapitalist*, given that capitalism is understood to refer to the alliance between the state and the corporate elite, to social dominance by capitalists, to hypercommercialization, or to familiar economic arrangements that obtain in the contemporary world; the undesirability and, in many cases, the injustice of these arrangements is evident in light of the requirements of practical reasonableness. And a legal order adhering to the NAM would be, in an idiosyncratic but genuine sense, *socialist*, because of its emancipatory response to "the social question" through the undermining of privilege and the rectification of injustice. Thus, just legal rules and institutions in a stateless society could be said to embody clearly leftist, anticapitalist, and socialist values.

In some broad sense, anarchism is part of the *liberal* tradition, too, insofar as it opposes hierarchy, subjects tradition to careful scrutiny, and favors freedom and equality. At the same time, as I have argued already, it can create significantly more space than the liberal state is likely to allow for the flourishing of the given identities and constitutive attachments that the communitarian tradition prizes, as long as this flourishing is fostered through peaceful, voluntary cooperation. Mutual aid networks, which might be expected to flourish in a stateless society, can offer the sorts of solidaristic connections that communitarians value. And the absence of state subsidies for transportation infrastructure in a stateless society might enhance the stability of geographic communities, in particular, in a way likely to please communitarians.

Anarchism is also perfectly capable, I believe, of capturing important values treasured by the *civic republican* tradition. Certainly this is true if civic republicans are understood to value meaningful opportunities to shape communal institutions and attitudes, since anarchism offers just such opportunities. It rejects large-scale institutions propped up by state-secured privilege, and thus increases the worth of participation insofar as it boosts the frequency with which institutions operate at human scale. And by rendering legal institutions much more radically consensual than they are at present, it ensures that people who do not believe they are being afforded opportunities to participate in shaping such institutions can opt for others, thus both increasing their own immediate opportunities for participation and pressuring the institutions they have abandoned, and others as well, to offer more such opportunities. Civic republicanism often seems to assume not only that participating in public deliberation is a crucial aspect of flourishing but *also* that such deliberation needs to lead to action by the state. It seems as if these two assumptions could be disentangled, just as it seems as if the sorts of institutions with which civic republicanism is concerned could be deterritorialized and consensualized without excessive loss.

Anarchism can thus be seen as incorporating what's valuable in civic republicanism and as being a species not only of leftism, anticapitalism, and socialism but also of both liberalism and communitarianism.

Simple moral principles—rooted in a recognition of the essential equality of moral patients and the importance of respect—constrain the space of possibly just legal rules in tandem with a range of relevant facts. These principles, summarized in the NAM, leave no room for the state and none for the unjust dispossessions it licenses and commits or the unjust privileges it secures. Unnecessary and dangerous, the state can and should be replaced by a network of overlapping, consensual legal regimes and other social institutions that can safeguard peaceful, voluntary cooperation without the liabilities that accompany the existence and activity of the state. Such legal regimes should embrace the legal principles summarized in the NAM, substituting restitution for retributive and deterrent responses to aggression while eliminating the privileges characteristically secured by the state and remedying the wrongs committed under its aegis. In doing so, these regimes will lay the groundwork for liberation not only from aggression but also from deprivation, exclusion, and subordination, and so for a social order in which non-oppressive personal and subcultural diversity can flourish. Just legal rules—leftist, anticapitalist, and socialist—will pave the way for the flourishing of a society rooted in peaceful, voluntary cooperation, and so for the full embodiment of freedom.

Index

About the Author

GARY CHARTIER is Associate Dean of the Tom and Vi Zapara School of Business and Professor of Law and Business Ethics at La Sierra University in Riverside, California. He is the author of *Economic Justice and Natural Law* (Cambridge, 2009), *The Conscience of an Anarchist* (Cobden, 2011), and *The Analogy of Love* (Imprint Academic, 2007) as well as the co-editor (with Charles W. Johnson) of *Markets Not Capitalism: Individualist Anarchism against Bosses, Inequality, Corporate Power, and Structural Poverty* (Minor Compositions-Autonomedia, 2011) and (with Roderick T. Long and Ross Kenyon) *Libertarian Theories of Class* (forthcoming); *Economic Justice and Natural Law* was the focus of a session at the 2011 San Diego conference of the American Philosophical Association's Pacific Division. His byline has appeared over thirty times in scholarly journals including the *Oxford Journal of Legal Studies*, *Legal Theory*, *Law and Philosophy*, the *Canadian Journal of Law and Jurisprudence*, the *American Journal of Jurisprudence*, and the *UCLA Law Review*. He received the La Sierra University Faculty Senate's triennial Distinguished Scholarship Award in 2010. A keynote presenter at the 2012 Students for Liberty Philosophical Seminar, he was an invited speaker at the first Libertopia and Agora I/O events and at Individual Sovereign University's founding conference.

A member of the Alliance of the Libertarian Left and a trustee and senior fellow of the Center for a Stateless Society, he serves on the advisory board of the *Journal of Philosophical Economics*, the editorial board of *Libertarian Papers*, the advisory board of the Moorfield Storey Institute, and the board of directors of the North American Religious Liberty Association—West. He has discussed political and philosophical issues as a guest on *Reason TV* and *The Young Turks with Cenk Uygur*.

After receiving a BA in history and political science from La Sierra (1987, *magna cum laude*), he explored ethics, theology, Christian origins, the philosophy of religion, and political philosophy at the University of Cambridge, earning a PhD (1991) with a dissertation on the idea of friendship. He graduated with a JD (2001, Order of the Coif) from UCLA, where he studied legal philosophy and U.S. and comparative constitutional law and earned the Judge Jerry Pacht Memorial Award in Constitutional Law. A proud southern California native who wishes he had attended UC Sunnydale, he shares a slowly improving 1920 home in Riverside with his partner, Elenor Webb, and their two cats, The Kitty Madrid and Lysander Spooner the Kitty. He blogs at <http://liberalaw.blogspot.com>.

CPSIA information can be obtained at www.ICGtesting.com
Printed in the USA
BVOW02s1148110416

443784BV00008B/44/P